Genealogy and Identity:

The Genealogical Evidence for the Appropriation of Early East Greek Mythology by the Mainland Greek City-States in the Archaic Period

Zoe A. Pappas

Mytho Logic Inc.
Hastings-on-Hudson, NY

Αἱ γὰρ συγγενεῖς ὁμιλίαι φίλτρον οὐ σμικρὸν φρενῶν.

ΕΥΡΙΠΙΔΗΣ ΤΡΟΙΑΔΕΣ 51-52.

ISBN: 978-1-7339501-3-8 (hardcover)
ISBN: 978-1-7339501-4-5 (paperback)

Library of Congress Catalog Card Number: 2019915409

1. Ancient Greece – Mythology – Religion

2. Geography – History – Genealogy

3. Epic Poetry – Literature

4. Philosophy – Logic – Logical Analysis

2019. Second Edition.

Copyright © 2008 Zoe A. Pappas

All rights reserved.

Published in the United States by Mytho Logic Inc., Hastings-on-Hudson, New York

No part of this work may be reproduced or transmitted in any form or by any means, electronic or mechanical, including information storage and retrieval systems without permission in writing from the author.

DEDICATION

In Memory of:
Bernice and George
Anna and Demetrios
Nina and Samuel

TABLE OF CONTENTS

ABSTRACT ix

ACKNOWLEDGMENTS xi

INTRODUCTION xii
PREVIOUS SCHOLARSHIP ON THE AIOLIC ASPECTS OF THE HOMERIC POEMS
THE GENEALOGICAL APPROACH TO THE EARLY AIOLIC FEATURES OF GREEK MYTHOLOGY
SIGNIFICANT ASPECTS OF THE GREEK MYTHIC BACKGROUND
THE ANCIENT SOURCES

PART 1: STANDARD TECHNIQUES OF MYTHOLOGICAL INNOVATION 41
CHAPTER ONE: MYTHIC THEFT TYPE ONE 41
CHAPTER TWO: MYTHIC THEFT TYPE TWO 114
CHAPTER THREE: MYTHIC THEFT TYPE THREE 149
THE DAUGHTERS OF ATLAS 196

PART 2: THE POST-EPIC REEVALUATION OF MYTHOLOGICAL GEOGRAPHY AND THE DISTRIBUTION OF POWER IN THE PELOPONNESE 223
CHAPTER FOUR: GENEALOGICAL OVERCROWDING AND THE PROBLEM OF MYTHIC ARGOS 223
CHAPTER FIVE: THE PROBLEM OF MYTHIC ARGOS SUPPORTING EVIDENCE 270

CONCLUSION 351
CHAPTER SIX: THE LINEAGE OF THE SEER MELAMPOUS - A GENEALOGICAL CASE STUDY 351

BIBLIOGRAPHY 374

APPENDIX A: THE LEGEND OF THE TRIPARTITE DIVISION OF ARGOS 415

APPENDIX B: ARGIVE GENEALOGIES 447

ABOUT THE AUTHOR 451

ΑΡΧΑΪΚΗ ΕΠΟΧΗ

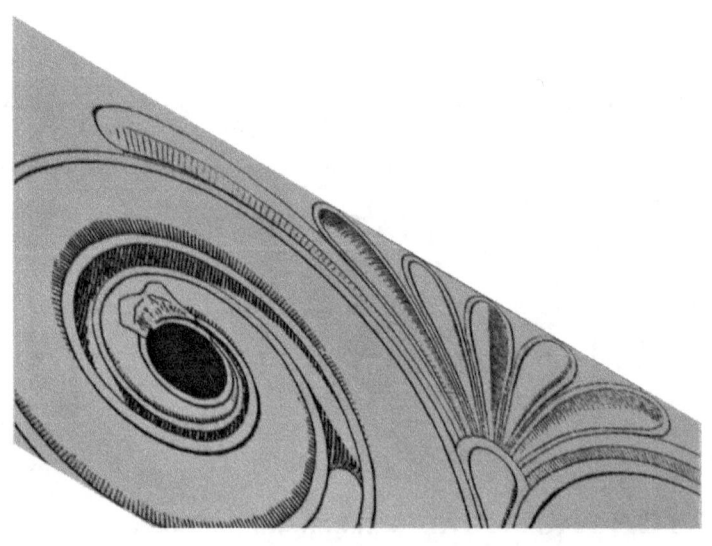

ABSTRACT

Genealogy and Identity: The Genealogical Evidence for the Appropriation of Early East Greek Mythology by the Mainland Greek City-States in the Archaic Period

This investigation is the result of extensive research into Greek mythological genealogy. Overall, it endeavors to demonstrate that in spite of the attention lavished on Greek mythology and the problem of myth as a historical source, there is an approach to this body of evidence based strictly on genealogical patterning that has not been adequately investigated to date. The genealogical approach gives chronological precedence to patterns first manifest in the Homeric poems, which by comparison with later mythic material delineate the outline of a genealogical template that initially emerged in Aiolic East Greece. This stands to reason on a number of counts, prominently, for example, because it explains the importance of Troy as the appointed target of a legendary Greek conquest in the east (Troy was located in Aiolic East Greek territory), and also because East Greek Asia Minor was the first point of contact between Dark Age Greek culture and Near Eastern metropoleis that deployed genealogy as a structural medium in the canonization of cultural pre-history.

Inasmuch as the later Greek mythic corpus readily divides into clusters of stories associated with major mainland Greek city-states, I determined, in view of the Homeric evidence, that these state genealogies in general relied on the use of recurrent manipulative techniques designed to supplant the early Aiolic structure, while at the same time retaining the most famous legends amidst a largely restructured genealogical framework. Tracing these patterns further, it turned out to be possible to distinguish and correlate post-Homeric genealogical emendations with political developments on the Greek mainland, where unified opposition to a legendary framework conceived and promoted initially in East Greece led to tangible ideological changes, detectable since they altered but did not destroy all vestiges of the inherited tradition.

This hypothesis demands quite detailed exposition because it cannot comfortably coexist with the leading approach to Greek mythogenesis. According to that view, separate regional mythic cycles were rather awkwardly fused together before the emergence of pan-Hellenic self-consciousness in the early Archaic Period. Still, the opposite view, this thesis argues, in which a meaningful whole was incrementally split up into an assortment of disjointed parts is the simpler, more logical explanation for the development of Greek mythic tradition, and is, moreover, capable of comprehending random segments of Greek mythological testimony. What follows, therefore, is a blow-by-blow account of the most pivotal evidence to this effect on the mythical and the historical side, reinforced, in conclusion, with a case study of a single major genealogical line that was largely preserved in its original form, as verified by its coverage in the Homeric poems and in surviving texts by seven later Greek authors[1].

---

[1] viz. Bakchylides, Pindar, Herodotos, Diodoros, Strabo, Apollodoros, and Pausanias.

ACKNOWLEDGMENTS

There have been many impediments arrayed against the publication of this analysis in book form. Gladly, however, without further ado, it is here: a significant piece of an ephemeral life's work. May the lessons that need to be learned be learned widely. May whatever warnings still require acknowledgment be broadcast. It is well-known that the truth is often stranger than fiction; that it is also stronger is not as well-known.

INTRODUCTION

PREVIOUS SCHOLARSHIP ON THE AIOLIC ASPECTS OF THE HOMERIC POEMS

Philologists had long recognized an Aiolic substratum in Homeric hexameter verse when in 1883 and 1886 in his respective editions of the *Odyssey* and the *Iliad*, August Fick sought to demonstrate that the Homeric poems were originally composed in the Aiolic dialect, and only later transposed into Ionic, generating the familiar mixture of forms. However, as J.L. Myres explains, "subsequent revisions of Fick's data in light of more copious and earlier examples of Aiolic and Ionic speech[2], by more trustworthy methods of philology, and with a more scientific text of the poems, shows that the problems of Aiolism are very much more complicated than he [Fick] supposed (1958: 144[3])." Fick's work nonetheless contributed significantly to the preoccupations of Homeric scholarship that came to the fore in the late nineteenth century. The major issues at stake were provenance and chronology, which at the time hinged on whether Homeric poetry was an Ionic artifact with Aiolic roots, backed by a long-standing, yet still proximate tradition, antecedent to the historical period, or the surviving product of an altogether pre-Iron Age poetic culture[4].

Following George Grote, and later, William Geddes[5], Fick believed that the Aiolic dialect substratum harked back to northern Greek mainland traditions that had proceeded from there to Asia Minor, where imported stories about the life of Achilles were substantially expanded upon[6]. This was the argument that was lodged against the archaeological findings of Heinrich Schliemann, first at Hissarlik from 1870 onward, where Schliemann championed the site as the ancient city of Troy, and at Mykenai from 1874-1876[7], where he claimed to have unearthed the treasures of Agamemnon. From the publication of Schliemann's excavation reports into the first decades of the twentieth century, intense polarization infiltrated the discipline. On the one side, scholars such as Paul Cauer, Erich Bethe, Richard Jebb, and Ulrich von Wiliamowitz[8] adhered to the standard Ionian context for the provenance of the Homeric poems, advocating their Aiolic mainland Greek heritage before the Greek migrations to coastal

Anatolia[9]. On the other, in Britain led by William Gladstone[10], Walter Leaf[11], Andrew Lang[12], and a string of successors, Schlieman's discoveries engendered a complete shift in the contextualization of Homeric poetry. Henceforth, the widely accepted Iron Age dating was abandoned in favor of the preceding Bronze Age[13]. This intervention would ultimately control the direction of subsequent Homeric studies.

In his account of key developments in Homeric scholarship from antiquity to the early 1950s, J.L. Myres describes this remarkable shift with the subtle benefits of retrospection[14]. For while in keeping pace with the latest research on the oral transmission of the Homeric poems, Myres departed from his predecessors' conviction that Bronze Age lore had passed down into the succeeding period through the survival of actual Bronze Age texts[15]; his confidence that Homeric poetry embodied a genuine Bronze Age inheritance, which vindicated the content of early Greek myth, exemplifies the tenacity of the point of view that arose in the wake of Schliemann's discoveries[16]. For Myres, among others, the Bronze Age equation offered a sober correction to all previous theories, silenced unwarranted conflict on the unity of the poems, and endowed them with concretely proven truth value[17].

Most remarkable, looking back from the twenty-first century, is the relative brevity with which this heated debate resolved into the near-universal acceptance of a Bronze Age origin for Homeric narrative content, which was tied to a factual ancient conflict between Trojans and Greeks over the city of Troy. This is especially so in light of the fact that just prior to Schliemann's grand declarations, the highly skeptical reading advanced by George Grote had achieved broad-based consensus. Grote classed Homeric poetry as narrative fiction of historical value primarily for the insights it offered on contemporary customs and cultural practices. Emphasizing the poetic nature of the evidence, Grote divided Greek history into two separate periods: legendary and historical Greece. He considered it impossible to realistically distinguish early Greek history from early Greek legend any time prior to the date traditionally assigned to the first Olympiad (viz. 776)[18]. Against this, Schliemann's discoveries did not displace the composition of the Homeric poems from coastal Asia Minor in the pre-Classical period. Rather, they transformed Homeric poetry from a robust contemporary cultural artifact into a conduit for the preservation of actual events that had nothing to do with the poet's own lived reality, and yet, still ostensibly reproduced the realities of a long-bygone age.

    This extreme reversal from fiction to fact in terms of the status of the Homeric poems is particularly striking since the medium at issue was an inherently mythological one, and this was notably a factor the new theory itself sought far more to accommodate than to deny. It is interesting for this reason that contemporary theorizing on the cultural status and function of myth (likewise a major sub-discipline at the time), was not exactly conducive to the type of commensurability that Schliemann's findings would appear to require. And this was the case whether myth was conceived as the expression of humanity's intellectual childhood[19], as the primitive antecedent to modern religion[20], the basis for community ritual practices[21], or any of the array of interpretive suggestions that have waxed and waned down to the present time[22]. Mainly, the notion that legends are reliable arbiters of accurate historical information has always posed certain gnawing, if subliminal, difficulties. It is possible, however, to a degree, to observe ways in which such subtle difficulties were effectively mitigated till the mid-twentieth century, when the Grotean perspective regained a foothold in the analysis of early Greece[23].

    It would seem that the advent of European Hellenism from Johann Winkelmann's admiration for Greece[24] to the upheaval associated with the two great world wars facilitated a number of analytical blind spots that could not be detected anywhere within range of the fervent commitment to the idea that ancient Hellenic culture was the inspirational source of the finest attributes of Western Civilization[25]. In this context, the slightly ironic divergence between the dominant tenets of "Homeric archaeology" and the vehement contemporaneous search for a valid universal theory of myth indirectly invokes more recent complaints against Classical Archaeology's long entrenched reliance on the reportage contained in surviving ancient texts, in contrast to other archaeological disciplines where material analysis has not been subject to comparably influential external constraints[26]. This late twentieth-century professional objection offers some added insight on the momentous shift that took hold of the discipline one hundred years earlier because of the way it provisionally suggests the subordination of archaeological data to information extracted from the literature that inspired the archaeological quest to begin with.

By the mid-twentieth century, in certain quarters, the pendulum was beginning to swing back toward the Grotean myth / historical divide. The oral poetry research of Milman Parry and Albert Lord, followed by Michael Ventris and John Chadwick's penetration of the Bronze Age syllabic script known as Linear B, irrevocably affected the truth value equation that arose in the wake of Schliemann's discoveries by demonstrating quite incontrovertibly that a Bronze Age Homeric poetic tradition would have had to traverse a cultural divide roughly half a millennium in duration, remaining fundamentally unscathed in the process, in order to accord with the demands of that model. Meanwhile, oral tradition was concomitantly shown to be more of a living organism in a state of flux, which was vital to sustaining its cultural relevance, than a static instrument bound by verbatim repetition, and, therefore, believably frozen intact at a remarkably distant point in time[27].

THE GENEALOGICAL APPROACH TO THE EARLY AIOLIC FEATURES OF GREEK MYTHOLOGY

The following analysis begins with the acknowledgment of an Aiolic substratum in the Homeric poems, as proposed by August Fick and refined by his successors. It also takes a programmatically skeptical stance on any of the leading truth value equations that have linked Homeric poetry with historical events, as exemplified by George Grote in the 1850s, and revitalized after the Second World War by Rhys Carpenter[28] and pre-eminently by Moses Finley[29]. Here the Aiolic substratum is addressed mythologically rather than with a view to linguistic concerns, whereas the body of data under consideration throughout consists of the genealogical patterns present beneath the surface of the Greek mythic stories. The notion that Greek mythology refers to past-time events that actually happened is programmatically excluded in the present context so as to permit other potential dynamics that may have informed relations between Greek myth and Greek history to come to the surface[30].

The point of this analysis is to show that Greek mythology bears the imprint of a genealogical structure originally promoted by the Aiolic east Greeks, who emigrated from the mainland to coastal Asia Minor in between the Bronze Age and the Archaic Period[31]. The idea is that in the beginning, so necessarily beginning with the Homeric poems, an all-inclusive Aiolic family structure commanded the most famous traditional stories that constitute Greek mythology as we know it. This early Aiolic cultural manifesto ultimately became the national charter that was adopted by all Greeks regardless of their provincial affiliations, and in no small part due to the virtuosity and successful dissemination of the Homeric poems.

The demonstration breaks down into a short list of topics integral to substantiating this theory, namely: 1) the impetus for an elaborate mythological repertoire built upon an Aiolic genealogical framework; 2) a detailed exposition of the reasons why, as well as the systematic ways in which, the original Aiolic genealogical structure was partially, yet not altogether dismantled by ensuing generations of Greeks with no vested interest in Aiolic identity since they were not Aiolic Greeks themselves; 3) a detailed account of the evidence to the effect that the Homeric poems followed the Aiolic genealogy, although at length the early Aiolic framework was incrementally reconfigured by creative representatives of the most powerful archaic mainland Greek city-states. This last observation makes it possible to demonstrate that the most influential structural changes imposed on the early Aiolic framework mirror the rise of the mainland Greek poleis as understood independently from other sources.

This project came about pretty much unexpectedly and has turned out to be larger and more comprehensive than I could have ever imagined at first. During the course of my graduate studies I happened to notice something that was not typically cited as a characteristic of Greek mythology, though it certainly seemed to be the case: the major Greek heroes were blood relations. This led me to start charting heroic Greek genealogies – a preoccupation that grew increasingly intense – to the point where I have by now charted virtually the entire early Greek mythic corpus backward and forward numerous times. In the course of so doing, I began to notice conspicuous patterns that were not addressed in the standard bibliographies dealing with the subject. Foremost among these was the observation that the major Greek heroes were not only related, but they also traced back, more often than not, to a specific set of Aiolic families. These connections held true across the full spectrum of the most famous heroic stories, the majority of which were clearly well-known to Homer, raising a number of logistical problems for the dominant theory of Greek mythogenesis.

Essentially, if indeed, as is widely supposed, the Greek mythic corpus developed gradually as the result of the fusion of discrete mythic cycles that first emerged in separate regions of Greece[32], these recurrent genealogical links connecting individuals from presumably separate cycles become notably difficult to explain. On the other hand, seeing that the separate-cycles-hypothesis necessarily acknowledges the convergence of cycles prior to the time of the Homeric poems, since the poems bear witness to a number of such cycles, this hypothesis necessarily also assigns the close kinship relations among the Greek heroes to the same process of pre-Homeric convergence. The problem is that the suggested convergence is not held to result in a seamless alignment (since it would scarcely be possible for this to be the case), or even a provisionally coherent one, but is rather described as an ad hoc process responsible for the conceptual dissonance characteristic of Greek mythology. This picture leaves the repeated identification of heroic Aiolic family roots across the Greek mythological landscape in need of explanation precisely because patterning of this sort is not liable to result from the type of random causation proposed, in turn, raising the specter of inductive fallacy. However, since the proponents of the coalescence hypothesis also frequently acknowledge Aiolic mythic preeminence[33], it looks like, one way or another, the theory in its totality has exerted a measure of inadvertent control over the assessment of its component premises and the consequences such premises are held responsible for.

Along similar lines, it is customary to acknowledge an extensive underlying collection of stories that the poet and his audience presupposed. Yet it is not customary to emphasize that audience knowledge of such depth and such scope could potentially signal the influence of an operative infrastructure that tacitly guided mytho-poetic communication in a far more immediate and more meaningful way than the previous coalescence of disparate traditions would be conceivably capable of. Tipped off in this way by the discrepancy between important family links among the major Greek heroes and the concept of originally separate cycles, after a long drawn out survey of Greek genealogical patterning, I have been led to conclude that mythological genealogy served precisely this type of organizational function by providing a robust conceptual infra-structure for the dissemination of collective cultural history. Thus, the celebrated traditions of neighboring eastern metropoleis that likewise deployed genealogical structure ultimately inspired the unique adaptation of symbolic genealogical precedents by the Aiolic Greeks of coastal Asia Minor.

It is definitely worth noting in this regard that this alternative hypothesis does not preclude the existence of similar contemporaneous initiatives undertaken by other contingents of Greeks, just as it does not preclude the integration of legendary material of greater antiquity than the Aiolic synthesis itself. The point is that, as the data repeatedly show, it was the Aiolic synthesis that rose to prominence and became the cultural legacy for all of Greece, whether it eclipsed other competitive efforts, or whether it was, in fact, powerfully unique, and whether it subordinated traditional material to the project of Aiolic self-promotion, or whether all the material that it embraced was developed specifically on behalf of the Aiolic lineage structure[34].

The analysis that follows sets out the supporting evidence for a qualitatively simpler version of the development of Greek mythology from the emergence of the Homeric poems through the Archaic into the Classical Period. By that time the early genealogical framework had undergone a dramatic structural transformation driven by regional political objections to the priorities of the dominant early structure – that is, to the Aiolic genealogical heritage of all the major heroic protagonists, and to the fact that the early mythological system that elevated the status of Greek culture *per se* was a testament to Aiolic East Greek identity and excluded alternative geopolitical claims. On this last point it is evident that the Ionic Greeks who flourished south of Aiolis on the Anatolian seaboard, and who counted the poet Homer as one of their own did not register early on among the system's detractors. Therefore, in spite of the legends later devised to describe Greek migration to Asia Minor (specifically, in this case the Athenian legends[35]), judging from the perspective of the Homeric poems, the Asia Minor Ionians in this early period rather considered themselves distinguished beneficiaries of the Aiolic mythological framework, which inasmuch as it served as a national charter for Aiolic habitation in the north, could by extension equally serve the interests of the Ionians to the south with minimal creative elaboration[36].

The proposed model represents the simpler view because it begins with an organized structure that deployed genealogy for specific purposes. These purposes correspond with genealogy's contemporary cross-culturally symbolic use, backed by ancient precedents in the environment that evidently inspired a specifically Greek mytho-genealogical charter developed by the Aiolians of Asia Minor. The foremost objective was to define the fundamental significance of being Greek (viz. Achaian, Danaan, and Argive in this context[37]) through a succession of unforgettable stories that would, successfully, in the same breadth, justify the Greek right to control territory in the shadow of powerful eastern nations equipped with elaborate prehistorical legacies. Thus, in line with the alternative model proposed, the story of Greek mythological dissonance is the story of a progression from unity to discord, rather than from inherent isolation to a state of conditional accommodation, as a consequence of increased interaction among discrete Hellenic populations. The most persuasive evidence to this effect cuts both ways from the vantage point of an Aiolic mytho-genealogical charter.

On the one hand, it can be shown that the early Aiolic genealogical framework was in due course largely reconfigured by various special interests that made it their business to redistribute the glory the Aiolic framework monopolized. As set out in chapters one through three, this breakdown of the evidence traces the ways in which new structural formations were repeatedly developed using the same manipulative techniques to reorganize the inherited structure. Moreover, based on the resulting genealogical patterning, the special interests at issue can be readily identified as the most powerful mainland Greek city-states that set out individually, using similar methods, to cut themselves a significant piece of the action, while at the same time, at least to a degree, preserving the integrity of the tradition – a subsidiary concern that sheds additional light on the manipulative tactics that became standard.

As described next, in chapters four and five, it can reciprocally also be shown that when Homeric mythic geography is taken seriously – that is, as meaning quite literally exactly what it says – while by no means consistent with later mythic geography, it is entirely consistent in and of itself, and it is also consistent with what can be discerned of the early Aiolic genealogical structure. In conclusion, chapter six conducts a brief case study of the lineage of the famous seer, Melampous, that brings together these two interpretive strands: the first concerned with the gradual dissolution of a once comprehensive mythological vision, and the second concerned with the attributes of that vision as manifest in the Homeric poems through comparisons with extant later mythology. Cumulatively, then, parts one and two of this thesis demonstrate how recurrent manipulative techniques mesh with identifiable geopolitical motives to vindicate the existence of an early Aiolic framework that became less and less visible to the naked eye.

This leads to the main reasons that the Aiolic framework is not generally identified as a framework at all, but rather identified as a prolific branch of the legends that constitute Greek mythology. In general, this situation ricochets back to the pervasive supposition that it is futile to look for organizational structure in the Greek mythological narratives – a feeling that is enhanced by the related belief that genealogy played a culturally conditioned role in the narratives of Homeric epic, and was, therefore, more ornamental than programmatically meaningful. So, for example, R. Rutherford states, "Genealogy is important in the *Iliad*, but principally in self-assertive speeches, in which the heroes can declare themselves and define their status. There is little hint that Homer's audiences found special satisfaction in the exploits of their supposed ancestors…[38]" On this basis it is generally observed that Homeric genealogies certainly reinforce a strong ancient Greek interest in this area, yet contrast with genealogy's overtly prominent role in Hesiod's *Theogony*, in the first instance, and later in the Hesiodic *Catalogue of Women*. Finally, embedded in the separate-cycles-account there is a predisposition to categorize stories associated with particular places as products of storytelling tied to those places, to the effect that such stories are linked by default to a narrowly patriotic frame of reference even when they are recited very far from home base.

    Notably, these interpretive guidelines are inhospitable to the prospect that the Homeric poems could have been narrated from the viewpoint of the Aiolians of Asia Minor. However, inasmuch as the Aiolic genealogy, as it has been preserved from later sources, radiated from a single eponymous progenitor of the Aiolians of Northern Greece, and expanded via numerous lineage trajectories that from the beginning evidently embraced at least six sons and five daughters, fanning out to encompass the whole of Greece by means of a memorable sequence of stories, it follows in the event that such a system was already sovereign at the time of the composition of the Homeric poems that its poetic adherents could speak with authority about virtually any region of Greece. On these grounds, the prospect of a holistic systematization that was at once geographically comprehensive in scope, and profoundly biased in its authority over the structure of Greek prehistory makes it possible to account first, for the form and function of Greek mythology as it existed at the time of the Homeric poems, and second, for the outbreak of subsequent fragmentation in the wake of the initial systematization's meteoric ascension to the position of pan-Hellenic cultural charter[39].

    In conjunction with the foregoing it is also possible to interpret the two major surviving genealogical poems in terms of how they fit into the suggested schema. Regardless of whether Hesiod's *Theogony* is held to precede or postdate the Homeric poems[40], it is safe to say that poem was designed to address vital aspects of the tradition that were related to, but also distinct from, the subject matter addressed in the *Iliad* and the *Odyssey*. Hesiod's topic was, namely, the birth of the gods. In this regard, it may be maintained that, acknowledging the development of alternate cosmologies[41], there was, as a rule, far greater consensus concerning divine honors and divine genealogies than there was by comparison in the heroic realm. Accordingly, in a sense Hesiod's *Theogony* became canonical in certain ways that Homeric poetry all told did not, since there was no end to conflict and regional disagreements over the possession of the Greek heroes, while the same level of conflict was not reproduced when it came to the origin of the gods. The explanation for this appears to derive from the most outstanding feature of the Greek system: that the heroes were considered the descendants of gods, whereas contemporary Greeks considered themselves the hereditary descendants of the Greek heroes. This premise is as consistent in Homer and Hesiod as it is in later Greek authors[42], and as such amounts to the linchpin in the analysis of the Greek mythological mentality.

Mainly, divine genealogies were inherently apolitical – detached for the most part from the topography and the familiar constraints of the empirical world[43]. The heroic genealogies were another matter for there was nothing metaphysical that was more politically charged than the geographical origins of the Greek heroes, since it was directly via heroic descent that the Greeks arrived at the origin of their communities, and by extension, their hereditary forebears, and by extension, ultimately themselves. Given, therefore, the overwhelming importance of mythological heredity in the Greek context, stemming from the specifically Greek formulation that linked the human present with the heroic past, it is possible to perceive that heroic genealogies, even when surrounded by the accoutrements of elaborate and seemingly irrelevant narratives, were at no time superfluous to the Greek cause. On the contrary, lineage statements expressed in passing invoked major constituent parts of the story, which was fundamentally, at least in the beginning, a single, if remarkably long-winded account, replicated by genealogical structure that could, therefore, cross-reference large swaths of narrative through genealogical abbreviation. In this sense, it is clear that the Homeric poems exemplify early Greek genealogical poetry as much as more obvious instances of the genre. They offer, in addition, by way of passing asides, enough raw-material to verify the authoritative conceptual structure of the Aiolic genealogy.

These circumstances set the stage for the competitive struggle over control of the greatest heroic personalities that the genealogical record suggests accompanied the diffusion of the Homeric poems and inspired great feats of manipulative ingenuity that aimed to rectify critical errors in the Aiolic perception of the map of Greece. The political battleground was well defined. Its inextricable dependence on Greek mythology illuminates succinctly why the Greeks had no choice when they claimed that Greek myth was tantamount to Greek history and reinforces the absence of any concrete divide between political pragmatism and ritual piety[44].

In all this, the Hesiodic *Catalogue of Women*, which was conceived as an extension of Hesiod's *Theogony* and deals specifically with the Heroic Age, stands at an intermediary juncture between the Homeric and Classical permutations of the heroic mythological canon. Most importantly, the *Catalogue* is not just intermediary from a chronological point of view, but conspicuously also on a structural level. A close look at the genealogical changes the *Catalogue* makes to early Aiolic legend confirms that by the time of the *Catalogue's* composition the techniques deployed by the mainland Greek city-states to diminish the influence of Aiolic mythology had long since become standard procedure. Based on these key features the *Catalogue* documents the emergence of a second mythological canon, created and popularized in southern Greece, and consisting of the most powerful reinterpreted stories acknowledged by the most powerful Greek city-states.

SIGNIFICANT ASPECTS OF THE GREEK MYTHIC BACKGROUND

The initial intent of the Aiolic framework and the structural transformation it subsequently inspired may be assessed with much greater clarity when the genealogical evidence is situated within the traditional cosmogonic system that served as an overture to the Heroic Age[45]. In this light it is clear that the Greek birth of the cosmos replicated a mode of self-representation current in the Levant and Mesopotamia in the first millennium BC, with roots going back to second Millennium Sumer[46]. Moreover, this broader context reveals critical aspects of the genealogical continuum that informed the Greek concept of prehistorical time. Competitive and mutually exclusive narratives specializing in cultural history took the primordial cosmos as their point of departure, focusing on the rise of *one* civilization in a world manifestly populated by many. A key aim of such narratives was to depict a particular culture as preeminent above others, a feature clearly expressed in each extant case. Common to all was the role of prehistory in prefiguring the lives of indigenous audiences and the use of genealogy as a schematic aid in the ideological construction of the cultural past[47]. Above all, such accounts institutionalized sacred rituals, galvanized public patriotism, and promoted social cohesion. They were powerfully real in the realm of religious practice, cultural consciousness, and lived experience, but they openly coexisted with equivalent proposals that told the origin stories observed by neighboring peoples, which was in some sense transparent to participants on all sides, if scarcely intuitive from a modern standpoint. Apparently, for example, birth-of-the-cosmos narratives could be taken seriously without being taken literally, which is such an anti-modern idea that it is easily liable to misunderstanding[48].

On account of the function they served by convention, high order national charters of the type at stake here, were exempt from normative standards of rationality and granted a special invincible status, which they sustained for all intents and purposes. This meant that they were, in a formal sense true, quite apart from the fact that much of their content was incompatible with lived experience, or for that matter, with common sense. The reason for this appears to stem from such narratives' jurisdiction over an extraordinary formative world held to precede contemporary lived reality and vital to the mystique of the rise of the nation[49]. So while the nature of this approach to the past embroiled culture in certain untenable truths, if untenable, such truths remained unassailable, partly since they were set back into the mists of time, but otherwise due to the preeminent status of the stories which followed this ancient paradigm and their vital role in everyday life[50].

Evidently, early Greek mythic tradition also abided by this popular paradigm and became, for this reason, so indispensable to any operative concept of Greek cultural history that it was in a sense fundamentally immune to the attacks of later critics and analysts. On this basis, it could be argued that these individuals, like Xenophanes of Kolophon in the sixth century[51], the Sophists in the fifth[52], or Plato in the fourth[53], were primarily interested in clearing some ground for their own agendas and calling attention to their own aims. These critics, at any rate, got a great deal of leverage from the limitations inherent in the traditional canon, which they were perhaps not, on close inspection, actually seeking to dislodge. However, to the extent that symbolic mytho-genesis was a cultural imperative, not a religious dogma, played out in a bygone alternate world, it tacitly delineated an expanse of free space for alternative modes of philosophical inquiry. Along these lines, by contrast, it is plausible to suggest that the work of the sixth-century Ionian rationalists arose in response to, but was not directed against the traditional narratives on the birth of the cosmos. Rather, since the traditional narratives on the birth of the cosmos provided the customary point of departure for the cultural origin of various peoples and, therefore, in a sense, were not really meant to account for the birth of the cosmos at all, a group of Greek intellectuals were evidently inspired to address the problem on empirical grounds. Meanwhile, notwithstanding, from an ethical standpoint, symbolic mythogenesis was almost bound to inspire a measure of critical disapproval because its reliance on mythic motifs in conjunction with its commitment to structural hierarchy (that in turn relied on memorable and fantastic deeds on the part of the gods as on the part of the heroes) challenged normative social and moral precepts and favored the use of extravagant misconduct as a leading narrative catalyst[54].

Symbolic mytho-genesis created the nation. It was the aitiological source of Greek state religion and the arbiter of piety between the Greeks and their gods. In complete consistency with its internal logic it harked back to a time when humans were more like gods and gods were reciprocally very much like humans. Symbolic mytho-genesis commanded allegiance, regulated civic and political identity, and established the basis for pious behavior in the realm of accepted ritual practice, but it did not barter in abstract ideas, it did not favor virtue over vice, nor did it even purport to explain how it was that the cosmos came into existence. Beyond this, seeing that symbolic mytho-genesis made no attempt to explain or to justify the unknown, if for no other reason than such concerns lay outside the scope of its main objectives, it is reasonable to conclude that the dynamics involved are very far from akin to the conflict between science and theology as we know it.

In adopting the venerated eastern mode of genealogical representation that created civilization metaphorically and traced it from its inception down to the period that immediately preceded the present-day, the Greeks of Aiolis conceived of themselves both in relation to, and competitively against, the inhabitants of the hinterland and the Levant. In this respect, it is important to emphasize that the Greeks were the underdogs in this early period and in terms of discernible historical content, this is the sort of political actuality that can be detected in Greek mythic reportage. The Iliadic characterization of Troy is imbued with admiration and awe for the wealth and prestige of Trojan culture. Phoinikians and Egyptians surface in the same vein. The caveat to this as construed in the *Iliad* is a pre-destined shift from Trojan to Greek supremacy signified by the sack of Troy. The force this shift commands throughout the course of the story rests on its impending inevitability, which is all the more remarkable given the fact that Troy is still standing at the end of the *Iliad*'s book twenty-four. The greatness of the Greek victory, predicted time and again, is intimately connected to the manifest greatness of the enemy of Greek enemies, the city of Troy. Relative to this emphasis it is also worthy of notice the way that various off-shoots of the Aiolic line interacted with two illustrious foreign families, depicted as immigrants to Greece from the East: the lines of Kadmos and Pelops, respectively[55]. The high profile status of these immigrant lines again corresponds with the initial tenor of *east – west* relations in the early epic period.

By contrast, a clear shift in Greek attitudes toward the East crystallized in the post Persian War period, replete with culturally chauvinistic innuendo and a series of antithetical *east – west* stereotypes that become standard shorthand for Greek superiority[56]. Also relevant to this perceptual shift was the decline of the Greek cities in Asia Minor following a botched attempt at rebellion from Persia in the fiasco known as the Ionian Revolt[57]. Henceforth, the leading cities of the Greek mainland and prospering colonies further a field became the bastions of political power and centers of intellectual and artistic trends. The literary evidence from the ensuing period is widely acknowledged for its Athenocentricity. This documentary bent is intensified by retroactive Athenian reinterpretations of history that justified Athenian imperialist aims[58]. As exemplified on the Athenian stage, the reinterpretation of history in this period was tantamount to the reinterpretation of legend. This was mainly because Greek legend held sway over the bulk of historical time, but also because civic identity hinged on the famous exploits of the Heroic Age.

The diminishing reverence for eastern culture was a gradual process bound up with the rise of Greek self-confidence in the Archaic Period. The greater the prestige of Greek centers of culture, the less the deference to venerable eastern legacies. Still, clear vestiges of early Greek admiration for eastern antiquity and eastern achievements remained influential in the later fifth century as Herodotus shows, by way of example, with his controversial insistence that Egypt was the source of most if not all Greek religious tradition. Herodotus' convictions evidently derived from a profound awareness that Greek culture was most notable for its relative youth (Hdt.2.53[59]). At the same time, however, Herodotus articulates a major fifth century shift in Greek attitudes abetted by the victories in the Persian Wars. The ascendance of Greece under Athens and Sparta informed every aspect of Herodotus' report. His text, like all texts, was a product of his age, and his age was the age of a new Greek supremacy in contrast to circumstances of bygone days and an assortment of intermediary configurations of power.

Homer and Herodotus, in this light, register different outlooks on the East roughly three hundred years distant from one another. The two texts in question legitimately suggest two definitive points on a time line with respect to prevailing popular opinions about the Greeks themselves and their eastern neighbors. Homeric Greek glory was a survival strategy; an instance of bold and competitive thinking among Greeks in a volatile political situation on the western fringe of eastern civilization. Herodotean Greek glory was a *fait accompli* viewed from the perspective of Athenian sovereignty.

Using Homeric epic and fifth century literature as two points on a chart of mythological developments the former commands authoritative status by virtue of being the earliest testimony to the tradition that has been preserved, while the latter represents the intervention of Athens as a power eventually powerful enough to commandeer the fate of the mythological record. Between these two extremities a stream of events occurred, involving distinct lead players among the Greek city-states, each intent on self-serving political aims, which conventionally demanded mythological backing. Before Athens' involvement in politics outside Attica, states like Argos, Corinth, Sparta, and Megara jockeyed for prominence throughout the Greek world and competed for mythological recognition. Economic and political inter-state competition was, in this regard, consistently paralleled by competition in the realm of myth.

These intervening events left decisive imprints on the surviving mythological record often corroborating independent evidence on the interests and fortunes of the states involved. New state-sponsored initiatives in the mythic arena tended to acknowledge the latest emendations put forth by other influential centers of power. Depending on their capacity to direct public opinion, the mythological novelties advanced by various states were accepted or rejected by their contemporaries. The former were fit into the revised mythic canon, the latter were either forced out of circulation, or contributed to the white noise in the background created by dissenting provincial claims. Amidst all this activity, legendary innovation never ceased to depend on the early epic foundations that originally set the whole process in motion with the establishment of a Hellenic cultural creed. The underlying idea has been frequently stated: mythological narratives must keep in step with changing times otherwise they are destined to extinction[60].

Throughout my encounter with the Greek mythic evidence, I have seen that the only really effective way to make contact with the dissemination of meaning attributed by the Greeks to Greek mythic tradition is through observations directed at the construction of the entire Greek mythic system as opposed to any particular part. As it happens, questions of structure and questions of function do not generate comparably coherent results through the analysis of Greek myths in isolation, in conjunction with similar or dissimilar myths, or based on the characteristics of any set group of stories selected according to any criteria. I am by now convinced the main reason for this is that the fundamental objectives assigned to Greek mythology were implemented initially on a systemic level so that inquiries concerning the nature of those objectives can only be accessed from a systemic viewpoint based on diachronic genealogical patterning. To use the schematization of Claude Lévi-Strauss, an active deep mythic structure can indeed be identified. That structure was genealogical and took the form a web of symbolic interrelations strategically organized by design[61]. But, in playing the role of deep mythic structure, far from exhibiting semantic autonomy with respect to the workings of narrative surface structure, genealogy and narrative – the deep and surface structures, respectively – operated in tandem on behalf of a single appointed systemic objective, namely, the aggrandization of Greek prehistory and the reputation of the Greeks.

In this situation it is important to bear in mind that each constituent myth in the overall framework was always in a sense more a means to an end than an inherently meaningful end in itself. This observation, however, only holds true when Greek myth is addressed on a systemic level – thus, in terms of the narrative-genealogical synthesis that governed the construction of Greek cultural identity. In this respect, the construction of Greek identity made no claims against its constituent legends' serviceability in other venues as objects of contemplation, objects of worship, objects of criticism, or objects of art, which also partly explains why the project itself lies buried in the expanse of its systemic structure and is, in this sense, difficult to ascertain.

Incorporating the study of mythic motifs, their conventional use and their conventional attributes, with the idiosyncracies of the Greek Heroic Age, and the systemic emphasis under consideration, conspire to undermine the use of Greek mythology as a source of historical information and shed light on the distortion of normative codes of conduct on behalf of a greater cultural cause. This is not to suggest that the Greek mythic stories were devoid of meaningful aesthetic or sociological resonance. But to suggest rather, that emphasis on considerations like these generates a smoke screen that in turn obstructs access to the bare-bones operation of genealogical structure deployed in the service of cultural identity.

The suggested working hypothesis would seem to recommend a few slight adjustments to the leading definitions that respond to the question: what is a Greek myth[62]? For the purposes of this analysis I would incline toward something along the following lines. A Greek myth is any one of the collection of stories devoted to the telling of Greek prehistory – that is, the period from the birth of the gods down to the end of the Heroic Age. These stories, in general, were never generic, but cite specific places and named protagonists, and in so doing participate in the larger project of mapping legendary ancestries onto the contemporary political landscape. A Greek myth is essentially a constituent element in the ancient Greek definition of being Greek, whereas the ancient Greek definition of being Greek was a long drawn out genealogically structured story subject to change in accordance with changing times.

THE ANCIENT SOURCES

A few words on the sequence of chapters that follow in terms of the treatment of the ancient evidence. The leading premise of this analysis is that Greek mythological emendation was a fundamentally reactive impulse, inspired by Homeric mythological precedents and, in this regard, politically motivated. Toward this end, two perspectives break down the ancient evidence qualitatively into parts one and two: first, a detailed look at select genealogies from the fully developed Greek mythic corpus (in the fragmented form that it has passed down to us) in comparison with their Homeric counterparts; and second, a detailed look at Homeric mythology (reinforced by the outlook of Hesiod's *Theogony* and, presumably, other lost epic accounts that circulated in the earliest period) in comparison with popular later myths. In this context, the aim of the first three chapters is to survey recurrent patterns of mythological change that surface in southern Greece in the Archaic Period, and stand at odds with the outlook of the Homeric poems. The verification of these patterns relies on material drawn from all available sources, thus from the Homeric Hymns, the lyric poets, the fifth-century historians (with the fragments of their contemporaries and their successors), the surviving work of the Attic playwrights and orators, and valuable statements preserved in later authors, with those of anonymous commentators and analysts.

The following two chapters build upon the first three by way of a survey of Homeric mythology that corroborates specific distinctions between Homeric and post-Homeric mythological thinking. These distinctions are shown to stem from the fact that the Homeric versions of the Greek myths predate the political integration of subsequently powerful southern Greek city-states into the Homeric mythological system, which was, evidently, derivative of early East Greek Aiolic patriotic initiatives. The last chapter synthesizes both perspectives by taking a final look at the mythological problems that result from the clash of political priorities current in these two phases of Greek mythic development. The concluding synthesis details the interpretive changes that were brought to bear on an old and venerable heroic lineage in order to bridge the conceptual divide[63].

Here then, the Homeric / post-Homeric division spotlights two distinct phases in the history of Greek myth, and is in essence the most important distinction as far as the Aiolic hypothesis is concerned. Still, this temporal division no doubt fails to account for the complexity of the historical continuum that the term post-Homeric necessarily implies. The post-Homeric Period is therefore broken down further into three distinct periods: 1) that of the earliest mainland response to the dissemination of Homeric poetry, which surfaces first in the Peloponnese; 2) that of the influential Athenian response to prior Peloponnesian mythic creativity, including Athenocentric amendments and additions; 3) and lastly, that of retrospective mythic chroniclers who frequently interject post-Classical innovations, yet fundamentally still abide by the mythological claims of the Classical Period after the intervention of Athens.

It is clear this third-category could be broken down further and traced chronologically into the Byzantine Period when ancient texts coexisted with Christian doctrine for the education of the literary elite. Yet doing so lies beyond the scope of this project and is also unnecessary for present purposes. In short, while Greek mythology remained vulnerable to creative enhancements down to the time when ancient tradition ceased to be a factor in everyday life, it can also be observed that all subsequent work relied on mainstream Archaic and Classical contributions that were superimposed onto Homeric foundations, resulting in a second canon of sorts. Common to all third-category authors was a retrospective relationship to early Greek myth. Thus, the main preoccupation of third-category authors in terms of the transmission of early Greek myth was primarily editorial decision making. On this basis these authors may be addressed as a group, zeroing in on the preferences expressed in their work through their respective treatments of the Greek mythic canon.

Given the fragmentary nature of the evidence, it has long been customary to use later authors to offset huge gaps in the early mythological evidence. It is also widely acknowledged that later authors frequently transmit significant early data, having many more texts at their disposal than the number that have survived to this day. These authors, moreover, lived and worked at a time when Greek mythology was still a living tradition or, at the very least, still fulfilling the role of the ultimate discourse on Greek prehistory. So by way of example, Diodoros of Sicily, writing in the 1st century BC, was still actively engaged in the systematization of the elaborate mythological tangents that had developed in Sicily and southern Italy and derived from the dominant canon in Greece. Pausanias, by contrast, roughly three centuries later, exemplifies a perceptibly more detached mindset that can best be described as antiquarian. Still, the reality was, even in this period that the level of interest remained very high because the whole Greek prehistorical era was still couched in terms of the most famous stories that had been recited from Homer onward[64]; accordingly, the entire Greek landscape was strewn with manifest traces of their ancient occurrence.

In terms of the general practice of consulting later authors, it will become clear in due course that this procedure is somewhat less of a problem in the present context, since the Aiolic hypothesis sorts all later material according to a single leading criterion, namely whether a given story is Aiolic or not. And this is actually a fairly reliable criterion because the political influence of the Aiolians was generally negligible in the historical period[65]. What requires greater attention in this particular case are the ways in which later authors navigated their way through the quagmire of conflicting accounts to create reasonably coherent myth-historical narratives. This inevitably required a complex selection process that was on the one hand, purely idiosyncratic and yet on the other (if not precisely for this reason) led various ancient authors time and again to make reference to deviant legendary traditions (viz. traditions that contradicted the fifth-century canon) that stemmed back to the reign of Aiolic legend.

In the end, therefore, post-Classical testimony reflects the constant demand for editorial choices as to which traditions to excise and which traditions to favor, and how to address the most glaring contradictions so that they could be effectively processed and, ideally, to some degree resolved.

² Fick dated the dialect transposition to Kynaithos of Chios in the late sixth century.

³ Cf. C.D. Buck, *The Greek Dialects* 1910; H.M. Chadwick 1912; C.M. Bowra 1930. For more recent work on the subject, see L.H. Jeffrey 1961; J.A. Davison and L.R. Palmer in Wace and Stubbings, eds. 1962: chs. 4, 6-7; R. Janko 1982; J. Bennet and G. Horrocks in I. Morris and B. Powell, eds. 1997; M. Finkelberg 1994, 2005.

⁴ viz. an Iron Age versus a Bronze Age tradition.

⁵ George Grote, *History of Greece*, 12 volumes 1846-1856. William Geddes, *The Problem of the Homeric Poems* 1878. Related propositions may be traced to the work of Giambattista Vico (e.g. *La Scienza Nuova Seconda* 1730) and Gottfried Hermann (*De interpolationibus Homeri* 1832)

⁶ The Aiolic Greeks inhabited two regions: in northern Greece, Boiotia and Thessaly; in Asia Minor, the region around the city of Troy, roughly from the island of Lesbos to the Hellespont, and extending somewhat to the east from there.

⁷ In 1886 the work at Mykenai was taken over by the newly founded *Greek Archaeological Service* under the direction of Christos Tsoundas, cf. C. Tsoundas & J.I. Manatt 1897.

⁸ E. Bethe *Thebanische Heldenlieder* 1891; P. Cauer *Grundfragen der Homerkritik* 1895; R. Jebb *Homer: an Introduction to the Iliad and Odyssey* 1887, *JHS* 3 1882; U. von Wiliamowitz-Moellendorf *Homerische Untersuchungen* 1884.

⁹ That is, tracing the origins of Homeric tradition to the period immediately prior to the composition of the Homeric poems.

¹⁰ *Studies on Homer* 1858; *Homeric Synchronism* 1876;

¹¹ *Companion to the Iliad* 1892; *Troy: A Study in Homeric Geography* 1912; *Homer and History* 1915.

¹² *Homer and the Epic* 1895; *Homer and His Age* 1906.

¹³ viz. placing the origins of Homeric poetry at least four hundred years earlier than the emergence of the poems themselves. I. Morris describes the gradual conversion of a few prominent skeptics during the first half of the twentieth century, J.B. Bury providing the most graphic example in his publications over two decades' time (1997: 108-110).

¹⁴ So also, for example, A.D. Momigliano's portrait of George Grote and his role in the study of Ancient Greek History (Univ. College London 1952), reprinted in G.W. Bowersock and T.J. Cornell, eds. *A.D. Momigliano Studies in Modern Scholarship*, Berkeley 1994.

¹⁵ This conviction was based on Arthur Evan's discovery of non-alphabetic inscriptions on Krete presented at Oxford in 1894. Evan's discovery was subsequently enhanced by Mykenaian – Egyptian synchron-ologies based on the work of the Egyptologist, Flinders Petrie, in the late 1880s and early 1890s (including the inscriptions of Ramses III – c. 1184-1153 – carved into the temple of Medinet Habu, which initiated the theory of the so-called Sea Peoples, associated with the chaos and widespread destruction that took place the end of the Bronze Age). The presumed existence of Bronze Age written editions of the Homeric poems surfaces, for example, in the work of Andrew Lang and T.W. Allen. This viewpoint, however, was soon rendered obsolete as a result of two groundbreaking developments that came to light in the first half of the twentieth century, namely: Milman Parry and Albert Lord's formulation of oral poetry theory based on their work with south Slavic bards, and Michael Ventris' decipherment of the Linear B script, which J.L. Myres promoted for publication shortly before his death in 1954 (Myres put Ventris in touch with J. Chadwick at Oxford, see D. Gray's epilogue in J.L. Myres 1958: 265).

INTRODUCTION

---

[16] Cf. Myres' *Who Were the Greeks?* New York: 1930.

[17] Thus, Homeric poetry was a recollection of an actual ancient conflict in which a host of Greek warriors from the mainland attacked and defeated the city of Troy.

[18] Prior to Schliemann's excavations, Homeric poetry was typically situated between the end of the Trojan War (generally dated 1184 via the calculation attributed to Erotosthenes of Kyrene) and the mythological *return of the Herakleidai*, which was popularly identified with the infiltration of Hellenic Dorians from the north. Ignorance of this "invasion" in the Homeric poems in contrast with its top billing in later Greek literature was held to be a decisive chronological factor, just as the Homeric absence of Greek habitation along the Asia Minor coast was understood to reveal manifest ignorance of subsequent Greek migrations into that region. In the period after Schliemann's discoveries Homeric composition was still placed in this period. Yet, the poetry itself, from that point onward, was understood to reflect real life situations associated with the palatial culture administered from great Bronze Age strongholds such as Pylos, Mykenai, and Tiryns. Thus, the same basic chronological scheme maintained its position in the service of primarily Bronze Age poetic content, however, giving new weight to the intervening period between the Bronze Age and the historical times (defined by the emergence of the Homeric poems) that became known as the Greek "Dark Ages." The Dark Ages were essential to Bronze Age theory as the scarcely known era that one way or another Homeric poetry had to pass through in order for professional bards to recount outstanding Bronze Age events hundreds of years later in eighth century Ionia. This theory of long-term survival and transmission has only recently begun to attract further scrutiny (e.g. J.M. Hall 1997). Basically, on either side of the rift generated by Schliemann discoveries, the distinct lack of a functioning critical apparatus to address the relationship between Greek myth and Greek history is conspicuous in much of the secondary literature. Whereas the straightforward treatment of myth as history is more obvious in the nineteenth-century texts published before Grote's *History of Greece*, and again, after the intervention of Schliemann, the notion of legendary kernels of truth that facilitates endless interpretive permutations remains influential to this day (e.g. J.K. Anderson in J.B. Carter and S.P. Morris, eds. 1995).

[19] A popular concept of the European Enlightenment as anticipated by Thomas Hobbes (*Leviathan* 1651), and exemplified in the works of John Locke (e.g. *Second Treatise of Civil Government* 1689), David Hume (e.g. *The Natural History of Religion* 1755), and Jean-Jacques Rousseau (*On the Social Contract* 1762), among theorists committed to grounding their work on the concept of man in a state of nature. The notion took on a life of its own in the realm of mythological interpretation, where its influence can be identified in such diverse authors as C.G. Heyne, K.O. Müller, Sigmund Freud, and Ernst Cassirer.

[20] A concept that frequently played a role in the popular theoretical antithesis held to distinguish Science from Religion. According to this view, anything mythological is firmly placed in the second category and stands in opposition to the first (so, especially, Edward Tylor and James Frazer).

[21] Most notably represented by the *Cambridge School* with James Frazer (*The Golden Bough* 1st ed. 1890) and Jane Harrison (*Themis* 1912) at the vanguard. For an incisive critique of the ensuing debate on the relationship between Greek myth and Greek ritual, see H.S. Versnel in L. Edmonds, ed. 1990; compare, however, W. Burkert 1970.

[22] This is equally true of historicist treatments which capitalized on the ancient *communis opinio* that Greek myth was equivalent to Greek prehistory. As Fritz Graf points out, theorists who choose to endorse this view are forced to negate Greek mythology's most important characteristics, often resorting to allegoresis and various quasi-Euhemerist tactics (1993: 30). For accessible basic surveys on the intellectual history of mythological thought, see for example, F. Graf 1993; R. A. Segal 2004.

²³ There were in the interim a few prominent exceptions to the dominant historicist point of view. So, for example, J. Beloch (*Griechische Geschichte* 1893), who denied the historicity of the *Dorian Invasion* (contra E. Meyer, *Geschichte des Alterums* in the same year), and J. Burckhardt, who advanced the (at that time) eccentric approach of tracing influential historical attitudes over historical events and personalities.

²⁴ *Geschichte der Kunst des Alterums* 1764.

²⁵ See especially, I. Morris 1994: 15-35; and now, K. Vlassopoulos 2007; also, A. Momigliano's biographical portraits of E.A. Freeman and J.G. Droysen. For a more polemical account, see M. Bernal 1987. Not surprisingly, Hellenism took on various forms in the course of its historically formative role in Classical Philology as a discipline. Thus, it was as vehemently supported by political conservatives (e.g. William Mitford, *History of Greece* 1784-1810; Fustel de Coulanges, *La cité antique* 1864, A. Momigliano and S.C. Humphreys, ed. 1980; Jacob Burckhardt *Griechische Kulturgeschichte*, posthumous lectures 1872-1885, O. Murray, ed., trans. S.Stern 1998;), as by those with markedly liberal sympathies (paradigmatically, G. Grote), naturally resulting in very different perspectives on the legacies of Ancient Greece and Rome. Conspicuously, given the ideological cachet of "democracy" in current American parlance, the dominant consensus on that aspect of the Greek legacy was predominantly negative till the late twentieth century all the while European Hellenism was at its height (see also, M. Herzfeld 1981; R. Clogg 1992, including relevant coverage on the Greek War of Independence). The main issue here is the use of the ancient texts and the types of evidence they can be held to support. For a finite analysis that judiciously negotiates between the indispensable value of textual sources and the level of caution they also demand, see W.A.P. Childs 1993; More generally, R. Osborne 1996.

²⁶ I. Morris 1994; A. Snodgrass 2006; B. Trigger 1989/2006.

²⁷ e.g. Albert Lord 1960; A. Parry 1966.

²⁸ *Folk Tale, Fiction and Saga in the Homeric Epics. Sather Classical Lectures vol. 20.* Berkeley: University of California Press 1946. Notably, however, by way of comparison, see D.L. Page, *History and the Homeric Iliad. Sather Classical Lectures vol. 31.* Berkeley 1959.

²⁹ So especially, *Historia* 6 1957: 133-159 repr. in *Economy and Society in Ancient Greece* New York: 1982; & (1964) with J.L Caskey, G.S. Kirk and D.L. Page in "The Trojan War" *JHS* 84 1-20; *The Use and Abuse of History* 1986: ch.1.

³⁰ On this topic, E. Hobsbawm and T. Ranger 1983; E. Gruen, *TAPA* 123 1993: 1-14.

³¹ The work of Filippo Cassola (1953) on Greek myth, genealogy, and Greek identity seems to come closest to the perspective advanced in this analysis.

[32] So, especially, M.L. West 1978: 29-30, 137ff.; also, M.P. Nilsson 1932: ch.1; H.J. Rose 1959: 182; G.S. Kirk 1962: 40-41, 121; J. Bremmer in J. Bremmer, ed. 1987: 2; G. Nagy 1990: ch.3; C. Brillante in L. Edmonds, ed. 1992; K. Dowden 1992: 69; J.M. Hall 1997: 97; R. Fowler 1998; J.S. Burgess 2001: 173; M. Finkelberg 2005: ch.2. Traces of the current separate-cycles-hypothesis can be identified in certain previous contexts, stemming back to the work of C.G. Heyne and J.G. Herder and their emphasis on the connection between specific groups of myths and specific peoples and places. This is no doubt a valid and extremely important point. Yet, when applied to the Greek historical context, this formulaic connection comes up against a nexus of distinct ethnic and regional identities in contrast to a coherent national consciousness. As argued here, this perspective becomes problematic when applied straightforwardly to the Greek case, since the historical circumstances of the Archaic Period worked to conceal the influence of an antecedent mytho-political landscape. The correlation suggested by Heyne and Herder was more comprehensively evaluated by Karl Otfried Müller, who associated the process of Greek mythic dispersal with the political development of the Greek city-states, and eventually with the Greek recognition of a common identity as Greeks or Hellenes. Thus, Müller's perspective can be understood to anticipate the current separate-cycles hypothesis (*Prolegomena zu einer wissenshaftlichen Mythologie* 1825; cf. W.W. Briggs and William Calder III 1990; F. Graf 1993 22-23; on Greek ethnicity / nationality cf. F.W. Walbank *Phoinix* 5 1951: 41-60, and more recently I. Malkin, ed. 2001).

[33] e.g. M.L. West 1978: 41; J.M. Hall 1997: 48, 56, 64; R.L. Fowler 1998: 8-9. Among contemporary analysts concerned with the status of the Aiolic genealogies of northern and central Greece, this region is variously described as the source: of the Hellenic genealogy (viz. that stemmed via Deukalion to the eponymous Hellen, e.g. J.M. Hall 2002: 134-171; I Rutherford in R. Hunter, ed. 2005); of the Hesiodic *Catalogue of Women* (R.L. Fowler op.cit); and of the Homeric poems themselves (R. Drews 1979a; B. Powell in Morris and Powell, eds. 1997).

[34] Background circumstances of this order cannot be conclusively determined.

[35] The stories that gave the city of Athens a prestigious intermediary role in the Ionian migration to Asia Minor.

[36] It is notable in this context that the Ionians of the *Iliad* evidently hailed from central Greece just south of the mainland-Greek Aiolic territories (Il.685-688). This point is dealt with at length later in this report.

[37] The Homeric use of these terms is also dealt with below. Suffice it to say, in the present context, that the Achaians were equivalent to Aiolians from a genealogical point of view.

[38] R. Rutherford continues, "The Hesiodic Catalogues illustrate a widespread interest in mythical genealogy, but firm evidence that families traced their ancestry back to mythical heroes comes from a later period, when heroic epics are already assuming canonical status. For Homer and his predecessors, the glorious past matters more than reflected glory in the present (1996: 4-5)." Also, on this topic, M.L. West 1978: *ch.1 The Nature of the Catalogue*.

[39] See L. Edmonds in I. Morris and B. Powell, eds. 1997: 418, for the acknowledgment of a shortage of analysis on the function of myth in Homer (in contrast to questions of mythic origins and issues of religious and historical significance). See also, A. Henrichs for a critique of the value of a "mythographical approach" to the Greek mythic data (J. Bremmer, ed. 1987).

[40] Though, I personally side with those who place Hesiod after Homer (e.g. R. Janko1982; I. Morris 1986; J.P. Crielaard 1995; R. Fowler 1998; K. Dowden in R. Fowler, ed. 2004: 195-6).

[41] M.L. West *The Orphic Poems*, Oxford 1983.

⁴² viz. contra Rutherford as quoted above, e.g., Hesiod, *Works and Days* 299; Hdt.2.143 on Hekataios of Miletos, 5.57-58 on the Gephyraioi (viz. descendants of the Phoinicians who sailed with Kadmos): two of the numerous cases in which prominent clans derived their origin from heroic ancestors. Thus the Agid and Eurypontid Spartan kings considered themselves descendants of Herakles. The Athenian family of Miltiades and Kimon (that included Thucydides, the historian), promoted connections with the line of Aias, the Peisistratids and the Alkmaionidai with Neleids from Pylos; the Eteobutadai with Erechtheus, the Thymoitadoi with Theseus and so on and so forth. Likewise, according to later biographical traditions, Epaminondas of Thebes was considered one of the Spartoi, Philip the II a descendant of Herakles, his wife Olympias, and later, Pyrros of Epeiros were acclaimed descendants of Achilles, Plato was judged a descendant of Poseidon, Aristotle a descendant of Asklepios (cf. J. Burckhardt 1998: ch.2).

⁴³ Notwithstanding certain contradictory claims, such as the various descriptions of the city of Nysa – the alleged birthplace of the god Dionysos (notably born to a mortal mother) – to the effect that it is completely unclear where such a place was traditionally located.

⁴⁴ So, A. Giovannini in J. Emlen, A. Molho, and K. Raaflaub, eds. 1991.

⁴⁵ viz., the system set out in Hesiod's *Theogony*. Within the Greek cosmos, it may be observed that the farther into the past an ancient narrative setting, the more intense the mythical symbolism, which is to say, the more prehistoric the more phantasmagorical and the less deferential to plausibility or to historical protocol. While there is correspondingly, no guarantee that mythic narratives set in the more recent past were any more accurate for being less miraculous (see C. Calame in Buxton, ed. 1999). In terms of the more distant mythological past, C. Sourvinou-Inwood offers an astute analysis of divine aggression against heroic malefactors who abused their close contact with the gods (1986). The more proximate past is well represented by the most famous stories of the Heroic Age.

⁴⁶ With or without a literal scriptural corpus. On Greece and the Near East, cf. J. Boardman 1964; W. Burkert in Bremmer, ed. 1986; R. Mondi in L. Edmonds, ed. 1990; G. Kopke and I. Tokumaru, eds. 1992; S. Morris in I. Morris and B. Powell, eds. 1997; M.L. West 1966, 1997; M. Finkelberg and G. Stroumsa 2003.

⁴⁷ viz. A cultural cannon with or without the authority vested in scriptural texts, compare R. Lamberton in M. Finkelberg and G. Stroumsa.

⁴⁸ There are two main points here: that the literal interpretation of sacred tradition popular now in the twenty-first century was not standard practice in antiquity (even in the presence of revered written scripture); and that the religious aspects of a given cultural creed could well provoke intellectual controversy (so, especially in the Greek case), but evidently did not provoke violent aggression under ancient polytheistic conditions. This supports the idea that the type of religious dogma that rose to prominence in the current era was not in effect in pre-Christian antiquity. For additional observations on counter-intuitive aspects of the ancient Greek outlook on issues such as these, see, for example, J. Gould in Easterling and Muir, eds. 1985; A. Henrichs in T.H. Carpenter and C.A. Faraone, eds. 1993; C. Calame in Buxton, ed. 1999. For another assessment of these types of issues, see S.C. Humphreys 1978: ch.9.

⁴⁹ *Genesis* offers a familiar comparison.

⁵⁰ In Plato's *Hippias Major*, Hippias emphasizes the continuous demand for genealogical stories about great heroes and the founding of ancient cities among his Spartan clientele (285e). At *Poetics* 14606b Aristotle remarks that people, in general, inevitably follow the traditional (poetic) accounts of the gods.

[51] Xenophanes' notorious accusations against Homer and Hesiod's portrayal of the gods were evidently based on ethical objections, which also seem to have been the main impetus for the philosophical critique of popular tradition. The Greek historians, by contrast, were more concerned with finding rational ways to limit the impact of especially fantastic traditional stories, whereas Xenophanes' contemporaries on the Ionian seaboard advanced a non-mythological mode of inquiry that removed divine agency from explanatory hypotheses in the name of empirical observation. While the sixth century Ionian rationalist movement is often described as a scientific revolt against traditional Greek religion, there are persuasive reasons to view the movement instead as entirely compatible with Greek tradition, however, operative on a completely different plane. In this regard, the Ionian rationalists focused on major issues that Greek tradition made no satisfactory attempt address (ironically, for example, the origin of the cosmos). Unlike thinkers concerned with ethical issues, the natural philosophers apparently saw no reason to acknowledge the traditional poetic cosmos at all. This would tend to support the hypothesis that the real clash between poetry and philosophy was fundamentally played out over ethical issues (notably including theological ethics, viz. the status and behavior of the gods). Even so, it would seem, the traditional canon was at no time exposed to any serious threat. On Xenophanes, E. Diehl *Anthologia* vol. 1; A.B. Drachmann 1922; C.M. Bowra 1960; More generally, G.S. Kirk & J.E. Raven 1964; L.P. Gerson 1990. On the Homeric portrait of the gods, see W.K.C. Guthrie 1950; A. Lesky 1961; M.M. Wilcock 1979; E. Kearns in R. Fowler, ed. 2004. On Hesiod's mentality, in particular, see W.G. Thalmann 1984. For Herodotus' point of view, cf. N. Luraghi, J. Romm, and S. Scullion in C. Dewald and J. Marincola, Cambridge, 2006.

[52] cf. W.K.C. Guthrie 1971.

[53] e.g. Republic 377a-398b. Plato's chief concern was divine perfection. It was strictly in violation of this ideal that he was moved to censor the gods and heroes (demi-gods) of the poets. So for example at 391d, in Socrates' Πολιτεία it will not be permitted to say that Theseus, son of Poseidon, and Peirithoos, son of Zeus, engaged in any kind of dreadful kidnappings. Socrates rejects their bad deeds, but not their existence, nor the authority of heroic tradition (cf. S. Halliwell 1984, particularly in terms of Plato's use and investment in sustaining a great rivalry between poetry and philosophy). On the rationalization of traditional myths, cf. R. Drews 1973, on Hekataios of Miletos; J. Stern, in R. Buxton 1999, on the work of Palaiphatos, with G. Most's contribution in the same volume. On the dominant early status of mythological speech, see B. Lincoln 1997. The remarks of Herodotus (3.122) and Thukydides (1.4) on King Minos of Krete are also instructive.

54 Notably, the idea of a religious framework that was not accompanied by an ethical code (at least not in a familiar or straightforward way) represents another counter-intuitive phenomenon essential to making sense of the Greek situation. I do not mean to suggest that Homeric epic was devoid of coherent ethical standards, but rather to suggest that conspicuous aspects of the Homeric epic world view were necessarily incompatible with real life conditions and cultural norms. For this reason I favor A. A. Long's perspective in the field of Homeric ethics (1970) over the contributions of A. Adkins (1960, 1971), and in general maintain a more skeptical view than theorists engaged in the reconstruction of Homeric society from the Homeric poems (e.g.. M. Finley 1954; I. Morris 1986; K. Raaflaub in I. Morris and B. Powell, eds 1997). So, for example, the designation *heroic* in some sense corresponds to the term *aristocratic*, however, inasmuch as the poems depict a thoroughly homogeneous distribution of power among illustrious leaders of great households / clans (not excluding the widely denigrated Thersites, cf. B. Lincoln 1994: ch.2), they do not provide an accurate reading of genuine socio-economic conditions and, in particular, do not represent the kind of class conflict associated with the emergence of the Greek city-states. Rather, this idealized picture that was meant to unfold prior to the onset of the contemporary human era may well provide a measure of insight on the competitive behavior of real-time Hellenic elites, yet its idealized ethos was likewise responsible for its transcendental appeal across class or status, political, and geographical boundaries, as a folk tradition charged with the preservation of a comprehensive collective cultural identity. For a concise account of what can be discerned of the operative social structure in the Homeric poems (consistent also with Hesiod's *Works and Days*), based strictly on the available poetic evidence and, thus, cautiously excluding preconceptions derived from later political circumstances, see W. Donlan 1985. Donlan's insights concerning the epic use of such terms as: οἶκος, δῆμος, λαός, ἔθνος, φῦλον, and, φρήτρη make it possible to anchor heroic idealization within a realistic cultural setting that preceded the emergence of the Greek polis as a coherent and functional political entity, and makes sense of the anonymous contingents of followers that devoted their allegiance to the respective chiefs. Cf. J. Lenz, diss., Columbia, 1993.

55 For another assessment of the role of Kadmos, see R. Buxton 1994: 184-193. For another assessment of the role of Pelops, see J.M. Hall 1997: 89-91.

56 e.g. E. Hall 1989; T. Harrison, ed. 2002.

57 Hdt. 5.30-38, 40-51, 55, 97-126. In comparison with the evidence on mainland Greece, there is significantly less archaeological data on the East Greek city-states in the Archaic Period (see J.M. Cook 1962, whose general assessment for the most part still holds true today; A. Snodgrass 1971 and J.N. Coldstream 1977 remain invaluable sources of archaeological information). On coinage, see D. Kagan 1982. For a compelling analysis of extant information on East Greek worship of the goddess Athena, see A. Villing in N. Fisher and H. van Wees. The work of H.W. Parke is also indispensable, so esp. 1985a and b, 1988.

58 See, for example, J. Boardman 1975; U. Kron 1976; W.R. Connor 1987; V.J. Rosivach 1987; E. Kearns 1989; F.J. Frost 1990; J.J. Winkler and F.I. Zeitlin, eds. 1990; H.A. Shapiro 1992; W.R. Connor, F.J. Frost & H.A. Shapiro in P. Hellström and B. Alroth, eds. 1996; A.L. Boegehold and A.C. Scafuro, eds. 1994; S. Mills 1997.

59 On Herodotus and ethnicity, see R. Thomas in I. Malkin ed., 2001. See R. Drews 1973 on Hekataios of Miletos, Hellanikos of Lesbos, and other scarcely known predecessors of Herodotos, who like Herodotos, himself, hailed from the East (Hellanikos, like Herodotos, relocated to Athens). See R. Drews 1965 on Herodotos' successors, the universal historians, and their continuing reverence for eastern antiquity. On the attihdographers cf. L. Pearson 1942; F. Jacoby 1949; On the Ionian historians, L. Pearson 1939. On the development of Greek historiography, C.W. Fornara 1988; S. Hornblower, ed. 1994.

60 e.g. J-P Vernant 1980: 258; C. Brillante in L. Edmonds, ed. 1990; F. Graf 1993: 3.

[61] The deep mythic structure in the present context does not, therefore, involve conceptual oppositions native to the workings of the human mind (cf. C. Lévi-Strauss 1955).

[62] G.S. Kirk 1974: ch.1; J. Bremmer, ed. 1987: ch.1.

[63] This is the lineage of the seer Melampous, who migrated from Pylos to Argos, though his family roots trace back to Thessaly.

[64] On the continuing role of ancient literature as the source of definitive educational texts, see N.G. Wilson 1983.

[65] Evidently their glory-days lay back in the scarcely knowable era that prefigured the emergence of Homeric poetry.

PART 1: STANDARD TECHNIQUES OF MYTHOLOGICAL INNOVATION

CHAPTER ONE: MYTHIC THEFT TYPE ONE

PREFACE: TWO STANDARD TECHNIQUES OF MYTHOLOGICAL INNOVATION

1. The Regenerative Strategy

Two related techniques for mythological emendation corroborate the idea that the early Aiolic legendary framework was dismantled by powerful southern Greek states during the course of the Archaic Period. The first technique is called the *regenerative strategy* because it involved the development of new genealogical sources from scratch, and subsequently deployed these new lineage sources to make competitive claims against the heritage of traditional heroic personalities. This procedure worked in collusion with the split of established genealogical trajectories, horizontally, into two parts: one part above and one part below, slicing each affected vertical line. Doing so made it possible to disrupt the distribution of Aiolic genealogical origins as defined in the upper lineage zones, where major heroic stemmata initially branched off from the early eponymous progenitor, Aiolos. Likewise, the split made it possible to append the disembodied lower portions onto newly created genealogical artifacts that show no signs of acknowledgement in early epic poetry. In this regard, the *regenerative strategy* spotlights the development of local Greek genealogies, which, all told, create the illusory impression that the indigenous mythologies of the Greek city-states had existed from time immemorial.

That numerous genealogical lines familiar from the surviving Greek mythic corpus did not exist as such in the early Epic Period can be established if it can be shown that Homeric mythology worked in accordance with the Aiolic genealogical paradigm, and, on this count, demonstrates no awareness of these influential later formations. Inasmuch as this proposition is not readily acknowledged it must be substantiated throughout this report. It is thus invoked at this stage as a working hypothesis to define the significance of the *regenerative* designation. The *regenerative strategy* in essence explains how a once-comprehensive Aiolic framework could have existed at first, but was later effaced, to the point where its initial structural influence was no longer manifestly self-evident in any general encounter with Greek mythology. The pyramid shape of the Aiolic genealogy, whereby multiple lines branched off from a single progenitor, diagrammatically illustrates how the upper lineage zones became a virtually self-appointed target in the eyes of non-Aiolic political interests. Also significant is the hierarchical nature of genealogical representation *per se*, for genealogical hierarchy, as a rule, granted the man at the top (or the men up above, as new lines branched off to new locations) credit for the descendants that would ensue, while in this case, the descendants that ensued were none other than the great Trojan war heroes.

The following reconstruction restates the case. At some obscure point in hoary mythic antiquity when the stabilization of the Olympian pantheon gave rise to the Greek heroes or demigods, Aiolos and his progeny established a monopoly in the East Greek concatenation of stories, fanning out in the course of a few generations to plant sovereign trajectories throughout mainland Greece. From the perspective of later political developments, the undesirability of this formation is immediately tangible in terms of local pride and highlights the issue that faced many Greek cities – namely how to best refute the efficacy of Aiolic genealogical supremacy. The resolution developed across the board was to wrench control of Aiolic authority through the substitution of indigenous origins for the Aiolic account of the Heroic Age. In this light, the promulgation of indigenous lines was at once a declaration of political autonomy as well as an assertion of local control over the vitality of local prehistory. That numerous city-states felt driven to take locally rehabilitating creative action underscores the political grievances inspired by Aiolic mythology in the West. There, fervent indignation arose from the fact that the leading mytho-political description of Greece did not harmonize with lived reality from the point of view of the actual inhabitants of influential mainland Greek cities.

What happened relates closely to Martin West's observation that genealogies tend to grow backward[66] and hones in more specifically on why this was so in an Archaic Greek mythic context. The Aiolic legacy fostered the development of a spate of new genealogical lines essentially for the following reasons: 1) the closer to the source the weaker the canon, that is, the farther into the upper lineage zones the greater the obscurity of the figures involved, since their status was primarily etiological in contrast to the status of their descendants who were major protagonists in the most popular stories of the traditional poetic repertoire[67]; 2) the pre-eminence of early Aiolic origins was perceived as objectionable in non-Aiolic Greek territories, while the creation of alternative lineage sources neutralized the dominant status of the inherited genealogical structure and facilitated a mass redistribution of honors; 3) the genesis of indigenous genealogies was set back into the mists of primordial time so that they could provide the prerequisite structures onto which famous heroes from the lower lineage zones could be grafted by acts of appropriation, namely via the second strategy, identified here as mythological theft (see below).

Moreover, new genealogies were commonly launched by way of a visibly standard procedure using geopolitically meaningful eponymous names for anthropomorphized native natural phenomena. Taygete, Sparte and Amyklas register as examples designated by Sparta, just as Lykaon and Arkas surfaced in Arkadia, and the River Inachos was promoted in Argos[68]. These are all mythic personas that fit into this category, and they are, in addition, all founding figures promoted in the developing mythic landscape that created numerous replacement upper lineage zones. Like mythological eponyms, generally, they are lacking in character and legendary depth when compared with the cast of epic protagonists, while the provincial lines sparked off by such figures typically proceed down to a point where they suddenly break this mold and begin to interact with otherwise established and well-known legends. A number of curiosities arise at this juncture which is a kind of transitional mythological zone. Foremost among these is the occurrence of figures bearing familiar names – names familiar, however, upon reflection, since they are famous in other legendary contexts, an observation that oftentimes goes along with the eerie recognition of peripheral stories that have been told differently, elsewhere, before. The foregoing sense of reduplication is understood here to be symptomatic of regional encroachment on the Aiolic line. The technique at stake was a kind of cutting and splicing: cutting away from Aiolos and splicing onto home territory. Yet, it was a technique that could not be performed without causing significant repercussions in the broader arena of pan-Hellenic prehistory, that is to say, the set corpus of mythic events acknowledged virtually anywhere in Greek territory at the beginning of the historical period[69]. That these repercussions can be observed and to a large extent traced lends further support to the fundamental idea that the traditions acknowledged throughout the Greek world first spread abroad under the auspices of the Aiolic genealogical model.

The conditions that inspired mythic emendation varied from state to state, at least inasmuch as individual states responded in kind to the coverage they received in the *Iliad* and the *Odyssey*, and presumably, in the earliest versions of the lost poetry identified with the *Epic Cycle*[70]. The majority of states were not reacting out of utter poetic deprivation though this was clearly the problem in Megara's case. They were rather responding to epic coverage that was not perceived as commensurate with their political aspirations and collective self-image, or to perceived injustices and distortions in their Homeric epic portrayal[71]. The epic depiction of mainland Greece was in general at odds with geo-political realities and state identity on the Greek mainland, and often, what is more, alarmingly inaccurate from a contemporary mainland Greek point of view[72]. Given the early evidence from Korinth, Argos, and Sparta, mainland Greek response to East Greek epic poetry must have commenced posthaste upon its arrival in the West[73]. The tenor of the response inspired on the Greek mainland was evidently influential for centuries, gathering momentum as successive states rose to power, prompting them to address the ubiquitous issue of local mythology versus early epic legend.

The isolation of the *regenerative strategy* as a standard procedure for creating new lines identifiably linked to their creator states makes it possible to analyze the resulting innovations as historical data based on mythic phenomena, particularly in terms of available information concerning the individual poleis involved. The validity of the *regenerative strategy*, that is – the early epic-inspired promulgation of locally rooted genealogical lines as a means of circumventing early epic authority over the underlying lineage structure – gains further support through related activities once again common to all such regional lines, thereby bridging the gap between the structure and function of the earliest Greek genealogical template and the state of the Greek mythogenealogical edifice after centuries of accumulated amendments proposed on behalf of various special interests. The transitional zone associated above with strangely reminiscent stories and personalities is a critical locus of manipulative activity where regionally fabricated mythical genealogies make contact with traditional epic poetics. In and around this special juncture another standard technique surfaces with great frequency. This technique is best described as mythological theft.

2. Mythological Theft

Under close scrutiny, it is possible to observe the development of mythological dissonance in action. In conjunction with the formation of indigenous lines, mythological theft is a key source of evidence concerning the deconstruction of the Aiolic lineage. Mainly, the process involved programmatic new claims to already established heroic protagonists who were targeted for political transplantation. Whenever ideologically ambitious Greek states seized and appropriated mythological figures already renowned and contextually situated within the framework of Aiolic saga, an incremental discrepancy was the result. Such acts of appropriation fall into three major categories, each of which is corroborated by a few choice examples that constitute the focus of the first three chapters.

There is, first of all, the simple re-allocation of an eminent mythological name. This name was then endowed with a whole new identity, and consciously integrated into an all-new context, which capitalized on its inherent prestige and either, prompted the eclipse of the original figure or forced the acknowledgement of more than one of them. This procedure is dubbed mythic-theft-type-one. There is, secondly, the seizure and relocation of an eminent mythological name, replete with it attendant legendary identity. In this case, an established mythic figure was forced to compete against the popularity of an innovative upstart namesake, or succumb to their influence altogether. This procedure is dubbed mythic-theft-type-two. Thirdly, there are instances of outright mythic invention that can be identified because of the way they work to supplant the coherence and authority of the Aiolic lineage framework. This procedure is dubbed mythic-theft-type-three. The underlying impetus for this activity was the rise of powerful Peloponnesian states, gradually, from the late eighth century onward. In due course, the diffusion of East Greek epic poetry led to the perception throughout the region that the inherited mythological structure was geopolitically obsolete, engendering efforts to render it so. Common to all three methods of emendation was the motivated effacement of the Aiolic lineage, which arose from the impulse to mold the tradition in order to correspond more palatably to regional distributions of political power.

The upshot of these efforts, cumulatively, was the restructuring of major segments of the early epic tradition. Instances of mythic-theft-type-one and type-two created competing mythological figures at odds on the basis of bearing the same name and often in conjunction with errant renditions of formerly definitive epic stories. Notwithstanding, the recurrence of mythological names was already a far from unusual phenomenon. Multiple figures bearing the same name surface frequently in the Homeric epics, especially the *Iliad* where duplicate names were par for the course as the fighting intensified, excluding high-order legendary figures, the likes of Achilles, Agamemnon, Hektor, or Helen. This would, on the face of it, render mythical doubles a dubious criterion for tracing mythical change. And yet, quite unlike the doubles at issue later on, Homeric doubles stand up to scrutiny as either multiple references to the same individual, or as meaningfully distinctive personalities, including numerous cases where the figures named were battlefield extras, as opposed to full-fledged personas, deployed to authenticate the unfolding conflict.

The great care that is taken throughout the *Iliad* to distinguish Aias, son of Telamon, for example, from Aias, son of Oileus, is representative of consistent attentiveness to such details. Battlefield confrontations between two mighty armies demanded a steady stream of accessory participants, peripheral to the central plot[74]. This demand brought forth a veritable onslaught of names along with named warriors destined to perish scarcely the moment after they were invoked. The repetition of names is thus by no means surprising, yet the remarkable lack of narrative disjuncture that occurs in addressing them, is surely one of the great feats of Homeric poetry.

In brief, two observations are most significant. The first is that the duplication of names in the *Iliad* is frequently distributed between the two sides with the same name occurring among Greeks and Trojans. This is in itself yet another example of the meticulous treatment of duplicate names in Homer, and demonstrates, furthermore, that duplication is not symptomatic of confused identities. Second, the recurrence of names in Homeric poetry, generally speaking, does not occur in contradiction to the unfolding plot, for instance, to the effect that assertions are made concerning named individuals, which are undermined elsewhere in the story. On the contrary, distinctive figures emerge whenever it is logically impossible for the same name to indicate the same individual. The poet is in command of his cast of characters.

Against this premise, which has always had its adherents and a host of detractors as well, there is the famous example of Pylaimenes, Lord of Paphlagonia and ally of Troy[75]. This man is killed by Menelaos in book five (575-579) only to reappear in book thirteen (643-659) tearfully accompanying his son Harpalion's funeral after Harpalion was killed by Meriones of Krete. Though it may not be far-fetched, particularly in view of Achilles' interaction with Patrokos' ghost (Il.23.65-1-7), that when Homer states that Lord Pylaimenes will receive no "man-price[76]" for the death of his son, Homer means he will not, because he can not, namely because he is dead already, and therefore joins the procession not as a man but as a spirit. However, even excluding this possibility, which could perhaps be accused of special pleading, in light of the great demand for named warriors in the *Iliad*, this rare and notorious contradiction is likely to be somewhat overrated. If indeed it ought to be considered as such, it is the kind of exception that serves to prove the rule: viz. an astounding lack of conceptual dissonance in terms of character casting in the Homeric poems. Given the length of the poems and given their oral heritage, a remarkable level of architectural clarity places Homeric poetry in a class by itself. Thus, duplicate naming in its Homeric context provides a foil against which duplicate naming may be assessed in later Greek mythological narratives.

Returning to the underlying idea that mythological emendation on a grand scale gained its initial momentum on the Greek mainland in response to the undesirable fact that the ultimate Greek epic cultural charter was based on an East Greek Hellenic worldview, the account of what next transpired, presently under review, postulates the reworking of the Homeric edifice to accommodate mainland Greek cultural politics. This was accomplished by specific techniques that took root and spread because of their effectiveness in straddling the divide between mythological change and the preservation of the Homeric cultural charter. The validity of this concept needs to be established, so the remainder of Part One of this analysis surveys a few choice examples of mythological theft to demonstrate that it was standard Greek practice.

In the first category, mythic-theft-type-one (ch.1), the simple re-allocation of a pre-eminent name, the following examples will be summarized: Hypermestra and Lynkeus' appropriation by the state of Argos from the Aitolian branch of the Aiolic line and the line of Perieres, son of Aiolos, respectively; two potential appropriations of the heroine Sterope, from the Aitolian branch of the Aiolic line; and the Arkadian appropriation of Atlalanta who was formerly situated in Boiotia. In the second category, mythic-theft-type-two (ch.2), the wholesale transplantation of heroes and their stories with augmentation and adjustments in their new mythic settings: the transplantation of Aiakos from Thessaly to Aigina and the Spartan appropriation of certain sons of Perieres (son of Aiolos) are presented as paradigmatic examples. In the third category, mythic-theft-type-three (ch.3), which deals with sheer mythic innovation, the invention of the Argive hero Danaos and the re-characterization of the daughters of Atlas offer demonstrative examples of that particular strategy.

All told these examples lend substantial support to the prospect of a coherent early Aiolic mytho-genealogical vision of Greece that essentially gathers strength on a case by case basis and only cumulatively gains any real force at all. Likewise, no single example is remotely compelling until it has been shown to play an integral part in a consistent array of re-interpretive patterns that illuminate Greek mythological change in terms of the conceptual self-definition of individual Greek city-states. The same re-interpretive patterns further suggest that narrative contradiction was not an inherent Greek mythic attribute from the start[77]. Here, the prolific level of mythological dissonance acknowledged throughout the Greek mythic corpus is traced to the activities of separate Greek states in their efforts to promote flattering and competitive local prehistories. Though no doubt the antithesis of the influential idea that mythological dissonance arose unavoidably from the artificial consolidation of previously isolated regional narratives, the alternate view that moves from unity to discord follows rationally from the Aiolic hypothesis and repeatedly garners cogent support from random subsets of extant Greek mythic data. In sum, if in the beginning the Aiolic line held a monopoly on heroic glory, the one clear-cut route to the redistribution of glory was through the manipulation of the Aiolic line. The manipulative activities that furthered this objective at no time receive explicit acknowledgement, but they were nonetheless normative and vigorously applied in a kind of omniscient cultural silence.

EXAMPLE ONE: HYPERMESTRA AND LYNKEUS

The name Hypermestra is famous in the context of the upper reaches of the Argive line. This segment of the line, the portion that lies closest to its native progenitor, the river Inachos[78], is often recognized as a suspicious entity. As exemplified by such exotic figures as Libya, Agenor, Belos and Aigyptos, its international character is anachronistic with respect to conditions in early Archaic Greece[79]. By the fifth century these figures were portrayed as descendants of the Argive River Inachos and, in this context, came to represent a major backward extension of the regional Argive line[80]. Zeroing in on its chronological parameters, this genealogy documents a Hellenic worldview that was alien to early archaic perspectives, yet meaningful by the late seventh century and evidently canonical by the fifth[81]. In its full-blown form the line of Argos gives key roles to one Hypermestra, daughter of Danaos, and to her husband, Lynkeus, Aigyptos' son, whose story is partly told in Aischylos' *Suppliant Maidens*, the sole surviving first play of a trilogy devoted to the adventures of Danaos' daughters[82]. This drama sets the stage for the famous wedding night bloodbath in which Hypermestra's forty-nine sisters kill Lynkeus' forty-nine brothers rather than consummate marriage to their first cousins. In this situation, Hypermestra alone among her numerous sisters is famous for compassionately sparing her mate, and thus permitting the line to continue on down to the illustrious births of Perseus and Herakles[83].

The objective here is to simply note that both of these names have important antecedents in the Aiolic lineage structure[84]. Hypermestra, like Leda as well as Althaia, was a daughter of Eurythemiste and Thestios, two significant if scarcely celebrated figures in the Aitolian branch of the Aiolic line that stemmed from Kalyke, daughter of Aiolos. Althaia's most famous offspring were Meleagros by Ares, and Deianeira by Oineus (son of another wife of her grandfather, Porthaon[85]). Leda's were Helen, Klytaimestra, and the Dioskouri either by Tyndareos or by Zeus[86]. Hypermestra was known as the mother of Amphiaraos, and the wife of Oikles, a hero who hailed from Argos via a genealogy that stemmed back to the *Odyssey* (15.225ff.), and which was also vital to the plot structure of early epic legendary events. This Hypermestra was evidently a woman of substantially greater mythological depth than her ingeniously crafted Argive double (viz. daughter of Danaos), who took up residence with a great deal of fanfare in the upper reaches of the Argive line[87]. Essentially, she was an Aiolic woman who married into another major Aiolic stemma: namely, into a Thessalian branch of the family that stemmed back to Kretheus, son of Aiolos. This family included the instigators of the Argonauts' voyage, a Neleid offshoot that migrated to Pylos, and a further contingent that later migrated to Argos led by the brothers Melampous and Bias, whose descendants played indispensable roles in the famous wars between Argos and Thebes. Hypermestra, it may be observed, was a progenitrix of considerable stature in the old Aiolic account of the Aitolian line.

Lynkeus, likewise, was a name associated with a one-time high profile Aiolic stemma. He was the son of Aphareus (son of Perieres, son of Aiolos), who with his twin brother Idas came into conflict with the Dioskouri (Kastor and Polydeukes), either over possession of Phoibe and Hilairia (viz. daughters of Leukippos, Aphareus' brother and, therefore, first cousins of Lynkeus and Idas, Aphareus' sons) or over possession of prize cattle herds[88]. This conflict, at any rate, spiraled out of control and led to the deaths of all four heroes concerned, including Helen's twin brothers whose absence on the battlefield below the ramparts at Troy Helen pauses to contemplate out loud (Il.3.236-242). Lynkeus, in addition, was the uncle of Kleopatra, the daughter of Idas[89], who married Meleagros, and who is mentioned by Phoinix in *Iliad* book nine during his attempt to coax Achilles into striking a deal with Agamemnon (Il.9.556). Further, in line with certain data presented below[90], Lynkeus was initially very closely related to the offspring of Tyndarios and Ikarios: namely, Kastor and Polydeukes, Helen, Klytaimnestra, Penelope, and others. This outlines, in summation, the early legendary profiles of the Lynkeus and the Hypermestra whose status, it would seem, predated the advent of their named rivals in later mythology.

This example indicates that later Archaic Greek mythic narratives often featured protagonists whose names carried with them famous ulterior associations. Logically, such duplication was a deliberate choice made instead of promoting new figures from scratch. Nothing, in any case, stood in the way of populating new myths with new star protagonists whose names were not laden with established meaning. Notably too, the antecedent figures, who bore names that became so desirable elsewhere, tend to trace back to the Aiolic lineage in instances where their history can be traced. This pattern suggests something special about the early Aiolic genealogical framework that is worthy of further investigation.

EXAMPLE TWO: STEROPE

The Arkadian line is a classic example of the establishment of an aboriginal framework onto which well-known figures were strategically joined (viz. the regenerative strategy). The resulting amalgam was then promoted against recognizable, traditional precedents. A figure named Lykaon invokes the great mountain of central Arkadia. He emerges to rule over the inhabitants, engendering many sons whose eponymous names designated key settlements throughout the region[91]. The Arkadian line begins to diverge from its initial aboriginal framework with the descendants of the sons of the state eponym Arkas, son of Lykaon's daughter, Kallisto, and Zeus. Arkas' descendants initiate a progression out of primordial time into the distant prehistory of the Arkadian state. Of the three sons of Arkas: Elatos, Azan, and Apheidas, Elatos is yet another duplicate name originally associated with the legendary Lapith clan. Evidently, Elatos was transported to Arkadia from northern Thessaly, along with a cache of famous stories that subsequently competed with established precedents[92]. Azan invokes the northwestern Arkadian territory known as Azania[93], while via the progeny of his son Aleos[94], Apheidas provides the main link to well-known epic material, including Arkadian dealings with Herakles and Arkadian involvement in the Trojan War[95].

Sterope, the daughter of the Arkadian Kepheus, a son of Aleos (son of Apheidas, grandson of Arkas), provides a discrete example amid a broader field of manipulative Arkadian mythic activity. The Arkadian Sterope's main claim to fame was the defense of her native city, Tegea, when her father Kepheus led her brothers into battle in alliance with Herakles (e.g. DS 4.33.6; ApB 2.7.3). Sterope miraculously defended her city using a lock of hair from the gorgon Medusa, which Herakles had provided in exchange for support on his campaign to restore king Tyndareos who had allegedly been ousted from the Spartan throne. Sterope's father and most, if not all, of her brothers were said to have died in this confrontation[96], and though Sterope herself remained safe in Tegea, at that point, her biography meets a sudden dead end in the extant sources.

It is, therefore, unclear whether Arkadian mythic narratives ever connected her with Oinomaos, the central figure in the most famous legend where the name Sterope occurs, most frequently in the role of Oinomaos' mother. Oinomaos was one of those notorious kings who set up a contest for the hand of his daughter, having no real desire to give her away[97]. Therefore, by way of extraordinary or supernatural powers he ensured that no suitor could conceivably win, killing them in succession and keeping their skulls as trophies. But this cycle was bound to be disrupted by the one suitor destined for victory, and that suitor was Pelops, who arrived from Asia Minor[98] and gave his name to the Peloponnese[99].

The Arkadian Sterope is classified here an instance of mythological-theft-type-one because her story does not resemble the most famous narratives her name invokes. Evidently, her name was chosen on behalf of a brand-new Arkadian legendary initiative. Yet, since as we shall see, there were two other Steropes vying for control of the most popular story that was connected with the name, it is not inconceivable that the Arkadian Sterope attempted to compete for those honors as well (albeit unsuccessfully from a pan-Hellenic perspective). In general, the fate of local idiosyncrasies depended on their ability to gain widespread acceptance further afield. Therefore, in the event they were rejected elsewhere, they were liable to be excluded from the mythological record. Such circumstances, however, by no means forbid their continued livelihood in the region which first conceived and promoted them. In terms of relative mythic chronology, the well-developed collection of Arkadian legends that occur in the ancient sources can be readily identified as post-Homeric in that the Homeric portrait of Arkadia is characterized through an Aiolic lens and is markedly underdeveloped by contrast. As a major contributor to regionally influential mythological activity in the Peloponnese, the Arkadian line was largely, if not completely, successful in captivating allegiance elsewhere in Greece, notably including the city of Athens, which is primarily why we hear so much about it[100].

In this context, the real basis for the comparison that categorizes the Arkadian Sterope as an example of mythological theft is the fact that she had a significant namesake in the Aitolian branch of the Aiolic line. The Sterope in question was one of three daughters of Porthaon and Laothoe, as was Eurythemiste, who with her first cousin, Thestios, bore Leda, Althaia, and Hypermestra (viz. the same Hypermestra cited above). This places Sterope one rung further up in the Aitolian branch of the Aiolic line[101], while, in general, the further up in the Aiolic lineage a particular mythic figure resides, the more obscure their persona tends to appear to us now, regardless of how familiar such persons may have been to early epic listening audiences. Colorful personalities the likes of Phrixos or Sisyphos tend to register on the basis of their memorable exploits. Details concerning their genealogies, however, do not necessarily spring to mind[102], whereas many, if not most, of their near contemporaries or close descendants are frequently far from familiar at all.

From a present-day point of view, this observation is partly the result of and partly what facilitated the systematic dismantling of the Aiolic lineage, since new initiatives were apt to zero in on figures located in the upper lineage zones. Such figures were ideal targets for mythic redactors, on the one hand, because they were often free from explicit Homeric statements, to which the whole Greek world was closely attuned[103]. And, in addition, because the appropriation of mythological figures situated high up in any lineage sequence granted the new beneficiaries of their personas control over all progeny born into that lineage and located accordingly further down in the sequence[104]. Moreover, Aiolic mythic figures of the upper lineage zones generated the participants for such legendary adventures as the voyage of the Argonauts, the hunt for the Kalydonian boar, the Argive–Theban wars, and ultimately, the war against Troy. Sterope and her sisters, Eurythemiste and Stratonike, their father Porthaon, and his sister Demodike were all characters that were genealogically important, yet, at the same time, comparatively obscure, and destined to become more so as time wore on.

In any event, each one of these sisters enters a liaison that yields significant offspring. As previously noted, the daughters of Eurythemiste[105] and Thestios were Althaia, Leda, and Hypermestra. This couple also engendered a number of sons, active in the quest for the Kalydonian boar, and if they survived that, in the ensuing conflict between Pleuron and Kalydonian over the boar's hide[106]. Stratonike, a sister of Eurythemiste, was evidently selected by the god Apollo as a wife for his son, Melaneus, ultimately giving birth to Eurytos (father of Iphitos and Iole, among others), king of the ancient city of Oichalia, which was sacked in due course by Herakles[107]. This narrative complex certainly goes back to Homer, where there is no shortage of evidence to its antiquity. Thus, Odysseus' possession of Eurytos' bow is explained as a gift of friendship from Iphitos, who had inherited the bow upon the death of his father (Od.21.13ff.). One of the world's greatest marksmen in his day, Eurytos was notably both a descendant as well as a victim of the god Apollo, whom he had once dared to challenge in a marksmanship duel (Od.8.223ff.).

Sterope, the third daughter of this particular union, has more tenuous ties to genealogical notoriety. First and foremost, her membership in this family is in itself plainly a high-status affair. Yet the pertinent fragments of the Hesiodic *Catalogue of Women* that testify to the marriages of her two sisters break off before the report as to Sterope's match[108]. Nevertheless, a woman named Sterope, who bore illustrious offspring, is not hard to find in the surviving Greek corpus, namely, Sterope, mother of Oinomaos, or alternatively, sometimes his wife[109]. Oinomaos was, by consensus, fathered by the god Ares, and was also the father of Hippodameia, the woman who first drew Pelops into Greek country to compete for her hand in chariot racing. All in all, Pelops' victory was intimately bound up with the death of Oinomaos, on the one hand, and on the other, through his chariot victory, with the integration of his descendants into the mythic topography of the Peloponnese. Notably, Ares happened to be a god who repeatedly engaged in intimate dealings with the female members of the Aitolian line, namely with Demodike, Sterope's paternal grandmother, as well as with Althaia, Sterope's niece. This layout easily accommodates Oinomaos, who as a son of Ares and Sterope, would wind up to be a man with a heavy dose of Ares running through his bloodstream.

Alternatively, if Oinomaos hailed from some parallel stemma and arrived in Aitolia to seek the hand of Sterope, he would bring yet more Ares to an Ares-laden line in a mythological system where divine power was deemed to flow through veins of demigods and deemed to be transmitted to subsequent generations with ever-diminishing quantitative potency, unless a given lineage was infused yet again with another divine-mortal coupling[110]. The suggestion here is that the Aitolian line represents the most favorable legendary context for Oinomaos and Sterope, of old[111], even though this setting was ultimately dispatched and its heroine, Sterope, dwarfed by two personalities, neither of which bore any resemblance to the venerable daughter of Porthaon and Laothoe. Of Sterope's two celebrated successors, neither the Arkadian daughter of Kepheus, nor Sterope, the daughter of Atlas who later captured the role of Oinomaos' Sterope, fit organically into the genealogical landscape that can be pieced together from early epic material. Specifically, neither of them bear any connection to the mythology of the Aiolic line.

It is perhaps curious that the Homeric epics make no reference whatsoever to the famous chariot race in which Pelops won the hand of Hippodameia. On the other hand, though, the absence of early epic acknowledgment is not a uniformly reliable factor in determining the antiquity of a given myth. Moreover, from the point of view of mythological time, the contest for the hand of Hippodameia took place generations prior to the events selected for coverage in the Homeric poems[112]. Pausanias witnessed the contest on the chest of Kypselos in the temple of Hera at Olympia (Paus.5.17.7[113]), so no doubt the story was standard in the sixth century. Beyond this, the story's indispensable role in prefiguring the conditions of the Trojan War suggests that its roots went back further still.

The *Iliad* was well-acquainted with Pelops, who received a royal scepter from Zeus via Hermes, which passed down through his family until it became the prized possession of Agamemnon, commander of the Greek forces at Troy (Il.2.99-108). This passage says nothing about Pelops' origins or, for that matter, his appointed destiny other than to confirm that they were well accounted for. But there was an old story that dealt with the matter of Pelops' immigration to Greece from the East, which though later reduced to a rather eccentric version, managed to survive in a few obscure notations. This story speaks of one Killos, Pelops' charioteer[114], who died in Lesbos on the journey westward, but, who endowed Pelops with great power and fortune in gratitude for elaborate funeral honors that Pelops took the time and trouble to offer him[115].

Though quite contrary to later mainstream versions, this tangent offers an interesting parallel to the suggested eclipse of the Aitolian Sterope. The story itself suggests its Aiolic roots, since the island of Lesbos was a crucial stopover on Pelops' route to the Peloponnese, and a major Aiolic stronghold in historical times, even though at this stage in the Heroic Period, Lesbos was not yet completely under Greek control. Like the Aitolian Sterope, whom the present argument suggests was later eclipsed by other contenders, Killos, Pelops' erstwhile charioteer was eventually replaced by one Myrtilos, son of Hermes[116], who dominated all later canonical versions, while the island of Lesbos fades away altogether.

The island of Lesbos is a pivotal datum. Historically speaking, the island loomed large as a prosperous stronghold in eastern Aiolis. Mythologically speaking, as with the island of Lemnos, where Jason the Argonaut's son Euneos, resided (e.g. 7.468[117]), Lesbos seems to have had a share of Greek inhabitants from back before the Trojan War period (Il.24.544; H.Hymn 3.37[118]). This is particularly important in comparison with the non-Greek pro-Trojan pattern of habitation on the Anatolian mainland.

The ahistorical nature of the Iliadic depiction of the Anatolian seaboard has been subject to long-standing speculation[119]. The solution that appears to carry the most weight when it comes to explanatory consistency is the idea of deliberate chronological distancing[120], which holds up under scrutiny as a technique that is globally utilized throughout the Homeric poems. A distinction, however, needs to be made regarding the function of Homeric distancing, for while it is often linked to the studied depiction of conditions associated with the Heroic Age (viz. a distinctively mythological era[121]), and from there often granted historical analogues held to reflect aspects of Greek society at the time the poems were composed[122], the Heroic Age is not generally linked to a genealogical reckoning of the mythic present that led back step by step deep into the mythic past. As the conceptual basis for the spread of Greek culture in the Eastern Aegean in the pre-historical period, such a reckoning surely mingled with Greek reality, at least inasmuch as it was designed to validate the advent of Greek sovereignty in Asia Minor, which was believed to take place in the post Trojan War period, illuminating the function of the Trojan War. The ancient interpretive use of chronological distancing gains clarity and momentum as this investigation progresses. Currently, the objective is to simply to point out that the *Iliad*'s depiction of the northeast Aegean acknowledged nascent genealogical sources for the potential development of Hellenic authority, which coincides with the notion that Hellenic authority was a preordained future eventuality[123]. In this regard, the marginality of the outlying islands off the coast of the Troad coincides with the Greek and Trojan catalogues in depicting an environment of mixed allegiances inhabited both by Greek and non-Greek peoples.

It seems, for example, at first glance, that Imbros and Tenedos were understood to lean toward the Trojan sphere of influence, seeing that Eetion of Imbros ransomed Priam's son Lykaon, after he had been sold on the island Lemnos (Il.21.40-42), while there is some mythic evidence to the effect that a son of the Trojan Kyknos, who surfaces in the *Kypria* was held to have given his name to the island[124]. This information, however, is offset by stories of a Greek feast that took place on Tenedos when the Achaians were first making their way to Troy[125], and by King Priam's lament that Achilles sold his sons on the islands of Samos (Samothrace), Lemnos, and Imbros (Il.24.751-753). Focusing on Imbros in particular, this list of markets suggests a more complex rendering of northwest Aegean poetic demographics than, for example, M. Dickie's assumption that all these islands were aligned with Troy[126]. For while Achilles sells Lykaon on the island of Lemnos where Greek habitation is explicitly confirmed, if Trojans were also sold on the island of Imbros, where Lykaon was ransomed and sent back home, either Imbros' population was more diverse, or commerce in captives is not an accurate gauge of Trojan War political sympathies.

These factors appear to be connected. Wine is transported to the Achaian camp, on the one hand, from Lemnos (Il.467-475), but also from Thrace (Il.9.71-72; Od.9.39-61), although Jason's son Euenos presents a large portion to the Greek commanders, apparently free of charge (viz. motivated by patriotic allegiance?). Achilles boasts that he stormed twelve cities by sea and eleven by land throughout the Troad (9.328-329). Those stormed by sea create the impression of looting raids, rather than attacks bent on total destruction, whereas judging from the reports of two surviving victims (viz. Briseis and Andromache[127]) and the absence of their cities among the allies of Troy, several of the land conquests led to thorough devastation. The sea raids are exemplified by three women: Hecamede of Tenedos (Il. 11.623-624[128]), Diomede of Lesbos, and Iphis of Skyros (Il. 9.663-668[129]). This last place is a particularly unlikely candidate for pro-Trojan diplomatic relations, and yet it was also stormed by Achilles. In this context, the story of Herakles' sack of Kos offers an even more cautionary example. Koan mythic ancestry readily traces back to a set of prominent Aiolic genealogies, which at once clinches the case for their synchronic importance and dramatizes their usurpation at the hands of a fellow Greek (Il.2.676-679[130], 14.249-255, 15.26-30). It seems reasonable to conclude from the *Iliad*'s perspective that Hellenic influence was already substantial on Rhodes and Krete and the Dodekannese (Il.2.653-680[131]), yet was not evidently fully established on the islands in close proximity to the kingdom of Troy.

Achilles' sack of Lesbos is no doubt relevant to Agamemnon's possession of seven Lesbian women (9.128-130, 9.270-272). In light of auxiliary patterns, however, these circumstances do not negate the possibility of a nascent Greek presence on the island of Lesbos as well. The Homeric portrait of the northwest Aegean does not, as it happens, cogently abide by an easy political polarization derived from the hostilities that unfolded at Troy. This landscape, on the contrary, seems to provide a deliberately peripheral legendary setting imbued with a mixture of ethnic identities that, through the existence of scattered Greek enclaves, also contained the seeds of a future landscape in which the Greek element would rise to distinction. Thus the contemporary landscape, like the rest of the *Iliad,* effectively worked to create the illusion that the future still hung in the balance, insinuating all the while the conceptual basis for the predestined outcome that was incontestably already well-known.

The notion that Aiolic Greek habitation of east Greek Aiolis radiated from Lesbos was a notion retained, albeit with embellishments, by latter-day mythic chroniclers[132]. An appropriate early context therefore exists within which Killos' involvement in Oinomaos' journey (whether the man was believed to be Asian or Greek) fits more suitably than it would as a more recent tangent leveled out of the blue against the dominant version of the story. The Killos version was distinctive geopolitically, but aside from this factor, it essentially reproduced, if it did not set the stage for, the later popular story and its cluster of variants that explained how it was that Pelops came to be counted among the great magnates of heroic Greece.

Returning to the place where the fragments of the *Catalogue of Women* break off leaving Sterope, daughter of Porthaon, in a state of suspended animation, the existence of this lacuna is certainly a great pity because it is believed that this composition made reference to another Sterope as well. In addressing this genealogy, Martin West acknowledges the trio of sisters in the Aitolian line, but focuses mainly on only two, namely, Eurythemiste and Stratonike, whose marriages and progeny are recorded[133]. This is entirely reasonable on account of the lacuna, yet West goes on to portray another Streope as the woman who united with the god Ares and gave birth to Oinomaos. He grants this role to yet another Sterope, namely the daughter of the Titan god, Atlas.

No doubt, Sterope, daughter of Atlas was a prominent member of the collectivity consisting of seven sisters who were in due course equated with the star cluster known as the Pleiades[134]. As the evidence stands, Sterope's presence along with the presence of her sister Merope are not concretely attested in the *Catalogue* fragments, and must, therefore, be inferred from Hellanikos who specifically acknowledges all seven sisters (FGrHist 4F19)[135]. If, however, as it seems on the balance, Hellanikos' presentation of the Atlantids stemmed back to the *Catalogue,* which, likewise, claimed Oinomaos for the Atlantid Sterope, the missing marriage and progeny of the Aitolian Sterope raise a number of interesting questions.

Following Apollodoros' *Bibliotheka*, West suggests that the *Catalogue of Women* addressed the genealogy of Atlas' daughters directly after its treatment of the Arkadian genealogies, but reserved Sterope for separate coverage in connection with the line of Pelops[136]. He states in this regard, "the Pelopid stemma was probably associated with the Atlantid stemma, since Pelops' wife Hippodameia, was the daughter of Oinomaos, who in the *earliest* tradition was the son of Ares and the Atlantid Sterope (1985: 43)."

Elsewhere, however, West remarks that "Atlas' family is clearly a rather artificial construct (1985: 156)," an appraisal that is echoed by Gantz (1993: 212). In this regard, West's chronology is somewhat difficult to get a handle on inasmuch as the artificial nature of the Atlantid sorority would seem to contradict the idea that the Atlantid Sterope represents the *earliest* genealogy for Oinomaos[137]. At any rate, the definitive novelty of the Atlantid sisterhood puts a certain emphasis on the problem of Atlas' daughters' mythological development, suggesting, in addition, that there was a time when Atlas' family did not exist in the form that we eventually find it.

The genealogical evidence seems to suggest that the roster of seven sisters developed in stages inspired by the characterization of

Maia and beginning with three heroines in particular, namely, Taygete, Elektra and Alkyone. The daughters of Atlas are dealt with below as an exemplary case of mythic-theft-type-three since there is considerable evidence that they represent a major post-Homeric structural innovation. A few preliminary remarks should thus suffice at this juncture. The *Catalogue of Women* seems to have focused primarily on Taygete and Electra, a pair who created a striking parallel between the line of Sparta and the line of Troy[138]. Next to these, Alkyone received considerable attention. Pausanias reports that he witnessed Alkyone together with Taygete on the Amyklai throne (3.18.10[139]). This image is telling because Alkyone played a major role in the Spartan effort to appropriate the family of Perieres, son of Aiolos[140]. Thus, she was described as Perieres' wife, a marriage that is acknowledged in the *Catalogue* (fr 49 MW[141]). Alkyone, however, competed in this role against a preference for Gorgophone, daughter of Perseus, who first surfaces in Stesichoros. Though Gorgophone gained a considerable edge (e.g. ApB 1.9.5, 3.10.3), Alkyone's mythic status in southern Greece was inextricably bound up with the genealogy of Sparta[142].

The Hesiodic *Catalogue* explicitly emphasized Alkyone's union with Poseidon which apparently invoked the typical formula whereby a given heroine generated two stemmata, one with a mortal, one with a god[143]. Notably, this union was responsible for a number of conspicuous central Greek figures with discernible early Aiolic connections[144]. Under the auspices of the Spartan lineage, however, any such protagonists would be subordinate to the Perieres-Alkyone-Poseidon arrangement, whereby Perieres was transformed into a Spartan magnate and Alkyone, originally a daughter of Aiolos, was cast as a daughter of Atlas instead.

There are therefore a number of key indications that the personification of the daughters of Atlas was at first a specifically Spartan affair, augmented by the time of the Hesiodic *Catalogue* to include all seven sisters known to posterity. Notably, the expansion of the collectivity would not only conveniently complete the equation of seven sisters = seven Pleiades, but would have had the added effect of broadening their collective mythological range to include heroines rooted in other locations. In this way the Atlantid sisterhood became attractive and viable from a pan-Hellenic perspective[145].

On the one hand, the earliest data confirm the existence of Maia, daughter of Atlas, who was a goddess (as opposed to a mortal heroine) and, as such, mated with Zeus and bore the god Hermes. On the other hand, the star cluster known as the Pleiades was understood mythologically, early on, as the result of the metamorphosis of an anonymous group of Boiotian heroines who were pursued by the Boiotian hero Orion, though his effort to overtake them was thwarted by the gods[146]. The further transformation of the Pleiades into a stellar representation of the daughters of Atlas as they were acknowledged in the fifth century reflects a process that is conspicuously akin to the transformation of Erechtheus' daughters in accordance with the development of Athenian mythology. The daughters of Erechtheus, legend had it, collectively gave their lives for their city in connection with the Eleusinian War. In due course, notwithstanding, they were characterized as significant individual heroines who engendered great Athenian heroic lines[147]. The most straightforward approach to these contradictions is to see them as symptomatic of the clash between early and later mythic developments, since it is clearly impossible, on both counts, for both sets of circumstances to coexist.

In accordance with numerous indications that the full-blown Atlantid sorority was a mythological development of the sixth century inspired by certain major Spartan innovations, it remains to observe that the only recorded identification of the offspring born to the Aitolian Sterope that could be applicable to the *Catalogue* (if indeed, Sterope, daughter of Atlas, claimed Oinomaos in that text) describes them as the Sirens who threatened Odysseus with the supernatural power of their voices (e.g. Od.12.39-46). These, legend had it, Sterope engendered with the Aitolian River god, Acheloos (ApB 1.7.10).

The problem here is the difficulty of viewing this genealogy as a genuine early archaic formation. It was rather an expedient genealogical fantasy akin to the citation in fragment 10a (OCT) that portrays the Nymphai, the Satyroi, and the Kouretes as the offspring of the daughters of tribal eponym Doros. It is a pity, in this regard, that Hesiod's *Theogony* does not provide a genealogy for the Sirens, and yet this is likely a related point[148]. It was no doubt the prerogative of Greek mythology to freely generate extraordinary beings whose relationship to their genealogical surroundings was an altogether arbitrary affair[149]. Nonetheless, the genesis of extraordinary beings operated within certain cosmic parameters which the *Theogony* implicitly delineates. Notably, as time wore on, it was far from infrequent for these first principles to fall by the wayside in favor of advantageous new mythological formulas that abandoned such principles with impunity. Consequently, however, on a comparative basis, such activities often reliably signal the popularization of new mythic initiatives.

    Thus aside from the fact that this genealogy stands out like a sore thumb in the Aitolian line, it can also be said that the birth of the Sirens, no less the Nymphai, Satyroi or Kouretes was not the type of thing that was supposed to take place in the middle of the Heroic Era, nor via relations between mortal women and gods[150]. On the contrary, according to early Greek thinking, the origins of super-numinous beings harked back to the prior cosmogonic era. In general, there was no bleeding into the Heroic Age[151].

    If it was, therefore, this attribution that filled the *Catalogue*'s gap in the Aitolian line, it amounts to a very ingenious substitution evidently designed to replace something else. Whereas if it did not (and we have no way of knowing), the notion that this genealogical juncture was Oinomaos' early epic location is no less commensurate with the remarkable silence concerning this major heroic genealogy.

    Other than Sterope, daughter of Kepheus, who surfaces in mainstream mythic narratives with regard to Herakles' dealings with Tyndareos of Sparta, and does not tangibly surface in the *Catalogue*[152], there are no other high-order assignments that were reportedly linked to the name. During the course of the sixth century the Atlantid Sterope became preeminent. Her connection with Oinomaos in later tradition distracts from a more venerable legendary context that may not be verifiable in isolation, but which becomes more persuasive as it is shown to abide by recurrent patterns of Greek mythic change.

    Much information is left to be desired concerning the facts of this particular case. Still, a significant measure of revisionist activity can be seen to revolve around the redeployment of famous mythological names. In this light, the three Steropes in question were not, as it happened, created equally. For, to the extent that they were invoked under various circumstances by various interest groups, they do not reproduce the type of distinctions that characterize homonymous names in the context of Homeric poetry. Instead, the tendency of post-Homeric authorities to fabricate new personas and call them by the same names as older and well-known mythological figures stands out against the data on bona fide early figures wherever such data exists for comparison. Here, the jockeying for possession of multiple Steropes emphasizes the proposed link between Oinomaos and Porthaon's daughter - a once illustrious heiress in the Aitolian line - on the basis that, unlike her competitors, the Aitolian Sterope was organically connected to a solid and well-known early epic stemma.

Basically what we have here is a series of leads. In the case of a figure such as Oinomaos that is nonetheless quantitatively more than the background material available on a number of his heroic peers at the time of the spread of Homeric poetry (e.g. the likes of Aiakos, Telamon, and Perseus among others). In the case of Sterope, at its most basic level, we are certainly dealing with a name that commanded genealogical gravitas. On such an analysis, neither the daughter of Kepheus nor the daughter of Atlas, were named Sterope without precedent or without motivation. What took place instead was a shifting of honors achieved through the use of homonymous names. In the end, the most prestigious life story was captured by Sterope, the daughter of Atlas, who ostensibly claimed the early personal history that was once allocated to Porthaon's daughter[153].

On the available evidence, as Apollodoros records, whether by the time of, or subsequent to, the Hesiodic *Catalogue of Women*, Porthaon's daughter was granted a surrogate life story as the woman who united with the River Acheloos, and consequently, gave birth to the Sirens. Notably, Apollodoros himself does not place much faith in this genealogy, but his report of its existence coincides with the transfer of the Aitolian Sterope's identity[154]. Accordingly, at this stage it still remains to be seen whether the legendary deployment of homonymous names can be unraveled in a meaningful way using Aiolic connections as the leading criterion. Again the notion of mythological theft is only credible on cumulative basis.

EXAMPLE THREE: ATALANTA

There are two Atalantas in Greek mythology. They are associated with two different regions of Greece: one from Boiotia, and one from Arkadia. They have different life stories, respectively. One was a runner capable of defeating a multitude of suitors who competed against her in order to win her hand in marriage, that is, until one Hippomenes came along and raced with the blessings of Aphrodite[155]. The other was a huntress, who passed her time in the wilds, yet finally fell in love with her first cousin Melanion[156]. Not too surprisingly, a degree of confusion as to which was which and who was who surfaces in the mythographical testimony. The general interpretation of this is that two previously separate Atalantas naturally generated conceptual static as regional Greek traditions began to interact in an increasingly pan-Hellenic milieu[157]. This outlook is consistent with a broader policy of interpreting disputed mythological claims as the result of the fusion of originally separate legends with originally separate genealogical roots[158]. Here, the prospect that disputed claims of this sort could have resulted, just as well, from a reversal of circumstantial conditions, whereby a once-comprehensive body of legends was deliberately fragmented as time wore on, is presently under review.

Applying this logic to Atalanta, one Atalanta in due course became two. The Arkadian at once mimicked and distinguished herself against the established Boiotian heroine[159]. She mimicked her name and her ruthless courage, but distinguished herself by way of possessing a slightly different heroic mystique and an entirely different genealogy. The two Atalantas together present two oddly analogous, yet irreconcilable heroines. Because each in essence commands her own special story, the case of Atalanta registers here as an example of mythological-theft-type-one. The issue of precedence and the license to use *mythological-theft* as a valid description of the source of confusion between these two heroines gains support on primarily genealogical grounds.

Like Sterope, daughter of Kepheus, the Arkadian Atalanta belonged to the lineage that stemmed from Apheidas, son of Arkas, eponym of the region. This lineage, first off, is ridden with adaptations of expressly the sort that involved mythic figures who were already well-known from other legendary contexts, but whose characterization featured all kinds of novelties under the auspices of the Arkadian line. In this context, Atalanta was described as a granddaughter of the Arkadian Lykourgos (son of Aleos, son of Apheidas), who was credited with a number of sons. These were notably, Iasios, Atalanta's father, Amphidamas the father of Melanion (Atalanta's first cousin who also became her mate), and Ankaios the father of Agapenor[160], who though traditionally associated with the lineage of Kalydon (Il.2.609, 23.635), appears here as a bona fide Arkadian native. In this way, it was furthermore claimed, that the Arkadian Agapenor was the man who led the Arkadian contingent to Troy. The Arkadian genealogy as we have it, however, plays no perceptible part in early Greek epic.

The Arkadian Atalanta, daughter of Iasios, makes two early appearances in Greek art that coincide fairly well with other manifestations of Arkadian legend in the same period. On the *Chest of Kypselos* (Paus.5.19.2) and on the *François Vase* (ca.570[161]) Atalanta is paired with Melanion, a pairing that indicates the Atalanta in question is the daughter of Iasios of the Arkadian line. This same Atalanta surfaces in Theognis (1287-1294), Xenophon (Kynegetikos 1.7), Palaiphatos (13), Kallimachos (H 3.215-216), Apollonios (1.769-773), Ovid (*Ars Amatoria* 2.185-191, 3.771-777[162]), and Statius (*Thebaid* 6.563-565). Yet in the Hesiodic *Catalogue of Women*, which antedates the above listed sources, with the possible exception of Theognis, this woman's Boiotian double is cited instead, namely: Atalanta, daughter of Schoineus, who was a son of Athamas, a son of Aiolos (ApB 1.9.2). There, Hippomenes' race against Atalanta was one of the selected narrative interludes in an otherwise densely genealogical text, giving the story a kind of special emphasis (Hes fr 72-76 MW)[163].

The snippets of evidence preserved in subsequent authors indicate that there was a movement to replace the Boiotian with the Arkadian, which was mainly tripped up by the problem of suppressing a potent and unruly cognizance of the Boiotian Atalanta, daughter of Schoineus, and her well-known suitor, Hippomenes. According to this view, the impression that there were two distinct Atalantas was precisely the intention of the redactors who created and promoted the Arkadian one, for they did not do so casually, or just for entertainment, but to diminish the status of the model in favor of the status of the replica.

Overall this initiative was extremely successful, but for the persistence of the Boiotian's persona, which prompted an ad hoc array of solutions, in which the proclivities of each interpreter guided their interpretive approach to the dual Atalanta dilemma. Some favored Atalanta, daughter of Iasios, others insisted that she was the daughter of Schoineus. Some avoided any reference to her parentage, while a few mixed and matched Melanion with Hippomenes, and other elements of her two stories, drawing attention to the synthetic nature of the mythic distinction between the two. The Arkadian Atalanta and Melanion were as a rule overwhelmingly favored, although they never completely suppressed the legacy of the Boiotian Atalanta in the realm of Greek mytho-cultural consciousness. Thus, Apollodoros' abridgement, which blended both personalities[164], did not do so without taking note of a number of countervailing opinions including Atalanta's Boiotian lineage, which he cites as the preference of Hesiod and others (ApB 3.9.2). Ovid's strategy too warrants separate mention because he avoided the whole sticky issue by addressing the Arkadian in the *Ars Amatoria* and dealing with the Boiotian in the *Metamorphoses*.

In this regard, it is important to emphasize Atalanta's exceptional role in a number of collaborative heroic quests. She was known, for example, as a competitor in the funeral games held in honor of Pelias, son of Kretheus, son of Aiolos, as well as uncle and adversary of the hero Jason, leader of the Argonautic adventure[165]. Remarkably, in this context, she competed in wrestling, specifically against Peleus, father of Achilles[166]. More remarkably still, she was held in some quarters to have been the victor[167], though there are, notwithstanding, accounts of the match that ignored Atalanta altogether and gave Peleus more traditional adversaries[168]. Atalanta was again known as the only female participant in the hunt for the Kalydonian boar, where, at least in some versions, she prompted the further conflict between Meleagros and his uncles either by winning the boars's hide as the boar-slayer[169], or by receiving the hide as a gift from Meleagros[170], who some late authors assert was also her lover[171]. Evidently, it also became customary to include Atalanta on the Argonauts' voyage. Apollonios, however, rejected this notion by having Jason dissuade her on account of the danger of a lone beautiful woman in a crew full of men. Here Apollonios emphasizes guest-friendship ties forged between Jason and Atalanta during Jason's visit to Mt. Mainalos and Atalanta's reciprocal gift of a spear, which is enough to establish that Apollonios had the Arkadian Atalanta in mind (AR 768-773)[172].

The antiquity of Atalanta's participation in each and/or all of these adventures cannot be conclusively gauged due to the absence of early epic testimony. It is as likely, however, that such a heroine - a kind of independent Amazon archetype[173] - was a bona fide fixture of early Greek tradition, as it is likely that her story gradually expanded in accordance with emerging mytho-political trends[174]. Though the Kalydonian boar hunt may be the best bet, it cannot be determined with concrete certainty which of these episodes featured her early on. On the other hand, it would seem prudent to doubt that the myth of Atalanta materialized out of nowhere, and cogent to speculate that of these three legends the Argonaut's voyage is most likely to be an inference based on her performance at Kalydon and/or at Iolkos in the days before her eventual marriage, which given her personal characterization, was hardly an ordinary nuptial event. The salient observation, in this regard, is the link between Atalanta and these heroic adventures, along with a named preference for the daughter of Schoineus in the authors who choose to make mention of them[175].

Given then that a measure of uncertainty surrounds the chronological accumulation of episodes that became a part of Atalanta's story, the evidence, as it stands, can be seen to accord with a concerted effort to re-create and relocate a mythological figure named Atalanta. Such an effort *a priori* suggests there was something substantial to be gained in so doing, even if Atalanta's initial portrayal cannot be straightforwardly extricated from the buildup of traits that in due course attached to her dual personality. It is plain, in addition, that the heroic adventures in which Atalanta played a part all belong to the old Aiolic repertoire. They were acknowledged as such by ancient antiquarians, whereas nothing Arkadian traditionally played a part in any of these prominent early stories. Taking a closer look at the extant evidence reveals a fairly self-conscious geo-political shift and indicates that the premier Atalanta was an Aiolid who hailed from Boiotia.

Notably, various methods were used to transform the Boiotian Atalanta into an Arkadian heroine. The most obvious method was the deployment of the Arkadian genealogy outlined above. A second strategy was less straightforward and requires a close reading of some of the more subtle literary assertions. Its identification, however, goes a long way to show that the Arkadian designation became predominant, in spite of mixed opinions as to how the shift should best be accomplished. Apollodoros (1.9.16), for example (like Diodoros 4.41.2), states that Atalanta, daughter of Schoineus, sailed along on the Argonautic adventure, yet when dealing with the Kalydonian boar, he states that Atalanta, daughter of Schoineus, was an Arkadian not a Boiotian (ApB 1.8.2), which would seem to be a contradiction in terms. Yet, Pausanias also agreed with this idea and provides a vital piece of added information, namely that the Arkadian plain known as Schoineus[176] was named after Schoineus, a Boiotian, after he immigrated to the Peloponnese (8.35.10). The name Schoineus traditionally referred to a Boiotian district in between Thebes and Anthedon[177]. Here Pausanias expands upon Schoineus' eponymous influence in order to invoke not one site but two: a Boiotian homeland and an Arkadian resettlement[178]. Taken together, these passages show that the phrase *daughter of Schoineus* was not necessarily taken to mean that the Atalanta in question was the Boiotian Atalanta of old. Instead, they demonstrate that the authors cited above used the phrase to describe the Arkadian Atalanta in lieu of acknowledging her Arkadian genealogy, evidently because, one can only suppose, they were reluctant to characterize the Atalanta who participated in well-known heroic events as the daughter of Iasios, son of Lykourgos, in contradiction to established tradition. Pausanias again shows that this was the case through a slight but significant modification to the Arkadian genealogy.

To coincide with the fact that his Atalanta was a daughter of Schoineus, a Boiotian who migrated to the Peloponnese, Pausanias removes the Arkadian Iasios (Atalanta's designated Arkadian father) from his normative place in the Arkadian line. Indeed, Pausanias grants Lykourgos, son of Aleos only two sons against Apollodoros' four (ApB 3.9.2). He retains only Epochos and Ankaios, annihilates Iasios, and makes Amphidamas Lykourgos' brother instead of his son, thus recasting but maintaining Melanion and his father, who notably comes up elsewhere in Pausanias' text (8.4.10, 3.12.9)[179]. As for Epochos and

Ankaios, the former dies off without much fanfare, while the latter was said to have sailed with the Argo and to have subsequently met his death in the hunt for the Kalydonian boar (8.4.10, 8.45.2). As mentioned above, according to the *Iliad*, the Aitolian Ankaios' son, Agapenor, represented the Arkadian contingent at Troy (2.609-614)[180]. Against the *Iliad*, however, the Arkadian Agapenor, son of Ankaios, was descended from Ankaios, son of Lykourgos, rather than from Ankaios, son of Oineus, a member of the ruling house of the city of Pleuron, known to Homer as the Kouretes (Il.9.529-587, 23.635).

Thus, in contrast to the substantial roster of Arkadian mythological thefts, the point here is to note how Pausanias' adjustment permits the Boiotian Atalanta to become an Arkadian independently of the enhanced Arkadian genealogy, which is all the more interesting given the degree to which he accepts Arkadian innovations. Apparently, a persistent strain of thought refused to deny Atalanta's descent from Schoineus of Boiotia, with her legendary ties to Boiotian territory, even though, at least in Pausanias' case, Hippomenes was supplanted by Melanion, and even though, in more general terms, her Arkadian identity eclipsed her Boiotian roots. So while Pausanias modified the Arkadian genealogy, expressly it seems, to exclude Atalanta, he still gives the line considerable credence. He just refused to acknowledge Atalanta as a legendary possession of the Arkadian line.

In general, Pausanias was committed to internal consistency in his own work. He was sensitive to, and at pains to ward off jarring mythological contradictions to the greatest extent it was possible to do so, given the nature of his material. Thankfully, for the sake of documentary evidence, Apollodoros did not have the same scruples. He readily reports pieces of information that cannot coexist and at the same time be true. In so doing, time and again Apollodoros reports valuable data that would have been censored by other writers, who used strategic omission, among other tactics, to maximize coherence in their own narratives. Diodoros and Pausanias, for example, neglect the fact that Schoineus was well-known as a son of Athamas (son of Aiolos ApB 1.9.1) and of Themisto (daughter of Hypseus ApB 1.9.2), two old and prestigious Aiolic figures[181]. This is quite understandable if, as it seems, they aimed to minimize Atalanta's Aiolic background[182] in favor of an Arkadian *mise en scène*.

Apollodoros fundamentally shared the same goal, though he readily adopted the Arkadian account of Atalanta's genealogical heritage (3.9.2[183]). With respect to this preference he accordingly set about conflating the life stories of both figures[184] at once, admitting that others addressed her heritage differently, and making a subtle genealogical nod to the notion of her Boiotian origins. Thus, Apollodoros declares that Iasios' wife was a woman named Klymene, daughter of Minyas, which could well have been another Arkadian claim, but which quite transparently, in any case, gives the Arkadian Atalanta Boiotian roots on her mother's side of the family[185]. Apollodoros has Melanion win Atalanta's hand in a foot race, a role commonly associated with Hippomenes and Boiotia, while he has her father, Iasios, expose her at birth, has her suckled by a bear, and raised by hunters, attributes commonly assigned to the Arkadian. Then after noting that Hesiod and others describe Atalanta as the daughter of Schoineus (son of Athamas and Themisto), Apollodoros cites Euripides for the idea that she was, alternatively, a daughter of Mainalos (eponym of an Arkadian mountain) who, as it happened, married Hippomenes. Therefore, although the Arkadian Atalanta surfaces on the chest of Kypselos, in the company of Melanion, in the early sixth century we witness a fair measure of critical resistance to the Arkadian genealogy that embodied this claim, as well as a diversity of sustained commitments to aspects of Atalanta's Boiotian identity. So, evidently, Euripides too, preferred an Arkadian Atalanta, whom he reportedly assigned an autochthonous birth and paired with the Boiotian Atalanta's Hippomemes[186].

The key observation with regard to all this is that the politically motivated desire to upstage the Boiotian Atalanta not only involved an Arkadian double who was a good deal like her, though at the same time quite different, but alternatively involved an interpretive twist to her established heroic legacy that rejected the split in her personality and simply transported her to Arkadia, at times substituting her old lover Hippomenes with the Arkadian Melanion in accordance with contemporary mytho-political trends. Moreover, once these tactics have been sorted out, it is not inconceivable that the relocation approach, minus the preference for Melanion, may well have informed the Hesiodic *Catalogue*. But whether or not this was the case, the miscellaneous documentary strands depict a tension between two partly distinct, yet competing, identities, those of two separate heroines from two separate regions who happened to be graced with the same given name. The issue of the fate of Atalanta with the related question of heroic offspring corroborate the idea that the trouble stems back to the promotion of a quasi-duplicate figure, whose new roots were established genealogically, but who was, as it happened, unable to foster a peaceful coexistence with her more ancient namesake, who first commanded the honors that elevated the name.

ATALANTA AND PARTHENOPAIS

Atalanta and her husband, according to legend, were transformed into lions by an act of divine vengeance for the impropriety of having sex in a temple[187]. It is important to note with respect to this story that metamorphosis features among the types of mythic motifs useful for terminating a genealogical lineage. Metamorphosis essentially functioned as a supernatural form of extinction in contrast to more straightforward methods of death[188]. In this regard, it was somewhat akin to being chosen for perpetual service to the gods, as in Zeus' famous seizure of Ganymedes (Il.20.232-235; HHAphrodite 202-217) or Eos' seizure of the old Arigive hero Kleitos (Od.15.250)[189]. Notable too, is that Greek mythology generally granted equal acclaim to admirably famous and infamous acts[190].

It is worth asking next whether this astonishing fate was attached to Atalanta and Hippomenes or to Atalanta and Melanion? The answer is that it was applied to both, first, however, as Palaiphatos reports, to Atalanta and Melanion, but later, and thereafter, predominantly, to Atalanta and Hippomenes. This patterning is important. Since the chest of Kypselos provides the *terminus ante quem* for the emergence of Arkadia's Atalanta, Palaiphatos' account shows that the metamorphosis story was at some point attached to her legendary persona[191], which, in turn, suggests that it was either an original feature of the biography of the Arkadian Atalanta[192] or that it represented a strain of resistance to the offspring attributed to this couple, a sentiment that comes up in other sources. In due course, this fate was evidently transferred to Atalanta and Hippomenes whose progeny remain a conspicuous blank. In any event, by the Classical Period Atalanta and Melanion were awarded a son named Parthenopais. Presuming, as it seems most reasonable to do, that the marriage of Atalanta and Hippomenes, which involved a great and perilous tournament for her hand[193], initially also led to the birth of children, the transfer of the metamorphosis story from Atalanta and Melanion to Atalanta and Hippomenes was an adjustment strategically capable of discrediting the existence of any such offspring.

This notion gathers strength from three related factors: 1) that by the late fifth century Atalanta and Melanion were exclusively credited with a son; 2) that no evidence whatsoever survives concerning the offspring of Atalanta and Hippomenes (nor is there any data until the time of Ovid concerning the lineage of Hippomenes); 3) that the metamorphosis story seems to have shifted from Atalanta and Melanion to Atalanta and Hippomenes, as recognition of the Arkadian Parthenopais became the dominant mythological doctrine. The suggestion here is that the attribution and reattribution of the metamorphosis story, viewed in conjunction with Atalanta's biography, and the evidence concerning her only recorded child, collectively forward the present working hypothesis that the oldest Atalanta was the Boiotian and that the business of the Arkadian was to cipher off and to repossess a considerable number of her ancient honors, more and more of them actually, as time wore on.

As for Parthenopais[194], whenever he was associated with Atalanta, which was, as it happens, not always the case, he was considered to be the son of Melanion or Ares, a joint attribution entirely typical of heroic progeny engendered by gods[195]. Notably, by comparison, Parthenopais is never associated with Atalanta and Hippomenes. His link to Atalanta and Melanion, however, is complicated by a streak of popular opinion that knew him already as a son of Talaos (son of Bias, son of Amythaon), of the Aiolic line of Kretheus and Tyro[196].

This is an especially old and venerable lineage. It generated the main heroic protagonists involved in the legendary Argive wars against Thebes. This series of conflicts was acknowledged by Homer[197] and commemorated by Aeschylos in his *Seven Against Thebes*, originally the conclusion of a trilogy on the subject[198]. The Argive-Theban Wars were also addressed in the lost epic poem entitled the *Thebais*[199], and in a number of other fifth-century dramas that, unfortunately, have not survived[200]. As the evidence stands, Aeschylos' extant remarks and the relevant statements in Sophokles and Euripides, all acknowledge Parthenopais as a soldier in the first Argive assault against Thebes. In this context, he is described, either, simply as an Arkadian, or as the son of the Arkadian Atalanta.[201] Hekataios, however, in the early fifth century (FGrHist 1F32), with fragments of Philokles and Aristarchos (two scarcely known fifth-century tragedians), all weigh in on the side of the old figure Talaos (against Melanion) whom they explicitly cite as Parthenopais' father[202]. By the end of the century, however, Hellanikos maintained that Atalanta, daughter of Iasios, and Melanion, son of Amphidamas, were the mother and father of Parthenopais (FGrHist 4F99), throwing considerable light on the more oblique references in the works of the major Athenian tragedians. Accordingly, on the balance, it seems that Parthenopais, son of Atalanta, rose to prominence sometime between Hekataios and Hellanikos.

A preference for the Arkadian Parthenopais also occurs in Apollodoros (3.9.2) with the added proviso that earlier in his text he readily acknowledges that the Parthenopais who participated in Argive assault against Thebes was, as recorded elsewhere, the son of Talaos (ApB 1.9.13). Pausanias accepts the main implication of Apollodoros' dual testimony: namely that on account of the popular trend, represented explicitly by Hellanikos, chroniclers who were thereafter unwilling to make the Argive warrior a son of Atalanta (and Melanion) were accordingly forced to entertain the idea of two distinct figures named Parthenopais in light of the advancement of public opinion. Thus, Pausanias knows the deeds of the son of Talaos (e.g. 9.18.6), and knows of the existence of the son of Melanion (e.g. 3.12.9), and therefore, with due regard for his predecessors' remarks, orchestrates a clear demonstration of yet another set of conditions that led to the duplication of Greek mythic figures.

The doubling of Parthenopais in this instance resulted from the refusal on the part of mythographers to exclusively credit the new mythic figure with the great deeds and attributes of a same-named, but genealogically different predecessor[203]. Pausanias exemplifies this predicament since he declined to corroborate the fifth-century novelty that altered the lineage of Parthenopais and transferred his identity to the Arkadian line by replacing the son of Talaos with the son of Atalanta through the technique labeled here mythological-theft-type-two[204]. Though unwilling to actively go along with this theft, Pausanias felt obliged to acknowledge its impact. His response took the form of a diplomatic concession inasmuch as he admitted that under the circumstances there had to be two separate Parthenopais. Apollodoros, by contrast, was all out in favor of the genealogical amendments sponsored by the theft (ApB 3.6.9, 3.9.2). Nevertheless, he was not apt to enforce the type of self-censorship that would have concealed it, leaving no trace either of its existence, or for that matter, its motivation. The relatively late doubling of Parthenopais contrasts in a number of interesting ways with the earlier doubling of Atalanta.

In the case of Atalanta, the division of one into two personalities was apparently part of the initial aim, which set up a same-named yet distinctive competitor, in order to capitalize on the ambiguity as to which was which and who was who. The objective was for this new competitor to secure her own special place in the limelight and potentially upstage her esteemed namesake. The career of the replica may have started out modestly, but almost inevitably, in due course, began to encroach on the heroic feats traditionally associated with the original. No doubt this development gathered widespread acceptance, but fell short of commanding public unanimity because there were those whose knowledge of tradition forbid them from casually playing along. This contingent developed a less radical strategy, one which made the Boiotian Atalanta Arkadian without a complete genealogical makeover. This compromise tactic, in addition, implied that there was only one Atalanta, not two.

But the Arkadian innovation, in the final analysis, was more influential than the compromise strategy, to the effect that the dominant Atalanta was hands-down the 'pure- blooded' Arkadian one[205]. Moreover, in the absence of published access to the logic behind this less radical view, and in the absence of telling contradictory data, it would be impossible to reconstruct the ongoing conflict over this heroine, and it would be equally difficult to determine, whether stripped of all subsequent emendations, Atalanta was really one person or two. Yet the data exists in this case and in others because Greek mythic change confronted serious problems when it came to exercising control over the reception of Greek mythological changes. And all such emendations came up against a tacit awareness of the antecedent structure wherein the great protagonists of the Heroic Age were affiliates of the Aiolic account of Greek prehistory.

Reciprocally, Atalanta and Parthenopais illustrate the kind of tension provoked by invasive anti-Aiolic activity. Atalanta, daughter of Iasios, a case of mythic-theft-type-one, was championed as a second same-named protagonist. The skeptics insisted there was only one. She was the Boiotian, yet at the same time Arkadian in response to contemporary political actualities. The skeptics made their case, but still and all, it succumbed to the overall dominance of the 'pure-blooded' Arkadian who triumphed as the unified Atalanta amidst the chatter of dissenting voices. At a distance in time and a sea away, perceiving the clash between the two personalities, Ovid thought it best to treat each Atalanta in her own separate literary context.

Parthenopais was an instance of mythic-theft-type two and a post-script attached to Atalanta's persona. He was championed as the one true Parthenopais against the reputation of his illustrious namesake. The skeptics insisted on two separate Parthenopais, preserving the Aiolic legacy of the first, while accommodating the second as the son of the Arkadian Atalanta.

THE BOIOTIAN ATALANTA AND
THE LINE OF ATHAMAS

Turning to the genealogical heritage of the Boiotian Atalanta so often glossed over in the extant reportage, Atalanta, daughter of Schoineus, was a descendant in the third line of Athamas, a son of Aiolos, who married three times. Homer demonstrates an awareness of Athamas' first two marriages, both of which involved awesome and tragic events that distinguished the life stories of his offspring as significant benchmarks in the Heroic Age[206]. It is clear that the genealogy of the Athamas branch of the Aiolic saga underwent considerable adaptation from the early Archaic to the Classical Period, at which point it received considerable attention from the Athenian tragedians[207], whereas between the Classical Period and Pausanias' Περιήγησις further interpretive rearrangement took place. It is also clear that key elements in the saga stem back to the earliest Greek mythic repertoire, a factor that contributed to its popularity as a subject for dramatic exploration and to its standard inclusion in synoptic texts that addressed the highlights of Greek prehistory.

Athamas fathered two children, Phrixos and Helle, with an obscure goddess-type woman named Nephele (viz. the cloud). Persecuted by Athamas' second wife Ino, they escaped from Greece on the back of a golden ram, which their mother provided for their rescue[208]. Helle fell off the ram to meet an untimely death, falling into the sea at the Hellespont, which was thereafter thus named in her honor. Phrixos landed successfully in Kolchis and established himself in the kingdom of Aeetes in exchange for the fleece of the golden ram. He was said, in addition, to have married the king's daughter[209]. Aeetes' possession of the Golden Fleece later prompted the Argonauts' quest to the east.

Athamas' second wife, Ino, was a daughter of Kadmos, who gave birth to Learchos and Melikertes. These two sons also met an untimely death when their parents were seized by divinely inspired madness. The madness was said to have been prompted by Hera, who aimed to avenge the couple's dedication to the vulnerable infant god Dionysos after his mother Semele (viz. Ino's sister and paramour of Zeus) was consumed by fire[210]. Thereupon, in a frenzy Athamas killed Learchos. Ino grasped Melikertes and leapt into the sea whereby they were transformed into sea deities (Od.5.331-353; ApB 1.9.1, 3.4.3). After regaining his sanity Athamas married Themisto, daughter of Hypseus. She was therefore a sister of Kyrene, whose son Aristaios by the god Apollo married a daughter of Kadmos as well (viz. Autinoe, Ino's sister).

Tales of Phrixos' descendants returning to Thessaly from Kolchis surface in the mythographical testimony (e.g. Paus.9.34.6-8[211]), though Diodoros apparently found it expedient to suggest that the family ultimately died off (4.46.1-2, 47.5). And while the destruction of the line of Athamas and Ino evidently stemmed back to early epic, which also presupposed Phrixos and Helle's escape, Euripides evidently engineered the destruction of the line of Athamas and Themisto as well, using a plot line that Timothy Gantz observes looks very much like his own unique contribution. In any case, whenever Athamas was granted any sustained genealogical influence, it stemmed from Phrixos' progeny conceived in Kolchis (homeland of King Aeetes and his daughter Medea), or from the children of Themisto, daughter of Hypseus.

Regarding Athamas' three marriages, Timothy Gantz remarks that such an unusual collection of stories associated with this one mythic figure suggests that Athamas may well represent "two or even three separate persons (176)" by way of "the conflation of traditions (177)." But the fact remains that the three main stories in question were explicitly and repeatedly linked to Athamas[212]. Moreover, Athamas' first two marriages established two key prerequisites relevant to ensuing mythic events: a geographical signpost en route to the Black Sea that recalled the demise of Phrixos' sister, Helle, and king Aeetes' possession of the Golden Fleece, the object that prompted the Argonauts' voyage. In this light, Athamas' third marriage was the only source capable of sustaining the continuity of his family lineage on the Greek mainland. As for the blood connection with the line of Kadmos, although it led nowhere genealogically since Greek legend killed off the offspring of that union, the goddess Leukothea (the name Ino assumed after her transformation), as Homer tells us, rescued Odysseus from great peril at sea, while Ino's son, Melikertes, in the role of the numinous, idealized youth Palaimon, was worshipped as a hero at the Isthmian games (cf. Paus.1.44.8, 2.1.8, 2.2.1, 2.3.4, 8.48.2) [213]. Athamas' life story appears to break down into two kinds of constituent elements.

There is, on the one hand, a basic cast of characters and their prescribed fates. There are, on the other, various cause and effect explanations that elaborate on the basic plot structure and interpret its progress in different ways, toying, at times, with the fate of major protagonists against a background of audience knowledge that rendered such deviations perceptible for their deviance[214]. Though the buildup of embellishments generates the impression of arbitrary renditions mired in confusion, an impression intensified by the loss of most of the literature that dealt with Athamas' biography, it is still possible to perceive that these emendations depended on the same basic underlying story. In this sense, they mainly suggested new ways of interpreting cause and effect relations. Upon close inspection, this re-interpretive work has, for the most part, very little effect on the outcome of the story in question. Thus, for example, it is of no great significance whether Phrixos and Helle were rescued by Nephele from the woods, from the sea, or from a sacrificial altar, nor whether a corrupt oracle or a famished populace demanded that Athamas sacrifice his son Phrixos, nor whether Ino's plot against her stepchildren was contrived out of jealousy, or instead, out of vengeance after her stepson spurned her sexual advances, or even whether this role is transferred to Themisto, and so on and so forth. Indeed, it doesn't even really have much effect if the order of Athamas' liaisons is reversed so that Nephele gave birth to Phrixos and Helle after Ino gave birth to Learchos and Melikertes[215], as long as Phrixos and Helle set off on the ram and Learchos, Ino, and Melikertes all perish, paving the way for Athamas' third marriage.

No doubt these variations cause interpretive static, but they basically amount to creative variations on the same fundamental family drama. Thus, the observation that such variations worked within the parameters of a single plot structure makes it possible to separate the wheat from the chaff. Mythological emendations of consequence structurally, which is to say of consequence genealogically, stand out in comparison to other forms of creative reinterpretive work that mainly sought to explain strange and violent traditions in terms of viable mythological causes and their respective mythic effects. In contrast to the variants listed above, the surviving account of Euripides' *Ino*[216] indicates that this play deviated considerably from the established legendary plot structure, altering the outcome of the story. For although the line of Athamas and Themisto was an acknowledged source of heroic progeny from the time of the Hesiodic *Catalogue of Women,* which was almost certainly guided by earlier precedents (Hes fr 70 MW), Euripides invokes the jealous-mother-motif to have Themisto attempt to kill Ino's children in much the same way that Ino was said to have plotted to kill the children of Nephele. Themisto, however, according to this account, wound up killing her own children instead of her rival's and, upon that discovery, took her own life. This version stands alone in staging the extinction of an otherwise viable branch of the family through the clever application of a stock motif[217], while the development of this plot line is only unique in that, in defiance of established tradition, it altered the outcome of the whole Athamas saga by eliminating the progeny of Athamas' third marriage. Notably, in so doing the story eliminated the birth of the Boiotian Atalanta.

Needless to say, there was no authoritative agency in existence to regulate or prohibit such deviations, so the very existence of this plot structure effectively illustrates a number of things. It illustrates, first, a measure of interest in the complete destruction of the line of Themisto. It demonstrates, secondly, that genealogical alternatives of this magnitude competed with established traditional tales much like commodities on the free market. Accordingly, just as nothing stood in the way of radically counter-conventional versions of the way ancient stories were supposed to run, the effect of such novelties depended upon public recognition of their aberrant status, and subsequently, on whether there was sufficient interest in the transformation of a brilliant novelty into a popular standard. Thereafter, the selection process boiled down to the political influence of professional storytellers whose work was linked to the status of their native states, which along with the exigencies of testimonial survival generated the Greek mythological record. Third, it emphasizes a qualitative distinction between structural and circumstantial amendments and reveals that the confusion about Athamas' persona was primarily of the circumstantial variety, though Euripides' *Ino*, an exception to this trend, as far as the legacy of his progeny was concerned, indicates that in fifth-century Athens there were structure-altering initiatives at large relevant to the fate of the Boiotian Atalanta. Still, there is ultimately no deeply compelling reason to attempt to deconstruct Athamas, son of Aiolos, into several distinct previous personalities, as opposed to viewing the man as a heroic ancestor with a traditionally eccentric personal life.

EARLY BOIOTIAN GENEALOGIES: THE OBSCURE LINE OF MINYAN ORCHOMENOS

The inter-relations of Athamas' progeny within the early Aiolic genealogical structure can only be assessed as if through a glass darkly on account of the level of manipulation imposed on Athamas' family later on. Another obstacle to any real sense of clarity is the extensive reconstruction of the legendary history of Minyan Orchomenos to which the line of Athamas was apparently also linked. This situation is exemplified by Pausanias' remarkably complex and manifestly synthetic genealogical portrait of that Boiotian city. Essentially, Pausanias describes the Minyan line as a sequence of kingships that alternated between the descendants of Sisyphos, son of Aiolos, and the descendants of Athamas, son of Aiolos[218]. There may well be some long-standing truth to the matter, though it is difficult to access genuine early details. The later reconstruction of the Minyan line is further exemplified by the redefinition of the word Minyan in common parlance, which was fully in force by the Classical Period. It is clear that the word Minyan came to be used as a catch-all term for the cohort of heroes who participated in the Argonauts' voyage, and applied, by extension, to their descendants (e.g. Hdt.4.145[219]). But this usage was only superficially relevant to the legendary genealogy of Boiotian Orchomenos and did much to increase its genealogical obscurity.

In his detailed analysis of the remaining fragments of the Hesiodic *Catalogue of Women*, Martin West recommends the eponymous figure Minyas as a candidate for the seventh son of Aiolos whose identity has been lost in a textual lacuna (West 1985: 64-66; Gantz 1993: 182-183). Undoubtedly, Minyas became a prominent member of the lineage of Orchomenos. Looking back at the Homeric evidence, however, it seems that, early on, Iasos or Iasios, of Orchomenos, was the regional figure of the greatest stature in the upper reaches of the Minyan line (Od.11.281-285). And while times had changed, and mythic favorites along with them by the composition of the *Catalogue*, Minyas, son of Aiolos is not an attribution favored in the mythological sources, which is surely another relevant factor[220]. Notably, no other son of Aiolos, was identified by an eponymous name, so if indeed Minyas ascended to this post (as opposed to reigning further down in the sequence), his ascent would register as another key indication of the mythological changes that were imposed on the genealogy of Orchomenos in the post-epic period.

What can be discerned from the evidence, as it stands, is that the progeny of Athamas were deeply engaged in a complex web of inter-relations among Aiolic stemmata in central Greece, and especially in Boiotia. These connections logically mirrored the connections between the line of Athamas and the line of Thebes, except for the fact that their genealogical organization is now, by contrast, barely discernible[221]. Major early legends associated with the region are preserved in a kind of disembodied form, that is, minus a clear-cut concept of their schematic layout in the upper lineage zones, and oftentimes challenged by competitive claims made by distant Greek principalities. So, for example, the deeds of Orion and the great master builders, Trophonios and Agamedes, were certainly native to this region, even though they were later re-assigned: the former to Krete,[222] the latter to Arkadia[223]. Famous legendary conflicts survive in shadowy form, often under layers of reinterpretation, such as initiatives against the mysterious Phlegyans[224] and ongoing hostilities between Thebes and Orchomenos[225]. Notably, two granddaughters of Iasos (of the old Minyan line) were held to have married the two most famous magnates of the Aiolic line of Iolkos, namely, Pelias and Neleus, respectively[226]. And it is clear that this line forged important connections in the northwestern Peloponnese[227].

By contrast, interactions with the Theban line directly affected Athamas' biography and have been preserved with much greater clarity because the main figures of the line of Kadmos sustained notoriety in their own right. The preservation of Themisto's heritage was reinforced by the status of her sister Kyrene, who gave her name to the prosperous North African city[228]. In subsequent generations things get a good deal more hazy, but the link between Athamas' line and Boiotian Orchomenos persists in the evidence, in spite of increasing emphasis on the eponymous figure Minyas, which is often accompanied by a reluctance to address Minyas' heritage whatsoever. Minyas and the descriptive adjective Minyan apparently provided a useful barrier that made it unnecessary to delve further into the Aiolic identity of the venerable families whose legacies dominated the prehistory of the region. Nonetheless, Athamas' line is often linked to Orchomenos, which suggests marriage ties to early Minyan families, including, perhaps, as Pausanias suggests, marriage connections with the line of Sisyphos. It was this nexus of stories, at any rate, that animated the ancestral background of the Boiotian Atalanta.

No siblings are attributed to the Boiotian Atalanta. Yet if she ever had any, this is hardly surprising, inasmuch as Atalanta's Boiotian identity was essentially transmitted against the odds. Schoineus' brother Leukon, however, was credited early on with a number of daughters, who ostensibly married into illustrious lines, one of which at least commands a valid early provenance since it involved Kopreus, the herald of Eurystheus, whose son, Periphetes, according to Homer, took up residence at Mykenai (Il.15.636-640)[229]. It is difficult to gauge the early authenticity of figures such as Presbon and his son, Klymenos the alleged descendants of Phrixos who returned from Kolchis and took over the kingship at Orchomenos. But it is not inconceivable that persistent reports to the effect that Phrixos' descendants also enhanced the genealogical landscape out of which the Boiotian Atalanta and her lover Hippomenes first arose were based on a well-known early tradition. Essentially in terms of mythic antiquity, Atalanta's Arkadian genealogical context is far from equivalent to its Boiotian counterpart, where we witness the confluence of great old epic families in a rich, if fragmentary, legendary environment.

OTHER RELEVANT NOVELTIES IN THE ARKADIAN LINE

The foregoing discussion of Atalanta leaves a few loose ends relevant to the rise of post-Homeric Arkadian mythology. In books six and seven of the *Iliad* two men named Lykourgos play a part in the narrative. The first, a son of Dryas, was described according to *Iliad* 1.263 as a member of the northern Greek Lapith clan (Il.1.263). In book six, as reported by Diomedes, this Lykourgos was ultimately blinded by Zeus and did not live long after that brutal incident, which he had apparently brought upon himself by terrorizing Dionysos and his followers (Il.6.130-`40). Another Lykourgos appears shortly thereafter amidst one of Nestor's frequent reminiscences (Il.7.123-160). Accordingly, it is clear that the poem was working with two distinct individuals named Lykourgos. The first Lykourgos died prematurely because his outrageous deeds had offended the gods[230]. The second Lykourgos lived to old age in the halls of his palace (Il.7.132-149). And though his lineage is not specified, the second Lykourgos was an

Arkadian hero. Recounting a confrontation between Pylians and Arkadians that took place in his youth, Nestor boasts that he killed a warrior named Ereuthalion, who wore the armor of one Areithoos. Lykourgos, it is stated, obtained this armor at the time when he ambushed and killed Areithoos. He later left it to his henchman Ereuthalion, who wore it into battle against the Pylians.

As mentioned above, the Arkadian line laid claim to Agapenor, son of Ankaios, whom the *Iliad* identified with the Aitolian lineage that evidently stemmed back to Aiolic sources. It does not seem like a matter of mere coincidence that in transforming Ankaios and his son Agapenor into Arkadian heroes, the new link was forged via a man named Lykourgos whose Arkadian identity could be traced to the *Iliad*. Thus, once the *Iliad*'s Lykourgos was interpreted as a major progenitor for the Arkadian line (son of Aleos, son of Apheidas, son of Arkas), he successfully negated Ankaios' and Agapenor's early association with Aitolia, while taking on a few additional sons (viz. Iasos and Amphidamas), he further accommodated Atalanta and Melanion into a family that significantly enhanced the legendary mystique of contemporary Arkadia.

Meanwhile, as we have seen, Lykourgos' brother, Kepheus, Kepheus' daughter, Sterope, and a cohort of sons, linked Arkadia with Herakles' Peloponnesian activities[231]. Beyond these examples, it is worth summarizing a few further attributes of the Arkadian line before proceeding on to other material. Mainly, Kepheus and Lykourgos had a sister named Auge. One rung further up, their father, Aleos, had a sister named Stheneboia. These two heroines invoke major early legends, though these legends' early attachment to the genealogy of Arkadia is a very dubious prospect at best.

Auge was the mother of Telephos by Herakles. Their story was one of considerable antiquity, though later subject to considerable elaboration. The legend at issue is the first allied Greek expedition to Troy that ran awry on the coast of Mysia[232]. Providing the background, Auge's life story explained how it happened that the allied Greek forces in their initial attempt to reach the city of Troy came up against the army of an Asian prince who was actually a Greek ex-patriot. In his effort to defend his kingdom, Telephos of Mysia was wounded by Achilles[233]. This wound later forced him to travel to Greece in search of Achilles, because only the spear with which he was wounded had the power to heal his wound. In exchange for Achilles' cooperation, Telephos, legend had it, was coerced into directing the Greek fleet to Troy in the second, more famous, expedition[234].

Although the Mysian prelude to the Trojan War does not surface explicitly in the Homeric poems, it prefigures a number of major events traditionally associated with the sack of Troy that are presupposed throughout the *Iliad* and referenced selectively in the *Odyssey*[235]. In particular it prefigures the slaying of Eurypylos, Telephos' son, by Neoptolemos, son of Achilles, in the course of the final struggle. This arrangement mirrors Achilles' wounding of Telephos in the initial engagement at Mysia. From what can be gleaned from the Arkadian account, which was certainly dominant by the fifth century when it inspired a number of Athenian tragedies[236], Auge, Aleos' daughter was impregnated by Herakles while on some business in Arkadia[237], whereupon, Aleos, in anger, put his daughter and grandson into a chest and set it out to sea[238]. Ultimately, they wind up in Mysia[239]. In an alternate version that became very popular, Auge exposed Telephos on Mt. Parthenion and was sent off by ship reaching Mysia alone[240]. There, she was either adopted as king Teuthras' daughter, or was otherwise taken as his wife. Various sequels to the exposure version inevitably also lead Telephos to Mysia, after growing up ignorant of his heritage. This setup offered the ideal set of conditions for a dramatic clash of mistaken identities.

Yet it is plain from the Hesiodic *Catalogue of Women* that at one time Auge made her way to Mysia, independently, in her youth. There, she was adopted and reared by King Teuthras and later encountered Herakles when he came into port en route to or from Laomedon's Troy (Hes fr. 165 MW). Without reference to other significant tales that feature the integration of major Greek heroes into illustrious eastern ruling houses, one might be tempted to wonder whether, in the beginning, Auge was not simply an unmarried daughter of the Mysian king. But given the life stories of Phrixos and Bellerophon, Auge's biography appears to play on the irony of Greek aggression against a great eastern city under the control of a native Greek hero. This perspective furthers the less than foregone conclusion that Auge was always portrayed as a Greek, but it does not necessarily promote the idea that she was also Arkadian from time immemorial. For Auge, the prospect of an Arkadian origin stemming all the way back to early epic is called into question by the impoverished status of Arkadia in the Homeric poems. Aside from border skirmishes with the Pylians, Arkadia on the whole is remarkably underrated. So, Agamemnon supplied their ships, while the contingent's leaders hailed from Aitolia. Bringing this information to the layout of the developed Arkadian genealogy where the majority of figures are demonstratively imports adapted to Arkadian specifications, makes it seem most unlikely that the Auge of early epic, if she was, indeed, a displaced Greek heroine, was also, of old, an Arkadian native.

This prospect is reinforced by the Arkadian Stheneboia, alleged daughter of Apheidas, son of Arkas. From a chronological standpoint, the respective development of these two heroine's stories is definitely striking. For in dealing with Auge, the Hesiodic *Catalogue* reports what may well be the earliest version of her life story. When it comes to Stheneboia, however, the *Catalogue* reports a remarkable novelty, which can fortunately be judged with reference to Homer. Stheneboia was the wife of king Proitos of Argos and undoubtedly the same woman whom the *Iliad* calls Anteia[241]. Once adopted, the new name successfully stuck. But Anteia / Stheneboia was also said to be the daughter of King Iobates of Lykia, where according to some accounts, Proitos lived for a time before the couple took up residence somewhere in Argos, possibly at Tiryns[242]. As the *Iliad* reports, when Bellerophon was a guest in their house, Stheneboia falsely informed her husband Proitos that Bellerophon had attempted to seduce her. This accusation led Proitos to send Bellerophon off to Lykia, requesting Iobates to put an end to him. Iobates, however, did not kill Bellerophon, who ultimately married a sister of Sthenoboia and became a Lykian ruler through marriage. In the present context, the point is to emphasize that according to the Hesiodic *Catalogue of Women*, the line of Arkadia evidently attempted to blot out Stheneboia's Lykian heritage and to make her an Arkadian native instead, namely, a daughter of Apheidas, rather than Iobates (Hes fr. 129 MW; ApB 3.9.1, however, by contrast ApB 2.2.1).

Thus, the Arkadian involvement with these two women highlights the remarkable success achieved by the Arkadian claim to possession of Auge, with a reciprocal failure to gain consensus when it came to possession of Sthenoboia. For while the *Catalogue* describes Sthenobia as a daughter of Apheidas of Arkadia, the remains of Euripides *Sthenobia*[243], for example (in accordance with a number of other texts), continue to describe her as a Lykian princess. And while the *Catalogue* situates the romance between Auge and Herakles in Asia Minor with respect to Herakles' dealings with Laomedon of Troy, subsequent sources place that encounter in Arkadia, ostensibly in conjunction with Arkadian legend, which also endeavored to promote precisely this kind of relocation in the case of Anteia / Sthenoboia. The connection between the widespread rejection of Stheneboia's Arkadian heritage and the *Iliad*'s coverage of this woman's life story cannot be quantified but cannot be dismissed. In this regard, the data seem to suggest an initial attempt on the Lykian material, which made some headway at first, but then came up against a wall of resistance underwritten to some degree by the Homeric account of Anteia's biography. The appropriation of Auge attracted no such resistance, and indeed, attracted such thoroughgoing approval that her early epic characterization is impossible to access or to reconstruct.

As mentioned above, the Arkadian eponym Arkas was granted a son by the name of Elatos, although this name conjured up a famous mythic figure associated with the northern Greek Lapith clan[244]. Up until now we have been looking at figures that occur in the parallel line of Apheidas. A few comparable claims made on Elatos' side also deserve brief consideration to round off this survey of Arkadian innovations sparked off by the problem of Atalanta. First, there is little doubt that the southern Greek use of the name Elatos suggests an instance of mythological theft, since the man was granted a son named Ischys. Ischys was the name of an established Lapith hero, famous for his role in the northern Greek legend about Apollo, Koronis, and the great healer, Asklepios, whose sons were the healers on the battlefield at Troy[245]. Further confirmation comes from the fact that in the Arkadian version of things, via his son, Aiptyos, it was said that Elatos was the grandfather of Peirithoos, a man otherwise known as a famous Lapith hero, and also as the revered companion of Theseus, who became the great mascot of the Athenian state[246].

In addition to the emphasis on famous Lapith protagonists, by way of Stymphalos, son of Elatos, and eponym of the Arkadian town[247], the Arkadian genealogy also moved in on another prestigious piece of Boiotian lore, namely, the story of Trophonios and Agamedes, two famous architects from the line of Orchomenos. In Boiotia, as Pausanias records, Trophonios and Agamedes were regarded as sons of King Erginos of Orchomenos, of the line of Athamas, son of Aiolos (9.37.2-7). However, following a typical genealogical pattern, Trophonios was considered to be a son of Apollo. Though as emphasized above, the lineage of Orchomenos was subject to considerable adaptation between the early Archaic and Classical periods, these brothers' descent from the Minyan King Erginos is attested in the Pythian Hymn to Apollo, an affirmation of relatively early provenance. Overall there are adequate indications that this pair of gifted heroic brothers belonged to the earliest strata of Minyan lore[248]. They were traditionally awarded numerous cult honors, of which Trophonios' underground oracle at Lebadeia is certainly the most conspicuous example[249]. In Arkadia, notwithstanding, the assertion was made that Agamedes was the son of the eponymous Stymphalos, whose wife Epikaste united with Apollo and gave birth to Trophonios[250]. She also bore Kerkyon to Agamedes, a figure who was associated with the Eleusinian mysteries and subject to competing Athenian claims[251].

ATALANTA IN RETROSPECT

Taking a step back from the roster of duplicate figures that make an appearance in the Arkadian line, the line demonstrates a conspicuous lack of genuinely old indigenous figures. Essentially it was a contrived pastiche, mainly composed of recast mythic heroes whose roots can be traced back to the Aiolic Greek heartland. In this regard, the mere proposition of competitive genealogical arrangements camouflaged the derivative origin of these heroes' newfound Arkadian identities by creating an atmosphere of indeterminacy that reverberated throughout the greater corpus. Though the strategies exemplified by the Arkadian genealogy were reproduced by each major southern Greek state, the case of Arkadia is particularly transparent. On the one hand, this is because the Arkadian appropriations are quite well documented, which as already proposed, bears a close connection to their positive impact on influential Greek poleis outside Arkadia. On the other hand, this is because of the scarcity of genuine indigenous mythology within the Arkadian lineage itself. Aside from its primordial and eponymous progenitors, the bulk of the lineage was composed of originally well-known Aiolic figures, making Arkadian manipulative tendencies rather more clear-cut than those of other state genealogies. The appropriations of other contemporary city-states were to some extent either more intricately imbedded in local legendary lore (e.g. the Athenian genealogy), more effectively suppressed older Aiolic data (viz. the genealogies of Korinth, Aigina, and Sparta), or surrounded by distracting genealogical eccentricities (e.g. the genealogy of Argos), making them somewhat more difficult to visualize.

A number of the patterns that surface here have been detected by David Henige[252]. His cross-cultural work deals specifically with politically motivated accounts of the past under changing historical conditions, in societies grounded in oral tradition where symbolic genealogy was standard fare. Henige, for example, identifies a phenomenon which he calls *genealogical parasitism* and defines as "the imputation of filiation with earlier prestigious dynasties (41)." Genealogical parasitism is clearly akin to the kinds of activities described here under the rubric *mythological theft*. The difference primarily consists in that, instead of asserting straightforward filiation with long established genealogies, the Greek quest was directed at pulling away parts of established genealogies, so as to affiliate selected excerpts with autonomous regional self-representations. Henige lists this tactic among common strategies that surface when "a society is exposed to the exigency of creating a remote past which sanctions the present (ibid)." Backed up by Henige with supporting examples taken from diverse historical settings, these dynamics coincide remarkably well with the genealogical evidence from the Arkadian line and with post-Homeric innovation in general.

Also relevant to the present discussion is the impulse to exclude intervals of foreign domination from the official historical record, explicit with regard to authorized King Lists. Expanding this basic concept to include the repudiation of foreign control over the form and content of legendary culture, not just sovereignty over a given realm, and identifying the foreigners at stake in this instance as north and east Greek ξένοι of bygone days, a strikingly comparable situation arises in terms of the southern Greek deployment of what Henige describes as the "amnemonic process" or the deliberate encouragement of cultural amnesia; an obvious catalyst to documentary change (30ff.). In the context of Greek legend, the *amnemonic process* focuses on a specific category of people and places that were deemed advantageous to disguise, or to discredit, or to forget. This is precisely the process subliminally at work when new lineage constructs were proposed with the aim of supplanting their erstwhile antecedents.

But as we have seen, the *amnemonic process* was by no means altogether successful in the realization of every appointed goal. Coming from diverse sources at different times, sanctioned forgetfulness met with uneven reception. Evidently, the body of cultural knowledge targeted by such efforts was greater in scope than the jurisdiction of specialized bids to promote disregard for embarrassing or undesirable memories, and, in so doing, to cultivate widespread favor for new improved versions of the distant past. Such initiatives' substantial, if partial, achievements are amply preserved in the mythological record. The motivation can also be historically traced. Changing political conditions in the early Archaic Period saddled emerging centers of power with a veritable host of "useless ancestors (27)" whose hegemonic monopoly over Greek prehistory was experienced as an alien regime. In light of similar globally recognizable strategies provoked by present demands to change the face of past history, the Arkadian genealogy is paradigmatic of the ways in which this basic cultural impulse was played out in Archaic Greece.

In pursuing the double Atalanta dilemma into its surrounding Arkadian context in order to illustrate these broader connections, the focus has veered away from the distinction between different types of mythological theft. These are actually fairly nuanced distinctions. However, inasmuch as Greek mythic-theft-type-one and type-two delineate strategies that created duplicate figures and transplanted them into select new environments, these designations also shed some light on the mentality that stood behind these frequent acts of appropriation.

Addressing the personalities encountered thus far, Hypermestra and Lynkeus, Sterope, and Atalanta were all figures endowed with new characteristics when their names were co-opted and situated within emerging maverick state genealogies. Agamedes can best be added to this list, since once he was relocated to Arkadia, he was no longer considered to be Trophonios' brother, but regarded as his father instead. Trophonios, however, without further specification, can only be recognized as a reincarnation of the great architect known to central Greek myth. This dynamic whereby the original image of a mythic hero was also transported along with his or her name actually represents the more frequent mode of Greek mythological relocation. This pattern embraces Sthenoboia (her mythic persona intact, in spite of her name change), Auge, Lykourgos, Elatos, Ischys, and Trophonios, placing them under the aegis of mythic-theft-type-two, which denotes continuity of characterization. It is therefore appropriate to consider a few further examples of mythic-theft-type-two.

---

[66] 1985: 27.

[67] Namely, in the repertoire as we know it from the Homeric poems and surviving subsequent literature. Five of Aiolos' daughters and at least six of his sons are worth acknowledging in this context, since a number of them commanded memorable personalities that were integral to early Greek myth (see M. West fr 10a OCT. Three out of five daughters and six out of seven sons are identified in the Hesiodic *Catalogue of Women*, where the seventh son has been lost due to a lacuna. ApB 1.7.3 offers two missing daughters). The continued existence of these main Aiolic arteries is essential to any Aiolic reading of the organization of early Greek legend. It is accordingly clear that Aiolic influence was not diminished straightforwardly through the eradication of founding family members. For if indeed this had been the case, any tangible sense of early Aiolic sovereignty would have been eradicated along with them. Still, the surviving biographical fragments that deal with upper lineage Aiolic figures (the likes of Sisyphos, Ixion, Otos and Ephialtes, Tyro, Iphimedia and Koronis) suggest considerable atrophy in this area. This in turn suggests that upper level protagonists did not suffer from personality deprivation in early Greek oral tradition. They were subject to changing times and often to faded glory.

[68] Concerning eponymous names, see for example C.M. Bowra 1930 repr. 1977: 77-79 on their Homeric usage particularly in identifying minor heroes; more generally R. Drews 1973: 8-10; D.P. Henige 1974: 25-26, 46-68; C. Calme in J. Bremmer ed. 1987; A.J. Graham 1992: 45; J.M. Hall 1997: 77, 87; for their tribal role in Athens under Kleisthenes, cf. R. Parker 1996: 117-121.

⁶⁹ The poems of Homer and Hesiod are classed as *pan-Hellenic* by consensus. G. Nagy, however, who supports this idea, goes on to elaborate on the term as a synthesis of diverse local traditions "that suits most city-states but corresponds exactly to none (e.g. 1990: 37)." This assessment of accords well with the widely accepted view that the Greek mythic corpus, as a whole, resulted from the confluence of regional mythic cycles at some point in the prehistorical period (e.g. K. Dowden, M. Finkelberg, M. Nilsson, and M. West, among others). Here, the operative understanding of *pan-Hellenic* works with a different account of mythological development, visualizing, instead, the widespread aggrandization of a regionally exclusive mythological program (i.e. Aiolic) that became *pan-Hellenic* in spite of its biased form, prompting *post eventum* regional efforts to compensate for its inherent features. That early epic mythology was consistently adapted to meet the needs of local political interests is, in general, taken for granted and stands behind a compendium of interpretive work, minus, however, acknowledgement of the Aiolic genealogical framework in the earliest strata of Greek mythic stories. At present, a specific geo-political outlook is only rarely attributed to early heroic legend (e.g. B. Powell in Morris and Powell eds. 1997), though (as mentioned above) the Aiolic orientation of early Greek epic poetry was a major concern in the nineteenth century before the matter was reduced to a strictly linguistic consideration (cf. J.L. Myres 1958). The term *pan-Hellenic*, at any rate, essentially quantifies public recognition.

⁷⁰ See, M. Davies 1988, 1989; J.S. Burgess 2001; K. Dowden in R. Fowler ed., 2004. The assumption here is that the legends later ascribed to the *Epic Cycle* were long since well-known to Greek listening audiences. As the neo-analytic method has shown, they were part and parcel of the tradition that inspired the composition of the Homeric poems (hence, the question of precedence ought to be discarded, e.g. B. Fenik 1968). It is, in addition, frequently observed that "the narratives of Homer and Hesiod already presuppose a long tradition (C. Brillante in L. Edmonds ed. 1990: 14)." In some quarters the origins of this tradition are still traced back into the Bronze Age (e.g. A.J.B. Wace & F. H. Stubbings 1962; M. Lejeune in J-P Vernant ed. 1968; E. Vermeule in D. Buitron-Oliver ed. 1991; J. Latacz 2001; M. Finkelberg 2003 & 2005). The present report has nothing to offer concerning the status of Greek tradition before the proposed mythic systematization on coastal Asia Minor in the so-called "dark ages." For due emphasis on our limited access to pre-Homeric oral tradition, see, B. Fenik 1968: 122; A. Heubeck in B. Fenik ed. 1978.

⁷¹ As noted, for example, by F. Frost in B. Althroth and P. Hellström eds. 1993.

⁷² viz. particularly in terms of the distribution of kingdoms and the political allocation of cities and provinces, see ch.2, below.

⁷³ Following, G.S. Kirk in his acknowledgement "that the *Iliad* and the *Odyssey* were widely known by the middle of the seventh century B.C., if not earlier… (1985: 4)" cf. R. Fowler in R. Fowler ed., 2004. And also necessarily following those who insist on early textual fixation (e.g. J. Crielaard, M. Haslam, A. Heubeck, R. Janko, I. Morris, and, generally speaking, the neo-analysts). Without fixation it must be assumed that the early genealogical structure would have been altered, on demand, spontaneously, via oral transmission. This would preempt the basis for structural controversy before structural controversy ever arose (so, especially I. Morris 1986: 85-87; also A.B. Lord 1960). These topics remain the focus of ongoing debate.

⁷⁴ Noted, for example, by F.M. Combellack (1976: 47) and C.R. Beye (1964: 351, 356). Beye looks closely the *Iliad*'s major and minor characters in terms of Homeric naming conventions, but rather oddly assumes that each instance of the same name necessarily involves the same individual. This notion generates a host of active warriors that the text insists must be presumed dead already, hence a battery of unreasonable inconsistencies (cf. C.B. Armstrong 1969: 31). A glance at any good index to the *Iliad* indicates that this outlook is untenable. On military considerations, see, B. Fenik 1968; H. Van Wees 1994 and 1996 in A.B. Lloyd ed.; H.W. Singor in J.P. Crielaard, ed. 1995 *contra* van Wees; On characterization cf. C. Whitman 1958 in H. Bloom, ed. 1987; J. Griffin 1986; O. Taplin 1992.

75 The quest for Homeric narrative inconsistencies stems back to K. Lachmann in the late nineteenth century. Following F.A. Wolf, Lachmann considered the epics to represent an amalgamation of poems composed individually and accordingly prone to internal contradictions. Further advanced by such scholars as Fick, Bethe, and Wilamowitz, the process of identifying internal contradictions became the keystone of the *Analyst* doctrine. For the *Unitarian* treatment of this particular "inconsistency," see J.A. Scott 1965: ch.5; C.M. Bowra 1930: ch.5. The work of B. Fenik is also extremely useful. For more recent analysis of perceived contradictions, see for example, M. Edwards *CA* 9.2 1990; M. Nagler in M. Griffith and D. Mastronarde eds. 1990; L. Edmonds in I. Morris and B. Powell eds. 1997. As O. Taplin, however, definitively remarks, "the high degree of *consistency* in the plot and narrative generally far outweigh the correspondingly sparse inconsistencies (1992)" cf. E. Havelock in H Bloom ed. 1987; J-P. Vernant 1980: 45. Meanwhile, perceived inconsistencies of another order have encouraged a prominent group of scholars to deny the validity of Homeric poetry as a source of empirical information on Greek society in any period e.g. G.S. Kirk 1962; A. Snodgrass 1971, 1974; J.N. Coldstream 1977; J. Whitley 1991; C.J. Ruijgh in J.P. Crielaard, ed. 1995. No doubt, such an equation raises certain problems, yet the perceived inconsistencies have been powerfully countered by members of another prominent group who advocate thoroughgoing conceptual consistency (e.g. I. Morris 1986; G. Herman 1987; L. Muellner 1990; R. Seaford 1994; C. Ulf 1990; H. Van Wees 1992; K. Raaflaub in N. Fisher and H. Van Wees, eds. 1998).

76 ποινὴ δ' οὔ τις παιδὸς ἐγίγνετο τεθνηῶτος.

77 *Contra*, for example, L. Edmonds in L. Edmonds, ed. 1990: 6.

78 See Gantz 1993: 198-199 for details on the development of the indigenous line of Argos. It is clear, for example, that Io was considered the daughter of one Peiren, or the daughter of a hero named Iasos, before she became generally known as the daughter of Inachos, the Argive river. This was evidently a simplified version that was adopted outside of Argos and dispensed with a fair number of local Argive claims. The River Inachos and an eponymous Argos were nonetheless perceptibly central to the genesis of the Argive state genealogy, which cannot, on the evidence, be reconstructed with clarity.

79 e.g. Gantz ibid. 202; The developed formation ran: Io -> Epaphos -> Libya+Poseidon -> Agenor of Phoinicia / Belos of Egypt. **Belos** -> Aigyptos / Danaos. **Aigyptos** -> fifty sons. **Danaos** -> fifty daughters.

80 e.g. Bakchy. 19; Aischy. *Prometheus Bound* 589-590, 663; Hdt.1.1. On this mythological complex, see Gantz 1993: 198-203, 208-212. Its extension greatly exceeds the length of standard Aiolic lineage trajectories, which although not necessarily equal, do not go beyond seven generations from Aiolos to Troy. This lineage charts thirteen from Io (daughter of Inachos) to Herakles. On lineage lengthening and backward growth, see D. Henige 1974: 38-42; M. West 1985: 27.

81 This genealogy essentially presupposes the foundation of Kyrene from Thera, ca. 630 and the establishment of the Greek trading post at Naukratis in Egypt under Psammetichos I (664-610). See Hdt.2.178-179 with J.M. Cook 1937 and C. Roebuck 1951. Still, it more than just presupposes these developments, but more aptly reflects their subsequent impact since a full-fledged symbolic artifact of this order requires a retrospective state of mind. The Hesiodic *Catalogue of Women* demonstrates that the whole new narrative complex was standard by the time of its composition (fr 127-129; M. West 1985: 76-68). The fifth century currency of this formation is dealt with below under mythic-theft-type-three, example one.

82 The first explicit reference to this Hypermestra occurs in Pindar (*Nem*.10.1-6; also *Pyth*. 9.109-116), but the story was known to the Hesiodic *Catalogue*, recorded in a lost epic poem the *Danais* (see, G. Huxley 1969: 34-38), and addressed, for example, by Pherekydes (FGrHist 3F21). Later sources include, Paus.2.19.4,6, 3.12.2; ApB 2.1.4-5; Hyg.*Fab*.170;

⁸³ e.g. *Prometheus Bound* 774, 858-867, 991-997. On the subsequent re-marriage of Danaos' daughters, a few of which achieved some notoriety (So, especially, Amymone, who bore the Argive eponym Nauplios in union with Poseidon. She was the subject of one of Aischylos' satyr plays which is generally associated with the *Danaid Trilogy*; see R.P. Winnington-Ingram *JHS* 81 1961: 141-152; Gantz: 1980: 134; 1993: 206-208). It is clear that the murder was followed by a sequel whereby, in spite of their crime, Danaos' daughters married eligible Argives who competed for their hands in an athletic contest (Pind.*Pyth* 9; Paus.3.12.2). On this count, however, it is equally clear that this sequel was more an accessory to the crime that reinstated Danaos and his family in Argos than a salient genealogical vehicle for the perpetuation of Danaos' line. That role was preeminently commanded by the sole surviving original couple, namely, Lynkeus and Hypermestra, the designated perpetuators of the Argive line (cf.Winnington-Ingram ibid. 143).

⁸⁴ This genealogy is addressed again in greater detail in ch.3.

⁸⁵ Notably, Porthaon's second wife, Eurite, was a descendant of Perimede, daughter of Aiolos. Oineus and Althaia were first cousins once removed via two converging Aiolic stemmata. An alternate tradition (and not necessarily an old one) claimed that Deianeira was actually the child of Althaia and Dionysos, rather than the child of Althaia and Oineus (ApB 1.3.1; Hyg.*Fab*.129). Tydeus, Oineus' most famous son, was considered to be his youngest. He was attributed to Oineus' second wife whom he married after Althaia's death in connection with the war between Pleuron and Kalydon (neighboring Aitolian cities) that began with the hunt for the Kalydonian boar. This conflict divided Althaia's allegiance between her natal family (i.e. the Pleuronians under Thestios) and the family she married into (i.e. the Kalydonians under her husband and son, Oineus and Meleagros, respectively). Following Althaia's death (which is most often described as a suicide driven by the realization that she had killed her son to avenge the death of her brothers), Oineus was said to have married a woman named Periboia, from the Protid branch of the Argive line (i.e. sister of Kapaneus of Argos cf. Hes fr 12 MW). This woman gave birth to Tydeus whose heroic life story was intimately bound up with the Argive wars against Thebes and documented as such as early as the *Iliad* (4.365-410,14.110-125). The early Argive genealogies are addressed in detail in the next two chapters. Deianeira was Herakles' second wife whose actions unintentionally led to his death out of jealous feelings toward Iole of Oichalia whom Herakles' captured when he sacked her father's city. Herakles' death drove Deianira to suicide (see especially, Sophokles *Trachiniai;* and Gantz 1993: 434-437, 457-460 on the antiquity of this story). The main point here is that all of these figures were blood relations in the Aiolic line.

⁸⁶ Timandra, Phylone, and less frequently Phoibe also surface as offspring attributed to this family.

⁸⁷ Apparently in response to the rise of Hypermestra, daughter of Danaos, Pherekydes, notably, in the mid-fifth century mentioned only two daughters of Eurythemiste and Thestios. He named Leda and Althaia, yet omitted Hypermestra subtly contributing to the suspicions at issue with regard to the reallocation of names (FGrHist 3F9). On Pherekydes, see F. Jacoby, Mnemosyne 30 (1947) 13-64. See Paus.2.21.2. for the tombs of the two Hypermestras located in the Argive agora.

⁸⁸ Aiolos -> Perieres + Alkyone -> Leukippos / Aphareus / & others. **Leukippos** -> Phoibe / Hilaria / Arsinoe. **Aphareus** -> Lynkeus / Idas. **Idas** + Marpessa (of Euenos of Aitolia -> Kleopatra. **Kleopatra** + Meleagros (of Oineus + Althaia + Ares). cf. Gantz 1993: 324-326.

⁸⁹ The match between Idas, Lynkeus' brother, and Marpessa, daughter of Euenos (brother of Thestios and therefore an uncle of the three sisters in question here, viz. Hypermestra, Althaia, and Leda) represents yet another set of interactions involving old legendary Aiolic stemmata, spiked with interventions by Olympian deities and revealing that early Greek mythic protagonists turn out to be consanguine relations.

[90] cf. mythic-theft-type-two, example two, below.

[91] See Martin West's treatment of the Hesiodic *Catalogue of Women* (1985: 91; Hes fr 160-161 MW) for Pelasgos, the autochthonos figure who rose from the earth to engender Lykaon (cf. Paus.4.1.4-6). Pelasgos was essentially a generic name used to denote an aboriginal status. So, for example, in Aischylos' *Hiketides,* Pelasgos is the name of the ruling king at the time when Danaos and his daughters (including Hypermestra), arrive in Argos as suppliants seeking protection from their first cousins (i.e. the sons of Aigyptos, Lynkeus among them). On the *pelasgian* designation, see J.L. Myres 1907. It is evident that all indigenous lines were, in a general sense, functionally autochthonous.

[92] It is not possible to embark on a full-scale treatment of the diminishing status of Lapith genealogy, which is, as a result, preserved only in fragments. Notably, M.L. West remarks that "if the Lapiths counted as Hellenes they must have been Aiolids not Xouthids or Dorids (1985: 72)." Though I, personally, would not count these two latter named groups within the early Greek genealogical structure (see chs. 4 and 5 below). The evidence that exists is sufficient to show that prominent figures with Lapith roots who were widely known in early epic contexts were appropriated by the Arkadian line according to the patterns of mythic-theft-type-two. Arkadia, for example, claimed the Lapith Elatos (eponym of Thessalian Elateia) by honoring a son of Arkas with the same name, and giving Arkas a grandson named Peirithoos (cf. Hes fr 160-166 MW), though the *Iliad* stated, in no uncertain terms, that Peirithoos was a son of Zeus and the wife of Ixion (Il.14.317-318, another figure with northern Greek ties). Whether the man who made love to Koronis (daughter of Phlegyas, another Thessalian eponym in HHymn 16: 1-5, or, alternatively, the daughter of Azeus, as in HHymn 3: 211, another figure associated with Minyan Orchomenos cf. Paus.9.37.1; Rocher 1965: s.v. Azeus), while she was pregnant with Asklepios by Apollo, was actually an Arkadian, or a Thessalian, offers a case in point. M. West's rejection of Ischys (son of Elatos, and the name of the man who was said to have done so) in an Arkadian context (as cited by Pausanias 8.4.6; West 1978: 93), on the grounds that this man was clearly rooted in Thessaly, is definitely a point well taken, yet the nature of the confusion is left unexplained. The competition that Pausanias' testimony implies, tied to the very existence of two figures named Elatos, attached to two separate sons by the name of Ischys, and linked to two distinct and distant locations, suggests an instance of mythological theft. In terms of antiquity and legendary depth there is scarcely a contest between the two pairs. The Arkadian version is no doubt the innovation. The migration of Ischys is more intricate still, in that an effort to claim the birth of Asklepios on behalf of other Peloponnesian interests surfaces in the Hesiodic *Ehoiai* (Hes fr 50 MW; ApB 3.10.3; cf. West 1985: 69-70; Gantz ibid. 91, 181). There Asklepios' mother is not the standard Koronis, but rather Arsinoe, daughter of Leukippos, son of Aphareus (son of Perieres, son of Aiolos), who was traditionally associated with Messenia (though an Arkadian Ischys could no doubt work very well with an Messenian substitute for Koronis). Some of these machinations are bound to come up again, but here, the bottom line is that as far back as Homer, the Lapiths were a prominent legendary clan with established roots in northern Thessaly. They included such figures as Kaineus, Peirithoos, Dryas, Exadios and Polyphemos, of old (e.g. Il. 1.263-264), and Polypoites, Leonteus, Podaleirios and Machaon, in the Trojan War era (e.g. Il. 2.730-746, sons of Peirithoos, Koronos and Asklepios, respectively). The extant outlines of the early Lapith heritage are sufficient to indicate that it was heavily tampered with as time wore on.

[93] e.g. Paus.8.4.2-3.

[94] i.e. of Alea, outside Tegea, Apheidas' domain.

95 Lykaon -> Kallisto + Zeus = Arkas. Arkas -> **Apheidas / Elatos / Azan**. **Aphdeidas** -> Aleos / Stheneboia. **Aleos**-> Lykourgos/ Kepheus/ Auge. **Lykourgos** -> Iasos / Amphidamas / Ankaios. **Iasos** -> Atalanta. **Aphidamas** -> Melanion. **Ankaios**-> Agapenor. **Kepheus** -> Sterope & sons. **Auge** + Herakles = Telephos -> Eurypylos. **Stheneboia** + Proitos of Argos.
Elatos -> Ischys / Stymphalos and others. **Ischys** + Koronis + Apollo = Asklepios.
Stymphalos -> Agamedes -> Kerkyon / Trophonios.
Azan -> Kleitor (Arkadian eponym).

96 Diodoros cites three survivors out of seventeen brothers, which certainly decimates the extent of the family, but also implies that some of Kepheus' male offspring were granted subsequent legendary roles. So for example, Echemos of Tegea was identified as a grandson of Kepheus (son of one Aeropos) who married Timandra, daughter of Tyndareos (e.g. Paus.4.5.1; Hdt.9.26). Apollodoros, by contrast, opts for the annihilation of Kepheus and his sons. Whether or not he still regarded Echemos as a descendant of Kepheus of Tegea, therefore, remains an open question (cited at 3.10.6 as Timandra's husband). He could well have been thinking along the same lines as Pausanias at 8.44.7-8 where Aeropos is a son of Ares and Aerope, evidently, another daughter of Kepheus.

97 In his commentary on Lykophron's *Alexandria*, the twelfth century Byzantine scholar J. Tzetzes reports six mythic figures ostensibly known for erecting skull temples from the severed heads of the losing contestants for their daughters' hand in marriage (viz. Oinomaos, Euenos, Kyknos, Diomedes of Thrace, Phorbas and Antaeus, the first four were definitively known as sons of Ares). No doubt, the story was a popular early motif (R. Janko 1986: 51).

98 Pelops' father, Tantalos, was traditionally associated with the Anatolian kingdom of Phrygia (prosperous until sacked by Kimmerians from the north, sometime in the early seventh century, e.g. Hdt.1.14 on King Midas of Phrygia; and so, for example, T.J. Dunbabin 1957: 62-71) and later, with Lydia, alternatively. Tantalos is sighted in book eleven of the *Odyssey* (582-592), which aptly verifies his legendary antiquity (cf. Gantz 1993: 531-536).

99 For a comprehensive treatment of the Pelops legend, see W. Hansen 2000.

100 The Arkadian genealogy was quite well-developed by the time of the Hesiodic *Catalogue of Women*. See, M. West 1985: 91-93.

101 Porthaon + Demodike = Eurythemiste/ Stratonike / Sterope. **Eurythemiste**+Thestios = Althaia/ Leda /Hypermestra. **Stratonike**+Melaneus=Eurytos of Oichalia. **Sterope** + ? = ?.

102 viz. Phrixos, son of Athamas, son of Aiolos, who, as the result of family strife, fled Greece for the Black Sea with his sister Helle on the back of a magical golden ram: later, the object of the Argonauts quest (obliquely: Od.5.333-335; Il.12.30, 15.233, 17.433; Pind.Pyth.4.155-162; also, Palaiphatos 30; ApB 1.9.1; Hyg. *Fab.* 1,2,3 & 4. cf. Gantz 1993: 176-180). Sisyphos, son of Aiolos, who one way or another managed offend Zeus, and, therefore, wound up in Hades condemned to perpetually roll away a great boulder that inevitably fell back upon him (Od. 11.593-600; Gantz 1993: 173-176).

103 Not that Homeric statements were not outright contradicted whenever it was deemed necessary or expedient to do so.

[104] In this context, R. Fowler's statement that "the lower end of the genealogy is always contemporary with the genealogist (PCPS 44 1998: 16)" is difficult to interpret or apply. Assuredly, the lower end of any lineage sequence was diachronically closest to the lived existence of any actual ancient Greek writer. This observation, however, does not produce (if this was the intention) a reliable equation for detecting the novelty or antiquity of Greek mythological material, since novelty was apt to infiltrate Greek tradition at any point in the heroic continuum. In terms of molding the past to suit present purposes, there were also certain strategic advantages to working sequentially higher up or further into the depths of pre-historical time.

[105] i.e. the first sister.

[106] Though the present example focuses exclusively on Porthaon's daughters, the antiquity and importance of Porthaon's male descendants, including Oineus, Agrios and Melas, as well as Meleagros, Tydeus and Diomedes, all of whom surface in the *Iliad* (e.g. Il.9.529-599, 14.113-125) testify on behalf of the early prestige of the entire Aitolian clan. The list of lost Attic tragedies on related subjects corroborates the enduring prestige of this family, e.g. *Meleagros* plays by Euripides, Sophokles, a *Pleuroniai* by Phrynichos and coverage on the topic by Stesichoros.

[107] Gantz 1993: 457-461.

[108] Gantz 1993: 197.

[109] From Hellanikos onward Oinomaos was generally known as a son of Ares and Sterope (FGrHist 4F19). Not Sterope, daughter of Porthaon, however, but a woman described as a daughter of the god Atlas, who was ultimately credited with seven daughters. Yet in viewing the frieze on the Temple of Zeus at Olympia, Pausanias regarded the Sterope depicted as the wife of Oinomaos (5.10.6). This assertion is supported on art historical grounds by N. Tersini's close analysis of the frieze (CA 6 1987: 139-159). Either way, the prospect that the heroine involved was initially the Aitolian Sterope, who was, at length, overshadowed by same-named competitors remains unaffected by these two options. Pausanias' account, in any case, represents a viable and potentially early view of Sterope's relationship to Oinomaos. Moreover, Pausanias' conviction that Sterope was not Oinomaos' mother, but rather, his wife corresponds well with his further report that Oinomaos was the son of Ares and Harpina, daughter of the River god Asopos (5.22.6, attributed to the Eleians and the Phliasians and promoted earlier by Diodoros viz. 4.73.1-2). Naturally, this assertion may have nothing to do with Oinomaos' original genealogy, in which case, however, beyond his paternity, Oinomaos' early background remains completely obscure. Nonetheless a persistent tradition maintained that Sterope was Oinomaos' wife against the prevailing notion that she was his mother. The daughters of Asopos, like the daughters of Atlas, represent another female collectivity specializing in mythological change (see below). The bottom line is that both formulations reveal mythological adjustments relevant to the early status of Porthaon's daughter and the decline of her persona in the ancient sources.

[110] See G. Ferrari 2003 for an analysis of Greek vase painting based on the importance of zeroing in on the operative underlying cultural order, viz. the way in which a society thinks. Her conclusions aptly apply to genealogical analysis, and particularly to the concept at stake here, which addresses the Greek genealogical mentality. M. Broadbent's description of Greek genealogy as "a work of ordered imagination," is also apropos in this context (1968: 1) as is J. Griffin's statement that "everybody knows that the world of the heroes, in which the action takes place, is explicitly declared to be different from the world of the singers themselves. 'Such as men are nowadays,'οἷοι νῦν βροτοί εἰσι, they are not at all the same as men were in those days, when kings were sprung directly from the loins of gods, and a man could lift with one hand the weight that now two stout fellows can barely hoist onto a wagon (1986: 37)." See also, A. Snodgrass 1998: 4, 9.

111 It is perhaps not insignificant that another son of Ares in the same family also staged a tournament for his daughter's hand, which many attempted, but no one could win (at least not until the appointed occasion), and in which each contestant paid with his life. This contest's sponsor was known as Euenos (son of Porthaon's sister Demodike and thus, the brother of Thestios who married Eurythemiste); its object was the hand of his daughter, Marpessa. The victor was Idas, son of Aphareus (son of Perieres, son of Aiolos), ostensibly equipped with horses from Poseidon. Euenos pursued the couple to the Lykormos River, where he committed suicide because of his loss, and the river became the Euenos in his honor. Marpessa was the mother of the Aitolian Kleopatra who surfaces at *Iliad* 9.543-599 as the wife of Meleagros of Kalydon (viz. son of Althaia and Ares). The main evidence comes from the lyric poets and the scholia to Il.9.557, see Gantz: 1993: 196.

112 The Homeric poems offer intermittent coverage of major bygone legendary events, yet the presentation of data is incomplete, if generous and sufficient from the point of view of a constituency steeped in legendary knowledge. On this topic, see, for example, R. Fowler and D. Lateiner in R. Fowler, ed. 2004.

113 The Temple of Hera at Olympia is generally dated ca. 590. The most famous depiction of Pelops' chariot race for the hand of Hippodameia was carved into the frieze of the Temple of Zeus at Olympia, completed in 457 B.C. (again, see Paus.5.10.6-7).

114 Killos was evidently an eponymous name associated with Killa, a coastal town in Aiolis directly opposite the island of Lesbos. It is noted by in Homer at Il.1.38, hence the scholiast's remarks on this passage (see Hansen 2000). Here the point is the localization on Lesbos of a major component in Pelop's migration story, since historically speaking the island of Lesbos was the most important Aiolic off-shore territory.

115 cf. Theopompos FGrHist.115F350; Str.13.1.63-63; Paus.5.10.7.

116 Likewise, a name with Anatolian roots, e.g. T.J. Dunbabin 1957: 70.

117 And where Philoctetes was left to nurse his wounds (Il.2.716-728).

118 See also, Paus.10.38.4. These passages invoke the ancient Lesbian ruler, Makar/Makareus, who was either an original son of Aiolos (HHymn 3.37), or presumably otherwise an early affiliate of one of the major Aiolic families. In the *Iliad*, Lesbos apparently delineated the southern extremity of King Priam's kingdom at its height (Il.24.543-546). Thus it seems to have functioned as a kind of latitude marker that circumscribed the extent of the satellite kingdoms that owed political allegiance to him. For a later account of Makar's lineage where he is no longer portrayed as a son of Aiolos, but as a scion in another old Aiolian line (viz. the line of Alkyone, daughter of Aiolos, later daughter of Atlas), or later still as a grandson of Zeus who ruled the city of Olenos in the northern Peloponnese, see fr 184 MW; M. West 1985: 98, ZPE 61 1985: 1-4; for a further tangent, Ael. *VH* 13.2.

119 e.g. H.M. Chadwick 1912: 174; T.W. Allen 1921: 36ff.; J.B. Bury 1937: 37ff.; M.P. Nilsson 1932: 54ff.; C.J. Emlyn-Jones 1980: 14ff., where the general approach to this phenomenon is to invoke the Bronze Age Mykenaian landscape, and then to argue in various ways that Homeric geography manifestly pre-dates the Greek (Aiolic/ Ionic) migrations to Asia Minor. For an alternative interpretation in which the Bronze Age component is vehemently dismissed, see M.I. Finley 1963, 1978, 1981. For an overview of the archaeological evidence available from East Greece (notoriously meager in contrast to the Greek mainland), see J. Boardman 1999: ch. 2.

120 e.g. I. Morris 1986: 89, 97; On some of the more remarkable features that must be attributed to the Heroic Age, see, for example, E. Kearns & M. Clarke in R. Fowler ed. 2004.

121 Although granted, not always treated as such.

122 In this context, social hierarchy is often a major focus. So, for example, one may compare A.G. Geddes' extremely skeptical view of the historical value of Homeric class structure (*CQ* 34.1 1984: 17-36; cf. A.A. Long *JHS* 90 1970: 121-139; A.M. Snodgrass *JHS* 94 1974: 114-125), with I. Morris' confidence in the poems' clear depiction of contemporary social norms (following M.I. Finley with certain modifications), with special emphasis on aristocratic ideology (Morris 1986: 120-129; also a prominent theme in Morris 1987 and in the work of K. Raaflaub and J. Whitley). Neither interpretation is altogether adequate. Essentially, Morris does not give enough weight to the fictional ethos of the *Heroic Age*, while Geddes is too often inclined to insist on confusion and inaccuracy on the part of the poet. At any rate, it is no doubt impossible for creative composition to take place in a vacuum – that is, in a state of complete detachment from the conditions of everyday life (so, M.I. Finley 1978; J.M. Redfield 1975).

123 This acknowledgment is expressed through the existence of Aiolic trajectories in the region associated with legends that had already brought Aiolic forebears to the east. The voyage of the Argonauts may be considered the clearest example of this phenomenon.

124 On the relevant cluster of stories, see Gantz 1993: 588-594. See also Il.13.169-173 for Imbrios, son of Mentor, a Trojan ally from Pedaios. By contrast, the story of Orion of Boiotia and Oinopion of Chios offers yet another significant case of pre-Trojan War Aiolic activity off the coast of Asia Minor (see Gantz 271-272).

125 Not necessarily the result of aggression or conquest, Gantz ibid. See, Il.8.229—235 for the banquet on Lemnos.

126 *The Geography of Homer's World* in Anderson and Dickie eds. 1995: 45. This is a difficult presentation on a number of counts when it comes to the issue of Homeric geography, not least in its commitment to the down-dating movement that endeavors to place Homer in the late seventh century (here, on particularly tenuous grounds that inadvertently invoke A.M. Snodgrass' conviction that archaeology must be severed from literary analysis, so especially, 2006: ch. 2). On the other hand, Dickie's treatment of the Heroic Age and the problematic equation that links the Homeric poems with Bronze Age Mykenai is very well stated.

127 Il.2.688-693, 19.295-296; Il.1.366-367, 6.414-428.

128 Gift of Achilles to Nestor.

129 Iphis was a gift to Patroklos from Achilles. Diomede of Lesbos is called a daughter of Phorbas, which suggests that her lineage was of some significance. For what it is worth the name Phorbas invokes a series of competitive mythological referents, a number with strong Aiolic associations (e.g. Roscher s.v. Phorbas).

130 As stated in the catalogue passage, Kos was formerly Eurypylos' city, although it is represented at Troy by two grandsons of Herakles, Pheidippos and Antiphos. Eurypylos was the son of Poseidon and Mestra, a woman known as a daughter of Erysichthon, scion of the Aiolic line of Kanake (Hes.fr 43a MW; Gantz 1993: 444-445).

131 *Odyssey* 19.172-183 confirms Greek predominance specifically with regard to the mixed population that was held to exist on the island of Krete. We know no more of Nireus (son of Aglaia and Charopos), the contingent leader from the island of Syme than we do of the stories that may well have explained the absence of Greek contingents from the northwest Aegean in typical mytho-genealogical fashion. However that may be, there are concrete indications of Aiolic forebears at large in the region, camouflaged by the presence of others, with or without discernible Trojan War sympathies. We are also dealing with scraps of information derived from a context that, in its own day, was doubtless familiar to East Greek audiences.

[132] e.g. DS. 5.81.2-8; Str.9.2.3-5, 13.1.3; Paus.2.18.6, 3.2.1, 5.4.3. On a slightly different note it is worth mentioning also that the ruling elite of seventh-century Lesbos traced themselves back to Penthilos, son of Orestes, whom they honored as a leader of the Aiolian migration from the Greek mainland in the post Trojan War era (See, G.L. Huxley 1969: 88; L.H. Jeffrey 1976: 237-340). The Aiolic post Trojan War migration charter, which is vaguely perceptible in the Homeric poems and via East Greek poets, such as Mimnermos (so, fr 10 Edmonds), contrasts conspicuously, in any case, with accounts of the Greek settlement of Asia Minor that was codified later on the Greek mainland (see ch.2. below). Extant testimony to the effect that the daughter of one King Agamemnon of Kyme married Midas of Phrygia, presumably, therefore, in the late eighth century, sheds further light on the sorry state of our knowledge concerning East Greek politics and traditions in the early Archaic Period (see, for example, H.T. Wade-Gerry 1952: 6-8, where king Hektor of Chios is also addressed; on another relevant tangent, G. Huxley 1969).

[133] West 1985: 46-48 (Hes fr 26.5); On Sterope and the Pelopid line: 43, 90, 99, & 109.

[134] The seven sisters are: Maia, mother of Hermes; Electra of Troy; the Spartan mountain, Tayegete; Merope wife of Sisyphos; Alkyone, lover of Poseidon, ditto Kelaino whose son Lykos was removed to the Isles of the Blessed, and Sterope, mother of Oinomaos. They are treated separately as a group under mythic-theft-type-three, example two, below.

[135] viz. in the later fifth century. Maia and Elektra are explicitly attested (fr 170, 177, 180). The presence of Taygete may be inferred from the marriage of Eurydike, daughter of Lakedaimon to Akrisios, of the Argive line, which suggests complete coverage of the line of Sparta (fr 177). There is, however, no reason to believe that the Spartan mountain Taygete was first conceived as a daughter of Atlas. The presence of Alkyone is confirmed by the extensive genealogical coverage on the children she bore with the god Poseidon (fr 188A), supplemented by an additional reference that mentions her son Halirrhotios with Perieres (fr 49). Kelaino surfaces in Philodemos in a string of genealogies attributed to Hesiod (Most fr 157). The list of seven also occurs in an un-attributed scholiast's fragment (fr 169 MW; West 1985: 94; see also Gantz 1993: 212-215).

[136] There are evidently also some spatial issues involved (West 1985: 99). In Apollodoros the daughters of Atlas are introduced in relation to Maia, the mother of Hermes, who, legend had it, made love with Zeus in a cave on Mt. Kyllene in Arkadia (HHymns 4, 18; ApB 3.10.1-2). Maia is the earliest heroine (a goddess, in fact) to be identified as a daughter of Atlas who was also a member of the full-fledged sorority. Odysseus' captor, the island queen, Kalypso also shared this title early on, though she was never adopted into the sorority (On Kalypso, Od.1.52, 7.245; On Maia, compare, Od.14.436 and HHymn 4, especially the latter, where she is curiously never invoked as such, with *Theogony* 938-939 and HHymn 18, where she is). Interestingly enough, Apollodoros does not mention Sterope in connection with Oinomaos when he records the genealogy of the Pelopid line (ApE 2.1-9). Out of the seven sisters, four are addressed in a single summary paragraph. The rest of his coverage focuses exclusively on Maia, Taygete and Elektra.

[137] Since West presupposes the early existence of independent regional mythic cycles that were eventually fused together, he tends to situate major mythological developments in the pre-historical period. This coincides with the fact that close interaction between the designated regional cycles is already perceptible in the Homeric poems. This reading thus seems to place the Atlantid construct well before the beginning of the Archaic Period. No matter, there is sufficient reason to doubt that Oinomaos affiliation with the Atlantid Sterope actually represents the *earliest* tradition.

[138] As noted by M. West 1985: 157, 160.

[139] A. Faustoferri convincingly dates the throne (against influential down dating proposals) to the latter first half of the sixth century (in W. Coulson and O. Palagia eds., 1993). The likelihood that the Atlantid heroines existed independently before a formal relationship was forged between them makes it unreliable to interpret this image as testimony to the existence of the complete Atlantid sorority. Nonetheless, at some point in the sixth century the Atlantid formation was finalized and disseminated, as *Catalogue* fragments attest (West 1985: 94-99, 155-164).

[140] On this see below, mythic-theft-type-two.

[141] Curiously, the son of this union that surfaces in the fragments is not Ikarios, Tyndareos, Aphareus, or Leukippos, four major Aiolic figures who became contested members of the Spartan lineage (see below), but the obscure figure Halirrhothios and his equally obscure sons, Semos and Alazygos (though Pindar links the former to Mantineia in Arkadia Ol.10.70-75). The name Halirrhothios turns up again in Athens where he was considered a son of Poseidon, notably Alkyone's alternate mate (Gantz 1993: 81, 180-181, 234). Otherwise, this genealogy is extremely obscure.

[142] Gantz 1993: 180-181; and ch. 2 below.

[143] It seems to be the case that both of these families were attributed to the same Alkyone, which, in turn suggests they were both part of the program associated with the line of Sparta.

[144] Renner 1978: 287-289; West 1985: 99; Gantz 1993: 215-216.

[145] Compare the daughters of Asopos, so, for example, Paus.2.5.2, 9.1.1, 9.20.1; Gantz 1993: 219.

[146] Gantz 1993: 212-214, 273.

[147] These dynamics encouraged constant reevaluation concerning how many daughters and which ones were sacrificed. Moreover, new daughters were added on demand to compensate for the fact that those who became famous lineage bearers could not possibly be the same individuals as those who gave their lives for their city in their youth. Matters were much the same with the daughters of Kekrops, who leapt off the Akropolis to meet their deaths at the sight of the divine child Erichthonios, though each one was also credited with a divine liaison and divinely sired offspring. Still, Kekrops' three daughters seem eminently more likely to have received their new identities at the same time, instead of via some kind of developmental process. On these topics, see Gantz 235-238; 242-243; cf. C. Collard, M.J. Cropp and K.H. Lee, eds. 1995 on the remains of Euripides' *Erechtheus*.

[148] Providing, as it did, the ideal opportunity for this type of elaboration.

[149] e.g. Gaia + Ouranos = Kyklopes/One-Hundred-Handers/Titans.

[150] This second criterion is examined further in the section on the daughters of Atlas, below (ch.3, example 2).

[151] Again, see mythic-theft-type-three, example two, for the exceptional birth of the god Dionysos.

[152] Though the Arkadians, themselves, could have deployed her to make a bid for possession of Oinomaos.

153 It may not be insignificant in this regard that Pausanias cites the Hesiodic Corpus for one Alkathoos, son of Porthaon, among the suitors who lost their lives competing for the hand of Hippodamia (6.21.10). No doubt Pausanias' list, like all such lists attached to great collective legendary events was subject to embellishment over time with contestants put forth on behalf of various interests. Alkathoos, nonetheless, was one of the few figures repeatedly cited in this context (Gantz 1993: 540). Notably Alkathoos is not included among the sons of Porthaon named in the *Iliad* (14.109-120). Still, this reference is striking inasmuch as it spotlights a suitor closely related to Sterope and family. The notion that Oinomaos' wife's brother (Alkathoos) competed for the hand of his sister's (Sterope's) daughter (i.e. following Paus.5.10.3) may well be an early, if post-Homeric idea, later eclipsed by Sterope, daughter of Atlas. The uncle/niece coupling, in any case, was a frequent arrangement in Greek mythology. Interesting also is the *Iliad*'s portrayal of a Trojan Alkathoos called the son of Aisyetes, who married Hippodameia, daughter of Anchises, who was therefore a sister of the hero, Aineias (Il.13.429-431). It is doubtful that this reference escaped the notice of subsequent Greek mythic chroniclers, while it certainly mirrors the reuse of the name, since an added son of Porthaon named Alkathoos, who perished in his quest to win the hand of his niece (or less credibly the hand of his nephew's daughter) links the name Alkathoos with the name Hippodameia in a potential relationship that was never realized. It is significant, in addition, that though the surviving *Ehoiai* fragments do not offer much coverage on Pelops' sons, the Theognid corpus names one Alkathoos, who occurs repeatedly in this fairly volatile category (Theognis 773-774; Gantz 1993: 544; Paus.2.6.5 on Sikyon, son of Pelops). For if Sterope, daughter of Porthaon, married Oinomaos, yielding Hippodameia, a son of Pelops named Alkathoos would have inherited a maternal family name, essentially the name of his mother's (Hippodameia's) mother's (Sterope) brother, that is, in the event that Porthaon's Sterope was the wife not the mother of Oinomaos and was credited with a brother named Alkathoos (i.e. this patterning is simply clearer and more typical than the case in which Oinomaos is Sterope's son). Moreover, Alkathoos, the alleged son of Pelops became a well-known Megarian hero on account of his marriage to one Euaichme, a daughter of the eponymous figure Megareus (e.g. Paus. 1.43.4). Mainly at issue here is the frequent occurrence of variant intermediary genealogical formations in between early epic and the later status quo. Overall, these snippets of information lend a modicum of auxiliary support to the basic genealogical premise that the premiere Sterope was the daughter of Porthaon.

154 Apollodoros preferred to credit the River Acheloos and the Muse Melpomene for the birth of the Sirens (ApB 1.3.4, ApE 7.18), while, notably, at 1.7.3 he acknowledges the union of Perimede, daughter of Aiolos, with the River Acheloos, three generations above Sterope in the lineage of the Aitolian line.

155 Aphrodite provided two golden apples which Hippomenes used to distract Atalanta making it possible for him to win the race (see Ovid *Met*.10.560-739 for a complete narrative). Hippomenes is an obscure figure in early Greek myth, although he is finally described by Ovid as a son of Megareus, son of the eponym Oinchestos (a Boiotian town at the southwest foot of Mt. Sphinx northeast of Askra and northwest of Thebes), and a grandson of the god Poseidon, as well (*Met*.10.611-612).

156 She was variously said to have been exposed by her father, who did not want a daughter, but only sons, suckled by a bear, and raised by hunters (ApB 3.9.2) or alternatively, to have taken to the wilds in order to escape the shackles of marriage (Theognis 1282-1294).

157 This viewpoint is put forth by Timothy Gantz in a chapter devoted to the problem (335-339). Gantz' argument, overall, is extremely compelling. It is only due to the research leading to this report, which primarily involved charting genealogies, that I am moved to present an alternative argument.

158 Exemplified by Martin West in a genealogical context (e.g. 1985: 29-30, 137ff.). As enumerated in the introduction above, the theory itself more subtly pervades a considerable body of relevant scholarship.

159 Back in the 1920s Carl Robert suggested that the Arkadian Atalanta was modeled on the Boiotian (*Griechische Mythologie* 2.84)

160 Apollodoros lists Epochos as a fourth son (3.9.2). Pausinas lists him along with Ankaios, excluding Iasios altogether, and making Amphidamas another son of Apheidas (8.4.3-10). This arrangement turns out to be quite significant. Epochos is excluded from the present discussion. He seems to have been a figure of strictly local significance. Pausanias identifies him on the front gable of the refurbished Temple of Athena Alea near Tegea (i.e. 4th century), where he is supporting his brother Ankaios, who has been wounded in the hunt for the Kalydonian boar (8.45.4-6).

161 Concerning this vase, cf. M. Robertson 1975; K. Schefold 1966; and A. Stewart in W.G. Moon, eds., 1983.

162 So also, *Amores* 3.29-31.

163 See, R Hunter ed., 2005 for a collection of recent papers on the Hesiodic *Catalogue*, reviewed by M.L. West in *CR* 56.2 2006.

164 This unavoidably required certain strategic choices to render two personalities into one. At a minimum it involved: a choice of location (aka mythic heritage) and a choice of mate. Blending the huntress with the runner was really no great obstacle. The issue of offspring remains to be addressed.

165 Pelias and his brother Neleus were sons of Poseidon and Tyro, who was the wife of Kretheus, son of Aiolos, as well as his niece, since she was the daughter of Salmoneus, another son of Aiolos. Evidence for the antiquity of these games includes a lost epic by Stesichoros entitled *The Funeral Games for Pelias* and Simonides' remark that they were dealt with by Homer which suggests antecedents to Stesichoros' work. As it is, Pausanias' description of the Chest of Kypselos (5.17.9-11) provides our earliest concrete evidence.

166 e.g. via fragments of a dinos from the Akropolis (Athens Akr 590) and the imagery on a Chalkidian hydria (Munich 596), see Gantz 193.

167 ApB 3.9.2.

168 e.g. Jason, on the Chest of Kypselos, and one Hippalkimos, on a Korinthian Krater (viz. the Amphiaraos Krater ca. 575) who Hyginus reports was an alleged son of Pelops (*Fab. 14*; cf. Gantz 194). T. Gantz considers the possibility that Atalanta originally wrestled with Peleus in Kalydon, rather than in Iolkos (viz. Pelias' kingdom), but that their match was subsequently transferred to the funeral games in honor of Pelias. Gantz' discussion focuses on mythological chronology, an issue that comes up frequently when tracing mythic change. Since Steisichoros and others depict Meleagros as a participant in Pelias' funeral games, this would necessarily place the games before the famous hunt for the Kalydonian boar which unconditionally led to Meleagros' death. Gantz, therefore, wonders whether this was the original order, or whether the boar story at one time came first, excluding Meleagros from events at Iolkos. On the whole, Gantz emphasizes the difficulties involved in confidently pinpointing the earliest sequence, and illustrates that sequential alterations were a common feature of Greek mythic emendation. Beyond the tricky business of sequencing in this case, the early existence of an extraordinary Atalanta capable of wrestling with her male contemporaries and also portrayed as an equal participant in a number of key legendary adventures comes across unequivocally in the extant sources. The problem that arises is, which Atalanta? This presentation detects two basic choices: a figure with perceptible Aiolic roots and a figure attached to an indigenous genealogy, in this instance, to the Arkadian line. Taken together, on a case by case basis, the recurrent manifestation of precisely this choice (albeit often involving more than simply two figures) substantiates the conclusions set forth here, and supports the method advanced in this analysis for determining mythological precedence.

[169] i.e. The first hunter to hit the boar ApB 1.7.10; Paus.8.45.2. The hide was the prize of valor.

[170] According to Diodoros, Meleagros was motivated by infatuation DS 4.34.4-5.

[171] In his *Life of Tiberius* (44.2), Suetonius reports that the emperor had a painting that graphically depicted an encounter between these two. Gantz feels that this depiction is representative of an artistic trend that stemmed back to the fourth century and considers this pairing likely to be a relatively late feature of Atalanta's biography (Gantz 1993: 337). The notion, at any rate, seems present in latent form in Diodoros' account of the matter.

[172] Mt. Mainalos is located in southeastern Arkadia (just north of modern Tripoli). It was west of Mantineia and northwest of Tegea.

[173] i.e. Particularly with respect to her heroic feats. Atalanta was a kind of cross-between the Amazon imagery of excessive female strength and the mystique of self-sufficiency in the wilds associated with the female followers of Artemis.

[174] In art, Lynn Roller documents a short lived fascination with the depiction of heroic funeral games, particularly those of Patroklos and Pelias (*AJA* 85.2 1981: 107-119). These emerge in the first quarter of the sixth century and remain popular till just after the mid-sixth century. Roller's paper locates the source of this movement in the northeastern Peloponnese, specifically radiating from Argos and Korinth (still, a number of key pieces hail from Lakonia), and suggests a connection between these representations and the pan-Hellenic games established in the sixth century (viz. the Pythian Games in 586, the Isthmian Games in 581, and the Nemean Games in 573. cf. Pauly-Wissowa *RE*). Of the athletic contests that appear early on in association with Pelias' funeral games, only the wrestling match between Pelias and Atalanta, who supersedes Pelias' other adversaries in the midst of this artistic movement, remains consistently popular down to the fourth century, gradually leaving its initial context behind to become an independent set piece.

[175] e.g. On the hunt for the Kallydonian boar: DS 4.34.4; ApB 1.7.8; Paus.8.45.2. On the voyage of the Argo: DS.4.41.2; ApB 1.9.16 vs. 3.9.2. Kallimachos poses a significant contrast in assigning Atalanta, specifically a daughter of the Arkadian Iasios, to the hunt for the Kalydonian Boar (3.215.221).

[176] Beneath Mt. Mainalos to the west.

[177] See, also Strabo 4.427; W. Hazlitt 1995: s.v. *Schoineus*. Anthedon is located north west of Chalkis on the Euboian Gulf. For its role as the ancient port of Thebes, see D.J. Blackman 1969: 11-22.

[178] Pausanias frequently used the explanatory power of mythic-migrations in his interpretive treatment of legendary events.

[179] viz. Arkas -> Apheidas -> Aleos -> Lykourgos / Aphidamas. **Lykourgos** -> Epochos / Ankaios. **Ankaios** -> Agapenor. **Amphidamas** -> Melanion.

[180] Agapenor was associated with the foundation of Cypriot Paphos on his return from the Trojan War (e.g. ApE 6.15), which may well represent an early epic claim.

[181] Hypseus was a son of the Peneios River and known as a one time king of the Lapiths, who were (as mentioned above) an old and prestigious clan, closely connected with, if not an offshoot of, the early Aiolic genealogy. In addition to Themisto, Hypseus fathered Kyrene, who mated with Apollo and gave birth to Aristaios, who marred Autonoe, daughter of Kadmos. In turn, Autonoe gave birth to Aktaion, who was notoriously killed by his own dogs. As noted in greater detail below, Athamas, son of Aiolos, married three times which embroiled him in series of family conflicts. His second wife was Ino, daughter of Kadmos, while his third was Themisto, daughter of Hypseus, an arrangement which placed both of Hypseus' daughters into close contact with the Theban line and the contemporaneous Boiotian line of Athamas: a web of interrelations quite typical of early Aiolic genealogical patterns. Kyrene, Aristaios, and Aktaion evidently first surface in the *Ehoiai* (Hes.fr 215, 217 MW; fr 217A OCT; T.Renner 1978; Gantz 1993: 93; Pind.*Pyth*.9 for Hypseus), which also recorded aspects of Athamas' family drama (Gantz 176-180). Ino, daughter of Kadmos and wife of Athamas, surfaces obliquely in the *Odyssey* (Od.5.333-335).

[182] Which was, it seems, anyway, extremely well-known.

[183] At least, in this passage. Compare, however, 1.8.2 where Atalanta, daughter of Schoineus, participates in the hunt for the Kalydonian boar and 1.9.16 where Atalanta, daughter of Schoineus, sails along on the Argonautic adventure.

[184] Statius' *Thebaid* (6.560-565) offers another example of the Boiotian runner in an Arkadian landscape.

[185] Granted this association is with Minyan Orchomenos and, therefore, with northeast, rather than, southwest Boiotia.

[186] The play Apollodoros refers to is unknown. Gantz suggests the *Meleagros* (338).

[187] This motif first surfaces with Palaiphatos (i.e. in the fourth century) where it is applied to Atalanta and Melanion (13). Apollodoros also preserves this attribution amidst his medley of competing claims (3.9.2), In Ovid, the metamorphosis describes the fate of Atalanta and Hippomenes (*Met*.10.681-704). cf. Hyginus *Fab*. 185.

[188] On metamorphosis in Greek myth, see C. Calame, ed. 1989; P.M.C. Forbes Irving 1990.

[189] viz. Removal from the world of genealogical procreativity. Notably, Eos' multiple abductions also generated heroic progeny, Memnon via Tithonos being the most famous case (Hesiod *Theogony*: 984-991; HHAphrodite 218-219; M.West 2003: 110-113). Yet a sense of permanent genealogical exclusion dominates the Kleitos reference in Homer, while earlier in the *Odyssey* Eos' seizure of Orion led to his death at the hands of Artemis (Od.5.121-124).

[190] Acknowledged, for example, by G.S. Kirk in *JHS* 92 1972.

[191] Palaiphatos, quite typically, doesn't believe the story. His whole vignette purports to explain why it was that this rumor was spread about. In the end, Atlanta and Melanion are left off in a cave in their original human form.

[192] viz. a grand finale in lieu of offspring.

[193] i.e. to the marriage of the Boiotian Atalanta.

[194] Parthenopais first surfaces in the epic *Thebais* via a citation in Pausanias (9.18.6), which states that contrary to local Theban tradition (which maintained he was killed by one Asphodikos), the Theban epic reported that Parthenopais was killed by the Theban, Periklymenos, in the first Argive attack against Thebes. At 9.9.5 Pausanias attests that the mid-seventh century elegiac poet, Kallinos of Ephesos, maintained that the *Thebais* was composed by Homer, and goes on to proclaim that he rates this poem best after the *Iliad* and the *Odysssey*. Taken at face value, this testimony suggests a very early date for the *Thebais*. While acknowledging the antiquity of the tradition of the Argive–Theban Wars, M. Davies (1989), however, takes a more skeptical view on the date of the text at Pausanias' disposal. In the present context, at any rate, the evidence is sufficient to support the relatively early existence of a mythological figure named Parthenopais, who fought with the Argives in the first Theban War.

[195] The one exception to this was the proposal that he was the son of Atalanta and Meleagros, which is likely to be a post-Classical trend (see Gantz 337; Hyg. *Fab.* 99), but if not, yet another compelling tangent.

[196] Accordingly, therefore, a brother of Adrastos, leader and perpetrator of the first unsuccessful Argive offensive against the city of Thebes.

[197] e.g. Il.4.364-400, 4.405-410.

[198] On this trilogy, see, for example, D.J. Conacher 1996; William Thalmann 1978.

[199] On the Theban Epics, see G.L. Huxley: 1969: ch.3. The main extant sources on this topic include: Hesiod *Works and Days* 160-165. Bacchylides 9; Pind. Nem.9; Hdt. 5.67; DS 4.65; Statius *Thebaid*; ApB 3.6.1-3.7.2. Of the surviving Athenian tragedies (in addition to Aeschylos' *Hepta*), Euripides' *Phoinissai*, and Sophokles' *Oidipous at Kolonos* provide additionally relevant coverage. They illustrate, in particular, for example, the fifth-century Athenian codification of the major combatants on either side, including the Arkadian Parthenopais.

[200] So for example, Aischylos was credited with a number of related plays viz., a *Nemea*, an *Epigoni*, an *Eleusinioi* and an *Argeiai*, the latter two dealing with the aftermath of the Seven's ill-fated attempt; Sophokles was credited with an *Eriphyle* and perhaps also an *Epigoni*. Parts of Euripides' *Hypsipyle* survive. Earlier Stesichoros wrote a poem called *Eriphyle*, and Herodotos mentions an epic *Epigoni* that some attributed to Homer. (cf. M. West 2003 for further testimonia).

[201] See, Aeschylos *Hepta* 532-547 for Parthenopais of Arkadia; Sophokles' *Oidipous at Kolonos* 1507-1513 for Parthenopais, again an Arkadian, with one Hippomedon cited as Talaos son; Euripides' *Phoinissai* 150 for Parthenopais, Atalanta's son, and Euipides' *Hiketides* 888-901, for Parthenopais, son of the huntress, Atalanta, who was an Arkadian reared in Argos, and who loyally supported Adrastos' war effort. Though conspicuously Parthenopais' father does not surface in any of these texts, Talaos is never paired with Atalanta (e.g. at 1.9.13 Apollodoros records Lysimache, daughter of Abas, as Talaos' wife. In Athens she was said to be a daughter of Kerkyon (cf. Gantz 1993: 336). Pausanias 2.6.3. reports Lysianassa, daughter of Polybos of Korinth. Σ Pind.Nem.9.30 gives this role to Lysimache). The Arkadian Atalanta's most frequent connections are with Melanion and also with Ares (alleged father of Parthenopais, ApB 3.9.2), though, as we have seen, Hippomenes remained a favored substitute in some quarters, implying that this omission was not incidental.

[202] See Gantz 1993: 336 for an overview of the relevant testimony. Judging from Paus.9.18.6, where Parthenopais is cited as a son of Talaos, Gantz considers it likely that the epic *Thebais* (mentioned in the same passage), also promoted this genealogy.

²⁰³ A case of such resistance can, for example, be traced to Argos. In describing a monument of the *Seven Against Thebes* that was set up by the Argives at Delphi to commemorate their victory against the Spartans at Oinoe with the assistance of the Athenians (in the late 460s or 450s, the period of Athenian/Argive alliance), Pausanias lists a group of seven warriors depicted to the exclusion of Parthenopais (10.10.3). Here Parthenopais was replaced with a figure named Hippomedon, allegedly another son of Talaos, who surfaces also in Athenian tragedy when Parthenopais, the Arkadian, is a favored protagonist (e.g. Soph.*Oid.Kol.* 1507, 1510). By contrast, another statue group that Pausanias witnessed in downtown Argos (2.20.5) portrayed the victorious sons of the initial combatants (who Pausanias maintains were more than seven in number, till they were reduced to seven by Aischylos), and included Promachos, son of Parthenopais, once again identified as a son of Talaos. The Argives, it is clear, left to their own devices, preferred Parthenopais, son of Talaos, who happened to be an Argive with Aiolic roots (more on this genealogy in chs. 4-6 below). Accordingly, it may be surmised that Parthenopais' exclusion from the Delphic monument was in some sense linked to the rising influence of his Arkadian double who is so prominent in Athenian tragedy. However, what comes across from the heart of Argos is a potent resistance to the Arkadian Parthenopais, a viewpoint, moreover, that would be consonant with the attribution of the metamorphosis story to Atalanta and Melanion. Viewed from another angle, L.H. Jeffrey reports that Hypatodoros and Aristogeiton, the creators of the sculpture set up at Delphi have been identified as Theban artists on epigraphical grounds (1965). She goes on to emphasize that Pausanias' claim that the Argives commissioned two Boiotians to create a piece in honor of this victory, when they had many renowned sculptors of their own in this period, is very odd, and quite likely mistaken. Consequently, she suggests that this monument of the *Seven* was rather war booty taken out of Boiotia and set up by the Argives along the Sacred Way, where an *Epigoni* statue group was later placed to accompany it. In the present context, Jeffrey's proposal would seem to affirm the increasing marginalization of the son of Talaos in favor of the son of Atalanta, conceivably here, from a localized point of view in light of the appearance of one Alitherses, who is otherwise completely unknown. Moreover, the Argives could well have been willing to tolerate Hippomedon over Parthenopais, since Hippomedon was also deemed a son of Talaos. It is conspicuous that the two statue groups do not coincide with one another, although by convention the *Epigoni*, who launched the second successful attack against Thebes, were identified as the sons of the previous aggressors. Thus, the hero Promachos, son of Parthenopais, appears in the *Epigoni* statue group, though his father is absent from the statue of the *Seven*. In any case, it is sufficiently clear that Parthenopais, son of Talaos, remained the dominant figure in Argos even as his Arkadian double was already remarkably popular elsewhere.

²⁰⁴ viz. the transfer of a figure and the story attached to them to an all new genealogical setting.

²⁰⁵ e.g. Kallimachos 3.215-224.

²⁰⁶ In the *Iliad* and the *Odyssey* this information is presented obliquely through acknowledgement of the Hellespont, or the crossing of Helle, Jason's son Euenos on the island of Lemnos, and Ino in the form of the sea goddess Leukothea. In each case, fleeting reference to these conditions acknowledged the occurrence of past time events.

²⁰⁷ So, for example, the roster of lost plays includes: An *Athamas* by Aischylos, two *Athamas* plays by Sophokles, an *Ino* and two *Phrixos* plays by Euripides. Hyginus' *Fabulae* 1-4 provide partial access to aspects of these treatments, primarily, it seems, those of Euripides.

²⁰⁸ The incident is referenced in the Hesiodic *Catalogue of Women* (Hes fr 68 MW; fr. 245, 255 and 299 are also relevant. These fragments also mention Phrixos' eastward journey and his marriage to a daughter of the king of Kolchis). Apollodoros offers a concise overview of Athamas' biography at 1.9.1-2.

²⁰⁹ She was given, as usual, an assortment of names, see Gantz 1993:183.

210 These events admit a number of variations. Ino's guardianship of Dionysos, son of Zeus and Semele, another daughter of Kadmos (who, remarkably, though a mortal, gave birth to a god), invokes a recurrent form of provocation of the wrath of the queen of the gods (early references to Semele, include Il.14.323-325; *Theogony* 940-942; Pind.Ol.2.22-27). In addition to a brief reference in the *Odyssey* (5.333-335), Ino's fate was addressed in the *Ehoiai*. (Hes fr 70 MW). The flight of Phrixos and Helle appears to depend on the vindictive actions of either Ino or Themisto. In the case of the former it involved a deceitful plot through which Ino turned Athamas against his first wife's children (e.g. Apollodoros 1.9.1 and Pausanias 1.44.8). In the case of the latter, it involved a wicked step-mother version of the so-called *Potiphar's Wife* motif, based on a young man's rejection of sexual advances made by an inappropriate woman (this motif is addressed in greater detail below). Pindar (*Pyth*.4.159-162), Pherekydes (FGrHist 3F98) and Apollonios (3.191) testify to the currency of the wicked step-mother version. Pindar, here, leaves the step-mother nameless, while there were other contestants in addition to Themisto, the preference of Pherekydes and the tragedians, see Gantz 1993: 177. Themisto's role in this conflict is redundant, however, and essentially substitutes for Ino's story, seeing that the demise of Athamas' first two marriages along with his two sets of children was already adequately accounted for, leaving Athamas available for a new liaison without the introduction of illicit activities on the part of his third wife. A superlative overview is provided by Gantz, 1993176-180.

211 Here, Pausanias includes them in his detailed and characteristically synthetic account of the genealogy of Boiotian Orchomenos. Herodotos recounts an apparently well-known story in which Athamas for some reason wound up in Achaia (viz. the northeastern Peloponnese) and would have been murdered by the Achaians, if not for the arrival of Phrixos' eldest son from Kolchis (namely, one Kytissoros) in the nick of time to save his grandfather (7.197).

212 In this regard, it is interesting to note that before the intervention of Attic tragedy, evidently, Oidipous too was credited with three marriages (see Gantz 1993: 500-501). However, as the evidence stands, this antiquity of this sequence is less well supported than the antiquity of the sequence attributed to Athamas, primarily because we do not know where the epic *Oidipodeia* stood on the subject. Oidipous' sequence was assigned to Pherekydes and runs as follows (FGrHist 3F95). First, he married Iokasta, his own mother, who in addition bore two other sons, but they were killed off by the Minyans of Orchomenos (cf. Od.11.271280). Second, he married a heroine named Eurygaenia, either a daughter of one Periphas or a sister of Iokaste (generally, the daughter of King Kreon of Thebes). Eurygaenia was credited with the birth of Oidipous' most famous children: Polyneikes, Eteokles, Antigone, and Ismene (also, Σ Euripides' *Phoinissai* 1760 where Peisandros of Rhodes is named as the source). Third, he married Astymedousa, daughter of Sthenelos, one of Perseus' sons, though unfortunately the matter receives no further commentary (the Hesiodic *Catalogue* likely addressed this marriage as well based on Hes fr 193 MW). Oidipous' early biography is very sketchy, mainly because it was overshadowed as a result of the attributes chosen for emphasis by the fifth-century Attic playwrights. Overall, they seem to have simplified a considerably more intricate family history, much of which likely stemmed back to the *Oidipodeia*. The idea, for instance, that Oidipous' children were born of his incestuous marriage is one of the novelties that can be traced to Athenian dramatic production. The significance of this pattern in the present context is the compelling prospect that triple marriages characterized the lifestories of two great protagonists from two legendary Boiotian families that were also genealogically linked.

213 By contrast, Athamas' union with Themisto first surfaces in the Hesiodic *Ehoiai* where there are indications that this family genealogy occurred in connection with the feature story of Hippomenes' race for the Boiotian Atlalanta. The name Themisto is first attributed to Pherekydes (FGrHist 3F98; West 1985: 49, 66-67; Gantz 1993: 179). The antiquity of this union must accordingly be judged by its apparently early genealogical importance via Schoineus to Atalanta and via a second son, Leukon, to a number of daughters who appear to have married heroic personalities, in addition to the line's Aiolic affiliation and persistent identification with Minyan Orchomenos.

214 Greek mythic tradition thrived on innovation while the legacy of Greek epic was programmatically sacrosanct. This situation throws some light on the qualitative difference between genealogical and aesthetic innovation. Greek audiences waited in anticipation for dazzling new presentations of the cultural canon, but the canon itself was deemed inviolate. Within this framework, storytelling was fluid and re-interpretation was a vital art form, but theoretically no injustice was done to the integrity of Greek tradition. With a cluster of stories the caliber of the genealogy of the house of Athamas, it is safe to assume that the annihilation of Athamas' principal line of descendants would not go unnoticed by a crowd of Greek spectators. The entertainment value of such a suggestion derived from its recognition as contrary to fact. Still the fate of such a suggestion when the performance was over was a considerably more complex matter. If it was seriously promoted, it would no doubt face resistance, but it is not inconceivable, as we have seen, for such a proposition to gather sufficient strength to eradicate the line of Athamas and Themisto from the mythological record (although, as it happens, it did not). Radical structural alterations like these were evidently facilitated by a cultural double standard. So though it was obviously quite well-known when the inherited framework had been breached, there was no accepted mode of acknowledgment for structural violence to epic tradition. Standard parlance employed the most neutral approach: so-and-so maintains it happened thus, whereas others insist it happened differently, all of which was only to be expected since creative ingenuity was the norm. In this way influential genealogical change was systematically shielded by aesthetic creativity.

215 An arrangement attested in the A scholia to Il.7.86. Philostephanos, a third-century writer is cited. See Gantz 1993: 178.

216 Via Hyginus' summary in *Fabula* 4.

217 A Homeric example of this motif involves the *Odyssey*'s Aedon, daughter of Pandareos and wife of Zethos of Thebes, who killed their son Itylos in a fit of madness (Od.19.518-523, 11.260-265). The scholia to this passage go on to explain that Aidon meant to kill the child of her sister-and-law Niobe. The Athenian story of Prokne and Philomela, daughters of Pandion, the Athenian king, looks like a takeoff on the Homeric reference and a related tale that was known to Hesiod (*W&D* 568; Gantz 239-241). In the Athenian version, at any rate, Prokne and Philomela kill Prokne's son Itys and serve him as a meal to Prokne's husband Tereus to avenge Tereus' rape of Philomela. This was likely the plot line of Sophokles' *Tereus* and surfaces obliquely in two of Aischylos' plays with considerable coverage in a number of later authors (Aischy.*Hiketides* 60-68, *Agamemnon* 1144-1145; Konon FGrHist 26F1; Ovid *Met.* 6.424-644; ApB 3.14.8). Euripides' staged version of Medea's revenge against her husband Jason by way of killing their children is likewise a variation on the same theme. These examples exhibit some variation in the relationship between intention and outcome, but they work with the same basic mythic motif.

[218] Pausanias' line of Orchomenos begins with one Andreas, whom he describes as a son of the Peneios River and the first inhabitant of the country. On the one hand, this assertion clearly resembles the standard method of launching post-epic regional lines via personified elements of the indigenous landscape. On the other hand, though, it more closely resembles the standard epic formula responsible for the creation of heroes or demigods by way of deified rivers and assorted nymphs, the latter often in union with Olympian deities. Notably, too the Peneios River runs through Thessaly, not through Boiotia. It is not inconceivable in this regard that this inaugural formula was actually quite old and implied a genealogical connection between Thessaly and northeastern Boiotia. Similarly, Kyrene, who mated with Apollo and gave birth to Aristaios, was a daughter of Hypseus, in turn, son of the Peneios and one-time king of the Lapiths (cf. Gantz 1993: 92; see further DS 4.69.3-4 for yet another high status lineage including the Lapiths, Ixion and Peirithoos, who are attributed by Diodoros to a third daughter of Hypseus). Aristaios married into the lineage of Thebes. Notably, In the *Iliad* the Sperchios River plays a comparable role in the generation of the Myrmidon soldiers who served under Achilles. This particular formula, at any rate, commanded an early alternate application that distinguishes it to some extent from the personification of elements in the landscape (rivers included) that were used for primordial state formation in the major communities of the Peloponnese (not that this factor precluded novelty in Pausanias' case). Moreover, in general, early on, the auxiliary genealogies that interacted with the major Aiolic stemmata appear to have arisen via this formula, hence the examples cited.

[219] So, for example, Apollonios (1.230-233) asserts that people gave the name Minyai to the Argonauts, since most of them, and, all the best, could claim descent from the daughters of Minyas. This assertion, however, is simply not true as there is plenty of evidence to the contrary. On the daughters of Minyas, see Gantz 1993: 736-737.

[220] So, for example, Pausanias portrays Minyas as a son of Chryses, a descendant of Sisyphos, son of Aiolos (9.36.4-6). Meanwhile, the eponym Orchomenos, a son of Minyas in Pausanias is described by Hyginus as a son of Athamas, instead (*Fab*.1). Granted, Hyginus' data frequently deviate from early mythological precedents, but in this case his suggestion simply reiterates the tendency to link Minyan Orchomenos with the Aiolic lines Athamas and/or Sisyphos when the city's Aiolic heritage is not truncated instead. These examples, therefore, highlight the alternative practice of subordinating *Minyas* and *Orchomenos* to established early Aiolic lines, as opposed to placing them at the head of a separate Aiolic lineage (viz. via Minyas, son of Aiolos). Apollodoros' treatment, to cite another example, seems to follow the same general trend (viz. no Minyas surfaces among the sons of Aiolos; the seventh son of Aiolos recorded is Magnes 1.7.3). The crux of the matter is that no information exists to illuminate the early connection between Iasos, son of Amphion of Orchomenos in the *Odyssey* and the relevant early Aiolic lines. We know nothing of the structure that existed above Amphion as far as the Homeric poems were concerned, so Pherekydes' suggestion that Amphion's mother was a daughter of Minyas (FGrHist 3F117) leaves Minyas' heritage once again unidentified. This furthers the impression that the objective was to put the focus on Minyas to the exclusion of his mythological roots. Minyas, moreover, may not have been an early mythic progenitor at all, but rather a subsequent eponym strategically placed in order to eliminate the need to invoke the old outdated Minyan ancestry. Overall this state of affairs was evidently a symptom of emendations imposed on the line of Orchomenos: an early Aiolic line of unknown derivation.

[221] The existence of two Amphions in the Nekuia, one linked to Orchomenos, the other to Thebes, is also worthy of notice in terms of the connections and parallels forged between these two cities (Od.11.160-265, 11.281-285). It is also clear, however, that they were later conflated (so, ApB 3.5.6; Paus.2.21.9-10, 5.16.4; and as noted by Gantz on page 539).

222 Via one Euryale, daughter of Minos, who it was said united with Poseidon and gave birth to Orion (e.g. Hes fr 148a MW; Pherekydes FGrHist 3F52), though Orion was firmly rooted in Boiotia where he was linked to the genealogy of Poseidon and Alkyone (daughter of Aiolos) and subsequently to the daughters of Atlas, who were immortalized with Orion as the constellation the Pleiades (Gantz: 1993: 213-214, 270-273). On Orion in Sicily and his appearance in the *Nekuia* (Od.11.309-310, 572-575), however, with no account of his genealogical heritage, see DS 4.84.1-7.

223 See below.

224 e.g. Il.13.301; HHymn 3.277-279; Paus. 9.36.1-3, 10.4.1, where they are included in the line of Orchomenos; cf. Rocher for further details.

225 e.g. DS 4.10.2-5; ApB 2.4.11.

226 Od.11.281-297; ApB 1.9.10.

227 Neleus' Minyan wife Chloris remained famous in connection with an alleged Minyan element in the Peloponnese as noted by historical chroniclers (e.g. Str. 8.3.19; Paus.9.36.8; on the tradition of Minyan inhabitants in Elis and Triphylia, in general, cf. Hdt.4.148; Str.8.3.3). Notably, Chloris, daughter of Amphion, in the *Odyssey* is later described as the daughter of Minyas. In addition to the Homeric connection between Pylos and Orchomenos via Chloris and Neleus' marriage, there is also evidence, assembled below, for a connection between Elis and Orchomenos via Aktor, son of Azeus (Il.2.511-515).

228 Hdt. 4.150-158; West: 1985: 85-88; Gantz: 1993: 93.

229 See, West 1985: 65-67.

230 See Gantz 1980: 140-141 on the Aischylean tetrology that concluded with a Lykourgos; also ApB 3.5.1.

231 viz. Pelasgus -> Lykaon -> Kallisto -> Apheidas -> Stheneboia/Aleos. **Stheneboia** + Proitos of Argos. **Aleos** -> Lykourgos/Kepheus/Auge. **Lykourgos** -> Ankaios/Iasos/Amphidamas. **Ankaios**-> Agapenor. **Iasos** -> Atalanta. **Amphidamas**-> Melanion. **Kepheus**-> Sterope/& brothers. **Auge** + Herakles -> Telephos-> Eurypylos.

232 See D. Obbink ZPE 156 2006: 1-9 and M.L. West: 11-17 for an important recent Archilochos fragment. The fragment confirms the early currency of the whole mini-saga that dealt with the first (misdirected) Achaian mission to Troy, resulting in a confrontation at Mysia. There, Telephos, who is described by the papyrus as a descendant of one Arkasos, as well as a son of Herakles, was the reigning king at the time. As Obbink points out, the identity of this Arkasos remains an open question, though there are key indications that the name was distinct from the eponymous Arkadian eponym Arkas. Notably, the same epithet also occurs in two papyrus fragments attributed to the Hesiodic *Catalogue of Women* and, plausible in this light that Arkasos' persona was readily absorbed by Arkadian mythic interests (fr 129, 165 MW). It is unclear whether the Arkas/ Arkasos dilemma will be resolved anytime soon. But for the moment it looks as if we are dealing with an East Greek rendition of the Telephos saga that antedates the Arkadian sequel. This chronology works well with other scraps of information that vaguely but tangibly illuminate a floruit of East Greek mythology in seventh-century Ionia. In the same volume, M.L. West emphasizes the overall impact of the revelation that Archilochos knew the whole Telephos story. West, however, is not convinced that Archilochos' knowledge confirms his acquaintance with the Homeric poems, dating their dissemination to after c. 630.

²³³However, only after he killed the hero, Thersandros, the son of Polyneikes of Thebes, who was known to have previously participated in the second Argive assault against his father's native city (as recorded in the *Kypria*).

²³⁴ See Proklos' *ΧΡΗΣΤΟΜΑΘΙΑ ΠΕΡΙ ΤΩΝ ΚΥΠΡΙΩΝ*, Oxionii 1810. M. Davies 1989: 42-43; K. Dowden in R. Fowler, ed. 2004. Also, Pind.*Isth*.5.41-42, *Isth*.8.49-52; ApE 3.16-20. Against Telephos' role in leading the Greeks to Troy, see, Il.1.71-2; Hyg. *Fab*.101; *Fab*. 99 and 100 are also relevant to this subject matter. Curiously, at first glance, Agamemnon's first expedition to Troy is often glossed over in analytical treatments of the Trojan War. Upon further reflection, this omission is most prominent in historically oriented interpretations, presumably for the same reasons that stand behind the low-profile of Herakles' Trojan adventure, which was said to take place in the reign of Laomedon (e.g. Il.5.632-642, 14.249-251, 20.144-148). Taking these prior initiatives into account has a conspicuously negative effect on the potential truth value of the Trojan War story, and begs, for example, that Herakles be considered as historical a figure as Agamemnon, that is, among those inclined to argue that underneath many layers of legend, Agamemnon was a historical figure. Moreover, viewing these adventures altogether in sequence, reveals that they exhibit characteristics that are typical and recurrent in Greek mythic plot structures.

²³⁵ On Neoptolemos and Eurypylos, see Il.19.325-327; Od.11.505-523; also Proklos' *ΧΡΗΣΤΟΜΑΘΙΑ ΙΛΙΑΔΟΣ ΜΙΚΡΑΣ*; M. Davies 1989: 65. For an overview of all relevant subject matter see Gantz: 1993: 428-431, 576-80, 640-641.

²³⁶ viz. Aischylos wrote a trilogy on the subject. The known titles include a *Telephos* and a *Mysioi*. Sophokles also wrote a connected Telephia. Euripides wrote a *Telephos* and an *Auge*. On the remains of the former, what is known of the trilogies, and the plays on this subject by scarcely known playwrights, see C. Collard, M.J. Cropp and K.H. Lee 1997.

²³⁷ Diodoros makes northwestern Arkadia Herakles' base of operations for a period after he returned from Ilion e.g.4.33.3, 8; Sophokles *Aleadai* had Herakles seek help from Aleos of Arkadia as he prepared to launch an attack on Augeias of Elis (Gantz 1993: 429).

²³⁸ This motif is perhaps more widely known from the story of Danae and her son Perseus. On both counts, the floating chest may well represent a post-epic addition to these stories. The motif, itself, is typically associated with a king's outrage coupled with disbelief that his daughter has been impregnated by a god (granted, a demi-god in Auge's case). This outrage prompts him to exile mother and son, sending them out to sea, which inevitably leads them to start life a fresh in some new country. In spite of more abstruse treatments of this plot structure (e.g. N.M. Holley 1949 with references), pragmatically speaking, its function seems to be to cultivate a great hero in a distant location in preparation for future events.

²³⁹ See, Strabo.13.1.69 citing Euripides, presumably his *Auge*, and Paus.8.4.8-9, citing Hekataios.

²⁴⁰ This version is attributed to Sophokles' treatments and is evident in the fragments of Euripides' *Telephos*. See, also DS 4.33.7-12; ApB 2.7.4, 3.9.1.

²⁴¹ The story is told by Glaukos, son of Hippolochos, ancestor of Bellerophon, who ultimately married into the Lykian line (Il.6.144-211). It is dealt with more thoroughly in chapter 4.

²⁴² e.g. ApB 2.2.1. The genealogy, geography, and mythology of Argos are covered in chapters four and five, below.

²⁴³ See, C. Collard, M.J. Cropp and K.H. Lee, eds. 1997. Euripides' *Bellerophon* is also covered. A lost *Iobates* is attributed to Sophokles.

²⁴⁴ Elatos was the father of Kaineus and Polyphemos mentioned at Il.1.264, cf. AR 1.40; ApB 1.9.16; Ovid *Met*. 12.497; Lucian 22.9; Hyg. *Fab*.14.4;

245 Il.2.729-732, Il.4.193-194; HHymns 3.211; 16.1-5; Pind. *Pyth*.3; Pherekydes FGrHist 3F3, 3F35; Euripides' *Alkestis* 1-7, 121-131; Ovid *Met.* 2.540-550. Paus.2.36.3-7; see also West 1985: 69-72; for a comparable case of mythological theft that targeted this same family, though conceived and promoted at Epidauros, see J. Bremmer 1998: 516-517.

246 So, especially, Plutarch's *Theseus*; West 1985: 42, 93; Gantz 1993: 277-282, 288-295.

247 The town of Stymphalos was especially famous for a marauding flock of birds that were subdued by Herakles as one of his labors in the service of Eurystheus of Argos (e.g. DS 4.12.2; ApB.2.5.6).

248 In the Pythian Hymn to Apollo, Trophonios and Agamedes ceremoniously carved and installed the stone threshold for Apollo's first temple at Delphi (287-299). Pausanias credits them with the construction of Amphitryon's house at Thebes (9.11.1) and later goes on to recount in detail what was certainly the most famous story about them, namely, their construction of a treasury for Hyrieus (son of Poseidon and Alkyone, daughter of Aiolos) with built in features designed so that they could later rob it (9.37.5-7). They continued their thievery until they were caught, at which point Trophonios beheaded Agamedes and was instantaneously swallowed up by the earth, presumably due divine intervention. This story's resemblance to Herodotos' tale of the Pharaoh Rhampsinitos' architect and his sons is frequently invoked in this context (Hdt.2.121). On Hyrieus, see Gantz: 1993: 215-216, 273, 484.

249 On the oracle and Boiotian cults of Trophonios see especially, A.Schachter vol. 3: 1994: 65-89. Also, Hdt.1.46, 8.134; Euripides' *Ion* 300-302, 392-393, 400-409; DS 115.53.4; Paus. 1.34.2, 4.32.5.; Ael.*VH* 3.45.

250 This alternate genealogy is attributed Charax of Pergamon via Σ 508 to Aristophanes' *Clouds* (FGrHist 103F5). It is also evident that the *Telegonia* substituted the treasury of Augeias of Elis for the treasury of Hyrieus of Boioita in addressing the story of Trophonios' and Agamedes' architectural ruse (also, M. Davies 1989a: 85-87). This adjustment was transparently custom scripted to accommodate the alternate genealogy at issue (e.g. M. West 2003: 166-168). Pausanias, however, refuses to acknowledge an Arkadian Trophonios, though he gives a good deal of press to the Arkadian Agamedes (Paus.8.5.4, 8.45.7).

251 e.g. Compare Paus.8.5.4 and 8.45.7 on Kerkyon, son of Agamedes, son of Stymphalos with the Athenian Kerkyon, son of Poseidon and the Attic eponym Alope, Paus.1.14.3, and 1.39.3. The two accounts of the Athenian Kerkyon are not exactly compatible with one another, but they seem to have been contemporary alternatives. Pausanias attributes the former to the Athenian playwright Choirilos who wrote a play called *Alope*. Euripides also wrote a play by that title, confirming a keen Athenian interest in the promotion of Kerkyon's genealogy. At 8.56.3 Pausanias declares his preference for the Arkadian claim to the Eleusinian Kerkyon, which quite likely indicates the priority of the Arkadian genealogy from a chronological standpoint. Apollodoros notably offers an unrelated genealogy, tracing Kerkyon to Branchous and Argiope (ApE 1.3). This assignment implies East Greek, specifically, Milesian, roots (On the Milesian priestly family, the Branchidai, see L.H. Jeffrey 1976: 211; H.W. Parke 19985a and b; and V. Gorman 2001, with further references. On Alope, Kerkyon and Tripolemos at Athens, see especially, E. Kearns 1989: 146, 147, 173, 176 and 201).

252 *The Chronology of Oral Tradition: Quest for a Chimera*, Oxford 1974.

CHAPTER TWO: MYTHIC THEFT TYPE TWO

The second main type of mythological theft differs from the first in that it transferred to new surroundings legends and mythological figures together without breaking the bond between heroic names and the heroic deeds traditionally attached to them. This tactic is distinguished from the disembodied re-utilization of famous names characteristic of type-one-mythic theft[253]. Most significant about type-two-mythic-theft is that it uprooted figures genealogically, all the while preserving and reallocating whatever those figures were most famous for. Accordingly, this technique also aimed at extinguishing the collective memory of such figures' former identities, more so, by contrast, than mythic-theft-type-one, which relied on the ambiguity of duplicate names to bolster new favorites.

The successful application of the second technique made transported figures more memorable by far in their new mythic settings, effectively supplanting their previous roots in older mythological contexts. To the polis-based sponsors of such innovations, the new would optimally drown out the old in accordance with widespread public endorsement of more acceptable and up-to-date storytelling. In consequence, previous genealogical histories were oftentimes thoroughly blotted out. When they have been preserved it is through an assortment of meager but tenacious alternative statements that tend to contradict more mainstream points of view. In light of these dynamics mythic-theft-type-two may be held responsible for tangible indications that the revised Greek mythic corpus contained numerous truncated genealogical lines, which is to say, excerpts that were derived from the original Aiolic lineage structure. Thus in addition to the formations they perceptibly define, these excerpts express contrary-to-fact conditions that reflect what once was, but was later no longer so. Elusive as this type of testimony may seem, taken together and assessed in connection with related forms of mythological patterning, such vestiges of a former state of affairs contribute to a roughly diachronic account of Greek mythic developments in the Archaic Period. This is critical when it comes to mythological theft, since the concept itself would amount to a dead end in the absence of a consistent method of judging early and filched legends and their protagonists from the further array of contradictory options.

It is first of all clear that the world of Greek legend was from the very beginning hospitable to multiple versions of traditional stories[254]. On to this situation, the Aiolic hypothesis identifies a sudden and dramatic rise in structurally oriented mythic emendations due to perceived mytho-political discrepancies that erupted in the wake of the dissemination of the preeminent version of Greek prehistory from the east to the west. Under these conditions, the sustained integrity of an original core collection of stories is in a way more remarkable than the prospect of the complete dissolution of the early mythological edifice, especially considering the general propensity for various interests to re-interpret tradition as they saw fit[255]. That the cultural production of tradition in Greece remained in a perpetual state of flux is widely acknowledged and has been assessed as of late using the term "plurality" to recommend the blanket acceptance of this vital aspect of the Greek approach to the past[256]. The characteristic Greek toleration for a fluid account of Greek prehistory is also often cited in direct contrast to the monotheistic doctrine of revealed sacred texts[257].

Witnessing, however, this perpetual state of flux, the question arises as to the circumstances responsible for the sustained continuity of the basic tradition, both in the absence of a revealed sacred text, and in spite of the seemingly infinite variations in the presentation of its constituent parts. On the other hand, in a sense, the Homeric epics are actually quite comparable to canonized sacred texts, at least inasmuch as such a comparison grants proper emphasis to their authoritative role in disseminating a major cultural charter, and further suggests the basis for their transmission essentially as they were composed in East Greek Ionia in the late eighth century[258]. Nonetheless, it would seem that unanimous reverence for early epic tradition does not altogether adequately explain certain stories' resistance to change in a situation where meddling and manipulation were by all means the normative state of affairs, and where a substantial proportion of manipulation and meddling were specifically directed at the rectification of premises set out in the Homeric poems[259].

Addressing this situation, the intimate link between Greek epic narratives and genealogical structure may well shed some light on the sustained preservation of a certain core collection of stories; interpretive variations notwithstanding. The early epic medium appears to have plotted heroic protagonists as individual points on an extensive grid. The structure of the grid work was genealogical. And though it may be imagined that this affiliation was once an invaluable mnemonic device, likely useful to bards and audiences alike in grasping the architectural ramifications behind any given installment of the heroic repertoire, in time this inter-relationship became a liability to anyone interested in making amendments to the original genealogical framework, while retaining the integrity of its narrative content.

The idea is that genealogy united mythological figures by way of specific linear sequences to the effect that when their characterization was also bound up with the procession of major legendary events, tampering freely with lineage constructs was liable to jeopardize narrative cohesion and wreak havoc on venerated plots and protagonists. In a word, tamper too much and the sequence is broken, vital narrative elements cease to match up, and events are suspended due to alienation from their established legendary prerequisites, and, likewise, from their anticipated sequels. According to this logic, certain concrete restraints inhibited wholesale mythic emendation where certain essential sequences were at stake, as for instance in the case of key lineage sequences that not only provided key personnel in the triumph of Greek triumphs, the Trojan War, but also provided key participants in famous events previous to that conflict whose roles were recorded in early epic. It follows that the more integral a genealogical sequence and the more explicitly documented early on, the greater the likelihood of the preservation of its original structural elements. It also follows, and is surely the case, that the strategies developed to circumvent the tradition primarily sought to work around it, minimizing direct adversarial claims.

Taking this point of view in line with the notion that the operative early genealogical structure was a fundamentally Aiolic artifact makes it possible to identify reliable criteria for detecting the relative chronological status of various mythological elements. The main reason for this is the observable fact that the stories that are verifiably oldest turn out to have Aiolic roots, which links up with the attendant, if less obvious, fact that the early Greek heroes were blood relations.

Moreover, that the Aiolic genealogy claimed the greatest events and the greatest protagonists in the entire Greek mythic corpus, and has survived in fragments to reveal this was so after centuries of mythological change, suggests that genealogy played a significant role in thwarting certain types of mythic amendments, and also suggests that stray Aiolic assertions, when they can be identified, deserve priority consideration.

    The evidence concerning mythological change along with patterns of legendary survival is linked to genealogy in a number of ways[260]. In terms of sorting through conflicting lineage claims: if the original framework was Aiolic and subsequent initiatives tried to subvert that fact, in a face-off amongst miscellaneous versions, the Aiolic version, if it can be pinpointed, would be, generally speaking, the strongest candidate for first place in a given relative chronology. The remaining versions must therefore be assessed with reference to the development of respective polis mythologies as far as they express any telltale signs of their post-epic geo-political provenance. The basic procedure is applied here in addressing the issue of mythological theft, and now, in particular mythic-theft-type-two.

EXAMPLE ONE: AIAKOS

    The lineage of Aiakos, grandfather of Achilles, presents a curious situation. The key legends attached to Aiakos and family situate them in Thessaly, in the Sperchios River valley, yet according to standard mythic reports, Aiakos was rather a native of Aigina, the Saronic Gulf island that lies between the west coast of Attica and the northeastern Peloponnese[261]. The island, legend had it, was previously called Oinoe until Aigina, a daughter of the river deity Asopos, captivated the attention of Zeus. By way of divine abduction to its fair shores, the island took on her name and became her homeland, where in due course she gave birth to Aiakos, initiating the prehistory of this island state[262].

    This narrative, first off, is recognizable as a typical indigenous lineage charter out of which patriotic legendary prehistory can be expected to flow. Conspicuously here, without further ado, the major epic forebear Aiakos is born. Jarring, however, to the informed observer is not only the fact that an Aiginetan origin is at odds with the geo-political character of Aiakos' mythological family line, but that the Homeric epics characterized Aigina as an offshore component of the province of Argos, under the leadership of Diomedes and two colleagues associated with Argive legend (Il.2.559-566). Shifting from myth to historical reality, after a period of political domination, first under Argos and then Epidauros, by the mid-seventh century Aigina was an independent island polis that rapidly became a major seafaring power and leading regional entrepreneur in overseas transport and exchange[263].

The status of Thessaly as a Greek mythic heartland that comes up time and again in a multitude of stories has often confounded analysts of Greek myth, primarily because Thessaly was peripheral to the main theatres of cultural activity in the Archaic and Classical periods, and, in this regard, even more so because Thessaly was peripheral to the focus of the surviving ancient texts. According to the thesis under review, this discrepancy was the result of the smoke screen created by the cumulative impact of mythic emendations composed and promoted in various city-states during the course of the Archaic Period. These emendations, the hypothesis runs, obscured the original Aiolic structure, which radiated from northern Greece, by promoting an assortment of genealogical lines that emanated from non-Aiolic territories and, in so doing, purported to be the source of a multitude of illustrious Aiolic heroes. Here, the importance of Thessaly as a mythological heartland is understood to derive from the Aiolic roots of the premier collection of Greek mythic stories, whereas the test to determine if this was actually so, depends on whether the sum total of Greek mythic material responds to the principle of Aiolic precedence, so that the smoke screen disintegrates in the process of viewing the evidence in accordance with this idea.

The case of Aiakos meets the general criteria earmarked as standard by virtue of their occurrence in major southern Greek genealogies. Thus, a key segment of northern Greek lore was transported to a southern Greek location via the transplantation of Aiakos, in conjunction with the promotion of an indigenous line onto which his legacy could be appended. In consequence, Aiakos' previous heritage all but disappears from the mythological record. This is often the case with uprooted figures to the extent that their new identity succeeds in securing public approval. Also, in general, such relocations provoke a measure of residual incongruity perceptible in the wake of the shift. Often, as we have seen, such incongruity takes the form of irreconcilable same-named mythic figures. But this was not reproduced in Aiakos' case because his relocation was unanimously approved by subsequent mythic chroniclers.

Instead, Aiakos' transplantation exhibits a symptom that can best be termed *reverse migration*, since the assertion that Aigina gave birth to Aiakos necessitated a viable narrative link to facilitate the return of Aiakos' descendants to their proper traditional sphere of activity, so that Aiakos transplantation to the island of Aigina could still aptly accord with the old northern Greek legends that made him a worthy target to begin with[264]. All of these legends took place in Thessaly. Finally, there is a valid historical context in which Aigina, an ascendant southern Greek state, subordinate to Argos in heroic tradition, wound up at a loss for a prehistorical legacy commensurate with its rising political influence. As with contemporary Greeks from neighboring states, the Aiginetans were, therefore, driven to appropriate a significant piece of early epic prehistory through the transplantation of a major progenitor from an old and venerable genealogical line.

Aiakos' affiliation with the island of Aigina logically dates to the island's ascendance as a major sea power and trading state in the second half of the seventh century. This date is probably best regarded as a *terminus ante quem*, since Aigina's mythic charter could well have developed under Argive or Epidaurian control[265]. In the second half of the seventh century Aigina was the only powerful city-state closely associated with the Greek mainland involved in the otherwise East Greek *emporion* established at Naucratis in Egypt (Hdt. 2.178)[266]. Like its early seafaring neighbors, Corinth and Megara[267], Aigina became a competitive naval power significantly prior to the rise of Athens – eventually its archrival, and ultimately its nemesis (e.g. Thouky.I. 105,108, II.26). It was not until after the Persian invasion of Greece under Darius that Themistokles managed to persuade the Athenians to use revenues from the Laurion mines in order to build a substantial fleet (Hdt.7.142-144). Though preoccupied with the danger of a renewed Persian threat, Themistocles was said to have used Aiginetan hostility as a pretext to gain consent and support from the Athenian *demos* for this naval initiative (Hdt.7.144; Thouky.1.14). The main point is to emphasize the connection between Aigina's rise to power and the dissemination of the genealogy that derived from the island's eponymous progenetrix.

Two further factors stand behind the proposal that Aiakos and his family were Aiginetan imports uprooted from Thessaly: first the fact that the Homeric portrait of Aigina was less than flattering to Aiginetan prestige (Il.2.559-566), and second the existence of a narrative opening due to the lack of an explicit description of Aiakos' mother in the Homeric poems, although, as stated, his father was Zeus (Il.21.189[268]). The first of these points addresses the motivation, the second highlights an unspecified genealogical link onto which Aiginetan mythic chroniclers saw fit to impose their personified homeland. Aigina thereby achieved possession of a remarkably famous northern Greek lineage, leaving posterity at a loss for any indication whatsoever of the previous genealogy this adjustment suppressed beyond the eccentricity of Aigina's intervention when viewed from an early epic perspective. It is significant also that in due course the *daughters of Asopos*[269], Aigina among them, became a metropoleis-bearing female collectivity,[270] since this was clearly a type of figural group that specialized in facilitating mythological change, while the daughters of Asopos, in particular, did so largely through the use of eponymous names. In sum, it is essentially on a comparative basis, with keen attention to innovative formations like these that the artificiality of Aigina's genealogy can be convincingly substantiated and Aiakos' role at the head of Aiginetan prehistory can be productively judged against prior conventions.

The Homeric depiction of the island of Aigina as an off-shore component of the province of Argos – Diomedes', Sthenelos', and Eurylaos' joint domain – evidently, lay at the heart of the matter, for this portrait of the island was markedly incompatible with the most basic notion of local pride. Meanwhile, Achilles' epic portrayal as a hereditary king of Thessalian Phthia and commander of the Myrmidon army, a formidable fighting force composed of individuals who all hailed from strongholds in and around his kingdom (Il.2.684, 16.15, 16.171-197), presented the greatest challenge to mythological revision. The heroic tenor of Achilles' epic portrayal extended backward a generation in time to the legendary reputation of his father Peleus. But, conspicuously, as things stand, the Thessalian exploits of this great family do not extend back beyond Peleus' biography. Aside from his birth on the island of Aigina, later Greek myth was mainly concerned with Aiakos' eminent virtue and wisdom on which basis he was presumably qualified to sit in judgment of the dead[271]. In the nature of things, it is altogether abnormal for a Greek hero to exist without a definite homeland, yet, if deprived of Aigina, on the extant evidence that is exactly what Aiakos would be.

The famous stories about Peleus, son of Aiakos and father of Achilles, such as his involvement in the Kalydonian boar hunt, and various dealings around Thessalian Iolkos, including Peleus' participation in the funeral games for Pelias, and his later reputed sack of Pelias' city are matched by the antiquity of these legends, their central Greek provenance, and their Aiolic heritage[272]. Moreover, Peleus' divinely mandated marriage to the sea goddess Thetis, giving rise to Achilles[273], which the Olympian deities attended as guests was viewed by the Greeks as the occasion that ultimately triggered the Trojan War[274]. Initiating an inevitable string of events, the wedding feast of Peleus and Thetis was the site of the quarrel that arose between Hera, Athena, and Aphrodite concerning the virtues of their respective powers, and prompting the solicitation of the judgment of Paris, the impressionable son of king Priam of Troy (Il.24.28-30[275]). Paris' judgment in favor of Aphrodite essentially granted him license to steal Homer's *Helen of Argos* from hearth and home, planting the seed of Greek vengeance against his country. With much of this subject matter embedded in the *Iliad*, where Peleus rules a great kingdom from a palace in Phthia (e.g. Il.9478-495, 18.432-434), it would require a very ingenious argument to persuasively claim that the island of Aigina inhabited the subconscious of these traditions.

The tale of Aiakos' birth on the island of Aigina is thus more aptly conspicuous as a foil to Aiakos' family's central Greek sphere of influence. A key sign of this is that Aiakos' birthplace inspired a novel interpretation of the Myrmidon cohort, understood from the *Iliad* as a loyal infantry unit committed to the service of this great family (e.g. 16.168ff.). The solution to this problem was already entrenched by the time of the Hesiodic *Catalogue of Women*, where according to an alternative story, the Myrmidons were not warriors from around the Gulf of Malis but, by way of a clever etymological twist, were originally ants that Zeus transformed into humans in order to furnish Aiakos with subjects because he was born on a desolate island (Hes. fr 205 MW[276]). As for the relocation of the whole clan from Aigina back to Thessaly, where they were traditionally expected to reside, this was readily accomplished using the standard motif of heroic murder which inevitably led to heroic exile[277].

The murder in question was the murder of Phokos, son of Aiakos and Psamathe, as reported in Hesiod's *Theogony* (1004-1007). Though the number of Aiakos' offspring increased in due course, to include Telamon, father of Aias, and in some quarters, Menoitios, father of Patroklos[278], in the *Iliad*, Achilles, alone, commands the title *Aiakides*[279]. Phokos makes no appearance in the Homeric poems, yet his descendant Epeios surfaces conspicuously. He is acknowledged in the *Iliad* as a well-known, if minor, warrior, and in the *Odyssey* for his involvement in the construction of the Trojan horse (Il.23.669ff; Od. 8.493, 11.524). Regarding Phokos, it can at least be said that the *Iliad* and the *Odyssey* do not contradict the *Theogony*'s account of his genealogy, particularly not in the way these texts problematize the popular later claim that Telamon was a son of Aiakos as well. In this light, Phokos, who was by consensus a son of Aiakos and the Nereid Psamathe, antedated the initiatives sponsored by Aigina, which made Aiakos a native, and Peleus and Telamon both Aiakos' sons, as well as co-conspirators in a plot against their predecessor Phokos, ostensibly born of a previous marriage[280].

Phokos, in addition, was well integrated within the Aiolic lineage framework, marrying a daughter of Deion, son of Aiolos (viz. Asterodeia[281]), which linked him by marriage to a very prestigious line[282]. Notably, Phokos' mother, Psamathe, was a Nereid just like Thetis, whom Apollodoros maintains Aiakos had to subdue in a frenzy of resistance driven by animal metamorphoses (ApB 3.12.6). Elsewhere, Apollodoros reports that Peleus struggled in the same way in order to win the Nereid Thetis (ApB 3.13.5)[283]. The antiquity of this double metamorphosis cannot be concretely assessed[284], yet it seems to conform to certain distinctive early symbolic genealogical patterns. So, for example, as mentioned above, there was a propensity for the women of Aitolia (viz. the line of Kalyke, daughter of Aiolos) to have intimate relations with the god Ares. A more provocative example of this kind of thing occurs in the Aiolic line of Kanake, where a granddaughter of the god Poseidon unites with Poseidon, once again, generating two mortals so fearsome that they had to be eliminated by the gods (viz. Otos and Ephialtes, e.g. Il.5.382-390; Od.11.305-320; ApB 1.7.4[285]). This curious type of hereditary idea was integral to archaic genealogical thinking and, for what it is worth, invokes the possibility that Peleus and Phokos were not always half-brothers but together the progeny of Aiakos and Psamathe, which would render Achilles the exceptional outcome of Nereid matings in successive generations.

Be that as it may, the accepted heroine for the role of Peleus' mother, who became widely known as Telamon's too, was a woman named Endeis, daughter of Skeiron of Megara, the notorious robber that Theseus slew on the road to Athens from Troizen (Plut.*Thes*.10)[286]. Ultimately, the Megarians, as Plutarch attests, were at pains to deny Skiron's negative reputation so his daughter might seem worthy of her union with Aiakos. But Plutarch's account of Skiron, it should be noted, was influenced by a series of Atheno-centric narratives promoted after the Athenians under Solon were victorious against Megara over possession of the island of Salamis. Plutarch's overall outlook, in this regard, was affected by Athens' victory, on the one hand, and by subsequent Athenian history, on the other[287]. Suffice it to say that given Aigina and Megara's rise to power while Athens was still an introverted state[288], the Megarian protest "against all antiquity[289]" could well have been more of a protest against the Athenian disparagement of Megara's hero, Skiron, who had already been granted an illustrious genealogy by Megarians and Aiginetans in collusion with one another on the adoption of the Aiakid stemma[290]. Yet regardless of Skiron's character traits, his lineage does not readily qualify for venerable early epic status[291].

The only other suggestion that appears in the sources describes Endeis as the daughter of Cheiron and Chariklo[292]. Timothy Gantz reports that Chariklo surfaces first on a number of early sixth-century vases depicting the wedding of Peleus and Thetis (1993: 148). Yet these images offer no guarantee that she appeared in the role of

Cheiron's wife[293]. And while Pindar mentions Endeis in one ode, and Cheiron and Chariklo in another (viz. *Nem*.5.11-12; *Pyth*.4.102-103[294]), he offers no parentage for Endeis[295]. It is, therefore, unclear whether this genealogy antedated Endeis' alleged descent from Skiron, or rather represents a reaction to it that insisted on a more fitting geographical context, and so substituted Skiron with Cheiron, who was traditionally associated with northern Greece, especially the region around Mt. Pelion. It is also unclear how far back in time the centaur Cheiron was given a wife, while the ambiguity of Chariklo's connection to Cheiron is only increased by Plutarch's account of the complete family genealogy. Plutarch reports that Chariklo was a daughter of Kychreus, King of Salamis, who married Skeiron of Megara and gave birth to Endeis. Endeis, in turn, married Aiakos of Aigina and bore two sons, Peleus and Telamon[296]. This genealogy essentially combines Aiginetan and Megarian mythic formations and is eminently likely to stem back to the time when Salamis was under Megara's control (i.e. to the seventh century)[297].

Clearly, in this context, as Gantz points out, there was a measure of confusion between Cheiron and Skiron (ibid. 220)[298]. However, whether this was because some individuals (and with good reason) considered Cheiron to be the better choice based on his Thessalian connections (or for ulterior political reasons), or whether there was any substantial depth to Cheiron's association with a heroine named Chariklo in traditional Thessalian lore, it is evident that the main figure involved, as far as the Saronic Gulf region was concerned, was Skeiron of Megara, who married the daughter of Kynchreus of Salamis. Salamis was yet another personified island state, and likewise, a daughter of the Asopos River who was abducted by a god, though this time, as it happened, by Poseidon (DS 4.72.4; ApB 3.12.7). Pherekydes made Chariklo the seer Teiresias' mother (FGrHist 3F92), while Euripides' two Melanippe plays featured a daughter of Cheiron, originally named Euippe, who became known as Hippo after the gods turned her into a horse[299]. The mythic history of Endeis is notably a vexed question. However, the case for her legendary antiquity is not, on the balance, particularly strong.

Like Aiakos himself, Telamon also, was likely to have been an Aiolic potentate with solid early mythic credentials, and logically from the very beginning, a native of the island of Salamis[300], whether as a descendant of Salaminian Kychreus whose lineage was subsequently adjusted, or via some unrecoverable ancestral formula that linked him to the operative early framework. However, once roped into the Aiginetan fold, the great ruler of Salamis, like the great ruler of Phthia was forced to commit murder simply to reclaim authority over his traditional kingdom. By way of exile for homicide this joint filial murder brought Telamon to Salamis and Peleus to Phthia, the very places where Greek tradition apparently located them to begin with. These geo-political adjustments to their legendary heritage was a great boon to Aigina's acclaim and to the reputations of her closest neighbors, who, either collaboratively, or at Aigina's behest, became prominent participants in the genealogy devised to recast these old epic heroes[301]. In spite of the popularity of this lineage scheme, the extant traces of early epic thinking that pertain to the lives of Peleus and Telamon do not link these figures either as brothers or, for that matter, as close companions, and least of all on the island of Aigina.

Although at first glance, the adventures assigned to Peleus and Telamon appear to include various joint exploits[302], on close inspection the data seem to reflect two separate spheres of legendary activity that were programmatically fused together. Telamon was active in association with Herakles. In this regard, his main claim to fame was participation in Herakles' sojourn to the East[303], which, above all, included the first sack of Troy in which Herakles granted Telamon a Trojan princess as war prize[304]. This Trojan woman gave birth to Teukros, Aias' half-brother and close comrade in the *Iliad*, whose Trojan heritage was imbued in his name. Herakles, moreover, though born in Thebes, returned to his family's ancestral Argos to perform his assigned tasks in the service of Eurystheus[305]. Henceforth, Herakles' base of operations was for the most part in the south. The further association of the hero, Oikles, son of Antiphates of Argos[306] with Herakles' sojourn to the East serves to distinguish this southern set of adventures from an initially northern Greek series that was Peleus' native sphere of activity.

Peleus, by contrast, was a dominant figure in the hunt for the Kalydonian boar and events that took place in Thessalian Iolkos prior to his marriage to the Nereid Thetis[307]. He was known, for example, to have resisted the sexual advances of Akastos' wife during the funeral festivities in honor of Pelias – Akastos' father, former King of Iolkos, and instigator of the Argonautic adventure. Akastos' wife was an Aiolic heiress who, quite typically, embroiled Peleus in a string of events through an illicit attempt to seduce him[308]. Pelias' son Akastos, as the story goes, in the hope of causing Peleus' death on account of his wife's false accusations against him, abandoned Peleus in the wilds of Mt. Pelion where he was attacked by a vicious tribe of centaurs. Peleus, however, was rescued by Cheiron.

Additionally, somewhere amid this cluster of episodes, Peleus' first marriage must also be placed. From the *Iliad* it is clear that a woman named Polydore was the offspring of such a marriage. She was, evidently, Achilles' half-sister, who gave birth to the Myrmidon warrior, Menesthios (Il.16.173-178). And while it became popular to assert that Peleus' first wife was the daughter of Eurytion, king of Phthia[309], who purified Peleus after he murdered his half-brother Phokos (allegedly in collusion with his "brother" Telamon), it is fairly obvious that this construction was devised to make Peleus king of Phthia once his birth on Aigina had become standard. Another tradition of potentially greater merit described Polydore's mother as the daughter of Aktor, presumably the same man whom the *Iliad* identifies as the father of Menoitios, father of Patroklos (e.g. Il.1.307[310]). All and all these stories exemplify the Thessalian-based lore that clings organically to this family line and appears to command substantial antiquity. The effective eclipse of the distinction between two geo-politically distinctive fields of action (namely, Telamon's vs. Peleus' mythic spheres of influence) is, on this reading, fundamentally linked to the genealogical innovation that made Peleus and Telamon both sons of Aiakos.

The incremental expansion of heroes' heroic deeds is a related Greek mythological trend. Heracles' labors, for example, expanded from a circuit of the north-central Peloponnese (with a major foray into Asia Minor[311]) to essentially anywhere in the inhabited world where there was a demand for his legendary mystique. And Plutarch, for instance, in the same vein, highlights the augmented scope of Theseus' adventures (some of which he considered to be a little far-fetched), citing the popular ancient adage, "not without Theseus." Analogously, collective heroic exploits were extremely vulnerable to additions and substitutions in reports or depictions of their assigned cast of characters, albeit within certain parameters. Here, though there was leeway, and a good deal of it, tradition enforced certain basic dictates about who was necessarily associated with what. The visual depiction of mythic events, in particular, relied on the presence of certain established figures to insure recognition of the occasion at hand. Thus, the kinship bond forged between Peleus and Telamon took advantage of reinterpretive mythic prerogatives, fudging the boundaries between two sets of adventures without extraordinary offense to tradition. Likewise, the popular desire to include Herakles in the famous Argonautic expedition, although evidently he was not of old considered a participant in this adventure, shows how far such boundaries could be pushed. Though Herakles' inclusion was a fairly awkward affair, he became a standard participant in the voyage of the *Argo*.

  In the case of the Aiakid family stemma, later mythic material is distinctly earmarked as such based on clear incongruities with early epic. Yet, the main impediment to the analysis of this lineage is one that often affects high-profile genealogies that have been successfully manipulated to recast individuals of great prestige. This problem amounts to the impossibility of ever ascertaining the initial link that at one time led back to the line of Aiolis. Accordingly, such a link can only be hypothesized. If legitimate doubts surround Aiakos' conception on a desolate island in the Saronic Gulf, these doubts cannot be backed up by concrete indications of where Aiakos once stood in the early mythic paradigm. Legendary innovations of the kind and the caliber of Aigina's genealogical vision bolstered initially by political clout and leading in due course to their widespread acceptance represent the most serious obstacle to the reconstruction of the Aiolic lineage framework. For even though, for example, the antiquity of Aiakos' connection with the island of Aigina may well be suspect on broad contextual grounds and in terms of comparative Greek mythic trends, this formulation became so influential that it effectively blotted its antecedents out.

  The dislocation of significant genealogical blocks that were deliberately severed from Aiolic contexts and spliced onto autonomous regional lines was a process, which, by way of repeated enactment, camouflaged the frequency of its application as well as the very fact that it was typically done. Novel rearrangements were thereby intermeshed with excerpts from the oldest Greek mythic strata concealing these excerpts' derivative nature. The mystery surrounding the forebears of Aiakos, just like the mystery surrounding the forebears of a significant number of mighty ancient Greek heroes (e.g. Herakles, Perseus, Telamon etc.) is tantamount to an analytical barrier where genealogical alternatives cease to exist. Though barring access to knowledge as to how things once were, it is maintained here that barriers such as these do not likewise amount to deterrents against the substantiation of the former existence of the Aiolic genealogy. The elimination of data, as perceived in this instance, is a conspicuous pattern in and of itself, and one that coincides with patterns displayed elsewhere throughout the surviving body of evidence. Elimination and preservation on this basis converge, directing attention time and again at the antiquity and unparalleled status of the Greek legends with Aiolic roots.

EXAMPLE TWO: TYNDAREOS AND IKARIOS

A relatively similar rearrangement of figures, vital and well-known to early mythic tradition can be identified in the line of Sparta, once again, in subordination to an indigenous lineage framework[312]. A heroine named Taygete invokes the great Spartan mountain that borders the heartland in the west, dividing Lakonia from Messenia at the head of the peninsula nowadays known as Mani. According to legend, this woman mated with Zeus bearing the state eponym, Lakedaimon. She served in this capacity as the progenetrix of regional Lakedaimonian culture. The development of this scheme then united Lakedaimon with the even more localized eponym Sparte, portrayed as the daughter of the Eurotas River. Sparte gave birth to an eponymous son named Amyklas through whom Spartan control over neighboring Amyklai was symbolically affirmed[313]. Yet Sparte also gave birth to a daughter, Eurydike, who presents a subtle kink in the overall pattern, since she bears a heroic not an eponymous name. Eurydike is notable for her marriage to Akrisios of the line of Argos, father of Danae, the mother of Perseus. Their marriage forged a high-order Spartan connection with the ancient prestige of Herakles' family, though as it will become clear, this connection was based on the lineage of Perseus and Herakles in its revised post-Homeric form. Amyklas, meanwhile, was said to have married an equally contested Diomede, known in this context as a daughter of Lapithes (ApB 3.10.3), but elsewhere as the daughter of Xouthos and the wife of Deion, son of Aiolos (e.g. Hes fr 10a 20-24 OCT; ApB 1.7.3, 1.9.4; DS 4.69.1-5). The anthropomorphized Spartan landscape thus steadily perpetuated itself, simultaneously eliciting strategic ties with established legendary families.

The lineage continues with Amyklas' sons, Hyakinthos and his brother Kynortas, moving beyond Spartan landmarks to Spartan culture heroes. Hyakinthos' role is memorable enough, but slight from a genealogical standpoint, for he was one of Apollo's unfortunate lovers, famous for having perished from a blow to the head fatally inflicted by a stray discus[314]. Hyakinthos' story, therefore, represents a commemorative type of genealogical atrophy. For though a celebrated figure in Lakonian tradition, acknowledged at a major annual festival[315], the nature of his biographical drama undercut his potential as a mythic progenitor leaving this role to his brother Kynortas.

Kynortas remains remarkably obscure if presumably well-known to the citizens of Sparta[316]. Equally mysterious is a figure called Oibalos, who was later identified as the son of Kynortas (Paus. 3.1.3-4)[317], although in the earliest extant report attributed to Stesichoros by Apollodoros (3.10.3), Perieres and Oibalos were both evidently sons of Kynortas. Apollodoros, moreover, makes it reasonably clear that a popular alternative genealogical formation made Perieres the son of Kynortas, and Oibalos, in turn, the son of Perieres (e.g. ApB 3.10.4; Σ *Orestes* 457)[318]. Meanwhile, simultaneously, as Apollodoros attests, Perieres was well-known as one of the seven sons of Aiolos[319].

The appearance of Perieres in the Spartan line is the most critical factor in the analysis of the mix of assertions the ancient sources provide on the development of the Spartan lineage. It seems that Greek audiences were keenly aware that Perieres was an old Aiolic potentate, which turns out to be the crux of the matter when it comes to the variants on this genealogy. Further, though both Kynortas and Oibalos played major roles in the Spartan line, neither of them commands much in the way of narrative substance beyond the Spartan promotion of their existence.

At this juncture the Spartan line arrives at a point variously reproduced in each major southern city-state genealogy, namely the point where an indigenous framework begins to initiate appropriative acts against epic protagonists with Aiolic roots. Here, using the name Perieres, otherwise associated with a son of Aiolos, Stesichoros, the early sixth- century poet whose pro-Spartan sympathies are well-known[320], positioned four old and venerable heroes under the *aigis* of the Spartan state. According to Stesichoros, the Spartan Perieres was the father of Aphareus, Leukippos, Tynareos, and Ikarios, four famous heroes with overlapping biographies, all integral to the chain of events that ultimately led to the Trojan War[321].

A cogent interpretation of the ancient reportage dealing with the development of the Spartan line is possible based on two key premises: first, Apollodoros' testimony to the effect that Perieres, son of Aiolos, was appropriated by Sparta early on as a means to possession of four venerable heroes, Tyndareos, Ikarios, Aphareus and Leukippos, and second, the evidence provided by Apollodoros and others that suggests significant resistance outside of Sparta to Sparta's right to command the full extent of this claim. Due to this resistance, it seems that Spartan authority was eventually limited, by convention, to control over just two of these four protagonists (namely, over Tyndareos and Ikarios), whereas the remaining two (Aphareus and Leukippos) were restored to Perieres (son of Aiolos), who, needless to say, continued to exist in the presence of his same-named Spartan counterpart.

Again briefly regarding the stature of these four figures, Tyndareos was acknowledged, in conjunction with Zeus, as father of the Dioskouri (Kastor and Polydeukes) and also of Helen, who left Menelaos and sailed with Paris to Troy[322]. He was also the father of Klytaimnestra, Agamemnon's notoriously unfaithful wife, and a number of other daughters as well[323]. Ikarios was the father of Odysseus' wife Penelope, who settled with him on the island of Ithaka, home of Odysseus' paternal line. Aphareus and Leukippos held power in Messenia. Aphareus had two sons, Lynkeus and Idas, Leukippos, two daughters, Phoibe and Hilaria[324]. The sons of Tyndareos, Kastor and Polydeukes, vied with Aphareus' sons over Leukippos' daughters, and ultimately, it seems, the Dioskouri won out[325]. Their victory, however, was also the prelude to a subsequent conflict that resulted in the death of all four heroes, an eventuality Helen was strikingly unaware of as she gazed out onto the Trojan battlefield searching in vain to catch sight of her dead brothers (Il.3.236-244).

In addition to these four figures who are repeatedly associated with the name Perieres in the sources, there were early on two other sons of Perieres who eventually fade from the mythological record. Thus, in the *Iliad* Perieres was credited with a son Boros, who married Polydore, the daughter of Peleus, evidently the offspring of his first marriage (Il.16.173-178[326]). The name Boros suggests an eponymous point of reference for one of the East Greek Ionian tribes, potentially also standard in East Greek Aiolis. As it happens, the life stories of Boros and Polydore have not survived in the mythological record, though the basic association Boros – Boreis is reasonably well documented nevertheless. Further clarity comes from the parallel formula that was based on the Chiot hero Oinopion (son of Dionysos and Ariadne)[327], the eponymous ancestor of the East Greek tribe the Oinopes. Interestingly enough, neither of these two tribes, occur in mainland Ionian tribal structures though they were widespread in the East Greek cities where there were six major tribes to the mainland's four[328]. Given this situation, the *Iliad*'s Boros can at least be considered a potential eponymous tribal founder from a Homeric point of view.

The Hesiodic *Catalogue* also identified one Halirrhothios, son of Perieres and Alkyone, who engendered two sons Semos and Alazygos (fr 49 MW). These figures are, for the most part, completely obscure. However, Pindar's mention of Semos in connection with the Arkadian city of Mantineia (*Ol.*10.70-75), along with his descent from Perieres and Alkyone, suggest that these two brothers at one time played a part in a popular southern Greek genealogy and, on this count, quite likely, the genealogy of Sparta, where the names of Aiolos' son (Perieres) and Aiolos' daughter (Alkyone) were evidently put to new use.

But the name Halirrhothios surfaces again, notably in fifth-century Athens, in connection with a son of Poseidon who was notable in Athenian lore for the rape of Alkippe, a woman described as the daughter of the god Ares and the princess Aglauros, daughter of Kekrops, the early Athenian king[329]. To avenge his daughter, the story goes, Ares killed Halirrhothios, son of Poseidon, and at Poseidon's insistence was forced to stand trial before the twelve gods on the Areopagos. Apparently, he was acquitted as charged (ApB 3.14.2), though the accusation against him became the standard *aition* for that venerable Athenian political landmark[330]. If, indeed, this legend does not represent a genuinely separate local tradition, the Athenian use of the name Halirrhothios to illuminate events in the reign of King Kekrops is likely to postdate its Peloponnesian counterpart in accordance with diachronic mythic developments in the southern Greek city-states of the Archaic Period. Thus the Athenian version may well be responsible for the Peloponnesian version's eclipse. Moreover, judging from global mythological patterning, the Athenian Halirrhothios was quite likely set up as a foil to his Peloponnesian counterpart, who was, in turn, set up as a foil to an older northern Greek predecessor with ties to either Perieres or to Alkyone. No doubt, Halirrhothios' association with Perieres and Alkyone in the Hesiodic *Catalogue* would also casually accommodate an alternative claim that Halirrhothios was in fact a son of Poseidon, the god, notably also attached to Alkyone.

The *Catalogue*'s position concerning the controversy over the heritage of Perieres' sons cannot, on the evidence, be explicitly ascertained. But, the fact that Tyndareos is presented as a son of Oibalos in the Berlin papyrus (P.Berol. 9739 = fr 199 MW) is enough to establish that some permutation of the Spartan genealogy was reported. As stated, on the available data, it is fairly clear that the split in the family was the version that became standard outside of Sparta, where it gained considerable credence in response to the extravagance of the original Spartan claim known to Apollodoros via Stesichoros (3.10.3)[331]. This makes Apollodoros' second genealogy (or a permutation of it) the strongest candidate for the Hesiodic *Catalogue*[332]. Also relevant to this whole situation is the marriage of Alkyone, daughter of Aiolos, to a Thessalian hero named Keyx[333], which is not only attested for the *Catalogue*, but occasioned a separate poem on the subject from which very few fragments still survive (fr 263-269 MW[334]). As far as Alkyone and Keyx are concerned, the *Catalogue* provides the vital information that they were both transformed into birds, brilliantly actualizing the latent significance of their given names[335]. This story, moreover, eliminated them both from the realm of genealogical productivity.

As mythic analysts generally observe, the Hesiodic *Catalogue* confirms the existence of two Alkyones: the wife of Perieres and the wife of Keyx[336]. It is also apparent (even without the invaluable datum that Alkyone, daughter of Aiolos, married King Keyx) that the coupling of Perieres and Alkyone is not apt to reflect a valid early coupling, since the union of a son and daughter of Aiolos would amount to a union between two siblings, which militates against standard heroic protocol. This observation intensifies the novelty of this particular match, which involved a Perieres, who was not a son of Aiolos, and an Alkyone who was not Aiolos' daughter, in spite of the deployment of these prestigious names[337]. The only place where this situation occurred was in the genealogy of the Spartan line.

The Alkyone associated with the Spartan Perieres was considered to be a daughter of Atlas, when she was not supplanted altogether by Gorgophone, who was known as the daughter of Perseus of Argos. This second association in turn raised the question: who was the Spartan Perieres' wife? As Apollodoros testifies, Perieres' union with Gorgophone appears already in Stesichoros, becoming canonical as time wore on presumably due to the connection it forged with the legendary prestige of the Perseid line. Nonetheless, the formula Alkyone + Perieres clearly played a key role at some stage in the game as the various strands of evidence persuasively attest[338]. Since an early Aiolic setting must be excluded, three alternate formulations ultimately predominate, all three in connection with the Spartan line, namely: 1) Alkyone (daughter of Atlas) + Poseidon; 2) Alkyone (daughter of Atlas) + the Spartan Perieres; 3) the Spartan Perieres + Gorgophone (daughter of Perseus).

Given these permutations, it makes sense to suppose that Alkyone, daughter of Atlas was set up to outstrip Aiolos' same-named daughter, and was initially paired with the Spartan Perieres and simultaneously with the god Poseidon. But when at some point during the sixth century it became preferable to pair the Spartan Perieres with Gorgophone (the daughter of Perseus), rather than with Alkyone (the alleged daughter of Atlas), Alkyone's status was reduced by default and her offspring with Perieres fell to Gorgophone[339]. In this light, the pairing of Perieres with Alkyone looks like it was abandoned not all that long after it was championed as an attribute of the Spartan line. It was eclipsed by the impulse to give precedence to an even more advantageous marriage arrangement that left the Spartan Alkyone in the lurch. Under these circumstances it is possible to access a few further aspects of the mentality that informed these patterns of mythological change.

First, it is logical to witness here the deliberate marginalization of the Aiolic Alkyone through the introduction of Alkyone, the daughter of Atlas[340]. This quite neatly parallels her brother Perieres' incorporation into the Spartan line, where he notably ceased to be her brother at all and became the son of Kynortas or Oibalos. From here it is but a small step to take, backed up by similar patterning elsewhere, to detect that the underlying objective was to override the Aiolic Alkyone's legacy, which was *ipso facto* conspicuous enough to trigger a series of legendary adjustments. The upshot was a case of identity theft ingeniously vindicated by the metamorphosis of the traditional Alkyone, Aiolos' daughter, which at once negated her progeny with Keyx[341] and took the focus away from her progeny with Poseidon, by maintaining that Alkyone, daughter of Atlas bore children to both Perieres and to the god. This suggests that Alkyone, Aiolos' daughter, at one time presided over two separate stemmata: one with Poseidon the other with Keyx, each responsible for major heroic progeny. This prospect is supported by the Hesiodic *Aspis*, which bears witness to a daughter named Themistone, wife of Kyknos of Thessaly whom Herakles' killed (350-356). On comparative grounds, Themistone's very existence is more likely to be representative of an old lineage of considerable stature – that was ultimately consigned to obscurity by those who saw fit to deny its existence – than a chance reference to a solitary offspring in an otherwise non-existent heroic line[342].

Therefore, once the wife of Keyx was out of circulation and supplanted by a named double in the Spartan line, the old formulation that ostensibly ran Poseidon + Alkyone + Keyx, ran Poseidon + Alkyone + Perieres instead. This subsequent arrangement was the genealogy that rendered Perieres a Spartan native and Alkyone a daughter of the Titan god Atlas. This re-designation aptly coincides with the contemporaneous movement emanating from Sparta that capitalized on the very early idea that the Titan god Atlas sired heroic daughters, by claiming that Alkyone, onetime daughter of Aiolos, along with Electra, the source of the Trojan line, and the great Spartan mountain Tayegete, were all descendants of that great Titan god[343].

Into this configuration, the evidence suggests, came Gorgophone throwing a cog in the works by upstaging the ingenious previous Spartan coupling between Perieres and Alkyone. That relatively recent heroic match was thereby split asunder by the no-contest prospect of enhancing the Spartan state genealogy with a direct blood connection to the lineage of Herakles[344]. This connection provided genealogical backing that was used to authenticate the sovereign right of the descendants of Herakles (the Herakleidai) to oust the Achaians of early Greek myth from their allotted Peloponnesian kingdoms and take over the bulk of the Peloponnese[345].

The other salient observation with regard to all this is the mythological atrophy of two sons of Perieres, Boros and Halirrhothios, even though these protagonists at one time commanded significant mythological roles. The *Iliad*'s Boros practically disappears, at least in the annals of southern Greek lore[346], while Halirrhothios (whoever he was early on) debuts an all-new Athenian personality, reducing the focus of the family drama to the distribution or the right to possess Tyndareos, Ikarios, Leukippos and Aphareus.

The split in this family has been judged by Gantz to indicate a fusion of two originally separate families (viz. Perieres and sons: Leukippos & Aphareus, and Oibalos and sons: Tyndareos & Ikarios 1993: 181). As Gantz points out, this fusion must have predated Stesichoros, our earliest reference to its occurrence. The opposite, however, may more aptly account for the gist of the data in the surviving sources: a once-unified family torn in different directions by Spartan-sponsored amendments to the epic worldview. Aside from the contrived nature of the indigenous Spartan line, which militates against the antiquity of Sparta's contribution to the fusion proposed (i.e. Stesichoros' account), another reason to consider the suggested alternative is that the unity of this family was remarkably short-lived. Mainly, the thrust of the emphasis in the ancient sources is on the division of key family members into two separate clans with two separate ancestries. Thus in contrast to Stesichoros' report, which appropriates all four heroes on behalf of the Spartan state by way of Perieres, son of Kynortas, elsewhere only Tyndareos and Ikarios were typically allocated to the Spartan line. And although there is surely no guarantee that early epic was not aware of some more complex rendering of Perieres' family that was already simplified by Stesichoros, who presented four brothers and cut two others out, the four brothers in question were organically linked by way of an old collection of stories; so it seems stranger to doubt the antiquity of their kinship than to question their affiliation with Sparta.

    This notion is corroborated by Apollodoros who exhibits no discomfort with the idea that all four brothers shared an Aiolic heritage (viz. descent from Perieres), but was clearly ill at ease with the proposition that all four belonged to the Spartan line. Thus, though he first addresses the family in his account of the Aiolic genealogies (1.9.5)[347], there he remarks that since many people do not consider Perieres to be a son of Aiolos, he will reserve further treatment of the matter for his coverage of the Spartan line (viz. the line of Taygete, daughter of Atlas). The same reservation, however, occurs when he comes around to the Spartan genealogical setting, where he invokes Stesichoros' view of the matter and begins to outline the progeny of all four brothers (3.10.3-4). However, after his coverage of Aphareus and Leukippos, Apollodoros proceeds to divide the family. In so doing, he openly sides with "those who say" Aphareus and Leukippos were sons of Perieres, son of Aiolos, and gives equal credence to those who assigned Tyndareos and Ikarios (and Hippokoon) to one Oibalos, son of Perieres, son of Kynortas, of the Spartan line.

    As for this otherwise mysterious Oibalos, whom Stesichoros seems to have viewed as Perieres' brother (therefore, introducing a collateral line), but who surfaces in the *Catalogue of Women* as Tyndareos' and likely Ikarios' father (Hes fr 199 MW; echoed by Apollodoros at 3.10.4), Oibalos on the one hand served as a buffer that lessened the impact of Sparta's claim against Perieres' old Aiolic persona. On the other he played a significant role in regulating the length of the Spartan lineage, an issue that comes across in greater detail below. The interjection of Oibalos between Perieres and Tyndareos and Ikarios, at any rate, made it possible to invoke Tyndareos and Ikarios as Spartan natives without making reference to Perieres at all while in no way renouncing that claim[348].

Pausanias' solution to these problems provides a concluding measure of clarity. With a stroke of ingenuity, Pausanias asserts that Perseus' daughter, Gorgophone, was the first mythic heroine to ever marry twice (2.21.8). She first married Perieres, son of Aiolos and bore Aphareus and Leukippos (4.2.4). However, after Perieres died, she married Oibalos, son of Kynortas (son of Amyklas, son of Lakedaimon) giving birth to Tyndareos and, by convention, Ikarios, though Pausanias is conspicuously reticent here, about Ikarios' status in this formation (3.1.4). Pausanias, then, as usual, granted Sparta control over Tyndareos and Ikarios[349], but deprived the Spartans of Perieres altogether[350]. Perieres remained an Aiolic potentate and to an extent an Aiolic progenitor, preserved, as it were, by his untimely death.

In treating Alkyone, daughter of Atlas, Pausanias notably excludes her completely from any association with the Spartan line, although it is evident that Sparta was responsible for her conceptualization and her promotion in southern Greek mythological contexts. Again, focusing exclusively on her progeny with Poseidon, Pausanias places her back in Boiotia at the head of a genealogy that reflects modified versions of an important piece of Aiolos' daughter's original legacy (e.g. 2.30.8, 9.22.5; West 1985: 98-99[351]). Accordingly, Alkyone, daughter of Aiolos, has for all intents and purposes ceased to exist.

Stepping back from the data on the Spartan line, it is clear that each extant account of this family yields to analysis based on the coexistence of two competing traditions, one old and one new: a unified family and one split apart by exigencies of mythological change. Above all, it is clear that the Spartan state obtained its greatest heroes from the old Aiolic framework. These were transplanted fully equipped with a well-known repertoire of famous stories which continued to be their main claim to fame under radically different environmental conditions both mythologically and in reality. This wholesale mode of legendary appropriation is equally visible in other state genealogies and answers to the catch phrase *mythic-theft-type-two*.

---

[253] Though, as we have seen, at times the distinction is not altogether cut and dry.

254 Hence, the ongoing efforts to ascertain the ways in which Homer was an innovator: e.g. M.M. Willcock 1964; B.K. Braswell *CQ* 21 1971: 16-26; J. Griffin *JHS* 97 1977: 39-53; M. Lang in C. Rubino and C. Shelmerine, eds. 1983; L. Edmonds in I. Morris and B. Powell, eds. 1997; but also F.M. Combellack 1976.

255 On variants vs. continuity see C. Brillante in L. Edmonds, ed. 1990. So, for example, on page 120 "Greek myth, although undergoing continual modifications and adaptations, did not substantially alter its character during the entire period of antiquity (so too, J-P Vernant 1980: 219)." See also. page 119 for "the widespread opinion on the *heterogeneity* of Greek mythology" as reflected in definitions ascribed to Greek myth and akin to *plurality* noted below. On the limitations of such definitions cf. G. Lloyd in R. Buxton, ed. 1997.

256 e.g. R. Buxton, *Imaginary Greece: The Contexts of Mythology* (Cambridge 1994); also in the introduction to R. Buxton ed. 1999. For the *multivalency* of Greek myth cf. J. Gould in the same volume; for *multiplicity*, L. Edmonds in L. Edmonds ed. 1990. For a far less well-founded interpretive claim that posits "ideological uncertainty" in the Homeric poems, see M. Nagler in M. Griffith and D. Mastronarde, eds. 1990; M. Griffith also in the same publication.

257 e.g. W. Burkert 1985: 4 & in R. Buxton ed. 1999: 104; P.E. Easterling & J. Gould in Easterling and Muir eds. 1985; J. Bremmer 1994. On the comparative analysis of Homer and the Bible that came into vogue in the eighteenth century and continued to flourish well into the nineteenth, see F. Turner in I. Morris and B. Powell eds. 1997.

258 e.g. As mentioned above, in this ongoing debate, I follow, for example, J.P. Crielaard, R. Fowler, R. Janko, and I. Morris on the subject of early textual fixation. The reason for this is essentially based on consistent genealogical patterns tied to the piecemeal appropriation of major heroic figures and stories that were already well-known to the *Iliad* and the *Odyssey*, but were reinterpreted by emerging southern Greek states. This factor combines with the enduring remnants of the early Aiolic genealogical structure, and the evidence for its deliberate break down beginning in the early seventh century. These dynamics would logically seem to depend on a concrete and inviolable countervailing authority whose sovereignty could not be effectively breached. Otherwise it is very difficult to explain the strategic machinations of Greek mythic redactors whose activities indicate that they were operating under significant conceptual restraints. The only real candidate equal to such authority is the Homeric poems themselves, which places the evidence for the "Peisistratid Recension" in subordination to the evidence for the Homeridai of the islands of Chios and Samos in their role as overseers of Homeric tradition in early seventh-century Ionia (more on this issue in chs. 4 & 5 below). The interpretation of the Homeric poems as the national charter of the ancient Greeks goes back to C.G. Heyne in the late eighteenth century. In the nineteenth, various perspectives on the Greek nationalist ethos remained a prominent feature of German scholarship (e.g. J.G. Droysen, E. Meyer and J. Beloch). Mainly, stripped down to its most basic form this association explains the pan-Hellenic status of the Greek epic repertoire at the beginning of the historical period (at present, cf. W. Burkert in D. Cairns, ed. 2001, arguing, however, for a sixth century text; M. Finkelberg & Guy G. Stroumsa, eds. 2003: vol. intro.; and D. Lateiner & J.M. Foley in R. Fowler, ed. 2004). Here, the point being that the early epic tradition we are familiar with was initially brought into existence as the national charter of the Aiolic Greeks. The Aiolians of the Asia Minor seaboard lived in close proximity to powerful eastern nations that traditionally structured contemporary lived reality in terms of a structured genealogical past, beginning with the beginning of the terrestrial cosmos and proceeding down through exotic intermediate stages to arrive at a proto-empirical world.

259 These activities, for the most part, did not involve actual amendments to the Homeric poems, but were rather accomplished through the prolific expansion of the early epic mythological canon. In this context, R. Lamberton, for example, points out "evidence for accretions is easier to find than evidence for deletion, and the tradition seems to have been reluctant to remove or to suppress any received material (I. Morris & B. Powell eds. 1997: 34; also M. Haslam in the same volume; M.J. Apthorp 1980)." Again, with respect to the hotly debated topic of the proper dating of the Homeric poems, the genealogical evidence (although scarcely cited) definitely weighs in on the side of formalized written versions in circulation considerably prior to the acclaimed "recension" attributed to Pisistratos and his sons at Athens.

260 So, the fundamental observation that a genealogically constructed pre-historical framework was subsequently altered by genealogical means.

261 viz. off the coast of the Argolid. Bakchylides.13; Pindar.*Pyth*.8.96-108, *Nem*.7.80-84, *Nem*. 8.6-10, *Isth*.8.11-25; Hdt.8.46; DS.4.72; Ovid Met.7.472-480; ApB 2.9.3, 3.11.6; Paus.2.5.2, etc.

262 Pherekydes FGrHist 3F119. Pherekydes identifies the Sikyonian Asopos and situates the abduction in Philous. He identifies Sisyphos as the sole witness of the deed, which aligns with Eumelos' early popularization of Sisyphos' association with Korinth (Huxley 1969: 60-65). Pausanias testifies that it became customary to identify Aigina, Korkyra, and Thebe as daughters of the Peloponnesian Asopos. The Thebans, he explains, denied this, however, insisting that Thebe was a daughter of the Boiotian Asopos River (Paus.2.4.2). Though these dynamics are entirely typical of Greek mythological inter-state competition as played out in the historical period, it is clear that Herodotos (5.80) and especially Pindar (e.g. *Isth*.8.17-24), a native of Thebes, saw matters quite differently in the fifth century than Pausanias' later-day Theban informants. On Pindar's contributions to Aiakos' Aiginetan legendary heritage, see especially, T.K. Hubbard 1987.

263 Hdt.2.178, 3.59, 5.82-88; T. Figueira 1993: ch.1.

264 The dispersal of heroes in older Aiolic legends invariably radiated from the Aiolic heartland to populate outlying areas of Greece. So, for example, Neleus, son of Kretheus and Tyro, established a heroic lineage in Pylos. Melampous and Bias, scions of the same line, joined Neleus in Pylos, but later moved on to Argos. Major descendants in the line of Perieres settled Messenia and Lakedaimon (viz. Tyndareos, Ikarios, Aphareus, Lynkeus).

265 cf. T. Figueria ibid. 19.

266 On Naucratis cf. C. Roebuck 1951; J. Boardman 1964; *CAH* III.3 1982: ch.36b.

267 Though Aigina, by contrast, invested strictly in trade as opposed to extensive colonization.

268 Pindar's *Nem*.8 first explicitly names Aigina in this capacity.

269 Regardless of the issue of which Asopos. The Theban and the Sikyonian were the main contenders. The former commanded an older legendary persona, while the latter was implicated in most key innovations including the ancestry of Aigina.

[270] The earliest recorded daughter of Asopos was Antiope, mother of Amphion and Zethos, encountered by Odysseus on his journey to Hades (11.260ff). As mother of the builders of the foundations of Thebes, her father was logically the Theban Asopos. Antiope, however, unlike her sisters who surfaced in the course of the Archaic Period was, notably, a standard mythic personality as opposed to a geographical eponym. The daughters of Asopos, as a category, was thereafter expanded to include Aigina and Thebe, its two most famous twins (e.g. Pind. *Nem.* 8.6-12, *Is.*8.17-23), and also quite early, if not leading the trend, Sinope, courtesy of Eumelos of Corinth (fr 10 PEG), who was no doubt interested in the Sikyonian Asopos. The generative potential of this particular type of post-Homeric mythological group, viz. genealogically linked female collectivities available for insemination by gods, is succinctly expressed in Diodoros' list of twelve daughters notably attributed to the Peloponnesian river (4.72.1). The strategic flexibility of this type of construct is embodied in the resulting mix of geographical eponyms and traditionally named figures; notably of the former, the likes of Salamis and Nemea, and of the latter, the likes of Harpina (4.73.1), yet another rival for the title of Oinomaos' mother.

[271] So especially, Plato's *Gorgias* 524a and *Apology* 41a. Earlier inferences occur in Pindar, e.g. *Nem.*8, *Is.*8. cf. Gantz 1993: 220-221 for further references.

[272] On the Kalydonian Boar Hunt and the Funeral Games for Pelias, the bulk of the earliest data is lost but there is considerable testimony to its former existence. Peleus' association with these events is also sufficiently documented (see, Gantz 1993: 131, 191-194, for a comprehensive overview). Peleus' activities at Iolkos following Pelias' funeral games involved Pelias' son Akastos, heir to the throne, and the misplaced advances of Akastos' wife. Amidst, conflicting reports of her name and identity, she was evidently a member of the Aiolic line of Kretheus and Tyro, (Gantz 226). Also, the matter of Peleus first marriage, which surfaces as far back as the *Iliad* (16.173-178), was traditionally set in this period of time (cf. Hes fr 213 MW; Pind.*Nem.*4.51-61). Moreover, these events were said to have culminated in Peleus' sack of the city of Iolkos with the help of Jason and the Dioskouri (Pherekydes FGrHist 3F62; Hes fr 211 MW). Although on behalf of Aristokleidas of Aigina (pankration victor), Pindar proclaimed that Aiakos sacked the city alone (*Nem.*3.32-34). The sword that Peleus' used to survive these adventures is described by Pindar as the sword of Daidalos (*Nem.*4.58), yet earlier by Anakreon as a gift of the gods (fr 497 PMG). See also, ApB 3.13.1-3.

[273] e.g. Il.18.84-48, 430-434; Philodemos on the *Kypria* in M. West 2003: 82; Pind. *Isth.*8.26-47; Aischy. *Prometheus Bound* 755-768; ApB 3.13.5.

[274] Achilles' armor, donned by Patroklos, and seized by Hektor after Patroklos' death was, evidently, a gift from the gods presented on the occasion of his parents' wedding (Il. 17.192-197, 18.82-87). The text infers the same provenance for Achilles' immortal horses (Il. 17.441-447).

[275] cf. Proklos' summary of the *Kypria*.

[276] οἱ μυρμήκες -> μυρμιδόνες

[277] On this topic, see, R. Parker 1983 in conjunction with D. McDowell 1963.

278 Telamon's parentage is not recorded in the Homeric poems. He is not explicitly called a son of Aiakos until Pindar's *Nemean* 5. The tradition, however, is certainly somewhat older as indicated by a fragment from the epic *Alkmaionis* which mentions the joint slaying of Phokos (Σ Eur.*Andr.*687; Kinkel fr 1). Menoitios, son of Aktor and father of Patroklos in the *Iliad*, was evidently promoted as a fourth son of Aiakos somewhere within the Hesiodic corpus and known to Eustathios in the twelfth century C.E. (Hes fr 212a MW; Gantz 1993: 222; On Eustathios, see N.G. Wilson 1983). Pindar, however, preferred the arrangement in which Menoitios was the son of Aktor and Aigina, while Aiakos was the son of Aigina and Zeus (*Ol.* 9.69-70). Evidently, this tradition identified Aktor as a son of Myrmidon and Peisidike, daughter of Aiolos (Hes fr 99-101; ApB 1.7.3). This formation could represent an established genealogy, but, in any case, it is clear that the Myrmidon Aktor was transported to Aigina just like Aiakos, thereby providing an alternate *aitia* for the origin of the Myrmidons (i.e. in contrast to the *Ehoiai*'s version).

279 Gantz 1993: 221.

280 The formation whereby Peleus and Telamon were considered half-brothers of Phokos, a son of Aiakos from a previous marriage, was, evidently, canonical before Pindar, e.g. *Nem.* 5.7-18.

281 Gantz 1993: 223.

282 Namely, the line of Deion, son of Aiolos, which via Phylakos and his son Iphiklos spawned the *Iliad*'s Protesilaos and Podarkes (Il.2.695-710; Hes fr 62 MW; ApB 1.9.4), and via Philonis to the lineage of Odysseus and the line of the legendary musician Thamyris (Il.2.591-596; Pherekydes FGrHist 3F120).

283 See also Ovid *Met* 11.222-259. Gantz notes that this story would aptly explain the birth of a son whose name means "the seal" (1993: 220. The tale of metamorphosis and resistance to capture could thus indicate a legendary identity independent of the later use of Phokos as the eponymous ancestor of the province Phokis. Asios of Samos and the *Ehoiai* both presented Phokos as the eponym of Phokis in a popular genealogy that associated Phokos with two eponymous rival sons, Krisos and Panopeus (ibid. 223). The pair of two rival sons is a mythic motif that occurs, for example, in Argive mythology in the story of Proitos and his brother Akrisios. The evidence that Akrisios was inserted into Proitos family by means of this standard mythic motif is presented in chs. 4 and 5 below. Such an addition is perhaps also likely in Krisos' case. Krisos and Panopeus personified Krisa and Panopeus, the two rival cities at odds for control of the Delphic oracle in the First Sacred War. This genealogy, therefore, probably became standard in the aftermath of that conflict which is generally dated to the early sixth century (Asios providing a *terminus ante quem*, cf. Huxley 95). The *Iliad* acknowledged Panopeus as a Phokian city, and elsewhere as the name of Epeios father. Krisa or Krisos do not appear in either the *Iliad* or the *Odyssey*. But in the Homeric Hymn to Apollo, "Krisa beneath the fold of Parnassus" was the place where Apollo built the foundations of his first Delphic temple (HHymn 3.269). The *Iliad*'s account of the Phokians at Troy is populated with an assortment of unknown personalities (though Schedios was a son of Panopeus Il.17.304-305). Still, they were certainly meaningful in the poet's mind's eye and do not necessarily constitute evidence that Epeios was not viewed as a man from Phokis, though he was not a designated contingent leader. The line of Deion which Phokos married into certainly had roots in and around Parnassos (Od.11.84-86, 19.386-475; Pherekydes FGrHist 3F120; Gantz 1993: 109, 181-182). In any event, the Homeric understanding of the heroic lines from Phokis apparently atrophied fairly quickly, while the post Sacred War version of the line of Phokos became the dominant lineage associated with the region. Basically, though it cannot be confirmed that Epeios, son of Panopeus, grandson of Phokos, great-grandson of Aiakos was a standard sequence known to early epic, the sequence does not pose any serious contradictions and also shows signs of considerable antiquity, whether initially assigned to Phokis or to some other proximate region. See Gantz 1993: 223 for additional testimony on Phokos, as well as the genealogy that made Krisos' son Strophios the father of Pylades: Agamemnon's son Orestes' closest companion.

284 At 5.18.5 Pausanias' reports Peleus' struggle with Thetis on the Chest of Kypselos.

285 viz. Kanake + Posedon = Aloeus/Triopas. **Triopas** -> Iphimedia. **Aloeus + Iphimedia +** Poseidon = Otos and Ephialtes.

286 Pind.*Nem*.5.11-12; Bakchy.13.96-99, ApB 3.12.6, Paus.2.29.9. Plutarch, Apollodoros and Pausanias explicitly report her lineage as stated.

287 e.g. The unmistakably Atheno-centric tenor of his *Solon* and his *Theseus*, which were written roughly five hundred years after the Athenian acquisition of Salamis.

288 See, for example, amidst a vast bibliography, *Athens Comes of Age: From Solon to Salamis*. Princeton: 1978; A. Andrewes in *CAH* 3.3 1982: 360-416; E. Robinson, *The First Democracies Historia* 107, Stuttgart 1997; F.J. Frost, *Politics and the Athenians*, Toronto 2005. For a thorough account of the Athenian use of Aiakid genealogy derived from epigraphical sources, see, W.S. Ferguson *Hesperia* 1938: 1-74, see p. 18 for the some more positive testimony on Skiron's identity.

289 τῷ πολλῷ χρόνῳ πολεμοῦωτες (*Thes*.10).

290 On this point I cannot agree with John Wickersham's assessment of the effects of the war for possession of Salamis on the genealogical content of Megarian pre-history (1991: 16-31). Essentially, though I wholeheartedly agree with his description of the dynamics that governed the relationship between Greek myth and Greek history, I do not think it is likely that the Megarians developed their contribution to Aiakos' southern Greek genealogy in response to the Athenian conquest of Megara. Rather, in spite of their victory, the Athenians were obliged to work within an already established framework of genealogical emendations, so chronologically speaking it worked the other way around. It seems that prior to the escalation of hostilities, the Athenians had already adopted Philaios and Eurysakes (i.e. two alleged sons of Aias, alleged grandson of Aiakos) for purposes of local aggrandization. Thus, in general, while Athens was by default forced to cope with the genealogical artifacts promoted earlier on by neighboring poleis, surely nothing prevented Athenian strategists from degrading the character of key Megarian notables or insisting on certain advantageous adjustments. The political tension between Athens and Megara stemmed back at least to the Kylonian conspiracy ca. 650 (Hdt. 5.71; cf. R. Legon 1981; T. Figueira and G. Nagy 1985).

291 The Homeric epics do not acknowledge Megara as an autonomous state. In fact, they do not acknowledge Megara at all.

292 Σ Nem.5.12; ΣA Il.16.14; Σ AR 155.4; Gantz 1993: 220.

293 This is rendered more problematic by Plutarch assertion that Chariklo was the daughter of Kychreus of Salamis, see below.

294 In *Nemean 3* Pindar mentions Cheiron and his mother Philyra in a domestic setting with no mention of Chariklo at all.

295 Not unlikely to be a deliberate omission.

296 Asopos -> Salamis + Poseidon -> Kychreus -> Chariklo + Skiron = Endeis. **Endeis +** Aiakos = Peleus / Telamon.

297 R. Legon 1981: 22.

298 I would doubt, however, that any Greek in that period considered them either mythically or linguistically equivalent (J. Wickersham in Wickersham and Pozzi, eds. 1991: 20).

[299] viz. Melanippe's mother, see C. Collard, M.J. Cropp & K.H. Lee, eds. 1997: 241; Gantz 1993: 146, 530.

[300] cf. Il.2.557, 7.219ff., 8.281-291; T. Gantz shares the suspicion that Aias was of old a native of Salamis, ibid. 222.

[301] The fundamental innovation at stake is Aias' descent from Aiakos of Aigina. Beyond this, the evidence seems to affirm that Telamon's and accordingly Aias' domain was traditionally the island of Salamis. This datum is aptly reinforced by Aias' entry in the Homeric Catalogue of Ships (Il.2.557-558), which although no doubt modified in the form that we find it, was primarily modified to emphasize the Athenians proximity to Aias' contingent, if not perhaps, also, to efface undesirable information concerning the heritage of Aias' family (cf. W.S. Ferguson 1938: esp. 15-24, and quoting E. Bethe on p.17). The brevity of the entry stands out, at any rate, among its generally noted anomalous features, while in the absence of any information on the hexameter lines this entry supplanted, more cannot really be surmised. As Ettore Cingano has recently shown (in R. Hunter ed. 2005, following Walter Leaf in 1910), the Hesiodic fragment relevant to the case that describes Aias' bid as one of the suitors who gathered to compete for Helen's hand in marriage, certainly took its cue from the *Iliad*'s *Catalogue of Ships* as we know it, making clever use of that material. Nonetheless, this fragment essentially reiterates the abiding premise that Aias' kingdom was traditionally the island of Salamis (Hes fr 204.44-51 MW). An earlier analysis by Margalit Finkelberg (*CQ* 38.1 1988) is effectively critiqued by Cingano. In the present context, the main objection to Finkelberg's reading is the suggestion that the Hesiodic passage was somehow apolitical in terms of its significance and its reception, while Aias' emended entry in the *Iliad*'s catalogue was politically relevant and well received across a broad band of southern Greek territory. First of all, in accordance with Cingano's analysis there is no profound incongruency between the two, whereas what was true for one must be true for the other in as much as geo-politically specific Greek mythic assertions were necessarily political artifacts. To cite a further example of this type of misunderstanding, in assessing Kleitias rendition of the funeral games for Patroklos as depicted on the François Vase, Steven Lowenstam asserts that two of the contestants, Damisippos and Hippothoon, who played no part whatsoever in the *Iliad*'s book twenty-three were merely bystanders and as such unimportant (1992: 176). This is eminently unlikely to be the case whether or not the identity of these figures can be ascertained from the surviving evidence. But as things stand, the Damasippos in question is, at least conceivably, the brother of Penelope who appears in the sources, accordingly providing a competitor from Sparta (Str. 10.2.24; ApB 3.10.6). Perhaps with greater certainty, Hippothoon was the eponymous hero of an Athenian tribe known as a son of Poseidon and Alope, daughter of Kerkyon, and as a major affiliate of the Athenian version of Eleusinian lore (cf. E. Kearns 1989: 73, 78, 176 and D. Whitehead, *The Demes of Attica*). Here the emphasis lies with the practical impossibility of a neutral or apolitical move involving the rearrangement of mythic protagonists, and hence, their relationship to the legendary map of Greece. All signs indicate that the southern Greek version of the Aiakid stemma caught on like wild fire in the Saronic Gulf region in the late seventh century.

[302] So, for example, Apollonios and Apollodoros included them as brothers in their augmented lists of Argonautai (AR 1.23-337; ApB 1.9.16). Neither, however, are included in the earliest extant list in Pindar's *Pythian 4*. Consequently, it is unclear whether either of them were traditionally participants, although from a geo-political standpoint Peleus represents the more qualified candidate. In a number of contexts, Diodoros, most prominently, it is clear that Telamon's role in the Argonauts' voyage hinged on the inclusion of Herakles (DS 4.40.2). Hyginus' *Fabula* 273 offers a comparably augmented list of athletic contestant at Pelias' funeral games.

303 Telamon is first attested as an accomplice of Herakles in the poetry of Peisandros of Rhodes (via Athenaios, M.West 2003 fr 10). With the ambiguous exception of *Isthmian 5* where the descendants of Aiakos are said, rather vaguely (viz. with respect to exactly which ones), to have accompanied Herakles on his mission to Troy and to have subsequently sailed with the Atreidai, Pindar's poems vindicate the proposed distinction with Telamon paired off with Herakles and Peleus linked to northern Greek mythic contexts. Compare, *Nem*.3.33-39 (where the presence of Iolaos is also notable), *Nem*.4.25-30, *Is*.5.34-39, *Is*.6.25-30.

304 viz. The daughter of Laomedon of Troy. She is unnamed in Sophokles' *Aias* (1299-1303) but was most commonly known as Hesione, e.g. Xen. *Kynegetikos* 1.9; DS 4.32.5, 4.42.2-4; Ovid *Met*. 11.211-17; ApB 2.6.4.

305 e.g. First appearing in the *Iliad* at Il.8.358-365 &19.107-136.

306 For Oikles' genealogy, see, Od.15.222-157. On his involvement with Herakles and Telamon at Troy, DS 4.32.3 (although cited in error as the son, as opposed to the father of the hero Amphiaraos); ApB 2.6.4.

307 See Gantz 1993: 225-228.

308 viz. Hippolyte of the line of Kretheus (i.e. Kretheis), son of Aiolos (Pindar *Nem* 5.36 plus scholia; also Σ *Nem*.4.92; Σ AR 1.224). This designation notably corresponds with Σ AR 1.287, which cites Ibykos for a heroine named Hippolyte, sister of Jason. Neleus, Pelias, Aison, Pheres and Amythaon were, by consensus, all designated sons of Kretheus and Tyro, the two former were notably fathered by Poseidon (cf. ApB 1.9.8 &11). Apollodoros calls Akastos' wife Astydameia (3.13.3), but offers no genealogy for her. No other Astydameia in the *Bibliotheka* adequately qualifies for this role, on which count, it is probably reasonable to conclude that he was working with some alternative genealogical assignment.

309 e.g. ApB 3.13.1-2 following Pherekydes FGrHist 3F1b, 3F61.

310 cf. Gantz 222 for Aktor, son of Myrmidon and Peisidike, daughter of Aiolos, and 227 for further details. The relevant genealogy basically runs as follows: Aktor -> Menoitios/ Polymele or Eurydike. **Menoitios** -> Patroklos. **Polymele or Eurydike** + Peleus = Polydore. Patroklos and Polydore were thereby first cousins. This straightforward analysis based on the *Iliad* excludes a great deal of later creative work. Again, it should be noted, in this regard, that via Aktor, Patroklos' grandfather, this line was also transported to Aigina, where Aktor became Aigina's mortal husband in contradistinction to her liaison with Zeus. The post-Homeric proliferation of heroes named Aktor is another sign of emerging re-interpretive trends.

311 Herakles' sack of Troy was variously attached to the eastern episodes associated with his fully developed heroic biography. His interaction with Troy conventionally took place in two installments. Apollodoros, for example, links Herakles' first adventure at Troy with the ninth labor performed in the service of Eurystheus, viz. to obtain the belt of the Amazon queen (2.5.9). He links Herakles' subsequent sack of the city with his servitude to the Lydian Queen Omphale (2.6.4). Diodoros, by contrast, links Herakles' initial encounter at Troy with his participation in the Argonauts' voyage, and accordingly, situates his sack of Troy after his servitude to Omphale.

312 For a previous treatment of this genealogy, see C. Calame in J. Bremmer, ed. 1987.

313 ca. 760

314 So, ApB 3.10.3 and also 1.3.3, which gives a different genealogy for Hykinthos (viz. Son of Pieros, son of Magnes, and the muse Clio).

315 cf. M. Petterson, *Cults of Apollo at Sparta* (Stockholm 1992).

316 His name has been associated with the Spartan township (oba) of Kynosoura (C. Calame in J. Bremmer ed., 1987: 166). Mt. Kynortion in the Argolid, near Epidauros perhaps offers a closer etymological match, if, no doubt, more problematic vis a vis its location.

317 Amyklas -> Kynortas -> Oibalos (no Perieres).

318 viz. Amyklas -> Kynortas -> Perieres -> Oibalos -> Tyndareos/ Ikarios /Hippokoon. It seems that this became a widely accepted sequence, though there is more variation when it comes to Hippokoon. For another account of Apollodoros' assessment, see M. West 1985: 95.

319 On the known seven, see Hes fr 10a OCT & ApB 1.7.3; Perieres' Aiolic heritage is specifically stated by Apollodoros at 1.9.5 & 3.10.4. Apollodoros' account of Stesichoros implies that the poet presented Oibalos as a son of Kynortas, thus Perieres' brother. Stesichoros version presumably runs: Amyklas -> Kynortas -> Perieres/ Oibalos. **Perieres** -> Tyndareos/ Ikarios/ Aphareus/ Leukippos. **Oibalos** -> Arene + Aphareus = Lynkeus/ Idas.

320 e.g. C.M. Bowra *CQ* 18.2 1934: 115-119.

321 These were accompanied as early as Alkman's poetry by a half-brother (or brother) named Hippokoon who also looks like a product of the emerging mythology of the Spartan state (P.Louvre E3320 = fr 1 PMG). Hippokoon, legend had it, was responsible for ousting Tyndareos from his Spartan kingdom (either in cahoots with Ikarios, so Paus.3.1.4, or against both Tyndareos and Ikarios, so DS 4.33.5; Str.10.2.24; ApB 3.10.2). Tyndareos' expulsion was said to have prompted the intervention of Herakles, who restored Tyndareos to the throne. But Herakles' assistance also established a Spartan debt to Herakles' descendants, which served as the operative justification for the post Trojan War claim on the Spartan realm invoked by these descendants, known as the Herakleidai. The Herakleidai, according to the sequel, invaded the country from the north in alliance with a Dorian army, ushering in a new era in Peloponnesian prehistory. This story is dealt with further below where it is assessed as a post-epic addendum created in the Peloponnese and tacked onto established epic lore.

322 For the data on Helen, see Gantz 1993: 319-321. On the Dioskouri, 323.

323 viz. Timandra, Phylonoe, and less frequently, Phoibe surface in the ancient sources, see Gantz 321-322.

324 A third daughter Arsinoe was a later addition. See West 1985: 68-70; Gantz 91, 181.

325 Gantz 324-327.

326 Gantz 225-228.

327 Gantz 116, 271-272.

328 On this topic, C. Cassola 1957; C. Roebuck 1961; W.R. Connor 1993.

329 On the Athenian Halirrhothios cf. Hellanikos FGrHist 4F38; Euripides' *Elektra* 1258-1262; West 1985: 67, 104; Gantz 1993: 168, 180. The question, as usual, is whether these two same named figures were competitive permutations of the same tradition or unrelated manifestations of autonomous streams of thought.

330 cf. Paus.1.21.4, 1.28.5; See, E. Kearns 1989: 144-145 and T. Gantz ibid. 81 for additional references; On the Areopagos cf. D. M. MacDowell 1963; R. Sealey 1983; M. Visser 1984.

331 Thus Stesichoros, active in the early sixth century, provides a *terminus ante quem* for the Spartan appropriation of all four heroes: Aphareus, Leukippos, Tyndareos and Ikarios.

332 viz. Amyklas -> Kynortas -> Perieres -> Oibalos -> Tyndareos & Ikarios (ApB 3.10.4).

333 e.g. Hes fr 16 MW.

334 The extant fragments are few and do not provide further genealogical information. Nor do they bear witness to the *Catalogue*'s metamorphosis, so there is no way of knowing where that composition stood on the matter. They do portray Herakles as an Argonaut, however, and also make reference to his dealings with Keyx which ultimately became a key feature of the story of the *Return of the Herakleidai*.

335 ἡ ἀλκυών / ὁ κῆυξ both predatory sea birds. For an elaborate version of their story, see Ovid *Met*.11.410-747.

336 West 1985: 61, 94; Gantz 1993: 168, 180.

337 For the non-Spartan genealogies attributed to Alkyone, see T. Renner 1978: 287-289; M. West 1985: 97-99; T. Gantz 1993: 215-216. Evidently, Alkyone, daughter of Aiolos, stood at the head of a major central Greek lineage that ostensibly included the Euboian Abantes, as well as the famous hero Orion.

338 See especially, Paus. 3.18.10 for Taygete and Alkyone, daughters of Atlas, pursued by Zeus and Poseidon, respectively, as witnessed on the throne of Amyklaian Zeus, created by Bathykles of Magnesia. On the date of the throne, see A. Faustoferri in W. Coulson and O. Palagia 1993. Faustoferri argues for the mid-sixth century. Southern Greek references to Alkyone invariably invoke the daughter of Atlas.

339 The genealogies associated with Alkyone and Poseidon are significant, early, and Aiolic. On this basis, they persuasively stand behind the Spartan appropriation of the Aiolic Alkyone in the guise of the daughter of Atlas. This issue is treated further below under mythic-theft-type-three, example two.

340 Essentially, a case of mythic-theft-one, since Alkyone takes on an all new identity, whereas the Spartan Perieres was clearly involved in the appropriation of mythic figures with established traditional reputations.

341 Whose existence is confirmed by independent testimony.

342 Meanwhile, Keyx (or certainly, the name Keyx, minus the Alkyone association) was apparently rescued from metamorphosis on behalf of another cause: namely, the episode in the story of the *Return of the Herakleidai* in which the descendants of Herakles (reduced to fugitives by Eurystheus, Herakles' great-uncle) sought refuge with King Keyx in the city of Trachis (see Euripides' *Herakleidai* for the Athenian version). There also, according to a fragment of the *Megalai Ehoiai* two sons of the hero Boutes married two daughters of Hyllos, Herakles' son (fr 251 MW; cf. fr 71A OCT). As M. West observes (1985: 109) these Boutidai logically do not have any connection to the Athenian Eteoboutidai, the alleged ancestors of the Athenian Boutes (viz. son of Pandion I who married his brother Erechtheus' daughter, Chthonia) and the family in charge of the hereditary priesthood of Poseidon in Attica. Though the extant data leaves much to be desired, this is, once again, the type of situation that in a sufficient number of cases can be shown to reflect two competing legends that derive from conflicting political claims to a single old and illustrious hero. Thus, in this case, it looks like Boutes (just like Halirrhothios as suggested above) was an old and venerable northern Greek hero who was the target of two separate appropriations: one spearheaded by Peloponnesian Dorians and the other (likely later) by the Athenians. This resulted in multiple figures named Bootes. It seems the Peloponnesian Bootes was in some way also related to Keyx, which could actually reflect an older relationship (e.g. see DS 4.69.3, 4.70.3 for the marriage of Hippodameia, the daughter of Boutes to Peirithoos, the famous Lapith hero). Diodoros' report at 5.50.2-5 where he describes Boutes' rape of the heroine Koronis may well have played a part in the Peloponnesian version providing the lineage of the two sons of Boutes held to have married two daughters of Hyllos. Accordingly, this vignette may be viewed as a possible candidate for the Koronis *Ehoiai* as it appeared in the Hesiodic *Catalogue*. In this regard, it is now acknowledged that the *Catalogue* offered a divergent genealogy for the famous northern Greek hero Asklepios (viz. son of Arsinoe, daughter of Leukippos, son of Aiolos or of the Spartan Perieres, see also ApB 3.10.3), who was traditionally the son of Apollo and Koronis: a situation that renders Koronis' role in that text somewhat of a mystery (West 1985: 67-72; Gantz 1993: 181). Looking at the data from the perspective of Apollodoros' portrayal of the Athenian Boutes (3.14.8, 3.15.1), illuminates a legendary division between a set of related Peloponnesian claims (i.e. Dorian) and an alternative set of Athenian claims: both, however, arising from the same name and ostensibly from the same mythic figure, who otherwise traced back to northern Greece. The upshot was two entirely distinctive Boutes and, it seems, two entirely distinctive Keyx: the metamorphosed husband of Alkyone and the appointed host of the Herakleidai.

343 On this topic, specifically, see mythic-theft-type-three, example three, below.

344 Notably, this connection served in addition to the union of Eurydice (of Sparte and Lakedaimon) and Akrisios (father of Danae, in turn, mother of Perseus) mentioned above. It was a qualitatively more powerful claim because it was located further down in the sequence, that is, in the thick of the Heroic Age.

345 So, for example, Paus.2.18.7. For more on this topic, see chs. 4 & 5, below.

346 At 3.13.1 Apollodoros reiterates Boros' genealogy as it appears in the *Iliad*.

347 viz. The considerable spread of Aiolic stemmata that remained influential in spite of major amendments to the Aiolic framework.

348 viz. since he was now their grandfather instead of their father.

[349] Pausanias unequivocally viewed Ikarios as a Spartan and excluded him from any association with Perieres' union with Gorgophone (e.g. 3.1.2-4, 4.2.4; 3.20.10-11, 3.15.3-5 are also relevant). His refusal to list him along with Tyndareos in connection with Gorgophone and Oibalos seems to indicate that in line with his insistence that Ikarios sided with Hippokoon in usurping Tyndareos' right to the throne, he rather subtly preferred to group Ikarios with Hippokoon as the offspring of Oibalos' previous marriage to an unidentified heroine. Here, it is important to bear in mind the likelihood that the Hippokoon story was Spartan invention in and of itself, especially, for example, when reading an analysis like that provided by Strabo at 10.2.24. In this passage the key figures involved are embroiled in a complex migration narrative that depicts Arkanania as a Lakadaimonian colony.

[350] Evidently, Pausanias' lineage ran as follows: Amyklas-> Kynortas-> Oibalos. **Oibalos** + ? = Ikarios / Hippokoon. Gorgophone (of Argos) + (Perieres son of Aiolos) = Aphareus / Leukippos. **Gorgophone + Oibalos** = Tyndareos/Arene. (Arene of Oibalos + Aphareus became generally standard, so ApB 3.10.3, again citing Stesichoros).

[351] Namely, the Euboian stemma that proceeds as follows (via P. Michigan inv. 1447 ii 7-9, T. Renner, ed. =188A OCT; *HSCP* 82 1978: 277-293): Alkyone + Poseidon -> Hyperes -> Arethousa+Poseidon-> Abas -> Chalkodon -> Elphenor.

CHAPTER THREE: MYTHIC THEFT TYPE THREE

Two final examples, addressed under the rubric of mythic-theft-type-three conclude the present synopsis of the kinds of evidence that illuminate the Greek practice of mythological theft. The widespread deployment of this technique and its motivational affiliation with the concerted effacement of the Aiolic lineage is only barely substantiated by the instances outlined here. Together these represent the tip of the iceberg as far as the practice itself is concerned. Type-three-mythic-theft is in its own way distinctive from its related counterparts, types one and two. Mythic-theft-type-one and mythic-theft-type-two represent two methods that were widely used for the appropriation of mythological figures, whose prior existence in Aiolic contexts stands out against the roles they later came to play. Type-three-mythic theft differs from these two categories because rather than uprooting heroic figures per se by duplicating them in, or transplanting them into, entirely new genealogical settings, type-three-mythic-theft invented new mythic figures and positioned them over established lineage sequences. Such maneuvering made it possible to detach substantial portions of heroic material from the Aiolic lineage framework. The severed excerpts were then repossessed by ambitious and influential upstart lines. In addition, the advancement of new mythic figures appointed to play vital genealogical roles was enhanced by extravagant and memorable stories that solidified the impact of their legendary personas. Each such contribution effectively reorganized targeted areas of the Greek mythic corpus, which moved incrementally further away from what can be discerned of its earliest structure.

As already emphasized, as a general rule, the upper mythological lineage zones were exceptionally vulnerable to invasive activity, lying in closer proximity to primordial time and farther from the great feats of the heroic age. Type-three-mythic-theft takes full advantage of this by fabricating protagonists and situations empowered to subordinate venerable mythic narratives that wind up below, and consequently fall victim to the authority of forebears placed above them. This tactic thus fits the bill as a means of strategic appropriation or theft, and represents a strategy that was particularly ideal for relocating whole blocks of legendary material. Here the dubious antiquity of the mythic figure Danaos and the equally dubious antiquity of the female collectivity known as the *Daughters of Atlas* illustrate the effectiveness of this third technique.

EXAMPLE ONE: DANAE, DANAOS, AND THE DANAIDS

Danaos is suspect as an interloper in a genealogy that was at one time likely to have headlined Danaos' great-great-granddaughter instead of himself: beloved of Zeus, mother of Perseus, the ancient progenetrix named Danae (Il.14.319). Danae and Perseus were feature figures in the genealogical fabric of Homeric epic, whereas Danaos and his family were not. This observation reveals a strange rivalry for eponymous status within the same lineage; rivalry for the title of principal namesake behind the *Iliad*'s designation *the Danaan warriors*. This designation gets top billing in Homer, yet atrophies quickly on a practical level, particularly in the wake of the developing concept of Hellenic identity shared by Greeks or Hellenes. *Hellas* in the *Iliad* was a central Greek district of uncertain dimensions that included a portion of Achilles' kingdom (2.683-4, 9.478)[352].

Seeing that the later Hellenes were not, in the beginning, Hellenes at all, but *Danaans*, *Achaians* and *Argives* in Homer, the subordination of Homeric terminology to standard subsequent naming conventions remains controversial to this day and no doubt relates to the auxiliary problem of the original significance of the Danaan title[353]. While *Achaians* and *Argives*, the two other categories operative in the Homeric triad, could easily be adapted to mainland Greek politics (regardless of their prior signification), based on the fact that Argos and Achaia were actual provinces in the Peloponnese, this was not the case with the designation *Danaans*, since it was not a geo-political term. The term itself suggests that the early epic *Danaans* were the hereditary descendants of Danae, if not the descendants of her ancestor Danaos. And if Danae, not Danaos, what of Danaos? This is the thrust of the issue at hand.

The *Iliad*'s *Achaians* and the *Iliad*'s *Argives* were affected by a process of modernization based on post-script realities that geo-politically altered the perceived significance of these two terms.

Accordingly, in due course, the terms no longer signified the Greeks as a whole, as they did in Homer, but were re-designated to signify the inhabitants of two major Peloponnesian districts (viz. Argos and Achaia), with the proviso that on demand they were still acknowledged as antiquated synonyms that previously denoted all Greeks or Hellenes. In this context, the term "Achaians" became the preferred designation for the great heroes of the traditional heroic repertoire and was used to distinguish those heroes of old from the descendants of Herakles, who, allied with the Dorians (out of an enclave around Mt. Oita in Thessaly) seized the Peloponnese in the post Trojan War period, ushering in, as the story goes, a new era in the prehistory of the region[354]. Yet, the Homeric *Danaans,* as a designation, did not correspond to any tangible place, and apparently prompted by virtue of this, a modernizing initiative of a different order. Danaos and his family were integral participants in an elaborate extension of the Argive line, replete with anthropomorphized foreign nations that purportedly traced their heritage back to Io, the daughter of the Argive River Inachos[355]. This mythic excursus conferred exotic prestige on the genealogy of the line of Argos, while the conspicuous role allotted to Danaos doubled the etymological basis for Argive authority over the line of Perseus[356] - a manifestly established mythological clan already endowed with a venerable namesake: daughter of Akrisios, beloved of Zeus, mother of Perseus, the heroine Danae[357].

    The case against Danaos in favor of Danae in the role of namesake of the Danaans gains credibility in accordance with the broadly observable tendency of Greek genealogies to expand backwards (M. West 1985: 27). The case is once again based on repetitive patterning. At the heart of the matter lies the extremely creative yet equally destructive genealogical synthesis readily identified as the Argive line. Even at first glance this line is distinguished by its remarkably elongated vertical extent (West ibid. 144-145[358]), which Danaos' ancestors and immediate descendants were, evidently, responsible for[359]. Above Danaos lay the great foreign eponyms construed as descendants of the Argive princess Io, whereas below Danaos, come Lynkeus and Hypermestra, who as earmarked above under mythic-theft-type-one introduced a synthetic albeit ingenious coupling of two old and venerable mythological names. Viewed from this perspective, the whole sequence in question begins to look more and more like innovative material that stands apart from the early heroic repertoire until the point where Akrisios, son of Abas (son of Lynkeus), in union with some curiously anonymous woman engenders Perseus' mother, Danae.

Later Greek mythographers amply illustrate that the elaborate lengthening of polis-based genealogies was by and by a burgeoning trend. Pausanias and Strabo offer special emphasis by organizing their reportage on geo-political grounds and recording diverse local legendary charters. These emerged from the depths of primordial time to articulate regional mythological histories that led down to the advent of the Trojan War where they inevitably meshed with established tradition[360]. In this light, the development of indigenous lines delineated within the malleable space between the hypothetical dawn of time and the most famous achievements of the heroic age constitute a root cause of lineage extension and in the end, of mythological dissonance by disrupting traditional inter-relations between major Greek heroes from established families, once these subsequently developed indigenous lines emerge from proto-prehistory to participate in the famous events of the Heroic Age.

Creative mythological elaboration fairly close to the source of a given progression and conducted independently, on a state-by-state basis, resulted in markedly uneven stemmata that logically strained interactions between heroes widely known to have been contemporaries. Surely it would be rash to assert that by contrast, the early Aiolic structure exhibited perfect synchrony. Still, given the legendary content of the whole enterprise, which afforded a measure of built-in flexibility, since the life spans of Greek heroes were not yet normative life spans[361], and siblings do not typically procreate simultaneously, the Aiolic charter appears to have facilitated markedly more harmonious lineage correspondence. Moreover, to the extent that it can be reconstructed, with obvious accretions placed to one side, the genealogies of the Aiolic line advanced from Aiolos' progeny to the Trojan War in roughly three to six generations. This stands in sharp contrast to the full-fledged Argive line, which maintained thirteen generations from Io to Herakles, a hero known to have died before the Trojan War.

The genealogy of Argos, therefore, exemplifies the art of creative lineage lengthening. Moreover, its relatively early development combined with its virtually unanimous acceptance highlights the status of the revised Argive line as a major trendsetting contribution to the early archaic emendation movement that gained momentum as various city-states promoted legendary changes based on local self-interests. Since such augmentation was extremely widespread and naturally generated uneven results, the rigid linear structure imposed by genealogy enabled radically altered lineage schemes to emphasize select points of contact with parallel genealogies and their respective heroes, but this was always accomplished at the expense of inconsistency in other areas. On a systemic or global basis, diachronic consistency was no longer possible. Logically, moreover, structural dissonance increased in proportion to the incorporation of genealogical amendments to the contemporary canon. Mainly, the greater the number of uniquely eccentric lines the greater the difficulty (difficult even under ideal conditions) of sustaining coherent correspondence among them.

The proliferation of dissonance throughout the corpus was therefore extremely difficult to control in any kind of thoroughgoing manner, and became, on this count, the single greatest challenge that faced Greek mythographers committed to an integrated account of Hellenic prehistory. Against the fully developed Greek mythic legacy, the economy and simplicity of the Aiolic lineage offers the most persuasive support for its early integrity and original mission. The flip side of the evidence for its early preeminence is the evidence that articulates the ways in which the early Aiolic genealogy incrementally faded from view; a process epitomized and, no doubt, abetted by Danaos' rise to power in the line of Argos.

DANAOS, GENEALOGY, AND THE HESIODIC *CATALOGUE OF WOMEN*

The *Hesiodic Catalogue of Women* was also known in antiquity as the *Ehoiai* since the invocation of heroines responsible for the generation of major heroic families was the text's leading organizational principle. Applied systematically on a repetitive basis via the introductory phrase ἢ οἵη ("such is she…"), each new heroine listed in this manner provoked the reiteration of a stream of protagonists vital to the mystique of the Heroic Age[362]. That Γυναικῶν Κατάλογος and Ἠοῖαι were alternative names for the same composition was conclusively established in the late nineteenth century[363]. Also in circulation, likewise, it seems, after the foundation of Libyan Kyrene, was a second text cited as the Μεγάλαι Ἠοῖαι. Since there are much fewer fragments assigned to this text, a good deal less is known about it, but it was no doubt an instance of the same genre[364]. Attributed, as they were, to the poet, Hesiod, and composed, as they were, in epic hexameter, these poems commanded a level of cultural authority shared by a certain collection of poems that were, by convention, though often erroneously, attributed to either Homer or Hesiod: the two definitive spokesmen on matters of Greek prehistory[365].

The catalogue genre is most notable for its preoccupation with genealogy. The genealogical presentation was thorough and intense. So, seeing that this was deemed normative and acceptable, we appear to be dealing with the ideal mode of expression with which to convey in abbreviated form the latest and updated roster of heroes whose great deeds epitomized the Greek cultural legacy. In this information laden poetic environment, selected narrative tangents intermittently provided a modicum of relief from the liturgical procession of figures and progeny with abbreviated references to their great deeds. Apollodoros' *Bibliotheka* recreates the sensation.

As the earliest examples of this type of reportage, the *Homeric Catalogue of Ships* and the *Odyssey*'s *Nekuia,* indicate that this genre was a mythological shorthand dependent on in-depth audience knowledge. Evidently, the object was to invoke intricate streams of legendary material through the mere act of listing illustrious proper names laced with telling descriptions and subtle allusions. Yet for such extreme brevity to resonate meaningfully, a great deal of information had to be supplied and this has additional implications. It suggests that the same body of traditional material could be expressed in two alternative ways, either by telling the stories that made up the tradition or enumerating their genealogical content. Each method entailed a measure of cross-referencing so that genealogical expression incorporated some narrative, and narrative incorporated genealogical references, but on the whole, we seem to be dealing with two equivalent forms of expression for the very same thing.

Accordingly, the *Ehoiai* provides a key piece of evidence that a concrete genealogical infrastructure was understood to direct mythological storytelling and could, consequently, substitute for it, notably, early on, in hexameter mode[366]. More specifically, the *Ehoiai* represents the overt expression of the inner substratum of the Greek mythic stories, which Homeric narrative left largely unspoken, but deployed as a guiding mnemonic device and invoked intermittently to remind the listening audience about vital events that took place in the past and that the unfolding action essentially presupposed. Beyond a doubt, it would be impossible to determine that the Homeric poems followed Aiolic lineage patterning if not for use of the catalogue genre, combined with more oblique methods of recounting past events, such as Nestor's tendency to wax nostalgic and heroes' penchant for boasting about their pedigrees[367].

From an aesthetic perspective, the *Ehoiai* represents a drastically impoverished literary genre in contrast to its narrative epic counterpart. Yet since genealogy abbreviated the legendary events that narrative programmatically expounded upon, the *Ehoiai* technique, which narrated structure over narrating story, could recount a huge chunk of Greek mythic tradition in, for example, far less space and less time than it took for Achilles to reenter the Trojan War. Yet the *Iliad* and the *Odyssey*, in all their poetic grandeur, are indispensable, if poor examples to use as grounds for comparison on this issue.

Judging from Proklos' summary of the *Epic Cycle*, it is obvious that narrative epic could likewise report great mythic events in a far more succinct manner than the *Iliad* or the *Odyssey*, with varying degrees of poetic quality. On this basis, however, it can be surmised that it was not just for reasons of economy of expression that genealogical poetry rose to prominence for the reiteration of Greek legendary history, thus expanding upon its exemplary role in telling the story of the birth of the gods for which it was certainly ideally suited[368]. The *Theogony* shows that the genre was documentary and ideally suited for the canonization of that which was already culturally well-known, but in need of definitive articulation[369]. It seems the genre's main function in the heroic milieu was to institute and disseminate the latest rendition of the heroic genealogical structure, including a multitude of innovations that had been at first locally proposed, but were subsequently widely adopted[370].

Around line 940 of the *Theogony*, following the list of goddesses whom Zeus subdued in the process of consolidating his kingship, and a brief list of unions among lesser divinities, the narrative shifts to sexual encounters that took place between mortal women and gods, namely the subject matter of the *Ehoiai*. Given the Greek genealogical continuum between gods and heroes and ordinary mortals, this shift in emphasis was by no means a non sequitur. However based on a number of anachronistic features, like the deification of Herakles (950-955) and the conspicuous eponyms, Latinos (1001) and Medios (1014), this final portion of the *Theogony* is frequently identified as an addendum to Hesiod's original composition (e.g. West 1966: 397-399, 417,429-437; 1985: 125-130[371]). Whether and if so, to what extent, the original *Theogony* saw fit to address the genealogies of the heroic era is, as things stand, not possible to establish[372].

What can be established is that the *Ehoiai* pursued this predictable mythological sequel down to the genealogies of the Trojan War heroes. As Martin West suggests, once again, based on mythological content, the *Ehoiai* was very far from original either, but rather designed to permanently supplant whatever early heroic material may have at one time concluded Hesiod's composition, or to otherwise serve as a definitive treatment of the ensuing block of mythological time (West 1985: 128). This actually makes a good deal of sense, since any authentic heroic genealogies that stemmed back to the early epic period were liable, according to the present hypothesis, to reflect the Aiolic *status quo*, and would therefore stand in need of a major adjustment as the Archaic Period progressed.

Moreover, by and large, the Greeks did not argue profusely concerning the provenance of the gods[373], but when it came to the provenance of the Greek heroes a greater bone of contention is hard to identify. Time and again, lineage patterns reveal that this preoccupation derived from serious objections to the inherited mythic structure, the dissolution and redistribution of which provoked high stakes, competitive, contemporary concerns and continuous creativity throughout this period. Clearly, this was because Greek identity hinged on the identity of the Greek heroes.

Although the fragments of the *Ehoiai* that have been preserved often provide the earliest references to major Greek mythological stories, including many that sustained permanent prestige and many that are likely to be very old, when viewed as a sixth-century composition with key indications of Athenian provenance, the *Ehoiai* represents an intermediary stage in the process of Greek mythological development. This is to say, the *Ehoiai* provides testimony at the lower end of the archaic spectrum[374], between early epic mythological thinking and the Classical and post-Classical versions of the Greek myths, some of which took their cues from the *Ehoiai* (e.g. Aischylos' *Danaid Trilogy*). Concerning the *Ehoiai*'s linguistic characteristics and their relationship to early epic diction, it is necessary to acknowledge a conflict between where the poem registers diachronically from the point of view of such criteria[375], and where the poem registers from the point of view of its mythological characteristics. Since mythological criteria cannot be ignored, on which count they receive priority status in West's seminal analysis of the extant fragments, it can perhaps be hypothesized that the *Ehoiai* was largely composed by substitution, using an earlier genealogical text as a guide for the replacement of outdated lineage patterns[376]. Beyond this, the problem must be left to the experts, yet the mythological data speaks for itself.

Thus the comparatively early date of the *Ehoiai* when compared to the bulk of extant mythic material should not inadvertently obscure the fact that there was ample time for major enhancements to the premier East Greek genealogical charter during the course of the Archaic Period, yet prior to the *Ehoiai* as we know it. Given a time lapse between inception and spread, and making allowances for incremental additions, the *Catalogue*'s acknowledgment of a revamped Argive line, inspired by, yet at odds with epic notions of Argos, diachronically speaking, must presuppose the prior development of Argive mythology and its affirmation in neighboring states. Other indigenous city-state genealogies that were, by the same token, advanced in the *Catalogue* must have reached the same stage of widespread popularity. These features in conjunction with the *Ehoiai*'s account of the genealogical version of Greek tribal identity – which signals the widespread proliferation of the tribal migration narratives that reconfigured the patterns of habitation in southern Greece after the Trojan War[377] – altogether amount to a very strong case for a sixth-century date for the *Ehoiai*.

Finally, the very production of an extensive catalogue based on the female reproductive principle again highlights the importance of the Greek mythic precept that the Greek heroes were descendants of gods. In this regard, the basic lineage scheme was driven by a set of sporadic unions between Olympian deities and primordial women[378], who though inhabitants of early mythical time were destined to die like ordinary human beings[379]. On this count it is important to emphasize that in terms of genealogical structure, and therefore, in terms of systemic function, in the tangential world of Greek mythic genealogy men and women commanded equally vital roles. The fact that women alone were eligible candidates for insemination by leading male deities is relevant at the most basic level to the importance of the *Ehoiai* as a mytho-cultural document. Genealogy as a symbolic medium deals fairly straightforwardly with its raw material mainly because of the strict limitations on what a lineage framework can represent, and the limited ways of going about it where human reproduction is concerned. Genealogical equality between the sexes can, therefore, be seen as a direct result of the thoroughgoing deployment of genealogy as the organizational framework for Greek legendary history[380].

In general, Greek mythology is a risky place to go looking for concrete information on historically socio-cultural norms, in spite of the fact that Greek mythology was an indispensable aspect of Greek culture. The biggest problem arises from the temptation to extract select data from legendary contexts to support independent analytical claims external to the world of Greek myth itself[381]. So, for example, a recent proposal that is in the end, masterful and yet untenable, links mythological statements about jointly ruled cities to inheritance practices in the Bronze Age, when kingship was apparently often transmitted by way of marriage to the kings' daughters and passed to their husbands on a rotational basis [382]. Against this proposal, it can be shown that mythological references to shared kingship in Argos (to cite a prime example) meant just what such statements literally seem to mean: multiple simultaneous rulers, and hence the division of the Argive kingdom.

On the other hand, though it would be rash to deny viable points of contact between the world of Greek myth and the world of Greek reality, it is necessarily prudent to bear in mind that the Greek legendary landscape was artificial and operated according to rules of its own that had nothing to do with lived reality and can only be identified on systemic grounds. As an example of just such a systemic phenomenon that exists for entirely pragmatic reasons, the genealogical equality of heroic men and women has not attracted much attention in this vein. The relationship of this factor to lived reality is, notwithstanding, a totally separate issue. Still, it is likely to have some explanatory bearing on the status of women in Greek myth[383].

The expanded version of the Argive line, which included the life stories of Danaos and his daughters was acknowledged in the Hesiodic *Catalogue of Women*[384], and presumably also featured in the lost epic *Danais*, which is believed to have been an important source for Aischylos and Akousilaos of Argos[385]. The story also surfaces in Hekataios and Pindar[386] so that by the time of Aischylos' *Hikitides*[387], which provides our earliest access to the basic plot[388], it is clear that the story was already well-known for quite some time[389]. Depending on individual dating preferences, one of these poems provides a *terminus ante quem* for the popularization of Danaos' legendary biography. Following M.L. West's late sixth-century date for the Hesiodic *Catalogue of Women* suggests that the *Danais* could well have informed the *Catalogue's* references to Danaos and family[390]. West's dating mainly relies on the mythological content of the *Hesiodic Catalogue* itself, and although it has not been unanimously accepted[391], his dating has a great deal to recommend it.

Essentially, the most persuasive factor is the significant number of indications that Athenian mythology had achieved a fairly advanced state of systematization prior to the *Catalogue's* composition. Its Athenian emphasis in certain areas works to support West's further proposal that the *Catalogue* poet was an Athenian[392]. It is argued in greater detail below that the Athenian contribution to the Greek mythic repertoire was profoundly influential but rather late in the offing in contrast to post-Homeric lineage schemes promulgated in other southern Greek states[393]. This chronological factor is extremely important, since as late competitors on the scene, the Athenians acknowledged and incorporated earlier innovations promoted by others and often structured Athenian innovations around them[394]. In this sense the Athenians looked to already prominent city-state genealogies in determining the content of their own synthesis with an eye to strategic one-upmanship[395]. Though clearly a mix of old and new elements, the development of Athenian mythology seems to have accelerated under Peisistratid rule, yet it was scarcely a factor outside of Attica before Solon's archonship in 594/3. The number of inferences in the *Catalogue of Women* that highlight Athenian re-interpretive work, accordingly, coincide with the well-attested fact that Athens was not involved in external affairs for the most part until the Peisistratid Period[396].

Supplementary dating information relates to the eponymous foreign figures that appear in this portion of the Argive line, as exemplified in this branch of the family by Libya, Aigyptos, and Arabos: Danaos' grandmother, brother, and nephew, respectively. It is generally thought that the presence of these figures indicates that this genealogy must postdate the foundation of Libyan Kyrene (ca. 630)[397]. This is sound reasoning and seems to coincide with Greek activity at Egyptian Naucratis, as well as with the revival of Argive fortunes in the last quarter of the seventh century after political setbacks in the previous decades[398]. The rather audacious claim of this genealogy to the effect that personified foreign nations traced their lineage back to the Argive princess Io bears an interesting relationship to the fact that Argos was not a colonizing polis. This suggests a rather ingenious genealogical means of symbolic Argive competitive compensation in lieu of actual Argive foreign policy initiatives.

The extended genealogy of Argos was quite well developed in the Hesiodic *Catalogue*, though a certain measure of disagreement persisted concerning the genealogies that stemmed from Libya's progeny. Among the main protagonists Belos and Agenor assumed control of the lineage of Egypt, as well as the lineage of the Levant, respectively. And with varying levels of testimonial clarity, these two parallel branches of the extended family incorporated a number of old heroic protagonists[399]. So, for example: Europa, the daughter of

Phoinix, whom the *Iliad* reports was abducted by Zeus (Il.14.321-322), the famous seer, Phineus, from the Argonauts' voyage, and Kepheus, Perseus' father-in-law[400] were evidently old figures whose proper positioning in the new formation were points of ongoing genealogical negotiation.

So while the genealogical progression from Io to Herakles seems to have quickly achieved canonical status, certain points of recurrent indeterminacy reveal the upper reaches of the Argive line in a state of ongoing analytical synthesis, particularly, and probably not by chance, when it came to integrating old traditional figures within the international lineage matrix[401]. This observation reinforces the idea that, excluding such figures, the matrix itself was recent and previously uncharted territory.

Again, in this regard, it is not surprising to witness certain striking sequential incongruities. So, for example, the major backward extension of Perseus' ancestry was at odds with the attendant assertion that Perseus married Andromeda, daughter of Kepheus. For whether Kepheus was considered to be a son of Belos, a son of Agenor, or a son of Phioinix, Perseus' wife, unanimously Kepheus' daughter (viz. Andromeda), remains four to five generations Perseus' senior. Whether or not any of these alleged identities matched Kepheus' legendary identity of old, in this case a potentially traditional coupling was preserved at the cost of considerable distortion with respect to surrounding innovations. The rift in essence boils down to the exceptional length of Perseus' stemma, which no parallel line could conceivably match. It seems exceptional length was an outstanding feature of Perseus' line as far back as Homer (e.g. seven generations from Akrisios to Herakles with necessary extensions on either end), so in terms of innovation we are looking at the buildup of an elaborate genealogical structure around an already exceptional genealogical line.

Though it is not really possible to coherently analyze the exceptional early length of the Perseid stemma, it shows that the Greek genealogical system at no time displayed completely uniform synchrony. The length of Perseus' line can perhaps best be regarded as an indication of special status, whether also the sign of a genealogical sequence that was older than its surrounding legendary affiliates, a tradition imported from an outside source, or simply an instance of unique augmentation with no significant further qualifications. At any rate, in the revised line of Argos, incongruity was measurably intensified by the dramatic elongation of a family line that was already exceptional with respect to its length. The kinds of discrepancies that resulted are often taken in stride as entirely normative in the world of Greek myth, and this is certainly justified from the perspective of the later Greek mythic corpus. Still, it remains worth considering whether this situation was not actually tied to a dynamic root cause, namely, the tacit enactment of profound and permanent changes on a collection of stories that were at one time woven together within far more controlled conceptual bounds[402].

Argos, it would seem, was the primary beneficiary of these genealogies and their attendant narratives, which in an early archaic revisionist environment suggests their invention and promulgation in Argos[403]. Yet the extraordinary elevation of Greek culture that was effectively sponsored by the Argive line through the use of personified foreign nations was by no means lost on other Greek city-states. Such states evidently considered themselves surrogate beneficiaries of this great innovation. And, indeed, subsequent genealogical reports on the matter were hardly restricted to Argive chroniclers.

On the question of Argive lineage development, based on a fragment from the *Aigimios* that appears to conclude Io's misadventures on the island of Euboia, as opposed to on the banks of the Nile (fr 296 MW), one influential proposal sees a gradual process of geographical expansion with respect to this section of the Argive line (M.L. West 1985: 145-146[404]). It is alternatively possible that the Euboian version was devised in response to Argive Egyptian claims, and that it sustained a level of currency because it challenged the remarkable aggrandization of Argos. This line of reasoning emphasizes that while there was surely an indigenous Argive line before the promotion of the Egyptian interlude, and while an Euboian version would no doubt represent a less exotic conception of Io's adventures, and could therefore suggest an intermediate claim, the whole point of the promotion of the Argive Abas was to portray the man as an Argive, specifically, as the ancestor of Perseus and Herakles. This project involved severing the Argive Abas from any meaningful association with an eponymous ancestor of the Homeric Abantes (Il.2.536-545[405]). The existence of such a figure with Aiolic roots can be provisionally traced in the surviving fragments of the *Ehoiai* (244 MW; 188a OCT). Thus, as far as the Argive line was concerned, there was no attempt to make the Argive Abas Euboian, which stood at cross-purposes to Argive aims or, it would seem, to make Euboia Argive using some mythic colonization strategy. Rather, the whole initiative aimed to promote an exclusively Argive claim in place of a traditionally Euboian title.

Comparing later testimony with the *Ehoiai*, it would seem that these two heroes – the Euboian and the Argive – competed with each another until the Argive successfully usurped all relevant honors (e.g. Str.9.5.5; Paus.10.35.1). And it is probably also relevant that fr 188a is the last we hear of the heroic Euboian genealogy beyond the general run of independent references to the *Iliad*'s major Euboian heroes (i.e. Chalcodon and his son Elphenor). Considering the amount of prestige that accrued to the Argives from their connection with Egypt, it is worth wondering whether the Argives would have targeted Euboia as the ideal place to spawn their illustrious lineage, and likewise, whether they would have brought Abas, son of Lynkeus, of the Argive line into such close contact with Euboian lore[406].

The link between the name Abas and the island of Euboia comes across powerfully in the sources. But the Euboian version restricts the influence of that link by situating the origin of the Abantes at some hypothetical point in time before the main events of the Heroic Age. Basically, this arrangement eliminated the need for an ancestral Euboian Abas at all, and this is interesting because the Hesiodic *Catalogue* documented both the Egyptian version of the line of Argos, as well as key information on the ancestry of the Euboian leaders that sailed off to Troy. As reconstructed from the *Ehoiai* fragments, Abas was a son of Poseidon and Arethousa, via Hyperes, Arethousa's father. Hyperes, in turn, was a son of Poseidon and Alkyone, the repeatedly contested daughter of Aiolos. It is impossible to verify to what extent the *Ehoiai*'s portrait of the Euboian line mirrors the Homeric view of the matter (though there are some conspicuous traditional signs). Nonetheless, the *Iliad*'s heroes, Chalcodon and Elphenor, were evidently traced to this lineage at a time when the expanded Argive line had already achieved widespread recognition.

In fragment 296, Stephanos of Byzantium cites the *Aigimios* for the story that Io travelled through Euboia in the form of a cow. As a result the name of the island was changed to Euboia from Abantis in commemoration of this event. At 10.1.3 Strabo confirms the existence of such a version that may well derive from the *Aigimios*, in which Euboia, not Egypt, was Io's final destination, and where she gave birth to Epaphos in a cave. He also repeats the story that made Io's arrival in the form of a cow the basis for the name of the island, offering a number of other previous names, while noting that Euboia was the name used by Homer. Strabo further cites Aristotle for the idea that the old name *Abantis* derived from a group of migrating Thracians who made their way to Euboia via Aba in Phokis. This claim transforms the Abantes into Thracian immigrants which is certainly notable in itself. Yet, whether immigrant Thracians or native islanders, the island's alleged name change from Abantis to Euboia excludes either an Argive or an Euboian Abas from any traditional eponymous role. Mainly, the Abantes themselves gave their name to the island virtually at the dawn of mythological time, in a story that offered nothing of substance about the Abantes' heroic deeds, but simply acknowledged their existence when an Argive princess in the form of a cow arrived to confer her legacy on the island. This explained how Euboia came to be known as it was already ubiquitously known in Greek epic and in real life. Meanwhile, as far as the Argive line was concerned, Abas was not an ancestor, but a descendant of Io and, specifically in the Egyptian version, a descendant who was not destined to be born for another six generations (whereas to get to Perseus required further three).

The astute chronological marginalization of the greatest names in the history of the Euboian line, activated by Io's sojourn in Euboia, would work equally well with either version, varying only in the length of her stay. But, seeing that the removal of Io's Egyptian progeny[407], which an Euboian version would necessarily entail, in lieu of Io's immigration to Egypt, simply plants Argive progeny on Euboian soil and relies on a plot line that not only pales in comparison with the Egyptian story when it comes to the issue of Argive prestige, but raises questions of Argive motivation in light of the other dynamics involved.

These factors introduce the alternate possibility that the Euboian version arose in response to the grandeur of the Egyptian version before such efforts were squelched by Egypt's great popularity[408]. Either way, Io's passage through Euboia draws attention to an important matrix of stories that haunted the Argive Abas on account of his name. These stories represent the one viable lead concerning Perseus' family's ancestral origins prior to the development of the expanded Argive line[409]. Beyond this, Strabo's account confirms the existence of an Euboian variant that lived on independently of its far more popular Egyptian counterpart.

    For what it is worth, Abas happens to be the only name that is repeatedly used to describe Akrisios' father, whereas Akrisios himself goes back to the *Iliad* (Il.14.319-320). The *Aigimios* is one of a whole host of texts that invariably connect the name Abas with Euboia, and continue to do so under the rising influence of the Argive line. This is pretty much all there is to go on, but it does contain a seed of the idea that Perseus' line may have been connected to the early lineage of the Abantes. So whereas the Argive line depicts the hero Abas, Perseus' great grandfather, as a native of Argos, and the *Iliad* informs us that Perseus' family controlled Mykenai before the Atreidai (e.g. Il. 4.372-381, 15.636-643), in the present context, it is worth noting that although mythologically the name Abas invoked connections with Euboia and with Phokis, we are fundamentally left in the dark as to the early narratives that brought Perseus' family from either of those locations to the Peloponnese[410]. And according to the *Iliad*, this must have been done, if indeed this once was a valid connection.

    Whatever Perseus' ancestry was in the *Iliad*, his family ruled an extensive block of territory in the northern Peloponnese, on which count, it can only be said that this pattern of dispersal from north to south was typical of Aiolic genealogical patterns and may be as close as it is possible to get to Perseus' family's ancestral claims before the advent of the revised Argive line[411]. At any rate, by the time of the *Catalogue of Women*, Abas, his son Akrisios, and Akrisios' daughter Danae were all solidly situated in Argos, following their ancestors' prolonged residence in Egypt. Meanwhile, the *Catalogue of Women* is also the source of the genealogy of Euboia and its Aiolic Abas, which adequately confirms that Abas of Argos was a serious adversary, as well as a source of considerable confusion by virtue of bearing the same name (M. West 1985: 98-99; Hes fr 188A OCT). We no doubt witness here a set of conflicts provoked by the meteoric rise of the Argive line in its familiar form.

MYTH, POLITICS, AND THE LINE OF ARGOS

The Argive lineage in its full-blown form was an intricate blend of old and new elements cleverly fused together to enhance the reputation of the Argive state. The line of Argos also played a pivotal role in the early stages of the proposed movement dedicated to the modernization of the inherited epic legacy. The goal was to reconfigure the existing mythic structure so that it might more effectively represent contemporary political actualities. Developing early from a mainland perspective, Argos was a formidable power by the early seventh century, declined midcentury, and experienced a revival toward the end of the century[412]. Throughout this period Argos competed with Sparta for coterminous territories and political influence. In the mythic arena, this rivalry took the form of competitive legendary foundation charters that managed to achieve broad-based public approval in spite of their conceptually provincial bent.

A central premise throughout this report is that there is a discernible correlation between mythological productivity in the major Greek city-states and available information on their political development during the course of the Archaic Period. It is furthermore held that polis-based contributions to the emerging revised mythic repertoire were largely accepted by neighboring states so that significant locally generated claims cultivated increasing influence when they were favorably acknowledged beyond provincial borders. Roughly speaking, therefore, the relative sequence of political developments matches the relative sequence of mythological developments, since mythological influence was fundamentally tied to political influence of a certain magnitude. Moreover, states on the rise looked to their predecessors, who were, notwithstanding, often also their rivals, but who had set the standards as to the best methods of mythological emendation by creatively forging local mythic identities and co-opting great figures from old epic lore. For these reasons influential southern Greek states left indelible marks on the mythological record. Among them in particular, Argos and Sparta both rose to power relatively early on and vied for influence throughout the seventh century, with Sparta predominating later in the sixth[413]. Their efforts were accompanied in due course by the emerging state mythologies of Arkadia and Aigina.

Extant data suggest that the development of the Argive line took place in two stages, both prior to the composition of the *Ehoiai*. Stage one established the origins of mythic Argos, genealogically, in primordial time. Accordingly, an indigenous genealogy provided the framework which, down the line, informed Argive involvement in great epic events and the ancestry of the Argive heroes associated with those events. Stage two incorporated the Argive princess Io's extravagant genealogical saga that wedged five generations of foreign-born magnates in between the Argive foundation charter and recognizable epic protagonists. This segment included Danaos and his daughters whose story reinstated Inachos' descendants once again into the kingdom of Argos.

Traces of the first stage indicate that it was a standard exercise in local lineage building. This involved an array of primordial figures, the personification of a piece of the landscape, which was, in this case, the Argive river Inachos, and an eponymous Argos, namesake of the city. Accounts of the earliest sequence of progenitors are, as they stand, conflicting and meager. Yet the remnants suffice to show that such work had been done and continued to be actively reiterated by Argive chroniclers such as Akousilaos, whose fifth-century treatment was frequently cited by ancient antiquarians. Apollodoros preserves the sole coherent report on the earliest strata of the Argive lineage, but his report also differs to some extent from two of his key sources, namely, Akousilaos and the *Ehoiai*, since these two texts made Io the daughter of one Peiren, while Apollodoros asserts she was a daughter of Iasos (the son of Argos, who was a son of Niobe, daughter of Phroneus, ApB 2.1.1[414]).

Io was the appointed legendary vehicle through which stage two was developed and promoted. In this regard she may be held responsible for the eventual foreshortening of the indigenous Argive charter once it achieved widespread consensus. By the time of Aischylos, at any rate, the mythological machinations of the early Argive founders, the likes of Iasos, Peiren, and Phoroneus[415], had lost considerable significance outside Argos in the wake of the formula that rendered Io simply the daughter of the River Inachos, left the matter at that, and took the story from there. Io was the woman, it is to be remembered, who was transformed into a cow when Zeus attempted to conceal his passion for her from Hera. Though first imprisoned, as such, and put under surveillance by a figure named Argos with a number of eyes, the famous slaying of Argos by the god Hermes marked a new beginning for the cow-maiden's woes, since at that point Hera sent a gadfly against her, which drove her in flight across a great many nations until she finally reached the banks of the Nile. On the banks of the Nile, legend had it, Zeus finally restored Io to her true form. There she bore the child Epaphos to the god, and he, consequently, became the forebear of a great brood of exotic Argive ex-patriots. The North African branch of Io's family prospered abroad until the appointed hour, when the daughters of her descendant, Danaos, fleeing from the sons of her descendant, Aigyptos, prompted the reunification of her wayward line with traditional epic genealogical material, and leading, subsequently, to the conception of Perseus, son of Danae daughter of Akrisios, aka the great-grandfather of Herakles.

This mythological interval stands behind the story dramatized by Aischylos in his *Suppliant Maidens* and mentioned briefly in his *Prometheus Bound*, about the flight of Danaos and his fifty daughters from Danaos' brother, Aigyptos and his fifty sons, to the city of Argos, which granted them refuge, yet was still, evidently, unable to protect them from their predestined marriages to their first cousins. This marriage became a very famous affair, and justifiably so, given its bloody outcome, since forty-nine out of fifty of Danaos' daughters, killed forty-nine out of fifty of Aigyptos' sons, notably leaving a single surviving couple, whose role it was to perpetuate the Argive line (namely, Lynkeus and Hypermestra, addressed as an example of mythic-theft-type-one[416]).

As for the enigmatic mythological plot that features Danaos' daughters' violent resistance to a standard betrothal to their first cousins, common to Greek mythology and acceptable in real life[417], a good deal of attention has focused on ascertaining the deeper (and potentially sociological) meaning behind the dramatization of such resistance[418]. Once again, genealogy, if permitted to intervene, offers a far more mundane explanation for an otherwise baffling situation. This storyline based on resistance to marriage that was so intense it resulted in murder stands in a cause-and-effect relationship to the need to cut a huge family down to size once it had provided sufficient narrative grandeur. This requirement was connected to the further objective of bringing Io's descendants back home to Argos and restoring their suspended Argive identity.

The mating of fifty sons with fifty daughters, or even a far less, if still prodigious number, represents an untenable situation from the perspective of lineage management. The perpetuation of such a family, even just as far as the next generation, is a prospect of overwhelming proportions, inimical to symbolic genealogical aims. Such an unmanageable number of individuals, let alone the result of their respective unions, was altogether counterproductive to the Argive state-aggrandization initiative that prompted the extension of the Argive line to begin with, since this lineage, though engaged in an elaborate tangent, was nonetheless bound to reconnect with the general run of well-known heroic stories. And so we witness in two simple strokes, first, the flight of Danaos' daughters from Egypt, which brought Io's lineage back to Argos, and second, their murder of their Egyptian husbands, which slimmed the family down to two appointed progenitors, by way of the standard sole-survivor motif. Moreover, this was accomplished through a minor adjustment to the standard motif of exile-for-homicide, generally used to move people around, that is, to lead them from one place to another[419].

Following the outline of Aischylos' version, though various permutations could surely also suffice, pursuit and flight took the place of the standard function of exile-for-homicide, while the murder was postponed to the appointed destination. The attendant expectation that the Danaids then face exile from Argos on account of the murder was ostensibly mitigated by special pleading for a just cause, namely, acquiescence by force[420]. Purification and reintegration ensued[421]. And though, no doubt, from the standpoint of jurisprudence, this plea involves a variety of ponderous issues, the Danaids had reached their appointed destination so their resettlement elsewhere simply had to be stopped. The ingenuity with which certain standard motifs were custom-scripted to facilitate this outcome does not require an elaborate theory. The Danaids remarriage to Argives in Argos privileged their naturalization over their crime[422]. This outcome, too, was symbolically important, yet at the same time peripheral to the status commanded by Lynkeus and Hypermestra, who were, for all intents and purposes, the unrivaled perpetuators of the main artery of the Argive line. Beyond this, as G.S. Kirk once remarked, "myths are not interested in the ordinary" actually, "the stranger the better," which relates to the fact that Greek mythic plot structures adhered to the logic of their own alternative world[423].

It is curious that discussions of this subject matter frequently miss the point of the hierarchical structure that stands behind this whole strange drama. Io, was a Greek woman driven abroad for provoking a conflict between Zeus and Hera, and therefore, in some sense, by the will of the gods, subordinated powerful foreign populations to the hereditary dominance of the royal line of Argos. All the protagonists in question, here, including the assortment of foreign eponyms, were Greeks by blood by virtue of being the hereditary descendants of Io of Argos. Danaos, Aigyptos, and their immediate forebears were merely living and ruling in foreign territories until the appointed plotline sent them back home to enrich and perpetuate Argive prehistory. The message inherent in this formation is tinged with an element of chauvinistic Greek thinking that is something quite different from the notion of Greek competitive merit in a multicultural landscape that comes across in the Homeric poems.

The full-fledged line of Argos accordingly illustrates a significant change in prevailing Greek attitudes toward the legendary treatment of foreign cultures[424]. For whereas the interactions of the Achaian warriors with foreign guest-friends and enemies alike was infused with a sense of deference and respect that extended to foreign nations in general, in terms of the layout of this genealogy, the symbolic buildup of Greek prestige is no longer presented as the result of economic transactions, alliance, or conquest. Instead, the genealogical subordination of others is accomplished by way of a lineage claim that made foreigners Greek by association, negating their identity as distinct peoples. This amounts to a very conspicuous fantasy.

Traditionally Greek mythology imported high-profile foreign personas, such as Pelops and Kadmos, established them on Greek soil, and had them foster great lineages[425]. The line of Argos, however, at this subsequent stage has reversed these dynamics and exported a Greek persona in order to dominate a trumped-up cluster of figures distinguished by exotic eponymous names. Again by contrast, but in a similar vein, the dispersion of Greek heroes and Trojan survivors in the aftermath of the Trojan War was evidently a notion as old as epic itself and signaled the termination of the long drawn out saga that began with the birth of the first demigods. In the course of succeeding post Trojan War generations, Greek tradition was thrown open to improvisation on the part of all interested chroniclers. In this regard, from the very beginning, a fundamental objective of the whole enterprise was to generate a multitude of outstanding personas whose descendants could be founders of real-life communities based on their illustrious ancestral credentials. Here, we see a variant form of mythic colonization at a different point in the progress of mythological time, and one that was developed to achieve different if, by no means, incomparable ends.

Beyond its own special brand of cultural bias, the most significant feature of the Argive line is its promotion of Io as a genealogical emissary at a point near the top of the extended sequence, which on account of its extraordinary subsequent length situated Io and her immediate descendants well before the onset of the Heroic Age, as if part of some hypothetical twilight zone. This arrangement sets the scheme off as an interpolation: a kind of eccentric twist inserted between the indigenous origins of the Argive state and the well-known legends of the Heroic Age. Moreover, once this elaborate extension achieved widespread acclaim, its ubiquitous influence made it impossible to determine where, within the old epic lineage framework, Perseus and Heracles originally resided. Heracles, notwithstanding, though born in Thebes, came from a family that was well established in "Argos" by the time of Herakles' immediate forebears; this much as far back as early epic tradition[426]. It nonetheless seems misguided to place much faith in the genealogical information situated above that fact, since above it lies the very mythic interlude presently under consideration.

The particular type of cultural chauvinism exhibited genealogically in the line of Argos is worth noting in another context as well, since the bulk of the publicity on the subject is generally associated with Athenian propaganda created and spread abroad in the post Persian War Period. Mainly, here is a patriotic supremacist vision that certainly antedated the Greek conflict with Persia and must, therefore, be viewed independently of the frequently emphasized psychological impact of the victories of 490 and 480 B.C. on the conceptualization of Greek identity. The effect of the Persian Wars was without a doubt profoundly significant in this area[427], yet this antecedent shows, by way of example, that the relationship between Athens' rise to power and the ideology of Greek supremacy is pertinent also in other Greek contexts where the effects of power and wealth were realized and experienced at an earlier date[428].

According to Herodotos, in 490 and again in 480 B.C., the effort to ward off invading Persian armies was jointly spearheaded by Athens and Sparta with help from as many allies as they could muster though commitment to resistance was very far from unanimous[429]. Yet in his numerous flashbacks to earlier times to account for rise of these two powerful states, Herodotos shows that their joint leadership role, especially the status of the Athenians, was an eventuality that at length replaced other earlier distributions of power not all that long before Xerxes' invasion (Thouky.1.1ff.).

Looking critically, then, at the international segment of the Argive line, it seems that Argive mythographers sought to compete on mythological grounds with states such as Korinth, Megara, and Aigina that were actually involved in international trade and/or colonization in a major way. So while Argos actually did not engage in seafaring ventures of any significant consequence, Argos nevertheless vicariously aspired to appropriate a portion of the mystique that surrounded international entrepreneurship through the genealogical enhancement of the public image of the legendary Argive state. The island of Aigina stands out, in this regard, as a catalyst to the Argive mythic vision.

Argos' affiliation with the island of Aigina during the period of Aiginetan maritime prosperity and after Aigina's independence from Epidauros, provides a suitable context for this genealogy[430]. Aigina was the only mainland Greek state in the company of East Greek trading metropoleis (Hdt.II.178)[431] seriously involved in Egyptian commerce centered at the Greek trading post of Naucratis[432]. The alliance between Argos and Aigina in this period, was based on the union of complementary assets. Argos specialized in agriculture and military strength, Aigina in overseas economic transactions[433]. As allies, Argos and Aigina were antagonistic toward Sparta and wary of Spartan expansionist motives at the conclusion of the Messenian wars (c.600). They sustained a mutual enmity toward Corinth as well, an enemy of Argos since the Kypselid period, a naval competitor from Aigina's point of view, and also a longstanding ally of Sparta[434]. With respect to the mythological segment at hand, the sixth-century affiliation between Argos and Aigina provides a persuasively solid context for an Argos-inspired, Argos-generated account of Io's flight to the banks of the Nile, including the misadventures of her descendants that reinstated her line back in the Argive heartland.

KYRENE AND ARGOS

There is another factor that also has some bearing on the mythological narratives under consideration. For the North African city of Kyrene, established from Thera ca. 630, was portrayed in a number of legends that seem to bear no organic relation to the genesis of Libya in the Argive line, though the state of Kyrene flourished in its midst. First, the poet Eugammon, a native of Kyrene, was famous for an account called the *Telegonia* after Telegonos, a legendary son of Odysseus and Kalypso (elsewhere a legendary son of Odysseus and Kirke[435]). Eugammon's poem dealt with post Trojan War exploits and dates to the reign of Arkesilaos II (viz. after 570). It notably traced the lineage of the Kyrenian kings back to one great legendary Arkesilaos, an alleged second son of Penelope and Odysseus[436].

Second, there is the story that the Kyrenean kings were the descendants of an Argonaut named Euphemos, elaborated at length in Pindar's *Pythian* 4[437]. This tale represents the standard fifth-century mainland Greek view and was also treated at length in Herodotos' *Histories*, where the foundation of Kyrene from the island of Thera is traced back to a group of Spartan ex-patriots accompanied by Minyans from the island of Lemnos toward the tail end of the Heroic Age

(4.145-159). A third report that occurs in Pindar's *Pythian 5* (77-84), refers to a stopover in Kyrene by Menelaos and his comrades on their way home from Troy, with Helen, at long last, again in his possession[438]. The returning Greek victors in this party were accompanied by the Trojan warrior Antenor and his surviving family members, who were spared by the Greeks for their abiding conviction that Helen should be returned to her rightful husband[439]. In this context the Antenoridai are conspicuously poised to make a fresh start in distant territory, embodying the Greek notion of fleeing Trojan survivors that was later adopted by Roman chroniclers as the basis for the foundation of Rome[440]. Fourth, a few free-floating lines from the Hesiodic *Ehoiai* (Hes fr 215 MW), backed up and filled out by Pindar's *Pythian 9* (9-16) relate how the city came to be named after a Thessalian nymph who could wrestle with lions. Abducted by Apollo and transported thither, the god awarded Kyrene, for her trouble, title and dominion over the territory[441].

As far as the interaction of these varied strands and the attendant issue of their development, seeing that all but Eugammon's patronizing tribute to the origins of Kyrenean royalty appear or reappear in Pindar's victory odes, which also acknowledge Io's Egyptian born progeny[442], it would seem that these strands might somehow work together according to some kind of ingenious synchrony.

Pindar's *Pythian 4* sets out the basic framework. After the successful theft of the Golden Fleece, and following a twelve-day journey across the Libyan desert, Medea, Jason, and the returning Argonauts set sail once again, making a stop on the island of Thera. There, a clairvoyant Medea makes the prophesy that the Argonaut Euphemos, son of Poseidon, and his Lemnian bride-to-be[443] will become the ancestors of the kings of Kyrene, seventeen generations into the future (*Pyth*.4.1-8, 47-54 with 247-261). Libya, specifically, the daughter of Epaphos, alias the great country, already exists, and will wait metaphorically for the prescribed time to pass before receiving the cities destined to be implanted in her (viz. the Kyrenean cities, *Pyth*. 4.9-16).

Like *Pythian 4*, Pindar's *Pythian 5*, also commemorates the chariot victory won at Delphi in 462 by Arkesilas IV of Kyrene. Here we learn that in the course of time between Medea' prophesy and its realization, Kyrene welcomed the Trojan sons of Antenor who were honored henceforth by the citizens of the city. We are reminded also of Apollo's role in granting Lakedaimon to the descendants of Heracles and prompting their descendants to claim the island of Thera. Adding to this remarks made in *Pythian 9*, it is possible to detect Pindar's working chronology[444]. This poem reveals that Kyrene, namesake of the city, was a Lapith princess from Thessaly. She was the daughter of Hypseus, son of the Peneus River, one of the myriad offspring of Okeanos (*Pyth*.9.9-25[445]). Her destiny, as it happened, lay in North Africa where queen Libya is prepared to greet Apollo's lover as foundress and domatrix of Kyrene, and where she will be honored in perpetuity as the fearless pioneer heroine of a great city-state[446].

Thus, as unrelated as these trajectories may seem, they can be perceived as one long unfolding story. This is not to say that they were composed all together, belong to the same time, or even to the same place. Yet they have been brilliantly processed and assimilated by Pindar, but not, however, by Pindar alone. As an epinician poet, Pindar spoke to the mind's eye of a greater Hellenic audience. This was an audience steeped in the latest mythological trends, thoroughly adept at piecing together entire mythic scenarios from a few cryptic remarks.

There is no doubt, first of all, that Pindar is operating with the legacy of Io firmly in mind. He is almost certainly, therefore, presupposing the thirteen generations from Io to Herakles standard in the Argive lineage by the midfifth century[447]. It is clear from *Pythian 9* that he is also treating Medea, Euphemos, and Herakles as contemporaries. This too was standard by the fifth century, though in addition it is reasonably clear that Herakles was not an original Argonaut. No matter, it follows that Pindar was placing seventeen generations between the Argonauts voyage (via Medea's remarks on the island of Thera) and the accession of Battos I, the first Theran king of Kyrene. These seventeen generations followed in direct sequence from the preceding thirteen that led from Io to Herakles. This sets Battos I and his companions' arrival at Kyrene from the island of Thera well over the figurative threshold between the between the Heroic Age and historical times[448]. And although Medea describes Battos and company as Kyrene's pre-destined founders, Apollo himself was the city's founding father (*Pyth*.60-62), and indeed, Kyrene had long since been in existence at the time of the accession of Battos I. For the city was there in the age of the Argonauts, and while it necessarily follows that the city was there when the surviving heroes made their way home from Troy, this particular point is explicitly emphasized (*Pyth*.5.74-84). Battos and his compatriots were, therefore, portrayed as the real-life founders of a North African city that was actually founded by Apollo and Kyrene at the beginning of the Heroic Age.

Critical too, is the contrary-to-fact statement that occurs midway into Medea's prophesy. This statement refers to a clod of earth, a token of Libyan hospitality that was handed to Euphemos by the sea god Triton, who appeared as Eurypylos, son of Poseidon[449], at the end of the Libyan leg of the journey[450]. According to Medea, had this clod been protected and had it not, as it happened, disappeared overboard, and had Euphemos deposited it in due course at the entrance to Hades known as Tainaros (in Lakedaimon), his descendants would have claimed Libya in the fourth generation instead of, as things now stand, in the seventeenth. In the fourth generation, again, had this been possible, the foundation of Libya would have coincided with the flight of the "Danaans" from Lakonian territory. And though the point is, emphatically, that this did not occur, the allusion is vital to Pindar's mythography. Using the term "Danaans," Pindar here had in mind the heroic population of the Peloponnese prior to the so-called return of the descendants of Herakles[451]. In this connection, Pindar simultaneously invokes the arrival of a group of marauding Pelasgian refugees on the island of Lemnos. These Pelasgians succeeded in expelling the Minyai, who had long since established themselves on the island in conjunction with the voyage of the *Argo*[452]. When the hostile Pelasgians drove the Minyai out, the Minyai subsequently sought refuge in Sparta. This story is recounted in greater detail in the fourth book of Herodotos' *Histories* (4.145 and 6.136 -140[453]).

A few conspicuous features characterize the tale concerning the expulsion of the *Minyai*, a term by this time synonymous with *Argonautai*, and which, by implication, also invoked a group of old venerable Aiolic heroes. Herodotos' Minyai arrive homeless in Sparta after the designated descendants of Herakles have already successfully established themselves as the ruling family of Lakedaimon[454]. The plea of the Minyai based on kinship ties, is, in this situation, a trifle ironic, seeing that their arrival in Lakadaimon takes place after the Achaians (i.e. the Danaans) of heroic legend have been already thrown out of the country and replaced by Dorians, aka Herakleidai. This radical change in the mythological constituency of the Peloponnese ranks among the most important post-epic innovations devised and promoted by southern Greeks. Due to the predominantly Dorian population of the Peloponnese in the Archaic Period, this legend provided a complete mythic history for this influential Hellenic subgroup, a history which quite typically worked in and around the established tenets of early epic tradition[455].

Mainly, the legend explained how it came to pass that the Dorians replaced the Homeric "Achaians" as rulers of the great Peloponnesian cities, thereby enabling the contemporary Dorians to distinguish themselves from the old epic heroes who were traditionally members of the Aiolic line, and in accordance with that distinction, to claim Achaian tradition, also, as their own[456]. It is evident in this context that the Homeric "Achaians" initially raised a number of problems for the contemporary inhabitants of the Peloponnese, while their semantic affiliates, the epic "Argives," at least outside Argos, were, in a way, even worse. Herodotos, however, explains, nonetheless, that the Dorian/Heraklid rulers of Sparta waxed nostalgic at the thought of Kastor and Polydeukes, the old Achaian participants in the Argonauts' voyage, who were known as the sons of Tyndareos of Sparta[457]. Accordingly, as the story goes, the Spartans gave refuge to the Minyai in honor of Tyndareos' illustrious sons, which as Herodotos also points out was an altogether uncharacteristic accommodation for the Spartans to make and one that they had cause to regret in short order[458].

What followed was that a man named Theras, a descendant of Oidipous via his son Polyneikes, who had allegedly married into the family of the descendants of Herakles[459], was on hand to negotiate a peaceful solution between the arrogant Minyai and the disgruntled Spartans that was also advantageous to himself. His solution involved coaxing the Minyai off Mount Tayetetos and out of the country, to seek their fortunes with him on the island of Kallista, which was henceforth known as the island of Thera[460]. The rehearsal of this story along side Pindar's remarks, yields the following observations. Pindar and Herotodos are both working within a standardized mythological framework that was firmed up by the early fifth century. One of the most striking features of the fifth-century canon (also visible in the *Ehoiai*[461]) is the integration of the story of the *return of the Herakleidai* into the original epic repertoire, since this story exhibits no signs of currency in either the *Iliad* or the *Odyssey*. The most astonishing aspect of the Heraklid story is the way the story shows that it was deemed necessary to force the epic population of the Peloponnese to flee the country in a wave of migrations that played off one another in a domino effect initiated by the seizure and resettlement of the island of Pelops by the descendants of Herakles[462].

Focusing on the relevance of this phenomenon to the international segment of the Argive line, the canonization of the Heraklid story and its reiteration in subsequent authors shows that the first priority of Greek mythic thinking was to create the most plausible alignment between the inherited mythological stories and the avant-garde glosses that redefined that material on behalf of contemporary Greek identity. The coalescence of actual and mythological strands concerning the prehistories of Kyrene and Argos stand out perceptibly against this background. The story of Kyrene and her Lapith heritage seems like the earliest element in the mix. She was a Thessalian heroine, the mother of Aristaios who married Autonoe, a daughter of Kadmos, and fathered Aktaion who was killed by his own dogs[463]. This story was part of the original mythic repertoire, a notion corroborated by the fact that once Apollo's tryst with Kyrene was relocated to North Africa, it was necessary to send their son Aristaios posthaste back to Greece to reunite with his family's prescribed mythic destiny[464].

Subsequently then, the line of Argos in a sense replicated Kyrene's transplantation from the northern Greek heartland to North Africa on a considerably more grandiose scale through the peregrinations of Io. Taking a modest prototype a good deal further, Argive mythology left Kyrene intact, presumably in deference to the story's familiarity, yet one-upped her as well, by staking an even earlier claim that dealt with the genesis of the whole country in which the Greek state of Kyrene was situated, and breaking new ground by having Io's progeny fan out across the civilized world. Thinking in terms of the sequence of composition, it certainly looks like the legendary foundation of Kyrene from Thessaly antedated the development and promotion of the international segment of the Argive line. Such a dating scheme would furthermore coincide with Kyrene's foundation ca. 630, as well as with the extension of the Argive line in conjunction with Argive - Aiginetan relations in the immediately ensuing period.

     Eugammon's testimony tends to suggest that Kyrene itself was perhaps late to acknowledge the mainland Greek legend that was devised to account for the city's Dorian origins, unless he was simply committed to dismissing it, or it did not exist in the early sixth century. Eugammon's manifest interest in the latest and most fashionable Arkadian myths such as the story of the Arkadian Trophonios who robbed Augeias' treasury instead of Hyrieus'[465] seems to suggest that the combined Minyan / Dorian foundation story as understood by Pindar and by Herodotos was not yet current in early sixth-century Kyrene. No doubt, Eugammon's very different account of the genealogical origins of Kyrenean royalty was a transparent political ploy. However, Arkesilaos, son of Odyssseus and Penelope, reflects the standard old-fashioned mode of extending epic tradition into historical times and amounts to a far more rudimentary claim than the complex machinations of the Dorian charter known as the *return of the Herakleidai*.

     In this light, it seems neither necessary nor advisable to attempt to connect the mythic figure Kyrene with the upper reaches of the line of Argos simply on account of Libya's feature role in the Argive genealogy and the fact that Kyrene was located in Libya. A hypothesis of this order was proposed by Martin West, who, based on a Pindaric scholiast's reference to one Childanope, wife of Hypseus, felt that this datum should somehow be attached to the upper reaches of the Argive lineage, where he perceived that Kyrene was disconcertingly missing (West 1985: 85-89[466]). Though perhaps, from a modern perspective, it might seem natural to expect Kyrene and Libya to reside in the same mythological stemma, close examination reveals that this kind of thinking does not harmonize with ancient Greek mythic thinking as expressed in Pindar's victory odes.

     Beyond the ordinary objections to this suggestion, such as the problem that Childanope does not surface either as a daughter of Phoinix or a daughter of Agenor (viz. West's hypothetical recommendations) in the multitude of statements concerning these figures that have survived from the post-epic period (with Phoinix stretching back as far as the *Iliad* 14.321), the point is that this suggestion, though attractive in some ways tests the mythological logic at work. Kyrene's involvement with the line of Kadmos, through the marriage between her son Aristaios and Kadmos' daughter, Autonoe, places Kyrene along side Kadmos toward the beginning of the Heroic Age. In addition, the union of Aristaios and Autonoe is the only available signpost that might anchor Kyrene in mythological time. But when Libya's sons, Belos and Agenor (father and uncle of Danaos, respectively), and indeed Danaos himself, are viewed as participants in an innovative vignette wedged between the genesis of the Argive line and the succeeding heroic era, and designed to incorporate a slew of great foreign families through the insinuation of this sequence of stories above anticipated legendary events, a number of loose ends fall into place. It is clear, for example, that in this location these figures were limited to prefiguring the conditions of the Heroic Age, for they lay out of reach of participating in it (i.e. above it). This limitation was reinforced by the manifest lack of heroic pedigrees available to substantiate most of these figures' existence.

The line of Argos from Io down to Akrisios[467], father of Danae, attested in the *Iliad* and on this count, incontrovertibly old, stands out, once again, as contrived and more recent when the Childanope proposal is seriously considered. On the one hand, this section of the Argive line rendered Kadmos a living contemporary of Danaos, namely his first cousin, once removed. On the other hand, Kadmos and by extension, Kyrene, had no conceivable business being alive at this juncture, which works well as a stretch of primordial time, but fails as an early stretch of the heroic period. Standard heroic chronology would situate Kadmos' migration to Greece round about the time of Akrisios, who was Danae's father, and would situate Kyrene there along side him poised to have her son marry one of his daughters.

Anyone interested in charting the effects of Kadmos' appropriation by the line of Argos, which made him a son of Phoinix, the son of Agenor, in turn, a son of Libya, granddaughter of Io, in contrast to his likely epic portrayal as a son of Phoinix, that is, from a

Phoinician family, will see that the line of Argos has the effect of moving Kadmos up by two generations. Moreover, when he is moved up by two generations, the standard six generations from Kadmos to Troy wind up terminating two generations before the time of Trojan War. Notably, if one abides by the Argive genealogy and also perceives that it would be fitting to situate Kyrene's mother within it, no doubt the most logical way to describe her would be as a daughter of Agenor and a sister of Phoinix so that Kyrene and Kadmos would still align[468]. However, while it is obvious that Pindar acknowledged the genealogy of the Argive line, he was presumably also well aware of the negative side effects that it produced. These, Pindar successfully steered clear of emphasizing by otherwise operating according to a heroic chronology that was unaffected by the modification of the Argive line, as if no such modification existed[469]. Basically, when it came to these kinds of details Pindar preferred to deal in abstractions. In a sense, therefore, it can be said that beyond this new twist in Kadmos' line of descent based on the machinations of the line of Argos, Kadmos, the Phoinician founder of Thebes retained his established legendary integrity to the extent that any listening audience refrained from in-depth lineage calibration, which was apt to reveal the contradiction between his restructured background and his heroic legacy.

So, aside from the fact that Kyrene's abduction from Thessaly had been, it would seem, in circulation since sometime in the late seventh century, and, in and of itself, generated little offense to the architecture of heroic tradition, the introduction of Childanope in order to link Kyrene with the Argive genealogy, would quite unnecessarily attract attention to the very discrepancy Pindar, it seems, was committed to warding off. The insinuation of Childanope therefore registers as the type of emendation that a later redactor might conceivably be inclined to make, but her proposed genealogy does not seem to reflect the coordination of old and new elements first devised in response to the modified Argive line as treated by Pindar and by Herodotos.

Accordingly, Pindar portrayed a personified Libya waiting patiently for an unspecified block of time for the foundation of Kyrene to take place in her midst, although by all indications Libya's characterization postdated Kyrene's immigration to Africa. And accordingly, Pindar portrayed Kyrene as waiting out the entire heroic period, when she hosted a number of heroic visitations, till seventeen generations beyond the Argonauts voyage and well into the normative human era, for the communities of the poet's athletic patrons to be implanted on Kyrenean soil.

Still, a major amendment to the line of Kadmos that facilitated the plot line of Euripides' *Antiope* and looks like it was invented around (if not at) that time bears an uncanny relationship to the case[470]. This mythological strand cleverly reconfigured the old Aiolic story of the heroine Antiope, originally a daughter of the Asopos River (Od. 11.260-265), who mated with Zeus and bore Amphion and Zethos, the twins that built the foundations of the city of Thebes prior to Kadmos' arrival from the East. The fifth-century version of Antiope's life story transformed her sons from the first founders of Thebes into members of a curious and rather forced interregnum inserted smack in the middle of Kadmos' lineage sequence. The well-known mythological connection between the city of Argos and the city Thebes is enough to suggest that this strange interregnum effectively offered due compensation for the underlying two generation discrepancy that resulted from the standardization of the international segment of the Argive line. And though inasmuch as the interregnum itself was wedged into the midst of the heroic era, and was, therefore, bound to create a new set of problems as far as mythic chronology was concerned, seeing that it evened out the line of Thebes in relation to the revised line of Argos, it can at least be said to have established conditions more conducive to the overt designation of an Argive mother for Hypseus' daughter Kyrene[471].

Reviewing the relevant mythological narratives in line with documented external evidence shows that the legendary biographies of Io and Kyrene developed at different places and at different times for fundamentally similar reasons. Moreover, both these biographies rose to command considerable publicity and extremely wide circulation, playing significant roles in a conceptual synthesis that treated them separately, yet simultaneously, emphasizing the way regional mythic innovations could potentially change the face of Greek prehistory. This potential was either realized or it was not, depending on a whole host of external variables that controlled the reception of Greek myths in real life, beginning with relative political authority. On a case-by-case basis, new mythological themes were either accepted or disqualified from staking a place in the revised mythic canon, and likewise, on a case-by-case basis, accepted in some quarters but disqualified in others, or accepted for a period but later supplanted, disqualified but nevertheless remembered, and so on and so forth.

In this context: the underlying idea of an originally Aiolic genealogical template, the broadening of Greek overseas initiatives during the course of the Archaic Period, and the primacy of southern Greek mythic amendments, converge to support the basic claim that the Homeric Danaans were the descendants of Danae, rather than the descendants of Danaos with considerable force and specificity.

THREE GENEALOGIES BY WAY OF EXAMPLE

Fig. 1 Danaos: Stage 1 – Foundation Mythology of the Argive State.

Inachos: typically a son of Okeanos (e.g. Aichylos *Prometheus Bound* 635 -636) / Interesting variant: *Inachos*, son of Oineus (Hesiodic Corpus – unknown location, Hes fr 122 MW).

Inachos -> Phoroneus... Niobe (Akousilaos, the epic *Phoronis*) ...Peiren -> Io (*Ehoiai*).

Inachos -> Phoroneus -> Niobe + Zeus -> Argos -> Iasos -> Io. (Apollodoros).

Fig. 2 Danaos: Stage 2 – International Version of the Descendants of Io.

Io + Zeus -> Epaphos + ? -> Libya + Poseidon -> Belos & Agenor.

Belos + ? -> Danaos & Aigyptos & Thronie & Damno.

Danaos (+ Melia via Pherekydes) -> 50 daughters Aigyptos (+ Isaie via Pherekydes) -> 50 sons.

Thronie + Hermes -> Arabos via Pherekydes + ? -> Kassiepeia + Phoinix-> Phineus / Phoinix + Alphesiboia -> Adonis (via Ehoiai).

Agenor + Damno (1) -> Phoinix & Melia & Isaie / Agenor + Argiope (2) = Kadmos (& Europa?) via Pherekydes.

Agenor -> Phoinix + Kassiepeia (1) ->Europa (& Kadmos) & Phineus/ Phoinix + Alphesiboia (2) -> Adonis (via Ehoiai) In Homer, however, in the *Ehoiai*, in a Homeric scholion, and in Bakchylides: Phoinix -> Europa / Kadmos ?/ Phineus?

Whereas in Apollodoros and Hyginus as in Pherekydes: Agenor is the father of Kadmos & Europa and Phoinix, additionally, earlier on, Phoinix was the father certainly of Europa, and, presumably, of Kadmos too.

Fig.3 Danaos: 13 generations from Io to Herakles.

Io -> Epaphos -> Libya -> Belos -> Danaos -> Hypermestra -> Abas -> Akrisios -> Danae -> Perseus -> Electryon -> Alkmene -> Herakles.

EXAMPLE TWO: THE DAUGHTERS OF ATLAS

The case of the Pleiades or the daughters of Atlas mirrors Danaos' case as a mythological novelty that brilliantly reconfigured earlier legends along with their genealogical corollaries. As preliminarily referenced above, the dominant stories concerning these figures include indications of their manufacture for contemporary ideological purposes with special emphasis on the likelihood that their initial development stemmed back to Sparta[472]. Concerning the earliest association between the daughters of Atlas and the Pleiades, the question has been raised as to whether the star cluster that Hesiod identified as a sign of the right time to reap and the right time to sow (*W&D* 382-383), was, in addition, understood by the poet to represent the daughters of the Titan god Atlas, particularly in the way they later came to be known (Gantz 1993: 212ff.).

There was, in any case, an old legend that told of an impassioned Orion[473] pursuing these women through the hills of Boiotia, till a merciful Zeus turned them into stars[474]. They were admired thereafter as the constellation the Pleiades. This story, however, stands in contradiction to a subsequent portrait of the daughters of Atlas that featured seven distinct alter egos (viz. Maia, Sterope, Alkyone, Kelaino, Taugete, Electra, and Merope): six who mated with gods, and one with a mortal, to the tune of producing six heroic lines[475]. Orion's early quarry were unnamed and generic, and made it into the heavens as numinous *parthenai*, while the daughters of Atlas, in their popular incarnation, were seven distinguished primordial women, who played a part in seven distinguished seductions and bore a slew of distinguished mythical progeny.

The sorority known as the daughters of Atlas is generally viewed as a synthetic development on account of the geographical strain involved in uniting an assortment of heroines who hailed from distant geographical regions altogether into one family (Gantz 1993: 213; West 1985: 136). Geopolitically speaking, the daughters of Asopos also present a similar problem[476]. Indeed, taking stock of both sets of daughters suggests that these two female collectivities were major instruments of mythological change. The oddest thing about the daughters of Atlas is that though they were in some sense synonymous with the Pleiades, the only known story concerning the Pleiades makes such an association absurd. The Pleiades were catastericized virgins, the daughters of Atlas were prolific child bearers. Yet the formula, Pleiades aka the Atlantids, was evidently proverbial nevertheless. Was this merely symptomatic of mythological culture or linked to some more pragmatic initiative?

Well aware of an identity metamorphosis at some point on the lifeline of the daughters of Atlas, Timothy Gantz experiments with the notion that the Pleiades might not, in the beginning, have been thought of as daughters of Atlas at all, and might, for that matter, have been simply stars without also being mythological figures (certainly a viable possibility). Along these lines he speculates that the term *Atlageneis,* as it appears in Hesiod's *Works and Days* (383), might have first been a geographical reference, having nothing to do with the Pleiades' paternity, yet mistaken as such as time wore on[477]. Therefore, once the association was made, linking the Pleiades with the daughters of Atlas, the second title, the Pleiades, needed an explanation. And because manifestly it was not a patronym, although originally it could have been, the idea developed that it was a matronym. Hence the daughters of Atlas likewise became the daughters of Pleione (daughter of Okeanos), furnishing a fine source for their collective title[478].

So while it is possible to detect explanations arising from the mythological connection between the Pleiades and the Titan god Atlas, it is also clear that this early connection was oblivious to the characterization of the daughters of Atlas famous by the fifth century[479]. It was, moreover, precisely this old and intimate link that posed the thorniest obstacle to redactors interested in promoting an all-new depiction of this once generic group of female Titan offspring whose metamorphosis yielded the Pleiades star cluster. Mainly, if not for this well-known early mythic equivalency, no identity conflict would have ensued when the daughters of Atlas were recast as new characters and placed at the head of seven prestigious lines. Yet the daughters of Atlas in this latter persona did not, it seems, altogether suppress the influence of their discarded identity wherein they were associated with the Pleiades by way of an entirely different story. This tension sheds some light on the order of things. Dissonance seems dependent on precedent, here, for in the absence of precedent the daughters of Atlas would not have wound up at odds with themselves, straddling two distinct mythic identities.

Both Homer and Hesiod acknowledged the Pleiades[480], but were they merely stars or were they daughters of Atlas? Not too unreasonably, it could well be the case that the term Atlageneis, meant precisely Atlageneis, which works well with Hesiod's further remark, that at the time when the Pleiades are seen fleeing Orion, it is best to haul your ship out of the sea for the season (W&D 618-629): a comment that suggests mythological roots[481]. Another salient factor that colors these brief remarks zeros in on the logic inherent within the conceptual structure of Hesiod's *Theogony*[482], and also, more generally, in this regard, on the early epic delineation of the structure and function of the Heroic Age[483]. For Atlas' daughters' fate in the Orion story, namely, becoming the Pleiades without so much as bearing a single child was particularly fitting to their Titan heritage as depicted by Hesiod in his *Theogony*. Traditionally, Titan deities, it is to be noted, played no part in the genesis of the world population after the dawn of the Olympian era, though they were not only the ancestors of the Olympians themselves, but responsible for an astounding combination of natural, abstract, and legendary elements that together invoked the empirical world (or a recognizably familiar version of it[484]). The main challenge to Zeus in consolidating his power was to subdue any wayward remnants of superior primordial strength, through a mixture of diplomacy, reverence, and brute force[485], while the divine procreation of heroic lines was, by that time, the special prerogative of the Olympian rulers of the world[486].

But then again, there were two daughters of Atlas attested in the *Odyssey* and the *Theogony*, who seem to stand apart from any such group. The first of these was Maia, mother by Zeus of the god Hermes, the immortal messenger of the Olympian gods (Th.9.38; HHymns 4, 18 to *Hermes*). The second was Kalypso, the beguiling "dread goddess[487]" who detained Odysseus on her remote island kingdom for seven years, greatly delaying his return home from Troy (Od.7.244ff.). The last lines of the *Theogony* attribute two obscure offspring to Odysseus and Kalypso[488]. The goddess Kalypso in Hesiod though, is not a daughter of Atlas at all, but rather a daughter of Okeanos (Th.359[489]), while the Titaness Maia's conception of Hermes occurs after Zeus' defeat of his Titanic rivals, in conjunction with his sexual pacification of autonomous, immortal, feminine forces (Th. 881ff.). If, then, the Atlantid Pleiades pursued by Orion were a contemporary mythological sideline, acknowledged and at large, along with these two goddesses, these two goddesses, notably, stood apart from their sisters, one on her own island, the other in her own cave. And while the former was excluded from the ranks of the sorority that, in due course, achieved great acclaim, the latter looks like that acclaimed sorority's one and only early bona fide member. A few further factors illuminate the disjunction between the Titan god Atlas' earliest daughters and the later collectivity that took charge of the title. Once again the desire for mythological change inspired by contemporary political realities left certain discernable tracks in its wake. In this instance one of the ways that such tracks are perceptible is the second Atlantid sisterhood's overt defiance of certain early cosmological principles.

Kalypso's union with Odysseus - a mortal hero - differs from Maia's union with Zeus, because according to standard Greek mythic custom, a goddess, in general, regardless of her origins, would bear a mortal in union with a mortal, but bear a god in union with a god. One basic maxim accordingly runs that sexual interaction between goddesses and mortals, just like such interaction initiated by gods, was bound to generate mortals, not gods. This maxim is taken for granted in early Greek epic poetry and it is in every way vital to Greek genealogy, since it governed the perceived hereditary relationship between humanity and the gods through the intercession of the Greek heroes (οἱ ἡμίθεοι), who were literally part human and part god. The second basic maxim accordingly runs that two gods together were bound to generate gods, which is readily identified as a guiding principle in Hesiod's account of the birth of the cosmos[490]. A notably a striking exception to this equation occurs in the line of Phorkys and Keto (Th.270-335)[491], which was specifically devoted to the generation of monsters. These monsters, though the products of divine generation were, for the most part, defined as mortal beings[492]. In context, this was obviously the case so the great mortal heroes could eventually kill them. They were, in this sense, created to be destroyed. Taking this observation a step further, the line of Phorkys and Keto demonstrates that mortality could be arbitrarily assigned to a specific subset of semi-numinous beings. This is certainly something to bear in mind.

That as a general rule, Maia's union with Zeus would be expected to generate further deities is amply attested in Hermes' case[493]. And though Hermes allegiance to the Olympian order is linked to his conception by Zeus, on the one hand, as well as to his birth into Zeus' established dominion, it is clear, overall, that the Greek cosmic system left the door open to the potential overthrow of its supreme ruler for some obscure period of mythological time following Zeus' official enthronement and during the period when his reign was still new[494].

Therefore, in accordance with Hesiod's cosmic patterning Maia and/or Kalypso in union with other deities[495] would presumably engender deities once again, while as immortals of the generation prior to Zeus, the offspring of such goddesses (more so than the offspring of less ancient mates) would embody within them the latent potential to upend the sovereignty of the ruling king[496]. Yet no such threat was involved when it came to a tryst between such a goddess and a mortal man, which leaves Kalypso and Odysseus in a separate category: one match in a cast of innumerable others, characteristic of the Heroic Age, excluding the anomaly of Kalypso's Titan origins. Both the birth of Hermes to Maia and Zeus, and Kalypso's infatuation with Odysseus, harmonize well enough with the genealogical structure and the distribution of power in Hesiod's cosmos. The point is that by contrast, it may be maintained that the Pleiades in their second incarnation, namely the group of six (excluding Maia) that became forebears of major heroic lines[497], do not harmonize on a conceptual basis either with the suppression of Titan authority that accompanied the establishment of the kingdom of Zeus[498], or with standard Greek principles of cosmo-genesis operative in *Theogony* and in the Homeric poems[499]. If so, this suggests another telltale sign (in addition to geographical range) of later archaic mythic redaction.

The main problem with the Atlantid sisterhood is that it maintains against standard tradition that sexual relations between Olympian deities and the female descendants of the Titan god Atlas is an acceptable formula for the institution of mortal heroic genealogical lines. No doubt, applying the two formulas mentioned thus far, namely, god + god = god and god + mortal = mortal, leaves the origin of humanity entirely unaddressed, but this is just how things stand in Hesiod's texts, though they consistently presuppose human existence[500]. Moreover, Hesiod's cosmos itself conveys a serious need for human activity on at least two counts: first, to terminate the perpetual creation of gods, and second, to fulfill the important condition that a world ruled by deities entails live mortal subjects.

Seeing that the whole quandary about human genesis is limited in its relevance to the Atlantid problem, just a few brief remarks will be made on the subject[501]. Mainly here it suffices to show that the later archaic Atlantid genealogy, first perceptible in the Hesiodic *Ehoiai*, and generally standard from that time onward, was anomalous in its generation of mortals from the sexual union of powerful deities.

Hesiod gives no recipe for humanity either in the *Theogony* or in the *Works and Days*. Yet the poet acknowledges human existence at least from the reign of Kronos onward. At the beginning of his parable on the *Ages of Man* the poet implies that his aim in presenting this story is to explain how it was that Greek men and Greek gods were related by descent (*W&D* 105- 201)[502]. Yet reaching the end of the whole *Ages* passage, the modern reader is apt to feel more confused than enlightened as to the poet's meaning or his use of metaphor, and especially, as to his satisfaction at having addressed the ponderous issue that he invoked at the start of the passage[503]. The bottom line is that no clear solution concerning the materialization of the demigods is forthcoming in this passage on the ages of man, or anywhere else in Hesiod's poems. Here, the race of bronze men simply kill themselves off, just as the gold race and the race of silver had been permanently dispensed with before them[504]. Next, Zeus made the heroes and that is that.

Was it then that he made them by a wave of his hand? Or was it by way of a thought or by way of an utterance? This is all pretty much any spectator's guess. These heroes, however, are clearly the linchpin with respect to the poet's whole *Ages* discourse, for they are the bridge between humanity and divinity that informs the identity of the poet and his peers (*W&D* 299). The phrase, Zeus made the heroes, is the crux of the matter[505]. And though Hephaistos made Pandora out of a slab of clay (*Th.* 571), and Zeus made the bronze warriors ostensibly out of ash trees (*W&D* 145), if Zeus, in fact, made the heroes in some similar fashion no valid blood line of descent would exist between the Greek divinities and the Greek heroes, and between the Greek heroes and contemporary Greeks[506].

On this count, it may be worth considering whether the poet was not simply playing with his audience concerning a matter well-known to one and all. Given a ubiquitous body of cultural knowledge, a professional poet, it stands to reason, could well afford to indulge in perceptual games, twisting and toying with information that virtually everyone took for granted. That this prospect is more than a mere flight of fancy can be substantiated by other occasions where poetic omissions also correspond with mythological knowledge elusive to us, but at the same time transparent to ancient Greek audiences[507]. This type of mythological sleuth work, though necessarily often driven by *argumenta ex silento*, is as unavoidable as it is indispensable to any competent simulation of the world of Greek myth. It is, for example, precisely the type of Greek mythic cross-referencing that has successfully illuminated the organic connection between the plot structure of the Homeric epics and the legendary content of the *Epic Cycle*. Such cross-referential or neo-analysis (ie. motivforschung) has, at the very least, established incontrovertibly that Homeric poetry drew on a much greater body of legendary material that professional bards essentially took for granted, summoning up elaborate mythological episodes via semi-cryptic remarks that dealt with aspects of the greater corpus[508]. The practice was not unique either to Homer or to Hesiod[509].

To cite an example from Hesiod's *Theogony*, the poet offers a list of fifty Nereids[510] at the beginning of the poem. He does not take his account of them any further, although one in particular, the sea goddess Thetis can hardly be considered an accidental omission, or a figure whose life story the poet was unaware of. Thus Hesiod sets the stage, but subsequently omits the story of Nereus' most famous daughter, namely Achilles' mother, the sea goddess Thetis. In the imminent future, from the *Theogony's* standpoint, it would be predicted that the Nereid Thetis was liable to bear a son capable of robbing Zeus of his kingship[511]. Though wildly attracted to this particular goddess (a feeling also shared by Zeus' brother, Poseidon[512]), getting wind of the oracle concerning his downfall, Zeus countered his passion (Poseidon followed suit) and resolved the whole problem by forcing Thetis to marry a mortal man: Peleus, son of Aiakos, a Thessalian king[513].

Along similar lines, the suggestion here is that early Greek myth tacitly utilized a rudimentary formula that everyone knew and therefore nobody stated, to account for the origin of the demigods. This formula understood them as diluted divinities, arising from a vast multitude of extraordinarily long-lived, yet not quite immortal, female nature spirits[514], who united with local rivers or with Olympian divinities under the aegis of Olympian Zeus. On this analysis, when Hesiod says that Zeus made the heroes, he is speaking of Zeus as ruler and procreator, and he is citing only a part of a broader scenario and letting it stand in place of the whole.

This conceptual basis for the genesis of humanity is well supported throughout Greek literature generally. In the *Iliad*, for example, there are certainly plenty of Nymphai at large available to mate with assorted heroes, just as the daughters of kings mate with river deities[515]. These couplings, of course, simply beg the same question as to the primeval source of differentiation between immortal and mortal beings. The crux of the matter is clearly the need for a formulaic reduction of divine power sufficient to produce not gods but demigods. Inasmuch as the *Odyssey* describes the Nymphai specifically as the daughters of Zeus[516] (a premise echoed by Alkaios and Pherekydes[517]), one cannot go much further than to surmise an operative formula comparable to Zeus' spate of Titan / Okeanid matings listed at the denouement of the *Theogony* with a notable variety of results. Nonetheless, exact knowledge of the formula deemed responsible for the genesis of the Nymphai is for the most part inconsequential[518]. The critical issue is the Nymphai themselves, and their ubiquitous presence in the heroic landscape[519]. For once they had their Nymphai, the Greeks had their demigods. They had arrived at their concept of themselves.

Thus, via some prescribed reduction in numinous strength assigned to this ancient race of female beings, genealogical continuity was effectively realized. Bridging the gap between endless and finite existence, the Nymphai embodied the missing link that obscures the

Greek recipe for humanity. In this sense, they essentially stand behind heroic genealogy in its totality, spawning the original Aiolic line and all of its contemporary legendary affiliates, just as they later sparked off the indigenous lines devised to dismantle early Aiolic authority[520]. In this respect the formula nymph + Olympian deity was the ultimate genealogical source.

Returning to the sorority of the daughters of Atlas, the point here is that their synthetic nature is more fully substantiated by a close look at the underlying genealogical principles that consistently informed the earliest strata of ancient Greek mythological thinking. Their alleged generation of major heroic lines, even though they were Titan goddesses and took gods as their partners, is a phenomenon that stands in violation of early Greek mythological protocol. The god Dionysos, to cite another example, of a similar, though not quite comparable, deviation, was conversely a god held to have arisen from the union of Zeus and Semele, the mortal daughter of King Kadmos of Thebes. The two cases are parallel as reverse deviations[521], but they are not exceptions of the same kind. The god Dionysos possessed an antique pedigree[522]. His very existence at once critiqued and upheld the archaic genealogical system. Dionysos thrived in the role of the god, who, small wonder, people didn't believe in, to their inevitably violent and fatal demise[523]. No such pedigree testifies to the antiquity of the daughters of Atlas as they came to be known. Quite unlike Dionysos, the daughters of Atlas are not the type of exception that proves the rule, but they are rather the type of exception that shows that the rules have begun to unravel[524].

Along the same lines, a strong case can be made that the genealogical roles ultimately awarded to Atlas' Titan brethren, Prometheus and Epimetheus, were also innovations developed between Hesiod's *Theogony* and the *Catalogue of Women*. In the *Theogony* and the *Works and Days* these two get top billing in the story that pits the will of Zeus against all other interests with special emphasis on the earthly fate of mankind. Yet their role in the poems is basically allegorical and not genealogical in any standard sense[525]. Prometheus' actions lead to his punishment, which renders him effectively out of commission like the notorious members of the rest of his family (*Th.* 507-534; M. West 1966: 313-315). Epimetheus, who, first off, may be regarded as a clever invention of the poet himself[526] simply embodied the meaning of his name. He functions semantically as the designated recipient of the deceptively beautiful woman, Pandora, the product of divine workmanship and conspiracy. Thus, Epimetheus wholeheartedly accepts Pandora in spite of Prometheus' ominous warnings against an anticipated gift from the gods. This skillfully orchestrated etiological error heralds the dawning of a new era, when men cannot rest assured of the virtue of women but must forever stand guard against beautiful women invisibly ridden with ruinous traits[527]. If this is held to imply a genealogical stemma it is far from the ordinary heroic type. Moreover, in context, it functions far more straightforwardly as a simple *aitia* devoted to the genesis of the type of woman that Hesiod feared and disdained. By the later Archaic Period, in any event, Prometheus and Epimetheus had been transformed into celebrated progenitors of the Hellenic race[528].

This leads to one further systemic justification for a skeptical reading of the daughters of Atlas in their developed second persona: namely, the genealogically structured portrayal of the Titan family of Iapetos. Of the genealogical family portraits that constitute Hesiod's theogonic poem, with the single exception of the line of Phorkys and Keto [529] devoted as it was to a great brood of monsters, Iapetos and family are unique inasmuch as each family member in some way fits the image of antagonistic malefactor inimical to the dominion of Zeus. This consistent characterization is particularly striking given the often arbitrary distribution of attributes among even the closest family members in Hesiod's genealogical landscape. There is nothing intuitive, for example, about the fact that the 100-handers, the Cyclops, and the Titans are siblings, or the Graiai and the Gorgons, to name a comparable instance[530]. The poet's narrative states it and his narrative makes it so. Moreover, the primary interest of the poem was the dispensation of divine honors toward an ordered hierarchy of cosmic powers, specifically, in relation to the ascension of Zeus whose quest to vanquish and propitiate preexistent forces potentially greater or equal to himself is vital to the establishment of equilibrium. This progression is at once portrayed as the fulfillment of a prescribed destiny and an eventuality still subject to the prospect of unforeseen intervention.

In this light, the creation of a spate of free agents arising from the bloodline of Iapetos and sons is a notion that is more than a little at odds with the overall emphasis of the poem. The innately arrogant tendencies attached to this lineage combined with the specter of its Titan heritage was not an admixture conducive in context to a batch of new progeny from this line. This judgment accords well with the general observation, that excluding later genealogical tangents and the potential exception awarded early on to offspring in the line of Hyperion and Theia[531], the role of the Titans was restricted by design to extinguish their influence as independent progenitors. Indeed, their awesome potential as autonomous agents was synonymous with a vision of extreme cosmic crisis, hence their imprisonment in perpetuity, either on earth, or in the dark depths of Tartaros, that scarcely fathomable underground penitentiary that arose out of *Chaos* ostensibly to contain them. Viewed from this perspective, Hesiod's *Theogony* provides an indispensable gauge for the evaluation of the later Atlantid stemma. The verdict as to its novelty is concretely upheld.

The daughters of Atlas in their second persona reveal that the demand for mythological change was greater than the demand for conceptual adherence to established mythological principles. Like other such deviations that later became popular venues for genealogical change, the abandonment of the story that defined the Pleiades as a generic group of Titan progeny whose ephemeral period of existence on earth was memorialized through their transfer into the starry heavens signals a pressing need to redefine these figures so they could serve far more pragmatic purposes. Accordingly, an established genealogical *telos* was annulled and revitalized as a genealogical opening that aptly facilitated the political interests of a number of leading mainland Greek states seeking illustrious origins for their regional prehistories. In these terms, the latter day Atlantid stemma exemplifies the intrinsic manipulative power of an upper-lineage insert seven women in breadth designed to supersede prior hereditary sources and to redistribute the heroic descendants freed up by these previous sources' eclipse.

MYTHIC THEFT TYPE THREE

THE DAUGHTERS OF ATLAS

1. Maia + Zeus = Hermes

2. Sterope + Ares + Oinomaos

3. Kelaino + Poseidon = Lykos

4. Merope + Sisyphos = Glaukos. Glaukos + Mestra (of Erysichthon <- of Triopas <- of Kanake <- of Aiolos) = Eurypylos of Kos. Eurypylos + Koan Woman = Chalkon / Antigores. Glaukos + Eurynome (of Nisos) = Bellerophontes. Bellerophontes + Philonoe (of Iobates of Lykia) = Isandros / Laodameia / Hippolochos. Laodameia + Zeus = Sarpedon. Hippolochos + Lykian Woman = Glaukos.

5. Alkyone + Poseidon = Hyrieus / Hyperes / Anthas. Hyrieus + ? = Orion / Krinakos / Nykteus / Lykos. Krinakos + ? = Makar of Lesbos. Nykteus + ? = Antiope. Antiope + Zeus = Amphion / Zethos. Antiope + Epopeus (of Kanake <- of Aiolos). Hyperes + ? = Arethousa + Poseidon = Abas. Abas + ? = Chalkodon. Chalkodon + ? = Elephenor.

6. The Line of Sparta.
Taygete + Zeus = Lakedaimon. Lakedaimon + ? = Amyklas / Eurydike. Eurydike + Akrisios (of the "Argive" Abas). Amyklas + ? = Hyakinthos / Kynortas. Kynortas + ? Oibalos. Oibalos + Gorgophone (of Perseus) = Ikarios / Tyndareos / Hippokoon.

7. The Line of Troy.
Elektra + Zeus = Eetion / Dardanos. Dardanos + ? = Ilos / Erichthonios. Erichthonios + ? = Tros. Tros + ? = Ganymedes / Assarakos / Ilos. Assarakos + ? = Kapys. Kapys + ? = Anchises. Anchises + Aphrodite = Aineias. Ilos + ? = Laomedon. Laomedon + ? = Tithonos / Priam. Priam + Hekabe = Hektor / Paris / Kassandra etc.

[352] This topic is addressed further in chapters 4 and 5.

[353] The original meaning of *Hellas* and *Hellenes* and the curious matter of their transformation from regionally circumscribed designations to the signification of Greece and all Greeks is also addressed in greater detail in chapters 4 and 5 below. The earliest use of the word *pan-Hellenes* occurs in the *Iliad* and Hesiod's *Works and Days* (Il.2.530; W&D 526-528). The term in both instances seems reflect the regional definition that was derived from the Central Greek province known as Hellas (there are, in addition, different opinions on the early extent of the district called *Hellas*). By the time of Alkman, however, the transformation begins to materialize, since it is clear, in context, that Greece as a whole has started to replace the limited prior meaning (fr 77 PMG; cf. Hes fr 130 MW). For a diachronic account of the relevant sources that illustrate the development of these terms, see J.M. Hall 2002: 125-134; On the "great puzzle" of "how the name of a small tribe in north central Greece came to be applied to all of the inhabitants of the peninsula," see R. Fowler, 1998.

[354] The updated definitions described the Dorian *Argives* of the province of *Argos* and the descendants of the Homeric *Achaians*, who were held to inhabit the province of *Achaia* in the period that bled into historical times (e.g. Hdt.1.145; Strabo e.g. 5.495, 8.1.2, 8.6.10, 8.7.1; Paus. 7.1.5). In this capacity, the *Achaians* of *Achaia* signified the surviving remnants of the venerated heroic population that the Dorians and Heraklids reputedly forced from power and confined to the north coast of the Peloponnese. This region was thereafter known as *Achaia* in commemoration of these events, which also imbued the term with a sense of continuity. Continuity, however, did not likewise apply to the meaning of the word "Argives" in common parlance, since the term *Argives* came to denote the post-Achaian (viz. Dorian) inhabitants of the Argolid, explaining the bifurcation of the two terms. The reasons for concluding that this nexus of stories represent a major mythic addendum created and spliced onto early epic tradition by the inhabitants of the Peloponnese are addressed more extensively in Part 2, below. In the meantime, the point is that these citations and others express the conditions according to which the designation *Achaians* continued to signify all the great protagonists of early Greek legend (viz. those who lived prior to the return of the descendants of Herakles and their Dorian allies). Notably, Strabo states specifically that the heroic *Achaians* were an *Aiolic* tribe (8.1.2), an equation that is worthy of special emphasis in terms of the thrust of the present report, but also in light of M. Finkelberg's publications that persistently equate the Homeric *Achaians* with the *Mykenaians* of the Bronze Age (M. Finkelberg 2003, 2005, reviving an otherwise waning trend). That the Greeks of the historical period were meaningfully acquainted with the Bronze Age Mykenaians is by no means a foregone conclusion. Powerful arguments to this effect have been put forth by such scholars as M.I. Finley, A. Snodgrass, I. Morris and W. Burkert to name a few (so also J. Bennet covering the Bronze Age in the *New Companion to Homer* 1997: 532). By default the present thesis asks its readers to judge which of these two equations the evidence best supports: the traditional Achaian-Aiolian correspondence or the Achaian-Mykenaian theoretical equivalency.

[355] viz. Io, daughter of Inachos, abducted by Zeus and persecuted by Hera. Transformed into a cow and pursued by a gadfly across Asia, and finally, into Egypt. At last, restored by Zeus to her original human form she perpetuated the lineage of her native Argos. See, for example, Aeschylos' *Prometheus Bound*: 561-886; Hdt. 1.1-5.

[356] e.g. Strabo 8.6.9.

[357] M. West among others also considers Danae the eponymous ancestor of the Danaans in a no contest comparison with Danaos (1985: 144-145). On the precedence of Danae, see also, M. Nilsson 1932: 42, following E. Meyer, *Forschungen zur alten Geschichte*, vol. 1, 1892.

[358] Moreover, in noting the exceptional length of the line of Argos (viz. the line of Inachos) West notes that in terms of lateral extension "there is nothing to match the breadth of Aiolos' family," cf. R. Fowler 1998: 8.

[359] 1. Io + Zeus -> 2. Epaphos -> 3. Libya + Poseidon -> 4. Agenor/Belos -> **Belos** -> 5. Aigyptos/Danaos -> 6. 50 sons/ 50 daughters including Lynkeus + Hypermestra -> 7. Abas -> 8. Akrisios/Proitos -> **Akrisios** -> 9. Danae + Zeus -> 10. Perseus + Andromeda -> 11. Sthenelos/Alkaios/Elektryon. **Alkaios** -> Amphitryon/ **Elektryon** -> 12. Alkmene + Amphitryon -> 13. Herakles.

[360] This pattern is most evident in Pausanias and may be witnessed at random for any given locality.

[361] The *Iliad*'s Nestor (Il,1.246-252) provides a paradigmatic example of demigods who enjoyed extraordinary long life spans. B. Fenik called attention the same trait in the characterization of Idomeneus of Krete (1968: 137). These are notably also the shortest stemmata in the early heroic repertoire. The phenomenon itself is even more explicit in the genealogical saga of the Biblical *Genesis* vis-à-vis the comparative length of ante vs. post-deluvium life spans. The length of post-diluvian life spans, however, still situate the initial post-deluvian period well within the bounds of the *Heroic Age* (viz. prior to onset of lived reality). On Nestor as a vehicle for the invocation of significant past time mythic events, cf. F. Graf 1993: 63.

[362] Following M. West's analysis of the phrase as a signal of resumption and/or sequential shift as the text turned to address a collateral lineage after concluding a progression within the same stemma (West 1985 31-39).

[363] F. Leo. 1894 *Hesiodea*. Göttingen: *Ausgewählte kleine Schriften* 11 1960: 343-363.

[364] fr 135 MW; Pind.*Pyth* 9; I.M. Cohen argues that the Μεγάλαι Ἠοῖαι was simply another addition of the same poem (*Phoenix* 40.2 1986: 127-142; cf. A. Casanova 1979). Reinforcing Martin West's original interpretation, G. Battista D'Alessio once again concludes that this text was an independent example of the same genre (in R. Hunter, ed. 2005).

[365] e.g. Hdt. 2.53.

[366] Subsequently, the genealogical genre was taken over by the prose historians, who thereafter became the authoritative purveyors of contemporary genealogical trends. See I. Rutherford in Depew & Obbink, eds. 2000, on the evidence that such catalogues deserve to be considered representative of a very early genre and were recited orally before committed to writing.

[367] A more casual source of information on the genealogies of the major Greek heroes was the customary identification of individuals with reference to their paternal lineage in addition to their given names. This traditional nomenclature likewise provoked audience familiarity with established heroic pedigrees. On lineage boasting, see M. Lang *CQ* 44.1 1994.

368 The genealogical structure of Hesiod's *Theogony* is a superlative example of symbolic representation based on a lineage-driven hierarchy. The birth of the gods and the dispensation their respective prerogatives is in this text symbolically linked to simultaneous progress from primordial chaos to the Olympian *status quo*, which is to say, toward the cosmic balance understood to exist in contemporary times. By incorporating the notion of processual movement from the primitive to the civilized world and documenting this movement genealogically in relation to the ascension of Zeus, the narrative format of the birth of the cosmos can be said to surpass the genealogical depiction of the Heroic Age in terms of the magnitude of its symbolic content. The reason for this is essentially that the heroes were all together one type of being and existed in the same phase of cosmic development, on which basis they were fundamentally equals, except for the fact that divine blood was unequally distributed among them. The genealogical depiction of the *Heroic Age*, therefore, ceases to exploit the hierarchical potential of symbolic genealogy to its full extent. These observations notably coincide with comparative data from the Near East (particularly the Mesopotamian theogonies e.g. *Enuma Elish*) to suggest that the genealogical paradigm was first deployed in cosmopolitan polytheistic contexts to describe the emergence of different national pantheons, out of primordial forces, at the beginning of time, to the point of epiphany in cultural present. Like the Greek interpretation of this paradigm, the Hebrew interpretation was also adapted to suit specific cultural priorities (as was likewise the case on other Near Eastern contexts). So, in *Genesis*, for example, the hierarchical potential of genealogical symbolism is, once again, fully exploited, though in this case transferred to the early human era, to map out the supremacy of God's chosen people in relation to neighboring ethnic groups. The Greek claim to uniqueness in this milieu seems to be twofold. First, the use of the genealogical paradigm not just into the early *Heroic Age*, but throughout the entire length and breadth of it (viz. down to the first few post Trojan War generations) and including all constituent genealogical branches, which were, at any rate, exclusively Greek (excluding a few celebrated immigrant lines). And secondly, the deployment of human descent from great national deities (needless to say, abandoned in the Hebrew charter, excluding the famous passage in *Genesis* 6) to underwrite the ancestry of all Greeks (or at a minimum, all Greek elites), instead of restricting divine lineage claims to the ancestral right of kings. As far as I can tell, these were the defining factors of the Greek mythological system, which was conceptually based on a genealogical continuum between the Greeks and the Greek gods. The profound significance of this connection makes it difficult to agree with James Whitley's assessment (in N. Spencer, ed. 1995) that "the Greek past was discontinuous (p58 based on Hesiod *W&D* 106-201 viz. *The Ages of Man*)," and that "some heroes could be ancestors, but not all ancestors were heroes and not all heroes were ancestors (p.53, however, see R.K. Hack 1929)." On the contrary, the Greek past was above all continuous and unfolded as a structured diachronic continuum based on the underlying principle that the heroes were at once descendants of gods and the ancestors of ordinary human beings. Whitley's remarks must be understood as part of the reaction to J.N. Coldstream's proposal (1976) that the archaic Greek hero cults developed in response to early Greek epic poetry, (cf. C. Antonaccio 1995). Coldstream's proposal became a contentious issue when further archaeological findings illuminated the worship of individuals with no explicit heroic (viz. legendary) connections. Accordingly, from an archaeological standpoint, the interpretive use of the term *hero* opened up a much larger semantic field and came to require greater specificity. For such specificity cf. I. Morris 1988: 752-755. In the present analysis, the heroes addressed are strictly synonymous with the Greek demigods.

369 In this regard it is important to note the indispensable role of descriptive narrative in creating symbolic genealogical hierarchies. Thus, for example, in the Greek cosmic setting, there is nothing intuitive in the genealogical formula that describes the Titans, the Kyklopes, and one-hundred-handers as siblings (ditto the Graiai and the Gorgons, let alone the idea of two immortal and one mortal Gorgon). Narrative exclusively makes it so. For this reason it is appropriate to characterize the relationship between early epic narratives and genealogy as a mutually interdependent symbiosis.

370 For an alternate explanation that includes certain recent suggestions of others, once again, see I. Rutherford in Depew & Obbink eds. 2000. Curiously, Rutherford's analysis is based on the idea that at a previous point in time, the catalogues of great heroic women had an "aretological," not a genealogical function.

371 This much by general consensus, cf. H. Fränkel 1973: 108-109; R. Hamilton 1989: 14-15.

372 Following the poet's statements concerning his subject matter (viz. *Th.* 29-35, 104-105), H.T. Wade-Gerry concludes that the poem was restricted to the treatment of the immortals (1958: 9).

373 On alternative cosmologies in circulation, see, M.L. West, *The Orphic Poems,* Oxford 1983; H.S. Schibli, *Pherekydes of Syros* Oxford 1990.

374 Lower, numerically, in terms of dating on a time line.

375 viz. R. Janko, *Homer, Hesiod and the Hymns: Diachronic Development in Epic Diction*, Cambridge 1982.

376 For commentary on this issue, I. Rutherford 2000: 82; P-J Shaw 2003: 126-127.

377 By compilation I refer here to the combined Dorian and Ionian contributions to the overall tribal migration sequence (fr 10a OCT). The latter very persuasively seems to have been tacked onto the premises of the former under Athenian creative influence. This point is argued below in chs. 4 and 5.

378 viz. divine/mortal unions engaged different male deities (primarily Zeus, Poseidon and Ares), and some lines boasted more divine unions than others. As a rule, divine/mortal unions did not occur in successive generations. Unions between goddesses and mortal men was generally a far less frequent phenomenon, albeit also important to the Greek mythic repertoire.

379 At least in the early Archaic Period, the fundamental difference between gods and mortals boiled down to the distinction between finite vs. infinite periods of existence (viz. οἱ ἀθάνατοι vs. οἱ θνητοί). Needless to say, there was a good deal more to it, as expressed in the genealogical hierarchy enumerated by Hesiod in his *Theogony*. The absence of an explicit account of the origins of humanity in that text has been a source of considerable confusion (acknowledged, for example, by C.W. Querbach *CJ* 81.1 1985: 10; F. Graf 1993: 85, and J. Strauss Clay in *GRBS* 29.4 1998: 323-333; W. Burkert in R. Buxton, ed. 1999). In my view, at least, this omission is due to ubiquitous knowledge concerning human origins, which stemmed back to primordial women and gods. A vast collection of literature exists on the subject, primarily dealing with the role of Pandora (*Th.*535-616; *W&D* 42-105), and the parable of the five ages of man (*W&D* 106-202). For further references, see W. Blümer 2001.

380 For another interpretation of "theogeniture," see J.M. Hall 1997: 87-89, 95-96.

381 See especially the concerns, suggestions of C. Sourvinou-Inwood in *Reading Greek Culture,* Oxford 1991; also, A. Henrichs in J. Bremmer, ed. 1987.

382 So, M. Finkelberg "Royal Succession in Heroic Greece" *CQ* 41.2 1991: 31-41; *Greeks and Pre-Greeks* Cambridge 2005: ch.4. Finkelberg advocates the transmission of kingship through the female royal line in a setting otherwise governed by patrilinear descent (i.e. Greece), citing evidence for this practice in the Hittite royal archives. It is inappropriate to embark on a thorough critique of Finkelberg's interpretation of the genealogical data. Suffice it to say, by way of example (via 2005: 68-70 and each example she cites must be addressed individually), that since Penelope was not a native of Ithaka, she cannot be considered an eligible candidate for kingship transmission through the female line, which, if it existed, would presumably run from Laertes' mother to Laertes sister etc. (compare H. Van Wees' description of the situation in J.P. Crielaard, ed. 1995: 161-162). On the inheritance status of Kastor and Polydeukes, it does not make very much sense to maintain that they were not rightful heirs to Tyndareos' kingdom, when the mythological fact of the matter is that they were killed off in the prime of their lives in a confrontation with the sons of Aphareus (cf. I. Malkin 1994: 25). Consequently, their territorial assets were in some way distributed among Tyndareos' daughters. It is also important to bear in mind the absence of primogeniture in the Greek context (cf. M. Broadbent 1968: 200ff; J. Goody and S.J. Tambiah 1973; J.M. Hall 1997: 94). Moreover, the basic concept of a divided realm with often far from specific territorial boundaries is vital to a number of Greek mythic stories, and may be evaluated, alternatively, in strictly mythological terms.

383 These dynamics are in some sense relevant to the high-profile discussions on the position of women in Ancient Greece that peaked before the turn of the millennium. In a particular body of work this topic basically took on a life of its own, accentuating the ancient oppression of women as a point of departure in a discourse that seems more deeply rooted in the present day than in ancient sociological contexts (especially, for example, S. Pomeroy, *Goddesses, Whores, Wives and Slaves*, New York 1975; E.Keuls, *The Reign of the Phallus*, Berkeley 1985; F. Zeitlin, *Playing the Other*, Chicago 1996; by way of comparison, see D. Cohen, *Law, Sexuality and Society*, Cambridge 1991; U. Kron in B. Alroth and P. Hellström, eds. 1996; and A.W. Gomme 1937 which demonstrates how far back such discussions actually go). For a bibliographic account on progress made in social history during the eighties and nineties with special emphasis on marginalized social groups, see K. Raaflaub in S.M. Burstein et al., eds. *Ancient History: Recent Work and New Directions* 1997. See now, J.B. Connelly 2007. The pendulum swings in the other direction.

384 e.g. Hes fr 137, 138 MW.

385 e.g. G.L. Huxley 1969: 34-37. It is likely enough that the two lost epic poems *Phoronis* and *Danais* were post-Homeric Argive compositions.

386 FGrHist 1F9; *Pyth*.4.14-15; *Nem*. 10.1-6; cf. Bakchy. 11 & 19; Pherekydes FGrHist 3F21, 86; Hdt.2.91, 171,182.

387 See D.J. Conacher 1996: 75-76 for the now widely accepted dating for Aischylos' *Danaid Trilogy* to the late 460s. Before Aischylos' rendition, the playwright Phrynichos is credited with two relevant titles: an *Aigyptioi* and a *Danaides*. A few fragments exist from Sophokles lost *Inachos*.

388 cf: ApB 2.1.4.

389 See Gantz 1993: 201-202. For Pindar and Bakchylides' reliance on the Hesiodic *Catalogue of Women*, see G. D'Alessio in R. Hunter ed. 2005.

390 e.g. Hes. fr 127-129; *Danais* fr 1 Davies.

391 e.g. R. Janko 1982 & 1986 42: 85-87, 221-225; R. Fowler 1998; and I. Rutherford in R. Hunter ed. 2005.

[392] West's dating criteria are stated in the last chapter of his critique on the *Hesiodic Catalogue of Women* 1985:125-136. In summary form, the evidence, as I see it, consists in the following. 1,2,4,7, and 8 are also cited by West. He treats the material in 3 and 5 also one way or another, if not necessarily as dating criteria. 6 and 10, however, do not accord with his mode of analysis. 9 is not prominently emphasized.
1) The eponymous Kyrene, addressed in detail below (fr 215 MW). 2) Sikyon, son of Erechtheus (fr 224), as opposed to Ibykos' Sikyon, son of Pelops (308 PMG = Paus.2.6.5). West associates this genealogy with political interaction between Kleisthenes of Sikyon and the Athenians, beginning with the alliance in the First Sacred War. See Herodotos 5.68 for the Athenian finalists in the grand competition that Kleisthenes held for his daughter Agariste's hand in marriage. 3) Athenian interest in the Aiolic figure Erysichthon, son of Triops from the Aiolic line of Kanake and Poseidon. As the *Catalogue* records, Triops' daughter, Mestra, was traditionally Sisyphos' son Glaukos' first wife (Poseidon, however, intervened, generating the Eurypylos of *Iliad* 2.677). In the *Catalogue,* however, Mestra and Erysichthon were apparently situated in Athens (fr 43a, b and c MW; cf. West 1985: 105; Gantz 1993: 175). 4) The promotion of a second marriage for this same Glaukos to Eurynome, daughter of Nisos, son of Pandion. Contingent on whether, as it seems likely, this man was an Athenian Pandion (later Athenian genealogy featured two Pandions), his appearance is associated by West with Peisistratos' seizure of the Megarian port of Nisaia ca. 565. This formation is, at any rate, a scarcely viable candidate for the hero Bellerophontes' early epic heritage. And while it could conceivably have Megarian roots, this genealogy also signals the emergence of the family attributed to the Athenian king later known as Pandion II, namely, Aigeus, Nisos, Pallas, and Lykos, who surface in the work of the Atthidographers (cf. Gantz 1993: 247). 5) Sporadic and more conjectural indications that Kreusa, daughter of Erechtheus (and wife of Xouthos, son of Aiolos, fr 10a.20-24 OCT), was accompanied elsewhere in the text by some of Erechtheus' other famous daughters, who together secured some major old genealogies on behalf of the Athenian state. Among them, one fragment identifies Prokris (fr 332). The appearance of Boutes perhaps suggests the presence of Chthonia, his wife and his niece (fr 223). Together they generated the ancestors of the Athenian family that presided over the Athenian priesthood of Poseidon, though Boutes was identified otherwise elsewhere (fr 251a,b MW attributed to the *Megalai Ehoiai,* cf. West 1985: 109). The coverage on Phineus suggests the potential presence of the Athenian Oreithuia, who, as the alleged mother of Zetes and Kalais, provided the Athenians with an Argonautic connection (fr 156 MW). The antiquity of this link is again highly questionable. Another stray comment attributed to Hesiod seems to acknowledge the story of Prokne and Philomela, ultimately the daughters of Pandion I. This story was, evidently, an adaptation of an old story known to Homer (fr 312; Od.19.518-523; Gantz 1993: 239-241; Fontenrose 1948, offers some valuable background). 6) The acknowledgement of developed state genealogies for Sparta, Argos, Aigina, and Arkadia. So for instance, the extensive coverage on the expanded version of Argive line, presently under consideration (e.g. fr 127, 129, 135). The evidence on this is presented throughout this document, so I will isolate only the next two examples because they are also singled out by West, plus a third piece of evidence that would seem indispensable. 7) The idea that Pleisthenes, son of Pelops, was the true father of Agamemnon and Menelaos, who were adopted by Atreus after Pleisthenes' death (fr 194 MW). This proposal was also made by Stesichoros (209, 219 PMG), and followed later, to some extent, by the Athenian tragedians. 8) The marriage of Eurydike, daughter of Lakedaimon, to Akrisios, son of Abas of Argos (fr 129 MW). On this point, however, I do not agree that this marriage subordinated the line of Perseus to the authority of the line of Lakedaimon (West 1985: 132). It is rather more straightforwardly a strategic connection that linked two major autonomous state genealogies. As inferred above, this link was quite possibly devised in Sparta in response to the development of the Argive line, but it was generally acknowledged from that time onward regardless of its initial provenance (Argos is clearly another contender) 9) The Catalogue's description of Aias' domain which functions as an expanded replacement of Il.2.557-558 (fr 204.44-51 MW). 10) Finally and most persuasively, given the rest of the evidence: a fully developed account of the Hellenic genealogy (viz. the lineage that stemmed from the eponymous Hellen; fr 9 MW), including the Dorian story of the *Return of the Herakleidai* (fr 10a.6-10 OCT), and the Athenian account of Ionian identity that worked in collusion with the Dorian charter (fr 10a.20-24; more on this issue in chapters 4 and 5. West also emphasizes the deification of Herakles which is widely regarded as an Athenian innovation (fr 229 MW).

³⁹³ See especially, R. Parker "Myths of Early Athens" in J. Bremmer, ed. 1988. Parker's opening remarks emphasize the inescapable fact that Athenian stories are exceedingly rare in both Homer and Hesiod, while they assume pride of place in the mythological repertoire from the fifth century onward, and consequently, abound in later authors such as Apollodoros and Ovid. Pursuing this phenomenon in greater detail, Parker's article primarily focuses on systematic Athenian mythological refinements of the fifth and fourth centuries, which can be seen as a second phase of the process initiated in the early sixth century. This second phase corresponds with the zenith of Athenian political influence and cultural creativity, serving on that count as the long-term guarantor of Athenian mythic dominance in perpetuity. A standardized king list, along with a set canon of extraordinary Athenian legendary achievements were fleshed out and disseminated during that period (cf: FGrHist Marmor Parium; Isoctrates' *Panegyricus* 54-70). On the contributions of the *Attidographers*, see F. Jacoby 1949; L. Pearson 1942; also U. Kron, *Die Zehn attischen Phylenheroen*, Berlin 1976; N. Loraux in Y. Bonnefoy, ed. Paris, 1981. On earlier developments, see for example, W.R. Connor in A.G. Ward ed., London, 1970; J. Boardman *JHS* 95 1975; E. Kearns, London, 1989; H.A. Shapiro, Mainz 1989; F.J. Frost *Ancient World* 21.1 1990. For a historical overview, see R. Sealey 1976: chs. 4-6; A. Andrewes in *CAH* 3.3 1982: 360-402.

³⁹⁴ e.g. Prominently, for example, the Athenian account of Ionian Migration to Asia Minor was molded to fit the Dorian account of the *Return of the Herakleidai* (This point is developed at length in Part 2, below). It was also designed to supersede previous (namely, East Greek) Aiolic and Ionic migration narratives (e.g. H.A. Shapiro in W.G. Moon ed. 1983 on the Ionian narratives). Concerning the provenance of the Hesiodic *Catalogue*, central Greece with special emphasis on Boiotia, Lokris and Phokis is the most popular alternative that has been proposed to counter M. West's Athenian hypothesis (So, R. Fowler 1998; I. Rutherford sup.cit.; also S. Larson 2000 and J.M. Hall 2002: esp. ch.5). Interestingly enough, this interpretation is based on the predominantly Aiolic character of the major central Greek genealogies, the presumed antiquity of the Deukalionid lineage, and then further, given this mytho-geographical focus, a tendency to attribute mytho-political authority to the influence of the Delphic Oracle.

³⁹⁵ e.g. Athenian concept of autochthony, which does not actually differ all that much from the underlying concepts involved in the creation of local indigenous lines out of personified elements in the landscape. On this topic see, for example, N. Loreaux in *Enfants d'Athena*, Paris 1981; V. Rosivach *CQ* 37.2 1987: 294-305, which includes an appendix on Arkadian authochthony.

396 Beginning with the conflict with Megara over Salamis and Athenian participation in the *First Sacred War*, both associated with Solonian leadership (Plutarch's *Solon*; Isocrates's *Plataikos* 14.31). This is not to suggest an underlying endorsement of the so-called "Peisistratid Recension" theory concerning the transmission of the Homeric epics and currently experiencing something of a revival. The observation is simply that the early systematization of Athenian myth must be dated to Solonian and Peisistratid times. The First Sacred War was a conflict of the late 590s / early 580s for political control over the Delphic Oracle. The amphiktyonic alliance led by forces from Thessaly, Sikyon, and Athens seized the oracle from Phokis. Victory games were held in 586. The Pythian Games were established in 582. See, for example, J. Boardman & H.W. Parke, *JHS* 77 1957: 276-282; L.H. Jeffrey 1976: 71-84; G.A. Lehmann's response to N. Robertson *CQ* 28 1978: 38-73 in *Historia* 29 1980: 242-246; W.G. Forrest in *CAH* 3.3 1982: 312-313; H.A. Shapiro, *AJA* 88.4 1984: 523-529 and in H.A.G. Brijder ed. 1984; J.K. Davies in S. Hornblower, ed. 1994. Boardman, Parke, and Shapiro establish the evidence for the mythological and artistic impact of the First Sacred War in Peisistratid Athens. For a basically apolitical reading of Hesiod's *Aspis* that arrives at the same general dating results, see R.M. Cook *CQ* 31 1937: 204-214. For an intricate treatment of the literary evidence that more questionably, however, seeks to attribute the Pythian *Hymn to Apollo* to the Sacred War victors and the Hesiodic *Aspis* to the losing side, see R. Janko *CQ* 36.1 1986: 38-59. This conclusion is based on perceived internal evidence for an anti-Theban perspective in the *Hymn* and a pro-Theban perspective in the *Aspis*. In this regard, it is important to note that though the data on Theban sympathies is quite slim, Herodotos depicts the Theban authorities in cooperation with Kleisthenes of Sikyon (5.67). For more on this topic see, L.H. Jeffrey 1976.

397 Gantz 1993: 202.

398 Argos this period is associated with the decline of the "Temenid" dynasty under the successors of Pheidon. See, T. Figueira 1993: 16, 31-32 with references; and more generally, R.A. Tomlinson 1972: chs. 7, 18 . On Naucratis, see C. Roebuck 1951; J. Boardman 1999: 118-133. Also Gantz 1993: 202.

399 The formation: Io -> Epaphos-> Libya -> Belos / Agenor is consistent in the ancient sources. See M. West 1985: 77; Gantz 1993: 202-203.

400 The earliest genealogical information on Phineus and Kepheus comes from the Hesiodic *Catalogue* itself (e.g. Hes fr 151 MW, Hes fr 135 MW). Their antiquity, therefore, is entirely based on the *Iliad*'s acknowledgment of the Argonauts voyage, in conjunction with Perseus' role in the text (e.g. 7.468, 21.40-41;14.320, 19.116), and prominently also, in Hesiod's *Theogony* (280-281). Clearly, no concrete inferences can be made about these figures' early genealogical identity beyond the observation that they were both high-status foreign figures with traditional roles in early Greek legend, hence, reasonably enough, their incorporation into the foreign installment of the full-fledged Argive line. Notably, the story of Perseus' marriage to Andromeda, daughter of Kepheus, abides by the same plot structure as the story of Herakles' claim to the Trojan princess, Hesione, whereas the latter was well-known to the *Iliad* (Il. 5.638-651, 8.281-284, 20.144-148). Hesione was the daughter of King Laomedon of Troy. And she was also the prize Herakles received in exchange for killing a great sea monster that had laid siege to the city. Herackles gave her to his comrade Telamon, and she gave birth to Teukros, Aias' half-brother. Perseus won Andromeda in the same way, though her father's early ancestry and his designated realm are impossible to identify. He was typically placed on the Levantine coast or otherwise situated in Ethiopia. Suffice it to say, that neither the tale's plot structure, nor its illustrious foreign marriage, are alien to the early epic milieu.

401 So Kadmos was variously a son of Phoinix or a son of Agenor, Phoinix' father. Europa shifted accordingly. Phineus and Kepheus, typically presented as brothers, vacillated even more dramatically between Belos, Agenor, and Phoinix. For the details see Gantz 1993: 208-209, 211. Concerning Kepheus' origins, M.L. West suggests that Andromeda's father was originally the Arkadian Kepheus, thus, the son of Aleos, father of Sterope addressed above (1985: 84, 147). According to the present analysis, however, such a suggestion must be disqualified due to the innovative nature of the Arkadian line.

402 So, for example, in ZPE 61: 3, M.L. West cites the frequency of such incongruities as grounds to support a genealogical reconstruction where a wife is three generations her proposed husband's junior (viz. Euboia & Hyperes). The line of Aitolia, where West locates his main supporting examples, was an old Aiolic line, lengthened in later sources through the insertion of gratuitous eponymous names (viz. Aitolos, Pleuron, and Kalydon cf. ApB 1.7.5-7). The insertion of eponyms was no doubt widespread, but when viewed as a sign of strategic emendation, the genealogies that exhibit such symptoms can be productively viewed against earlier epic patterns. It is most unlikely in this regard that the early epic line of Aitolia acknowledged the eponyms that surface later on.

403 According to the present hypothesis, however, this type of myth-to-city-of-origin correlation did not hold true in the previous period, since the Aiolic structure embraced all of Greece and dealt with all principalities from a single perspective. In the post-epic period, generally speaking, this type of equation was more frequently valid, so especially in the case of indigenous lines for which there is a great deal of supporting evidence. Nonetheless, there remains considerable risk in the blanket assumption that the site of a story suggests the identity of the story's creators because it is clear that mythic emendation did not always function along these lines. As a rule of thumb in attempting to identify the geopolitical emphasis of individual narratives it is most effective to restrict analysis to major political and mythological trends as opposed to equating specific stories with specific or finite historical events in order to arrive at the source of the story. This latter method is a frequent snare in the political analysis of Greek mythology. Apparently the main problem stems from the fact that granting the coexistence of local mythologies, on the whole, the mythological record reflects mainstream contemporary distributions of power (rather than autonomous local ad hoc initiatives), which universally affected the content and reception of the evolving Greek mythic corpus. Accordingly, the most prolific mythological innovators aka the most influential Greek states (needless to say, a chronological variable) effectively maintained jurisdiction over the most important legendary events, regardless of where they were held to unfold, in much the same way the early Aiolic Greeks espoused a mythic vision that embraced all of Greek territory. Thus the most prolific era of Greek mythic productivity may be divided into three periods and three respective distributions of power. The mythological record bears the mark of each one: 1. The initial cultural/political base that informed the inherited mythic structure viz. early Archaic Aiolic / Ionic authority. 2. The competitive and often cooperative dominance of Peloponnesian city-state mythologies. 3. The Athenian domination of mainland Greek tradition from the Classical Period onward. In as much as throughout the time span in question a certain level of conceptual stability kept the rudiments of the tradition in tact, the institution of changes as time wore on consistently reflect the distribution of power at the time of their promulgation. For this reason the practice of zeroing in on a specific mythological story in order to expose the political interests that lie beneath the mythic veneer can easily produce erroneous results when setting and/or protagonists and finite real-life events are utilized as the leading criteria, especially when the setting or the leading participants do not represent major political players in the contemporary distribution of power (e.g. when southern Greeks discuss northern Greek cities or northern Greek heroes in the post-epic period). In a word, the Greek mythological record was subject to the same forces of hegemonic regulation as other contemporary historical phenomena.

404 cf. Gantz 1993: 203. On the peregrinations of Io from a fifth-century standpoint, see M. Finkelberg 1998.

405 Or more generally from the Euboian line.

406 If, however, the *Aigimios* was a Spartan text (which is in fact quite likely) the motivational issues behind the Euboian version readily fall into place.

407 viz. the removal of Epaphos -> Libya + Poseidon -> Belos -> Danaos/Aigyptos. Lynkeus and Hypermestra are already accounted for as prominent Aiolic legendary figures and may be likewise omitted due to the fact that their role as the parents of the Argive Abas is inextricably tied to the Egyptian version.

408 The *Aigimios* was no doubt a Dorian poem, in spite of its ascription either to Hesiod, or via Athenaios to Kerkops of Miletos (503d; see G. Huxley 1969: 107-110). The poem's title indicates that it dealt with the subject of the Dorian allies of the descendants of Herakles. Accordingly, it is far from inconceivable that the ostentatious international character of the revised Argive genealogy elicited an initially negative reaction from non-Argive Peloponnesian Dorians. On this reading, and provided as West suggests, this text terminated Io's adventures in Euboia, and therefore excluded the Egyptian genealogy, whether it proceeded or followed the proliferation of the international segment of the Argive line, it confirms a widespread awareness of the old established connections between Abas, Euboia, and the Abantes. The Argive Abas made these connections untenable from a genealogical standpoint. So, once the Argive Abas, whose ancestors lived in Egypt, drowned the Abas-Euboia,-Abantes connection, this connection had to be sustained by other means. This led to the development of reverse migration stories (so, Paus.10.35.1).

409 A major concern in Part 2, below.

410 On the Oracle of Abai in Phokis, see Str.9.3.13; Paus. 10.35.1.

411 Thus in deference to the revised Argive line, Strabo (9.5.5) and Pausanias (10.35.1) propose *reverse migrations* that bring Abas from Argos to northern Greece. Thus Strabo has him found a northern Greek colony to explain the origin of the term *Pelasgian Argos* as deployed in the *Iliad* ((Il.2.681-684). Pausanias makes him founder of Abai in Phokis, the site of the well-known oracle at that location. The suggestion here, is that early epic migrations consistently went the other way round (that is to say, southbound, from northern Greece).

412 Via T. Figueira's reconstruction (1993: 30-31). Alternatively, R. Sealey, maintains that Argive history between the reign of Pheidon of Argos and the sixth-century confrontation with Sparta, known from Herodotos (1.82) as the *Battle of the Champions* is essentially a complete blank (1976). For others, the issue of Pheidon's dates and accomplishments is also a far from straightforward matter (so, T. Kelly 1976; P.J. Shaw 2003). Still, while Figueira's reconstruction rests to an extent on speculative grounds, the status of Argos in the seventh century is on the whole adequately attested and spotlights the issue of political tension between Argos and Sparta in the period prior to the *Battle of the Champions*. This matter is revisited in chapter 4.

413 See Hdt. 1.65-68 on the conflict between Sparta and Arkadia in the first half of the sixth century. General historical treatments include: R.A. Tomlinson 1972; L.H. Jeffrey 1976, R. Sealey 1976; P. Cartledge 1979; *CAH* 3.3 1982. Korinth was also a vibrant early competitor, though early trendsetting Korinthian contributions were later dwarfed by developments in other Greek states (see below).

414 Notably, the same name as the father of the Arkadian Atalanta, son of Lykourgos, son of Aleos, son of Apheidas, son of Arkas. Iasos was also the name of the son of Amphion of Orchomenos whose daughter Chloris married Neleus of Pylos (Od.11.281ff.). It was also an epithet used to describe a district in the northwestern Peloponnese (Od.18.245-249; T.W. Allen *CQ* 1909: 86-88).

415 In the *Ehoiai* an unnamed daughter of Phoroneus of Argos marries Doros, son of Hellen, son of Deukalion: eponym of the Dorian Greeks. She bears five daughters who in turn give birth to the Nymphai, Satyroi and Kouretes (Hes fr 123 MW, a notable innovation itself). In Akousilaos, Phoroneus, son of Inachos is portrayed as a survivor of the great flood (FGrHist 2F23). He was, therefore, by that time a co-flood survivor and contemporary of the northern Greek figure, Deukalion, whose wife Pyrrha gave birth to the eponymous Hellen. At what stage the Near Eastern flood motif became a feature of Greek genealogical history cannot be gauged with great precision, though it was certainly known to Pindar (*Ol.*9). The *Ehoiai*, notwithstanding, with or without the flood, connects the indigenous line of Argos to the Hellenic genealogy through the marriage of Phoroneus' daughter to Doros, son of Hellen, son of Deukalion. These facts relate to a particular question raised in a number of studies on Greek ethnicity, namely, *Why* is it that no attempt was ever made to link the line of Inachos to the Hellenic genealogy so that Inachos' descendants would register as Hellenes (cf. M. Finkelberg 2005: 36-39 with references)? The answer to this question seems to boil down to the chronological precedence of the Inachid stemma over the development of the Hellenic genealogy (or, at least, its widespread canonization), though both were well entrenched by the time of the *Ehoiai*. The indigenous Argive line gave Perseus and Herakles a highly elaborate and thoroughly Argive ancestry, which was, first of all, incompatible with, and secondly, seems to have adamantly resisted the prerogatives of the Hellenic genealogy. Consequently, Phoroneus ultimately became an autonomous contemporary of Deukalion as opposed to a blood relation in the Deukalionid line. Essentially the developed Argive edifice was far too much to forfeit merely in exchange for membership in the Hellenic stemma, which would require the subordination of Argos. A marriage connection would therefore suffice.

416 e.g.. Bakchylides 11; Pind. *Nem.*10; Aischy. *Prom.* 848-869.

417 On the mythological side cf. M.West's acknowledgement in *ZPE* 61 1985: 3 and the corpus itself. On the historical side cf. W.E. Thompson *Phoenix* 21.4 1967: 273-282.

418 A few ancient sources introduce a quarrel between Aigyptos and Danaos, which clearly played no part in Aischylos' drama, but indicates that a causation dilemma was also perceived in antiquity (e.g. ApB 2.1.4; Hyg. *Fab.* 168 cf. Davies *Danais* fr 1). As for discussions concerning the Danaid's motives, cf. A.F. Garvie 1969: 204ff; J.K. Mackinnon 1978; H. Friis Johansen & E.W. Whittle 1980 I.30-42; R. Seaford 1987: 110-119; For a concise, pragmatic, and persuasive reconstruction of the Trilogy's format and primary concerns see R.P. Winnington-Ingram 1961.

419 R. Janko reports eleven occurrences of the exile motif in the Homeric poems (G.S. Kirk ed., *The Iliad: A Commentary* vol. 4: 387 cf. N. Richardson vol. 6: 175). Presumably his figure is based on the following: 1) Meges 2.625-630 2) Tlepolemos Il.2.661-667; 3) Bellerophon Il.6.155-202; 4) Phoinix Il.9.430-495; 5) Medon Il.13.694-700; 6) Lykophron Il.15.429-432; 7) Epeigeus Il. 16.569-576; 8) Patroklos Il.23.80; 9) Odysseus in disguise Od.13.258-573; 10) An Aitolian Od. 14.379-81; 11) Theoklymenos Od.15.224ff. 272-276. The majority, although, not all of these cases are specifically exiles for homicide. In any event, the function of the motif is remarkably well documented in Homer. In addition to treatments of specific mythical cases (e.g. L. Slatkin in J.P. Euben, ed 1986, cf. R. Parker 1983), there is also a considerable bibliography concerning Greek exile as a real life phenomenon including the analysis of its legal application (so, for example, J. Roisman "The Image of the Political Exile in Archaic Greece." *Ancient Society* 15-17: 1984-1986: 23-32; D.M. MacDowell 1963).

420 See Winnington-Ingram sup.cit. Also relevant to Aeschy. *Prom.*851-858.

421 See Gantz 1993: 206-207 for the popular postponement of the Danaids' punishment until their arrival in the underworld.

422 Pind. *Pyth.*9.111-116; ApB 2.1.5; Hyg.*Fab.*170. Earlier renditions of the Danaid saga that are now lost include the epic *Danais*, Phrynichos' *Aigyptioi*, and the missing details from the *Ehoiai*.

⁴²³ G..S. Kirk 1972: 81; cf. R. Lattimore 1964; V. Propp 1968. On the analytical fascination with the scandalous aspects of the Greek myths, see M. Detienne 1981; For a variety of astute applications of the concept of structure vis-à-vis Greek mythic content, largely excluding genealogical structure, however, cf. C. Lévi-Strauss 1955; P. Vidal-Naquet 1986; J.-P. Vernant 1988 ; M. Detienne and J-P. Vernant 1989. J. Gould's emphasis on frequent misunderstandings of Greek myth and religion as a system of thought that permeated all aspects of everyday life is also instructive in this context (viz. in Easterling and Muir, eds. 1985 & S. Hornblower, ed. 1994).

⁴²⁴ Something similar, granted on a smaller scale, was pioneered by Eumelos of Korinth who claimed the lineage of Aeetes, King of Kolchis on behalf of the Korinthian state (see G. Huxley 1969: ch. 5. The work of Asios of Samos outlined in ch.7 is also relevant).

⁴²⁵ Scholarship on the subject of Pelops and Kadmos' early eastern origins has by no means unanimously endorsed this view. Against Pelops' generally acknowledged Anatolian roots see J.M. Hall 1997: 91. The case of Kadmos (for which the earliest evidence is not very early) has inspired a long and complex debate. In 1913 A.W. Gomme advanced the view that Kadmos' Phoinikian identity was a mythographic invention of the fifth century. His conclusion was extremely influential (e.g. followed in various contexts by F. Vian 1963, E. Vermule 1972, and T.K. Hubbard 1992, among others. However, see T.J. Dunbabin 1957, as well as work of the theorists who have focused on the development of the Greek alphabet from the Phoinikian script (c.g. H.T. Wade-Gerry 1952; L.H. Jeffrey 1961; E. Havelock 1982; W.V. Harris 1989; B. Powell 1991; C.J. Ruijgh in J.P. Crielaard, ed. 1995). In 1979 R. Edwards critiqued Gomme's argument in a text that offers full coverage on the topic from the nineteenth century to the late 70s. While in the interim major progress was made through (for, example) L. Wooley's excavations at Al Mina in the thirties and the work of Popham and Sackett at Lefkandi in the sixties, the question of Iron Age interaction between Greeks, Phoinikians, and other neighboring populations was again revitalized in the late 80s thanks to the controversies sparked off by M. Bernal. A great deal of invaluable work has ensued (e.g. G. Kopke & I. Tokumaru, ed. 1992; & the ongoing contributions of the authors involved; for a close look at the Phoinikians, themselves, see M. Aubet 2001). From a mythological standpoint, the roles awarded to Pelops and Kadmos make the most sense when viewed as part of the earliest legendary stratum (viz. early epic). This chronology also accords with the overall ethos of the Homeric poems, and with external data concerning the prominence of the East Greek cities in the early Archaic Period (again, a point of view that has not always held sway). At that time, the Greeks were the underdogs in a cultural setting that was dominated by eastern urban centers. Notably, Greek admiration for eastern culture and wealth is a leitmotif in the Homeric poems (e.g. B. Knox 1990), and is certainly relevant to the status attached to the long-drawn-out yet predestined Greek conquest of Troy (namely, one such metropolis). In depth eastern influence on Greek mythology is no longer subject to reasonable doubt (cf. P. Walcot 1966; W. Burkert 1985 & in Bremmer, ed 1987; R. Mondi in L. Edmonds, ed. 1990; M.L. West 1997).

⁴²⁶ Herakles' parents' (viz. Amphitryon and Alkmene's) exile from Argos is covered in greater detail in chapter 5, below.

⁴²⁷ cf. E. Hall 1989; J.M. Hall 1997: ch.3; and now T. Harrison, ed. 2002.

⁴²⁸ See S. Said in T. Harrison, ed. 2002 for a thorough appraisal of Euripides' decidedly negative reaction to the Greek chauvinist attitudes of the post Persian War Period.

⁴²⁹ Argos notably ranks among the Greek states that refused to participate in the resistance movement.

⁴³⁰ cf. T. Figueira 1993: ch.1.

431 Among the commercial participants at Naucratis, the Aiginetans, the Samians, and the Milesians alone erected their own state-sponsored temples (to Zeus, to Hera, and to Apollo respectively). These functioned independently of the Hellenium, shared by a consortium of East Greek trading states. The temples of Aigina, Samos and Miletos are believed to predate the Hellenium on archaeological grounds (*CAH* III.2.3.37-43).

432 Following Figueira 1993: 10. Initial traces of interaction from 635 BC.; foundation period: ca. 610-594; official concentration of trade under Amasis ca. 570.

433 Figueira 1993: 32; also R.A. Tomlinson 1972.

434 Sparta and Corinth allied with Chalcis in the eighth-century confrontation known from Thoukydides as the Lelantine War. Fierce hostilities between the Euboian cities, Chalkis and Eretria, over land and power, managed to polarize a slew of other Greek states, which took sides, as Thoukydides' reports, in the first post Trojan War conflict of any such magnitude (I. 15). Greek legend gives way to early Greek history with reference to this event, which remains a very hazy affair since its influential lineup of allies and enemies must for the most part be reconstructed. This conflict is addressed in greater detail below, the point here being that in due course Spartan sympathies lay with the Korinthian side of the Lelantine polarization. Friendly relations between Corinth and Sparta were alive and well throughout the sixth century, spawning the *Peloponnesian League* toward its close. Notwithstanding, Corinthian misgivings about increased Spartan power surface as well, as in, for example, the Corinthians refusal to endorse King Kleomenes' violent intervention in Athenian Politics in 508. Epidauros and Athens in the sixth century generally sympathized with Corinth and Sparta, while Megara gravitated toward Argos and Aigina, as an enemy of Corinth, and of Athens as well. Protracted antagonism between Athens and Aigina also had its roots in this period. This conflict, in the long run, would be Aigina's undoing as a prosperous independent commercial entity (in 459/8), while contributing to the development of Athenian interests in seafaring power that led, in due course, to the defeat of the Persians, and to the naval imperialism of the Delian League.

435 *Theogony* 1011-1018.

436 Attributed to Eugammon by Eustathios see G. Huxley 1969: 172; cf. Paus.8.12.6 for Ptoliporthes, son of Odysseus and Pelelope conceived after Odysseus' return from Troy.

437 cf. fr 253 MW for an antecedent reference in the *Megalai Ehoiai*. Though as Pindar also reports, this fragment places Euphemos in the line of Tityos, who was evidently an old epic transgressor (Od.11.576-581) and appears in the Odyssey on the island of Euboia (Od. 7.322-324). Tityos was known as the father of a woman named Europa, which might seem anomalous at first glance, but which upon reflection does not contradict typical Homeric naming protocol, whereby numerous Greeks and foreigners alike answered to the same given names (cf. Il.14.321-322 for Europa, daughter of Phoinix). This fragment, at any rate, makes Euphemos the son of Meikonike and the god Poseidon. Pindar calls him the son of Europa, daughter of Tityos and Poseidon (*Pyth*.4.40-46). Strikingly also, the *Megalai Ehoiai* has Euphemos marry an otherwise unknown sister of Herakles. Pindar makes no reference to this previous marriage. Whether he presupposed it or not is an open question. Pherekydes emphasized Euphemos' Minyan origins by describing Tityos as a son of Elara, daughter of Orchomenos (FGrHist 3F55). The use of this eponym pointedly signals the later revision of the Minyan line, which remains fairly hazy, but clearly diverged from the Homeric conception of Minyan identity. Pindar and Herodotos use the term Minyai as a synonym for the heroes who sailed on the Argo.

438 Menelaos' leadership of this expedition is tacitly inferred by the presence of Helen.

439 e.g. Il.7.345-353.

440 On this topic see, for example, E. Gruen 1993: 1-14.

441 "The position in the *Catalogue* of the Kyrene-Ehoiai, of which the opening lines are preserved as fr 215, is quite uncertain." West 1985 p.85. cf. Gantz 1993 p93.

442 e.g. *Pyth*.4.9-16; *Pyth*.9.109-116; *Nem*.10.1-6.

443 Pindar has reversed the standard order of things. The Lemnian adventure typically takes place on the way to Kolchis rather than on the way homeward. But here what is normally the first adventure is saved for last since it suits Pindar's purposes.

444 *Pythian* 9 was composed in 474 for Telesikrates of Kyrene, victor of the foot race in full armor.

445 So, *Theogony* 337-370.

446 *Pyth*.9.51-58, narrated in the present at the time of the abduction.

447 e.g. Aischylos' *Prometheus Bound* 774.

448 By way of comparison, see Hdt.1.143 for Hekataios' account of his family genealogy.

449 That is, in the guise of an old Aiolic hero and fellow son of Poseidon. Eurypylos was the son of Poseidon and Mestra, the daughter of Erysichthon, a son of Triops of the Aiolic line of Kanake and Poseidon. He established his lineage on the island of Kos, though his descendants were later ousted by Heracles on his way home from the first sack of Troy. So, *Iliad* 2.676-679, 15.13-30.

450 viz. The homeward journey, which apparently runs Libya, Thera, Lemnos in Pindar.

451 e.g. the main protagonists of Euripides' *Herakleidai*.

452 "Pelasgian" was a generic term widely used to denote non-Hellenic aboriginal peoples (see, J.L. Myres 1907: 170-225). These Pelasgians, legend had it, came to Lemnos from Attica as Herodotos reports at 6.137. It seems that the story was initially told by Hekataios of Miletos, who attributed their expulsion to Athenian mistreatment. But the story was later revised by the Athenians who described their expulsion as a justified response to sexual misconduct and criminal activity on the part of the Pelasgians. At any rate, the story has two prominent functions. It gives the city of Athens a conspicuous role in a narrative that had nothing to do with Athens. And it sets off a migratory chain reaction that leads to the foundation of the island of Thera and later to the foundation of the city of Kyrene. Conspicuously, moreover, in terms of the story's content is the blending of the Aiolic Argonaut legend with the later archaic legend that came to define the Dorian ancestry of the Spartan state and all southern Greek Dorian principalities. Accordingly, Thera and Kyrene are characterized as Dorian cities.

453 So also, for example, Paus.3.1.6-8.

454 This accords with Pindar's nuanced synchronization of the return of the Heraklids and their Dorian allies, which led to the flight of the old epic Achaians, with the expulsion of the Minyai from the island of Lemnos (*Pyth*.4.47-50, *Pyth*.5.68-74).

455 The Herakeidai narratives epitomize the gray area that lay in between the later Heroic Age and the onset of lived reality. Imbued with much typical mythological content, they also exhibit a number of clear indications of post-epic Peloponnesian provenance that are dealt with at length in chapters 4 and 5 below. These stories' historical status in the eyes of the Greeks was not qualitatively more or less potent when compared to the rest of the heroic repertoire. Nonetheless, this cluster of stories has been singled out as a source of evidence for historical events, second only perhaps to the Trojan War. On close inspection, the significance of the Herakleidai stories appears to have been the novel link that they forged between the distribution of power in the Peloponnese in the immediate aftermath of the Trojan War, as depicted in early epic, and the distribution of power in the archaic Peloponnese as experienced by Peloponnesian Dorians. Their main function was, therefore, aitiological: like Greek mythology as a whole, they vindicated the present through the construction (in this case the manipulation) of the (inherited) legendary past. These stories' critical role in the reinterpretation of the legendary history of the Peloponnese comes across, for example, in Ephoros' decision to begin his universal history with the *return of the Herakleidai*.

456 cf. Hdt.1.67-68 on the discovery of the bones of Orestes. For scholarly analysis, see, for example, D. Boedeker in C. Dougherty and L. Kurke, eds. 1993.

457 On close inspection, Herodotos' claim that the Spartans were moved by the suppliant Minyai on account of their ancient kinship connections essentially boils down to this single link.

458 cf. Hdt.9.33-35 on Tisamenos, son of Antiochos of Elis, known as the only outsider who was ever granted full citizenship privileges in the Spartan state. The passage is essentially an historical account ridden with mythological features. See Herodotos 4.146 for the reasons behind the swift souring of relations between the Spartans and the Minyai.

459 At 4.147 Herodotos gives the following genealogy: Oidipous -> Polyneikes -> Thersander -> Tisamenos -> Autesion -> Theras. The marriage connection runs as follows: Autesion -> Theras/ Argeia. Argeia + Aristodemos -> Prokles/ Eurysthenes = members of the founding family of Spartan Heraklid kings.

460 Herodotos makes the point that a contingent of Minyans proceeded to Triphylia in southern Elis instead. This assertion played a part in a standardized supplementary narrative, so, for example, Str.4.8.3, 4.9.3; Paus.7.2.2.

461 Though on the extant evidence it is hard to say whether the Pelasgian (Athens) -> Minyan (Lemnos) -> Sparta -> Thera -> Kyrene sequence that dovetailed with the *return of the Herakleidai* story in the accounts of Pindar and Herodotos was also current at the time of the *Ehoiai*.

462 See, in addition, for example, DS 4.57-58; Str.8.5.4, 8.6.10, 8.7.1; ApB 2.8.1-5; Paus.7.1 & 3.1.5-8 in line with Pindar and Herodotos in the present context.

463 Aktaion was turned into a stag and killed by his own dogs, a fate that was attributed to divine vengeance. Though it is clear that Aktaion's transgression became more generic with the passage of time (DS 4.81.4-5; Kallimachos 5; Ovid *Met*.3.138-152; ApB 3.4.4; Hyg.*Fab*.180), the earliest testimony describes his transgression as falling in love with his mother's sister, Semele, who had been chosen by Zeus to bear the god Dionysos (Hes. fr 217A MW; Stesichoros 236 PMG; Akousilaos FGrHist 2F33, with the fragments of Phrynichos' *Aktaion*, see Renner 1978; Gantz 1993: 478-481; West 1985: 88). Needless to say, this must have happened at Thebes.

464 e.g. West 1985: 87.

465 Addressed in Proklos' summary of the *Telegonia*, cf. G. Huxley 1969: 171.

466 West suggests that the Kyrene-Ehoiai was positioned under the auspices of Childanope, namely via her mother's potential connection to the Levantine branch of the Argive line. In note 123 on page 86, West acknowledges two alternate names for this woman, namely, the two Thessalian eponymns, Trikka and Larissa. On page 89, he goes on to state that "The most awkward feature of this hypothesis is Childanope's transfer from the house of Agenor (in the Near East?) to that of a northern Lapith, a rather extreme case of exogamy. But of course it was not simply a matter of choosing any handy fellow to marry her. *Some tradition or persuasion, the basis of which lies outside our understanding, dictated that Kyrene came to Libya from Thessaly."*

467 Thus, including eight of the thirteen generations from Io to Herakles standard in the fifth century. Interestingly enough, the line of Perseus represents the longest genealogical sequence that can be traced back to early epic mythology (i.e. six generations from Akrisios to Herakles, viz. roughly seven to Troy; with an entirely inaccessible genealogical history that necessarily extended upward from Akrisios). This fact, however, is impossible to effectively analyze, since Akrisios' early genealogical roots do not go back beyond his father Abas (at least, potentially Akrisios' father of old) precisely on account of the popularization of the international segment of the Argive line.

468 And indeed M. West's preference for Childanope.

469 This situation brings to mind the title of an article by B.E. Perry written for *TAPA* in 1937, called "The Greek Capacity for Seeing Things Differently." Though the piece itself was not particularly helpful, the capacity cited was clearly very important, not so much psychologically or in the abstract, but as a strategic method of coping with the ramifications of genealogical change.

470 See Gantz 1993: 483-488 for comprehensive coverage on the development of Antiope's story; cf. Hyg. *Fab.* 7 & 8.

471 On purely mythological grounds, the location of the Kyrene-Ehoiai (fr 215 MW) which on the extant evidence remains unknown could conceivably fit into one of three contexts. Either in conjunction with the line of Athamas, whose wife Themisto was like Kyrene, also a daughter of Hypseus (fr 70). Or in conjunction with coverage on the Lapiths of Thessaly, so, for example, the story of Kaineus (fr 87-88). Or alternatively in conjunction with the line of Kadmos, which is to say, in the section on the Inachids of Argos in a listing that dealt with the daughters of Kadmos, one of whom married a son of Kyrene.

472 So, especially, the genealogical layout, which conspicuously places the line of Sparta in juxtaposition with the line of Troy by way Taygete and Electra.

473 Orion was the great mythological huntsman and major constellation visible from both hemispheres (viz. he straddles the celestial equator; Il.18.486; Od.11.572-575). He was said to have rid the island of Chios of wild beasts (and other places as well, according to the Boiotian poet Korinna 673 PMG), getting into trouble on account of his passion for the Chiot king's daughter (Hes fr 148a credited, to Hesiod's *Astronomia*). He was also renowned for the remarkable ability to walk on (or through) water as if on dry land (ibid.), and as a lover of the goddess Eos, though he was eventually killed by the goddess Artemis (Od.5.121-124) for one of a number of offenses against her attributed to him by miscellaneous authors (cf. Gantz 271-273). Genealogically, Orion was linked to Boiotia via Hyrieus, a son of Poseidon and Alkyone (of Aiolos). A particularly unique account of his birth survives in Palaphaitos (*Met.* 51), Ovid (*Fasti* 5), Hyginus (*Fab* 195), and the A scholia to *Iliad* 18.486 (viz. from the buried semen of Zeus, Hermes and Poseidon). The *Ehoiai* (fr 148 MW) and Pherekydes (FGrHist 3F52), however, notably situate him in Krete as the son of Euryale (daughter of King Minos) and Poseidon. The superior antiquity of Orion's Boiotian heritage (albeit preserved in later sources) is probable on a number of counts. So, for example, the parallel transfer to the island of Krete of the *Iliad*'s Sarpedon, likewise, an illustrious member of major Aiolic line (viz. Sarpedon, son of Glaukos, son of Sisyphos, son of Aiolos. cf. Il.6.152-2-06; Pindar *Ol.*13.63-92 vs. Hes fr 140 MW (attributed to Hesiod and Bakchylides); with Gantz 1993: 210 on Aischylos' lost *Kares*). See L.H. Jeffrey 1976: 211 for a sculptural dedication made by the "sons of Orion" along the sacred way from Miletos to Didyma. The "sons of Orion" were evidently an influential Milesian family who traced their lineage back to him. Complementing his legendary Boiotian origin, Orion was a major East Greek hero.

474 Σ A to Il.18.486 attributes this story to the *Epic Cycle*. A number of passages address Orion's pursuit of the Pleiades (daughters of Atlas and Pleione, cf. Ovid *Fasti* 5.81-84; ApB 3.10.1; Hyg *Astr.*2.21.3) in connection with their stellar transformation and notably in a Boiotian setting (Athenaios *Deipnosophistai.* 11.490.d-e; Σ AR 3.225; Σ Aratos *Phainomena* 254; Hyg.*Astr.*2.23.4). Elsewhere, Orion pursues Pleione (or first pursues Pleione), which, in any case, still somehow provoked the transformation of her daughters (Pind.*Nem.*2.10-12 plus scholia; Hyg. *Astr.* 2.21.4).

475 Subtracting, Maia + Zeus = the god Hermes.

476 Gantz 219ff.; West 1978 162ff.

477 Atlas was understood to hold up the heavens where the Mediterranean meets the Atlantic, viz. in the west. Yet apart from a blood link with the great Titan figure, the westward location does not make that much sense when applied to the genesis of the Pleiades, since like other heavenly bodies viewed from the earth, they rise in the east and set in the west on account of the earth's rotation. Od.1.52-54 and Th. 517-519 provide early testimony as to Atlas' burden.

478 As in the case of the *Moliones,* mythic figures were sometimes identified in this manner. Molione was their mother who mated with Poseidon and bore these two sons. They were known individually as Kteatos and Eurytos and belonged to the generation of heroes whose valor Nestor repeatedly praises and whose past days of glory he repeatedly laments (Il.655ff.). These brothers were also known as the Aktoriones, thus alternatively after their mortal stepfather. As Gantz points out, in the case of the Pleiades and the Titan god Atlas, these questions of designation evidently arose from the connection forged between the two. They are in this sense genealogical questions that inspired genealogical answers, though the sequence of developments remains somewhat obscure.

479 As J. Bremmer points out, Porphyry in his *Life of Pythagoras* relates that the early Pythagoreans called the Pleiades "the lyre of the Muses." (Bremmer, ed. 1987: 75).

[480] Il.18.483-489; Od.5.272-274; W&D 383, 619-20; Sappho fr 94 Diehl.

[481] The first literal confirmation of a solid link between the daughters of Atlas and the Pleiades occurs in a fragment of Simonides (555 PMG). Again, Hellanikos is the first to offer a complete list of seven Atlantid sisters (4F19), a number of whom were already addressed in the Hesiodic *Catalogue of Women* (e.g. Hes fr 169-171, 177, 184-185 MW). As mentioned above, Alkyone and Taygete, two lineage-bearing daughters of Atlas were depicted on the early/mid-sixth century throne created in honor of Amyklean Zeus by the architect Bathykles of Magnesia (Paus.3.18.9ff.) Though, Pindar's *Nemean 2* mentions the Pleiades and Orion strictly as constellations (as did Homer and Hesiod) with no overt indication of genealogical thinking, it is nonetheless clear from the *Ehoiai* that by Pindar's time the daughters of Atlas who united with gods and produced heroic families were to some extent already en vogue.

[482] For a comprehensive bibliography on Hesiod's poetry, see W. Blümer 2001.

[483] Addressed as a topic in its own right by H.M. Chadwick in 1912. Chadwick, incidentally, believed that the *Heroic Age* of the Homeric poems reflected the period of the poems' composition (that is, to the extent the poems reflected reality, they reflected the poet's day and age), which he situated in the later "Dark Ages" and associated with the Aiolic Greeks (for persuasive argumentation in support of the poetic historic present cf. I. Morris 1986; K. Raaflaub in I. Morris and B. Powell, eds. 1997). More recently, cf. E. Havelock 1963 on "historical fantasy;" I. Redfield 1975 and I. Morris 1986 on "epic distancing;" A. Heubeck 1989 for "the mythical idealized past;" E. Kearns 1989 and in R. Fowler, ed. 2004 on the merely part human status of the Greek heroes; C. Brillante 1990 on the form and integrity of Greek mythological time, notwithstanding, its generally abstract nature (*contra* M.I. Finley 1975; cf. B. Knox 1979: 10); J.M. Foley 1999 on "traditional referentiality". The Greek characterization of the Heroic Age is crucial to any clear understanding the Greek mythological system, and it is apt to invalidate, quite indiscriminately, any historicist reading of Greek mythology on account of its essentially fictional nature (though its tendency to do so is often ignored). By historicist, I refer to the type of analysis that collects assorted historical and archaeological "evidence" to make erratic and generally unfounded claims concerning mythic figures or mythic events. So, for example, that Danaos was actually a Greek mercenary serving in Egypt during the Hyksos period (P. Walcot 1966: 71 citing N. Maranatos). This notion conspicuously mirrors the case of Charaxos, brother of Sappho of Lesbos, who likely served in Egypt roughly one thousand years later, just as the poet Alkaios' brother, Antimenidas, was said to have served with the Babylonian army, cf. D.A. Campbell 1982); that the Dorians should be equated with the so-called "Sea Peoples" identified in stone carvings from the reign of the Ramses III in the late 12th century and linked to widespread chaos at the end of the Bronze Age (popular briefly, so E. Vermule 1972, but now generally discounted), or otherwise, literally with a horde of invaders that migrated southward from northern Greece in the post-Homeric period (e.g. J.B. Bury 1937; T.J. Dunbabin 1957, and still extremely influential); or likewise, that the wars between Argos and Thebes represent a bona fide series of ancient conflicts as opposed to a myth-historical construct driven by the Aiolic genealogical structure that reinforced the narration of the *Heroic Age* at the time when it first comes to light (for a more skeptical view of the Theban Wars cf. A. Schachter 1967; K. Dowden 1992). The intellectual history relating to the question of the historical content of the Homeric poems demonstrates that the material evidence has often been problematically used to validate Greek legendary tradition. That Greek legendary tradition was universally granted historical status in the eyes of the Greeks (due to its authority over Greek identity), though widely acknowledged (e.g. A.E. Wardman 1960; M.I. Finley 1964; F. Graf 1993) has not actually had a sufficiently rigorous theoretical impact. For while it is manifestly self-evident that any composer must compose with reference to a personal lived reality, the Greek *Heroic Age* presents certain special difficulties in this area. Though necessarily historical to the Greeks, it was altogether distinguished from any historical era ever known in real life (if equally imbued with empirical traits and often subject to studied rationalization, as exemplified, for example, by Thukydides). This is, in my opinion, is enough to destabilize any analysis that does not acknowledge these fundamental considerations. Certainly, also, for the same reasons, fictionally embellished historical sagas the likes of *The Song of Roland* and the *Nibelungenlied* do not easily fit into the same genre as the *Iliad* and the *Odysssey*. For a recent critique of historicist thinking, see J.M. Hall 1997. Still a number of Hall's archaeologically based conclusions show that he is not entirely out of the loop (cf. M. Nilsson 1932: 31).

[484] e.g. H. Fränkel 1973: 98. Th.337-521.

485 e.g. S. Said 1977; C.W. Querbach 1985: 11; J. Strauss-Clay 1989; Gantz 1993: 48-49. Contemporary emphasis on literary and conceptual unity in Hesiod's poetry contrasts with the formerly influential conclusions of A. Rzach (*Hesiodi Carmina* 1902). Rzach felt that Hesiod's work was heavily interpolated and devoid of cohesive conceptual structure. Similar allegations lodged against Pindar have been aptly overridden by A. Köhnken and T. Hubbard, revealing a close explanatory connection between theories of textual interpolation and recourse to the notion of the creative and erratic poetic mind. With Pindar, this connection comes to the fore since as a fifth-century author in an age of artistic literacy, much of whose work has been preserved intact, interpolation is scarcely an issue. Thus the work of the scholars mentioned above who have assessed Pindar's thinking with clarity (against the ambiguity of the poetic mind), shows that creative incoherence exists largely in the eyes of the beholder. At this point the whole issue pivots back to the intimate connection between Greek poets and Greek audiences based on mythological knowledge. Mainly, wherever Greek legend is concerned it is entirely irrational to visualize poets talking in circles or impenetrable abstractions. This is not to deny that interpolation occurred or that creativity has its idiosyncrasies, but merely to emphasize that Greek mythical poetry was rooted in the architecture of Greek cultural heritage, and, in this regard, necessarily involved an intelligible system of communication.

486 An important exception to this general phenomenon is the activities of the goddess Eos, who was renowned for her passion for mortal men (Eos, daughter of the Titans, Hyperion and Theia, who likewise produced Helios and Selene Th.371-374). Whether or not, as Apollodoros maintains (1.4.4-5), Aphrodite originally stood behind Eos' proclivity in this regard, her lovers, namely: Orion, son of Hyrieus (Od.5,121-124, 272-274, 11.572-575; Gantz 1993: 271-273), Kleitos, son of Mantios (Od.15.249-251), Kephalos, son of Deioneus (Th. 986-987; Paus. 3.18.1), and Tithonos, son of Laomedon (Il.11.1, 20.237) all possess significant ancient pedigrees (a few of which became subject to intense competition). While the major events from various sources that were connected with Orion's life story do not suggest a definitive sequence, as the *Odyssey* indicates his early biographical profile included a feature encounter with the Pleiades, at the time, a generic collectivity. Notably, Homer does not credit any heroic offspring to Odysseus and Kalypso or to Odysseus and Kirke. However, the former, as a daughter of the Titan god Atlas (Od.1.14, 15), and the latter, as a daughter of the Titan god Helios (second generation) and the goddess Perse/Perseis, a daughter of Okeanos (Od.10.135-139; Th. 956-957), would have both qualified as full-fledged divinities (as explicitly stated in the Homeric passages). In this regard, their unions with Odysseus would be expected to generate mortal offspring, as indeed they did in subsequent texts that chose to enumerate those genealogies. The mortal status of such offspring would amount to a workable, if unique situation, since Greek heroes were not typically awarded Titan genealogical origins. Their mortality would ostensibly counterbalance the potential threat of their Titan heritage, and would, therefore, not necessarily yield individuals destined to disrupt the greater cosmic equilibrium (a major concern of the *Theogony* as a whole). The insubordination of powerful demigods was notably a recurrent mythic motif exemplified, for example, by Otis and Ephialtes (sons of Iphimedia and Poseidon in the Aiolic line of Kanake), as by Asklepios (son of Apollo and the Lapith Koronis), as well as a slew of other malefactors such as Sisyphos, Tityos, Tantalos and Ixion (cf. C. Sourvinou-Inwood 1986; and note Orion's introduction at the head of this group in *Odyssey* book eleven 572-574). On the early genealogy of Kirke and Aietes the data suggests that they were at first regarded as minor divinities, but were later granted heroic status instead. Thus Aietes became king of the eastern Black Sea kingdom known as Kolchis, rather than the sovereign ruler of a fantasy kingdom identified as Aiaia or Aia (So, A. Heubeck 1989: 4, dating the first signs of transformation to the early seventh century). This transformation appears to be connected to the early mythic ambitions of the Korinthian state (see Gantz 1993: 340-341; Huxley 1969: ch.5).

487 δεινή θεός.

488 Th.1017-8. These were one Nausithoos and one Nausinoos, ancestors of the Tyrrhenians (viz. the Etruscans), noted at the tail end of the concluding section that enumerates unions between mortals and gods. As already noted, the authenticity of this section is generally disputed (cf. M. West 1966: 436, 1978 130).

⁴⁸⁹ Apollodoros includes "Kalypso" in his catalogue of Nereids (ApB 1.2.7). Yet "Kalypso" appears again as a daughter of Atlas, this time supplanting Kirke as the mother of Latinos by Odysseus (ApE 7.24; Th.1011-1014). Accordingly, Homer's Kalypso, daughter of Atlas, though often ignored was also keenly remembered.

⁴⁹⁰ On these two maxims in relation to what can be understood of the Greek mythic mentality, see especially, C. Sourvinou-Inwood 1979: 18-19). It is worth noting that the very existence of any such mentality, especially one equipped with a sense of logic and coherence of its own is quite frequently point- blank denied (e.g. G.S. Kirk 1974: 277) or otherwise interpreted beyond recognition through the importation of external premises. With respect to the analysis of Hesiod's texts, it seems that the main impetus for such denial is the inability to make sense of what the poet is saying strictly in terms of the poems themselves, which has led to theorizing aimed at the justification of the cultural centrality of a poetic genre perceived to be ridden with contradictions (C.J. Rowe *JHS* 103 1983; R. Mondi *GRBS* 25.4). So to cite a very finite example, the two sets of fates (Moirai) in Hesiod's *Theogony* (211-222, 904-906) have been a source of considerable confusion, although it seems fairly clear from a textual standpoint that the first set of Morai (daughters of Night) commanded a level of cosmic sovereignty that restricted even the destinies of the most powerful gods, whereas the sovereignty of the second (daughters of Zeus) addressed the civilized world and its human inhabitants under the jurisdiction of Zeus (cf. C.J. Rowe ibid. F. Solmsen *HSCP* 86 1982).

⁴⁹¹ The only pure-blooded Pontid + Pontid line.

⁴⁹² Clearly the English word mortal with its emphatically human implications is an inadequate rendering of the Greek θνητός and its cognates.

⁴⁹³ cf. *Homeric Hymn to Hermes*.

⁴⁹⁴A major theme in Aischylos' *Prometheus Bound*, set out vividly in the prologue.

⁴⁹⁵ Or Kirke, for that matter, at least, as depicted in the Odyssey, viz. as a daughter of Helios (son of the two Titans, Hyperion and Theia) and the Okeanid, Perse / Perseis.

⁴⁹⁶ Generally, Thetis provides a paradigmatic example. In the Theogony comparable roles are played by Hekate, Metis, and Styx, among others.

⁴⁹⁷ And essentially excluding Kelaino too, whose only son Lykos was selected for immortality thereby excluding her lineage from the arena of genealogical productivity. Kelaino's Lykos, whoever he may have been, accordingly remains completely obscure.

⁴⁹⁸ Culminating in the Titans' imprisonment in Tartaros (Th.705-720); logically, however, to the exclusion of vital personified natural phenomena the likes of Helios, Eos and Selene, progeny of the Titans Hyperion and Theia.

499 Acknowledging the existence of slight variations between Homeric and Hesiodic cosmogonic reportage, it is still clear that their thinking was fundamentally compatible. Though naturally concerned with highlighting these distinctions, M. West's detailed study on alternate cosmogonies also lends support to this basic premise (1983a). This topic is complex and impossible to treat here, yet there seems to be some kind of underlying connection between ethical priorities and cosmogonic structure that developed as time wore on in reaction to the traditional framework. Nonetheless, and particularly at this early stage the discrepancies are slight and the general outlook quite comparable, although the evidence suggests that Okeanos and Tethys commanded a greater role from a Homeric perspective than Hesiod gives them in the *Theogony*. More generally, as analysts have observed, the *Iliad* and the *Odyssey* presupposed the basic content of the *Theogony*, just as the *Theogony* filled a significant void by definitively recording mythological conditions deemed antecedent to the emphasis of the Homeric poems (cf. M. Clarke and K. Dowden in R. Fowler, ed. 2004). It is furthermore clear that the subsequent promulgation of alternative cosmologies (whether philosophic, empirical, or mythological) did not negate the mainstream traditional views, which these poems peerlessly exemplified.

500 As cited above, acknowledged, for example, by C.W. Querbach 1985; J.S. Clay 1998 (also 2003); F. Graf 1993; W. Burkert in R. Buxton, ed. 1999.

501 Though presented here in simplified form, a comprehensive argument can be made that Homer and Hesiod were working with the same recipe for humanity, which was traditionally acknowledged yet not explicitly stated. The operative recipe apparently depended on another class of intermediary beings, namely, the *Nymphai* of the mountains, woodlands and streams, who lived exceedingly long, yet not infinite lives and were, therefore, classified as mortal beings, in spite of the fact that they were also divinities. From what can be gleaned of their genealogical heritage, they were considered to be the offspring of Zeus. The feminine protagonist in this mating, as it happens, cannot be confirmed, but Zeus' paternity seems to register as a vital ingredient. The ubiquitous early currency of such a formula: potentially overrides the frequent misunderstanding that Hesiod's Pandora (like the Biblical Eve) was considered by the Greeks to be the first mortal woman, effectively addresses the peculiar logic of Hesiod's widely contested *Ages of Man*, and is, in addition, globally compatible with the major poetic works attributed to each author (viz. the *Iliad*, the *Odyssey*, the *Theogony*, & *Works & Days*). On Pandora, see for example, N. Loraux, *Arethusa* 11 1978; J-P Vernant 1980: ch.8; P. Leveque, *Kernos* 1 1988; E.D. Reeder, ed. *Pandora: Women in Classical Greece* Princeton, 1995; W. Blümer 2001: 239-395. These assessments generally follow J. Fontenrose's statement "the Pandora myth demands that we look upon Pandora as ancestress of living men and as archetype of womankind (*CP* 69.1 1974: 2)." At this point, however, I am convinced that it is far preferable to view Pandora as the source of a particular type of woman, of special concern to Hesiod, personally, (i.e. beautiful on the outside, deceitful within) – ἐκ τῆς γὰρ γένος ἐστὶ γυναικῶν θηλυτεράων *Th.* 590 – as opposed to either the archetype or the source of all women, and, consequently, thereafter, of humankind.

502 He entreats his listening audience to bear this issue in mind as they experience the vignette that follows: σὺ δ'ἐνὶ φρεσὶ βάλλεο σῆσιν, ὡς ὁμόθεν γεγάασι θεοὶ θνητοί τ'ἄνθρωποι.

503 For a set of references on the premiere contributions to the analysis of Hesiod's *Ages of Man*, beginning with A. Lebegue in 1885 and including the opinions of F. Nietzsche, J. Harrison, E. Meyer, U. von Wiliamowitz-Moellendorff and T.A. Sinclair see K .von Fritz *Review of Religion* 11 1947: 227-260; cf. P. Walcot *REG* 74 1961: C.W. Querbach *CJ* 81 1985. On the Near Eastern origins of Hesiod's *Ages* parable, as well as numerous other textual features see P. Walcot 1966; C. Penglase 1994; M. West 1997; A.S. Brown 1998; for further bibliography R. Hamilton 1989; W. Blümer 2001; and now J. Strauss Clay 2003.

504 Here, the vital point is there is no continuity between the first four races that occur in succession: the gold, the silver, the bronze, and the heroes. Noted, for example, by T. Rosenmeyer *Hermes* 85 1957: 266-267. J. Fontenrose notes the contrasting continuity between the Greek heroes and the subsequent iron race (*CP* 69.1 1974: 10). Against this, however, cf. B.C. Dietrich 1988: 21; J. Whitley in N. Spencer ed. 1995: 58.

505 αὐτὰρ ἐπεὶ καὶ τοῦτο γένος κατὰ γαῖα κάλυψεν αὖτις ἔτ' ἄλλο τέταρτον ἐπὶ χθονὶ πουλυβοτείρῃ Ζεὺς Κρονίδης **ποίησε** δικαιότερον καὶ ἄρειον ἀνδρῶν ἡρώων θεῖον γένος οἳ καλέονται ἡμίθεοι προτέρῃ γενεῇ κατ' ἀπείρονα γαῖαν (W&D 156-159). Throughout the Ages passage the verb ποιέω accounts for divine creative activity: notably, an exceedingly general description.

506 For supporting evidence, see P. Walcot 1966: ch.3 on the Babylonian genesis of mankind. W. Burkert's distinction between *biomorphic* and *technomorphic* creation is also relevant (in R. Buxton, ed. 1999). In addressing this matter J.S. Clay suggests that Hesiod's race of gold consisted of men only and, therefore, atrophied of its own accord, having no means to perpetuate its existence (2003: 81ff.). She believes, on the other hand, that the race of bronze warriors came about by means of sexual reproduction, specifically with the Melian nymphs, rather than asexually, via the will of Zeus directed at ash trees and, by extension, upon the animate spirits attributed to them (Th.187). No doubt, the cultural assumptions that lurk beneath this narrative are extremely challenging to ascertain, however, of the named races of mortal men, the bronze race, by description, would seem to be the most likely to represent an exclusively male population created by Zeus in the role of demiourgos rather than in the role of procreator. The bronze warriors perished by their own self-destruction. But, likewise, since they were exclusively male, they would have expired inevitably anyway, doubly affirming the discontinuity between the race of heroes and their bronze predecessors. As for the generation of the golden race (viz. the men created during the reign of Kronos), it may be preferable to visualize their creation via standard sexually reproductive means (by way of some unspecified genealogical formula), and to view them, accordingly, as a gendered population (like the race of silver, the heroes, and the race of iron) that perished during the great cosmic struggle between the Titans and the Olympians. A change in divine sovereignty, at any rate, could well be held to necessitate a change of human subjects. Interestingly enough, the race of heroes is the only race referred to as *men* (ἀνδρῶν ἡρώων θεῖον γένος) not *mankind* (e.g. χρύσεον γένος μερόπων ἀνθρώπων), when we can, in this instance, at least affirm that the population at stake was a gendered population. This testifies to the intricate level of communication between poet and audience that we are only partially privy to.

507 On similar grounds, it is argued below that the Homeric *Catalogue of Ships* represents another example of the deployment of elusive mythological knowledge that can be reconstructed cross-referentially Once again references to peripheral episodes effectively exert a figurative influence in contexts where they are not literally re-told.

508 cf. M. Wilcock in I. Morris and B. Powell, eds. 1997 for a concise history of the neo-analytic approach and methodology (going back to the work of J.T. Kakridis in the 1940s), as well as a catalogue of key examples that have been conclusively shown to negate the idea that access to the significance of certain key passages is restricted by dependence on *argumenta ex silentio*. For further reference, E.R. Dodds in M. Platnauer, ed. 1954; M. Edwards 1990.

509 It was paradigmatically sustained by Pindar and likewise deployed by the tragedians especially through the medium of the choral ode.

510 viz. daughters of Nereus (a son of Gaia and Pontos) and Doris (of the line of Okeanos).

511 As dramatized in Aischylos' *Prometheus Bound* 750-785. Again, quite strategically, Thetis' identity is left unstated in the presence of a knowing listening audience on hand to witness now the lost remainder of Aischylos' *Prometheus Trilogy* (on this topic cf. C.J. Herington and J. Scully 1975; M. Griffith 1983). The story of the marriage of Peleus and Thetis goes back to the earliest Greek epic poetry (e.g. Il. 1.413-420, 18.429-443, 24,531-541, Th.1006-7).

512 Following L.R. Farnell, T.K. Hubbard argues that Poseidon's involvement was an invention of Pindar's (1987). If so, Pindar's interjection nonetheless abides by the same genealogical logic.

513 On Thetis, specifically, see L. Slatkin 1991.

514 See especially, HHymn to Aphrodite 256-275; Hes fr 304 MW; also Hes. Th. 129-130; Il. 20.8-9, Il.24.615-616. And, it would seem, they were extinct by the end of the Heroic Age.

515 See Il.6.21-26, Il.14.444-445, Il.20.383-385 for heroic unions with naiad nymphs; Il. 16.173-176 for Peleus' daughter and the Sperchios River.

516 e.g. Od.6.105-108, 122-124, Od.9.154, Od.13.356.

517 Alkaios fr 343 Lobel and Page; Pherekydes FGrHist 3F16 where Zeus and Themis are cited as parents. Pindar, by contrast, in *Pythian 9* makes the naiad nymph Kreusa a daughter of Gaia, likely, as Gantz points out, in accordance with *Theogony* 176-187. However, Hesiod's Melian nymphs who arise from the blood of the castrated Kronos seem to relate to *Works and Days* 145, rather than to the general nymph population. For an overview of the evidence on the Nymphai, including the generic meaning of the word, see Gantz 1993: 139-143.

518 Whatever the formula, it necessarily involved an arbitrary, if systematic, breach in the sexual perpetuation of deities. The formula therefore followed the precedent set when Phorkys and Keto spawned a line of monsters.

519 For an alternative but in some ways comparable reading, see, J. Strauss-Clay 2003: ch.4.

520 e.g. Sparta's Taygete; Aigina's Aigina; Korinth's Antiope; the wife of Pelasgos in Arkadia and so on and so forth.

521 deviation 1) god + god = mortal, e.g. the daughters of Atlas. deviation 2) god + mortal = god e.g. Dionysos.

522 He is acknowledged on Linear B tablets from Krete (E.& B Hallager and M. Vlassakis *Kadmos* 31 1992: 75-80). This is not to imply a clear cut relationship between Bronze Age and Iron Age religious practice (for which the evidence is very meager at best), but to emphasize that the only thing "new" about the god Dionysos was his relative date of birth according to standard Greek mythic chronology.

523 Also worthy of notice by way of comparison is the alternate genealogy for Dionysos in which the god was derived from Zeus and Persephone (daughter of Zeus and his sister Demeter at Th. 912-913). This featured in certain later circulating theogonies; the antiquity of the claim is difficult to judge (M.West 1983a).

524 The ensuing manifestation of the god Pan whose genealogy was a highly contested issue lends further support to the dissolution of traditional conceptual / structural boundaries. Against Pan's derivation from Hermes and Dryope (HHymn 10), and either Hermes (e.g. Hekataios FGrHist 1F371) or Apollo (e.g. Hdt 2.145) and Odysseus' wife Penelope, Apollodoros at one point has him arise from Zeus and Hybris (ApB 1.4.1, however, see, ApE 7.38), while a fragment of Aischylos connects him in some capacity both with the reign of Zeus and the reign of Kronos (fr 25b Radt). A key aspect of the dispute was evidently the very existence of yet another god born to a mortal heroic mother (for further citations, see Gantz: 1993: 110-111). On the fifth-century integration of Pan into the Athenian Pantheon see, Hdt. 6.105-106; R. Garland 1992: 9, 18-21, 60-61; R. Parker 1996: 163-168.

525 Mankind (θνητοί ἄνθρωποι), for one thing, already exists at the time of the gathering at Mekone.

526 M. West 1966: 307-309 with select bibliography on Prometheus; 1978: 166; 1997: 295.

527 ἐκ τῆς γὰρ γένος ἐστὶ γυναικῶν θηλυτεράων, [τῆς γὰρ ὀλοίιον ἐστι γένος καὶ φῦλα γυναικῶν,] πῆμα μέγα θνητοῖσι, σὺν ἀνδράσι ναιετάοθσαι, οὐλομένης Πενίης οὐ σύμφοροι, ἀλλὰ Κόροιο (*Th.*590-593).

528 The genealogy that eventually became standard made Deukalion and Pyrrha the sole survivors of a great deluge initiated by Zeus. These two, in turn, were the parents of Hellen (among others), the eponymous ancestor of the Hellenes. Deukalion was considered to be a son of Prometheus (and an obscure woman variously named e.g. Klymene, Pryone cf. West 1978 50), while Pyrrha was the daughter of Epimetheus and Pandora (e.g. ApB 1.7.2; Ov. *Met.* 1.390 and via the scholia to W&D 158; Pind.*Ol.*9; & Plato's *Timaios* 22a.), a notion no doubt derived Hesiod's *Works and Days* (By contrast, Aischylos, in his *Prometheus Bound* 554-560, cites one Hesione – evidently a fellow Titan – in the role of Prometheus' wife. No offspring are mentioned, yet if any ever existed, they would certainly represent a formidable threat to Zeus. The key quote on the subject attributed to the *Catalogue* made Deukalion the son of Prometheus and Pyrrha, which adequately substantiates, in any case, that text's promulgation of some such genealogy (Hes fr 2 MW = Σ.AR 3.1086). Interestingly enough, Pyrrha was an old name associated with the Aiolic island of Lesbos (e.g. P. Green 1984), a fact that suggests potential mythic antecedents independent of this genealogical scheme.

529 The only union between two offspring of Gaia and Pontos.

530 Likewise: Pegasos and Chrysaor; Orthos, Kerberos and the Hydra; the Sphinx and the Nemean Lion.

531 See Gantz 1993: 30-35 for evidence concerning the liaisons attributed to Helios, Eos, and Selene, offspring of the Titans, Hyperion and Theia (Th.371-374). It seems like Titan procreative prerogatives were initially unique to this particular lineage (in conjunction with the offspring of Okeanos), which therefore stands as a foil to the line of Iapetos. Two key passages occur in the Odyssey. In the first, Kirke and King Aietes are described as the offspring of the god Helios and the Okeanid Perse (Od.10.135-139; with Th.956-957). Here, Kirke is specifically classified as a goddess, which would logically apply to Aietes as well. In the second passage, by comparison, (Od.12.127-136), Helios is paired with one Naeira whose status is not further identified. This mating generates Helios' daughters, who are specifically described as nymphs, living with their mother on the far off island of Thrinicia. They are the shepherdesses responsible for the wellbeing of Helios' extraordinary cattle. In spite of the ambiguity of Naeira's status, these two matings, individually, appear to abide by the underlying principles at issue, namely: god + god = god / god + nymph (mortal) = mortal (including nymphs). Notably the *Theogony's* continuation of the story, in which Aietes unites with one Idyia, who is also a daughter of Okeanos (and Tethys?), would ostensibly make Medeia a full-fledged goddess as well. This may represent an early tradition, in some sense commensurate, at any rate, with some of Medeia's most famous activities (e.g. her rejuvenation of Aison attributed to the *Nostoi*, and her vital role in assisting Iason in his quest to obtain the golden fleece, see Gantz 191, 367, 358-361 for supporting testimony). Alternatively, Medeia's status could be easily adjusted simply by way of her mother's demotion from goddess to nymph, according to the distinction explicitly stated in the Homeric Hymn to Aphrodite (237ff.). This passage provides the most serviceable information relevant to the distinction at stake. Here, nymphs take after neither mortals or immortals, live very long lives, and eat immortal food. Conspicuously though, they do not live forever and, therefore, represent an intermediary race of beings, imbued with outstanding numinous traits, yet subject to death in the long course of time (viz. they no longer populate the terrestrial landscape after the end of the Heroic Age). Thus, they are ultimately θνητοί in a literal sense. A number of other unions in the same family conform to the operative formulas in question. So, for example, when the god Helios became especially popular on the island of Rhodes (e.g. Pind. *Ol.*7; DS 5.55.5, 5.56), in union with Rhode, an eponymous nymph, he spawned a second set of Heliades (viz. in addition to the *Odyssey's* who lived on Thrinicia), and also the hero Phaethon, who met his death recklessly driving the chariot of the sun. Phaethon was, therefore, necessarily mortal, which comes across just as well in the *Theogony's* version, where he is a son of Eos and Kephalos who attracted the attention of Aphrodite (Th.986-989). The identity of this Kephalos is a moot point (an Aiolian and an Athenian are the main contenders). In any case, it is clear the man was a mortal (for Helios' involvement in the genealogy of Korinth, see Huxley 1969: 63-65; Gantz 340; see ApB 2.5.5 for the claim that made him the father of Augeias of Elis). Eos, one of Helios' sisters, was renowned for her infatuation with mortals. So notably, her passion for Tithonos, son of Ilos, of the royal line of Troy, which generated the powerful hero Memnon, who arrived to assist the Trojans in the *Aithiopis* (Il.20.230-240; Th.944-985, HHymn 5). Memnon, therefore, claimed part-Titan ancestry on his mother's side, which made him a most fitting match for Achilles, who boasted part-Nereid ancestry via his mother Thetis. Additionally, Selene, sibling to them both, took a fancy for the hero Endymion (e.g. Sappho 126, Lobel and Page), contributing to the lineage of the Aitolian line that stemmed from Aiolos' daughter Kalyke. In sum, the Titan family of Hyperion and Theia provides considerable insight in terms of the parameters that defined the remarkably fluid boundary between mortality and divinity. This stemma straddled the terrestrial and extra-terrestrial worlds, and stands out as an original Titan source of heroic genealogical ancestry.

PART 2: THE POST-EPIC REEVALUATION OF MYTHOLOGICAL GEOGRAPHY AND THE DISTRIBUTION OF POWER IN THE PELOPONNESE

CHAPTER FOUR: GENEALOGICAL OVERCROWDING AND THE PROBLEM OF MYTHIC ARGOS

On page seventy eight of his commentary on the *Hesiodic Catalogue of Women*, Martin West discusses the recurrent myth about the madness of the daughters of King Proitos of Argos. The story of their affliction explains why it was necessary for Melampous, the famous seer from Pylos, to restore these unfortunate women to sanity, and how, in exchange, the seer insisted on claiming two-thirds of Proitos' kingdom: one-third for his brother and one-third for himself. West asserts that the settlement made with Melampous "was the origin of *a tripartite division of the Argive kingdom,* [a division] which persisted for some time[532]." He goes on to present a possible reconstruction of Melampous' descendants in association with Argos, as he believes they may have appeared in the *Catalogue*. He does the same for the line of Proitos, as well. The line of Bias, however, the third party involved by virtue of being Melampous' brother, is excluded from detailed genealogical treatment as West passes on to Proitos' brother Akrisios, ancestor of Perseus and Herakles. This rapid progression from family to family is par for the course given West's main objective: to make sense of the fragments that survive from this text in light of what is now known of the Greek catalogue genre[533]. Thus the manuscript's content and its organization take precedent over more tangential concerns. Still, the passing reference to such a division of sovereignty, along with the catchy tripartite name, leaves the curious reader pining for information about this great kingdom that was partitioned in thirds, and wondering too, how this story played out elsewhere within the Greek mythic corpus.

A strange inconsistency is already perceptible. Since with Proitos' brother Akrisios added to the mix, another ancestor/ruler commanded power in Argos, so the division among three must then be one among four. Followers of the Trojan War saga, moreover, are bound to think Agamemnon must share a place in all this as the "king of all Argos and many islands[534]." Could it be, therefore, that Argos was somehow split among five distinctive heroic families? How, logically, might such an allotment have worked? And do the Greek mythic narratives actually flesh this out?

Pursuing these telltale signs of some more intricate problem attached to Melampous' migration to Argos, this chapter sorts out the genealogical strands that converged in Argos according to Greek legend. Mythic Argos is, therefore, broken down genealogically to the point where its Homeric depiction stands apart from its later mythological portrait. Moreover, once this distinction comes into focus, the later genealogical portrait of Argos can be easily recognized as the result of deliberate acts of mythological change. Again, the method used to obtain these results hinges on two basic propositions. First the preeminent authority of the Homeric epics as the earliest source for the systematization of Greek mythology in the pre-Homeric period, and second, that although these stories take place all over Greece, it is misleading to assume that they were first recited in the Greek cities where they unfold, or likewise that they originated in those cities. Instead, the idea is to test the implication, ubiquitously preserved in the ancient sources, that all the great early myths that have come down to us were originally told and arranged in accordance with the interests of those whom they originally served, namely the Aiolians of northwest Asia Minor, whose legendary vision traversed all of Greece.

The value of this experiment either stands or falls on the results of this approach to the relevant data, but this is, necessarily, precisely the point of privileging all discernibly Aiolic evidence. In treating the evidence according to these criteria, either mythological clarity will emerge to show that this procedure is actually worthwhile, or it will not, in which case it should be abandoned. In this chapter and in the next these principles are applied in an attempt to demystify mythic Argos through a diachronic assessment of the mythological narratives that built up around "Argos" over time, causing a considerable amount of confusion as to the meaning of the word. The results pave the way for a text-driven study of Melampous' migration to "Argos" in the last chapter. There, the genealogical patterns that surround this old seer lend further support, by way of example, to the existence of an early Aiolic structure and to the methods employed to diminish that structure: the main points advanced throughout this analysis.

There are good reasons for choosing Melampous and Argos for a case study designed to test the strength of the proposed Aiolic hypothesis. First, the legend of the *tripartite division of Argos* involves the convergence of three old Aiolic houses[535] that are aptly described in the mythological record with an unusual degree of genealogical uniformity. Further, with a minimal buildup of lineage variations, all three lines in question lead back from the Troy saga to the eponymous progenitor Aiolos himself in a rare and notable instance of mythic continuity[536]. The story of Melampous and the *tripartite division* has also, as it happens, been preserved in an ample number of ancient sources, specifically: Homer, Bakchylides, Pindar, Herodotos, Diodoros, Strabo, Pausanias, and Apollodoros, with a number of other oblique references elsewhere[537]. There is thus adequate material for a case study, and it is possible to conduct one, quite systematically, by presenting the text from each source individually, followed by a close reading of the data contained in each – an exercise that will follow the present synopsis of major issues and findings concerning mythic Argos[538].

Another reason for choosing Melampous and Argos for systematic investigation has to do with the points of interpretive disagreement expressed by each relevant ancient author. As mentioned above, this series of accounts is remarkably stable in its genealogical coverage of major legendary events and solidly Aiolic in this regard. This spotlights the fact that textual disagreements in these narratives' dealings with the seer Melampous center instead on *where* and *when* key legendary events were said to have happened. This shift in emphasis is extremely important for it suggests that the *tripartite division* of "Argos," as understood from the ancient texts is relevant to unmasking the potential root cause of the notorious ambiguity of mythic Argos[539].

This set of ancient accounts has something further in common inasmuch as their shared objective was to update the antiquated Homeric definition of "Argos," so that the "Argos" of legend might more closely represent the "Argos" of post-Homeric mainland Greek lived reality[540]. That this motivation was responsible for the re-characterization of the place called Argos as it appeared in early Greek myth is the main focus of this and the following chapter. The key evidence cited in support of this claim is the addition of genealogical lines and their respective sagas into Argive terrain, where they had no native roots in early Greek tradition, and which placed them, moreover, in competition with the affiliates of the *tripartite division* whose sovereignty in Argos was integral to the earliest portrait of the Argive state.

Accordingly, the persistent tension between the epic world view and later Greek lived reality affected the definition of the place called "Argos" in a way that makes it strategic to address the legendary transformation of "Argos" *per se*, before assessing the collection of ancient remarks that deal with Melampous' migration to "Argos," since these date to the time when Argive mythology had already been significantly transformed. The proposed source of the problems that surround mythic Argos are, therefore, first presented and analyzed in detail, then examined against the Homeric uses of "Argos," which differ from patterns of later usage and also include a number of definitions that atrophied altogether under changing conditions and the passage of time. The line of Melampous is then revisited in conclusion[541], where its genealogical evaluation serves to support the overall line of reasoning that is set out in the course of this thesis.

THE CONTINUITY OF THE LEGEND OF THE TRIPARTITE DIVISION

The discrepancy between early epic mythology and its subsequent counterpart that developed on the Greek mainland, breaks down into two fundamental dilemmas as far as Melampous and Argos are concerned. First, why do the lines associated with Melampous exhibit a level of genealogical continuity unmatched by the majority of old Aiolic stemmata, which in general fall victim to more frequent intrusions of calculated mythological theft? And second, why are there so many mythological lines crammed into the place referred to as "Argos?" Is there, accordingly, some connection between this overcrowding and the problem of discerning what the word "Argos" really means (i.e. What is Argos? / Where is Argos?)?

As far as genealogical continuity is concerned, the argument runs that the reason for this is linked to the fact that heroes born into each of the lines that divvied up "Argos," according to the story of the *tripartite division*, participated in the two great legendary wars between the cities of Argos and Thebes. That these wars recruited descendants of all three magnates who ruled Argos jointly after Melampous' cure, situates his migration prior to those wars. Moreover, the legend of the *tripartite division* underlies the description of the three Argive leaders who marshaled troops against Troy in the *Iliad*'s *Catalogue of Ships* (Il. 2.559-568[542]). This means that the interaction between the lines of Proitos, Melampous, and Melampous' brother Bias, was, first of all, native to early epic, second, covered a length of heroic time, and third, by virtue of tracing back to Aiolos, involved three genealogies likely to represent three legendary trajectories integral to the original Aiolic lineage structure. The *tripartite division* was, therefore, an allocation sustained over a period of generations, namely, from Melampous' migration to Argos down to the period of the Trojan War, with two Argive-Theban wars intervening. Its status as such is consistently corroborated by the ancestry of heroic personnel cited in connection with these adventures[543].

The close relationship between the *tripartite division* and this canonical sequence of stories highlights the way early mythic narratives and heroic genealogies interacted in tandem. In this synthesis genealogy served as a practical shorthand for intricate full-blown stories. Thus, together, genealogy and narrative plot structures generated what can perhaps best be called a meta-language of culture that could be spoken at length, or otherwise inferred, simply by naming any of its constituent genealogies[544]. As a synthesis then, the early structure consisted in a concatenation of stories, diagrammatically replicated genealogically. Moreover, not any stories, but those that everyone knew, and constituted a body of communal knowledge needed to bring such a language to life[545]. The designation, however, *those that everyone knew* is evidently a shifting category. For the *knowledgeable audience* is, at all times, contingent and fluctuates with historical conditions at large. In the context of the Aiolic hypothesis, which looks back in time to late "Dark Age" Greece, when according to the investigation at hand, the traditions that stand behind the

Homeric poems were promoted to serve as a cultural charter, the initial group knowledge under consideration is that of the early Aiolic Greeks[546], while the stories themselves were more than sheer entertainment, but the essence of Aiolic pre-historical heritage[547].

Though the works of Homer, in retrospect, register as the body of Greek cultural knowledge with the greatest longevity and the greatest scope (pan-Hellenic in terms of their cognitive audience), it is clear that subsidiary bodies of knowledge increasingly coexisted, as time wore on, inspired by East Greek epic, in the first instance[548], yet based on new renditions of earlier stories and more restricted constituencies of those in the know. There were subsets of knowledge and subsets of adherents, some confined within local/regional borders, although others, while local in orientation, eventually managed to command allegiance over extensive parts of Greece. All told, these developments do not defy expectation when it comes to projecting what is likely to happen when a provincial charter becomes universalized and, therefore, ceases to be the exclusive possession of those who created it to begin with. As far as the present hypothesis is concerned, the early Aiolic lineage structure, as it spread abroad with the spread of East Greek epic became public property in just such a fashion. It was thereupon subjected to revision in fragments, inspired by various local self-interests which characterized its reception abroad.

One consequence of the interdependence of legend and genealogy in early archaic myth was a degree of structural rigidity based on the close-knit connection between specific protagonists and specific events. The genealogical mapping of individuals is, by and large, a linear progression, broadening horizontally, mainly on account of new ties formed by each marital union, and via multiple progeny born into the same family. Multiple progeny prompt new parallel lines that, in turn, proceed vertically, charting the passage of time in generations. A strong established connection between named personnel and explicit adventures, sustained over the course of multiple generations, creates a framework more resistant to change than unattached independent legends would be. In such circumstances breaking the bond between specific events and specific protagonists necessarily sets off a chain reaction dislodging key players vital to the sequence from locations where they were expected to be. The arbitrary removal of any protagonist acknowledged as a part of an established series suspends the progression of legendary events by creating a gap or missing link between well-known forebears and their descendants whose presence the series altogether depends on. The removal of a protagonist therefore arrests due progress from legendary point A to legendary point B, throwing all attached elements out of synchrony. Such dynamics, moreover, infer the existence of an organized framework at large to begin with[549].

The triad of lines that converged in "Argos" seems to have been a part of a structural alliance that bound mythic narratives to genealogy during the heyday of early Aiolic legend. Yet this alliance was a fairly short-lived phenomenon, since the level of cohesion such an arrangement required could not be sustained in the subsequent era of mass emendations enacted by poets on behalf of miscellaneous Greek city-states[550]. While the concept of genealogical/narrative symbiosis could, as a principle, still be upheld when it no longer obtained in actuality (that is to say, when the two no longer actually meshed), and could well be imitated in order to authenticate new or adjusted legendary material[551], the concept is, in fact, only technically viable within a complete and cogent lineage structure, since once structural stability has been disrupted, and orderly patterns disfigured every which way, snippets of genealogical information are no longer capable of abbreviating substantial tracts of legendary narrative. Genealogy, henceforth, continued to play a highly politicized role in Greek myth, yet it did so as a comparatively vestigial element, a relic of bygone structural cohesion. Though still used and revered by cultural convention, later on each great deed and ancestral achievement had to be literally explained in words, as deliberate encroachment on Aiolic mythic terrain fragmented consensus among interested parties and sparked innovations with a vested interest in laying the early structure to waste[552].

Returning to the relative genealogical continuity exhibited by the trio of lines that traced back to Melampous' migration to "Argos," the hypothesis runs that this mythic block thwarted change on account of its engagement in a succession of vital legendary events[553]. These events unfolded in a linear sequence, based on canonical stories and their respective protagonists so that the damage disturbance to this sequence would cause prevented such disturbance from taking place. Accordingly, these dynamics may be held responsible for the maintenance of these lines from Melampous to Troy. And they add strength to the prospect that this segment of Greek myth was a bona fide piece of early Aiolic legend.

As for the second dilemma, the ambiguity of "Argos," the critical question that needs to be addressed is why, free from compulsion, any reasonable person would squeeze so many great lineages into so small a space, only to be saddled, as a result, with a virtually inexplicable landscape that demanded astute interpretive antics to sort out the resulting mythological entanglements? The response to this runs: first, that this state of affairs was not always the case, which is readily apparent with reference to Homer. And second, that the most likely instigator behind the promotion of such entangled mythological circumstances is the historical Argos, the archaic Greek city-state. With Argos as instigator, it is possible to detect how the advantages of such action could outweigh the liabilities. Namely, what is a dose of logistical confusion compared with the level of legendary prestige that would result from securing possession of five of the most powerful mythological lines? The prospect that it was Argos that stood behind these developments makes it readily possible to explain the otherwise perplexing mythological controversies involved in ancient discussions of the *tripartite division*, as well as the equally perplexing refusal of ancient writers to commit to a stable definition of mythic "Argos"[554].

THE HISTORICAL EVIDENCE ON EARLY ARGOS

The idea that Argos was the early source of certain permanent mythological changes gains support on historical and mythological grounds. First, the historical. Argos was the premier Peloponnesian land power to emerge in the early Archaic Period[555] and remained a force to be reckoned with until the early fifth century, when the Spartans under king Kleomenes defeated the Argives at the battle of Sepeia (494)[556]. From the mid-seventh century down to the fifth, Peloponnesian politics were dominated by competition for influence between Argos and Sparta in combination with shifting provincial interests of independent neighboring states. This polarization most likely emerged in relation to the Spartan conquest of Messenia, which perhaps began in the later eighth century but was not complete until around 600. The initial extent of Messenian subjugation is not explicit in the early period[557]. Based on Tyrtaios' oft quoted description from a poem composed in the mid-seventh century[558], of the plight of the Messenian helots, namely likening them to donkeys under great constraint and obliged to forfeit half of their agricultural yield for the benefit of their Spartan masters[559], it is safe to say that reducing Messenians to helot status had become Spartan policy before that time[560].

The first phase of the process was roughly contemporary with the emergence of Korinth as the foremost Peloponnesian seafaring power under the leadership of the Bakchiad clan[561]. Megara, at the time, had been attacked by Corinth, which seized a substantial block of Megarian territory. Autonomous Megarian colonization initiatives, first in the west and later in the east, were subsequently initiated as a result[562]. Likewise dated to roughly the same period[563] is the shadowy conflict known from Thoukydides as the Lelantine War, which was, in his opinion, the first organized military confrontation of significant scope since the Trojan War (1.15)[564]. Named after the open plain between Chalkis and Eretria, Euboia's two dominant entrepreneurial powers, the war was said to have mobilized major Greek states in favor of either of these two cities, whose early cooperation[565] degenerated into rivalry quite typical of bordering Greek metropoleis. Though we only know for certain, namely from Herodotos, that Miletos supported the Eretrian cause and Samos the interests of Chalkis (5.99), and from Plutarch that Chalkis obtained cavalry from Thessalian Pharsalos and assistance from Chalkidian colonies in Thrace (Mor. 760e-761b), it is customary to fill out the roster of participants to match Thoukydides' remarks on the scope of the war in accordance with two distinct groups of powers consistently hostile to one another and friendly among themselves in the ancient sources[566].

Retrospectively, based on subsequent information, Corinth[567], Erythrai, and Sparta are considered to be likely allies of Chalkis, while Megara, Chios[568], Messenia, and Argos are considered likely allies of Eretria[569]. If dated to the eighth century or even the early seventh, doubts may be raised whether the conflict in Euboia enlisted the sympathies of the Peloponnesian land powers[570].

The polarized opposition of allied states, perceptible later, in any event likely hung in the balance for quite some time, as far as the Peloponnesian states were concerned (with the likely exception of seafaring Korinth), at least until the impact of Sparta's conquest of Messenia galvanized Peloponnesian concern over Spartan supremacy in the region. Reaction to the specter of Spartan violence toward fellow Peloponnesian communities was tangible in the first half of the seventh century as the result of the "First Messenian War,[571]" whereas it was, in essence, the "First Messenian War" that defined the entity known as Sparta. Consolidation began around the mid-eighth century with the gradual incorporation of surrounding settlements, then increasingly distant perioecic communities, followed by incursions beyond Mt. Taygetos into the plain of Makaria, then to Stenyklaros in the heart of Messenia, and finally as far west as Messenian Pylos. The last advance listed took place later, however, in the course of the "Second Messenian War,[572]" while the submission of communities such as Pharis, and Geronthrai and the initial forays west of Taygetos appear to have been accomplished just prior to, if not after the onset of the first war[573]. The point is that Sparta was in a state of development in the late eighth and early seventh centuries, and had not yet become the formidable power that it would later turn out to be.

Serious opposition from Argos in the north was predicated on the manifest rise of Sparta. Thus the early *Lakonismos* of the town of Asine (in the Argolid[574]) that was subsequently destroyed by Argos in vengeance sometime before the year 700 may well document progress toward a face-off between two equally matched Peloponnesian land powers. However, to the extent that Asine is symbolic of the gradual escalation of conflict, it is the benefit of hindsight that makes it so, while with the benefit of hindsight it is also possible to discern how uncertain it was before the late seventh century how things were actually going to turn out.

A decisive display of Argive strength is credited to Pheidon, the Temenid dynast,[575] whose reign, though controversial, is now generally placed in the first half of the seventh century. Pheidon is unanimously considered to represent the apex of power for archaic Argos. His achievements, moreover, went down in history as a restoration of the Temenid inheritance that, according to legend, placed a large tract of territory under the control of the Argive state. Pheidon's reputation implies the re-conquest of places that had slipped out from under Argive control, and shows, in addition, that the famous legend that defined the inhabitants of Argos, Sparta, and also, Messenia, as descendants of a single ancient immigrant family was not only widespread and in full force at the time, but was also a phenomenon with a life of its own beyond the vicissitudes of interstate violence[576].

Though definitive proof of Pheidon's responsibility for the "crushing[577]" defeat of invading Spartan forces at the battle of Hysiai in 669 is not forthcoming in the extant evidence, Pheidon of Argos was known to Herodotos for promoting a standard system of weights and measures (6.127), and for seizing control of the Olympic games, which must have involved an overland campaign that drove Argive forces into Eleian territory (Paus.6.22.2) [578]. Aristotle regarded Pheidon of Argos as the one of the earliest of the Greek tyrants (Pol.5.1310b), and while Herodotos places him in the late seventh century, if not the early sixth[579], this time-frame discredits the possibility of Pheidon's leadership at the battle of Hysiai. On the evidence, as it stands, a late seventh-century Pheidon is not an altogether inconceivable prospect[580]. Still, one way or another, Argos successfully thwarted Spartan designs against Thyreatis[581] and discouraged Spartan aggression for roughly a century after the date associated with the Battle of Hysiai.

In this connection it has been additionally proposed that the humiliation of Sparta at the hands of the Argives at the battle of Hysiai[582] sparked off the second prolonged round of fighting by suggesting the opportunity for Messenian revolt[583]. Quite typically, this proposal has its share of detractors and controversies about dating are particularly acute[584], yet whether via this sequence or by way of some other cause Messenian resistance in the mid seventh century apparently fostered an anti-Spartan coalition supported by a number of Peloponnesian states. Pausanias lists Arkadia, Argos, Sikyon, and Elis as contributors to the defense of Messenia, none of which are unreasonable in the early seventh century[585]. Strabo, moreover, in this case cites Tyrtaios for Argives, Arkadians, and Pisatans allied on behalf of the Messenian cause (8.4.10)[586]. Herodotos mentions Samos as a supporter of Sparta, while Pausanias adds Korinth in the same capacity[587]. The first Messenian revolt or Tyrtaian War was not completely suppressed until the end of the century at which point Spartan sovereignty was firmly secured, precipitating the floruit of Spartan culture.

Here the point is not so much the impossibility that either Argos or Sparta sent military support to Chalkis or Eretria in the Lelantine War, but that the war antedates the crystallization of Spartan statehood and its effects throughout the Peloponnese. Logically such circumstances restrict the likelihood of participation in the Euboian conflict to the colonizing maritime poleis, already active beyond their own boundaries in the late eighth century, and politically sympathetic to either the Chalkidan or the Eretrian side[588]. In any event, from the time ascribed to the battle at Hysiai (i.e. 669) to the Spartan victory at the battle of the Champions in 546, and then conclusively at Sepeia in 494, Peloponnesian politics were influenced by a spirit of competition and underlying hostility between Argos in the north and Sparta in the south.

If the Lelantine War took place in the late eighth century or significantly prior to the Messenian revolt, it took place in the midst of a developmental period before shades of gray gave way to black and white[589]. It is in no way surprising that in the end, the political polarization of the Peloponnese aligned with the polarization of states established further a field at an earlier date. However, efforts to synchronize these events tend to negate a block of Peloponnesian history when state relations were somewhat more fluid and as such more conducive to common cultural consciousness and collective accounts of the distant past.

On a more concrete level, by way of example, although in some sense affiliated with Samos[590], Bakkhiad Korinth maintained reasonably amicable relations with Argos before the Kypselid tyranny of the early 550s, while Sikyon too, among nearby satellite states, remained within Argos' sphere of influence at least until the reign of the Orthagorid tyrants[591]. Megarian resistance to Korinthian expansion made lasting enemies of these two states, but it did not immediately or automatically make enemies out of Korinth and Argos or, alternatively out of Argos and Megara. Notably, sometime in the eighth century, the famous early state poet, Eumelos of Korinth, composed a hymn for a Messenian choir at Delos[592], which interjects a reminder that there was a time when Messenia interacted on par with other early archaic Greek city-states. Early political affinities and disaffections appear in this light to have been more complex than sweeping generalizations tend to allow, particularly in advancing a polarization of states before conditions that provoked polarization were met, while access to more nuanced motivations and outcomes is limited by the available evidence. The early preeminence of Argos, however, is stable regardless of constituent controversies, though eventually undercut by the rise of powerful tyrannies, and ultimately eclipsed by the ascendance of Sparta.

In all this it is clear that Argos was early on a formidable Peloponnesian power and in the position, as a result, to direct the contemporary invention of tradition. It is also evident that there was a time in the early Archaic Period when rivalries among the Dorian states had not yet surfaced as such or hardened into alignment, freeing a block of time in which to date the curious link in the legendary histories of Argos, Messenia, and Lakonia[593]. Equally curious is Korinth's omission from this triple association, since Korinth too was a powerful Dorian state situated just beyond Argive borders, and Korinth, like Argos, had emerged as such before the Spartan subjugation of Messenia.

THE STORY OF THE RETURN OF THE HERAKLEIDAI

In addition to the proposal suggested above that archaic Argos successfully appropriated the mythological lines of Perseus and Pelops, on top of the early epic allocation of stories associated with the *tripartite division*, another important piece of Greek legendary history that hinges on the status of archaic Argos is the story of the *return of the Herakleidai*, which culminated in a drawing of lots for control over Argos, Messenia, and Lakonia. Temenos, Kresphontes, and the sons of Aristodemos[594] (all descendants of Hyllos, Herakles' son), who, legend had it, penetrated the country with the help of a Dorian army, obtained their respective realms as the result of this drawing, through which they obtained regional ancestral status. Though notably restricted to three Dorian poleis, this charter was destined to have a lasting effect on

Peloponnesian group identity, gradually expanding to take account of all Dorian inhabitants of the Peloponnese. At the same time, however, there are indications that creative Peloponnesian local pre-histories were already unfolding in a very different manner, prior to the advent of the Heraklid claim. And this suggests a time when Peloponnesian Dorians had not yet defined themselves against the legacy of the early epic Achaians who controlled the island of Pelops in the Homeric poems.

On this count, Eumelos of Korinth reveals that his interpretive strategy did not acknowledge a major Dorian/Heraklid conquest, but proceeded in accordance with standard epic protocol, recasting established epic traditions to the advantage of the Korinthian state. And notably, it seems, Eumelos failed to distinguish the Achaian protagonists of the old epic stories from the Dorian ethos of historical times, at least, not in the way these rival claims were distinguished once the Heraklid charter rose to prominence. Instead, Eumelos mainly co-opted well-known adventures, like the story of Bellerophon and the Argonauts' voyage, and endowed them with distinctly Korinthian resonance[595]. Meager but telling evidence further suggests that Eumelos' poetry was not unique in its ignorance of the Heraklid vision of things.

The Aipytidai clan of Messenian Stenyklaros, which bordered on Arkadia to the east, early on, evidently, traced their lineage back to the Homeric figure by the name of Aipytos, whose tomb the *Iliad* situates in the vicinity (Il.2.604)[596]. Moreover, greater Messenia was by all means entitled to the illustrious family of Aphareus and Lynkeus, sons of Perieres, son of Aiolos, who was also credited, perhaps originally so, with the paternity of Ikarios and Tyndareos[597]. Though the family of Perieres, son of Aiolos was heavily tampered with in the post-epic period[598], it is sufficiently clear, in spite of such activity, that Perieres' family, like the family of Neleus (cf.Od.11.235ff.), was understood as a clan of Aiolic migrants to the western Peloponnese[599]. Aphareus' two sons, Lynkeus and Idas, died in combat with the Dioskouri[600] as the result of a showdown that centered around either the possession of a herd of cattle or the possession of Phoibe and Hilaeria, the daughters of Leukippos[601], or, in some cases, a combination of both[602]. Moreover, Aphareus' granddaughter,

Kleopatra (daughter of Idas, son of Aphareus and Marpessa, daughter or Euenos of Aitolia) married Meleagros, son of Oineus of Kalydon a match acknowledged by Homer in *Iliad* book nine (556)[603].

Thus, from an epic standpoint, early archaic Messenia was fairly well endowed with heroic lore, while Korinth by contrast faced a deficiency, which the Bakchiad Eumelos set out to fix by reinterpreting epic on Korinth's behalf[604]. In addition to the examples cited above, there is adequate evidence to the effect that in the early phases of Greek colonization the foundation mythologies devised by new Greek metropoleis also proceeded directly from established heroic lore. So, for example the prolific use of the *Nostoi* as an originally standard point of departure for new trajectories based on the heroic past[605].

Overall, this type of data suggests that before the Heraklid charter came into vogue, regional genealogies proceeded straightforwardly from Homeric antecedents, without making intermediary identity claims. This would additionally seem to imply that in this early period no great urgency was felt when it came to nuanced distinctions about Greek tribal identity. This meant that influential Dorian groups were quite content to align themselves with established Aiolic tradition without rewriting old myth to draw any such distinctions. Though the Heraklid story also relied on the same early epic legendary foundation, it unfolds in a markedly different fashion on account of its interest in Greek tribal identity (e.g. the Dorians vs. the Achaians) that required some complex narrative maneuvering to insure that a clan of Dorian ancestors could supplant the Achaians of East Greek epic tradition, yet preserve that tradition at the same time, no less, its greatest exploit: the Trojan War. By virtue of promoting this innovation the Heraklid story provides a *terminus post quem* for the abandonment of a more direct mode of epichoric creativity in the Peloponnese[606].

The provenance of the Heraklid story is fundamentally a speculative matter. However, based on a number of key indications concerning the mytho-political climate in the Peloponnese at the time of its inception, it is possible to identify a few probable factors involved in its development and subsequent spread. Toward this end, the story's analysis mainly relies on the content of the story itself, which, thanks to Tyrtaios (Str.8.4.10), may be confidently assigned a *terminus ante quem* in the mid-seventy century. Equally notable in this regard, is the absence of any trace of the Heraklid construct as far as the Homeric poems were concerned, though the source of its inspiration is tangible enough in the Homeric acknowledgment of Dorians on Krete (Od.19.177) and descendants of Herakles on Rhodes (Il.2.653-670) and Kos (e.g.Il.2.676-680)[607].

Among scholars prepared to entertain the idea that the highly influential modern theory responsible for equating the Heraklid legend with the actual southward movement of Dorian Greeks (consequently known as "the Dorian invasion"), may not be realistic, mainly on account of the mythological nature of the ancient reportage, Argos is currently viewed as the most probable source of a Heraklid "return" to the Peloponnese accompanied by a cohort of Dorian allies[608]. In support of this view, it has been pointed out that the Heraklid Temenos, who received Argos by lot in the narrated division of Peloponnesian territory is the only one of the participants involved in the drawing whose name directly invokes an actual clan of provincial Peloponnesian elites, namely the Temenids of the Argolid[609]. In Sparta, by contrast, it seems adjustments were needed to equate the designated Heraklid representatives with the regional heritage of the Spartan kings[610], whereas in Messenia, as mentioned above, the Heraklid legend came into conflict with already established Aipytid ancestors, who played an epic-based aitiological role[611]. That the implementation of the Heraklid charter required adaptation in Messenia and Lakonia in order to mesh with existing conditions, while it squared quite directly with conditions in Argos, supports the idea that the charter itself originally radiated from the Argolid.

The exclusion of Korinth from the allotment is yet another conspicuous factor, given Korinth's contemporaneous status as a high-profile Dorian state[612]. Indeed, the exclusion of Korinth from the legend's narrative core suggests that the story of the Heraklid return may have been influenced by mythological competition between the cities of Argos and Korinth, since both of these states were actively involved in legendary redaction very early on. It is sometimes proposed (although it cannot be decisively shown), that Eumelos associated the local hero, Aletes, who was also known as a descendant of Herakles, with Dorian identity in the Korinthia[613]. If so, such a narrative would have provided the impetus for a counterproposal developed in Argos, reasonably enough, to the exclusion of Korinth. If, on the other hand, Eumelos stuck strictly to the patriotic deployment of epic-based material, then the groundbreaking idea that Peloponnesian Dorians ought to devise their own abridgement to the early epic depiction of the Heroic Age would appear to default to Argive ingenuity, again quite justifiably, to the exclusion of Korinth, which, thanks to Eumelos, already possessed its own comprehensive and flattering account of the Korinthian mythic past.

Either way, the evidence indicates that in the early seventh century, the northeastern part of the Peloponnese was a locus of competitive mythmaking activity that spread rapidly throughout the rest of the region. Whether, in any case, the premier Dorian charter was first promoted in Korinth or first promoted in Argos, at length the Argos-based version dominated the field, strategically embracing the Dorian identity of Messenia and Lakonia as well. Thus, though an influential forerunner in the advancement of legendary redaction in mainland Greece, Korinth was consequently obliged to accept a subsidiary role in the standard account of the Dorianization of the Peloponnese[614]. That the mythological patterning visible here resulted from the jockeying for prestige between Argos and Korinth in the first instance, and in the second, from the fact that Argos' contribution won out in the end[615] is further corroborated by Argive activity in the Homeric epic milieu. It will soon become clear that the machinations of Argos, in terms of early epic political geography, altered the mythic layout of the Peloponnese in a way that matches up so remarkably well with the story of the return of the Herakleidai, as to raise serious doubts that this alignment could be a matter of mere coincidence. On the contrary, Argive treatment of Homeric tradition increases the plausibility that the Herakleidai story was also a product of Argive ingenuity.

THE ARGIVE GENEALOGY AND THE LINE OF PELOPS

Turning now to the mythological changes enacted by Argos against received epic wisdom that permanently altered the Greek mythic landscape and, in turn, paved the way for the widespread success of the *return of the Herakleidai* story. Here the argument runs that early archaic Argos in an application of actual power to myth managed to appropriate the kingdom of Agamemnon as described and allotted to him in the *Iliad*, in addition to the territory associated with Argos in the *Iliad*'s *Catalogue of Ships*[616]. This arbitrary expansion of mythological sovereignty defied the fact that the *Iliad*'s description of the domain shared by Diomedes, Sthenelos and Eurylaos far more accurately represented archaic Argos than the sum of that kingdom plus Agamemnon's. Further, in its absorption of Agamemnon's early epic domain, Argos ran roughshod over the mythic honors that should have accrued to neighboring states from Korinth to Elis along the southern coast of the Korinthian Gulf, at least to the extent such states would have been willing to associate their prestige with Agamemnon's[617]. Yet, nonetheless, in so doing, and with the help of a few keen mythological adaptations, the Argive polis laid claim to the line of Perseus and the line of Pelops along with it[618], in addition to the three lines she already possessed by virtue of Homeric emphasis on the seer Melampous' migration to Argos[619].

It is to be noted that in making this move to secure control over these genealogies, topographically speaking, archaic Argos remained just as it was, archaic Argos. For, in actuality, no political boundaries were expanded or redrawn[620]. Instead the lineages in question were simply imported into the state of Argos of everyday life. This is precisely why, the hypothesis goes, there was so much mythological overcrowding in "Argos," and why it was often so hard to figure out whether something was happening, or whether someone was ruling, in Argos, Mykenai, or Tiryns.

As for the mythic adaptations relevant to the case, the one that looms largest in the immediate context is the Argive adoption of the mythic figure Akrisios, father of Danae, the mother of Perseus. It is not that this figure did not already exist, for this is Perseus' genealogy in the *Iliad* (Il.14.319-320), but rather that it seems eminently unlikely that Akrisios' early lineage, whatever it was, made him the twin brother of Proitos of Argos[621].

PROITOS OF ARGOS

Proitos of Argos was an old mythic figure. He was famous for deporting the great hero Bellerophon (heroic master of Pegasos, the legendary winged horse) to the country of Lykia in Asia Minor, where Proitos' father-in-law Iobates was king (Il.6.152-170). Proitos charged Bellerophon to deliver a written message, which, unbeknownst to him, demanded that King Iobates attend to the murder of his new visitor, whom Proitos was reluctant to dispense with himself. A classic case of the so-called "Potiphar's wife" story was the motivating factor alleged in all this[622]. For during his stay as a guest at Proitos' residence, Proitos wife[623] attempted to seduce Bellerophon, and then, when most honorably rebuffed by him, she resorted to accusing the man of the transgression she herself had committed. Proitos therefore sent Bellerophon to Iobates, who, instead of killing him outright, as Proitos requested, decided to send him on an impossible mission, namely to kill the monstrous Chimaira. Bellerophon's success and return from this expedition next prompted Iobates to send him on two others (viz. against the Solymoi and against the Amazons). His successful execution of these in addition, magnified his stature to such an extent that Iobates offered Bellerophon his daughter's hand in marriage and granted him his own realm in the Lykian kingdom.

The story of Proitos' encounter with Bellerophon and Bellerophon's migration to Asia Minor comes to light by way of a battlefield confrontation between Diomedes of Argos and Glaukos of Lykia beneath the ramparts of Troy in book six of the *Iliad* (119-236). Relevant to interpreting the significance of this passage is a small but suggestive collection of data that records an alternate genealogy for Proitos of Argos: son of Thersander, son of Sisyphos, son of Aiolos[624]. This testimony suggests that Proitos, like Bellerophon, was a grandson of Sisyphos, son of Aiolos, to the effect that Proitos and Bellerophon were at one time considered to be first cousins: Proitos a son of Thersandros, son of Sisyphos, son of Aiolos, and Bellerophon, a son of Glaukos, son of Sisyphos, son of Aiolos. In line with recurrent genealogical patterning this tenacious alternative is likely to be genuine and equally likely to antedate the multitude of extant later accounts, which make Proitos and Akrisios both sons of Abas, who was a son of Lynkeus and Hypermestra, in turn, the son of Aigyptos and the daughter of Danaos from the international segment of the Argive line. As set out above[625], Lynkeus and Hypermestra were strategic agents in the post-Homeric reorganization of the Argive line[626]. Thus, the legendary heritage of Akrisios and his family have passed down to us in such a dramatically altered state that its early epic identity is largely obscured.

As for Abas, the father of both Proitos and Akrisios in all standard accounts[627], putting Proitos to one side in light of the prospect that he was once son of Thersandros, son of Sisyphos, it may well be that Abas was indeed Akrisios' father well before the advent of the revamped Argive line. If so, his former persona remains excruciatingly vague, though as argued above[628], not without potentially meaningful resonance in the name of the Euboian tribe, the Abantes (Il.2.536), or at the ancient oracle of Abai in Phokis (Str.9.3.13; Paus. 10.35.1). The problem here is that Perseus' heritage, both genealogically and mytho-topographically has been completely effaced by later mythic developments. Mainly, the promulgation of the revised Argive line rendered the former status of this great family unrecoverable back beyond Abas (viz. Perseus' grandfather). Still, there is little doubt that the genealogies that lead back beyond Abas in later Greek myth are substitutes for some unknown, older arrangement, which is likely, according to recurrent patterning, to have originally had Aiolic roots. On this count it is worth reviewing the Proitos/ Iobates/ Bellerophon story with Proitos' alternate genealogy in mind.

After Glaukos[629] recites his ancestry to Diomedes, confirming his status as the scion of a Greek line that took up permanent residence in Lykia (one of the *Iliad*'s most valued allies of Troy), Diomedes recollects the ancient ties of *xenia* binding his opponent to himself. For since Tydeus once hosted Bellerophon in Aitolia, Diomedes now extends a reciprocal invitation to host Glaukos at his home "in the heart of Argos[630]," contingent of course, on the conclusion, no less on their survival of the Trojan War. The bargain was sealed with the famous exchange of armor, and where the poet himself, in a striking *parabasis*, pauses to emphasize that Glaukos was duped, exchanging his gold armor worth one hundred oxen for Diomedes' bronze that was worth only nine. Aside from this passage's participation in the

Homeric ideology that extolled eastern wealth as part of a pre-ordained shift of power from Trojan to Greek sovereignty tied to the fall of Troy, it also makes certain genealogical inferences ostensibly meaningful to contemporary audiences. For example, since Diomedes was a commander from Argos[631] in the company of two descendants of Melampous' brother Bias, and likewise, in the company of a descendant of the very same Proitos, who banished Bellerophon from the country, his invitation to Glaukos is a special kind of truce – it is an invitation to Glaukos to be honored and welcomed in his forsaken homeland where a branch of his ancestral family resided.

Diomedes, himself, it is to be remembered, came from Aitolian stock on his father's side. His father Tydeus sought refuge in Argos after he was exiled for homicide. There he married one of the daughters of Adrastos of Argos at the very same time that Polyneikes, Oidipous' son fled the city of Thebes over a conflict with his brother and married a daughter of Adrastos as well[632]. These were the circumstances that stood behind the unsuccessful first Argive war against Thebes, yet they were also responsible for Diomedes' right to dominion in Argos to begin with. He reigned in cooperation with the descendants of Proitos, and with the descendants of Bias as well, while by the time of the Trojan War, the descendants of Melampous were long since out of the picture on account of a matricide, once again linked to the two great wars between Argos and Thebes[633]. Proitos' alternate genealogy, then, can at least be said to harmonize with other data advanced in the Homeric poems, but it can also be said to heighten the pathos and enhance the significance of Glaukos' deceptively foolish exchange[634].

AKRISIOS

Turning now to Akrisios, who plays a key role in the whole dilemma of mythic "Argos," mainly because his affiliation with either, the city, or the province of Argos (i.e. the Argolid) is upon close inspection remarkably weak. As far as the Homeric poems were concerned, this region was already completely full up. It was governed by a matrix of genealogies that covered a solid block of heroic time in a coherent and organized fashion. Moreover, when Proitos is severed from the line of Perseus on the basis of compelling alternate information there is no Perseid involvement in the region at all. Yet if the line of Perseus did not reign in the city of Argos or in the Argolid, the question arises where did his line reign?

Only one possible answer to this question ever surfaces in the extant testimony, and it surfaces consistently in spite of the fact that Akrisios was appropriated by the Argive polis and ultimately wedged into Argive domain[635]. At stake is the idea that the Atreidai were, one way or another, the beneficiaries of the kingdom that was once ruled by Perseus and his family[636]. Akrisios' and accordingly, Perseus' kingdom, if such a transfer of power were sufficiently old, would have therefore been equivalent to Agamemnon's domain as described in the *Iliad*'s *Catalogue of Ships*, namely the northern Peloponnesian coastline from Korinth to Elis, ruled from Mykenai, which lay further inland and bordered on Argive territory to the south and the east. From the texts that deal with Melampous it will be clear in due course that the citadel of Mykenai, Agamemnon's great stronghold, was unanimously thought to be founded by Perseus, which may well be an opinion based on early precedent.

Though the Homeric epics do not corroborate the transfer of power at issue explicitly, the *Iliad* sure seems to do so implicitly by way of a flashback that has the goddess Hera come down from Olympos and make her way to the district that was later Agamemnon's domain on a mission to speed up the birth of Eurystheus, grandson of Perseus and Herakles' famous rival[637]. The epics further express a keen familiarity with a number of characters and situations involved in the life stories of Perseus' descendants[638], and by way of a process of elimination suggest that Perseus' Peloponnesian domain, which was somewhere in "Argos" though it was not in the Argolid, nor in Elis, nor Pylos, nor Messenia, nor Arkadia, and certainly not in Lakedaimon, lurked behind the sovereignty of Agamemnon. If so, this transfer of power responds to the related question that asks: how Agamemnon, the grandson of Pelops, who immigrated to Greece from Asia Minor, managed to become the most powerful magnate in Peloponnese, and moreover, in all of Greece?

Again, Pelops' foreign status readily fits the mindset characteristic of early Greek epic thinking, for it reflects a time when

Greece was, by contrast, a fledgling Mediterranean power, and wealth and high culture were in general associated with great metropoleis to the east[639]. Thus, Pelops arrived as an emissary of eastern grandeur whose legacy was intimately entwined with the legendary prehistory of his adopted homeland[640]. But, how then, as a foreigner, who won the hand of a local king's daughter, did Pelops' descendants manage to amass sufficient authority in the course of just a few generations to make Agamemnon king of kings at the head of the Greek expedition against Troy? If genealogy is any guide, and if the case of Bellerophon a valid counter-example, showing as it does the reciprocal fate of a Greek who became a great eastern magnate, naturalization and landed wealth were most expediently acquired through marriage[641]. Menelaos' position as king of Sparta was likewise accomplished in precisely this way, yielding a formidable acquisition of territory[642].

According to the *Ehoiai* three sons of Perseus married three daughters of Pelops (fr 190.3-193.23 MW; cf. West 1985: 38, 110). This marriage is canonical from that point onward, however, taken alone, as we have seen, such an assertion does not suffice to conclude that this arrangement was necessarily old. For what it is worth, it is also true, that no other concrete suggestions arise, nor do the named figures involved in this context suffer from the kind of ambiguity raised by suspicious duplicate names[643]. Two further factors appear to be relevant. First, the collection of stories about the house of Perseus, a good number of which are verifiably old, lead collectively toward the extinction of that house. Moreover, they do so gradually, in the long course of time, through the buildup of discrete episodes in the family saga, that give the impression, overall, of an appointed transfer of power from the house of Perseus to the house of Pelops due to a consequent lack of Perseid heirs. The details on this will be set out below. Still, it is worth pointing out with respect to the alleged transfer, that as far as the *Iliad* was concerned, it seems the dynasty of Pelops, though destined to rule, was not as of yet entrenched in Mykenai at the time of the first Argive war against Thebes (Il.4.376-400).

Second, according to the present analysis, the most important post-Homeric mythic development that affected this segment of the Argive line was the move that made Proitos and Akrisios sons of Abas, and then pit these two brothers against one another over possession of sovereignty in "Argos." This development made good use of the marriage between the house of Perseus and the house of Pelops, since whether via this union[644], or some equivalent connection, the dominion of Perseus, administered from Mykenai, ultimately passed down to the house of Atreus, falling into the hands of Agamemnon, ruler of that kingdom in the *Iliad*, and likewise, the most powerful ruler in Greece[645]. This implicates the Proitos/Akrisios fraternity in a pivotal geopolitical change because it appears that Akrisios' claim to sovereign authority in the Argolid was absolutely dependent on it. But there, the kingdom assigned to Akrisios and his family (viz. the house of Perseus), and by extension, through the aforementioned marriage, later assigned to the house of Pelops, was a kingdom drastically diminished in size. In essence it was confined to Mykenai and environs, against the Homeric view of the matter, wherein Agamemnon ruled from Mykenai nearly the whole north coast of the Peloponnese (Il.2.569-580).

The presence of the line of Pelops in "Argos," and within "Argos," specifically at Mykenai, a site generally held to have been founded by Perseus, again suggests creative mythic activity on the part of archaic Argos. Of Agamemnon's early epic domain, realistically, only Mykenai, lay within the bounds of the historical Argive state[646]. Numerous strands of dispersed information fall into place by way of this simple datum. Putting the pieces together, it becomes more and more likely that archaic Argos appropriated Akrisios along with an ancient Perseid/Pelopid link for purposes of a revised mythic program aimed at the legendary enhancement of the Argive state. In essence, the Argive strategy simply annulled the greater kingdom these heroes traditionally ruled and swept the heroes themselves into contemporary Argos. The clearest manifestation of this initiative is the curious mythological overcrowding in "Argos," which on close inspection, evidently derives from a deliberate reworking of the Homeric geopolitical distribution of power. Moreover, this overcrowding is much less of an enigma once the Argive appropriation of Perseus, which made his grandfather brother of an old Argive king, is uncovered by way of a genealogical reading of the available mythological data, viewed, simultaneously, in light of the politics of archaic Greek mytho-poetic change.

That the dramatic downsizing of Agamemnon's domain stems back to Akrisios' conscription into the Argolid is tangibly corroborated by the space left un-ruled (viz. the northern Peloponnesian coast from Korinth to Elis), and hence mytho-politically left unaccounted for once these magnates and their lineages were crammed into "Argos." Yet, the void that resulted from the detachment and absorption of Mykenai by the Argive state, along with the great heroes who had links to Mykenai, was not left to languish thus unaccounted for. Next, the remaining expanse of territory beyond Mykenai that was formerly under Mykenaian control was reallocated through a combination of Argive mythmaking, in the first instance, and the creative impact of Argive mythology on contemporary poleis in the surrounding area. The way in which mythic sovereignty over this expanse of territory was first annulled and then reinstated again invokes the notion that throughout the Archaic Period the politically powerful southern Greek city-states basically took their cues from one another in terms of mythological protocol, building on one another's legendary amendments, regardless of whether friendship or enmity characterized diplomatic relations between them. Yet, before broaching the data concerned with filling the void, it is best to follow through with the evidence that such a void was created to begin with, in contradiction to received tradition.

---

[532] On the matter of duration, see below.

[533] After detailed examination of the papyrus fragments, Merkelbach and West concluded in the late sixties that the organizational structure of the Hesiodic *Ehoiai* was the prototype for the organizational structure of the Apollodoros' *Bibliotheka*. Apollodoros' text is largely extant and believed to have been composed in the second century B.C. or, alternatively, in the second century A.D. (*Fragmenta Hesiodea*, Oxonii 1967). Analyzing the fragments according to this discovery was one of West's main objectives in his 1985 edition of the Hesiodic *Catalogue of Women* (West 1985 31-50).

[534] Il.2.108

[535] 1. House of Proitos, 2. House of Melampous, 3. House of Bias, brother of Melampous.

[536] Melampous and Bias are consistently characterized as sons of Amythaon. Amythaon was a brother of Aison and Pheres and a half-brother of Pelias and Neleus. Like Aison and Pheres, Amythaon was a son of Kretheus and Tyro, a son and a granddaughter of Aiolos, respectively (Tyro was daughter of Salmoneus, son of Aiolos). Pelias and Neleus were also sons of Tyro, though the god Poseidon was held to have been their father. Proitos' early affiliation with the Aiolic line is given special consideration below. Though later affiliated with the ancestors of Perseus in the lineage of Argos, Proitos seems, nonetheless, to have previously been a grandson of Sisyphos, son of Aiolos (see below).

[537] e.g. Pherekydes FGrHist 3F33, 3F114, 3F117; Pindar *Nem*.9 scholia.

[538] In ch.6 below.

[539] e.g. F. Zeitlin, *Thebes:Theater of Self and Society in Athenian Drama*, in J.P. Euben, ed. 1986, S. Said, *Tragic Argos*, in Sommerstein, Halliwell, Henderson, & Zimmerman, eds. 1991.

[540] Clearly, excluding the Homeric passages.

[541] viz. specifically, by way of the relevant ancient texts.

[542] Namely: Sthenelos, son of Kapaneus, a descendent in the line of King Proitos, and Eurylaos, son of Mekisteus, of the line of Talaos, that ultimately stemmed back to Melampous brother Bias, and Diomedes, son of Tydeus, who immigrated to Argos from Aitolia. The absence of descendants of Melampous himself coincides with the famous string of events that prompted a matricide in that family (cf. *Od*.11.324-325).

[543] Argos vs. Thebes I: Line of Proitos = Kapaneus (son of Hipponoos), Line of Melampous = Amphiaraos (son of Oikles), Line of Bias = Adrastos (son of Talaos), plus Tydeus (son of Oineus) & Polyneikes (son of Oidipous) by marriage.
Argos vs. Thebes II (Epigoni): Line of Proitos = Sthenelos (son of Kapaneus), Line of Melampous = Amphilochos & Alkmaion (sons of Amphiaraos), Line of Bias = Aigialeus (son of Adrastos) & Euryalos (son of Mekisteus, son of Talaos), plus Diomedes (son of Tydeus) & Thersandros (son of Polyneikes) by marriage.
For a general overview of the Theban Wars see Gantz 1993: 502-528. For a critique of their historical status see Schachter, *Phoinix* 21 1967: 1-10. Mysterious, however, on the historical side, is the interpretive viewpoint that, counter to Greek tradition, acknowledges just one rather than two Theban Wars (Schacter ibid., Dowden 1992: 68-70). This view asserts there could be only one real war, if indeed either of them were, in fact, real. But tampering with tradition, in this regard, would seem to require clearer justification. Doing so, notwithstanding, is a fairly common practice where the historicity of Greek legend is concerned. No doubt, the same process is responsible for one potentially historical sack of Troy when Greek legend insisted that there were two, inasmuch as Herakles' conquest was held to precede that of allied Greek forces under Agamemnon. This second venture, moreover, was believed to have been preceded by a misdirected initial attempt in which the allied Greek forces were turned back at Mysia. Oftentimes these adventures are simply excluded from the analytical treatment of the Trojan War story.

[544] cf. R. Barthes 1972: 109-159.

[545] cf. E. Havelock, *The Homeric State of Mind* in H. Bloom, ed. 1987 for a superlative treatment of the cultural status of epic poetry in early Greece; cf: J.S. Burgess 1996: 93 on Audience Knowledge.

546 For an intricate account of *The Rise of Greek Epic*, going back as far as the thirteenth century B.C., see M.L. West, *JHS* 108 1988: 151-172. I have no particular problem with the idea that the Aiolic stories had Thessalian roots and were, therefore, adopted from central Greece and developed to fit an East Greek cultural context. Still, I take a strong stand against the convergence of previously isolated mythic cycles and theories concerning the transmission of myths based on the truth value of mythical claims such as the Neleid migration from Pylos to Ionia via Athens. As a matter of policy, I have refrained from thinking much back beyond Homeric epic, which provides the first evidence for the Aiolic structure. On the question of the existence of Mykenaian Epic, based on the near absence of definitive data (e.g. E. Havelock 1982: 168), I have formed no opinion on the matter beyond the basic implausibility of a culture devoid of traditional lore. The whole issue of Mycenaean epic mainly rests on two points: whether it ever became a literary tradition, and whether, really regardless of that, it influenced the traditions of Dark Age Greece. The degree to which early epic tradition was grounded in traditions that stemmed back to the Bronze Age is a question that on the evidence cannot be adequately answered. Though it is not impossible that the canon, as we know it, took its cues from a previous (even Bronze Age) repertoire, the point here is its Aiolic organization, which only makes sense historically after the foundation of Aiolic the cities on coastal Asia Minor at some point during the so-called Dark Ages (cf. I. Morris *Classical Antiquity* 5.1 1986; and in M. Golden and P. Toohey, eds. 1997).

547 As mentioned above, emphasis on the national character of early Greek mythology goes back to C.G. Heyne in the 18th century (cf. Graf 1993: 9-22). J.M. Foley stands out among contemporary theorists to reassess and articulate this point of view (e.g. Fowler, ed. 2004: 184-185). A nationalist ethos is also invoked in terms of Greek contact with Near Eastern cultures, either with respect to cultural competition (e.g. W. Burkert in J. Bremmer, ed, 1987: 11), or, with respect to the Greek importation of Near Eastern traditions and mythic forms, including the use of symbolic genealogy (West 1985: 11-27, 1988: 169, 1995: 213-217, & 1997). Here, the *Iliad* and the *Odyssey* are held to represent a transition from pure folk culture toward the formalization of a cultural creed. In my opinion, this transition is marked by the materialization of a named author (whether such an author ever existed or not). Though this point is not generally emphasized in presentations that attempt to distinguish folktales from myths (especially Greek ones), and to provide definitions for each of these categories, to my mind, at least, what defines anything folk is the absence of any specific composer. Not that this factor settles the matter of the definition of myth and its relation to folktales, which scholarly discussions over the years have succeeded in making unnecessarily complicated, but it certainly provides a welcome measure of clarity because it is universally valid. Two other key factors, it seems to me, affect the distinction between myths and folktales. The first is a given story's cultural status. Myths are high status, folktales are not (cf. Graf 1993: 7). The second concerns setting, and namely, consists of time and place and characterization. Myths are highly specific in terms of setting and deal with equally specific protagonists. Folktales are and do not. (For these reasons Greek myths are often compared to legend and saga as opposed to folktales. But this move is not satisfactory either because it demands the unwarranted exclusion of Greek cosmology and the birth of the gods). On this basis, clearly, it is entirely possible for a cultural charter to retain folk status and to still exert influence of the greatest magnitude. This is to say, that a national mythology can at the same time be a folk mythology, although composed of myths as opposed to folktales. In spite of this possibility, the Homeric poems are Homeric because they were associated with Homer, which simply means that Greek mythology abandoned folk status when an author was assigned to a major portion of the East Greek cultural repertoire. Other such assignments then followed suit. I am aware that on a number of points this synopsis runs contrary to the conclusions put forth by Bremmer 1987: ch.1, Burkert 1979: 1-5, Finley 1965: ch.1 and Kirk (1974: chs.1-2) among others (e.g. Peradotto 1990: ch 2.), the list is very long. On other points though there is clear compatibility. I am indebted to the analysts of this problem (who do not see eye to eye among themselves), for framing the issues and forcing me to address the buildup of confusion about terminology that stems back through the annals of mythological theory (cf. Graf 1993: chs. 2-3; Detienne 1981; On myth vs. Logos, see especially, B.Lincoln 1997; also, G. Lloyd and P. Murray in Buxton, ed. 1999). It is worth noting again, in the present context, that Homer was associated in antiquity with East Greek Aiolis and Aiolic legend as well (on the biographical tradition concerning Homer, cf. Allen 1912 & 1913; Kirk 1985: 1-4; Latacz 1998: 23-32).

⁵⁴⁸ It is now generally accepted that the Homeric poems were two preeminent works developed within a far more extensive mythological tradition. A myriad of oblique references in the *Iliad* and the *Odyssey* make it clear that the content of the *Epic Cycle* was contemporaneous with, and, indeed, integral to the tradition out of which Homeric poetry emerged. The Cyclic poems were, likewise, originally oral lays inspired by the same mytho-cultural repertoire, and, evidently, a part of the Aiolic edifice. Needless to say, before committed to writing, a range of variation would have been the norm, as well as the absence of any formal division of episodic material for public performance, or specific content associated with particular poets or particular poems. In this regard, it has been persuasively suggested that the Cyclic poems were considerably longer at the time when they were first recorded, but were truncated later to avoid duplication either among themselves, or in relation to the Homeric poems (J.S. Burgess 1996). Their commitment to writing may also be viewed as a response to the dissemination of the two master works attributed to Homer. This seems most likely to have taken place in the Greek East: the locus of culture in the early Archaic Period. Most of the poets, at any rate, assigned to the Cyclic poems, like Homeric tradition, also hailed from the East, where poetic, mythographic and philosophic activities remained at the vanguard through the late sixth century (ΗΠΑΙΣΤΙΩΝΟΣ ΕΓΧΕΙΡΙΔΙΟΝ ΠΕΡΙ ΜΕΤΡΩΝ ΚΑΙ ΠΟΙΗΜΑΤΩΝ, Oxionii 1810; cf. N.G. Wilson, 1983: 93-111 on Photios of Byzantium the ninth century source of Prokos' summary of the *Epic Cycle*. It remains uncertain whether the Proklos in question was a grammarian of the second century or a Neoplatonist of the fifth). So, the *Aithiopis* and the *Iliou Persis* were credited to Arktinos of Miletos, the *Little Iliad* to Lesches of Mytilene, the *Kypria* to Stasinos or Hegesias of Kypros. cf. T.W. Allen 1908; M. Davies 1989; R. Scaife 1995: 164-191; M.L. West 1995: M. Wilcock on *Neo-Analysis,* with bibliographic notes, and comments on the perspectives of J.T. Kakridis, W. Schadewalt and W. Kullman, in I. Morris and B. Powell, eds. 1997: 204; K. Dowden, in R. Fowler ed. 2004: 188-205. So also J. Griffin's extremely influential, *The Epic Cycle and the Uniqueness of Homer, JHS* 97 1977: 39-53.

[549] Likewise, Greek genealogy and Greek myth generated their own chronological framework. This chronology did not convert easily into a normative, real time dating scheme. Nonetheless, taken on its own terms it amounts to a valid relative dating scheme, albeit one that aimed to describe a distinctively non-empirical era. Although later attempts to translate myth time to real time exercised the ingenuity of ancient chronographers (so, for example, the *Marmor Parium*), Greek mythological time was, in essence, inscrutable, dealing as it did with prehistoric phenomena that were integral to a prior, alternate world. This world was a vital precursor to Greek lived reality, and could not be dispensed with except at the cost of the very foundation of Greek cultural consciousness. But because it was laden with supernatural beings (including the Greek heroes, in many ways) and defined by miraculous deeds and occurrences, it bore only a partial resemblance to its contemporary empirical counterpart. It was, in a word, a bygone era in which humans interacted very closely with gods, terminated thereafter, once and for all, giving way to the permanence of actuality (e.g. as acknowledged by R. Scodel, 1982; E. Kearns in R. Fowler, ed. 2004 64, and by M. Finkelberg, 2005: 24). The events ascribed to this remarkable era had a powerful bearing on present conditions because the denouement of received tradition bled directly into living history. The reason behind this was twofold. First, the extent of the role granted to genealogy from the primeval forces that emerged out of Chaos, down and over the threshold into historical times, and second, with this, the consanguine connection between mortals and gods based upon this continuum. These two attributes are particularly significant. First of all, they distinguish the Greek mythic edifice from other comparable narratives of the same type, such as the pre-historic national charters current in Egypt, the Levant, or in Mesopotamia. The distinction boils down to these same two attributes: the thoroughgoing use of symbolic genealogy (i.e. continuously throughout the Heroic Age) and human origins based on divine procreation. Secondly, they provide considerable added insight as to what made Greek myth tantamount to Greek history, even in the mind's eye of discerning empiricists, as Thoukydides' *Archaeology* pointedly attests. Thirdly, they suggest a fairly powerful argument against the truth value of the Trojan War story that, as far as I know, has yet to be made. Namely, although Thoukydides must be excused for his astute reduction of Greek legendary history to a brilliant piece of socio-economic theory, this justification does not extend to anyone unconstrained by cultural necessity, which means anyone other than the ancient Greeks. Beyond this, the crux of the argument asks: how might it be considered analytically prudent to insist on the historicity of events that according to the authority of Greek antiquity, specifically and emphatically did not take place in historical times? This strange inconsistency would seem to warrant the reappraisal of certain tenacious claims concerning the content of Greek epic poetry. M.I. Finley's dual proposal that Greek mythology was essentially a chronological void, and that the Greeks themselves had no real interest in history must also be countered on the foregoing grounds (1971: ch.1). Finley's viewpoint, however, does not mistreat the data as much as it relies on anachronistic standards of what was historical to make a judgment. For it was indeed rare that Greek interest in history stood apart from Greek interest in Greek legend, while the latter exceeded the former by far, in addition to being inseparable from it. Accordingly, it is not difficult to understand how such exacting criteria cut into the evidence and led Finley to the conclusions proposed. However, against the allegedly impoverished state of ancient Greek chronological thinking, a vast and well-organized lineage structure begs for credit where credit is due. That the structure itself was entirely ahistorical is adequately countered by the fact that it was created to serve historical purposes and was universally accorded historical status. And, though, in this capacity, it was subjected, time and again, to intense criticism, it was never deprived of either status or function. Thus, as Andrews among others, has observed, it was indeed possible, and moreover, quite common, to calibrate strictly in a lineage mode with no concern or intent to affect correspondence with specific real-time points of reference (1949 72-73). Sequential approximation was strategically useful, especially when applied to linear blocks of time that crossed the ambiguous boundary between coterminous stages of human history (e.g. Hdt. 2.143 on Hekataios of Miletos; Strabo 8.3.33 via Ephoros on Pheidon of Argos).

[550] G. Nagy's assertion that Homer and Hesiod synthesized "the diverse local traditions of each major city-state into a unified pan-Hellenic model that suits most city-states but corresponds exactly to none (1990: 37)" describes the subsequent situation quite well. Early epic poetry became pan-Hellenic because it was universally adopted as the ultimate source of Greek prehistory. By that time, however, the historical circumstances that informed its underlying organization were long since obsolete. The locus of power and influence in Greece had permanently and irrevocably shifted.

[551] The technique of mythological theft aspired to reproduce this effect, and to mitigate, in so doing, genealogical rifts through the promotion of new figures and stories using established genealogical protocol. The artificial impression that such a symbiosis was still in force is exemplified by the autochthonous genealogies created by various city-states as new foundations to graft venerable heroes onto, and overall, as a means of dissociating themselves from the early Aiolic map of Greece. Typically, however, the eponymous figures devised to fulfill this function were impoverished in terms of narrative substance when compared to their early epic counterparts (on eponymns as opposed to three-dimensional figures see, J. Hall 1997: 41, 50-51; for an acknowledgment of the role of local autochthony see C. Calame in Bremmer, ed. 1987: 152-166; for the coined phrase "land -genealogies" and yet another approach to this information, see I. Malkin 1994: 19-22).

[552] A comprehensive genealogical/narrative symbiosis was profoundly wellsuited to an oral tradition, that is, for composition in performance.

[553] A whole series as opposed to a few isolated happenings.

[554] So, for example, in Aischylos' *Oresteia*, Agamemnon's palace is located at Argos. In Sophokles' *Electra* it is placed at Mykenai. In Euripides' *Electra* the palace is apparently, again, at Mykenai as it appears to be also in his *Iphigenia in Aulis*, and yet, again at Argos in his *Orestes*. Likewise, Euripides' *Herakles* speaks of Eurystheus of Mykenai, whereas his *Alkestis* names of Eurystheus of Tiryns.

555 For a review of the archaeological evidence on the development of Argos in the Geometric Period see N.G.L. Hammond, *CAH* III.1 1982: 708-712; T. Kelly 1976: ch. 2; A. Snodgrass 1971: 56, 124, 233; R.A. Tomlinson 1972 : ch. 6. At 1.82, Herodotos reports extensive Argive land holdings down the east coast of the Peloponnese as far as Cape Malea and the island of Kythera. At 8.73 he describes the Kynourians as an indigenous people (like the Arkadians) who became Dorianized under Argive sovereignty. The veracity of these claims has often been doubted on the grounds that the geographical landscape made Argive sovereignty in these areas unrealistic at an early date (e.g. T. Kelly 1976: ch. 3; P. Cartledge 1979: 126; against H.T. Wade-Gerry *CAH* III.1: 521; N.G.L Hammond 1959: 77-78 and others, who've given Herodotos' testimony avid support. It has also been thought that Herodotos' claim derived from the *Iliad*'s famous statement that Agamemnon was "lord of Argos and many islands (Il.2.108)," i.e. K.J. Beloch *Griechische Geschichte*, I.1: 204). Indeed, direct control seems far-fetched in this light and the extent of it liable to be exaggerated. Still, provided that the idea of Argive sovereignty along the southeast coast of the Peloponnese is not merely, as Tomlinson suggests, a fiction devised considerably later on in order to explain Argive/Spartan antagonism (1972: 76), it is not inherently unreasonable that territories along the eastern seaboard as far south Kynouria were inhabited by settlers sent out from Argos, who identified themselves with Argive sovereignty. Epidauros, Aigina, and peripheral communities such as Sikyon, Kleonai and Phlious were traditionally associated with Argive preeminence in the region at an early date (cf. Figueira 1993: 11, 16-20, 31-33). Kelly singles out Aigina as an improbable satellite in the absence of a bona fide Argive navy, and censors Kythera on the same grounds. No doubt, Argos was never a major seafaring power, but it is questionable whether this indicates that, in a setting so profoundly influenced by the sea, early interaction between Argos and Aigina should be discredited out of hand (cf. Hdt.5.82-88 for such interaction in the sixth century). Kelly contests Argive influence in Kynouria anytime prior to 650, and restricts Argive sovereignty in the early archaic period to the immediate vicinity of the Argive plain. His views on early archaic Argos, however, seem unrealistically isolationist in an era defined by heightened communication and interstate economic transactions. Neither the Greek landscape nor the extant evidence would seem to warrant this point of view.

556 By the mid-sixth century it was already clear that Sparta had become the dominant power. The Battle of the Champions (c.546), in which Sparta won out after terrible losses incurred on both sides, foreshadowed Spartan supremacy and Argive decline. According to Herodotos, at the time of the battle, Kroisos of Lydia had determined that Sparta was the most powerful Greek state. Kroisos' request for Spartan assistance against the onslaught of Kyros and the Persian armies was stalled, and in the interim, his kingdom conquered on account of Argive/Spartan hostilities (cf. Hdt. 1.82-83; Paus.2.38.5; Hdt. 6.76-80 for the battle at Sepeia which devastated the Argive army). The legacy of hostility continued in the fifth century inasmuch as Argive resentment toward Sparta informed Argos' refusal to participate in cooperative Greek initiatives against Persian aggression (cf. Hdt.7.148-149).

557 Subjugation to the power of Sparta excluded the conquered from Spartan citizenship and defined them either as independent landholders with military obligations to the Spartan army (perioikoi) or as state-regulated agricultural slaves (helots). It is perhaps relevant, in this regard, that a subservient class of agricultural workers was evidently a feature of other early Greek states e.g. the Gymnetes at Argos, Konipodes at Epidauros, and the Korynephoroi & Katonakophoroi at Sikyon and the Isthmos, and the Penestai in Thessaly (*CAH* III 1 714,716,722-23, one might also consider the predecessors of the Solonian Thetes). Helots were the property of the Spartan state. They were inalienably tied to assigned plots of land and overall do not seem that dissimilar from subservient labor in other Greek cities. The difference, at any rate, would seem to involve definitions of state versus private property, in addition to the exceptional situation that placed free Messenians into Spartan servitude. It is not to be doubted that conditions in Sparta developed uniquely among the Greek city-states, and perhaps more specifically, failed to advance in step with developments in other Greek poleis due to the demands of institutionalized oppression. There is, however, good reason to doubt this was in fact the case to begin with, while the process itself remains largely obscure (on this topic, see, for example, P. Cartledge, *The Peculiar Position of Sparta in the Development of the Greek City-State*, in *Proceedings of the Royal Irish Academy*, 80.6 1980). The practical definition of helot status is at times difficult to comprehend, as in Herodotos' account of the battle of Plataia in 479, when Sparta allegedly marshaled an army in which seven helots were present to assist each of five thousand Spartan hoplites (Hdt.9.10.1). This scenario raises questions about loyalty and compulsion: how such principles interacted and how such lines were drawn (emphasized by R. Sealey 1976, 68). The battle at Plataia notably took place before the Messenian revolt of the 460s, which led Thoukydides to assess Spartan political motives in terms of the danger of helot rebellion (4.80.3). Perioeic status, alternatively (a form of subjection albeit less extreme), may well have been enough to inspire resistance, especially early on, when domination was new. Whether the word helot derives from the Greek word to seize (i.e. from αἱρέω cf. Forrest 1968: 31 cf. Cartledge 1979: 97) or from the town of Helos itself (e.g. Paus.3.20.6, Jeffery 1978: 118), is seems that the inhabitants of Helos were enslaved in the late eighth or early seventh century, either for attempting to collaborate with Argos (Paus.3.2.7, under Alkamenes), or simply for resistance to Spartan domination. Their enslavement was accordingly an act of vengeance that forecast Spartan policy in Messenia.

558 Tyrtaios' date depends on his statement that king Theopompos campaigned against the Messenians in the time of his father's father's (πατέρων ἡμετέρων πατέρες). Calculating from the later eighth century with reference to the Spartan king lists, a date around the mid-seventh century is reached. This was standard in antiquity and remains so today (cf. *Suidas* s.v. Τυρταῖος for the 35th Olympiad, 640/37 BC). A second calibration derives from Plutarch (Mor.194b), who cites Epaminondas for the declaration that he liberated Messenia after 230 years of Spartan domination (cf. Aelian.*VH*.13.42). Since the liberation took place in 369, this figure brings the Tyrtaian war to conclusion at the end of the seventh century which may down-date Tyrtaios to a degree (A. Andrews 1951: 44-45). But it is also emphasized, by R. Sealey, for example (1976: 66-68), that the delineation of two separate Messenian Wars looks like a belated historical construct. Two fourth-century orators also remarked on the duration of Spartan rule in Messenia: Dinarchos asserting it was 400 years and Lykourgos, for his part, preferring 500. These figures necessarily purport to refer to the onset of Spartan Messenian conquests, if they are not actually more symptomatic of popular retrospective exaggeration. In terms of distortion emanating from Athens, by the fourth century the Athenians had resolved that Tyrtaios was actually an Athenian native (e.g. Plato *Laws*.629a; Lykourgos *Leokr*.105; Paus. 4.15.6). A mid-to-late seventh-century date for Tyrtaios is reasonably solid, in any event, and generally preferable with regard to other historical comparanda (cf. E.N. Tigerstedt 1965: 44-57; G. Cawkwell CQ 43.2: 369; G.L. Huxley CR 56.1 2006: 148-151).

559 ὥσπερ ὄνοι μεγάλοις ἄχθεσι τειρόμενοι, δεσποσύνοισι φέροντες ἀναγκαίης ὕπο λυγρῆς ἥμισυ παντὸς ὅσον καρπὸν ἄρουρα φέρει (via Paus.4.14.5).

560 R.Sealey emphasizes the fact that very little is indeed known about specific events or about the chronology of the Messenian wars. It is customary to date the first war to ca. 736-715, and to date the second from the floruit of Tyrtaios to the close of the seventh century. Pausanias, however, dates the first war from 743 to 724 (4.5.10, 3.13.7) and the second from 685 to 668 (4.15.1,4.23.4), which contrasts, in turn, with the dating schemes offered by various other Greek authors engaged in what L. Pearson describes as "the ancient pseudo-science of chronology (1962: 400)." Sealey insists that all we really know is that the Spartan domination of Messenia was complete by c. 600 after a protracted revolt that began in the 660s (cf. G. Grote, *History of Greece* 2.7). It is clear in this context that parts of Messenia must have been claimed by force before Tyrtaios' time, since he was an eyewitness to the seventh-century revolt, and referred, in addition, to early Spartan conquests conducted under the leadership of Theopompos, two generations before his day (via Str.6.279). Sealey's level of skepticism is in a sense most welcome because of the difficulty of coming to terms with the various scholarly works on the subject where the chronologies offered are often incompatible and the presentation of facts, selective, to a degree (e.g. compare P. Cartledge, W.G. Forrest, N.G.L Hammond, G.L. Huxley, L.H. Jeffrey). One key issue is the use of Pausanias (mainly books 3 & 4), who provides the main extant continuous narrative, but whose account was heavily influenced by the revival of Messenian history after the liberation of the country under Epaminondas in 369 (e.g. Kallisthenes' 4th century *Hellenic History*, Rhianos of Krete's 3rd century epic *Messeniaka* notable for its highly romanticized portrait of Aristomenes, the great hero of the seventh-century revolt. Pausanias also mentions Myron of Priene (4.6.1), who wrote a prose history on the subject, but about whom not much is known. As an Ionian city, Priene was considered to have Messenian roots (e.g. Paus.7.2.1-9). Pausanias may well provide certain valuable data, albeit compromised by popular streams of thought that had become standard in his day (roughly one thousand years distant from the earliest incidents that he records, emphasized by Kelly 1979: 993). He is, notably, for example, the source of a number of valuable quotes from Tyrtaios, and by his own account, also made use of the Eleian *Olympic Victor List* (6.22.2-4). As Sealey emphasizes, the Olympian chronicle was more vulnerable to error and to fabrication as it moved further back in time, though all things considered, Olympic dating remains a valuable source of historical information (but see now P-J Shaw 2003). However, even taking a more skeptical outlook, especially in terms of absolute dating (as Shaw demonstrates is to some extent justified), Olympic documentation at the very least provides access to data current ca. 400 in contrast to later points of view. It is valuable also for more general information, so, for example, as G.L. Huxley points out, the late eighth century disappearance of Messenian victors ostensibly in connection with the First Messenian War (*CR* 51.1 2006: 148-151 in a brief response to Shaw's recent volume). Notably, Pausanias took great pains to present the romantic aspects of his account in a sober, pragmatic historical style, imitating the prose of Herodotos and Thoukydides (Pearson 1962: 412-414), which complicates matters to some extent even if no one thinks that they've been fooled. Yet since Pausanias' report was a composite work (drawn from various sources, many entirely lost), and was also interpretive in its treatment of Messenian ancient history, it is striking when his testimony is censored, on the one hand, but used to extract information, on the other (e.g. N.G.L. Hammond *CAH* III.3: 328; Huxley 1962: 56; Kelly, meanwhile, concludes in no uncertain terms that Pausanias' testimony is historically useless 1979: 992ff.). Nevertheless, this must in some sense be done. Modern reconstructions of early Spartan history at once reject and depend on Pausanias' data, which is symptomatic of the state of the evidence. It is, therefore, inevitable, if no less confusing, that each analysis is somewhat unique, although all of them are of considerable interest. Another issue arises from a slight variation evident in the two extant Spartan king lists (namely, that of Herodotos 7.204, 8.131 and that of Pausanias 3.8.11ff., 3.7.1ff.), because it is clear that Herodotos' version differed in its sequence of early Spartan rulers from other accounts later in circulation that made Polydoros and Theopompos contemporaries in association with the early Messenian conflict, while Herodotos places them two generations apart (cf. Huxley 1962: 19-20, Pearson 1962: 418-423). Pausanias' list is compatible with Herodotos' as far as the Aigiad lineage is concerned, but differs in its account of the Eurypontid line, mainly in its addition of King Sous (inserted as the grandson of Aristodemos). In Pausanias there is also some further confusion between Archidamos and Agasikles, that is, roughly from the mid-seventh to the mid-sixth century where he may be recording a collateral line, yet this does not alter the impact of the addition of Sous). Roughly a century earlier, Plutarch acknowledged Sous and also recorded one Patrokles above him (Lyk.6). These insertions suggest that they were contrived either simply to even out the number of rulers in each Spartan house (uneven as recorded in Herodotos, though Plutarch's double addition can hardly be classed as such), or (perhaps, more likely) to vindicate popular synchronizations based on precepts of diachronic compatibility (e.g. the reigns of Theopompos and Polydoros). It is, at any rate, clear that by Herodotos' time the dual Spartan kingship was codified and well-known, and it is equally clear that his fifth-century lists were not the last word on the subject. On the Spartan king lists, specifically, see P. Cartledge 1979: 104 w. Appendix 3. On the chronological methods of the Attidographers, see F. Jacoby 1949: 86ff., On ancient king lists in general, see Henige: 1974.

561 e.g. As exemplified by the colonization of Syracuse and Corcyra in the 730s (Thouky. 6.3,1.24ff).

562 Megarians first joined Chalkidians at Sicilian Leontini (founded from Naxos five years after Syracuse viz, 728). However, shortly thereafter the Megarians were expelled. They consequently founded Megara Hyblaia (Thuky.6.3-4). R. Legion explains that Korinthian encroachment on Megarian territory prompted Megarian colonization initiatives, which initially depended for resources and know-how on help from Chalkis, before Megara became an independent sea power. By the second quarter of the seventh century, Megara was a major colonizing polis, primarily active in the Propontis in areas free from Milesian control. The establishment of Selinus from Megara Hyblaia is also dated to c. 650 on archaeological grounds (1981: 69-76).

563 i.e. the second half of the eighth century.

564 cf. J. Boardman, *BSA* 52 1957; D.W. Bradeen, *TAPA* 78 1947; A.R. Burn, *JHS* 49 1929: 15-37, 223-241, W.G. Forrest *Historia* 6 1957, *CAH* III.1 760-764, *CAH* III.3 1982: 308-309 etc. The outcome of the Lelantine War is unknown, for both Chalkis and Eretria continued to prosper after the war. When a victor is advocated it is generally Chalkis (based on Hesiod W&D 654, Hdt.6.100 with 5.77, Ael.*VH.* 6.1 & Plut.Mor.298A-B), although Boardman argues on behalf of Eretria. Euboia's early pioneering role in overseas exploration and commerce, which had a profound effect on other Greek states, diminishes in the seventh century. Korinth, Megara and the East Greek states were effectively Euboia's successors. cf. J. Boardman *CAH* III 1 (1982) 18b.1. Aigina followed suit in the late 7th century, cf. Figueira 1993.

565 e.g. It is widely believed that Chalkis and Eretria cooperated in early overseas ventures including trade at Al Mina in the Levant for which the evidence is strictly archaeological (J. Boardman, for instance, 1999: 39-46, on Al Mina, see L.Wooley 1959). A. Snodgrass points out that Eretria itself shows no signs of settlement prior to 800 and, on this count, considers the possibility that the city may have been moved from an earlier site (1980) 40-41, cf. Boardman *CAH* III 1 (1982) 761,763. The most often noted joint enterprise of Chalkis and Eretria is the establishment of Pithekousai, the early eighth-century trading settlement on the island of Ischia off the Campanian coast. Shortly, thereafter, Chalkis alone becomes dominant, and Eretria, it is thought, was forced to focus attention on colonies in the northern Aegean (viz. Chalkidike), where Chalkis, again, was also involved (ostensibly prompted by political tension between traditional kingship and the aristocracy, viz. the ἱπποβόται, Arist. Fr. 603 Rose, cf. Theognis 891-894 Edmonds). Eretrians were also credited with early influence in the Kykladic islands, and more prominently associated with Kerkyra, where they were said to have been thrown out by Korinthians (c.735, Dion.Hal. 7.3.1; Strabo 5.4.9; Plut. Mor. 293a-b). Though sometimes discounted, Dionysos of Halikarnassos asserts (8.3.1) that Italian Kyme was also originally a joint foundation (e.g. accepted by Forrest, 1957: 161, as well as by Burn 1929: 15-16). Strabo describes a cooperative period disrupted by fallout over the Lelantine plain (10.1.11-12). Collaborative efforts generally seem to cease by the middle of the eighth century (Boardman ibid. 760). A thoroughly skeptical view of Eretria's status as an eighth-century maritime power, according to which, all of the credit rightfully belongs solely to Chalkis is offered by S.C. Bakhuizen (1976). However, cf. D. Ridgeway *Euboeans and others along the Tyrrhenian Seaboard* in K. Lomas, ed. 2004. The relatively recent discovery of extremely opulent graves at Euboian Lefkandi dated to the tenth century is also relevant inasmuch as such finds have called into question the level of darkness that ought to be attributed to the so-called Dark Age. cf. Popham, M, H. Sackett, & P. Themelis, eds. *Lefkandi I & II,*, also with E. Toloupa in *Antiquity* 56 1982: 169-174.

566 Specifically, in the late eighth and seventh centuries. The passage of time wrought significant changes, e.g. Korinth's shift toward Miletos from her allegiance to Samos through a pact between Periander and Thrasyboulos, respective tyrants of these two cities (Hdt.5.92).

567 via Thouky.1.13 where ca. 700, Ameinokles, a Korinthian shipwright built four battleships for the Samians, confirming early relations between these two states.

568 At 1.18.3 Herodotos describes Milesian support for Chios in a war against Erythrai.

569 Paros is sometimes cited, additionally, though the matter remains controversial, and perhaps, generally dubious in the late eighth century (cf. Burn 1929: 18. Burn was more concerned with early trading alliances than with the Lelantine War *per se*. On this basis he manages to include a remarkable number of widespread Greek poleis in his list of competitive political agents, yet his chronological framework is conspicuously loose). Burn is critiqued by Forrest for associating Paros with the Chalkidian side, but Forrest also discounts the opposing opinion that Paros should be classed with Eretrian interests (1957: 169-170).

570 L.H. Jeffrey agrees, explaining, in addition, that Athens, at times linked to the Eretrian side, with Thebes to Chalkis, are attributions based strictly on later history (1976: 64-67). J. Boardman exhibits skepticism as well (ibid. 763). R.P. Legion offers a sound critique on the involvement of Megara, which is certainly one of the more persuasive candidates in the overall reconstruction (1981: 83-84). A.R. Burn leaves the land powers out of the fray, merely commenting on their likely affiliations. Forrest and Bradeen, however give them top billing due to their commitment to a purported link between the Lelantine and Messenian Wars. cf. C. Roebuck 1959: 71-74.

571 It became even more tangible during the course of the "Second."

572 That is from 668 to the end of the century, according to the most widely accepted account.

573 The duration of the "First Messenian War" is described by Tyrtaios who states that the Spartans drove the Messenians from Mt. Ithome in the twentieth year and fought in the time of his father's fathers (via Str. 6.279). As noted above, Tyrtaios himself is generally placed in the mid-seventh century. It is hard to gauge when the poet's reckoning began, though incursions into Messenia would seem to be prerequisite, so his account of the war may well have commenced with the first conquests west of Mt. Tayegetos, though the number twenty, itself, may well be artificial. Pausanias attributes the subjection of Amyklai, Pharis, Geronthrai to Teleklos of the Agid line active in the third quarter of the eighth century (Paus. 3.2.6). Aristotle credits the subjection of Amyklai to the leadership of Timomachos from the elite Aigeidai clan, notable for their connections with Thebes (cf. Hdt.4.149). P. Cartledge suggests that Amyklai had been absorbed as early as 750. At some point, any rate, relatively early on, Amyklai was incorporated among the Spartan *obai*, or constituent villages, while the remaining populations of Pharis and Geronthrai along with other settlements in the Eurotas valley were allotted the lesser status of *perioikoi*. Teleklos was additionally credited with the first Spartan conquests in Makria along the coast of the Messenian Gulf (viz. modern day Kalamata, Strabo 8.4.4), which were likely also, initially granted *perioikoic* status. In addition, presumably, under attack, many Messenians simply fled. Tyrtaios names king Theopompos as the commander who drove the Messenians from Ithome. The historicity of other named Spartan rulers (not to mention their ancestors, cited on occasion, leading back even further into the mists of time), is problematized by Pausanias' coverage, which as L. Pearson convincingly argues "is no more an account of the (Messenian) war than the *Iliad* is an account of the Trojan War (1969: 418)." While the struggle for Messenia is not quite comparable to the epic struggle for the city of Ilion, Pausanias' account bears a resemblance to epic in its emphasis on heroic personas, semi-miraculous circumstances and semi-miraculous deeds. Such is the case especially with, Aristomenes, the Messenian hero, whom Pausanias admits was sometimes the hero of the early conflict (e.g. in Myron of Priene), though he found it more suitable to follow those (e.g. Rhianos of Bene 265FGrHist.) who assigned Aristomenes to the later war (Paus. 4.5.6; Diodoros corroborates the divergence of opinion on the proper context for Aristomenes, DS 8.7-9,12-13, 15.66.3). On this count, certain scholars have long regarded Tyrtaios as the only valid source of information (i.e. going back to K. Müller, G. Grote and E. Meyer, cf. R. Sealey, P. Cartledge and E. Tigerstedt). And while Tyrtaios has likewise been accused of attracting a buildup of subsequent legend (cf. R. Osborne 1996: 57), recourse to Pausanias also persists and is in some ways impossible to avoid. Accordingly, the following sequence of kings were linked with Spartan aggression and expansion once the tradition had solidified: Agiadai: Teleklos -> Alkamenes -> Polydoros. Eurypontidai: Nikandros -> Theopompos. (*CAH* III.3 323-324, 327-329, 351-352; Cartledge 1979: 75-129; Forrest 1968: 31-34; Huxley 1962: 22,31,33; Jeffrey 1976: 114).

[574] Asinean estrangement was likely provoked by Argive aggression in the first instance, cf. Hammond ibid. 716, Kelly 1970: 996-997, Tomlinson 1972: 75. In this regard, the incident evokes a common pattern in the history of the Greek city-states in which a beleaguered city seeks assistance further afield, oftentimes, from its besieger's enemies or surrogate opportunistic groups. A Spartan incursion into the Argolid, ostensibly, with help from the inhabitants of Asine was attributed to Nikandros of the Eurypontid line. Asine was said to have been destroyed in revenge under the Argive king Eranos. The town's destruction, at any rate, before 700 is corroborated on archaeological grounds. Asinean refugees were welcomed by the Spartans and settled in Messenia (Paus.2.36.4-5, 3.7.4, 4.14.3). Kelly plausibly questions direct Spartan involvement in the conflict between Argos and Asine. Instead, he emphasizes local antagonism over Argive supremacy in the Argolid that inspired the Spartans, after the fact, to grant hospitality to the victims of Argive aggression in the Argolid. Kelly extends the same skepticism to Argive involvement in the Spartan conquest of Helos (Paus.3.2.7), and again, later (i.e. late 7th C.), to Spartan involvement in the Argive conquest of Nauplia, ostensibly on the grounds of disloyalty to Argos (Paus.4.35.2), suggesting that Pausanias' account of violence at Asine, Helos, and Nauplia create the impression of a scripted narrative pattern, as opposed to straightforward historical data. The data are, indeed, late, and depend on Pausanias, while the data pool shrinks considerably when Pausanias' comments are stripped of their merit. In the same context, though, there comes a point where Kelly's vigorous skepticism attracts skepticism itself. For though it is clearly unreasonable to extend the "bitter enmity" between Argos and Sparta back into the barely historical period (viz. the ninth century), or, in my opinion, any time prior to the outcome of the "First Messenian War," commitment to the idea that any such enmity was a mirage built up from the fourth century onward and, as such, perpetuated by modern scholarship, is not quite an open-minded alternative stance. The main problem with Kelly's analysis is that it makes direct confrontation between Sparta and Argos a necessary criterion for "bitter enmity," yet then not only dismisses Pausanias' testimony - the only extant evidence for early, direct confrontation - but also negates the fundamental dynamics that proceed logically from key historical developments, that are adequately discernible, with or without Pausanias, though they may well require a looser concept of enmity. Kelly's critique is provocative and offers much food for thought, but it is nonetheless difficult to imagine how Argos could have remained oblivious to the Spartan conquest of the southwest Peloponnese, or how given, for example, the close ties between Argos and Tegea in the archaeological record (advanced by Kelly, himself, 1970b: 982), no joint efforts were adopted in the northeast to obstruct the threat of Spartan advancement. In this regard, it is simply unrealistic to down-date antagonism between these two states until the conquest of Tegea in the mid-sixth century, and especially curious to do so in the name of exposing the detrimental effects of an unfounded attitude that morphed into a legend during the Hellenistic period. Common sense, on the contrary, would suggest that though not immune to exaggeration, the idea of enmity arose from enmity; enmity that stemmed back to circumstances that were hardly conducive to either friendship or apathy. T.Kelly, "The Argive Destruction of Asine," *Historia* 16 1967, "The Traditional Enmity Between Sparta & Argos," *American Historical Review* 75.4 1970, "Did the Argives Defeat the Spartans At Hysiai in 669 BC?" *American Journal of Philology* 91.1 1970, *A History of Argos to 500 BC*, Minneapolis 1976.

[575] i.e. A member of the elite Argive clan that traced their lineage back to the Heraklid "Temenos," leader of the successful post Trojan War conquest of the Peloponnese, known in antiquity as the "Return of the Herakleidai," yet coined "the Dorian invasion," by modern analysts (cf. Tigerstedt 1965: 28).

[576] As set out below, the so-called *lot of Temenos* was part of the Dorian foundation charter that seems to have proliferated by the mid-seventh century. Again, Tyrtaios provides its *terminus ante quem* (fr 1 Diehl, Strabo 8.4.10) from which point on it became the dominant discourse on Peloponnesian cultural identity.

[577] See Kelly 1970a: 31, for the use of this and similar adjectives to describe the battle of Hysiai.

578 Paus.6.22.2. Pausanias' text, however, assigns this exploit to the 8th Olympiad, viz. 748 BC. It has become customary to interpret Pausanias as referring to the 28th Olympiad, rather than, that is, to 668, the year after the Argives, again according to Pausanias, defeated the Spartans at Hysiai (2.24.7 Pausanias is the only source for the battle, which he does not, however, explicitly link to Pheidon). The adjusted date for the battle of Hysiai is then associated with the *anolympiad* cited for that year in the Eleian Victor Lists (6FGrHist), and then linked, in turn, with the activities of Pheidon. Concerning these lists, the Anolympiad, and also a sound assessment of Pheidon, see R. Sealey 1976: 40-45.

579 Some kind of confusion is generally detected in Herodotos' assertion that Pheidon's son, Leokedes, entered the competition for the hand of Agariste of Sikyon, Kleisthenes' daughter (6.127. Though Kleisthenes' renowned hostility toward Argos may not, in fact, be sufficient grounds to outright disqualify the possibility of an Argive contender for his daughter's hand, as is sometimes proposed). Kelly's zealous defense of Herodotos' chronology is critiqued by Cartledge, 1979: 130. Nevertheless, it must be admitted that Herodotos' chronology works very well with Kelly's account of Peloponnesian state relations in which cross-communication and political competition are minimized early on, and consequently, down-dated (cf. 1976: ch.7).

580 Herodotos' dating, however, is problematized by other important aspects of Peloponnesian politics in the sixth and seventh centuries. Among the most persuasive surveys of the evidence is A. Andrews article, *The Corinthian Aktaeon and Pheidon of Argos*, where he convincingly demonstrates the existence of two distinct ancient chronologies for the reign of Pheidon, and goes on to make a strong case in favor of the earlier seventh-century chronology as opposed to the late seventh/early sixth. This judgment is mainly based on the difficulty of placing Pheidon's actions during the heyday of the Isthmian tyrannies. This view coincides with Aristotle's comments on Pheidon (Pol.1310b 19,27), and with the modified (i.e. gradual) conception of the development of the hoplite phalanx in the seventh century (cf. Sealey ibid. 29-30, 39-40). The title of Andrews' article (which is hardly transparent) refers to an obscure Korinthian myth in which the Boiotian Aktaion story (about the grandson of Kadmos who was torn apart by his dogs) turns up in a quasi-historical context that dealt with the fall of Bakchiadai at Korinth. Namely, in spite of the honor that accrued to Aktaion's family from thwarting an attack of Pheidon of Argos, Aktaion was torn to pieces at a Korinthian festival by unruly revelers from the ruling Bakchiad clan. This event is portrayed as the catalyst to the Kypselos' rise to power in Korinth. Andrews skillfully traces the remains of this story, analyzing the available information in terms of the career of Pheidon of Argos, and concluding that there may be some truth to the tale that he met his demise amid stasis in Corinth. He concludes, in addition, that the earlier date for Pheidon is preferable for historical reasons that are adequately supported by the ancient evidence. For an account of the period from another perspective, see Figueira 1995: ch.1.

581 viz. The northern plain in the district known as Kynouria, that Herodotos considered to be Argive controlled (Hdt.1.82), and which constituted a critical border region on the outskirts of Argive and Spartan territory. For what it is worth, Pausanias claims that the Spartans attempted to move in on this district in the reign of king Theopompos (3.7.5) and, indeed, even earlier (e.g. 3.7.1-3), which seems less likely. The prospect of Spartan control of this region no doubt represented a serious threat to Argos, since from Thyreatis direct access is gained into the heart of the Argive plain. When the Spartans finally seized control of this region (c. 545 in the battle of the Champions, Paus. 2.38.5), the Argives vowed to regain their ancestral landholdings. The Spartans lost Thryeatis under the Theban hegemony. In the Roman period, the Argives were again in control of the region.

582 Following H.T. Wade-Gerry (*CQ* 43.1-2 1949) it is widely believed that the Spartan festival known as the Γυμνοπαίδαι was first instituted to commemorate the disgrace of this defeat. Against this proposal see W. Den Boer 1954: 221-227.

583 e.g. advocated by Huxley 1962 p.53.

584 viz. Mainly, since at this juncture, the dating of Pheidon and his activities intercept the difficulties involved in the chronology of the Messenian wars.

585 Arkadia, with good reason, was consistently anti-Spartan out of fear of Spartan expansion, which would have concerned the Eleians as well, prior to the existence of a treaty with Sparta. Such an accord may have been established in response to Pheidon's interference at Olympia, but the data on this and related matters is exceedingly sketchy and difficult to interpret. A period of Pisatan control of the games dated to the 660s (Euseb.Chron.1.196) or the 670s (Str. 8.3.30), in which the Eleians were temporarily ousted, likewise, may be associated with Pheidon's initiatives and with an obscure line of Pisatan tyrants, though again the specifics cannot be ascertained. Andrews' theory that the alliance against Sparta was at first couched in terms of Argive/Spartan antagonism, and only later assigned by post-fourth century analysts, to the Second Messenian War seems to be incompatible with Strabo's claim to be citing Tyrtaios at 8.4.10, which names the Messenian conflict directly (1951: 43). Andrews' related theory (1949: 76-77) is, however, possible though, namely that Pausanias' Anolympiads that do not acknowledge any Pisatan interlude were based on Hippias' Olympic victor list, and only later transformed by subsequent authors into a period of Pisatan control, which thereafter became the dominant viewpoint (to the effect that only Pausanias transmits any viable early testimony). This cannot, however, be confirmed or denied. As for the question of Argive/Spartan enmity it was certainly likely to have surfaced in this period when Spartan aggression was a concrete reality, and more than a question of strictly local import, but rather, a situation of grave concern to all independent Peloponnesian communities. Prior to the Orthagorid tyranny at Sikyon, and perhaps simply prior to Kleisthenes' reign, concerted action of the part of Argos and Sikyon is not a patently unreasonable prospect, nor again is Eleian participation barring any potential pro-Spartan incentives. The ancient historiographical tendency to mythologize important actual events with the reciprocal tendency to superimpose contemporary perspectives onto popular legends reinforces the difficulties involved in sorting these claims. For a largely justifiable if intensely skeptical view of ancient chronological reckoning, including many astute insights on how such reckoning worked giving rise to the Olympiad dating system, see P-J. Shaw 2003. Shaw's book offers serious and well-supported warnings against the reliability of Greek dating assertions (with special emphasis on Olympiad-driven claims). At some point, however, a line must be drawn to bar the annihilation of all of Greek history. And while it is surely productive to understand and explore the fact that ancient Greek thinking about time and events is distinctively different from contemporary modes of thought, the suggestion that the ancient Greeks had no concept of absolute dating at all, I think, pushes the matter way too far.

586 This passage with a papyrus that came to light in the seventies (P.Oxy. 3316) adequately corroborate Argive / Spartan hostility in the mid-seventh century. In Tyrtaios, the absence of Sikyon altogether and the substitution of Pisatans for Eleians is notable. The latter may indicate that Pheidon's intervention at Olympia had already taken place, while Pausanias' combination of Argos, Elis and Sikyon aligned together on the Messenian side could conceivably be a retro projection of the Dorian legend of the *return of the Herakleidai* based on the notion of concerted resistance among participants in that foundation charter to Spartan oppression of the Messenians, who, according to the legend, were their Dorian kinsmen (There seems to be a trace of this kind of thinking in terms of the Kretan archers who appear on the scene to assist the Spartans in the "First Messenian War." Their presence seems to invoke ideological claims of an age-old connection between Sparta and Krete). Needless to say, if this was, in fact, the case, the connection between Pausanias' list of allies and any potentially historical circumstances would be coincidental rather than testimonial. His information, accordingly, could well be simply false.

587 See, Hdt.3.47, where the main topic is the Spartan decision to assist a group of exiled Samian aristocrats in their scheme to overthrow the tyrant Polykrates. The Spartans agreed to offer assistance ostensibly based on prior Samian aid given to Sparta against the Messenians. A strong case for the validity of the Samian claim to have assisted the Spartans against the Messenians is offered by P. Cartledge in *Sparta and Samos: A Special Relationship? CQ* 32.2 1982. Kypselos became tyrant of Korinth in this period (657-627), which made pro-Spartan / anti-Argive sentiments there a more tangible factor than ever before.

588 The emphasis is, therefore, on a certain improbability. Argive involvement is surely more likely than Spartan involvement during this period, but we are dealing with two separate theaters of war: one of considerable political scope and the other, at least, in the period in question, a regional southern Peloponnesian initiative. Notably, efforts to establish a correlation between the Lelantine and the early Messenian wars led Huxley to place Pheidon in the eighth century and led Bradeen to place the Leleantine War in the seventh. There are serious problems with both of these reconstructions. Forrest (1957) likewise upholds the link between the two wars, however, in accordance with the standard dating (viz. Lelantine in the eighth / Pheidon in the seventh), which aptly reaffirms the shortage of concrete data available to support this link. Forrest deployed Pausanias' statements on Messenia's allies versus those of Sparta to promote the connection. Though Pausanias list of allies for the Tyrtaian War pan-out, individually, as at least potentially viable, his assignment of allies for the early phase of the conflict, before Sparta was a definitively manifest entity, is clearly a more ambivalent issue. That extrapolation of this sort generates problems in this early period is basically the thrust of my argument here, whereas one of the pitfalls that highlights the risk involved is the desire to synchronize these two wars and to cast them as driven by congruent factors. That the rise of Sparta was not a *fait accompli* before the feat itself was actually accomplished is pivotal to acknowledging a period of time that we know little about, but which clearly preceded the political outcome we are all too familiar with. From the point of view of historical accuracy, it seems best to refrain from accelerating the development of such circumstances before their due (see C.G. Starr in *The Credibility of Early Spartan History*, *Historia* 14 1965). Forrest's main contribution is the astute observation that evidence gleaned from surviving Delphic oracles intelligibly corroborates the split of alliances understood to inform the Lelantine War. Namely, the states that were affiliated with Chalkis have left traces of Delphic consultation with respect to their colonization initiatives, whereas states presumably affiliated with Eretria must have consulted alternative oracles, for they have left no trace of seeking Delphic advice. This pattern contributes to an assessment of the two sides in the Lelantine War, but it remains inadequate for purposes of connecting the Lelantine to the Messenian conflict. That the Delphic oracle guided emigration from Sparta to Taras ca. 706 indicates the Spartans shared Delphic orientation with the Chalkidan group toward the end of the First Messenian conflict. It is still questionable whether this factor justifies the retrograde reconstruction of Spartan affiliations, no less, political activities outside the Peloponnese. On the significance of Taras in this context cf. I. Malkin 1994: 139-142.

589 cf. *CAH* III.1.730.

590 e.g. c. 700 Ameinokles of Corinth built ships for the Samians, Thucy.1.13.

591 ca. 665-565, the estimated dates for the Orthagorid dynasty, with Kleisthenes of Sikyon generally placed ca. 600-570.

592 cf. Huxley 1948: 67.

593 According to an assortment of ancient accounts the victorious descendants of Herakles divided these Peloponnesian kingdoms by lot (Pindar *Pyth*.5.70; Plato *Laws* 3.683c-d; Isocrates *Arch*.17-21; ApB 2.8.4; Paus.4.3.3-6). The stories concerning the *return of the Herakleidai* are viewed here as an archaic legendary addendum devised to correct the Homeric portrayal of the Peloponnese and its legendary inhabitants who were described as Achaians of Aiolic stock. Accordingly, this particular nexus of stories is understood as a mythological epilogue designed to account for the Dorian presence in the archaic Peloponnese. The idea that these stories in some way reflect the chaotic period of wanderings and migrations associated with the collapse of Bronze Age civilization has come under serious attack of late. The results of this project accord with the contention that the promotion of this cluster of stories was altogether ideologically driven, though it will become clear that the results obtained here differ in some respects from those of the leading thesis that has been advanced in this direction (viz. J.M. Hall, *Ethnic Identity in Greek Antiquity*, Cambridge 1997 / *Hellenicity*, Chicago 2002).

594 i.e. Eurysthenes and Prokles, e.g. ApB 2.8.2; Paus.3.1.5-3.2.1. They notably also boasted Theban descent on their mother's side, since their mother Argeia, was the daughter of Autesion, the son of Tisamenos, son of Thersander, who was in turn the son of Polyneikes (Hdt.4.147).

595 From what can be gathered of Eumelos' work, he used a number of prototypical techniques that doubtless had an impact on his successors in the field of patriotic polis-based genealogy. There was, for example, a primordial period, conspicuous for equating the city of Korinth with the place called Ephyra in Homeric epic (Il.6.152). Then came a mix of local notables and eponymous founders, aptly arranged so as to co-opt the lineage of Medeia, princess of Kolchis, and the line of Sisyphos, son of Aiolos (father of Glaukos and grandfather of Bellerophon). Especially jarring among the recorded fragments is the assertion that Leda, daughter of Thestios, and wife of Tyndareos in mainstream tradition (cf. Gantz 1993: 317), was really the daughter of Glaukos, the Korinthian (viz. son of Sisyphos), who mated with her mother, the Spartan Panteidyia, before Panteidyia married Thestios of Aitolia. Thestios' wife was otherwise known as Eurythemiste, daughter of Porthaon, of the Aiolic line of Kalyke. She was Thestios' mother's brother's daughter, and, therefore, his first cousin (cf. Hes. fr. 26 MW; ApB 1.7.10). Evidently, at least, one early Spartan poet followed Eumelos in making this claim (Huxley 1969: 60-68, 74-79).

596 There are no indications as to how the Aipytidai originally charted their descent from Aipytos. Nor is there any access to who Aipytos was in the mind's eye of the poet of the *Iliad*. Still, he must have been mythologically important enough to warrant the mention of his tomb. If comparative data are any guide, Aiptyos was a member of the Aiolic lineage.

597 As covered in ch. 2, above; e.g. Apollodoros cites Stesichoros to this effect (3.10.3), yet, his Perieres is no longer a son of Aiolos, but a son of Kynortas of Sparta, instead. T. Gantz sees this testimony as evidence for the synthesis of two originally separate families (181, 216). It is more fitting, however, to witness the fracture of an old Aiolic family into two trajectories, one of which was successfully claimed by the Spartans, and another which they were forced to surrender to Messenia. This is particularly persuasive, since, as emphasized above, the indigenous Spartan line is eminently unlikely to antedate the Aiolic lineage of Perieres. In terms of Perieres' early Aiolic status, it is not unreasonable to posit a large swath of territory under the divided sovereignty of his descendants before the rise of Spartan civic mythology. And while such an arrangement was apparently unacceptable from the point of view of Spartan expansion, the memory of Aphareus' and Lynkeus' control of Messenia proved impossible to extinguish unilaterally.

[598] As addressed in ch. 2 above, Perieres (son of Aiolos) was a major bone of contention, challenged by a number of Spartan claims on account of the status of his offspring. These included the transformation of his sister Alkyone (one-time daughter of Aiolos) into his wife, and her later replacement (Hes fr. 49 MW), with Gorgophone, daughter of Perseus, who married into the Spartan line either by making Perieres into a Spartan native (e.g. Hes fr 49 MW; Stesichoros via ApB 3.10.3, Σ Euripides' *Orestes* 457), or by having Gorgophone marry twice – a notable deviation from early epic protocol that Pausanias felt called for justification (viz. He claims that Gorgophone was the first woman to do so). In a brilliant assimilation of various strands Pausanias (2.21.8) asserts that Gorgophone first married Perieres (offspring: Aphareus and Leukippos, but later, upon his death married Oibalos (offspring: Tyndareos and Ikarios). The trend is also detectable in the *Ehoiai*, where Oibalos appears to have supplanted Perieres in the role of Spartan father of Tyndareos and Ikarios (Hes.fr.199.8 MW). This alternative genealogy, followed by Gantz (Table 9: Daughters of Atlas I), eliminated Perieres from the Spartan line altogether, which thus runs from Kynortas straight to Oibalos, to Tyndareos, Ikarios, and Hippokoon. Again, the split in the family looks very much like a compromise, advanced by those who rejected a Spartan Perieres, retaining the man in his original setting in deference to an older and well-known genealogy at odds with the novelty of his Spartan identity.

[599] e.g. ApB 1.9.9; Paus. 4.2.5; Though notably omitted by Diodoros, who tells of Meleager's passion for Atalanta (4.34.2-7) and lavishes attention on another Kleopatra, daughter of Oreithyia, granddaughter of Erechtheus (4.43.3-44.7). She likewise drops out of Ovid's account (8.262ff.).

[600] The story was narrated in the *Kypria* and surfaces obliquely at Il.3.236-238 and Od. 11.298-300.

[601] Or daughters of Apollo, alternatively, e.g. Paus.3.16.1, citing the *Kypria*.

[602] Pind.*Nem*.10; Σ *Nem*.10.112; Theok. 22.137-266; Ovid *Fasti* 5.699-702; ApB 3.11.2; Hyg. *Fab*. 80; Σ Il.3.243.

[603] And thereafter, e.g. Pind.*Nem*.10.55-72; Paus.4.2.7.

[604] Huxley 1969: 61.

[605] I. Malkin 1998 covers numerous instances. The role of the *Nostoi* in this regard was evidently a function of the earliest mythic framework. In this regard also, they can best be understood as the conceptual limit of the cultural manifesto that began when five primal deities first emerged from Chaos (Hes. *Th*. 116-125). Mythological trends in the early Achaian colonies are addressed in detail by J.M. Hall 2002: ch.3.

[607] The notion of a radical population shift, promulgated by the Dorian charter (aka the Herakleidai story), stands in contrast to genealogical adjustments aimed at spreading the wealth of the Achaian legacy by appropriating circumscribed portions of the inherited epic tradition.

[607] cf. Il.13.685 for *Ionians*, Boiotians Lokrians, Phthians, and Epeioi in cooperation on the battlefield. On these Ionians in particular, see the coverage on Argos in Homer below.

608 e.g. K. Dowden 1992: 71; J.M. Hall 1997: 61. Skepticism stems back to Grote and Beloch, but went out of vogue with the excavations of Schliemann (I. Morris 1997: 96-111 in Golden M. and P. Toohey, eds.). Skepticism is now, once again, on the rise. Dowden and Hall register among those who prefer an ideological reading and also believe that the signs point to Argos as originator of the Heraklid legend. J.T. Hooker, a specialist on Bronze Age Greece, took an intermediate stand in the late 70s. He felt that the legend stemmed back to Lakonia and ought to contain certain kernels of truth, while encouraging further research on the matter (1979: 353-360). A decade later, C. Calame advanced a strictly ideological approach to the matter, tracing the legend back to Sparta as well (1987: 177) with a useful account of the autochthonous Spartan genealogy: 153- 166. All told, however, the Argive attribution stands up more successfully to close analysis.

609 e.g. A. Andrews 1949: 72, 1951: 39-45; R.A. Tomlinson 1972: 60-63; J.M. Hall 1997: 61.

610 e.g. The Spartan royal lines were named after descendants of the founding Heraklids (viz. Agis & Eurypon), rather than the Heraklid founders themselves (viz. Prokles & Eurysthenes, son of Aristodemos). See J.M. Hall ibid. 61-61, P. Cartledge1979:104, 341-346.

611 Notably, by and by, the Messenian Aipytos was defined as a son of the Heraklid Kresphontes, which corroborates the mythic adjustments at issue. Nicholas of Damascus provides the *terminus ante quem* for Aipytos' revised Heraklid genealogy (viz. in the latter half of the first century BC, FGrHist 90F31-34). It is, however, reasonable to suppose that this lineage antedated Euripides' *Kresphontes* by an unknown, yet significant, block of time. Tyrtaios' testimony demonstrates that Heraklid thinking was rife by the mid-seventh century. On Euripides' play, see A. Harder 1985; C. Collard, M.J. Cropp, and K.H. Lee, eds. 1995.

612 J.M. Hall 1997: 56-66; J.B. Salmon 1984: 49-52.

613 cf. Dunbabin *JHS* 68 1948: 67 with J.B. Salmon ibid. 49, on the speculative status of this tradition.

614 cf. J.B. Salmon 1984: 49-52; J.M. Hall 1997: 56-66.

615 Making, as it did, more broadly appealing claims.

616 Il.2.569-580 describes the kingdom of Agamemnon as extending westward from Korinth to Elis along the southern coast of the Korinthian Gulf, yet including the fortified stronghold Mykenai, inland, and on the border of the province of Argos (aka the Argolid). The Argolid, notwithstanding, was also clearly defined (Il.2.559-568) and represented at Troy by the joint leadership of Diomedes, son of Tydeus (who married Deipyle, daughter of Adrastos, son of Talaos, son of Bias; therefore, into the line of Melampous' brother), Sthenelos, son of Kapaneus (a descendant in the line of King Proitos of Argos), and Eurylaos, son of Mekisteus (another descendant of Bias via his son Talaos).

617 Resistance to this prospect for reasons of civic pride was a major impetus for mythic emendation. Eumelos' detachment of both Korinth and Sikyon from Agamemnon's Homeric realm offers a case in point (the genealogy of Arkadia is also instructive). According to the argument under construction, Argos then took matters a step further by laying claim to Agamemnon's administrative stronghold. The remnants of early Korinthian initiatives, in contrast to the initiatives radiating from Argos, reinforce the idea (suggested above) of avid competition between these two states.

618 As outlined below, Agamemnon's authority derived from the legacies of these two great families: the house of Pelops succeeding the house of Perseus by proxy.

619 Namely, the lines of the *tripartite division*.

[620] The idea that real-life political boundaries would be redrawn on mythological grounds is fairly preposterous.

[621] Proitos and Akrisios are first attested as sons of Abas in a fragment of the *Ehoiai* (Hes fr 129 MW) and in Bakchylides' *Ode Eleven*.

[622] *Genesis 39* gives the prototype for this common motif. There the case involves Joseph, son of Rachel and Jacob, who was sold as a slave to Potiphar of Egypt, captain of the guard in the service of the Pharaoh.

[623] As noted above, Proitos' wife, the daughter of Iobates of Lykia was known as Anteia in the *Iliad* (Il.6.160), as Stheneboia, however, in subsequent texts. The name change appears to have been connected with an Arkadian genealogical initiative aimed at recasting Anteia of Lykia as a daughter of Apheidas, the son of Arkas of the Arkadian line. Although this alteration occurs in the *Ehoiai*, its intent was not altogether successful. This resistance is evident in Euripides, for example, who abides by the name change readily enough, yet sticks to the traditional lineage framework. It would seem, on this count that the appropriation made considerable headway in some circles, but stopped short of achieving complete consensus (cf. Gantz 311-316 with C. Collard, M.J. Cropp & K.H. Lee, eds. 1997 on Euripides' *Stheneboia*).

624 During his long digression on the paintings of Polygnotos commissioned by the Cnidians for their Lesche at Delphi (10.25-31) Pausanias sees Maira, the daughter of Proitos, son of Thersander, son of Sisyphos, sitting on a rock (10.30.5). Pausanias cites the *Nostoi* for this information with the added remark that Maira met her death when she was still a maiden (10.30.5). Odysseus encounters Maira's shade in the underworld, but no information on her life story is offered (Od.11.326-327). This indicates that her name was once a household word and did not require further elaboration. An *Odyssey* scholion to this passage states further that Maira was a devotee of Artemis, and specifically, a daughter of Proitos and Anteia of Lykia (i.e. in accordance with *Iliad* 6). The scholion names Pherekydes as yet another source and credits him with the story that Maira was seized by Zeus, and bore a son, Lokros, to the king of the gods (3F1790). She was then shot by Artemis for her betrayal. Given the other data, this eponymous offspring seems like a fresh twist tacked on to Maira's biography, which though scarcely recoverable, was certainly ancient and at one time well-known. In the *Nekuia*, moreover Maira is named along with Klymene and Eriphyle. Klymene's epic ancestry is somewhat problematic, though she was doubtless a high-status Aiolic figure. She appears in the *Ehoiai* as a daughter of Minyas (a favored candidate for the role of Aiolos' mysterious seventh son in that text cf. Gantz 182; West 1985: 65-66) and the wife of Phylakos (Hes fr 62 MW), the man in possession of the herd of cattle that Neleus demanded for his daughter Pero. The seer Melampous obtained this cattle on behalf of his brother Bias, before his predestined migration to Argos (Od. 11.281-297, 15.222-255). Eriphyle, the third heroine in this set of three, is identified by a few cryptic remarks consistent with her later mythological legacy (ἡ χρυσὸν φίλοθ ἀνδρὸς ἐδέξατο τιμήωτα). Suffice it to say that Eriphyle was an Argive woman from the line of Bias, who married Amphiaraos from the line of Melampous. This marriage led to disastrous consequences (see below), but more notable here is the way in which the passing mention of these two women invokes the legendary history of the Argolid as understood in the Homeric poems. Because Eriphyle, of the line of Bias, married Amphiaraos, of the line of Melampous, her name represents two out of three Argive lines. Maira represents the line of Proitos of Argos. Thus, Maira and Eriphyle when viewed as a duo, represent the three lines that were involved in the *tripartite division of Argos*. Together, Maira, Klymene and Eriphyle provide a synoptic rendering of the whole saga attached to the Aiolic seer Melampous that led in due course to the Argive wars against Thebes. This remarkably concise method of signification would perhaps seem far-fetched if not for the fact that its key mythic referents are meaningfully discernible. Further, this mode of expression is completely consistent with general principles of audience receptivity to a finite and reiterative cultural repertoire. Worthy of special emphasis in this regard, is this catalogue entry's invocation of a specific chain of events using the names of heroic female protagonists connected to that particular sequence of stories. See I. Rutherford in M. Depew and D. Obbink eds. 2000: 94, for an acknowledgment of "hidden genealogical connections" in the *Odyssey's Nekuia*. cf. Pherekydes FGrHist 3F170 for Proitos, son of Thersandros; Kastor FGrHist 250F3 for Akrisios, son of Proitos.

625 ch.1, example 1.

626 As presented above in chapter 1, they represent examples of mythic-theft-type-one, but also serve as catalysts in the reorganization of the Argive line as treated in conjunction with Danaos and his family (i.e. ch.3, example one).

[627] e.g. ApB 2.2.1-2, Paus. 2.16.2, 10.35.1. Proitos and Akrisios were pivotal figures in the revised version of the Argive line, which stretched from Io to Herakles (in thirteen generations cf. Aischylos' *Prometheus Bound* 774) via a genealogy that fanned out across Libya, Egypt and the Levant, winding its way back to Greece in time to facilitate Proitos' and Akrisios' fraternal conflict over control of the kingdom of Argos (Gantz 1993: 198-212; West 1988: 77-78, 144,145). Proitos' and Akrisios' status as brothers was canonical by the fifth century as Aeschylos' *Hiketides* attests in its dramatization of the chain of events associated with their shared family history. The same playwright's lost trilogy that dealt with Danae's life story no doubt treated the topic according to the same trend. Phrynichos also staged an *Aigyptioi* and a *Danaides* before Aischylos' treatment of these affairs (Gantz 203, 299). Both the Athenian dramatists and the early local historians (so, for example, Akousilaos of Argos) evidently relied on the lost epic *Danais*, which must have detailed the whole post-epic saga in its alleged 6,500 lines (fr 4 Kinkel; cf. Huxley 1969: 34-38).

[628] ch.2, example 1.

[629] viz. the second Glaukos in this family line which runs: Aiolos – > Sisyphos -> Glaukos -> Bellerophon -> Hippolochos -> Glaukos. Glaukos and Proitos are both descendants of Sisyphos.

[630] "Ἀργει μέσσω" 6.224.

[631] Here again, specifically the northeastern Peloponnesian province cf. Il.2.559-568.

[632] Customarily, Tydeus + Deipyle / Polyneikes + Argeia.

[633] The killing of Eriphyle by her son, Alkmaion, at the command of his father, Amphiaraos, was a vital event within the plot matrix of the two wars between Argos and Thebes. The matricide, itself, conspicuously resembles the more famous story of betrayal and revenge that afflicted the house of Pelops, as featured in Aischylos' *Oresteia*. In this antecedent case, a feud between Adrastos, of the line of Bias, and Amphiaraos, of the line of Melampous, was initially assuaged by Amphiaraos' marriage to Adrastos' sister, Eriphyle. However, offering up the fabled Theban heirloom - the necklace of Harmonia, divine progenitrix of Thebes - Polyneikes bribed Eriphyle to convince her husband to join the Argive attack against his native city, since his brother, Eteokles had ousted him from power. Amphiaraos, a great seer, in a great line of seers, was, therefore, forced to join an endeavor he knew, in advance, would end in disaster, driving him to extract an oath from his son to avenge his mother's crime by taking her life. The severity of this action and the severity of its consequences in terms of the blood guilt that attached to the murder (the suffering of Orestes affords the relevant parallel), aptly informs the lack of representation from the line of Melampous in the war against Troy. The *Odyssey* states that Amphiaraos had two sons: Almaion and Amphilochos (15.248). The latter was elsewhere known for the establishment of Amphilochia in northwest Greece. However, unlike Thoukydides (2.68), the Homeric poems do not acknowledge this man in the war against Troy. Whether, therefore, as Apollodoros suggests, the matricide was at one time a fraternal enterprise (3.7.5), or whether, of old, Amphilochos was embroiled in some other adventure that deterred him from Troy, it is clear that the man, just like Theseus' sons, later secured a place in that conflict (cf. ApE 6.2; Str.14.5.16; Theseus sons, Akmas and Demophon, first appear in the *ΙΛΙΑΣ ΜΙΚΡΑ* and the *ΙΛΙΟΥ ΠΕΡΣΙΣ*, respectively, cf. Davies 1988). With respect to Alkmaion's murder of his mother, beyond the general observation that what happens once in Greek myth, happens at least twice, the remarkable number of lost ancient texts that dealt with the calamities of this extended family indicate that the greater fame of the similar crisis that later afflicted the house of Pelops was by no means more famous in antiquity. Orestes' murder of Klytaimestra is accordingly more familiar to us due to the exigencies of literary survival (see Gantz 1993: 506-510, 525-528).

⁶³⁴ For an astute and compatible reading of this episode, with references to previous points of view, see W. Donlan 1989. On the ancient Greek institution of *xenia*, see G. Herman 1987. For the use of this episode as an example of the highly politicized local reception of the Homeric poems across the Greek landscape, moreover, clearly resulting from the transmission and negotiation with an early fixed text, see C. Higbie 2002.

⁶³⁵ i.e. As brother of Proitos, both sons of Abas.

⁶³⁶ e.g. Thouky.1.9; Isok.*Arch*.18; DS 4.58.2; cf. I. Malkin 1994: 24; J.M. Hall 1997: 89.

⁶³⁷ Il.19.115. See the treatment of *Achaian Argos* in ch. 5 below.

⁶³⁸ e.g. Il.8.358-363, Il.14.3.19.29. By contrast, as addressed above (ch.3, example 1), the Homeric poems show no signs of familiarity with the story of Danae's great-great grandfather, Danaos, as told by Aischylos, for example, in his *Danaid Trilogy*. On the trilogy, cf. R.P. Winnington-Ingram 1961, 1983.

⁶³⁹ e.g. Il.4.141-145, Il.6.289-296, Il.9.381-384, Il.24.228-237, Od.4.78-93, 120-130 etc. Hence, one might conjecture, the word *orientation*, viz. προσανατολίζω /προσανατολίζομαι via ανατολή to oriens.

⁶⁴⁰ In the role of eastern immigrant magnate, Kadmos parallels Pelops in central Greece. Yet, Kadmos was depicted as a city-lineage founder, whereas Pelops entered into an established Aiolic lineage located somewhere, quite unspecifically, perhaps in the western Peloponnese. Later mythographers placed Oinomaos' kingdom in the district of Pisatis where Olympia lies. Though this is not impossible from the *Iliad*'s standpoint, such a kingdom would be somewhat awkwardly wedged in between the Epeians to the north, and the Pylians, to the south. Still and all, Oinomaos no doubt possessed a designated kingdom in the early epic period, which subsequently became Pelops' domain and remained in that family from Pelops' time onward. Likely, as far as the Homeric poems were concerned, this kingdom did not warrant explicit mention, since it had been absorbed by Pelops' descendants long before the time of the poetic action. Poetic silence on the matter, however, left the early conception of Oinomaos' domain susceptible to reinterpretation. It is perhaps reasonable to suppose that Oinomaos' kingdom lay near if not within Agamemnon's, while Agamemnon's kingdom evidently extended well beyond the bounds of his designated realm (Il.2.612-614, 9.149-152). Yet there is no indication as to how it was that the kingdom Pelops won in winning Hippodameia was ultimately distributed among his heirs (and his progeny multiplied as time wore on, surfacing mainly, as eponymous names e.g. Hes. fr. 224 MW; Pind.*Ol*.1.89; Ibykos via Paus.2.6.5; Phereky.3F20, 132; ApB 2.4.5.). Oinomaos' kingdom, in any case, was the hegemonic point of departure for an increasingly powerful, if profoundly ill-fated family, in every way vital to Greek mythic history. The preeminent status of Kadmos and Pelops in early Greek myth makes good sense in the period when the Greek mythic corpus was in development in the Greek east. The importation of progenitors from overseas to enrich the portrayal of Greek legendary history mirrors the overall ethos of the *Iliad* with its reverence and admiration for exotic eastern metropolis. Throughout the *Iliad* also, Achaian control of western Asia Minor remains a future, if ever present eventuality based on the outcome of the Trojan War. For the curious notion that Pelops was really an indigenous Peloponnesian hero who was somehow transformed into an eastern immigrant see M. Nilsson 1932: 44, followed by J.M. Hall 1997: 91.

⁶⁴¹ M. Finkelberg 1991: 305; I. Malkin 1994: 24; E. Cingano in R. Hunter ed., 2005: 128.

⁶⁴² i.e. Helen's allotted portion of Tyndareos' realm.

⁶⁴³ Looking closely at the genealogies involved, one thing that conceivably weighs in against the antiquity of this particular union is the way in which it taxes the bounds of the accepted mythic chronology. Given the uneven lengths of the two lines in question (i.e. Pelops to Troy in two generations; Perseus to Troy, however, in four to five), matters would work more smoothly if the daughters of Pelops had married brothers, or even sons, of Eurystheus, as opposed to his grandfather Perseus' sons. Quite possibly then, the early epic connection initially ran along these lines. Clearly however, in terms of prestige, especially from a Peloponnesian standpoint, the choice between forging this vital connection at Perseus' level rather than Eurystheus' was pretty much a no-contest issue, regardless of the effects of this marriage on relative chronological synchrony. In any case, the marriage of three of Perseus' sons to three daughters of Pelops' was altogether authoritative from the time it first surfaces. Unlike J.M. Hall, I am not inclined to rank paternal over maternal descent formations, rather, viewing each option as integral to the workings of the genealogical system; alternately appropriate in various situations (cf. 1997: 64, 89, 91).

⁶⁴⁴ i.e. sons of Perseus + daughters of Pelops.

⁶⁴⁵ Mythological sovereignty in Mykenai is dealt with extensively in chapters 5 and 6 below.

⁶⁴⁶ With the consolidation of the Argive state, Mykenai became a part of Argive sovereign territory. After the Argives were defeated by Kleomenes at Sepeia in 494 (Hdt. 6.76-83) a brief period of Mykenaian independence ensued (e.g. Mykenaians assisted in the war against Darios). Strabo (8.6.10) and Pausanias (2.16.5) report that Argives conquered the city ca. 468. There was a revival in the third century.

CHAPTER FIVE: THE PROBLEM OF MYTHIC ARGOS SUPPORTING EVIDENCE

In order to establish the connection between the mythological reinterpretation of "Argos" by Argos and various standard features of later Greek myth that were devised and promulgated in neighboring poleis in response to Argos-sponsored re-interpretive strategies, it is necessary to consider the evidence for the gradual annihilation of the house of Perseus. This issue affects the line of Melampous by virtue of its relation to the problem of mythic "Argos" as it occurs in the ancient sources. The fate of Perseus' house is relevant to the case if it can be shown that Agamemnon's kingdom was actually equivalent to the kingdom of Perseus, as far as early Greek epic was concerned. For if these two realms were indeed synonymous, and, in addition, completely distinct from the province of Argos as it was known to Homer and as it was known to the archaic Greeks, then the Argos of King Proitos who summoned the seer Melampous from Pylos would cease to be a confused and indeterminate kingdom in which an excess of rulers obscured the basis for sovereignty.

First, the very idea of the systematic extinction of a famous mythological line presupposes a comprehensive mythological edifice. This is not to say that in an ad hoc environment where miscellaneous stories were strung together from diverse sources as it seemed fitting, a genealogical line could not be point-blank extinguished, but rather that it would be altogether misplaced to posit the preplanned rise and fall of a house in a setting where there was no preplanning. Needless to say, the Aiolic hypothesis is, in essence, an argument for such an edifice, but also, inasmuch as its conclusions derive from a strictly genealogical treatment of the familiar mythological data, methodologically, it is an approach that is fairly impoverished from the point of view of the more elaborate and more theoretical interpretations of the Greek mythological stories[647].

Whatever the disadvantages of this, it is probably the hypothesis' greatest asset. The genealogical focus cuts to the quick, zeroing in on the functional precepts operative in Greek mythological discourse, in the beginning and later on. The precepts that it isolates are genealogically driven and because genealogy is an organizational structure, the Aiolic hypothesis views all mythic events in terms of their effect on genealogical structure. Accordingly, the genealogical method confronts profound phenomena like Greek mythic death from a comparatively dry, common sense point of view, leaving grand psychological and moral dilemmas altogether out of the picture. For instance the mythic motif of exile-for-homicide, a major subcategory of mythological death, when viewed from a strictly pragmatic perspective, mainly serves to move heroes from place to place, though it clearly performs a double duty by orchestrating a killing in the same stroke. In a symbolic genealogical framework, death provides an indispensable regulatory function. For as families multiply and expand, certain trajectories may be earmarked to flourish, but others must be earmarked for extinction. If not, the ever increasing multitude of protagonists makes the symbolic project untenable; the genealogical framework spirals out of control. Conversely, the elimination of an individual hero affects the fortunes of their consanguine survivors and amounts, in this way, to a means of controlling cause and effect relations across a greater canvas where the main protagonists are all interrelated.

An exploration of the possible transfer of power from Perseus' family to Agamemnon's in the beginning and by design, must start off with Perseus' three illustrious sons[648], who were held to have married three daughters of Pelops[649]. This block of narrative is responsible for the birth of Herakles, Perseus' great-grandson, which, as far back as Homer was measured against the birth of Eurystheus, Perseus' grandson[650], in a contest of wills between Zeus and Hera over the next successor to the Perseid legacy. The queen of the gods trumped the king, on this occasion, and Eurystheus inherited Perseus' kingdom, forcing his younger relation, Herakles, son of Zeus, to execute a sequence of divinely appointed labors (Il.19.95-138)[651].

THE GRADUAL DISSOLUTION OF THE HOUSE OF PERSEUS: HERAKLES' BIOGRAPHY

The available testimony on Herakles' life, as well as on his ancestors and his descendants, falls into four categories[652]. There are, on the one hand, a collection of statements that go back as far as the Homeric epics, but there are at least as many testimonial gaps concerning the extent of Homeric knowledge on the family history of Perseus' line. Using later reports by way of comparison, it is more or less likely, on a case by case basis or sometimes simply impossible to judge, whether certain events in the family saga were equally old and tacitly presupposed in the Homeric poems, or embellishments added later on. There are, on the other hand, certain parts of the saga that were undoubtedly post-Homeric in origin, while there is also a set of clearly ancient components that were shuffled around by ancient authors so that their original sequential order is again hard to establish with any certainty. Given these variations in age and authenticity, the main features of the family saga may be summarized as follows.

Perseus' three sons had a share in his kingdom. Alkaios fathered Amphitryon. Sthenelos fathered Eurystheus. Elektryon fathered Alkmene, who became Amphitryon's wife, and, in addition, a number of sons. The first main event to affect this arrangement was the murder of all but one of Elektryon's sons[653] in a cattle raid by a group of marauders known as the Taphians and/or the Teleboians, who lived somewhere along the west coast of Greece. This tragic turn of events prompted Amphitryon, Elektryon's nephew, and suitor for his daughter's hand in marriage, to help lead his uncle's stray cattle back to his kingdom. This action, however, somehow went awry, and Elektryon was killed in the process, whether accidentally, when a fierce bull went wild or whether because Amphitryon wanted to seize the cattle for himself[654]. The killing of Elektryon, in any case, resulted in Amphitryon's exile to Thebes along with Alkmene, his betrothed, who vehemently insisted, the story goes, that Amphitryon avenge the death of her brothers with an expedition against their Taphian murderers[655].

Meanwhile, back in the Peloponnese, the kingdom of Perseus devolved on Sthenelos, and ultimately, on Eurystheus, his son. The family of Elektryon had been nearly extinguished, and his daughter Alkmene was co-exiled in Thebes with her husband Amphitryon, son of Alkaios. The one remaining potential claimant was Likymnios, son of Elektryon, who, legend had it, survived the Taphian raid, only to be killed off anyway, in due course, by Tlepolemos, son of Herakles (cf. Il. 2.653-670; Hes. fr 195 MW; Pind. Ol.7.20-26; DS 4.58.6-8; ApB 2.8.2).

In Thebes, the story continues, Amphitryon endeavored to organize a force to fulfill Alkmene's demand. He secured allies in Boiotia, Lokris, and Phokis and gained the endorsement of King Kreon of Thebes by endeavoring to kill the *Teumessian fox* that had become a great scourge on the country[656]. Amphitryon's successful return from the Taphian adventure was linked to the consummation of his marriage, since on the same night of his arrival, Alkmene attracted the attention of Zeus, who appeared to her in the guise of her husband[657]. This remarkable evening led to the twin births of Herakles and his brother Iphikles: the former fathered by Zeus, the latter by Amphitryon. Amphitryon and Alkmene lived and flourished in Thebes until Amphitryon met his demise in a military conflict against the Euboians, after killing Chalkodon, the famous Euboian warrior[658]. Thus, Alkmene evidently outlived Amphitryon. And the Boiotians honored her as both Amphitryon's wife, and in addition, rather mysteriously, as the wife of the Kretan hero, Rhadamanthys. She was acknowledged as Rhadamanthys' companion in death and immortalized with him on the Isles of the Blessed; otherwise this second union is fairly obscure[659].

Herakles' life story proceeds from auspicious signs of great strength in his childhood[660], to a series of adventures around Thebes in his youth[661]. His most notable exploit in this period was the defeat of the neighboring city of Orchomenos that had subdued the Thebans under King Erginos and oppressed the city with a harsh annual tribute. Next and perhaps, as a result of this victory, Herakles married Megara, King Kreon's daughter. He continued for a time to live prosperously in Thebes, until a sudden burst of madness caused him to go berserk and kill all the offspring from his marriage to Megara. This crisis prompted his departure from Thebes, and ushered in his long servitude to Eurystheus back in the northern Peloponnese.

As for the content of Herakles' biography thus far, the *Iliad* specifies Herakles' birth at Thebes (14.324) and his predestined servitude to Eurystheus (Il.19.95-129). The *Odyssey* gives his parentage as we know it (11.266) and also acknowledges his first marriage to Megara, whom Odysseus sees on his trip to the underworld (Od. 11.269). The killing of Elektryon by Amphitryon, however, in connection with the murder of Elektryon's sons does not receive explicit Homeric acknowledgment. Still, it is to be noted, in this regard, that the circumstantial consequences of this unverified episode are perceptible in the Homeric epics although the episode itself is not literally confirmed. Thus, Orchomenos is ruled by Askalaphos and Ialmenos, sons of Ares born to a woman named Astyoche, who was not, evidently, unknown to Herakles (Il.2.511-515). For Astyoche appears to have been the same woman, who just over one hundred lines later, bore a son with Herakles as well (Il.2.653-660). As already noted, this man, the hero Tlepolemos, ultimately slew Herakles' uncle, Likymnios, landing the final blow to the line of Elektryon[662], and typically, thereupon, abandoned his homeland, founding prosperous cities on the island of Rhodes (Il.2.661-670). He arrived with nine ships to assist the siege of Troy but is killed off by Sarpedon in book five (Il.5.628-669). As far as the *Iliad* is concerned, Eurystheus, like Herakles, is already dead. The text yields no trace of any of his descendants, nor of Elektryon's progeny, beyond Alkmene and Likymnios, while no children from the marriage of Herakles and Megara surface in subsequent mythic events.

In this situation it is pointless to dispute the antiquity of the events in this sequence that are absent from Homer but present in later sources. For if not for the stories that have been preserved, one would be forced to posit another set of stories that would lead to the same outcome by some other route, with no concept, however, as to what they once were. Yet when old mythic consequences are still maintained later on, in the absence of explicit early narratives, as there is enough evidence here to conclude[663], it is far less likely that the relevant later narratives were the products of sheer creative invention. The relevant principle is one of economy whereby full-scale invention was ostensibly reserved for select mythological situations, namely those deemed to require a major overhaul on behalf of specific innovative objectives, whereas when no great changes were in the offing, what was known to tradition served well enough. Episodes of this caliber, which is to say, those consistent with old epic presuppositions, and therefore quite likely to be that old, often exhibit low-grade embellishments of no great consequence to the basic plot structure but of some interest or to some advantage to contemporary Greeks in later periods[664].

The main point here is that though it is impossible to prove that Homer knew of Amphitryon's Taphian expedition launched to avenge the death of Alkmene's brothers, he knew of the Taphians (Od.1.105, Od.14.452) and he knew of Alkmene (Od.2.120, Od.11.266) and Zeus, and Amphitryon, and Herakles at Thebes (Il.14.324). He viewed Eurystheus as a descendant of Perseus and as a once great magnate in the Peloponnese, who lorded it over his great-nephew Herakles, and in so doing, built up Herakles' reputation through the series of tasks performed in his service (Il.8.358-363, Il.19.95-133). All told, these arrangements presuppose the deaths of Alkmene's father and brothers inasmuch as they prefigure the exile to Thebes and exclude Alkmene's male relations' potential claim to power. If they were at one time accomplished by some other means, the issue leads nowhere; the story is unrecoverable. Granting this possibility, the fact remains that the miscellaneous relevant Homeric statements are remarkably consistent with this story as we know it from later authors.

IPHIKLES

The fate of two other figures is also relevant to the gradual extinction of Perseus' line, namely that of Herakles' half brother, Iphikles, and Iphikles' son, Iolaos. There are at least three possibilities concerning Iphikles' death, which makes a fairly strong case for his death to begin with. Iphikles' heroic persona is notably vague as preserved in the sources. He was said to have accompanied Herakles on his expedition against Orchomenos (ApB 2.4.11) and in his dealings at Troy under king Laomedon (DS 4.49.3), while his name also surfaces in later lists of participants in the hunt for the Kalydonian boar (ApB 1.8.2, Ovid *Met*. 8.27ff, Hyg. *Fab*. 173). Yet it is difficult to judge the antiquity of these claims[665]. Oddly enough, the *Aspis* asserts that Iphikles abandoned his allegiance to Herakles and took sides with Eurystheus and his allies instead, although in time he lived to regret it (86-94). It perhaps follows from this account, unique in its portrayal of Iphikles' disloyalty that Iphikles' death in some version involved a confrontation between Eurystheus and company, and enemy forces marshaled against them[666]. The *Aspis*, however, does not elaborate.

Diodoros (4.33.5-6) and Apollodoros (2.7.3) link Iphikles' death to Herakles' expedition against Sparta. There, Tyndareos' alleged brother, Hippokoon, and his sons, were said to have seized the Spartan throne and cast Tyndareos out of his rightful kingdom[667]. Strengthening his forces through an alliance with king Kepheus of Tegea and sons[668], far from aiming at Tyndareos' restoration *per se*, Herakles' mission aimed first and foremost to avenge the death of Elektryon's grandson (Oionos, son of Likymnios), whom Hippokoon and his sons had murdered[669]. This confrontation thus posits and efficiently kills yet another descendant in Elektryon's line, whose ephemeral existence lends some credence again to the overall process of elimination, regardless of the novelty or the antiquity of the otherwise unfamiliar victim involved[670]. Though evidently a popular later setting for the orchestration of Iphikles' death, and though Tyndareos' alleged brother Hippokoon, along with his formidable cohort of sons, surface as early as the poems of Alkman[671], doubts may be raised whether this branch of the family stems back much beyond the time of Alkman's poetry[672]. At any rate, casualties were heavy on this occasion, a big day in the annals of mythological death, for in addition to Iphikles, Hippokoon and his sons were altogether eliminated, while Kepheus and his sons were either killed to a man (ApB 2.7.3) or otherwise graced with a few survivors (DS 4.33.5-7). Another account of Iphikles' death, however, makes a claim to considerably greater antiquity by virtue of involving an extraordinary pair of figures whose pedigree goes back to the Homeric poems.

Pausanias accounts for Iphikles' death in a confrontation between Herakles and the mighty sons of Poseidon and Molione (8.14.9). These two, often portrayed as Siamese twins, were both known after their mother, as the *Moliones*, and after their stepfather (viz. Aktor), the *Aktoriones*[673]. They were affiliated with the genealogy of Elis[674], and during their lifetime played the role of that city's most valuable military asset. It seems that their reputation, in this regard, was magnified by certain special powers derived from their direct link to the god Poseidon. From the *Iliad* we learn that one of the three Epeian divisions that sailed to Troy with Agamemnon embarked under the leadership of their respective sons (Il.2.615-621). Nestor reports facing off against them in a skirmish over cattle between Elis and Pylos

(Il.11.669-709[675]), and losing a chariot race to them as well, at the funeral games for Amaryngkeus of Elis, though Nestor was victorious in all other contests he entered (Il.23.626-650).

The only extant story on the demise of these twins asserts that it was Herakles who finally killed them at the town of Kleonai just north of Mykenai[676]. The motivations for the killing are as usual fairly numerous, and most of them, in addition, fairly suspect, since it became customary to connect their deaths with the story of Herakles' sack of Elis, an event that the *Iliad* does not seem to acknowledge[677]. Beyond this, a few authors refer to their initial defeat of Herakles' army[678]. However, to the extent that Herakles was invincible, such a defeat was apt to prefigure an impending reversal of fortune.

Unlike Herakles' dealings with Hippokoon and sons, Herakles' interaction with the Moliones receives solid Homeric contextual support, if not specific corroboration, whereas his role as their killer portrays a son of Zeus, at length victorious over two sons of Poseidon, whose father had once saved them from death on the battlefield (Il. 11.750-752) but who did not intervene to counter Herakles' wrath. Herakles, in this light, was a most fitting slayer for two heroes of particularly powerful stock, while on a more basic level, especially in the absence of an early and more streamlined version of these events[679], the conflict in question focused on great protagonists from coterminous states, each driven to act against the kingdom next door.

IOLAOS

Herakles' nephew, Iolaos, surfaces frequently as Herakles' loyal accomplice and his charioteer, but he is never depicted as a potential contender for sovereignty over the Perseid kingdom. On the contrary, he is associated with his native city of Thebes, or transported to Sardinia to found a colony manned by Herakles' sons born to the daughters of Thespios, the eponymous ruler of Boiotian Thespiai[680]. It is not clear when this assertion first became current[681] but it may well be a strictly mythological claim. In spite of the extent of Greek settlement in the west and Herodotos' testimony to the effect that when threatened with Persian domination, the Ionian cities of Asia Minor considered Sardinia a potential destination (1.170, 5.124[682]), there is not much in the way of concrete evidence for significant Greek settlements on the island, which was predominantly controlled by the Phoinikians[683]. These, circumstances, however, by no means negate the usefulness of the story that a group of Greek notables established themselves there during the heyday of the heroic age[684], whereas it seems that the tomb of Iolaos – originally an important Theban landmark – was later reduced to a cenotaph[685]. On this topic at any rate, Pausanias notes that in his day and age "even the Thebans admitted that Iolaos himself died in Sardinia with the Athenians and Thespians who made the crossing with him (9.23.1)[686]." It is clear that Iolaos, like Alkmene, was previously believed to have died at Thebes or at least laid to rest in his home country.

Whether, therefore in Thebes or in Sardinia, Ioloas had no stake in the Perseid succession in the northern Peloponnese. Still, he was nonetheless famous for one very great deed, in every way critical to Perseid succession, for Iolaos was reputedly responsible for the decapitation of Eurytheus in a battle where Eurystheus' sons also perished (*Pyth*.9.67-76, Str.8.16.9, Paus.1.44.10). This confrontation, however, was ultimately swept up in a mythic initiative that permanently altered the form and content of Greek legendary history. The initiative in question was the great clash between Eurystheus and the descendants of Herakles allied with the Dorians of northern Greece[687]. In spite of the emergence of the Herakleidai at this juncture, the foregoing survey of Perseid family fortunes makes it safe to posit an ancient *coup de grâce* that marked the end of an era for the Perseid legacy and welcomed the intervention of the descendants of Pelops. This is to suggest that there are sufficient grounds for viewing this pattern as part of the structure acknowledged by early epic as far back as we can go.

THE RETURN OF THE HERAKLEIDAI AND THE HELLENIC GENEALOGY

The aim of this synopsis is already in sight, so one can imagine how obvious it once was to individuals steeped in Greek mythic traditions. The point is to emphasize the situation in which the elimination of the lineage of Eurystheus would grant Perseus' kingdom to Herakles' line, whereas the elimination of both of these lines would necessitate some alternative arrangement, and thus potentially activate the affiliation between the house of Perseus and the house of Pelops. Early Greek epic appears to have opted for this latter outcome by engaging the link with the Pelopid line. Subsequent Greek mythology definitively opted for the former arrangement, while assuming the latter in the first instance, since according to later mythological canon, Herakles' son, Hyllos, with his allies, the Dorians, killed Eurystheus and Eurystheus' sons. Conspicuously, however, this conquest did not prevent the line of Pelops from inheriting Perseid power, while the Pelopid magnates[688] kept Herakles' descendants at bay for at least another three generations. This episode features in a string of events, evidently designed to bridge the gap between the denouement of the Heroic Age and the onset of contemporary lived reality, from the point of view and to the advantage of the inhabitants of the Peloponnese.

At this point, the study of mythic "Argos" intercepts another legendary phenomenon developed in southern Greece during the Archaic Period. This was, namely, the Greek tribal genealogy that mimicked the same format as the old Aiolic structure, beginning at the beginning of legendary time, and tried to outweigh the influence of that precedent in telling the story of the ancestry of leading contemporary Greek ethnic groups[689]. This goal was accomplished through a rather awkward attempt to situate Dorian and Ionian Greeks on par with the Aiolians, who, as it happened, monopolized the old legends (the hypothesis runs) since the Aiolian Greeks first conceived and compiled them.

We have arrived at a juncture where it is easy to see how the aforementioned Greek tribal genealogy was appended onto the Aiolic framework by taking advantage of a potential opening. As already stated this tribal genealogy was developed in imitation of old legendary patterns. Accordingly, it arose from procreative events set back in the primordial beginning of time. However, once this line makes it down to the juncture in question it is known as the myth of the *return of the Herakleidai*, which aimed to alter the outcome of the Cyclic Epics (viz. the whole story of the Trojan War) with a sequel that explained what happened next, and above all set out to reconfigure the heroic population of the Peloponnese in order to coincide with contemporary reality.

This initiative first acknowledged the transfer of power from the house of Perseus to the house of Pelops, and then set out to exploit the latent potential for Herakles' line to take back control of the Perseid inheritance which was Herakles' birthright, and accordingly, to take control of the Peloponnese. This was accomplished through a legendary revival of the Heraklid branch of the Perseid line, somehow truncated in the early epic account in order to pass the power to the sons of Atreus, but which obviously offered the most strategic route to elicit a subsequent reversal of fortunes that would redirect hegemonic supremacy in the Peloponnese in the post Trojan War Period.

The main point here is to note that the mythological narrative concerning the return of the Herakleidai exhibits certain structural features that could well be anticipated with reference to the genealogical observations at hand. Thus it involved the destruction of the line of Eurystheus and an elaborate legendary excursus on previously undocumented and unknown individuals who were championed as scions of Herakles. And it also involved a post-Trojan War confrontation over the right to power in the Peloponnese, between the Pelopids under the leadership of Agamemnon's grandson Tisamenos, and an unprecedented cohort of Heraklid compatriots. The Dorian / Heraklid seizure of power was further construed as justified retribution that aptly reversed the prior transfer of power from the Perseid to the Pelopid line. When taking a close look at the Perseid genealogy, these features are strictly those that suggest themselves as the best way to manipulate received tradition, given the annihilation of Elektryon's line, and given the ascension of the house of Pelops. From the same vantage point though, it is equally clear that the transfer of power from the house of Perseus to the house of Pelops that appears to inform Homeric thinking, also presupposed the elimination of the lineage of Eurystheus, and, in addition, relied on a manifest absence of available contenders from Herakles' line.

The rest of the details of the Herakleidai story[690] are basically unpredictable and idiosyncratic. Yet this set of genealogically scripted conditions is enough to confirm that we are indeed looking at a concrete opening in the established legacy that was readily acknowledged as exactly that. This opening and its actual exploitation furthermore vindicates, in an off-hand way, the principle of legendary conservation, since it shows that revisionist mythic initiatives tended to ground themselves in old epic traditions. This implies a strong force of resistance to change: a tangible countercurrent, though by no means as powerful as the political impetus to revise the inherited framework. Thus, in spite of the gaps in the ancient testimony, the established prehistory of Herakles' and his family, inasmuch as it was the point of departure for a legendary sequel that was devised to take the family heritage in an all new direction, can be said to exhibit a vested interest in preserving the integrity of the original legacy, at least to the extent that the original legacy did not obstruct the promotion of contemporary Peloponnesian ideological imperatives. Two further aspects of the story of the return of the descendants of Herakles are relevant to the problem of mythic "Argos" and, in this regard, indispensable to the mythological problems connected with the place to which the seer Melampous migrated.

The story of the return of the Herakleidai made a fundamental distinction between the "Achaian" inhabitants of the Peloponnese, who were understood as a group of affiliates of the Aiolic mythological edifice that established tradition had situated there[691], and the contemporary inhabitants of the Peloponnese, who considered themselves "Dorians" as opposed to "Achaians," and, therefore, felt the need to create a new charter in order to account for this hegemonic change. The Achaian protagonists of early Greek myth were ultimately replaced, the Dorian charter goes, by Dorians from an enclave in north central Greece, whose claim to the country was allegedly based on an ancient alliance with Herakles (e.g Pind. *Pyth*.1.61-65; Hdt. 1.56, 7.94, 943; Thuky.1.12; DS 4.37.3; Str.9.4.10; ApB 2.8.7; Paus.2.18.5-8). The awkwardness of this formula is hard to overlook, since, for example, the Dorian leaders this legend appointed to serve as commanders were killed off before the invasion succeeded[692], leaving the project of Peloponnesian resettlement to the leadership of the descendants of Herakles, who were clearly pure-blooded Achaians themselves (Str. 8.1.2)[693]. Be that as it may, what was said to have happened at least fifty years after the Trojan War[694] was that a Dorian cohort re-emerged on the scene allied with the descendants of Heracles. They drove the old

Achaians from their Peloponnesian homelands (particularly Argos, Messenia, and Lakedaimon) and sent them in flight to the province of Achaia, which they subsequently settled as their new home, naming the province after themselves (Str.8.7.1; Paus.2.18.8, 7.1.7-8).

It is not necessary to delve further into this matter to see that this narrative neatly corroborates the foregoing analysis of the evidence that the old epic Perseid/Pelopid kingdom had been shrunk down and swallowed up by the machinations of archaic Argos. Here the Dorian scheme is revealed to coincide with the mythological block of empty space left along the north coast of the Peloponnese, when Perseus' domain and thereby Agamemnon's was confined to Mykenai and placed under the auspices of the Argive state. The Dorian scheme coincides with this move since its migration pattern is predicated on it. The establishment of the historical province of Achaia, as it was known to all later Greeks, was now defined by the Dorian foundation story as a territorial depository assigned to accommodate the suddenly uprooted Achaians of Greek myth. Meanwhile, the notion that Achaians were uprooted at all traces back to the advent of the Dorian story, which, in this regard, manifestly exploited the earlier dissolution of the kingdom possessed by Agamemnon in the *Iliad*. Clearly, the province of Achaia known to all later Greeks was, in essence, the Perseid / Pelopid kingdom as understood in the Homeric poems. Moreover, this connection begins to expose the nature of the problem that faced ancient analysts when addressing the topic of Argive sovereignty.

According to the reasoning set out thus far, the deliberate mythological reinterpretation of the old epic kingdom assigned to Agamemnon concentrated an excessive number of lineages within the confines of the Argive state. This generated ambivalence about mythic Argos because it was difficult to distribute all of these lines in an orderly fashion throughout the Argolid where epic tradition had long since situated a specific set of high-profile families, including the two lines that stemmed back to Melampous. The situation created considerable confusion as to which lines held possession of the most famous cities, and issues such as *when* and *under whom* the key strongholds of Argos, Tiryns, and Mykenai were ruled from a legendary point of view.

Next a cursory look at certain elements attached to the story of the return of the Herakleidai confirms the actuality and the impact of the mythological reinterpretation of Perseus' kingdom, and, by extension, of Agamemnon's, as analyzed and presented here. It is clear in this context that the composers of the return of the Herakleidai story understood the kingdom of Agamemnon according to the changes attributed here to the machinations of the Argive state. It is equally clear that later Greek mythology unanimously placed Perseus' kingdom in Argos, in spite of indications that of old it lay elsewhere, and in spite of the logistical contradictions that stemmed from the act of situating it there[695]. Beyond this, moreover, the Herakleidai story also provides a concrete explanation for the otherwise astonishing tolerance toward such a mixed-up mythological / genealogical situation.

The level of tolerance to contradiction is explained by the fact that this news-breaking story rapidly traversed Greek regional boundaries, ultimately achieving pan-Hellenic status, so that feigned inattentiveness with regard to its flaws may be directly linked to the proliferation and general acceptance of the legend itself, which, as mentioned above, is already visible in the poetry of Tyrtaios and the political persona of Pheidon of Argos. The contagious influence of the Dorian charter eventually reached beyond Dorian states.

This further development receives explicit support from an Ionian copycat charter that was later wedged in to harmonize with it, thereby including all major southern Greek states in the altered denouement to old Aiolic saga. In this light, the tribal-oriented narratives in question can be collectively associated with the same movement that arose to address deep-seated concerns about the mapping of Greek identity onto the Greek landscape in the final phases of the Heroic Age. The effect of these addenda cannot be understated. Their profound significance to contemporary Greeks was no doubt the force that mitigated objections to prominent defects in the mythological interface devised to append excluded ethnic identities onto the inherited Aiolic structure. It is no surprise that the stories advanced to overcome the deficiencies of the inherited structure focused on the depiction of the dominant ethnic groups active in southern Greece in the historical period: the Peloponnesian Dorians and the Ionians of Athens.

It's worth asking briefly in the present context, how the Ionians fit themselves into the program, since the answer leads back to the main point of the present argument. What the Ionians did was to position themselves as the inhabitants of the province of Achaia, back in time before the Achaians' flight was precipitated by the arrival of the Dorians. The Ionians, in other words, filled up the empty space created by the original reallocation of the Perseid/Pelopid kingdom, whereby the old realm was swept into Argos. Achaia, they claimed, was no prehistorical wasteland, but was rather a region formerly called Ionia because it was inhabited by Ionians at the time (Hdt.145; Polyb.2.41; Str.8.7.1; Paus.7.1ff.). Accordingly, the north coastal Peloponnese was inhabited by Ionians until the time when the Dorians ousted the Achaians, forcing Achaian exiles to confront the Ionians and, as it happened, to drive them off to Athens and, subsequently, to Asia Minor, that is, to locations where Ionian Greeks were to be found in the historical period[696].

On the premise that the narratives concerning the Dorians were designed to mesh with old Aiolic tradition through the strategic extension of the lineage of Herakles – the most famous protagonist of the Perseid line – and conceived in conjunction with a debt of allegiance owed to Herakles' family by the Dorian peoples[697], the problem of mythic Argos in the present context concludes with a look at the end of Herakles' life. Herakles' death became a pivotal juncture between Aiolic and Doric mythic terrain, and because the confusion that surrounds mythic Argos turns out to result from the superimposition of new strains of thought onto established legends, it is important to review this mythological juncture in terms of the points made in the foregoing argument.

TRADITION AND INNOVATION IN HERAKLES' LIFE STORY

It is first of all clear that a number of stories that wound out the saga of Herakles' life predated the advent of his relationship with the Dorians of northern Greece. It is generally recognized that the deeds of Herakles were a magnet for legendary elaboration. They expanded with the expansion of the Greek world. Taken individually, some cases are more transparent than others, as when Diodoros of Sicily's report veers off on a tour of the Italian peninsula and Herakles' exploits on the author's native island. Diodoros was not unique in his devotion to the western installment of Herakles' biography, which was par for the telling in his day and age. Still, that elaborate chapter in Herakles' life did not go back to the early epic period[698]. The full-blown account of Herakles' adventures contains a mix of old and new elements that do not divide equally in terms of supporting data, or in terms of the ease or difficulty involved in establishing their chronological status.

    The best as well as the most stable criterion is whether a story stands in contradiction to declarations made in the Homeric poems. It would be a mistake to assess this criterion as inherently biased in any way, for it has no opinion on mythological change – that is, whether it is a good thing or a bad thing, which is nonsense, in any case, since change is inevitable – it is simply the most reliable way to detect new priorities and mythological trends. Regardless of controversy on their absolute dating, these poems are the oldest continuous narratives on the events of the heroic age[699]. It was once of course popular to dispute the aesthetic unity of the poems to begin with (the hallmark of the German analyst movement). And while that approach is really no longer tenable in the wake of the research of Parry and Lord[700], there are still those who insist that the poems as we have them were transmitted orally for many centuries, remaining, therefore, in a state of flux, even as late as the Hellenistic period[701].

    For the present purposes, at any rate, Homeric testimony is viewed as peerlessly authoritative because it is taken to represent a mythological state of affairs that is not just antecedent chronologically, but embodies an earlier cognitive view, against which later changes were devised and directed[702]. Comparison based on early epic assertions, accordingly, makes it possible to detect the difference between East Greek Aiolic mythology and the maverick mythologies devised by mainland Greek states during the course of the Archaic Period. The same process makes it equally clear that the latest great phase of Greek mythic activity involved the systematization of select contributions from all of these sources put forth at various times[703].

Without the *Iliad*'s testimony it would be tempting, and even more compelling to some[704], to doubt the veracity of Herakles' sack of Troy, which preceded the expedition led by Agamemnon. But the *Iliad* assures us of that legend's antiquity (Il.5.628-654, 20.144-148). Conversely, it can be shown that Herakles' sack of Elis under king Augeias did not feature in the Homeric vision of things[705]. Like Herakles' alliance with the Dorians, and a number of other legendary vignettes, the sack of Elis was apparently a by-product of the systematization of Herakles' deeds in between early epic and the later mythographers, who preserved his biography in fluid but final form[706]. The sack of Elis, however, can be textually substantiated as a deviation from Homeric thinking, whereas Herakles' Dorian alliance cannot. Since the Dorian episodes that were so popular later receive no mention at all in the Homeric epics, the case for these episodes' arrested development relies on the *argumentum ex silentio*. This species of argument is notoriously weak, but especially dangerous in Homeric contexts where it was neither possible, nor part of the agenda, to reference every aspect of mythic prehistory that stood behind the unfolding plot. On the other hand, though, silence about something that doesn't exist is a valid and concrete state of affairs.

With regard to Herakles' death, no Homeric testimony whatsoever exists about certain main characters who were involved (viz. Deianira, Nessos, Iole, Hyllos). Fortunately, however, most of them turn up shortly thereafter, and in a way that once again suggests that the fifth-century version we are familiar with represents a revision of a long- established story. In this light, the invention of the sack of Elis, which is notable since it can be supported, shows that such creativity was common procedure and is thus of some help in gauging the status of Herakles' association with the Dorians beyond the argument made from silence. Pinpointing comparable novelties that were later attached to the earliest strata of Greek mythic tradition sheds some light on the methods that were developed to introduce new traditions and adjust old arrangements. The use of such methods can then be applied to interpret the matter of Herakles' death, on the grounds that such practice was normative policy[707]. Moreover, the common thread that connects these three episodes (viz. Herakles' sack of Elis, Herakles' alliance with the Dorians, and ultimately, Herakles' death) and makes sense of the impetus for their development is once again Peloponnesian politics during the post-Homeric epoch.

HERAKLES' SACK OF ELIS

Epeian representation in the *Catalogue of Ships* depicts Augeias and collateral family members through the leadership status of their descendants at the time of the Trojan War (Il.2.615-624). Plainly, this arrangement is inconsistent with the occurrence of Herakles' sack of Elis[708]. Moreover, in the *Iliad*, Meges, son of Phyleus (evidently, both members of Augeias' family), rules in Doulichion and the Echinai islands (Il.2.629, 15.528-30)[709]. Notwithstanding, later mythographers report that after sacking Elis, Herakles made Phyleus king of that country once he killed off the rest of his family members (e.g. ApB 2.7.2; DS 4.33.4 & Paus.5.3.3[710]). This simply is not the case in the *Iliad*.

The standard later conflict between the Kalydonians under Herakles' leadership and the Thesprotians of northwest Greece is clearly also the product of post-Homeric thinking. The story of this war involves a concerted effort to change the identity of Tlepolemos' mother, who was an Epeian in Homeric epic, but is later a Thesprotian woman instead. Tlepolemos' mother in the *Iliad* was Astyoche of Ephyra on the river Selleeis. Given the protagonists involved in her portrait it is clear that Ephyra was an Epeian city. Astyoche bore two children by the god Ares in the house of Aktor, son of Azeus (Il. 2.511-513). She later bore Tlepolemos to Herakles (Il.2.657-659). As time wore on, this same Astyoche became the daughter of a man named Phyleus, who bore the same name as the *Iliad*'s Phyleus, the man who moved to Doulichion after a dispute with his father (Il.2.629), though this second Phyleus was the king of Thesprotia[711]. Still, the more famous Phyleus was Phyleus, son of Augeias, who also became known as Astyoche's father (a notion not incompatible with the *Iliad*), since the later mythographers are at pains to distinguish Phyleus, son of Augeias, who ruled Doulichion, and became ruler of Elis after Herakles' sack, from the second Phyleus, king of Thesprotia, who in assuming the role of Astyoche's father transported this woman from Elis to northwest Greece[712].

This paradox calls attention to a standard example of the doubling of Greek mythic figures, where the innovative introduction of homonymous names facilitates the split of an established identity, accompanied by the redistribution of honors that once accrued to one, among two individuals. The Thesprotian Phyleus not only contradicts Homer, but contradicts the story of the sack of Elis as well, if not for the intervention of a second Phyleus, since it is impossible for Phyleus to be ruling Thesprotia when he was ruling Elis after Herakles' sack, which is already a problem from a Homeric perspective because the man ruled Doulichion and the Echinai islands. Nor does is solve the problem to call the Thesprotian hero Phylas, instead of Phyleus, again under the assumption Astyoche was his daughter (though it is easy to see why one might want to do so)[713], since as Strabo points out, though there was an Ephyra in the land of Thesprotia, it was not an Ephyra on a river Selleeis. The main one on such a river lay in Epeian country[714].

A glance at the extant narratives on the subject, reveals that each author devised his own special solutions to the problems that stemmed from the substitution of the Thesprotian for the Epeian Ephyra and made Tlepolemos' mother a Thesprotian native. They did so, moreover, with a keen eye to minimizing the conflict these changes entailed with respect to the statements in the Homeric poems. Even though the rift could not be more than superficially neutralized, given the dissonant elements involved, the basic objectives of the new canon were accomplished with an admirable degree of finesse. These objectives would appear to have been the transfer of Astyoche from Elis to Thesprotia and the integration of Herakles' sack of Elis into his roster of illustrious deeds. As to the motivation behind the whole scheme, it is liable to rest with its main objectives and, therefore, discernible in terms of mythic results. Looking at the consequences of these adjustments, Elis was deprived of Herakles' son Tlepolemos, who happened to command more Homeric coverage than any other named scion of Herakles. Against this, however, Elis gained the distinction of experiencing one of Herakles' sacks, which was certainly a bona fide distinction of sorts, if hardly as distinctive as spawning one of his sons. But the sack of Elis was a boon to Herakles also, and by extension, likewise advantageous to certain high-profile groups of Peloponnesians who defined themselves as Herakles' descendants by way of a union that, as it happened, received no coverage at all in the Homeric poems. Thus, these two moves put the spotlight on Peloponnesian Dorians and their campaign to improve their heroic reputation, which was a fairly tall order inasmuch as Homeric poetry did not acknowledge them.

The *Catalogue* entries on Elis and Orchomenos suggest a connection between these two states that was typical of Aiolic mythic arrangements considering that the Aiolic lineage attributed the foundation of southern Greek cities to genealogical offshoots of north Greek Aiolic stemmata. The relationship between Elis and Orchomenos mirrors the relationship between Pylos and Iolkos, which was based on Neleus' migration southward[715]. It is true that the Orchomenos-Epeian connection is far less obvious than the Iolkos-Pylian one, mainly because it became customary to claim that Elis was founded from Aitolia (e.g. Str.8.3.33; Paus.5.1.3). Sticking to the *Iliad's* testimony, however, it is clear that Aktor, Augeias and Amaryngkeus were identifiably Epeian heroes and that prior to the time of the Trojan War a woman with connections to their patrimony (viz. Astyoche) bore semi-divine sons, who were sent to Orchomenos in order to lead the Minyan host to Troy. Herakles who was famous for "sacking many cities of god-supported fighters" was specifically famous for the sack of Orchomenos during the time he resided at Thebes. Indeed, his sack of Orchomenos works remarkably well with the *Catalogue*'s coverage of that Minyan city, for its destruction aptly explains why it was necessary to obtain naval commanders from the province of Elis to lead the Minyan contingent to Troy (Il.2.511-516)[716]. That they came from Elis does not seem like mere coincidence.

There are two further points that round off this example. Judging from a note on Archilochos in the scholia to Aristophanes' *Birds* (1764), augmented by the protagonists and location of the story, Herakles' cleaning of Augeias' stables seems to rate as an exploit of considerable antiquity. As it happens, this exploit is not represented in art or in literature until the fifth century, at which point it includes the standard justification for Herakles' decision to sack the city of Elis, namely since Augeias went back on his word and refused to pay Herakles for the job (e.g. Pind.*Ol*.10.; DS 4.33.1; ApB 2.5.5; Paus. 5.1.9[717]). The stables are thereby linked to the sack of the city. Moreover, the motif in which Herakles plays family favorite, sacking cities and placing the only clan member who advocated his interests back on the throne amidst carnage and rubble, is a later motif on comparative grounds. So much, by way of example, of results gleaned from textual comparison based on genealogy, with the obvious proviso that it does not work so smoothly in the absence of sufficient Homeric data.

Using the Homeric *Catalogue of Ships* as a valid source of mythological information (vital to clinch the case in the foregoing examples) warrants some explanation with respect to the *Catalogue*'s generally marginalized status in scholarly circles. The numerous discussions that have dealt with this document tend to agree, in spite of their differences, that the *Catalogue* should be viewed as a text unto itself, separate from the body of the poem that contains it. This conviction has discouraged a particular line of reasoning that nonetheless proves to be remarkably fruitful, although it relies on addressing the *Catalogue* as organically integral to the rest of the poem. Based on the premise that the *Catalogue* functions as a means to delineate background events that took place in the past and yet infuse the mythic present (roughly in the same way that personal reminiscences summon the past to the present throughout the course of the *Iliad*[718]), the *Catalogue* may be viewed as a mythological document with a pronounced mytho-geographical bent[719]. It is meant to reiterate to a listening audience thoroughly steeped in legendary tradition the underlying lay of the landscape and the origins of the personnel who came from specific centers of power to join Agamemnon's expedition to Troy. For what it is worth, this approach to the *Catalogue* is borne out repeatedly through investigative queries aimed at collecting all relevant information on persons and places that occur in the poems. What surfaces consistently as a result of such queries is a comprehensive and meaningful mythological setting provided for mythological purposes – that is, to conjure up by general consensus the broad conceptual canvas that enabled the poet to focus on a few days in the tenth year of the war and to leave off with the city of Troy still standing.

HERAKLES' DEATH

There is only one extant story about Herakles' death[720]. Sophokles' *Trachinai* is the first complete surviving account of it[721]. Herakles' death is fundamentally a matter of his second marriage to Deianira of Kalydon and his fascination with Iole of Oichalia. Herakles' association with these two women led to disaster when Deianira used a poison that she thought was a love charm in an attempt to shift Herakles' attention from Iole back to herself. Deianira applied this potion to a ceremonial robe which Herakles donned to pay homage to Zeus after his successful sack of the city of Oichalia. There he took the king's daughter, Iole, captive, her city destroyed and her family slaughtered. The potion itself has an interesting history. It was composed of a mixture of the blood of the Hydra, which Herakles used after killing that monster to heighten the deadly force of his arrowheads, blended with the blood (and/or semen) of a centaur named Nessos[722].

The poison, therefore, invokes another story. This was the one in which Herakles and Deianira, a recently married couple, crossed the Euenus river in Aitolia, aiming to seek their fortunes elsewhere after Herakles killed a servant in Deianira's father's household (viz. the household of Oineus of Kalydon)[723]. Apparently Nessos was in the business of escorting people across this river, and when it was Deianira's turn to cross, against all propriety, he attempted to rape her[724]. Comprehending this situation from afar, Herakles shot the centaur with one of his poisoned arrows. Whereupon, in a state of great duress, Deianira naïvely heeded the dying beast's declaration that the combination of substances linked to his death could serve as a love charm if she ever needed it.

Neither Nessos, nor Deianira, nor Iole are mentioned anywhere in the Homeric poems. The mythic history of Kalydon and of Oichalia, however, are frequently referred to and doubtless well-known[725]. Additionally, it is not insignificant that Iole and Deianira were close relations in the Aitolian branch of the Aiolic line, because Deianira's grandfather, Porthaon, was Iole's great-grandfather too. Namely, Porthaon's daughter Stratonike was the mother of Eurytos, Iole's father, and Porthaon's son Oineus (viz. Stratonike's half-brother –

since they had different mothers) was Deianira's father (Hes fr 26 MW). By way of these connections Iole and Deianira were first cousins, once removed[726]. Other notable members of this illustrious family include Meleagros and Tydeus (hence Diomedes), as well as Leda (the wife of Tyndareos), and possibly Oinomaos, as suggested above[727].

The *Iliad* situates Oichalia on the Peneios river just west of Mt. Titanos, thus southwest of Mts. Olympos and Ossa in north central Thessaly (Il.2.729-730[728]). The text is familiar with the kingship of Eurytos (Iole's father), who once entertained the itinerant singer Thamyris. Shortly after taking leave of Eurytos' household, Thamyris met his death at the hands of the muses in the Peloponnese for boasting of his skills in relation to theirs (Il.2.594-600). The *Odyssey* reports a similar fate for Eurytos himself. For the great marksman from Oichalia was killed by Apollo for excessive boasting about his archery skills (Od.8.223-229). Upon Eurytos' death, his son Iphitos inherited his bow, which turns out to be none other than the great bow that only Odysseus could successfully string. This was the bow that Odysseus used upon returning from Troy to kill Penelope's suitors, who had overrun his household and wrought havoc in his realm during his absence at Troy and his long delayed homecoming (Od.21.314-413).

Odysseus initially obtained this bow on a mission to the Peloponnese in his youth. For at the house of Ortilochos (not far from the source of the Alpheios river[729]), Odysseus once met Eurytos' son, Iphitos. Odysseus hoped to retrieve a stray herd of sheep and their missing herdsmen that had been stolen from Ithaka by a fleet of Messenians. Iphitos hoped to retrieve a herd of prized horses that Herakles had stolen out of his kingdom[730]. As a gesture of friendship on that occasion, Iphitos gave Odysseus Eurytos' bow which he had inherited from his father. This was apparently Iphitos' last noble gesture, for he was murdered by Herakles shortly thereafter, when Herakles having welcomed him first as a guest, he killed him with the intention of keeping his horses (Od.21.9-41).

We witness in all this considerable background knowledge concerning the house of Oichalia. And though the Homeric passages seem to imply that Herakles was well acquainted with Eurytos' kingdom, two of its rulers are dead and the city still standing when the Homeric poems abandon the subject. Still, it is equally clear the poems knew more of the story, since in the *Homeric Catalogue of Ships*, Oichalia has passed to the sons of Asklepios, while "Herakles fate and the wearisome anger of Hera have (already) beat him under the earth[731] by the time of the Trojan War.

With respect to the missing episodes at issue, there was an old epic poem that undoubtedly addressed them, attributed to one Kreophylos of Samos and aptly entitled the *Sack of Oichalia*. Kreophylos was an early Ionian poet closely associated with Homer in the sources or alternatively with the poet's alleged descendants known as the genos of the Homeridai. The Homeridai have been convincingly analyzed as an initially hereditary guild, centered, it seems, on the island of Chios but which subsequently branched out to include other professionals and devotees. Their mission was to protect and presumably to disseminate the *Homeric* compositions in their possession, as far as they were concerned, by hereditary right[732]. Though associated with Samos rather than Chios, it has been suggested and makes good sense to think that Kreophylos was in some sense affiliated with the broadening of this guild in seventh-century Ionia and its epic-oriented socio-cultural clique. Kreophylos, in any case, made a name for himself focusing on a topic that the *Iliad* and the *Odyssey* left incomplete, in accordance with typical ancient literary protocol.

Unfortunately, we do not know what his poem said much beyond the fact that it featured Iole. Pausanias claimed that Kreophylos was the first to place Oichalia in central Euboia, as opposed to central Thessaly where Homer placed it, which is significant because the Euboian location became a fairly popular standard[733]. In general, it seems that Kreophylos' work had considerable influence on other writers. It was likely, for example, a point of reference for authors such as Peisandros of Rhodes, Stesichoros of Himera, Ibykos of Rhegion, and Panyassis of Halicarnassos, all of whom composed poems that dealt with Herakles' life. The data appear to indicate that the sack of Oichalia was integral to the early epic repertoire, whereas the recorded version attributed to Kreophylos was, like the Homeric epics themselves, representative of the popularization of Aiolic epic in East Greek Ionia during the early Archaic Period[734].

From Panyassis[735], a contemporary and a relative of Herodotos, an interesting fragment survives to attest that quite unlike Sophokles' version of things, Deianira was actually in Oichalia with Herakles at the time of a feast hosted by Eurytos[736]. Looking back at the relevant Homeric reportage, that feast would have preceded the revenge of Apollo, and logically, would have been the occasion when Herakles duped his hosts and made off with their horses, after a disagreement with Eurytos. And though it was pretty well standard, as would be the case here, for this earlier visit to precede the sack, which was set up but delayed to a later occasion, later literary and artistic accounts alter the parameters of the Homeric version by replacing the feast with an archery contest with Eurytos presiding and Iole the prize (Gantz 435[737]). Here, Herakles was the victor but he was denied his due[738], setting off a sequence of violent reprisals which basically followed the same order implied by the Homeric statements on the subject (minus the premature death of Eurytos and the fact that the poems did not mention Iole), namely the killing of Iphitos in connection with his lost horses, followed sometime later by the sack of the city and the abduction of Iole.

Evidently, the advocates of this alternate version postponed Eurytos' death at the hands of Apollo so Oichalia's great king could establish a contest for his daughter's hand, and be present to experience Herakles' violence against his family and his realm. This postponement, however, also made it appropriate, if likewise a bit odd, for Eurytos to survive and flee the sack of his city in order to keep his *rendezvous* with Apollo in an unstated nod to Homeric tradition[739]. Equally compelling is Sophokles' decision to depict his star female characters in the *Trachiniai* as though they were actually total strangers. For when Deianira first lays eyes on Iole, she pities and admires her, but has no idea who she might be, beyond suspecting that she is the daughter of some noble family (*Trach.* 307-313, 316).

The snippet of information furnished by Panyassis is somewhat more interesting, given the fact that though he was a poet regarded with distinction, he was also accused by Clement of Alexandra of following Kreophylos rather too closely. This remark should be taken with a grain of salt, even coming from a critic with texts at his disposal[740]. Yet it does spotlight something that we already know emphatically with respect to Greek dramatic production where we can still experience it even now and need not just hypothesize on its nature or its impact.

That is the expectation of certain surprises by way of interpretive variation in each retelling of every well-known story. It is important to notice and to bear in mind that a predominantly aesthetic and apolitical mode of mythological adaptation flourished alongside more programmatic and highly politicized mythic initiatives. This alternate mode of mythic adaptation dealt more with pathos and personality than with structural (viz. genealogical) rearrangement. Still, there isn't exactly a clear-cut line between them because they generally functioned in tandem.

Oftentimes, at any rate, the rearrangement of things, as well as decisions about omissions and inclusions were made on behalf of aesthetic considerations, which the reception of a set piece relied on. This more aesthetically based *modus operandi* was the domain of the poets more than the domain of the historians and chroniclers, and it accounts for the fact that the great Athenian playwrights composed numerous plays billed under the same title. Obviously the audiences that packed the theatre on successive occasions were by no means expecting to witness the same thing twice.

And though it would be mistaken to claim that the poets were innocent of incorporating and astutely promoting the latest mythopolitical trends, the point is that an allegation of plagiarism takes on a meaning quite different from the meaning we are accustomed to nowadays in an environment where each practitioner was engaged in repeating the same well-known stories to knowing and expectant listening audiences. The operative definition of creativity is far from negligibly altered in this situation, given the limitations imposed by a strictly traditional body of material. Paying attention to this distinction offers some added insight on Clement's remarks because his critique may well imply that Panyassis' poem when compared with Sophokles' drama, which was bound to influence any such judgment, stuck disappointingly close to Kreophylos' version. These dynamics would heighten Panyassis' significance in terms of the transmission of early archaic precedents and accordingly distinguish Sophokles' version as memorably creative in the same vein.

In this regard, one sure innovation calculated to heighten dramatic effect was Sophokles' eclipse of the blood connection between Deianira and Iole, which no doubt struck his audience as an ingenious touch. Concerning the antiquity of the basic plot line, however, the involvement of Iole as far back as Kreophylos (Str. 15.1.18), the *Ehoiai*'s acknowledgement of the poisoned robe (Hes fr 15 MW), and Bakchylides' report, which accords with the *Trachiniai*, albeit with a display of brevity that renders his dithyramb pretty much unintelligible without adequate background knowledge, suffice to counter the tendency of later writers to make Sophokles their main source of inspiration. The array of early sources, obscure as they may be, nonetheless justify the conclusion that Herakles' death was intimately bound up with the lives of these two women as far back as early Greek epic tradition.

Likewise, the legendary history of Herakles' bow provides the epilogue in a concatenation of stories that placed Deianira, Nessos, and Eurytos and his family in a synthesis bent on Herakles' destruction. Once again, Sophokles first informs us that Philoktetes, son of Poias, was the beneficiary of Herakles' bow, if only inasmuch as in his play by that title, Philoktetes is discovered using Herakles' bow to kill live prey on the deserted island of Lemnos[741]. That Herakles' final act was to bequeath that bow, either to Philoktetes or to his father Poias, in exchange for lighting the pyre that put him out of his misery, is first preserved in Diodoros and Apollodoros (DS 4.38, ApB 2.7.7). Yet this piece of information not only sheds considerable light on what Sophokles expected his audience to supply when they gathered to view his portrait of Philoktetes, but also makes remarkable sense of Homer's cryptic remarks concerning the whereabouts of Philoktetes and his anticipated arrival at Troy (2.716-725). According to tradition, in any case, Philoktetes and his bow were indispensable to the sack of that city. Falling into the zone that lay in between the scope of the *Iliad* and the *Odyssey*, Philoktetes' persona seems as vital to the tradition as that of any protagonist involved in Herakles' death, which suffers from a deficiency of early extant coverage.

When, to the extent that it can be reconstructed, the one and only story concerning Herakles' death links back up with the question of his genealogical legacy, a few insoluble problems arise. Foremost among these is the question of progeny associated with Herakles' second marriage. It certainly seems as though Herakles' first marriage was created and destroyed from the very beginning, leaving no viable heirs to mythic posterity[742]. Meanwhile, the various sons who partook of his legacy and received acknowledgment in Homeric epic were born to women other than Deianira[743]. In a number of cases that are verifiably old, these sons established Perseid sovereignty abroad through a combination of emigration and conquest[744]. Tlepolemos, for instance, son of Herakles and Astyoche, slew Likymnios, son of Elektryon, and established Heraklid cities in Rhodes (Il.2.653-669), whereas Herakles' landing on the island of Kos on his way back from Troy through Hera's interference (Il.14.250-262), had the effect of displacing the authority of two prominent Aiolic lines, namely, Sisyphos' line and that of his sister Kanake, whose descendants apparently controlled the island up until the time of Herakles' arrival[745].

It is interesting that the sources generally treat Tlepolemos as a full-fledged family member, stationed somewhere in the family realms before committing the deed that led him into exile. Perhaps the fact that his destiny ultimately lay elsewhere made it unnecessary to emphasize Tlepolemos' status as a bastard son rather than a legitimate heir. More plausibly though, early epic conferred a good deal less weight upon this distinction than it was later granted in myth or in reality[746]. Thus, it is perhaps not unlikely that Tlepolemos could have commanded the right to inherit within the Perseid kingdom had he not been conveniently exiled for homicide. Meanwhile, as time wore on, Herakles' love life became an increasingly prolific source of new mythic trajectories by way of new liaisons albeit typically assigned to very distant locations. Still, it remains conspicuous nevertheless that early epic poetry names no obvious heir destined to take control of the Perseid territories in the northern Peloponnese. This factor heightens the mystery attached to Herakles' son, Hyllos, who was hands down the most significant offspring attributed to Herakles' second marriage – namely to Deianira of Kalydon.

HYLLOS

There is no early evidence on the existence of Hyllos whose main role in Greek myth was that of military leader for the joint Dorian/Heraklid initiative to seize control of the Peloponnese. The name Hyllos itself is a suspicious entity. It goes along with the names

Pamphylos and Dymas, two sons of the Dorian king Aigimios. Aigimios was responsible for recruiting Herakles to aid him in a war against the Lapiths (DS 4.37; ApB 2.7.7). He was thereby responsible by way of formal exchange for the ancestral pact between Herakles and the Dorians that allegedly justified Herakles' descendants' invasion and, at length, their conquest of the Peloponnese with the aid of Aigimios' descendants. More than invoking figures of any heroic depth, the names allocated to Aigimios' sons personified two out of three actual subdivisions associated with Dorian Greek identity, for the Dorians were composed of three constituent tribes (*phylai*)[747]. The three were identified throughout antiquity as Pamphyloi, Dymanes, and Hylleis, with an occasional added component specific to particular Dorian poleis (e.g. Hdt.5.68). Hyllos – Hylleis is thus the missing third formula vital to connecting the legendary past with the legendary harbingers of a new era, aka the Dorians in alliance with the descendants of Herakles.

Another point of reference connects the name with the river Hyllos located in Lydia. Herakles notoriously spent a block of time there in the service of the dowager queen of the country as punishment for the murder of Iphitos (viz. of Oichalia), which was considered to be a grave offense to the gods[748]. However, as it stands, the evidence for the Lydian episode involving Herakles' servitude to queen Omphale looks like a post-Homeric development, quite likely conceived in East Greek Ionia, since that region responds best to the question: *cui bono*? The main argument for the novelty of the Omphale episode is based on the fact that the kingdom of Lydia plays no role in Homeric coastal Asia Minor, just as numerous other East Greek states that existed at the time of the poems' composition do not appear where they would be expected to be.

Although often perceived as a reason to think that the poems replicated Bronze Age geography, this state of affairs was really quite programmatic, since it was dictated by conventional criteria understood to distinguish the Heroic Age from the subsequent onset of lived reality. The alternative perspective utilized here sees Homeric geography as a mythological artifact that superimposed a whole mythic idiom – that is, the early East Greek cultural state of mind onto the map of the Greek world[749]. When tested against the range of early epic testimony this approach to the data holds up more successfully than the long-standing theory that the Homeric poems worked with a flawed but factual template of the Bronze Age landscape[750]. This outlook, moreover, makes it completely unnecessary to look high and low for a reason why there were no Greeks living in Asia Minor at the time of the Trojan War because this arrangement was the by-product of a tangible and pervasive legendary chronology. From the vantage point of the Trojan War, the Greek colonization of Asia Minor was still a future eventuality, and one that was allocated by design to the descendants of the Greek survivors at Troy. This had nothing to do with historical memory, but was strictly a matter of chronological distancing – moreover, not on a casual or ad hoc basis, but based on a specific ideological plan[751].

Herodotos reports that in his day and age the Greeks claimed they ruled Lydia for twenty-two generations prior to the rise of the Mermnadai dynasty, initiated by Gyges, bodyguard of Kandaules, who murdered his master and married the queen (Hdt.1.6-7). This ingenious piece of propaganda was probably developed a good deal earlier by Greeks in the neighborhood of the Lydian kingdom, in response to the rise of Lydia in their midst. Herodotos dates Gyges to the late eighth century[752], yet whether Homer was acquainted with Gyges or not, he clearly did not participate in the later Greek program that claimed the wealthiest kingdom in western Anatolia had been governed by Greeks for five hundred years, on the basis of a sexual encounter that took place during Herakles stay in the country. Homer, on the contrary, does not acknowledge the kingdom of Lydia at all, though both his poems take place after Herakles' death. Again, in general, however, Homer does not acknowledge patterns of habitation in Asia Minor known to have been current in his day and age[753], yet taking this as a given, that is to say, as a deliberately retrospective approach to the issue of myth-historical time, this situation is not only consistent with the ethos, objectives, and specific details offered throughout the course of the poems, but it also makes it compelling to wager that, at the time of the poems' composition, Herakles' adventures had not yet reached Lydia[754]. As far as the *Iliad* was concerned, the territory controlled by the kingdom of Lydia was not Lydia, but Maionia. It was inhabited by Maionans, allies of Troy (e.g. Il. 2.864-866; Hdt. 1.7; DS 4.31.5-6; Str.13.1.8).

By the fifth century Herakles' sojourn in Lydia was viewed as the source of various genealogies[755]. It is interesting that the theme of penance through servitude was a form of punishment mainly applied to gods who defied the bounds of cosmic propriety[756]. By contrast, exile for homicide was the general prescription for heroic acts of violence against other heroes. And yet, perhaps it stands to reason, that if Zeus could force Herakles to submit to Eurystheus, he could force him to serve a Lydian queen. In any event, new innovations typically latched onto established material through the strategic mimesis of standard mythic tropes. More importantly, the Hyllos known to mainland tradition bears no connection to the Lydian episode, but was rather the son of Herakles and Deianira, whom his father commanded, according to Sophokles, to marry Iole after his death (Trach. 1219-1251). His prominent role at the head of the Dorians in the first unsuccessful pre-Trojan War effort to seize control of the Peloponnese, facilitated the passage of Perseid sovereignty into the hands of Atreus, son of Pelops, upon the death of Eurystheus, while Hyllos and company retreated from the fray to sit out the duration of the Trojan War (Thuky. 1.9; DS 4.57.2-4; ApB 2.8.2-3; Paus.2.18.7).

THE RETURN OF THE HERAKLEIDAI LEGEND REVISITED

A barrier materializes at this mythical juncture whereby the canonization of the Heraklid charter has permanently obscured key information from view. For example, it is impossible to determine, who, prior to the advent of the Heraklid story, the offspring of Herakles and Deianira might have been (albeit if not Hyllos), though a heroic marriage that did not produce offspring was, in essence, a contradiction in terms[757]. Nor is it possible to identify the situation that evidently prevented any such offspring from asserting their right to the Perseid territories that were bestowed on the house of Pelops, in the absence of any such claim. Hyllos, of course, aptly answers these questions, but if he was not a bona fide early epic persona, or played some role other than the one he became famous for, there are no available traces or leads concerning whom he supplanted, or what kind of stories at one time prevailed before the ones that we know. The previous circumstances of Eurystheus' death are likewise concealed behind the same barrier if he did not go down fighting against the Herakleidai.

Still, the assertions of Pindar (*Pyth*.9.79-83), Euripides (*Herakleidai* 680ff.[758]), and Pausanias (1.44.10) against Diodoros (4.57.6) and Apollodoros (2.8.1) that it was Herakles' nephew Iolaos who took the life of Herakles' great tormentor (and necessarily also the lives of his sons, unless they perished by way of some other ordeal), could easily stand independently of the specter of Dorian/Heraklid aggression and could, therefore, easily have played a part in some completely different narrative conflict (viz. who knows what?). In spite of this cluster of impenetrable mysteries, their impenetrability is at least sufficiently plain in terms of the rise of Dorian ideology in the archaic Peloponnese. In this light, it is possible to partially visualize the jagged edge of the boundary between old and new myth to the extent of perceiving strategically why the Dorian poets of the Peloponnese zeroed in on this juncture as the ideal place to splice on their account of Dorian ascendancy.

If in accordance with the available evidence, the development of the Heraklid story is a assigned *terminus ante quem* in the mid-seventh century and a *terminus post quem* in the late eighth, since the Homeric poems reveal no consciousness of it and if it is separated in point of origin from the main corpus of Aiolic legend, its spread and canonization can be readily grasped. For once these premises have been adopted, the content of the story harmonizes completely with the idea that it was composed in response to the proliferation of East Greek epic in southern Greece. There the politics of identity and state relations were vastly different from their political corollaries in Asia Minor in the preceding centuries. If we, therefore, place the crystallization of the Dorian ethnic charter roughly in this period, though it was very likely first conceived of somewhat prior to its *terminus ante quem* and perhaps even prior to the development of hostilities between the three major states that color the main narrative (viz. Argos, Sparta & Messenia), it took some time for the charter to gain ground farther afield and longer still to become a universalized concept replete with a developed Ionian subtext.

By the early fifth century when we begin to possess a substantial amount of literary testimony, the process of development was for the most part complete and the amalgamated result was mythological canon. Accordingly, the idea that Hyllos, Herakles' son, spawned a line of descendants who, either under his leadership or following his example, set out to conquer the Peloponnese with the help of their Dorian military allies but failed again and again before they succeeded in establishing themselves as the ancestors of the contemporary Peloponnesian inhabitants, was spreading around by the mid-seventh century. Catching on like wildfire, this same basic narrative expanded to incorporate the ancestry of every Dorian principality in southern Greece (Str.8.8.5[759]). It captivated the Ionians of Athens, no less, who responded by joining the movement themselves, apparently by the early sixth century (West 1985: 50-59, 113; Gantz 1993: 167[760]).

Among the more striking features of the *Herakleidai* story are the repeatedly unsuccessful attempts at conquest, which can best be understood in the following way. In order to integrate Dorian origins around the already extant heroic legacy, it was necessary to set the stage for the conquest in the period prior to the Trojan War, but quite impossible to have the actual conquest take place at that time, except at the cost of the Trojan War legacy. Thus, the Heraklid story insinuated itself during and at the end of Herakles' life, in accordance with the tradition that Herakles' actions antedated Troy by one to two generations, and, furthermore, antedated Agamemnon's ascension to the prerequisite position of power as sovereign beneficiary of the Perseid realm (Il.4.370-382). In this context, what could be more at odds with the whole point of the Heraklid story than to have the Dorians and the descendants of Herakles eject the Achaians from their Peloponnesian homelands before they could execute the war against Troy that stood at the pinnacle of Greek heroic achievements? It is self-evident that no one, at anytime, anywhere in Greece was remotely willing to forfeit that legacy, and so we witness a construct that works around it.

The first confrontation takes place before the Trojan War and succeeds in killing off Eurystheus, who dies at the hands of Hyllos or Iolaos. Consequent to this action, the kingdom of Eurystheus falls to

Atreus, son of Pelops, and through him, in due course, to Agamemnon. Variously sometime after these events, Hyllos orchestrates an all-out invasion, which fails, as it must, to oust the Achaians. So the Dorians retreat for a considerable length of time[761]. Following the war and the events of its aftermath, in the reign of Tisamenos, son of Orestes, the successful invasion ultimately takes place, at which time the great and great-great grandsons of Hyllos invade the country, expel the Achaians, and divide the land by lot amongst themselves.

    This summary captures the basic idea but necessarily fails to take account of significant variations characteristic of each ancient telling of the story. Suffice it to say, that even though each report is fundamentally comparable to every other, emphasis and omissions vary considerably and meaningfully also, from author to author. All told, these variations demonstrate that the most serious challenge in telling this story was to make its details work coherently with the already established mythic plot structures onto which it was superimposed. So, for instance, although the three generations from Atreus to Orestes' son Tisamenos accord with the number said to exist between Hyllos and his victorious descendants[762], Apollodoros' assertion that Hyllos led the invasion against Tisamenos, son of Orestes, though he was also the man who killed Eurystheus, throws off this alignment conspicuously and taxes the bounds of credibility. This is, of course, due to the difficulty of having Hyllos face off against both Eurystheus, and, later, Tisamenos, son of Orestes, in his role at the vanguard of the whole expedition, since asserting Hyllos' leadership on both these occasions against enemies four generations apart, thwarts the progression of generations in the line of the invading cohort (ApB 2.8.2). Nevertheless, this formulation is extremely attractive from the point of view of sustaining an adequate block of time between the Trojan War and the successful invasion. Calculating this interval at one hundred years that is roughly equivalent to the three generations, Apollodoros' report, in spite of its problems, deals successfully with this ambivalent period[763].

    A tug of war between vital but conflicting criteria is clearly discernible in this regard. On the one hand, the basic program demanded that the unsuccessful invasion precede the Trojan War. On the other hand though, in order to establish the requisite time frame between the first failed attempt and the successful invasion (as calculated traditionally in generations), the failed mission accords best with the reign of Orestes, which nicely enables Hyllos' descendants to fill the required chronological gap[764]. This prospect, however, stands in violation of the demands of the leading criterion that the first failed invasion precede the Trojan War. Thus, being pulled simultaneously in two directions, Pausanias first reports the Orestes' formulation (1.41.2), but is later moved to retract it for precisely these reasons, resituating the duel that turned back the invaders to the period prior to the Trojan War (8.5.1). One way or another, each ancient account is beset with some difficulty of this kind, whereby genealogical or narrative statements about one thing wind up clashing with narrative or genealogical elements vital to some other aspect of the story[765]. Mythological redaction was always imposed at some cost to mythological intelligibility.

Overall, the whole tribal-oriented genealogical edifice, which reinvented the wheel and the whole Greek world with it, using the old Mesopotamian myth of the flood, could never effectively correspond with the already extant Aiolic edifice that it attempted nonetheless to subsume. The Dorian branch of this genealogical artifact, the tail end of which we are dealing with here, was markedly underdeveloped and by all means too short to logically mesh with the legacies of its Heraklid accomplices or its Achaian (Aiolic) targets.

Viewed independently, the *Herakleidai* segment of the larger initiative is genealogically more convincing than the upper reaches of the Greek tribal genealogy, which basically relied on eponymous names to witness the origins of Greek tribal groups. But the fact that the *Herakleidai* story itself, an offshoot of the story of Greek tribal origins, came equipped with a lineage at pains to line up with the heroic traditions it was devised to leach off of, did not make it possible to fabricate a plot structure that could narrate this new genealogical artifact and seamlessly coincide with the Trojan War story or with established Greek mythic tradition in general.

The ambiguities that we are dealing with here, whereby various authors sought to present the most coherent picture they were able to formulate, cutting their losses as they saw fit by fudging the data and downplaying liabilities, are symptomatically comparable to the problems connected with genealogical innovation in the province of Argos. In the Heraklid story where the main objective was to stage interactions between old and new protagonists in relation to the Trojan War, ambiguity centered around the question: when? In the restructured portrait of mythic Argos where the main objective was to accommodate an overabundance of genealogical lines in a limited territory rich with legends and lineages, ambiguity centered around the question: where? So in the end it is as hard to establish when the various attempted invasions took place as it is to determine where in Argos a given lineage actually ruled.

THE HELLENIC GENEALOGY REVISITED

It is worth pausing briefly to recommend a particular way of viewing the so-called "Hellenic" stemma that differs somewhat from the leading interpretation that has most recently been proposed. For Jonathan Hall, the Hellenic genealogy "clearly" functions "to establish the degree of relatedness between the various Greek ethnic groups which are represented by their eponymous ancestors (Hellen, Doros, Aiolos, Ion and Achaios)." And, "More than simply providing an answer to the question of ethnic origins, however, the Hellenic genealogy employs the metaphor of kinship to construct a system of *ranked* relationships between the groups that are represented by their eponyms (1997: 43; 2002: 27)." While, "If from the fifth century, Greek self definition was *oppositional*, prior to the Persian Wars it was *aggregative* (1997: 47[766])."

The present analysis frames the matter quite differently. First, as emphasized by J.M. Hall, the Greek tribal genealogy was no doubt the product of cumulative thinking about Greek tribal identity during the course of the Archaic Period. In this sense one can certainly say that the Hellenic genealogy was an "aggregative" construct until the point it achieved a certain stability. However, rather than documenting the development of competitive feelings among specific Greek ethne, it seems the main purpose of this genealogy was to document the tribal-oriented additions to the inherited mythological repertoire devised in southern Greece in the post epic period. Thus, emulating the aforementioned conceptual symbiosis between the Aiolic genealogy and its constituent mythological narratives, these innovative Dorian and Ionian strands credited to the lineage of the eponymous Hellen, likewise reproduced mythological narratives in an abbreviated schematic form. In this sense the Greek tribal genealogy diagrammatically synthesized precisely the stories just encountered above, namely the cluster of narratives that were promoted by the Dorians and Ionians of mainland Greece in response to the epic lineage structure, which was, as it happened, overwhelmingly Aiolic.

Despite the general run of minor variations[767], when this stemma first surfaces in the *Ehoiai* it was conceptually fully formed, that is, replete with Dorian and Ionian referents, and also a number of other tribal-based stemmata tacked on to "non-Hellenic" collateral lines. This means that any gradual or aggregative development must have taken place prior to that composition[768]. However, if as proposed, this lineage functioned as a genealogical short-hand for the most popular stories that dealt with the issue of Greek tribal identity, then it stands to reason that the tribal lineage was brought into existence in response to the canonization of the stories it was deployed to represent. This indicates that it was the stories, not the genealogy that developed gradually, since the stories that were reproduced by the diagram *a priori* had to exist before the diagram could be symbolically meaningful. This illustrates why various Greek tribal groups that did played no part in the original narrative scheme were subsequently appended onto it according to the priorities of contemporary redactors by way of superficial eponymous names.

It is clear from their Dorian and Ionian emphasis that the relevant genealogies were devised and controlled by the most powerful Greek ethnic groups[769]. Proceeding from that premise, the suggestion here is that these genealogies were not designed to make qualitative or judgmental statements on the relative status of respective Greek tribes (although at times they were used to do so, e.g., Apollo's paternity in Euripides' *Ion*), but functioned iconographically to invoke in a flash the mythological narratives that had been advanced by the Dorians, in the first instance (i.e. *the return of the Herakleidai*), and subsequently embellished by the Ionians (e.g. *the Ionian migration from Achaia to Athens and subsequently from Athens to Asia Minor*). Accordingly, in collusion with one another these two groups rewrote post Trojan War Greek prehistory to reflect the southern Greek cultural and political priorities they were the dominant arbiters of.

From this point of view, the tribal lineage diagram articulates a significant accommodation between the major parties involved – once again, the Peloponnesian Dorians and the Athenians (aka the Ionians), the preeminent spokesmen for this particular cause, which aimed at discrediting a mutual enemy inimical to the stature of their mythic integrity, namely, the Achaians (aka the Aiolians) of traditional heroic legend. These stories excluded significant groups of Greeks, though not apparently on the basis of some kind of cultural chauvinism in a strict sense, but rather more simply, as a result of the fact that the initial creative enterprise did not consider the interests of others. This in turn sparked a process of assimilation to the dictates set out by the most dominant groups. In this regard also it seems to be the case that the concept of Hellas as opposed to that of Hellen was the authoritative force behind Hellenic identity, which therefore emerged one notch further up with the rise of Deukalion, the Hellenic first man, who embraced all subsequent genealogies.

This explains why the ranked relationship theory runs aground here and there in terms of clarity when attempting to treat the Deukalionid stemma. To take the case of Xouthos as an example[770], looking at a diagram of the standard version of the Hellenic genealogy, it is not self-evident why Xouthos, not Ion, is set up as the brother of Aiolos and Doros. Undoubtedly Xouthos stands out in that position as a non-eponymous figure surrounded by tribal eponyms. However, using later mythic data as a guide to the relevant background material (so, for example, Paus.7.1-2 with all relevant tangents), it is clear that Ion was portrayed as the grandson, rather than as the son of Hellen, because the standard account made it impossible for Ion and Doros to be contemporaries.

This relationship was impossible for no other reason than the *return of the Herakeidai* story involved the participation of Doros' grandsons (viz. Pamphylos and Dymas, sons of Aigimios, son of Doros), who provided the Heraklid expedition with its essential Dorian character. The expedition further required the generation of the descendants of Herakles, although it was also held to take place in the period that succeeded the reign of Ion. This meant that at a minimum another generation was needed to place adequate space between Doros and Ion (and likewise, Achaios) to accommodate Herakles' pact with Aigimios, as well as the generation of Heracles descendants, and still have the Ionians establish themselves in the north central Peloponnese before the successful Dorian conquest ousted the Achaians of Homeric epic forcing those Ionians to flee to Athens[771]. The genealogical arrangement was therefore dictated by criteria that stemmed back to the stories themselves. Without dwelling further on this phenomenon, the point is that it corroborates the stream of events identified here as pivotal to the substantial eclipse of early Aiolic mythology in favor of an alternative mainland Greek synthesis that was perpetuated and controlled by the most powerful states in the Classical Period[772].

THE ERADICATION OF THE PERSEID REALM

The foregoing review of certain major discrepancies between the mythological geography of Homeric Greece and the mythological geography that later replaced it, demonstrates that geographical conflicts, expressed mythologically in the ancient sources, represent real political conflicts of interest that can often be traced to known historical contexts. Above all, it is clear that the place called "Argos" to which the seer Melampous migrated on a mission to cure king Proitos' daughters was, traditionally, altogether distinct from the territories controlled by the old house of Perseus, which though coterminous, lay to the northwest in the earliest incarnation of all relevant stories. Homeric Argos, moreover, complicates matters further, since only two of its numerous early epic uses coincide with the subsequent use of the term. "Argos" in later periods strictly denoted the northeastern Peloponnesian province, which was known as Argos as well as the Argolid, and included within it the city of Argos that was also known by the same name. Consequently, there was an Argos in Argos, which may be compared to New York, New York (i.e. Argos, Argos). This latter day Argos included Mykenai, the administrative metropolis of Agamemnon's domain, which its Homeric counterpart explicitly did not, and by virtue of this political actuality, the state of Argos appropriated the Perseid legacy, thereby detaching that lineage from the territories over which it originally ruled. This action left the north coast of the Peloponnese available for other mythic initiatives.

THE PROBLEM OF MYTHIC ARGOS: ARGOS IN HOMER

Argos in Homer is a more complex matter, for the same term admitted a number of meanings in addition to those that remained current later. This problem has provoked some differences of opinion and occasioned innumerable remarks. Given the findings of this thesis, it is important to emphasize that the study of Homeric geography has been overwhelmingly directed toward the reconstruction of Greece in the Bronze Age. The crux of the matter, in this regard, is that Homeric geography doesn't make sense from the point of view of the historical period. As addressed briefly above, the main evidence to this effect comes from the *Iliad's Catalogue of Ships*, since there were numerous cities mentioned in the *Catalogue* that the historical Greeks could not easily identify. The division of provinces was also unfamiliar in certain ways, exemplified for instance, by the absence of Thessaly, the obscurity of Phthia, the nonexistence of Megara[773].

Highlighting the canonicity of the Homeric poems, the historical Greeks responded to these discrepancies by equating unknown Homeric metropoleis with familiar alternative contemporary communities, while reinterpreting unseemly Homeric districts, and frequently competing for jurisdiction over allegedly equivalent poleis[774]. One upshot of all this that could well be anticipated, was multiple claims to venerable ancient cities. Hence, the morass of Ephyras and Oichalias, and Strabo's report of the marvelous proverb concerning the ubiquity of the city of Pylos: "ἔστι Πύλος πρὸ Πύλοιο Πύλος γέ μέν ἐστι καὶ ἄλλος.

Consensus was greater on the provincial level where a tangible incentive to come to terms with a pan-Hellenic transcription of the Homeric kingdoms, in fact offset, at least to a degree, the vigilant egos of individual states. There was also a tendency, as we have seen, to accept the self-centered work of a powerful conspirator, based on the opportunity for other contenders to creatively graft themselves onto the scheme, counting themselves in sync with the latest greatest trend.

In all this it is clear that Homeric geography was unequivocally a description of Greece and very far from a picture of some alien country. But it was also less of an account of the landscape than it was a distribution of kingdoms: kingdoms assigned to specific heroes, heroes assigned to great hereditary lines.

The observation that the *Catalogue of Ships* does not depict Greece in the historical period is currently associated with two related theories. First, that the *Catalogue* was an isolated text created independently of the *Iliad* and inserted by the poet, or someone else, in the location where we currently find it[775]. And second, that since the *Catalogue* is not contemporary with the poetry that surrounds it, it is therefore a relic of the Bronze Age. It is worth briefly noting a few kinks in this logic. Putting archaeological research to one side, the rift between the *Catalogue* and the historical map of Greece by no means necessarily suggests a Bronze Age provenance for the *Catalogue*[776], nor does it recommend, in and of itself, that the *Catalogue* be treated separately, because this geographical rift could just as well reflect the passage of time in conjunction with an outdated rendering of mainland Greece current in Asia Minor in the Homeric Period. In this respect, a contemporaneous setting would adequately address the divergence at issue, while raising the prospect of diminishing correspondence with increasing distance from the Homeric Age. If, however, the *Catalogue* is completely cut off from the poetry that surrounds it, this kind of logic no longer applies.

The arguments used to uproot the *Catalogue* are not for the most part very convincing, and often seem to confuse the *Catalogue*'s true distinction as a special sub-genre of epic poetry with a justifiable cause for textual alienation. Observing, for example, that there are heroes in the *Iliad* who appear in the *Catalogue*, but not the rest of the poem, or that a cohort is fighting on the battlefield under the command of a hero other than the *Catalogue*'s designated group leader, or that the emphasis on Boiotia in the opening entry is not commensurate with the unfolding plot, is far from what is needed to incriminate a document that features more consistencies than inconsistencies with respect to the environment in which it occurs[777]. But really any discernible consistencies at all would seem to demand a very thorough reckoning before a major segment of poetry is dislodged from its place on the basis of inconsistency. It may not, moreover, be safe to assume that the muster list the *Catalogue* provides was driven by geographical first principles, as opposed to other first principles organized geographically[778] – this is to say, with reference to an interpretive mapping, as we do nowadays, for example, with representations of median household income or the distribution of religious adherents.

Neither of these issues is a closed case. Still, these two popular verdicts have dominated the field, bolstered by various archaeological findings, making it standard to equate Homeric geography with the political geography of the Bronze Age. Consequently, Homeric geography is not all that much of a hot topic of late, mainly, because it is irrelevant to the study of Greece in the historical period. For, if Homeric geography is Mykenaian, it stands apart from subsequent events, and is useful exclusively as a guide to the reconstruction of the lay of the landscape in a remote and scarcely knowable era. But also, this formulation pulls the Homeric data into a vicious analytical circle, since the Mykenaian world is understood by it, while it is understood as a reflection of lived reality in the Mykenaian world. Archaeological reliance on textual sources generates this analytical bind, for it is the *Iliad* that suggested to Schliemann that the great gold mask unearthed at Mycenae in 1877 was none other than the mask of Agamemnon, not an inscription carved into the mask itself[779].

More recently, the excavation of a handful of sites understood as equivalent to named Homeric cities has been alleged as proof of a Bronze Age *Catalogue*[780]. The prospect that these cities were initially inhabited, but then, abandoned at the end of that era, and remained uninhabited till the historical period may not suffice to prove the point. In any event, a very great burden is placed on a slim and tenuous collection of data[781]. Though there are a number of skeptics who have not been persuaded that the geographical question has been put to rest, the spell that goes back to the excavations of Schliemann is, for the most part, still in force. It is, therefore, really no wonder that Homeric geography does not weigh heavily on anyone's mind, since under such conditions it is strictly suited for the specialized study of Mykenaian times.

The present synopsis concerning Homeric Argos follows, by preference, the astute observations of T.W. Allen that date back to the beginning of the twentieth century. T.W. Allen's intense interest in Homeric geography can be attributed to significant changes in the intellectual climate between then and now. First, Allen was working just after Schliemann's discoveries began to reverberate throughout the discipline as demonstrative proof that the Trojan War story recorded an authentic Bronze Age event: the sack of Troy by allied Greek forces. Second, he was working before Milman Parry and Albert Lord demonstrated definitively that Homeric poetry was rooted in and inspired by oral tradition[782]. Based on the discovery of Bronze Age written inscriptions, it was frequently assumed in the early twentieth century that Homeric poetry was a response to long-standing traditions preserved in writing[783]. This made it possible to believe that the Homeric poems were written down as early as the tenth century BC (when Allen preferred to think Homer actually lived), developing into the text we possess, by the eighth century, at the latest, after an extended period of further transmission[784].

The intellectual climate in the early twentieth century inspired a level of confidence in historical continuity from the Bronze Age to the Early Archaic Period that has drastically disintegrated since that time. The establishment of the complete loss of writing[785], paired with an interval of comparative cultural decline during the intervening period, has jeopardized the immediacy of Bronze Age civilization, re-contextualized the Homeric poems, and overall, sapped the strength out of that point of view. Arguments in favor of historical continuity must now invoke the survival of age-old memories across a significant temporal divide, or alternatively insist, against evidence to the contrary[786], that oral tradition was a sufficiently static medium that it can be relied on to preserve obsolete information in unadulterated form. Ongoing archaeological excavation, moreover, has generated a picture less rosy than anticipated when it comes to the absolute correspondence between Mycenaean data and Homeric reportage[787].

Given these differences in the state of the discipline, Allen's pragmatic approach to the Homeric data remains one of the more serviceable interpretations of Homeric political geography. This is mainly because he thought the data were real, not just real in terms of accurately recording the outlines of a previous geo-political landscape, but real in terms of making logical sense and functioning globally throughout the Homeric poems. Allen insisted that Homer be judged exclusively with reference to Homeric poetry[788]. He further believed and frequently proved that the strict adherence to this policy was the best way to develop a clear understanding of the Homeric geo-political outlook, which occupied its own historical niche under conditions that later ceased to exist[789].

As it turns out, Allen's argument in favor of the authenticity of Homeric geography is well worth heeding, regardless of the fact that his approach to the topic is now outdated in a number of ways. Subsequent revelations between then and now suggest the Homeric epics should be down-dated. Yet, if as Allen detected, the Homeric world view is well represented by the *Catalogue,* the *Catalogue* should be down-dated as well, as part and parcel of the traditions that stood behind early Greek epic poetry. Toward this end, the block of time that succeeded the Dark Age Aiolic migration to Asia Minor receives consistent support throughout the Troy saga[790]. Moreover, this observation is nothing new[791].

As Allen saw it, the simplest test of the authenticity of the Homeric vision is that the Homeric epics depict "a state of things, political and topographical, which never recurred in later history; and which no one had any interest to invent, or even the means for inventing[792]." If, accordingly, Homeric geography can be deciphered in a way that makes sense in its native chronological setting, it should be judged a forerunner against its successors in a sequence of geographical interpretations, rather than as a relic of no dynamic import to the competitive ideologies of emerging archaic poleis. Along the same lines, Homeric geography is essentially a subset of information within the Greek mythological tradition.

Greek mythological genealogy, moreover, indicates that its attendant geographical counterpart, responsible for setting its every scene, is distinguished most by the quality it is most often denied, namely that it was genuinely mythological. Therefore, though this form of geography was uniquely deployed in the ideological description of the Greek past, the closest thing to the landscape that it described was mainland Greek territory in actuality. The confusion that stems from this nuanced distinction is not hard to fathom when observed in this way. And it is equally clear how misleading it is to mistake Greek mythic geographical data for straightforward information on the lay of the land.

As for the matter of Argos in Homer, both the city and the province known to latter day usage are well documented in the *Iliad*. The city of Argos was among Hera's favorites in the company of Sparta and Mykenai (Il.4.51-52). The province of Argos was delineated geographically as Diomedes', Sthenelos', and Euryalos' joint domain, a factor that remains constant throughout the course of both poems (e.g. Il.2.559-568; Il.5.405-415; Il.14.110-125; Od.3.180-182). In addition to these, there are four other meanings, one fairly straightforward, three, more subtly construed.

At its most general, the word Argos was synonymous with Greece as a whole. In this regard, it was equivalent to Achaia, which likewise designated all of Greece[793]. At the time, Hellas was a province near Phthia in central Greece. In accordance with these parameters, Argives and Achaians were both words for all Greeks regardless of their homeland, whereas the Hellenes, who later took on that role, were not conceived as such in the Homeric poems. Throughout the *Iliad*, the third designation, Danaans, also collectively characterized the members of the Greek cohort. This term differs from the other collective names by way of naming the whole by citing only a part of it. Inasmuch as the term, Danaans, invokes the lineage of Danae, mother of Perseus and paramour of Zeus, it derives from a specific genealogical eponym and puts the spotlight on people over place[794]. And indeed, it invokes the lineage of the family whose legacy devolved on Agamemnon, king of kings, and leader of the whole enterprise.

That Argos equals Greece receives clearest confirmation in passages where protagonists such as Nestor, Achilles, and Idomenos, who hailed from Pylos, southern Thessaly and Krete, respectively, all use the term Argos to describe their homelands, namely, as the place they may never return to if they meet their deaths on the Trojan battlefield. The ancient antiquarians, reasonably enough, did not make much of this use of "Argos," since no one in later times was remotely willing to use the word Argos to designate all of Greece. But this hardly has an effect on Homeric usage. Strabo notably acknowledges this usage in passing (8.6.5). However, generally speaking, the ancient writers preferred to equate Homeric Argos with the Peloponnese, which is a rather more delicate matter.

In the *Iliad* and the *Odyssey*, there is at times a vague sense that it is not quite appropriate for certain instances of "Argos" to indicate the whole of Greece. These instances of the word clearly do not infer either the city or the province, but they do not seem to invoke Greece as a whole either. In such cases the name appears to point to a unit other than either the city, or the province, but more circumscribed than the full expanse of Greek territory. And yet it is often difficult to ascertain whether this perception stems from the text itself, or rather from expectations of what it ought to be saying based on later historical conditions in Greece, or subjective impressions prompted by later attitudes. Still, there are certain cases that can be pinned down.

Four passages in particular mention an entity that is described as *Achaian Argos*. Two occur in the same scene in the *Iliad*'s book nine where Agamemnon attempts to win back Achilles' loyalty with an offer of marriage to one of his three daughters and the gift of sovereignty over seven cities, apparently under his command (Il.9.141, 283). In geographical terms, Agamemnon's proposal amounts to a southern Peloponnesian kingdom on the shores of the Messenian Gulf. Agamemnon's terms are repeated by Odysseus when he arrives in the company of Phoinix and Diomedes to convey the king's message to Achilles. Typically then, the second occurrence is a verbatim repetition of the first. The offer, moreover, is contingent on the outcome of the Trojan War, thus, "if we ever come back to *Achaian Argos*."

The third mention of a place called *Achaian Argos* occurs in book nineteen when the goddess Hera describes how she foiled Zeus' intentions for the succession of power in the Perseid clan. Coming down from Olympos to *Achaian Argos,* she managed to speed up the birth of Eurystheus, a deed that denied Herakles' claim to power, on account of an oath made by Zeus himself that the next born descendant in the Perseid blood line, would reign supreme (Il.19.115).

The fourth and final occurrence of the phrase *Achaian Argos* is spoken by Telemachos in the *Odyssey*'s book three (Od.3.251). On his visit to Pylos to inquire after his father, his host Nestor recounts a series of stories about the outcome of the Trojan War, including the slaughter of Agamemnon upon his return home by his first cousin

Aigisthos. Aigisthos had taken up residence with Agamemnon's wife, Klytaimnestra, during Agamemnon's long absence at Troy. Alarmed at the story of Agamemnon's grizzly death and amazed that Aigisthos could get away with such treachery, Telemachos asks whether Menelaos was out of *Achaian Argos* at the time. This question leads to the story of Menelaos' homecoming, which explains how it was that the two sons of Atreus did not return home together at the same time.

Three of the cases where *Achaian Argos* occur make reference to Agamemnon's domain, which, as argued above, was also the kingdom formerly held by the house of Perseus. The fourth occurrence, in which Hera intervenes to delay the progress of Herakles' birth is thereby explained according to the same premise, yet set back to a previous point in time (viz. before the Perseid kingdom fell to the house of Pelops). Making these observations in 1909, T.W. Allen suggested that *Achaian Argos* in Homer was equivalent to Agamemnon's domain, which is to say, the north coastal Peloponnese from Korinth to Elis, ruled from Mykenai. As for the seven cites offered to Achilles, Agamemnon, no doubt, commanded these auxiliary holdings and spoke with a view to their dispensation upon his arrival at his administrative stronghold. Though Allen did not acknowledge the prior Perseid connection, his conclusion as to the meaning of *Achaian Argos* is indeed well supported by the above listed passages.

As king of kings among the Achaian warriors, Agamemnon was the most powerful leader in Greece. This being so, on what basis, specifically? Though the *Iliad* notoriously describes Agamemnon as king of all Argos and many islands (2.108), he controlled no land directly outside the Peloponnese. Yet Agamemnon's offer to Achilles shows that in addition to his north coastal Peloponnesian base, between himself and his brother, Menelaos, who was no doubt the lesser of the two magnates, the sons of Atreus also ruled the bulk of the southern Peloponnese[795]. In Menelaos' case this was presumably due to his marriage to Helen, Tyndareos' daughter. In Agamemnon's, it would appear to be due to his inherited authority over territory controlled by his branch of the house of Pelops, before the strength of that house was profoundly augmented by the further acquisition of Perseus' realm and likewise through his marriage to Klytaimnestra. In conjunction with the assignments in the *Catalogue of Ships*, which place Pylos, Elis, and the province of Argos outside the control of Agamemnon, and depict Arkadia as a semi-dependent vassalage, Atreid sovereignty under Agamemnon's leadership, in essence, encompassed all the rest of the Peloponnese. Comparatively speaking, Agamemnon controlled the greatest of Achaian kingdoms. Hence, he was "lord of all Argos and many islands" since he was the most powerful Achaian king[796].

In the same publication, Allen also drew attention to a name for the west side of the Peloponnese in circulation in the Homeric period. This was the strange designation *Iason Argos* that, like *Achaian Argos*, was viewed later on as synonym for the Peloponnese[797], even though this usage is not corroborated by the relevant Homeric passages. The single appearance of *Iason Argos* occurs in the Odyssey in the form of a compliment on Penelope's beauty. This complement was addressed to her directly by the suitor Eurymachos, who states that if the Achaians in *Iason Argos* were to catch sight of her, a much greater crowd would be present the next day to join the competition for her hand in marriage (Od.18.245-249). Citing a few passages that point to close ties between the Ithakan islanders and the neighboring communities of the western Peloponnese, Allen concluded that the district in question must lie along the Peloponnesian west coast. Thus, Allen noted that certain Ithakan nobles customarily grazed their cattle in Eleian territory (Od. 4.635-637[798]). In an off-hand way this state of affairs relates to Telemachos' gracious refusal of Menelaos' gift of a horse-drawn chariot, on the grounds that his island home lacked adequate pastureland for such horses (Od.4.589-591, 600-608). Pasturing horses in Elis was hardly an option for Telemachos, given the situation with Penelope's suitors, whose interests were seriously at odds with his, and whose power and influence threatened his inheritance and his life.

Allen's reckoning of *Iason Argos* is further supported genealogically. There are a few mythic references that consistently link back to the Homeric portrait of the western Peloponnese. A figure named Iasos notably ranks among them, appearing in the *nekuia* of *Odyssey* book eleven (Od.11.283). This man is described as the father of Amphion, not to be confused with the brother of Zethos and their joint involvement with the city of Thebes, because these two figures appear independently twenty-one lines above (Od.11.262). Iasos' roots lay in Minyan Orchomenos, where his son Amphion once ruled as king.

He was the grandfather of Neleus' wife Chloris. Neleus and Chloris were Nestor's parents and ruled the kingdom of Pylos that became his inheritance[799]. Nestor's part-Minyan ancestry was never forgotten by antiquarians of later periods[800].

Another background pattern is also relevant. Neleus of Pylos and Pelias of Iolkos were known as sons of Poseidon and Tyro, daughter of Salmoneus, son of Aiolos. Apollodoros mentions a group of chroniclers who maintained that Neleus and Pelias both married daughters of Amphion of Orchomenos: Neleus to Chloris, Pelias to Phylomache (ApB 1.9.10). This is a meaningful pattern. It is also the kind of patterning that characterized interaction among Aiolic stemmata. Further, we witness here the clever facilitation of two distinct Amphions, in two nearby cities, famous for their hostility toward each another. What is most critical, though, is the muted outline of Iasos, in a lineage later dominated by the eponym Minyas (e.g. West 1985: 64-65). The eventual eclipse of Iasos in this context is very likely related to the later use of his name in the upper reaches of the line of Argos (e.g. Gantz 198) and, even more conspicuously, in the line of Arkadia, where he was the father of Atalanta (ibid. 335).

As mentioned above, the *Catalogue of Ships* suggests that at the time of the *Iliad*, the leaders from Orchomenos who sailed to Troy came from the Peloponnesian branch of that same Minyan family. These leaders were Askalphos and Ialmenos, sons of Astyoche and the god Ares, whom their mother bore in the house of Aktor. Along with Augeias and Amaryngkeus, Aktor was one of three Epeian magnates whose descendants led the Epeians to Troy (Il.2615-624). Astyoche's sons, who were conceived and born in Elis, returned to Orchomenos to lead the Minyans. Notably, the three relevant Epeian families lived in and around the same Epeian Ephyra where Penelope's suitors feared Telemachos went to obtain poisonous herbs with which to destroy them (Od.2.325-330)[801]. This comment relates to the further assertion that Augeias' daughter, who clearly dwelled in that country, was renowned for her knowledge of such preparations (Il.11.738-740). Iasos' role and persona remain obscure in all this, beyond the basic assertion that he was, of old, a key figure in line of Minyan Orchomenos. Yet, putting various snippets of information together, it can be reasonably inferred, as Allen suggested (though now somewhat more specifically), that *Iason Argos* was a term that referred to the combined kingdoms of Elis and Pylos by virtue of the fact that descendants of Iasos were ancestral members of both ruling royal families.

    Allen's take on the matter demonstrates that within the Argos that was also Achaia and therefore equivalent to all of Greece, there was a Peloponnesian province of Argos in the northeast quadrant of that great landmass, which contained a polis also known as Argos, while there was, in addition, an *Achaian Argos*, which was yet another distinctive Peloponnesian domain extending from the northeast to the northwest. It was the territorial heartland of Agamemnon. Moreover, in the far west there was *Iason Argos,* which was so-called for the foregoing reasons. The question that arises in terms of these designations is whether also, in addition to them, the Peloponnesian landmass, as a whole, was also called Argos in Homeric poetry. Or whether the practice of calling it so was actually a later Greek convention, and, as such, part and parcel of the movement to reconfigure Homeric mytho-political geography.

    Although it is clear that Argos and Achaia functioned in context as alternate words for Greece, just as Argives, Achaians, and Danaans functioned as alternate words for Greeks, it is tempting to interpret Argos and Achaia, especially where they appear side by side, as in *horse-pasturing Argos and Achaia land of fair women,* as a paired designation for two parts of Greece, one to the south and one to the north, rather than two names for the whole country. Such an auxiliary assignment would render statements about "Argos" spoken by Agamemnon, for instance, or any Peloponnesian for that matter, meaningfully referential in terms of their homelands and in terms of the territory under their control. It would, likewise, perform a correlative function with respect to north Greek protagonists speaking of Achaia. Yet for this terminological division to be convincingly valid it would need to occur without exception, or with marked consistency at the very least. For as soon as a southern Greek calls his homeland Achaia or a northern Greek calls his homeland Argos, the force of the dichotomy falls apart, and meaning defaults back to all of Greece. And if this is the case, it is worth considering whether all of Greece is not the more appropriate meaning, functioning uniformly on a global basis, to the effect that further specifications took their cues from the wellspring of common cultural knowledge, instead of from yet another meaning of "Argos."

The criteria required to establish the viability of the alternate meaning at stake are not well supported in the Homeric poems. It is not only, for example, Achilles' homesick feelings for *horse-pasturing Argos* (Il.19.329-332), nor those of Idomeneus who hailed from Krete (Il.13.221-230[802]), that make this formulation start to run awry, but issues such as Agamemnon's authority over "*all of Argos and many islands*," and Odysseus' fame "*throughout Hellas and mid-Argos*," that work against the further subdivision of Greece[803]. Mainly, passages that at first glance seem to equate "Argos" with the Peloponnese[804] become considerably less persuasive in light of counter examples.

A few key issues lead to the heart of the matter. Again, in the *Iliad* Agamemnon was championed as "lord over all of Argos and many islands" (Il.2.108). Yet although he controlled most, he did not control all the territory of the Peloponnese, and he controlled no territory whatsoever outside it. Therefore, since this assertion is simply untrue, no matter what definition of Argos one uses[805] (and equally untrue with respect to the islands), with the obvious caveat that the Peloponnesian meaning is proportionately truer than its all-of-Greece counterpart, the next order of business would be symbolic usage. Agamemnon is essentially defined by his status, and in this regard, as *primus inter pares* not just among his fellow Peloponnesian commanders, but among the commanders from all over Greece, including the islands addressed in the *Catalogue*[806]. From this point of view, clearly, it makes no sense at all to confine the "Argos" Agamemnon ruled over to any portion of the Peloponnese or to that landmass as a whole. For this kind of assessment based strictly on landholdings does not do justice to the variously worded mantra that places Agamemnon above his peers[807].

Second, there is the matter of what Penelope means when she says time and again that Odysseus' fame travels widely through Hellas and midmost Argos[808]? This statement only makes sense when Hellas is considered in accordance with Phoinix' fairly vague account of it (Il. 9.447-449, 478-485). Phoinix' description is at least enough to suggest that Hellas and Phthia were two separate districts[809], bordering also on one another, and to indicate in connection with a few other passages that Hellas was a province south of Phthia that included a number of central Greek kingdoms (Il.2.500; Il.10.266-271; Il.13.685-700), among them the region around Mt. Parnassos, where Odysseus' maternal family resided (Il.10.266-271; Od.11.84-85; Od.19.386-475; Od. 24.320-344).

In 1906 T.W. Allen reviewed the parameters of Peleus' and Achilles' kingdom in contrast with the district known as Phthia. He emphasized that Peleus' and Achilles' domain was defined by the term, *Pelasgian Argos*, though this term was later considered an alternate name for Thessaly. As the heartland of Peleus' and Achilles' domain, *Pelasgian Argos* was the Sperchios River valley and the Sperchios, itself, the national river[810]. As for Phthia, Allen most reasonably argued that the *Iliad* viewed this region as an extensive territory that stretched across much of latter day Thessaly. The key passage at issue, Il. 13.684-700, corresponds precisely with the Catalogue entries on Protesilaos' ((2.695-710) and Philoktetes' (2.716-728) domains. In book thirteen, however we learn, in addition, that Podarkes and Medon (these heroes' surrogate leaders) command men identified as Phthians, indicating straightforwardly that Phthia extended from Peleus' kingdom as far north as Pelion, which would certainly make it exceedingly strange if Eumelos' kingdom were not Phthian too, whereas Strabo speculates that Eurypylos' kingdom was quite likely Phthian also (9.5.7). Consequently, Allen concluded, "the Phthians are not Achilles' subjects only, but belong also to Protesilaos and Philoktetes (196)." And "Phthia was the property of no individual chief (198)."

Time and again the *Iliad* infers that the domain of Peleus and Achilles embraced part of Hellas and part of Phthia and was therefore considered a border state (Il.2.681-694; Il.9.395 etc., cf. Od.11.495-496). Hence, Achilles' subjects are Myrmidons and Hellenes. The former are primarily associated with Phthia, and the latter, who, inhabit the outlying areas, are accordingly associated with Hellas, which jutted into portion of the kingdom. Needless to say, both groups are likewise Achaians. However, just as Phthia was a greater entity that extended beyond *Pelasgian Argos*, the same was ostensibly true of Hellas[811].

In addition to the region around Mt. Parnassos, where Odysseus maternal family lived, Hellas evidently also included the territory represented by Aias, son of Oileus (Il.2.527-535) and, in addition, the Boiotian realm associated with Amyntor, son of Ormenos (Il.2.500; Il.9.447-449; Il.10.266-267). Looking at the passage in book thirteen (Il.13.684-700), it lists: "Boiotians, and Ionians with their trailing tunics, the Lokrians and the Phthians, with the shining Epeians." The Epeians were led by Meges, Phyleus' son, with Amphion and Drakios, so that takes care of them[812]. A good deal, however, is made of the fact that Podarkes and Medon lead the Phthians, in accordance with the kingdoms assigned to them in the *Catalogue*. And while the other named groups get no further description, a detailed explanation is put forth to explain why, Medon, a native of Lokris, was to be found commanding Phthians, rather than in the company of his half-brother Aias, thus, as to be expected, among the Hellenes[813]. It is by no means surprising to discover that Medon was exiled from Lokris for homicide[814]. What then, one may ask, do the Boiotians, the Lokrians, and Ionians with their trailing tunics (viz. the remaining groups) have in common? The logical answer is that they were all Hellenes and understood as such by the listening audience[815].

In the Homeric vision of things, Phthia and Hellas apparently designated two substantially greater districts, each of which embraced heroic dominions on either side of the kingdom of Peleus that, accordingly, straddled both. If Argos is understood as all of Greece in this context, then the phrase midmost Argos is another form of Hellas and refers to the region known as Στρέα Ἑλλάδα, namely: the horizontal band of central Greek territory (in between Thessaly and the Peloponnese) that, at the time, stretched westward from Attica, roughly, at least, as far as Aitolian border, where, it stands to reason, given his roots[816], Odysseus was indeed especially famous[817]. Moreover, placed side by side, Hellas and midmost Argos do not invoke two distinctive places, but like Argos and Achaia, present a pair of names that repeatedly emphasize the same location.

Once Hellas and Phthia are understood in this way, Allen's account of *Pelasgian Argos* appears to be somewhat less than adequate. Because if there was a phrase readily available to describe Peleus and Achilles' kingdom specifically, even though it traversed two separate districts, that phrase would have certainly come in handy, and, one would think, put to greater use. Presumably, it would have averted the ambiguity that prompts such close analysis of the relationship between

Peleus and Achilles' kingdom's and the districts of Phthia and Hellas. But *Pelasgian Argos* in the *Iliad* is not a term that is repeatedly used. It appears prominently, however, in the opening line of the Thessalian section of the *Catalogue of Ships*.

Looking closely at the syntax of 2.681, a number of scholars over the years determined that the purpose of this line was to introduce the concluding section of the Homeric *Catalogue*, which dealt with a region roughly equivalent to latter-day Thessaly, and called for a proem to redirect the progression once the *Catalogue* veered back from the Dodekanese. In 1979 Robert Drews compiled the evidence that registers in support of this interpretation, calling for a renewal of the once-popular theory that met its demise with the excavations of Schliemann and, which concluded, based on language and content, that the Homeric poems were predominantly Aiolic and that Thessaly was their original source (Drews *CP* 74.2 1979: 111-135).

Drews attaches a number of auxiliary theories to the revival of this mode of thought that seem less tenable than his leading premise, namely: that in Homer the phrase *Pelasgian Argos* signified the Aiolic heartland of northern Greece[818] and, therefore, included the district of Phthia. As noted, Peleus and Achilles' domain jutted into a portion of *Pelasgian Argos* because it included Phthian territory, though it likewise jutted into Hellas. Moreover, just as the *Catalogue*'s opening section named participating contingents from Hellas, its closing section named contingents from *Pelasgian Argos*. In *Pelasgian Argos,* the first series of contingents were also inhabitants of the sub district, Phthia, the second series, however, were not, hence the significance of the greater designation[819].

As J.L. Myres observed in 1907, the adjective *pelasgian* as deployed in Homer denoted superior antiquity. Accordingly here, the *pelasgian* designation may be conceivably understood to denote this region's status as the aboriginal source of the generations of heroes in the long-winded story that placed all of Achaia under the control of the descendants of Aiolos with the notable infusion of two illustrious lineages that hailed from the East via Pelops and Kadmos. The *Catalogue* is thus framed by the two mainland Greek districts (opening with Hellas, closing with Pelasgian Argos) where the offspring of

Aiolos carved out their kingdoms and set the great genealogical saga in motion.

Perhaps others would favor an alternate reading[820], but there are solid grounds for preserving the all-Greek sense of both Achaia and Argos. Doing so also seems to have the advantage of harmonizing each instance of either word, whether they surface together or independently, both in their immediate poetic context and in the overall context of the Trojan War story recounted in the *Iliad* and the *Odyssey*. When Argos means Greece, there is complete consistency, when the Peloponnese is substituted, there is not. The all-of-Greece sense of Argos may be also said to do justice to the idea of a national epic, where the opposition at stake was Argos versus Troy in the days before Argos was known as Hellas[821].

The foregoing survey of Homeric "Argos" has identified six locations that answered to the name. Together they delineate the mytho-political layout of Greece as a whole and certain southern Greek districts, as understood in the early epic period. If they are held to reflect prehistoric conditions, and likewise, held to resemble quasi-real-life geography, the missing cities and later-outdated provinces could well represent "Dark Age" conditions, from an Eastern perspective, through a mythological lens, considering that after the fall of Mykenai, Aiolic Greeks from the Greek mainland made east Greek Aiolis their permanent home. In summary, these six cases of Argos consist of: first, Greece itself; then, *Pelasgian Argos,* aka northern Greece from the Sperchios to the Peneios and westward into the Pindos range; plus three distinct Peloponnesian districts, namely: *Achaian, Iason,* and just plain Argos; and a city in the province known strictly as Argos which, evidently, like all of Greece, required no further epithet to identify it.

It was to this latter province of "Argos" that Melampous was summoned to cure king Proitos' daughters. The genealogical consequences of the seer's arrival as documented by various ancient authors provide major support for the Aiolic hypothesis, while the unusual amount of extant evidence on the topic offers an inside look at the dynamics behind the process of Greek mythological change.

647 e.g. W. Burkert 1979; J-P Vernant 1980; P. Vidal-Naquet 1986; Vernant & M. Detienne 1989.

648 Alkaios, Elektryon, Sthenelos.

649 Generally, Astydameia, Lysidike, Nikippe.

650 viz. Eurystheus and Herakles were first cousins once removed.

651 It is expedient here to exclude Herakles' labors in order to concentrate on a selection of family oriented, and hence genealogically oriented, incidents associated with Herakles.

652 On the legends of Herakles, cf. G.S. Kirk 1974: ch.8; W. Burkert 1979: ch.4.

653 This was Likymnios, son of Elektryon.

654 ApB 2.4.5-8 and *Aspis* 78-82 cf. Paus.911.1 for the fact, with no motivation. Motivational variations of this kind have no effect whatsoever on genealogical patterning. Virtually any explanation might well suffice, as long as the outcome is fundamentally unchanged. In terms of meaningful versus inconsequential amendments J. Fontenrose offers a useful distinction between mythic *versions* and mythic *variants* (1959: 5-6). He defines new versions as retellings that differ with respect to selective narrative details, yet maintain the same protagonists and the same general setting. He defines new *variants*, in contrast to new *versions*, as retellings of the same basic story with distinctive protagonists and distinctive settings. Since this definition of mythic *variants* addresses any occurrence of a similar story, it states the grounds for comparative mythological studies based on thematic cross-cultural comparison. Yet such *variants* also, in the present context, are clearly the province of mythological theft, which was frequently accompanied by narrative variations, and, in such cases, amounts to a blend of both categories. The main point is to note via these definitions that numerous emendations responsible for new versions and for aesthetic adjustments to mythic *variants* (according to Fontenrose's definition), were actually of no great consequence to the overall structure and impact of a story. The personal motivation of various protagonists provides a good example of this type of thing, for the miscellaneous reasons advanced to explain *why* it was that what happened happened the way it did were superfluous to the outcome of the story. Thus, the surprising claim that Menelaos' wife Helen sat out the Trojan War at a royal court in Egypt, on account of a quarrel among the gods, epitomizes the type of narrative variations that had no substantial effect on Greek tradition. Mythological *variants* as defined, on the other hand, had a profound effect on the status of Greek tradition, since new protagonists and new topographic locations signified acts of political appropriation that re-directed control over a given story. Such modifications reconfigured the links between protagonists and territorial realms that, although set back in mythological time, were inspired by current political initiatives. On this basis Fontenrose's distinction affords a valuable measure of clarity on essential and gratuitous narrative elements, while emphasizing the special importance of named characters and specific settings. Helen in Egypt, in this light represents a kind of limit to which emendation could go without affecting the dissolution of structure. This alternate version of Helen's life story mainly promoted an alternate explanation for *why* Helen behaved the way that she did or *why* it was that she did not really behave the way she was commonly thought to have done (cf. Euripides *Helen*; Gorgias' and Isocrates' *Encomia*; Plato's *Phaidros* 243a & Dio Chrys. Or.11. on Stesichoros' *Palinode*.). Yet the woman who was known as Helen at Troy and famous for instigating the whole Trojan War conflict, though strategically reduced to an illusory image in the aberrant versions that made this claim remained *causa sine qua non* of the Greek/Trojan conflict. Meanwhile, the outright denial of Helen's causal role by no means lessened the status of the Trojan War story (e.g. Thuky.1.9), nor did such a discerning empiricist's view put a dent in the general obsession with Helen. Whether, therefore, Helen's presence at Troy was deemed a legendary truth or a legendary falsehood, the Trojan War story remained unchanged. Fontenrose evidently drew these distinctions because he was interested in Greek mythic *variants*, specifically in order to demonstrate that a certain set of them could all be traced back to Apollo's slaying of the monstrous python that inhabited Delphi prior to the god's oracle. Accordingly, his project aimed at pinpointing a single prototypical mythic story on which basis a slew of similar stories could be understood to have arisen. Comparable quests for mythological origins stand behind a body of analytical work the conclusions of which are frequently hard to follow and the value of which is often difficult to ascertain (cf. Graf 1993: chs. 1 & 2 provides an overview; on Fontenrose, cf. B. Fenik 1968: 47; H.S. Versnel in L. Edmonds, ed. 1990: 42). For even taking Fontenrose's proposition as proven, its contribution to the understanding of Greek mythic thinking is not self-evident. It remains unclear, in practical terms, what discovering Delphic origins really illuminates? Exile for homicide and the Potiphar's wife story represent dynamic mythic motifs because they respond to cause and effect analysis in whatever context they happen to occur. Information of no cause and effect significance belongs to a separate peripheral category. True Greek mythic motifs can perhaps best be viewed as tools for the regulation of mythological structure. Their recurrent deployment indicates that such motifs were part and parcel of the language reserved for the narration of Greek prehistory. This genre demanded exceptional treatment, since it antedated the onset of lived reality, and consequently, abided by the conventions attached to a prior alternate world.

655 For a corroborative view of this sequence of events, some astute observations on the sole survivor motif (see below), and on deliberate as opposed to chance mythic violence, see P. Walcot 1979: 331-332.

656 These allies are cited in the *Aspis* 20-30. Amphitryon's raid against the Taphians occurs in Euripides' *Herakles* (60-62, 1076-1080), as well as, Herodoros (31F15), and Apollodoros 2.4.5-8; obliquely in the *Ehoiai* (Hes. fr. 195 MW) and Pherekydes (3F13b). Interesting too, is the appearance of Mestor, another son of Perseus in these accounts, who is at odds with Elektryon and perishes in the conflict. The story of the extraordinary Teumessian fox that became a great nuisance to the city of Thebes is rather more complicated due to the fact that the two main protagonists in the story were evidently appropriated by the Athenians. Thus, Kephalos, son of Deion (son of Aiolos) married a woman named Prokris (Od.11.321), who was later described as a daughter of Erechtheus, redirecting the focus of the story to Attica from its manifest roots in central Greece. Thus, a number of accounts send Amphitryon to Attika (when Kephalos is not simply exiled to Thebes), not only to obtain Prokris' magic hound to pit against the supernatural fox, but also in order to recruit Kephalos' aid in the impending offensive against the Teleboans. Moreover, Kephalos' name offered a convenient aitiology for the name of the island of Kephalonia (Epig.fr 2 Kinkel; FGrHist: Hellan. 4F169, Phereky. 3F34; Pind *Nem*. 10.13-18; Palaiph 2; ApB 2.4.7, 3.15.1; Paus.1.37.6). Without delving further into the various tangled strands, a simplified version set in and around Thebes seems to lie beneath a build-up of accretions and relocations. The main ingredients seem to involve a challenge to Amphitryon upon his arrival in Thebes that he addressed with the help of a miraculous hound supplied by the famous heroine, Prokris, who obtained the hound from king Minos on a venture to Krete (though, later, in some cases from the goddess Artemis e.g. Ovid *Met*. 7.672-862; Paus.9.19.1; Hyg. *Fab*. 189; also Od.11.321, where Prokris is mentioned in a Kretan context).

657 Pind.*Nem*.10.13-18; Euripides' *Herakles* 798-806; DS 4.9.3; ApB 2.4.8, however, cf. Pind.*Isth*. 7.1-5.

658 This is Pausanias' version which he is quite committed to 9.193, 9.17.3, 8.15.6-7; Apollodoros accounts for Amphitryon's death in the Theban war against the Minyans 2.4.11. Chalkodon was the Eubian leader listed in the Homeric *Catalogue of Ships*, Il.2.541.

659 e.g. ApB 2.4.11, 3.1.2; And Ant.Lib. *Met*.33 (viz. FGrHist.3F84) for the tradition attributed to Pherekydes that after her death, Alkmene was taken to the Isles of the Blessed and wed to Radamanthys. cf. Schachter, *Cults of Boiotia* v.1 p13-14. Schachter herein is inclined to believe that Rhadamanthys and the Kretan connection are late rather than early, relatively speaking.

660 viz. That as an infant he strangled two snakes either sent by Hera with evil intentions (ApB 2.4.8, DS 4.10.1), or sent by Amphitryon in order to determine which of the two infants, Herakles or Iphikles, was his son (again ApB 2.4.8 quoting Pherekydes).

661 e.g. The killing of the lion of Mt. Kitharon, a precursor to its famous Nemean counterpart. And Herakles' impregnation of King Thespios' fifty daughters, whether in fifty nights (ApB 2.4.10), or, as some said, in one night, oftentimes with one daughter refusing (Paus.9.27.2 where he remains deeply skeptical; notably, the one who refused was proclaimed the first priestess at the shrine to Herakles in Thespiai). The antiquity of this legend is suspect on the grounds of Thespios' purely eponymous persona, the claim that he was a son of the Athenian Erechtheus (DS 4.29.3), and the patently retrospective foundation legend ascribed to the island of Sardinia that made Herakles' nephew Iolaos the leader of a colony established there with the help of the sons of the fifty daughters of Thespios (DS 4.29.3-4), or as Pausanias more soberly explains, accompanied by Thespians and men from Attica (Paus.10.17.5-6).

662 Tlepolemos killed Likymnios, *scion of Ares and beloved uncle of Herakles* (Il.2.662ff). This same Likymnios is readily identified in the sources as a son of Elektryon, and therefore, brother of Alkmene, and notably, also, the sole survivor of the otherwise fatal Taphian raid. The sole survivor motif occurs frequently in Greek myth as in the *Iliad's* account of Nestor's escape, when Herakles attacked Pylos and killed all his brothers (Il.11.689-692). Complete liquidation and the case of the sole survivor are both symptomatic of genealogical regulation. They are two possible options relevant to population control and inheritance distribution. Likymnios and Tlepolemos, Herakles' son, remain key protagonists in all later accounts in deference to their status in the *Iliad,* on the one hand, but, on the other, due to the significance of a foundation charter for Dorian Rhodes credited to a descendant of Herakles.

663 i.e. With respect to the Theban defeat of Orchomenos and the elimination of the line of Elektryon: first in connection with Amphitryon's raid, and, later, Tlepolemos' killing of the sole survivor.

664 e.g. Amphitryon's alliance with the Athenian Kephalos and the contrived rise and fall of Hippokoon and his sons.

665 The roster of participants in the Kalydonian Boar Hunt was subject to a degree of variation. This was typical of occasions involving large groups of players, which easily accommodated the interjection of favorites and easily facilitated manipulative work. No list survives from the early archaic period. The first evidence comes from the FrançoisVase, created in Athens in the early to mid-sixth century, leaving plenty of time for interpretive innovation. The vase may indeed depict some fairly recent traditions (e.g. the Arkadian Atalanta and her beau Melanion) among potentially older and more venerable huntsmen (e.g. Peleus and the Dioskouri), but Herakles and his brother do not surface at all. It is quite likely that the hunt for the Kalydonian boar did not originally include Perseid family members. For like the voyage of the Argo and the funeral games for Pelias - magnets for diverse heroes as time wore on - the Kalydonian hunt was peripheral to Herakles' early sphere of activity, which centered first around Thebes and then the Peloponnese. Granted, Herakles eventually made his way to Kalydon in order to marry Deianira (cf. Bakchylides.5 & below), and was known early on for exploits in northern Greece (e.g. Kyknos, Diomedes). But he does not appear to be solidly grounded in the events at Iolkos or in Aitolia (though he once stopped off in Pherai and was received by Admetus) and neither does his half brother, Iphikles (cf. Schachter 1986 p17n.4). It seems that from the beginning, these collective events were designed to distribute heroic honors throughout the various branches of the Aiolic stemma, and did not, on this count, replicate or confuse allocations devised to spotlight major heroes from each constituent Aiolic line. Though a magnet for heroes from far and wide, these collective adventures have been perceived as separately manufactured regional cycles that later came into contact with one another. Nevertheless, a strong case can be made that these "regional cycles" were all part and parcel of the Aiolic genealogical framework, which took great care to build up its regional offshoots in the course of defining the heroic landscape across mainland Greece in the pre-Trojan War Period. The elimination, augmentation and transfer of personnel, as early criteria fell by the wayside, amounts to another predictable symptom of the disintegration of the Aiolic charter.

666 Not excluding the conflict deployed by old epic (whatever it might have been) to stage the destruction of Eurystheus and sons and initiate the rise of Pelopid power.

667 This story follows a pattern common in later authors (and particularly vivid in Diodoros), in which after his conquest of various cities Herakles placed his favorite on the throne. His conquests also left cities indebted to him with the expectation that his descendants would eventually return to claim a share in the country in compensation for his services. This pattern transparently anticipates the story of the *return of the Herakleidai* (cf. DS 4.33.5-6 for the case of Tyndareos & Gantz 1993: 436- 428 on Hippokoon and his sons).

668 Accordingly, integrating the post-Homeric Arkadian genealogy.

⁶⁶⁹ Additional allegations against them include: siding with Neleus against Herakles over Pylos (ApB 2.7.3) and refusing to purify Herakles for his murder of Iphitos of Oichalia (Paus. 3.15.4-5). Pausanias acknowledges the attack against Sparta, but does not link these events to Iphikles' death.

⁶⁷⁰ Whenever sons of Likymnios surface they are also killed off one way or another, e.g. ApB 2.7.7 where the otherwise unknown Argios and Melas (though these names are familiar from the Aiolic lines of Kalyke and Athamas), perish in Herakles' sack of Oichalia. Pindar mentions Oionos, son of Likymnios, among the first competitors in the Olympic Games (*Ol.*10.34-63, founded by Herakles after the sack of Elis; see also ApB 2.7.3), but, of course, as we have seen, his death was also accounted for.

⁶⁷¹ i.e. via the Louvre Papyrus from the 1ˢᵗ century A.D. discovered in 1855, fr 1 PMG. Further comments on Alkman's treatment of this story occur in the scholia to Clement of Alexandria's *Protreptikos* 36.2 (c.190 AD). cf. Malkin 1994: 20-21,24.

⁶⁷² According to the Suda (i 117 Adler), Alkman was alive in the twenty-seventh Olympiad (672/668 BC), when Ardys, father of Alyattes, was king of Lydia. Ardys ruled c.652-c.619. He was, however, the father of Sadyattes who was Alyattes' father (viz. Alyattes' grandfather). A remarkable amount of emendation occurs in the Spartan line at this particular juncture. As noted above, Tyndareos' descent from the Aiolic line of Perieres was superseded in a cut and paste operation that placed him and his brother Ikarios onto the indigenous line of Sparta via a Spartan figure named Oibalos. The existence of Hippokoon and his sons likely traces back to this development. They further exemplify the type of mythic figure that was basically created to be destroyed after serving a specific ephemeral function.

⁶⁷³ As explicitly noted in the *Ehoiai* Hes.fr 17 MW; cf. Gantz 1993: 424-426.

⁶⁷⁴ In Pausanias (5.1), though his genealogy of Elis differs dramatically from the Homeric account.

⁶⁷⁵ Nestor notes that they were still boys on that occasion, ibid. 708-709.

⁶⁷⁶ Herakles' defeat of the Moliones is basically standard in the ancient sources (Pind.*Ol.*10.22ff; Pherekydes FGrHist.3F79; DS 4.33.3-4; ApB 2.7.2; Paus. 5.2.1.). It was not, however, widely acclaimed as the incident leading to Iphikles' death. The Hippokoon version simply became the more popular.

⁶⁷⁷ Later authors portray the killing of the Moliones as a necessary prerequisite to Herakles' sack of Elis. This sack was construed as a matter of vengeance against Augeias whose dung-filled stables Herakles cleaned in a feat of remarkable ingenuity (viz. the diversion of the Peneios River, ultimately regarded as one of his twelve labors). Augeias, that story goes, went back on his word, and in the end refused to pay for the job, at the cost of his city and ultimately, his life (notably, payment was not customary for the labors performed in the service of Eurystheus). On the one hand, Herakles' dealings with the heroes of Elis, including his encounters with the Moliones, fit organically into the Aiolic mythic framework, which may well have addressed much of this material. On the other hand, though, it is also clear that the later organization of these stories, and, oftentimes, their content as well, differed substantially from their Homeric counterparts.

⁶⁷⁸ In Pindar's *Olympian*10, Herakles' attack against the Moliones is depicted as an act of vengeance for their previous attack and defeat of his army while encamped at Elis. In the same breadth, Pindar emphasizes king Augeias' callous mistreatment of visitors, which logically refers to that act of aggression. Pherekydes seems to acknowledge the same provocation and sees the Moliones as the only obstacle to Herakles revenge against Augeias himself (FGrHist.3F79b). Overall, certain incidents that cluster around Herakles' dealings with city of Elis would have worked well together independently of the sack of the city.

[679] i.e. minus the emphasis on the sack of Elis.

[680] ApB 2.7.6; DS 4.29; Strabo 5.223; Paus.1.29.5, 7.2.2, 9.19.3, 10.17.5.

[681] Schachter asserts that story of the expedition to Sardinia was canonical by the first century B.C., if not earlier (1981: 30).

[682] Sardinia is described as an ally of Carthage at Hdt.7.165.

[683] The Phokaians established the city of Alalia on the island of Corsica sometime in the 560s. In spite of reinforcements from Phokaian refugees fleeing Persian aggression in the 540s, however, their presence on the island was short-lived due to the joint effort of Etruscans and Phoinicians to counter Phokaian influence in the area. This was accomplished in battle of Alalia in 540 (Hdt. 1.163-167). Sardinia was settled by Phoinicians in the ninth century. It was controlled from Carthage from ca. 500 until it fell to the Romans in 238. It was then administered as a Roman province.

[684] Diodoros asserts that the island of Sardinia was developed by Greeks from the time of Iolaos' expedition. The island became the envy of the Carthaginians who fought long and hard to gain possession of it (4.29.5-6). Pausanias adds that native and Greek inhabitants were joined by refugees fleeing the sack of Troy (10.17.5-8).

[685] Paus.9.23.1. "ἡρῷον Ἰολάου." The original monument was a joint tomb in honor of Amphitryon and Iolaos. Pindar *Pyth*.9.67-76. Schachter 1981: 30-31, 1986: 24-25, 64-65.

[686] Diodoros reports the telling mythic datum that Thespios was considered to be a son of Erechtheus, the great legendary king of Athens (first cited in Homer, Il.2.547). Specific ties between Athens and Thespiai are noted in Herodotos (8.75, 9.30) and Thukydides (4.133, 6.95).

[687] It became popular to substitute Iolaos in his role as killer of Eurystheus with Hyllos, son of Herakles and Deianira. Certain authors, however, refused to comply.

[688] viz. Atreus / Thyestes, Agamemnon / Menelaos, Orestes.

689 The standard genealogy may be reconstructed as follows (cf. West 1985: 50-60, Gantz 1993: 35, 135-143, 164-170, 198-199, 242-243, 303-304):
Prometheus + ? = Deukalion / **Epimetheus** + **Pandora** + Zeus = Pyrrha.
Deukalion + *Pyrrha* = Thuia/ Pandora / Protogenia & Hellen.
Thuia + Zeus = Magnes & Makedon. Magnes + ? = Diktys & Polydektes.
Pandora + Zeus = Graikos (eponym of west Greek tribe)
Protogenia + Zeus = Aethlios. Aethlios + Kalyke (daughter of Aiolos) = Endymion (of Aitolia).
Hellen + Orthrys (eponym of mountain in Phthtia) = **Doros, Xouthos** & **Aiolos**.
Doros + daughter of Phoroneus of Argos = Aigimios + daughters.
Aigimios + ? = Pamphylos / Dymas (Dorian tribal eponymns)
daughters + Hermes = nymphai / satyroi / kouretes.
Xouthos + Kreousa (of Erechtheus of Athens) = **Ion** / **Achaios** / Diomede.
Ion + ? (Helike at Paus.7.1.2) = Geleon / Hopletes / Argades / Aigikores (Ionian tribal eponyms)
Aiolos + ? (Enarete at ApB 1.7.3) = 7 sons / 5 daughters (progenitors of the Aiolic line).

See, however, Euripides' *Ion* for the following structural variation (1552-1593):
Aiolos (son of Zeus) + ? = Xouthos.
Kreousa + Apollo = **Ion**.
Xouthos + Kreousa (daughter of Erechtheus) = **Doros** / **Achaios**.

As addressed above in the segment on the daughters of Atlas (ch. 3, example two), this genealogy appears to post-date Hesiod's treatment of its leading characters in the *Theogony* and the *Works and Days* (namely, Prometheus, Epimetheus, and Pandora; cf. West 1985: 50). I believe there is adequate evidence to conclude that Hesiod had no intention of portraying these three figures as progenitors at the head of any such lineage as the one which first surfaces in the Hesiodic *Ehoiai*. At some unspecified point in time, this lineage was associated with the Greek version of the famous Near Eastern story of the great flood. The Greek flood story first appears in Eparchamos (the early fifth century comic poet from Syracuse) and in Pindar (P.Oxy.2427; *Ol*.9.49ff). It could well have informed the Hesiodic *Ehoiai*, though this cannot be verified from the extant fragments. The Greek use of the flood story may be judged in comparison with its Biblical function, where it divided two stages of human existence (both heroic in nature from a real life point of view, e.g. compare, human longevity before and after the flood cf. R. Scodel 1982), and facilitated the emergence of a single new genealogy that superseded all prior relationships and conditions, effectively, as it were, wiping the slate clean. As the primordial couple in the wake of the flood, Noah and his textually anonymous wife were cast as the source of a new world population, interpreted from an Israelite perspective, and situated, as the narrative progressed, in a symbolic hierarchy based on the claims of God's chosen people. This hierarchy was expressed in genealogical terms. The Greek deployment of the flood story was as custom-scripted to Greek legendary interests, as any other occurrence of that motif, with respect to its indigenous cultural context (cf. the extant Mesopotamian versions whose roots go back to the dawn of Sumerian culture: the epic *Atrahasis* and the story of Utnapishtim in *Gilgamesh*). Evidently, in the Greek case, the main objective was to level the genealogical playing field, so that eponymous Dorian and Ionian delegates could compete on a par with the eponymous Aiolos. In this way, Aiolos, who, as it happened, monopolized the heroic lineage infra-structure by virtue of being its early appointed source, could be cut down to size through an invasive vignette that redistributed some of his assets and placed him beside eponymous representatives of the Dorian and Ionian Greeks. Thereafter, the deluge became a pivotal bench mark in the chronological reckonings of the Greek mythographers. There are two further factors relevant to the case. The first is that post-diluvian Greek genealogy depicted a landscape inhabited exclusively by Greek peoples, in contrast to the Hebrew post-diluvian scheme where symbolic genealogy defined the Israelites in contrast with other ethnic populations. The second is that occurrence of the Greek flood did not forbid the survival of human beings other than the appointed surviving couple, contemporaneously, elsewhere, across the Greek landscape. For this reason, the advancement of other first men and other first couplings that were never attached to the Deukalionid stemma did not represent logical inconsistencies (e.g. Phoroneus of Argos; see also Pausanias' regional genealogies), but rather worked in accordance with the general redistribution of legendary prestige that reduced the authority Aiolic charter, and, moreover, reflected the fundamental Greek interest in co-opting the flood as way to wipe the slate clean.

690 The story of the *return of the Herakleidai* is also generally known as the Dorian *invasion*. This designation reflects a tendency to strip Greek mythic migrations of their mythological content in order to treat the remainder as fact. For a paradigmatic example, see N.G.L. Hammond 1976 (From a different perspective, cf. W. Burkert 1977). Overall the approach is very widespread and has a very long history in the discipline, though it is currently subject to increasing scrutiny.

691 Strabo 8.1.2.

692 Pindar's *Pyth*.5 and Pausanias 2.28.6, however, indicate that there were other versions. Typically, as Apollodoros reports, Pamphylos and Dymas lost their lives in the successful attack against Tisamenos, son of Orestes, 2.8.3. Conveniently, therefore, it was unnecessary to include them in the distribution of the conquered territory. Major chronological problems in the "return" story are emphasized by J.M. Hall 1997: 60, 2002: 80-81. Hall emphasizes that the Dorians and the descendants of Herakles were originally two separate groups that were brought together for the sake of the story (in his view a conflation of two separate traditions).

693 In this way, the Heraklid legend at once promoted, yet tacitly underrated, the novel construct that granted Herakles' progeny Dorian status through a manifestly contrived military alliance with the Dorian King Aigimios and his sons, as well as by way of the manipulation of innovative eponymous names. This notion likewise underlies Herodotos' account of King Kleomenes encounter with the priestess of Athena on the Athenian acropolis. The event occurred in connection with the Spartan attempt to promote the initiatives of Isagoras, son of Tisander, over those of Kleisthenes, son of Megakles (the Alkmaionid), after the fall of the Peisistratid tyranny. When accosted by the priestess on the grounds that Dorians were forbidden to enter the temple, Kleomenes invoked his Achaian identity based on the Heraklid pedigree of the Spartan kings (Hdt.5.72).

694 DS 4.58.3 provides the lowest figure. Herodotos gives one hundred, 9.26. Thucydides gives eighty, 1.12. Pausanias (4.3.3) and Apollodoros (2.8.2) emphasize the third generation.

695 Strabo's testimony concerning Greek tribal heritage is pivotal here (8.1.1-8.1.2). On his personal mission to grant preeminence to the Homeric poems against the widely popular views of later writers, see 8.3.23 and 8.3.31.

696 On Achaia, specifically, see J.K. Anderson 1954. The first trace of the Atheno-centric account of the Ionian migration to Asia Minor surfaces in the poetry of Solon (Archon 594/3. Ath.Pol.5: πρεσβυτάτην ἐσοπῶν γαῖαν Ἰαονίας καινομένην). Mimnermos (fl. 632/629 *Suidas*) testifies that the basic concept of the Ionian migration ante-dated Solon (via Strabo 14.1.4). But Mimnermos is likely to have been working with a previous Ionian migration scheme that did not chart its course through the city of Athens. Notably, his reference to the foundation of Kolophon mentions Neleidai from Pylos, but nothing of the Athenians. A variety of signs point to the conclusion that the Athenian version that later became canonical does not go back beyond the early sixth century, though it was ultimately adopted in the Ionian East. As mentioned above, there is a good deal of evidence to support the idea that mythological foundations in the post Trojan War era were integral to the early epic structure, first involving the *nostoi* of surviving warriors, and then their descendants in the next two generations. On Lesbos, for example, the descendants of Penthilos, son of Orestes, were more than likely a part of the early migration scheme (and, in this regard, an Aiolic example cf. Str.13.1.3; G. Grote vol. 2 1899: 12-13,19-20; on Chios cf. Wade-Gery 1952: 6-8). The Athenian addendum to the Dorian charter sent the entire Ionian migration movement on a strategic detour through Athenian territory. Herodotos informs us that the tyrant Pisistratos also claimed descent from the Neleids of Pylos, in which regard, his name is also telling (i.e. reminiscent of Nestor's son, Peisistratos cf. Hdt.5.65; Od.3.36, 482). The Athenian sponsored migration scheme gained special significance under the Athenian leadership of the Delian League. Its impact on Greek mythography was thorough and permanent (cf. Str.14.1-2; Paus. 7.2-7.5; also, Plutarch & Diog.Laert. on *Solon*. cf. C. Roebuck 1959: 2,25; H.A. Shapiro in W.G. Moon, ed. 1983; V.J. Rosivach 1987: 296; E. Kearns 1989: 107; J. Bremmer 1997; J. McInerney in I. Malkin, ed. 2001: 57-59).

[697] For what it is worth, and it is rather astonishing since these events are often treated historically, the basis of the connection between Herakles and the Dorians was Herakles' aid to the Dorian side in a war between the Dorians, under king Aigimios (son of Doros), and the legendary clan known as the Lapiths (cf. DS 4.37; ApB 2.7.7). Concerning the latter, M. West's remarks, "If the Lapiths counted as Hellenes, they must have been Aiolids, not Xouthids or Dorids (1985: 72)." Yet, as Homer attests (Il.1.260-268, 2.738-747, 12.127-130), the Lapiths were around long before the advent of the Hellenic genealogy. Based on later accounts of their family members that also preserve early stories about them, there can be little doubt that they constituted a major branch of the Aiolic genealogy. The structure of the old Aiolic Lapith lineage, however, cannot be reconstructed with much clarity (especially in its uppermost range), because of the way that it was later worked over. Pausanias, for example, makes the eponym *Lapithos*, a decendant of the eponym *Epeios*, the alleged king of Elis, at the time when Oinomaos was king of Pisa. Strategically, these two eponyms were also said to be the ancestors of the *Iliad*'s Epeian Aktor. While a detailed assessment of the Epeian contingent in the *Iliad*'s *Catalogue of Ships* leads to the conclusion that Aktor and Augeas were linked to the Minyans and the Lapiths respectively, here Pausanias grants the city of Elis an altogether indigenous ancestry and makes the eponym *Lapithos* subservient to it. The upper Aiolic structure that led to the foundation of Homeric Elis, accordingly disappears into thin air (5.10-11). The Spartans, moreover, from quite early on, had Amyklas, the son of Lakedaimon, marry a woman named Diomede, the alleged daughter of yet another eponymous *Lapithos*, and bear sons to the indigenous Spartan line (e.g. *Ehoiai* fr 171 MW; ApB 3.10.3). Looking at the remnants of early Lapith prehistory it would be more than a matter of mere speculation to place Theseus and Asklepios among them. On another note, Herodotus reports that Eetion of Korinth was considered a descendant of the Lapith clan (5.92b).

[698] The same holds true for Herakles' exploits in Libya, see Gantz 1993: 416-419 for Antaios, Bousiris and Emathion. Like the detour through Sicily and the Italian peninsula, these exploits were attached to the quest for Geryoneus' cattle or to the quest for the apples of the Hesperides.

[699] This fact, at least, is incontrovertible. I personally side with Morris, who, among others (e.g. Janko 1998 & 1990; J.P. Crielaard 1995) supports a late eighth century date for the version of the *Iliad* that has passed down to us. Presently, however, there is a down-dating trend. So, H. van Wees 1994, especially p.145, where, admittedly, one potential chink in his argument is lack of material evidence from Ionia (also, M.L. West 1995, 1999; K. Raaflaub in Fisher and van Wees, eds. 1998, W. Burkert in D. Cairns, ed. 2001, and earlier, R. Sealey 1957). I am likewise persuaded that the late eighth century date reflects the historical outlook of the Homeric poems, which deployed the technique of *epic distancing* in order to depict a bygone Heroic Age (Morris 1986: 82, 97). The mythic traditions expressed in the poems would then trace back into the so-called "Greek Dark Ages," which coincides with the overwhelming impression that the versions we have were frozen in time at the beginning of the Archaic Age. Morris covers the key reasons for viewing the poems as a reflection of a contemporary poetic mind set, as opposed to a hodge-podge of historical periods (82-89, though admitting a few Mykenaian relics, such as the *Catalogue of Ships* in book 2 of the *Iliad*). Certain compelling reasons for the rejection of the Mykenaian origin of the poems were set out emphatically by M. Finley (e.g. 1964; 1971, 1981). As for the problem of writing technology, and whether the paucity of Greek inscriptions that have been recovered from the eighth century is at all consistent with the task of recording two monumental hexameter poems totaling 28,000 lines, I do not think we possess sufficient evidence to argue against this from a negative standpoint when we are in possession of the poems themselves. The notion that Greek alphabet was expressly created for the written recording of heroic poetry does not stand to reason and cannot stand alone (e.g. H.T. Wade-Gerry 1952; B. Powell 1991). There is one factor, however, that does not tend to feature in the general analysis of this subject, and notably so, given the increased interest in recent years in the Near Eastern influence on Greek culture. I would ask: how cross-culturally comparable literary content and related aesthetics, patterns, and motifs, ought to be emphasized to the exclusion of the highly developed record keeping traditions of Mesopotamian literary culture? In an excellent article dealing with the history of Mesopotamian scholarly archives, D.T. Potts debunks the popular notion that the famous library of Asurbanipal of Assyria (668-627) was the first bona fide great ancient library. Against this, he cites evidence and examples of "archival, curatorial, and registrational behavior" going back two-and-a-half to three thousand years prior to the vast and impressive collection compiled for Asurbanipal at Nineveh (R. Macleod, ed. 2002: 19-33.). Throughout this period, national epic poetry was among the key genres earmarked for preservation, and coveted by great cities and great rulers alike. The impulse to record high order oral epic was, in this light, already in the air at the time the technology of the written word became a feature of Greek reality. The preservation of literature was traditionally the domain of highly trained professional scribes, not pottery painters or entrepreneurs (E.A. Havelock 1982: 185-207). And though the Greek alphabetic script had more demotic potential than its hieroglyphic or syllabic counterparts, it is well-known that even centuries later, literacy was not a vital aspect of life for much of the general population (W.V. Harris 1989). No doubt, these same conditions in the Near East could have influenced or even inspired a Mykenaian literary tradition, although to date there is no evidence for one, whether it didn't survive or it didn't exist (excluding, of course, the Homeric poems). As far as Greek history is concerned, the political impetus for Aiolic legend harmonizes with one, and only one period, namely, the period prior to the recording of the Homeric poems as they have passed down to us, and when they were also not yet at odds with Greek political demographics. This would be the eighth century in the Greek east, where the evidence has it the poems were composed and would, therefore, generally place the tradition between the collapse of Mykenai and the early Archaic Age. By the early seventh century on the Greek mainland, conditions were already in serious conflict with the lineage infra-structure of the Homeric legacy. I simply cannot see how it could be possible that, if the versions we have were not preserved by that time, they would have been preserved the way that we have them (cf. A.B. Lord 1953; A. Parry 1966; R. Janko 1990, 1996; K. Raaflaub in N. Fisher and Hans van Wees, eds., 1998).

[700] cf. F.M. Combellack 1950; M. Edwards 1990; L.M. Slatkin 1991; M. Willcock in I. Morris and B. Powell, eds.

[701] This view is vehemently advanced by G. Nagy (cf. 1992; 1996; 2001) and has occasioned considerable debate under the rubric of "multiformity." The arguments against it are extremely powerful (cf. S. West 1996; H. Pellicia 1997; B. Powell 1997; M. Finkelberg 1995). His view in essence amounts to something of an idiosyncratic twist on the oral poetry research of Parry and Lord (e.g. A.B. Lord 1960; A. Parry, ed. 1971; cf. Janko 1990, 1998; M. Haslan in I. Morris and B. Powell, eds.). The more moderate view put forth by G.S. Kirk, is in some ways equally problematic (Kirk 1962 cf. A. Parry 1966). On another aspect of the whole heated issue, J.S. Burgess takes note of a recent revival of the *Peisistratid recension* hypothesis, which is certainly so, and perhaps all well and good, as long as the public role of Homeric Epic, in sixth century Athens, under the Peisistratids, is not (as it, unfortunately, often is) acclaimed as the source of the first recorded versions of the *Iliad* and the *Odyssey* (1996: 78). The latest wave of enthusiasm for this point of view (Nagy at the forefront) contrasts with long-standing arguments to the contrary, e.g. A. Lang 1906: 44-50; T.W. Allen 1913; J.A. Davison 1955 and in Wace & Stubbings, eds. 1962.

[702] On this topic, however, Mark Griffith remarks concerning Greek mythological contradiction (1990: 196-197): "At every stage of their history, as far as we can tell, the Greeks were well aware that different - and incompatible - stories could be told about almost any of their gods and heroes. By 'could be told,' I mean that they either had already been told and were known, or that the proliferation of alternative, interchangeable story-types was so common that a narrator could readily modify or invert any received version for his own particular purposes. Our oldest examples of Greek storytelling, those of Homer and Hesiod, demonstrate conclusively not only that their own central narratives have been radically reshaped out of preexisting stories and themes, but that other inserted stories may also be presented in quite unusual and lopsided versions. We are never entitled to assume that 'Homer's version,' just because it is earlier, is any more 'original' and intrinsically authoritative than a version attested for the first time a century or more later (e.g. in Stesichoros, or Pindar, or even Euripides); though its occurrence in Homeric epic will thenceforth tend to lend this version a peculiar authority, if only as a reference point for other versions." This outlook is not that uncommon of late, describing its position as one of *plurality* (cf. R. Buxton 1994). In the absence of intrinsic organizational principles or any operative hierarchy of significance it is suggested that the best thing to do is to come to terms with these conditions as normative to the Greek way of thinking and native to the Greek way of life. This thesis investigates another approach.

[703] This was the cumulative outcome of widely accepted regional emendations made to received tradition throughout the Archaic Period. It is quite uniformly manifest in the work of the later Greek mythographers in spite of the general run of interpretive variations.

[704] viz. Those committed to the truth value of the Trojan War story.

[705] Gantz, likewise, suspects this is the case (424-427).

[706] Diodoros and Apollodoros transmit comparable accounts that deal systematically with Herakles' life story. They differ frequently with regard to specific details and reverse each others' order for three pairs of labors: 3 & 4 (the Erymanthian boar & the Keryneian hind), 5 & 6 (the Stymphalian birds & Augeias' stables), and 11 & 12 (the capture of Kerberos & the apples of the Hesperides). Overall, their accounts brilliantly exemplify the type of variation from author to author that later Greek mythography readily accommodated within the parameters of the dominant canon that emerged to replace the early Aiolic framework. It is equally clear that Diodoros, Strabo, and Pausanias (authors of continuous surviving narratives) were working with the same standard collection of data. Their work exemplifies, in this regard, a second comprehensive mythic systematization consisting of select highlights derived from local initiatives developed to replace Aiolic tradition. This second systematization bears identifiable signs of organization, promotion, and control based on the tastes and ideological priorities of the most powerful mainland Greek states.

707 The entirely un-Homeric *apotheosis* of Herakles, which granted him residence among the gods, is another concrete example of this phenomenon (cf. West 1985: 169; Gantz 1993: 460-463; H.A. Shapiro 1989: 157ff.).

708 The Greek mythological sack of a city was not necessarily synonymous with the complete destruction of that city. Often a sack was more of a genealogical tactic used to disrupt and to reconfigure the basis of sovereignty in a given place. Toward this end, total destruction was not always desirable. So, for example, Herakles' sack of Troy surely did not annihilate the city, while the *Iliad* credits Herakles' sack of Pylos with Nestor's rise to power among the Pylians (Il. 11.689-694). The effectiveness of the paradigm inspired more frequent use of Heraklean aggression to control and to alter heroic regional leadership (e.g. Pylos, Elis & Sparta became a set sequence with some variation in the sequential order). Though the technique of the sack cleverly admitted degrees of destruction, the elaborate composition of the contingent from Elis in the Homeric *Catalogue of ships*, which included delegates from three great heroic families (viz. from the line of Augeias, cf. Il.11.669-701 / the line of Amarynkeus, cf. Il.23.626-633 / and the line of Aktor, cf. Il 11.702-761, 23.638-643), argues against the existence of any such sack as far as the *Iliad* was concerned.

709 In 1910 T.W. Allen suggested that Homeric Doulichion was equivalent to the island of Leukas (off the west coast of Greece just south of Aktion p305) though connected to the Greek mainland by a narrow promontory. Subsequently, however, W. Dörpfeld proposed that Lefkas was actually ancient Ithaka, whereas Homeric Same became Classical Ithaka, and Doulichion later became Kephalonia (1927). Of late and for surprisingly convincing reasons, R. Bittlestone has proposed that modern Kephalonia was originally two separate islands that were later geologically fused (R. Bittlestone with J. Diggle and J. Underhill 2005). His research suggests that Homeric Ithaka was really the western portion of Kephalonia, whereas the eastern portion was formerly known as Same and the two were divided by a water-filled strait. According to the same data, Classical Ithaka turns out to be Homeric Doulichion.

710 According to Pausanias, Augeias and his son, the *Iliad*'s Agasthenes are alive and well after Herakles' sack. Using the model of the Greek lawgiver, who sets things straight in a city and then departs (e.g. Solon & Lykourgos), Pausanias has Phyleus return to Dulichion after serving the Epeians at Herakles' bidding, making way for Agasthenes (son of Augeias), whose son, Polyxeinos, went to Troy in the *Iliad* (2.623-624). Not all commentators were quite so meticulous in making new facts line up with Homeric tradition. On the mystique of the Greek lawgivers, cf. A. Szegedy-Maszak 1978: 199-209.

711 cf. ApB 2.7.6; DS 4.36.1.

712 It is not stated point blank in the *Iliad*, who Astyoche's father was considered to be. She could conceivably have been a daughter of Phyleus, who stayed behind in Elis after his migration. Still, a fairly strong argument can be made that she was the daughter of Aktor, son of Azeus, from the point of view of the text. The *Iliad* informs us that Astyoche bore two sons to Ares in the house of Aktor (viz. Askalphos and Ialmenos. Il.2.511-516). This coincides with an arrangement that arises elsewhere in the poem, where a woman's father adopts and rears the offspring she conceived with a god. Thus at Il.16.179-192, Phylas rears Eudoros on behalf of his daughter, Polymele, who bore the child to Hermes, but then married Echekles, son of the *Iliad*'s Myrmidon Aktor (i.e. a second man who answered to the name), leaving her son in his grandfather's custody. This arrangement was plainly an alternative to the case in which a woman's husband adopts her divinely conceived children e.g.16.173-178. But the former arrangement is more appropriate to Astyoche, since she bears Tlepolemos to Herakles one hundred and forty lines later (evidently another extra-marital union, Il.2.657-658). At any rate, when the *Iliad* says (2.511-513): "Οἳ δ' Ἀσπληδόνα ναῖον ἰδ' Ὀρχομενὸν Μινύειον, τῶν ἦρχ' Ἀσκάλαφος καὶ Ἰάλμενος, υἷες Ἄρηος, οὓς τέκεν Ἀστυόχη δόμῳ Ἄκτορος Ἀζεΐδαο," the implication seems to be that Astyoche was the daughter of Aktor. Of course, if indeed, the *Iliad*'s Astyoche was the daughter of Aktor, son of Azeus, her transfer to Phyleus, son of Augeias, was an early step in the story's mythic development.

713 Thus, Apollodoros (2.7.6) uses Phylas and Phyleus in order to distinguish the ruler of Thesprotia from the son of Augeias who was recalled from Doulichion and made king of Elis by Herakles after he had ostensibly sacked the city (2.7.2). Diodoros, alternatively, settles for two Phyleuses: the son of Augeias, who Herakles placed on the Epeian throne and the king of the Thesprotians whose daughter (unnamed) bore Tlepolemos to Herakles. He also mentions one Phylas, king of the Dryopes, who committed acts of impiety against Delphi (4.37.1), thus preferring two Phyleuses to two Phylases (In any case, six of one to half a dozen of the other). Phylas in the *Iliad* was evidently a Myrmidon (16.181).

714 Strabo distinguishes four towns named Ephyra, two of which he associates with a river named Selleeis and two which did not lie near any such river (8.3.5). To sort out the contenders for the Eleian location, Strabo cites Il.2.659, Il.15.530, Od.1.261, and Od.2.328, which all told, provide an excellent example of Homeric consistency, leaving no doubt at all that Tlepolemos' mother was an inhabitant of the Eleian city. Neither the "Thessalian" Ephyra, which was actually located in northern Aitolia (viz. the Agraian district), nor the Thesprotian one, in southern coastal Epeiros, could, in his opinion, lodge a valid claim to Tlepolemos' mother as portrayed in the *Iliad*, for they simply did not possess a river Selleeis. The Korinthian Ephyra was the only other of four that also possessed a river by that name. But Korinth, he maintained, could not compete with Elis when it came to the matter of Herakles' adventures, since they clustered more around Eleian country. Whether or not the Korinthian Selleeis was a viable river of any force or renown, Eumelos made the Korinthian Ephyra a daughter of Okeanos and Tethys, and the first inhabitant of the country that stretched from the Isthmus into Sikyonian territory. From what can be gleaned of Eumelos' mythic program, his main targets were Aietes and Medea of the Argonaut's legend, Aloeus and Epopeus from the Aiolic line of Kanake, the Aitolian Leda, and the line of Sisphyos, which the *Iliad* situates in an Ephyra (in a corner of horse pasturing Argos) with no connection to any river Selleeis (6.150ff.). While there is no point in putting it past him, as things stand there is no sign that Eumelos conflated the two Homeric Ephyras and claimed Tlepolemos' mother for the Korinthians. Strabo's astute analysis basically just confirms what is already clear from the Homeric poems, namely that Tlepolemos, Herakles' son was a native of Elis in early Greek tradition.

715 e.g. Il.11.683-697; Od.11.281-287; Hes.fr 31 & 33a MW; Paus.4.2.5; ApB 1.9.9.

716 A more destructive sack, like that of Oichalia.

717 Gantz 332-333.

718 cf. J.A. Notopoulos 1951; E. Havelock 1978 ; J.M. Foley 1999; D. Lateiner and R. Fowler in R. Fowler ed., 2004.

719 The mythological significance of the *Catalogue* has been, for the most part, remarkably underrated. The work of E. Visser (1997) is a prominent exception. The scholarship on this topic is treated further below.

720 Emphasized by Gantz also, 458.

721 See M. Davies 1991, including further commentary and bibliography on the various strands addressed in this section. For further analysis cf. R.P. Winnington-Ingram 1980: 73-90, 330-333.

722 Archilochos, evidently, wrote a poem on this episode (fr 147 Lobel & Page). Other references include, ApB 2.7.6.; DS 4.36.4-5.

723 Eurynomos or Eunomos, son of Architeles and a relative of Oineus cf. ApB. 2.7.6.; DS 4.36.1-3.

724 The earliest extant account of these events comes once again from Sophokles' *Trachiniai*, followed by: DS 4.36; Ovid *Met.* 9.101-172; ApB 2.7.5-6; Hyginus *Fab.*36.

725 cf. On Kalydon: Il.2.640; 4.368-409, 5.412-415 & 14.113-125 for Tydeus migration from Aitolia to Argos; 9.529-599 for the attack of the Kalydonian boar. On Oichalia, see below.

726 Eurite + Porthaon = Agrios / Melas / Oineus. **Oineus** + Althaia (+ Ares) = Meleagros / Deianira. **Oineus** + Periboia (of Hipponoos of the line of Proitos of Argos) = Tydeus. **Porthaon** + Laothoe = Eurythemiste / Sterope / Stratonike. **Stratonike** + Melaneus (of Apollo) = Eurytos. **Eurytos** + ? = Iole + her brothers.

727 ch.1, example 2.

728 cf. G.S. Kirk 1985: 187, 234.

729 The information concerning the house of Ortilochos offered in *Odyssey* twenty-one is consistent with other relevant statements at Od.3.488-489 and Il.5.540-560. The family line apparently ran as follows: Alpheios->Ortilochos->Diokles->Orsilochos & Krethon. They were based at Pherai on the Messenian Gulf, specifically in the district of Messene, which the poet viewed as a portion of Lakedaimon. The city was included as part of the offer Agamemnon makes to Achilles in book nine of the *Iliad* (151). Diokles, son of Ortilochos, sent his sons along with Agamemnon to Troy where they met their deaths at the hands of Aineias. The situation exemplifies the system of patronage that stood behind the authority of Homeric βασιλεῖς. Their power was largely based on reciprocity and the personal acknowledgement of lesser regional rulers. The dynamics were based on cooperation, mutual allegiance and mutual respect within the context of unequal assets, and hence, unequal authority (on this topic, cf. R. Drews 1983; W. Donlan 1985; T.E. Rihll in H.V. Hurt and J. Pinsent, eds., 1992; J. Lenz 1993; N. Yamagata 1997).

730 The poet of the *Odyssey* may or may not assume that Herakles' robbed Iphitos of his horses in an act of vengeance against Eurytos and his family. The theft is not crucial to the chain of events that led from Eurytos' feast to Herakles' death, but it would certainly make the retrospective vignette that opens *Odyssey* 21 a good deal more meaningful if it were so. This suggests a case of well crafted subtlety aimed at bringing an established legend to mind. Herakles' robbery of Iphitos' horses surfaces widely in post-Homeric accounts, though Apollodoros advances the variant story that the horses were stolen by Autolykos, son of Deion, though Iphitos accused Herakles, and perished on account of it, so, all and all, he portrays the same result (2.6.1).

731 Il.18.117-119. οὐδὲ γὰρ οὐδὲ βίη Ἡρακλῆος φύγε κῆρα, ὅς περ φίλτατος ἔσκε Διὶ Κρονίωνι ἄνακτι ἀλλά ἑ μοῖρ ἐδάμασσε καὶ ἀργαλέος χόλος Ἥρης.

732 T.W. Allen, *CQ* 135: 1907, *JHS* 33 1913: 24-26; R. Fowler, in Fowler, ed. (2004): 231.

[733] See Gantz 1993: 434. Euboia was evidently Sophokles' choice. Kreophylos' assertion is noted by Pausanias at 4.2.3. The Euboians, not surprisingly, were in complete agreement, and so was, he informs us, Hekataios of Miletos. Yet Pausanias, himself, gave preference to the northeastern Messenian / southwestern Arkadian location, connected with Stenyklaros and Andania, where the locals claimed possession of Eurytos' bones (4.33.5). This opinion was also held by Demetrius of Skepsis, as reported by Strabo, who was inclined to agree (8.3.6). Strabo faults Apollodoros in this regard insisting there must have been at least two Oichalias, though Apollodoros acknowledged only one (apparently, also, the Euboian Oichalia 2.7.7). In taking this point of view, he was no doubt inspired by Il.2.591-601, where Thamyris met the muses in Nestor's domain, on his way from Oichalia, city of Eurytos. Homer, however, mentioned just one Oichalia, since Il.2.729 reinforces Il.2.596. And although Strabo, for the most part, vehemently promoted a narrow, literal approach to the Homeric material, he veers off on this occasion, siding with later critics who felt that the Thessalian Oichalia was simply too far from Pylos to have sensibly been Thamyris' point of departure, given the location where he met his death. Hence, there must have been two separate Oichalias, both of which, even if inexplicably so, were called "the city of Eurytos" (cf. Euripides, *Helen* 496-499). On top of this, Pherekydes suggests a fourth location, namely, near Tiryns, where Iphitos confronts Herakles about his missing horses (FGrHist 3F82a). In any event, Homer's Oichalia was equated with at least four different locations (cf. *H.Hymn to Apollo* 242 for a possible fifth). Kreophylos' relocation of Oichalia to Euboia documents the emergence of east Greek amendments that worked to endorse Ionian identity in an otherwise overwhelmingly Aiolic milieu. The promotion of such a strategic adjustment in early seventh century Ionia preserves an uncommonly clear remnant of the intermediary phase that stood in between the dissemination of Homeric poetry and the codification of mainland Greek response to it. In due course, the mainland Greek perspective seized control of the mythological record in accordance with the shift of political power from east to west in the later Archaic Period. As Matthews points out (1974: 29), works concerning the Ionian migration to Asia Minor were popular in the first half of the fifth century and appear to stem back to Solon in the late sixth. In this context, however, it is important to note that the accounts that were popular by that point in time favored the Athenian treatment of the Ionian migration, which bolstered the ideology of the Delian League (cf. J.P. Barron 1964), and, as Herodotos reports, was also applied to the circumstances surrounding the Ionian revolt (5.97). An early contribution from Kreophylos of Samos suggests an important source of inspiration for the Athenian conception of Ionian pre-history that shows signs of development in the sixth century. Yet, there must have been major distinctions between early east Greek thinking on the subject (presumably, in addition to local variants within Ionia from state to state), and its later Athenian counterpart, which first absorbed, and then superseded, antecedent east Greek points of view.

[734] cf. M. Parry 1932 on the linguistic data to this effect.

[735] See Victor J. Matthews, 1974 1*Panyassis of Halikarnassos: text & commentary.* 1-20 for his biography & 21-40 on his two epic poems, namely: a *Herakleia* and an *Ionika* that told the story of the Ionian emigration from Athens beginning with the death of Kodros (Huxley 1969: 177-188; *Sudias* s.v. Πανύασσις).

[736] "στεῖχε παρὰ μνστὴν ἄλοχον, κοίμιζε δ' ἑταίρους" via Athenaios 2.36d-37b. In this passage Eurytos' patience is tried by an increasingly inebriated Herakles. The scene seems to be escalating toward an outbreak of violence. Yet Athenaios' excerpt breaks off before its realization. In terms of content, the passage is quite similar to Lichas' edited account of events at Oichalia as reported to Deianira in Sophokles' *Trachiniai* (249-290). Though the truth of the matter in Sophokles' play turns out to be rather more complicated when Lichas is exposed by another eyewitness for the deliberate omission of Iole's role in provoking Herakles' wrath. That Herakles got drunk at Eurytos' banquet and prompted Eurytos to throw him out of the house, could well be a rendering of the oldest plot structure. As Gantz points out, Lichas' subsequent confession of the truth about Iole (472-489) does not damage the thrust of his original story, which seems to be the version that was reproduced on a red-figure cup attributed to Onesimos (435-436). Together, these examples appear to reflect the ongoing persistence of the old banquet story against the increasing preference for the archery contest (see below).

[737] This set up is inconsistent with the Homeric view, in which Eurytos dies while his city is still standing. Under such circumstances, the king of Oichalia could not be present at the time of Herakles' sack, which it seems was bound to take place, in any event.

[738] Whether Herakles was married to Deianira at the time of the contest for Iole's hand became a preoccupation of mythic chroniclers in a way that does not appear to have applied to the feast. Apollodoros and Diodoros went to considerable lengths to place the archery contest in between the dissolution of his marriage to Megara of Thebes and his subsequent marriage to Deianira of Kalydon. Accordingly, they required an explanation, other than that the victor was a married man, to facilitate Eurytos' rejection of Herakles. To this they offered the king's fear of the precedent set by Herakles' murder of his children with Megara. Earlier, Pherekydes had opted instead for the notion that Herakles entered the contest on behalf of his son Hyllos rather than himself, a notion which reinforces the evidence that Herakles and Deianira were already a couple in the early accounts of events at Oichalia.

[739] In Herodoros (FGrHist. 31F37) and Pherekydes (FGrHist. 3F82) Eurytos flees to Euboia after the sack, and then, presumably, on to the Peloponnese, unless Euboia also made some claim to have hosted the muses' revenge on Thamyris. Needless to say, neither of these authors favored the Euboian Oichalia. But, fleeing there would perhaps be the next best thing, in terms of heeding the prominence of that tradition.

[740] Especially seeing that Clement also accused Eumelos of Korinth and Akousilaos of Argos of transposing Hesiod's poetry into prose (fr 186 Kinkel).

[741] See also, however, the subtle statements made at *Trachinai* 1203-1215. Sophokles' portrait of a desolate Lemnos is another potential innovation of the dramatic pathos variety. Both Aischylos and Euripides are believed to have presented Philoktetes plays before the debut of Sophokles version (Gantz 459). According to Prolkos' summary of the *Epic Cycle*, Philoktetes' arrival at Troy from Lemnos was covered in the ΙΛΙΑΔΟΣ ΜΙΚΡΑΣ attributed to Lesches of Mytilene. He was famous for slaying Paris in single combat.

[742] cf. Euripides' *Herakles* 460-464 for Megara's contra-factual hopes for her children.

[743] Calling attention to Sophokles' *Trachiniai*, where numerous offspring (Hyllos' anonymous siblings) seem to be lurking in the background.

[744] These offspring generally perpetuated the lines of the mothers. Yet the case of Tlepolemos, son of Herakles and Astyoche, anchored as he was early on in neighboring Elis at a time when Herakles' exploits had a far more circumscribed range, comes closest to supplying a potential heir till he was sent into exile by subsequent mythic narratives.

[745] Herakles was said to have sacked the city and killed the ruling family except for the king's daughter whom he took to bed. She bore a son, Thessalos, who was the father of Pheidippos and Antiphos, leaders of the Koan contingent at Troy (Il.2.676-680). The previous ruling house consisted of the convergence of two Aiolic lines and can be charted as follows: Poseidon + Kanake (daughter of Aiolos) = Triopas. Erysichthon = a son of Triopas. Poseidon + Mestra daughter of Erysichthon + Glaukos (son of Sisyphos) = Eurypylos. Chalkon and Antagores = sons of Eurypylos, rulers of Kos before Herakles arrival. Gantz 1993 : 68, 169, 442-444; Il. 2.676.679, 14.245-256, 15.18-30; Hes fr 10a 102-4, 43a MW; ApB 1.7.4 (2.7.1, 2.7.8) Kallimachos 6.31-31, 96-100; Palaiph. 23; Lyk. 1391-1396; Ovid *Met.* 8.738-878. Another evidently early example is that of Telephos, son of Herakles and Auge, whose role as a potentate in Mysia was a major theme addressed in the *Kypria* (cf. Hes fr 163 MW; Gantz 428; Obbink and West: 2006).

[746] The portrayal of Teukros, bastard son of Telamon (Il.8.280-284), for example, and that of Medon, bastard son of Oileus (Il.13.693-698) make this point of view considerably more persuasive. cf. J-P Vernant 1980: 62.

⁷⁴⁷ The corresponding Ionian *phylai* (Geleontes, Hopletes, Argadeis and Aigikoreis) were also granted eponymous namesakes who were characterized as the sons of the eponymous Ion. On the coast of early archaic Asia Minor, however, the Ionian communities typically had six tribes. Thus, the East Greek Ionians acknowledged two (namely the Boreis and the Oinopes) that were never adopted on the Greek mainland (C. Roebuck 1961). This factor lends a measure of added support to the novelty of the Athenian version of Ionian migration and Ionian identity canonized under the auspices of the eponymous Ion. (cf. J. Bremmer 1997: 10-13; J.M. Hall 1997: 40ff.). On the role of the *phylai* in the socio-political structure of the Greek polis cf. N.P. Jones: 1980. On the religious aspects of these structures, C. Sourvinou-Inwood in O. Murray and S. Price, eds. 1990.

⁷⁴⁸ To Zeus Xenios, beyond all others, since the murder involved the betrayal of a guest. On this episode cf. DS 4.31.5-8; ApB 2.6.2-4.

⁷⁴⁹ e.g. E. Havelock 1978: 63-70; P. Veyne 1988: 2,18; K. Raaflaub in N. Fisher and H. van Wees eds., 1998.

⁷⁵⁰ Detailed discussions of Homeric geography necessarily involve the interpretation of the *Catalogue of Ships* in *Iliad* book 2. T.W. Allen 1921; V. Burr 1944; D.L. Page 1959; R. Hope Simpson and J.F. Lazenby 1970; and G.S. Kirk 1985 represent the predominant view that the Catalogue was based on Bronze Age geography. Notably too, a few vehement critics of the whole notion that Bronze Age civilization could have meaningfully informed the composition of the *Iliad*, nonetheless regard the *Catalogue of Ships* as one of the few potential Bronze Age survivals (e.g. M.I. Finley 1957; I. Morris 1986). This position accords with a general trend that stems back to the decipherment of Linear B, which led, in due course, to the realization of the magnitude of the difference between Bronze Age and Iron Age culture in Greece. Among those who view the *Catalogue* as a separate entity, Wade-Gerry is notable for his emphasis on the fictional nature of the epic world view, yet in terms of the significance of the *Catalogue*, itself, he preferred to invoke the theory of separate mythic cycles, characterizing the *Catalogue* as a set piece devised and contributed by a Boiotian poet (Cambridge 1952). In the minority, another group, B. Niese 1873 and A. Giovannini 1969, for example, have maintained that *Catalogue*, like the rest of the *Iliad* reflect the poet's perspective at the time the poems were composed (i.e. in the eighth or seventh century. W. Leaf (1915), notably, also, preferred a "post-Achaian" *Catalogue*, but placed the rest of the poetry in the Bronze Age). Niese's contribution notably antedates the profound impact of Schliemann's excavations. Giovannini advanced the compelling theory that the geopolitical sequence expressed in the *Catalogue* mirrors the routes of the itinerant θεωροδόκοι who traveled the Greek world as religious envoys. G.S. Kirk identifies "an undeniable element of late Mycenaean political geography in the Achaean catalogue in *Iliad* book 2 (8)," but he also insists that the *Catalogue* "formed a part of the epic as early as the seventh century; indeed it is too skillfully attached and developed to be any kind of post-Homeric addition (169)," a valuable deviation from the separatist doctrine. J.K Anderson more recently offered level-headed critique of the evidence utilized by those committed to a Bronze Age *Catalogue* (D.C. Pozzi & J.M. Wickersham, eds. 1991, however, see now, J. Latacz, 2001 & E. Visser in Latacz, ed. 2003). Yet he stopped short of renouncing the focus on historicity that binds these interpretations together. Alternatively, the *Catalogue* used a map of Greece that was intimately linked to early epic tradition for which Homer provides the *terminus ante quem*. The *terminus post quem* conceivably coincides with the Aiolic settlement of Asia Minor. In the case of the *Iliad*, this map facilitated the subtle enumeration of legendary events that stood behind the unfolding story of the tenth year of the Trojan War. In this sense the *Catalogue* had little bearing at all on conditions and circumstances that obtained in reality. It was rather a vehicle for informative reminiscence as it was practiced throughout the poem.

751 The priorities of the present report made it impractical to devote a continuous narrative to the analysis to the Homeric catalogues. The strongest evidence for this interpretive model is the way in which the proposed mytho-geographical principles accord with key examples of the catalogue genre embedded within the Homeric poems, namely, the *Odyssey*'s *Nekuia* and the *Iliad*'s *Catalogue of Ships*. These can be shown to coincide with the broader poetic contexts in which they occur, mainly in terms of their enumeration of presuppositions about the mythic past. Moreover, to the extent that their personnel can be traced, they turn out to link back to the Aiolic genealogy, on which count, this factor registers as one of the poems' leading structural principles, over other proposed factors and interpretations (e.g. S. Larson 2002). Here, *Catalogue*-based evidence is dealt with in light of a considerably broader collection of data and is therefore presented on a case by case basis. It would be good to eventually present this topic under separate cover. Nonetheless, I believe that the present arrangement adequately substantiates the idea that these catalogues were organically connected to the mythic world view of the poems that contained them. Time and again, their contents harmonize with Homeric remarks made elsewhere in the texts, dealing with mythic time and mythic geography. (See A.B. Lord 1971 for a few brief but valuable remarks on his experience with catalogues in Slavic epic poetry.)

752 This is, however, generally deemed too early. In coordination with Assyrian records and with the floruit of Archilochos of Paros, Gyges reign is more aptly dated to the second quarter of the seventh century cf. R.M. Cook 1946.

753 However, as emphasized above (ch.1, example 2) there was evidently a significant measure of latent Greek influence in the area linked to early Aiolic legendary families. So definitively, for example, on the islands of Lemnos, Kos, Krete, and Rhodes and potentially elsewhere in the northeastern Aegean.

754 See Matthews 1974: 96-99 on Panyassis fr 17K where he dates Herakles' adventures in Lydia after Kreophylos (early 7thC), but before Panyassis (ca. 505-450), with Peisandros of Rhodes a potential originator. Hellanikos (FGrHist 4F112) and Pherekydes (FGrHist 3F82b) also reported the story. Matthews raises the interesting possibility that the Omphale story was transplanted to Lydia from the region around the gulf of Malis (based on the appearance of the Kerkopes in both places), which though provocative, cannot be taken much further.

755 e.g. Hdt.1.7; ApB 2.7.8. Matthews (ibid.) cites a number of circulating proposals and concludes in addition, that according to Panayssis, Herakles named two of his sons Hyllos after the Lydian river in which he bathed: one of them, no doubt, the son of Deianira. The existence of two Hyllos in the fifth century could represent an east/west competition of sorts over the origin of the tribal Hylleis. In this context, a third Hyllos, son of Herakles and Melite, and ancestor of the Illyrian Hylleis, reaffirms that Hyllos was brought into existence to establish a tribal derivation, which by no means required a Hyllos river. It would not be surprising if eastern chroniclers, inspired by the proximity of the Lydian Hyllos, promoted a pedigree that, clever as it was, ultimately succumbed to the superior status of its mainland Greek genealogical counterpart. Herakles' Lydian interlude in the service of Omphale entered the Greek canon, in any case. We are no closer to unraveling the enigma of Hyllos.

756 So, for example, Zeus forced Apollo to serve Admetos, son of Pheres, for a year (Aiolic line of Kretheus and Tyro), allegedly in penance for killing the Kyklopes, after Zeus killed Asklepios for attempting to raise the dead (Hes. fr 51-2, 54-58.4; Stesichoros 194; Akousilaos FGrHist 2F18-19; Pherekydes FGrHist 3F35, Pind. *Pyth.*3.55-58; ApB.3.10.4. offers another explanation). Later testimonia report, in addition (e.g. the scholia at Il.1.399), that Apollo and Poseidon were forced to serve Laomedon, king of Troy, in retribution for a plot against Zeus. As it happens, this crime does not exactly square with the quarrels among the gods mentioned in the *Iliad* (see Gantz 1993: 59). But the premise illuminates, in a general way, what could have driven two powerful deities to pass their time, as if they were mortals, for an extended period in the city of Troy. Apollo's stay with Admetos replicates the same premise. The punishment, in particular, also accords well with the tumultuous state of divine relations that the *Iliad* at once documents and asserts Zeus has quelled (e.g. Il.8.1-28; Hesiod's *Theogony* and Aischylos' *Prometheus Bound* cf. E.R. Dodds repr. in H. Bloom, ed. 1987). At Troy, Apollo and Poseidon favored opposing sides, yet their joint prior affiliation with Troy is, at one point, specifically stated in terms of the construction of the city walls (Il.7.445-463). Poseidon's obsession with the walls of Troy and his abiding resentment against the Achaian wall are also germane at *Iliad* 12.15-36, where after Zeus reassures him of the magnitude of his power, Poseidon vows to obliterate the Achaian defenses as soon as the city has finally been sacked (cf. R. Scodel, 1982).

757 This once venerable rule was long since obsolete by the time Pausanias endeavored to enumerate the local genealogies of the major Greek poleis. In his text the number of progenitors who die childless, prompting the intervention of an auxiliary lineage shows that Pausanias relied heavily on this device in his effort to integrate strands of old and new myth. This technique likewise occurs in Apollodoros and others.

758 A deviation arises in Euripides' play, where Iolaos is, indeed, Eurystheus' capturer, but he is not his killer. Rather, to Alkmene's dismay, the "king" is turned over to the Athenian state. His death is imminent, in any event, though he must first submit to the due process of law. It is furthermore evident that Eurystheus will ultimately be buried in Attic territory and defend the city henceforth with apotropaic powers from beneath the earth. This twist represents a typical example of the ways in which Athenians insinuated themselves into established mythic traditions that originally had nothing to do with them. Although according to the present argument, the *return of the Herakleidai* must be considered a relatively new assemblage of myths, it had been in development for roughly two hundred years at the time of Euripides' production, and it was, once again, notably created and launched outside of Attica, namely, this time, in the Peloponnese. The Athenian version of the Heraklid story exemplifies Athenian political interests as well as any other dramatic example of traditional material staged for Athenian audiences. Of those that immediately spring to mind, Orestes' trial on the Areopagos at the conclusion of Aischylos' *Oresteia*, Oidipous death and burial at Kolonos at the end of Sophokles' play by that title, Medea's escape from Korinth to Athens at the end of Euripides' *Medea*, Theseus' role in Euripides' production of the *Hiketides* with the burial of the *Seven* in Attic territory.

759 Here, Strabo provides a convenient list. In ten books, Pausanias' Περιήγησις is the best source for the relevant claims of individual Dorian states.

760 The *Ehoiai* provides the earliest evidence for the complete synthesis (Gantz 1993: 164-167; West 1985: 50-60). The cited pages assemble the relevant fragments dealing with the Hellenic tribal genealogy originating with Deukalion and Pyrrha, including the evidence that the *Ehoiai* poet was aware of the saga of the *return of the Herakleidai* with the sons of Aigimios, son of Doros. In terms of the amount of early archaic coverage and the comparative depth of the Herakleidai theme, it is worth noting that Gantz reviews the whole topic in less than three pages, followed by twenty-nine pages devoted to the Aiolidai.

761 So, for example, Herodotos (9.26), Diodoros (4.58.3-4), and Pausanias (1.41.2, 8.5.1, 8.54.3, 8.53.10) report a duel to determine the outcome between Herakles' son Hyllos, and Echemos of Tegea (alleged husband of Timandra, daughter of Tyndareos e.g. Paus.8.5.1). Echemos is the victor and the Herakleidai are deterred. Apollodoros, by contrast, sees a successful invasion after the death of Eurystheus and sons, followed by a plague that gripped the Peloponnese, forcing the invaders to retreat, once again, as an oracle proclaimed, until the third generation (2.8.2).

762 The two lines run as follows: Atreus->Agamemnon->Orestes->*Tisamenos* || Hyllos->Kleodaos->Aristomachos->*Temenos/Kresphontes/*Aristodemos->*Prokles* & *Eurysthenes*, sons of Aristodemos (who was held to have perished in the invasion by everyone other than the Spartans themselves cf. Hdt.6.51-52, 7.204). The appearance of Pleisthenes in a number of texts (either as a son of Atreus or another son of Pelops) as an ephemeral surrogate figure in the Pelopid line (his most notable feature is his sudden death) seems to signify an ambivalent attempt to increase the length of the Pelopid lineage without disrupting the narrative framework (e.g. Hes fr 194 MW; Stesichoros 209, 219 PMG; Ibykos 282a PMG; Aischy. *Ag.* 1602; C.M. Bowra 1934: 118; Gantz 1993: 552-556; J.M. Hall 1997: 90-91). Logically, given Pleisthenes' premature death his interjection into the lineage would have no true impact on genealogical calibrations. Nevertheless, he would make it possible to add another figure into the sequence. His very existence is a prime example of the Greek mytho-genealogical mentality.

763 Precisely by having Hyllos confront both Eurystheus and later Tisamenos.

764 Albeit, covering two to three generations, against Orestes->Tisamenos in one (perhaps, a minor detail).

765 In addition to the foregoing, as J.M. Hall emphasizes (1997: 60; 2002: 80-81), the Dorian representatives, Pamphylos and Dymas, sons of Aigimos, a contemporary of Herakles, were often said to have perished in the successful invasion, which certainly attributes a remarkably long lifespan to two tribal eponyms who were not even considered the offspring of a god.

766 cf. 45, 48, 64 & 2002: 25-27, 83.

767 So, for example, as outlined above in terms of extant accounts of the *return of the Herakleidai* story. Additionally, it is worth comparing the *Ehoiai* with Euripides' *Ion* in terms of the layout of this genealogy (so, Hall 1997: 43). Notably, Euripides' adaptation makes Doros, Ion, and Achaios all sons of Xouthos (son of Aiolos) and his wife Kreousa (daughter of Erechtheus). Ion, however, claims superior status since he is actually a son of Apollo and this is, no doubt, a deliberately ranked relationship. Euripides' version is also conspicuous for its perceptible substitution of Aiolos for Hellen, who must, therefore, be visualized above Aiolos, if he is given a place in this genealogy, as he certainly must in the late fifth century. Moreover, Aiolos' role in this genealogy as the forebear of all major southern Greek ethnic groups is certainly a conspicuous adaptation, perhaps something of a metaphorical nod to the supremacy of Aiolos in the inherited tradition. While it may seem compelling to credit Euripides with this formation's departure from the *Ehoiai* where Hellen fathers Aiolos, Doros, and Xouthos, and Xouthos and Kreousa in turn give rise to Ion, the most conspicuous attribute of Euripides' version is surely its overt Athenocentricity, which he may not have conjured out of thin air, but may well have been generally symptomatic of the politics of the Peloponnesian War Period.

768 In *Ethnic Identity in Greek Antiquity*, J.M. Hall cites Naukratis as a potential source of the "aggregative construction" 49.

[769] The genealogy that originates with Deukalion and Pyrrha yields the lineage of Hellen and a number of lines that stemmed from Deukalion and Pyrrha's daughters (viz. Hellen's sisters). The latter bear the distinction of uniting with Zeus. This distinction is considerable and notably one that the Hellenic line could not reproduce (relying as it did on male progenitors). The lines that stem from Deukalion and Pyrrha's daughters have been accused of inferior status: first, on the basis of female descent, and second, by virtue of being un-Hellenic because they were not descendants of Hellen (so J.M. Hall 1997: 64, 2002 165, focusing on Thyia, mother of Magnes and Makedon, so, Hes. fr. 7-8 MW; M. West 1985: 53). Their inferiority on the first count is not self-evident. Their inferiority on the second presupposes that the whole point of this genealogical diagram was to promote qualitative distinctions among different geo-political contingents of Greeks based on competitive ethnographic representation. As Martin West points out, the genealogies that stemmed from Hellen's sisters were disbursed throughout northern Greece with an additional link to Aitolia. West also emphasizes that there were no traditional legends about them (1985: 53; an observation mirrored by Hall in terms of the tribal eponyms, generally, with the possible exception of Aiolos 2002: 27, 34), and states additionally that "Hellen in this context does not represent the Greek nation as distinct from barbarians, but the Hellenes of the *Iliad* 2.684 (ibid.)." In this regard it is clear that the Deukalionid stemma was designed to enumerate *Greek* genealogies even though some of its members were ultimately shafted by the formation's southern Greek bent. The problem, it seems, was that this genealogy did not arise from a straightforward decision making process. Rather it was the formation that emerged as a consequence of the stories developed by the southern Greeks to revise the inherited Aiolic legacy. And since these stories reflected the outlook and aims of the groups that first promoted their development, they necessarily excluded a whole host of compatriots, leaving numerous excluded subgroups clambering to get in on the action. These dynamics are exemplified by the efforts of Hekataios and Hellanikos to creatively integrate significant groups into the Hellenic scheme of descent, which shows that negotiations continued around the fundamental Dorian / Ionian core (FGrHist 1F15-16 with Jacoby's commentary on the Aitolians, Lokrians and Molossians, on the latter, also Thuky.2.80; FGrHist 4F125). As for the vexed question as to why the Dorians made themselves the descendants of an eponymous Hellen (here I mention the Dorians and exclude the Ionians in deference to the evidence that they acted first), I would suggest that the reason for this particular choice had to do with the fact that the southern Greek Dorians situated their pre-historical homeland in the northern district known as Hellas (see J.M. Hall 2002: 132 on the vexed question, 161 on the derivation of Hellen from Hellas). It further stands to reason, in this regard, that the original sponsors of the Hellenic stemma were also the sponsors of the movement that greatly expanded the semantic scope of the term *Hellenes* and the term *Hellas* (for other recent opinions cf. C. Ulf 1996: 250 ff; R. Fowler 1978; J.M. Hall 2002: 134ff.). I deal further with Hellas in the section Argos in Homer.

[770] So, also the case of Aigimios, to cite another example. Compare, J.M. Hall 2002 83.

[771] Albeit clearly not a conceptual priority in the schematization advanced by Euripides.

[772] The oppositional phase of Hall's interpretation follows along the lines of the famous antithesis between Greeks and Barbarians that is generally associated with post Persian War Greek thinking. Though it is not to be doubted that this mode of thought resonated widely during this period (cf. Herodotos; Aischy. *Persians*), it has also been frequently overrated (e.g. D. Castriota 1992), obscuring more complex factors from view (as brilliantly demonstrated, for example, by G. Ferrari 2000).

[773] See especially T.W. Allen 1921.

[774] Strabo, book 4 provides examples of each.

775 e.g. C.M. Bowra 1930: 70-74; H.T. Wade-Gerry 1952: 55-56; G. Huxley 1956; D.L. Page 1959: ch.4; R. Hope Simpson and J.F. Lazenby 1970: 153-175; M.M. Wilcock 1976: 22-38. There are those, however, who reject Bronze Age provenance for the Homeric poems, yet, nonetheless, regard the *Catalogue* as distinctive by way of an assortment of interpretations e.g.; B. Niese 1853; M. Finley 1957; A. Giovannini 1969; I. Morris 1986; J.K Anderson 1991; J.M. Hall 2002: 133-134. A minority of scholars do not acknowledge the requisite inconsistencies and do not think the *Catalogue* warrants separate treatment (e.g. T.W. Allen 1910, 1921; V. Burr 1944; G.S. Kirk 1985), again, according to very different chronological principles.

776 See especially, G.S. Kirk, A. Giovannini, & J.K. Anderson, ibid.

777 See especially D.L. Page 1959. The above listed objections recur frequently. Varying degrees of consistency are admitted. It is generally agreed that the *Catalogue* depicts the gathering of the Greek fleet at Aulis, listing the contingents that set out for war. This much, it would seem, adequately explains the role of the Boiotians at the start of the *Catalogue*, inasmuch as they were the appointed hosts. As A.B. Lord maintained (1971), it also makes sense that the *Catalogue* reflected catalogue traditions in circulation in the poet's day and age, which, therefore, stood behind the *Iliad*'s version. Since on close inspection the *Catalogue* corresponds with related assertions elsewhere in the Homeric poems, the blanket alienation of the *Catalogue* censors an important body of information.

778 e.g. A. Giovannini 1969.

779 Concerning archaeological and textual sources, see, for example, quite recently, C. Morgan in I. Malkin ed., 2001.

780 The research was done by R. Hope Simpson and J.F. Lazenby and published in 1970. Their report is often cited and reaffirmed, so, for example, by K. Dowden 1992: 60-62, and R. Osborne in Fowler, ed. 2004: 190-193, & 216-217. For a unique exposition that favors the Early Palatial Period against the later Bronze Age as the critical era for poetic production that influenced Archaic epic traditions (with the notable exception of the *Catalogue of Ships*) see E.S. Sherratt: 1990.

781 A. Giovannini, G.S. Kirk, and J.K. Anderson focus in on the problems involved. They also address the likelihood that numerous mainland Greek cities known in the Homeric period fell into obscurity during the time between the crystallization of Homeric tradition and its dissemination on the Greek mainland.

782 i.e. Working in southern Yugoslavia in the late 20s and 30s. The idea that Homer was an oral poet goes back to F.A. Wolf in the late 1800s. At the forefront of the German analytical movement that remained influential throughout the nineteenth century, Wolf was primarily interested in oral tradition as a means to justify the deconstruction of the Homeric poems into originally separate lays that the poets of the *Iliad* and the *Odyssey* had ostensibly stitched together. His interpretation set off the intellectual controversy that became known as the *Homeric Question*, which was finally quelled (or certainly, transformed) by the contributions of Parry and Lord. Wolf was notably also the first to develop the theory of the Peisistratid Recension, which is instrumental, to this day, in arguments devoted to the denial of an early written rendition of Homer. cf. Glenn W. Most and James E.G. Zetzel 1985, J.L. Myres 1958; J.A. Scott 1965; G. Nagy 1996.

783 This notion was inspired by the discovery of hieroglyphic writing on Crete by Arthur Evans in 1894. It was vehemently advocated by a number of scholars e.g. A. Lang 1906; Gilbert Murray 1907; H.M. Chadwick 1912; cf. Myers 1958: 159, 205-207.

784 e.g. T.W. Allen (1906): 199; (1909): 84; (1910) 307, 313, 318ff.; (1921): 21; (1924): 160,198.

[785] In connection with Michael Ventris' decipherment of the Linear B script in 1952. The Mykenaian documents that, therefore, became accessible revealed a radically different social structure from that of Greece in subsequent periods. cf. M.I. Finley 1957; J. Chadwick 1973; I. Morris 1997.

[786] e.g. A.B. Lord 1960; M.I. Lord ed. 1995; A. Parry 1966, which cites M. Parry's original publications; cf. J.M. Foley, R. Janko and J.A. Notopoulos for further contributions on this topic.

[787] Again, A. Giovannini; G.S. Kirk; J.K. Anderson; cf. I. Morris 1986. On Pylos, in particular, see, J. Chadwick in W.A. McDonald and G.R. Rapp ed., 1972.

[788] 1906: 193.

[789] 1906: 194.

[790] For the traditional dating of the ancient antiquarians, see C. Roebuck 1959: 26-27; F. Jacoby 239FGrHist. Archaeological evidence is uneven in Asia Minor and opinions on the date of the major migrations vary from the eleventh to the ninth centuries.

[791] As stated in the introduction to this analysis, before the excavations of Heinrich Schliemann redirected analysis within discipline, Iron Age provenance was widely accepted in conjunction with a contemporary *Aiolic Theory* inspired by August Fick's linguistic research, and furthered by the idea of a Thessalian Ur-*Iliad* that was derived from the conspicuous role of Aiolic mythology in the extant Greek corpus (viz. involving a hypothetical prior tradition that was set in Thessaly as opposed to Troy, and centered on the life story of Achilles). In this camp, moreover, there was considerable resistance to the perceived implications of Schliemann's findings (as exemplified by R.C. Jebb and U. von Wilamowitz-Moellendorff). In this regard, it is important to note that the link between Homer and the Bronze Age is the product of particular historical developments, and equally important, that Aiolic based thinking has a prominent history within the discipline.

[792] 1906:194.

[793] cf. R. Drews 1979.

[794] cf. Nilsson 1932: 42.

[795] As H.M. Chadwick pointed out (1912: 388), we are dealing more with a case of divided kingship than with two definitively separate kingdoms.

[796] With Achaia / Argos understood to mean all of Greece.

[797] Str.8.6.5.

[798] In the passage in question, Noemon, who has lent Telemachos his ship for the journey to inquire after his father, complains to Antinoos that he now needs the vessel to obtain one of the horses from out of his herd. In this way the most aggressive cohort of suitors are informed of Telemachos' absence from Ithaka, which up until that point they were ignorant of.

[799] cf. Il.11.722-723 & Str.8.3.19 for the Minyeios River that ran through Pylian country.

[800] e.g. Str.8.3.19, 14.1.3; Paus.7.2.3. The history and identity of the Minyans, however, was substantially reconfigured in the Archaic Period. The thrust of the new story is already perceptible in Herodotos (4.145-148; cf. Apoll.1.230-233; in contrast to ApB.1.9.16).

801 Again, that the Ephyra at issue was located in Elis is further advanced by the corselet of Meges. Meges sailed to Troy from Dulichion and the Echinai islands, since his father Phyleus, an Epeian noble by birth, had established a kingdom on these off-shore islands after a fall-out with his father, Augeias (Il.2.625-629). He went to Troy with the corselet he received from his father, who once brought it out of Ephyra on the River Selleeis, that is from his family's homeland in Elis (cf. Il.15.528-534). This Ephyra is also favored by Strabo in book 4 of his geography.

802 cf. Il.2.281-288; Il.11.758-760; Il.19.160, 175; Il.15.372, 376, 380; Od.1.272; Od.2.90; Od. 3.260-261.

803 Not to mention the recurrent, "Helen of Argos," e.g. Il.2.160-161; Il.4.19,174; Il.6.323; Il. 7.350 etc.; Od.4.296; Od.17.118; Od.22.218.

804 e.g. Il.2.352; Il.3.258; Il.7.363; Il.13.377-380; Il.15.29-30 etc. Od. 4.174-176, or Achaia with northern Greece, e.g. Il.11.768-769.

805 With the single exception of *Achaian Argos* which does not adequately justify the use of the phrase.

806 Euboia 2.536-545; Salamis 557-558; the Echinai 2.625-630; Kephallenia, Ithaka, Zakynthos, Samos 2.631-637; Krete 2.645-652; Rhodes 2.653-670; Syme, Nisyros, Karpathos, Kasos and Kos 2.671-679;

807 e.g. Il.1.442, 3.455, 4.335 etc. ἄναξ ἀνδρῶν Ἀγαμέμνων; 10.32 ὅς μέγα πάντων Ἀργείων ἤνασσε; 10.103 Ἀτρεΐδη κύδιοστε, ἄναξ ἀνδρῶν Ἀγάμεμνον; 13.111-112 ἥρως Ἀτρεΐδης, εὐρὺ κρείων Ἀγαμέμνων etc., but also, 7.180, 11.46 etc. βασιλῆα πολυχύσοιο Μυκήνης;

808 e.g. Od.1.344; Od.4.726, 816; and Od.15.79-85 where Menelaos offers to escort Telemachos on a traveling mission throughout this region to receive hospitality and collect gifts from the leading houses in various cities.

809 Str.9.5.6.

810 Likewise, a favorite local progenitor (Il.16.168-192).

811 Hellas has occasioned various definitions: e.g. central and northern Greece as distinct from the Peloponnese (Kirk 1985: 202); or the Sperchios River Valley but in the case of "Hellas and midmost Argos," northern Greece as opposed to the Peloponnese (Hall 2002 127). Hope Simpson and Lazenby come closest to the operative definition suggested here, citing a number of relevant passages (1970: 128-129).

812 Nonetheless, this passage is often considered disturbing. Mainly because, according to the *Catalogue*, Meges should to be commanding men from Dulichion and the Echinai islands (2.625-629). However, Meges was born into an Epeian line (Il.2.625-630). From the point of view of the text, this natural shift required no explanation. This prospect receives even further support from the explanations that were deemed essential with regard to this passage as a whole.

813 Podarkes, in this same context, warrants no further notice, cf. Il.2.695-710.

814 He was evidently received by Philoktetes.

⁸¹⁵ The word Panhellenes first occurs in two places: in Lokrian Aias' *Catalogue* entry (Il.2.530), and in Hesiod's *Works and Days* (528), a poem notably composed in Boiotia. Reportedly, it next occurs in Archilochos (via Strabo 8.6.5, viz. in the mid-seventh century): ὡς Πανελλήνων ὀιζὺς ἐς Θάσον συνέδραμεν. This is surely a more enigmatic usage. But if, as it seems likely, this statement is too early to abide by the developed all-of-Greece usage, it may well be based on the early East Greek notion of the mainland Greek source of the Ionian migration. For other current opinions on this topic, see R. Fowler 1998; J.M. Hall 2002.

⁸¹⁶ viz. grandson of Autolykos of Parnassos of the line of Deion, son of Aiolos (see Gantz Table 7).

⁸¹⁷ The modern περιφέρεια, which continues westward through Aitolo-Arkanania to the Ionian Sea, has evidently embraced these parallel western districts that the *Catalogue* chooses to address later with Elis and the Ionian Islands (Il.2.615-644). In conjunction with references elsewhere in the text, we may conclude that Hellas included the kingdoms listed in the opening section of the *Catalogue of Ships*, namely, the sequence that runs from Boiotia to Attica, where the list veers off to the northeastern Peloponnese. Whether by extension, in common parlance, Aitolia was casually included as well cannot be confirmed from the Homeric evidence.

⁸¹⁸ e.g. A novel separatist take on the Homeric *Catalogue* that curiously isolates one particular entry (viz. 2,559-568 Diomedes, Sthenelos and Eurylaos listing). Drews believes the northeastern Peloponnesian province of Argos conflicts with all other Homeric uses of "Argos" and, therefore, represents a later appropriation sponsored by the historical Argive state. On this count, he suggests that the early epic stories that dealt with the Peloponnesian province of Argos were not native to the Homeric repertoire, but were, rather, interpolations extracted from an original corpus of Pelasgian Argive lore, including the wars between Argos and Thebes.

⁸¹⁹ As discussed above, in addition to Peleus' and Achilles' domain, Phthia embraced the kingdoms of Protesilaos and Philoctetes and possibly Eumelos' kingdom also, since it lay in between. Eurypylos' kingdom (suggested by Strabo) was conceivably also included. Excluded then, are the northern Magnesians, the kingdom represented by Asklepios' sons, the kingdom of the Lapiths, and the kingdom of Gouneus.

⁸²⁰ e.g. Currently, e.g. R. Fowler 1998; J.M. Hall 2002.

821 The transition from Homeric *Argos* and *Achaia* to the universal usage of the word *Hellas* is enigmatic and largely unrecoverable. On the Greek mainland the change is first detectable in the poetry of Alman, who was notably a spokesman for the Lakedaimonian Dorians (fr. 5 Diehl). As Martin West noted, the collateral lines that stem from Deukalion included a constellation of northern Greek tribal groups. He further observes that "Hellen, in this context, does not represent the Greek nation as distinct from Barbarians, but the Hellenes of Iliad 2.684 (1985: 53)." As mentioned in the critique of this stemma above, the line of Hellen itself is an abbreviation of the stories devised by Dorians and Ionians to rework the denouement of the Heroic Age and distribute themselves in southern Greece. And while the line of Deukalion, as portrayed in the *Ehoiai*, included a number of northern Greek tribes that played no role in Homeric tradition, such as the Graikoi and the Makedonians, and notably also, a novel Epeian lineage (e.g. M.L. West 1985: 53 on the line of Protogeneia + Zeus = Aethlios – over and against their Homeric depiction), only the trajectory commanded by Hellen represented southern Greek tribal origin stories. This line was clearly the engine behind the whole enterprise. In pitting themselves against Aiolic tradition, the Dorians ensconced themselves in northern Greece, carving out a homeland around Mt. Parnassos in the region known as *Hellas* (I omit the full-blown circuit of Dorian migrations). From *Hellas* it is but a short step to Hellen, progenitor of the Dorian line, devised to embrace and subsume Aiolos (viz. another son of Hellen and brother of Doros), in a lineage that, as referenced above, ultimately accommodated the Ionians and Achaians, the latter in their reduced reinterpreted form. Inasmuch as this genealogy spotlights its perpetrators (the Dorians), and goes on to list its perpetrators' accomplices (the Ionians), and also includes their joint adversary (Aiolos), who embodied inherited heroic tradition (Achaian/Aiolic), and in as much as these two groups of conspirators (Dorians and Ionians) became the most powerful Greeks in Greece, it is possible to imagine them reappraising their edifice, and reappraising themselves with respect to its content, to the point where *Achaia* faded into *Hellas*, and became a north Peloponnesian asylum for displaced Achaian (i.e. heroic) refugees. Xenophanes of Kolophon mentions greater Hellas (fr.5 Edmonds), followed by Hekataios of Miletos (FGrHist.1.119). Hellanikos of Lebos occupied himself with grafting excluded groups onto the Hellenic stemma (FGrHist. 4F125). In a sense this activity reinforces the idea that the global use of *Hellas* was not the cause, but the consequence, of the Hellenic genealogy, which, in turn, was the consequence of the fusion of Dorian and Ionian aitiological narratives. Other indicators are perhaps somewhat less definite (e.g. the initial use of the term Hellenion at Naucratis cf. Hdt.2.178), and none of our sources speak for excluded Greeks, who were granted no role in the Hellenic genealogy. Nonetheless, it would seem the designation *Hellas* was well on its way to everlasting supremacy by the second half of the sixth century (cf. J.M. Hall 1997: 47-48 & 2002: 125-134; also F.W. Walbank 1951).

CONCLUSION

CHAPTER SIX: THE LINEAGE OF THE SEER MELAMPOUS - A GENEALOGICAL CASE STUDY

At this point it is possible to conduct a case study of the seer Melampous' migration to Argos as presented in a number of ancient texts, beginning with the Homeric poems. The passages reproduced in *Appendix A*, below, will be dealt with in light of the following premises extracted from arguments set out thus far.

- There are certain discernible discrepancies between the Homeric uses of the term "Argos" and the later use of the term. Notwithstanding, the province and the city were both known as Argos in early Greek epic and in later Greek myth.

- Argos, the Archaic Greek city state – whose influence extended, at least early on, as far as Sikyon in the northwest, Aigina in the east, Asine in the south, and likely, albeit for an ephemeral period, around the entire Argolic Akte and southward into Kynouria and eastern Arkadia – appropriated the line of the hero Perseus. The Homeric epics, by contrast, situate Perseus' line on the north coast of the Korinthian Gulf with political headquarters at Mykenai. This striking topographical alteration turns out to have genealogical roots in the contrived but permanent association that made the heroes Proitos and Akrisios brothers.

- In this connection, as we have also seen, the intervention of the line of Pelops, which evidently took over Perseid sovereignty upon the death of Eurystheus and sons, was apparently a feature of the earliest tradition, since the manifest, if curious, absence of an available Herakleid successor led the line to devolve on the house of Atreus, so that Agamemnon in due course became the single most powerful ruler in Greece. Yet once the line of Perseus, and by extension, the house of Atreus, and through him Agamemnon, had been swept into the real-life province of Argos, a very substantial tract of mytho-political territory was essentially rendered null and void. Once created, this space set off a chain reaction whereby contemporary Dorian and Ionian interests infused the post Trojan

War Peloponnese with a series of narratives that redefined the mythological significance of this region.

- The legendary space that opened up in the west (i.e. Achaia) was offset by overcrowding in the eastern sector (i.e. Argos). On this count, the absorption of Perseus line stands out as the root cause of the confusion that pervades the kingdom of Argos in the ancient sources. In Homeric epic, the province of Argos was already replete with mythological lines. Accordingly, the addition of the line of Perseus (i.e. the line of Akrisios), which subsequently morphed into the line of Pelops, turned out to be an accommodation that generated significant logistical side effects.

This case study approaches the ancient sources with the above listed factors in mind and, in so doing, seeks to demonstrate that the sources readily substantiate the same first principles.

Melampous' biography may be summarized as follows[822]. Melampous and, likewise, his brother Bias were grandsons of Kretheus and Tyro. Kretheus was one of the sons of Aiolos. Tyro was the daughter of Salmoneus, who was yet another son of Aiolos[823]. Tyro was therefore her husband's niece. As a mythic figure, Tyro was notorious for falling in love with the Enipeus River, a passion that was exploited by the god Poseidon who took the form of the river to seduce her (Od.11.235-259). This unique twist attached to Tyro's life story situates this union in eastern Thessaly, north of Mt. Orthrys, where the Enipeus arcs to the east of the territory associated with the lineage of Kretheus and Tyro[824]. Corroboratively, this mating produced the illustrious heroes Pelias and Neleus. The first assumed the kingship at Iolkos, and the second, consequently, migrated to Pylos. A parallel mating between Kretheus and Tyro produced the three heroes, Aison, Pheres and Amythaon[825]. The first two remained fixtures of Thessalian saga, while the latter gave rise to Melampous and Bias, who joined the Neleid branch of the family in the west central Peloponnese[826]. Again, from a Homeric standpoint it must be emphasized that the Pylos in question was the "Triphylian or Lepreatic Pylos," as Strabo vehemently argued against later public opinion that overwhelmingly favored the Messenian Pylos as the designated location of Nestor's kingdom, and hence Melampous' hometown before he set out for Argos (Str. 8.3.1; 8.3.26-29[827]).

Notably, in this regard, the Messenian Pylos, which lay opposite the island of Sphagia or Sphacteria in the bay of Navarino has garnered ample modern-day support, fueled by the discovery of a grand Bronze Age palace on the heights at Ano Englianos where a substantial collection of Linear B tablets was unearthed by Carl Blegen in 1939[828]. But since this site is equated with Nestor's kingdom only at the risk of textual distortion as far as the Homeric poems are concerned, this suggestion must be rejected for present purposes[829]. Meanwhile, mythologically, as already noted, Messenian Pylos was the domain of the Aiolic heroes, Aphareus and Leukippos. Moreover, upon the death of Aphareus' sons (Idas and Lynkeus), who perished in conflict with the Dioskouri, who were in turn the husbands of Leukippos' daughters, the Messenian kingdom evidently devolved on the line of Tyndareos of Lakedaimon, and from there subsequently, in one way or another, fell largely into the hands of Agamemnon, either because of his marriage to Klytaimnestra, his brother's marriage to Helen, or a combination of both[830].

In any event, the seer Melampous had roots in Thessaly but resided in Pylos where his brother Bias enlisted his aid in securing the hand of Neleus' daughter, Pero (Od.15.223-240; Phereky.FGrHist 3F33; ApB 1.9.12). Neleus had announced that the winning contender must drive a herd of cattle to Pylos from Phylake (again, in the same region, this time northwest of Iolkos), where the desired herd was in the possession of the Aiolic hero Iphiklos (son of Phylakos, son of Deion, son of Aiolos[831]), who was by no means likely to give it up[832]. Apparently on account of his mantic skills, Melampous was deemed the best man for the job and agreed to the task on behalf of his brother, knowing in advance that it would entail significant hardship and a period of imprisonment[833]. Overcoming all odds, Melampous' success secured Bias' marriage to Pero, whereupon shortly thereafter he was summoned to Argos on a mission to cure King Proitos' daughters who had been driven to madness for some offense they had committed against one of the gods (specifically Hera or Dionysos[834]). Whether, as Herodotos and Apollodoros describe, it was by way of a series of negotiations in which Melampous upped his price as the women's condition worsened that Melampous and his brother came to power in Argos, it is sufficiently clear from the Homeric poems that in one way or another, both Melampous and Bias eventually gained a share in the kingdom, since both brothers' descendants are well entrenched by the time of the Argive-Theban Wars, while the Trojan War personnel as portrayed in the *Iliad* may be traced to related cause and effect conditions[835].

The main significance of Melampous' migration was the resulting division of the Argive kingdom, specifically, as it were, into three parts. Additionally, two generations later, the tripartite arrangement further accommodated the heroes Polyneikes and Tydeus, exiles from Thebes and Kalydon respectively, who arrived and married into Bias' family line (via two daughters of Bias' grandson, Adrastos), thus completing the underlying genealogical structure that defined mythic Argos from Melampous to Troy in the mind's eye of early Greek epic. In this regard, as suggested above, the complexity and vitality of this nexus of stories protected them from extreme transformation, to the effect that the heritage of Melampous and Bias remained largely intact from its Aiolic origins all the way down to the Trojan War era[836]. Moreover, in its progression this lineage exemplifies the ways in which the genealogical landscape was dictated by mythological stories that brought on the destruction or sustained the good fortune of the various branches of each great house. So, in this case, the lines of Amphiaraos (i.e. the line of Melampous), Adrastos (i.e. a branch of the line of Bias), and Polyneikes (i.e. the line of Bias by marriage) were casualties of the wars that made them great to begin with, an eventuality that is concretely affirmed by the *Iliad*'s description of the Argive leaders at Troy.

In this sense, the *Iliad*'s account of the contingent from Argos presents a modified take on the *tripartite division* that resulted from the inherent narrative features of the relevant stories involved, namely the two wars between Argos and Thebes[837]. These stories explain the presence of Sthenelos (son of Kapaneus of the line of Proitos), Eurylaos (son of Mekisteus of the line of Bias), and Diomedes (a second representative of the line of Bias by way of Tydeus' marriage to Adrastos' daughter Deipyle), as much as they illuminate the absence of representatives from the line of Melampous (viz. the line of Amphiaraos, Melampous' great-grandson), the line of Adrastos (Bias' most conspicuous grandson), or the line of Polyneikes (who married

Adrastos' daughter, Argeia), whose family problems sparked off the whole saga. Mainly, in the line of Melampous, Amphiaraos' sons, Amphilochos and Alkmaion, were either jointly involved in slaying their mother, the duplicitous heroine, Eriphyle, or Alkmaion was single-handedly responsible, and Amphilochos was driven to Northwest Greece, ostensibly for some other reason[838]. In the branch of the line of Bias exemplified by his grandson Adrastos, Adrastos' son Aigialeus was the single Argive fatality in the second triumphant assault against Thebes, whereas Polyneikes' son Thersandros[839], a veteran of that battle, perished in the misguided first expedition to Troy, at the hands of the hero Telephos, the Greek ex-patriot king of Mysia[840].

This patterning and this logic are worth bearing in mind when reading the passages excerpted below, each of which represents a unique approach to the problem of the *tripartite division* from the Homeric period to the second century A.D. In light of the foregoing and in light of these passages, the remainder of this analysis seeks once again to identify the dominant mode of thinking that stands behind significant post- Homeric developments. In the case of Melampous and the *tripartite division*, this process reveals that all the relevant passages have a good deal in common in spite of the points on which they diverge.

Beginning at the beginning with the *Odyssey* passages, Melampous' life story is largely accounted for[841]. He is affiliated with the house of Pylos[842] and with the wars between Argos and Thebes. In particular, he is described as the great-grandfather of the hero Amphiaraos, who was compelled to participate in the first Argive offensive, even though he knew in advance the plan would lead to disaster. It is also implied, as later tradition tells us, that his participation was somehow the result of treachery on the part of his wife, who was unanimously identified as the "hateful Eriphyle," who "accepted gold for the life of her own dear husband," at *Odyssey* 11.326-327[843]. Somewhat more specifically later reports equate this gold with the necklace of the heroine Harmonia, the illustrious wife of Kadmos of Thebes[844]. It was, therefore, an heirloom of the Theban royal family, which was, in addition, generally known to have been brought to Argos by Polyneikes (Oidipous' son), the Theban expatriot with a vested interest in seeking revenge against his native city, having been ousted from the Theban throne[845]. The notion that Eriphyle accepted a bribe that worked in her brother Adrastos' favor in his efforts to muster a cohort of fighters, but that also resulted in her husband's death, and ultimately in her death as well, when Amphiaraos commanded their son Alkmaion to kill her in revenge for her betrayal, remained the standard catalyst in the sequence of events that prefigured conditions in the kingdom of Argos at the time of the Trojan War.

From the battlefield exchange in the *Iliad's* book four between Agamemnon, Sthenelos, and Diomedes (366-416), it is clear that the great wars between Argos and Thebes that spanned two generations and enlisted soldiers from the same illustrious family lines were already well-known to early epic communities. It is also clear, though it is nowhere stated, that Melampous' brother Bias eventually also migrated to Argos, seeing that the Homeric epics depict the convergence of all three lines in the province of Argos: the line of Proitos, and the lines of Melampous and Bias[846], and further emphasizes that bad blood between the line of Melampous (i.e. Amphiaraos) and the line of Bias (exemplified by Adrastos and Eriphyle) was a key motivational factor in the escalation of Argive aggression toward Thebes[847].

The *Odyssey* enumerates Melampous' descendants quite explicitly. His grandson Oikles was widely known to have married Hypermestra, daughter of Thestios, of the Aiolic line of Aitolia, thereby forging a link between Argos and Aitolia that antedated Tydeus' son of Oineus' eventual integration into the Argive line[848]. In this regard, it was generally acknowledged that Tydeus, son of Oineus, arrived from Aitolia seeking refuge in Argos at the very same time Oidipous' son, Polyneikes, arrived seeking refuge from internal conflict at Thebes. Accordingly, they both married daughters of Adrastos, sealing the pact that established Adrastos as the perpetrator of Polyneikes' revenge[849]. Amphiaraos himself, it is further implied with reference to standard later tradition, was swallowed up by the earth near the ramparts of Thebes in an act of divine acknowledgment of his painful awareness that the first expedition was as doomed to failure as it was bound to take place – inexorably by the will of the gods[850]. Legend had it, however, that in due course the Argives would triumph in a second assault, at which time Aigialeus, the son of Adrastos (leader and sole survivor of the first initiative), would be the only victim of

Theban defensive forces in the victorious second round. At least four of the victorious Argive veterans later joined Agamemnon's expedition to Troy[851].

The mythological patterns visible here are so tangibly orchestrated as such that it seems justifiable to relinquish all efforts to grant these wars historical status[852]. Nonetheless, in this regard, it is worth pointing out, that attempts to do so tend to deny the intricate legendary connections between the first and the second Argive / Theban conflicts.

Of the two collateral lines that stem from Melampous in the *Odyssey's* book fifteen, one generates a main artery integral to the story of the Argive-Theban wars, whereas the second leads down to Theoklymenos (yet another itinerant exile for homicide), who meets up with Telamachos on the coastline near Pylos and pleads to join his party en route to Ithaka. Theoklymenos' lineage exhibits four features that are worth noting in the present context[853]. First, that Theoklymenos' father (i.e. Polypheides), evidently left Argos after a dispute with his father (i.e. Mantios) and settled in Hyperesia instead. He thus settled on the north coast of the Peloponnese and so, by implication, within the realm ultimately controlled by Agamemnon. It is clear from *Iliad* 2.572 that Adrastos also left Argos, at least for a period, in his case for Sikyon, which was also a part of Agamemnon's domain in the Trojan War Period[854].

Yet, since it does not exactly stand to reason that Adrastos led Argive forces to Thebes from that city, there may be some substance to Pindar's report that he was forced to flee as a result of the feud between Melampous' descendants and those of his brother Bias, but later returned when Amphiaraos agreed to marry Adrastos' sister, Eriphyle, so that marriage produced a temporary resolution. In any event, two prominent members of Melampous' line took refuge in the Perseid/Pelopid realm, which therefore twice played host to an illustrious Argive lineage, first on Melampous' and then on Bias' side. Second, that Theoklymenos' uncle Kleitos was snatched up by Eos and consequently removed from the realm of normal human activity, which was an asset in terms of family prestige, yet likewise represented the termination of that branch of the family line. Third, that this passage depicts prophesy as a hereditary trait transmitted to members of a prophetic blood line.

    This is significant in generating support for other Greek mythic hereditary principles, a number of which were encountered above. Though often counterintuitive from the perspective of contemporary analytical practice, hereditary attributes of this sort become more perceptible and coherent when Greek myth is addressed as a discrete microcosm governed by its own prescribed set of rules. And last, though peripheral to the present case study, the collateral line of Theoklymenos, which stemmed from Melampous' son Mantios rather than from his son Antiphates, was taken up by prominent later mythographers and adapted to include a number of tangents; so, for example, as footnoted above, a venerable line of Korinthian seers, which at times involved Kleitos' convenient retrieval from his privileged seclusion in the realm of the gods[855].

    The Homeric passages cited below, in conjunction with testimony elsewhere in the poems, confirm the fundamental narrative structure of Melampous' genealogical heritage, the antiquity of his mission to Argos, his settlement there along with his brother Bias, and the mythological destiny of his descendants in generating the Argive-Theban Wars. Notably, in all this, there is no sign of Akrisios or any of his descendants in mythic Argos, though as the selected passages show he is Proitos' brother virtually everywhere else.

    Moving on to Bakchylides' *Ode Eleven*, its most immediately striking characteristic is Melampous' deprivation of any role in curing Proitos' daughters of their affliction. Here, instead, the goddess Artemis takes responsibility for the salvation of King Proitos' daughters, negotiating with Hera on Proitos' behalf[856]. Given this situation, the issue at hand is to what extent and on what basis this story may be considered meaningfully resonant, rather than just a cunning sleight of hand? And while this kind of question is intimately bound up with the poet's intentions and overall point of view, it may not be impossible to access his thinking given sufficient evidence for Bakchylides' reliance on standard contemporary mythological protocol in combination with standard epinician conventions.

    With reference to Bakchylides' *Ode Nine,* which is very fortunately also extant, it is clear that the poet was quite well-informed about the lineage of Melampous and Bias, especially in terms of their integral role in the circumstances that led to the Theban Wars[857]. And this is actually no great surprise given the level of coverage on this material, albeit dispersed, throughout the Homeric poems. In this light, the mythic content of Bakchylides' *Ode Nine* suggests that he had creative ulterior motives when in *Ode Eleven* he chose to supplant the seer Melampous with the goddess Artemis, a choice that was virtually guaranteed to attract the attention of his audience.

Bakchylides, however, was not alone in breaking the mythological bond between the seer Melampous and King Proitos of Argos, even though the intercession of Artemis may well be his own unique contribution. For in a number of passages cited below, Melampous does not cure the madness of Proitos' daughters, but rather the madness of a generic group of afflicted Argive women (so, Herodotos, Diodoros, and Pausanias, with Apollodoros at 1.9.12[858]). In the last two authors who offer more specificity, it is clear that Melampous migrates to Argos at a time when Proitos was no longer king.

Here, the Homeric poems are of little assistance, since Melampous' adventures after he moved to Argos were left to the poet's listening audience to fill in for themselves as tradition prescribed. And while perhaps it cannot be definitively proven, the persistence of the madness of Proitos' daughters, specifically[859], combines with the Homeric status of Proitos and a number of factors that will surface below to further the prospect that Proitos' daughters' madness antedated the madness of the generic Argive women, whose subsequent dominance thus needs to be explained.

In any event, because Bakchylides promoted Proitos' daughters over the generic Argive women, whereas those who preferred the generic Argive women as the appointed recipients of Melampous' cure also situated Melampous' migration in the period after Proitos' reign, it is quite conceivable that Bakchylides effaced Melampous for precisely this reason: namely, that he viewed Melampous' migration as a future eventuality, so that Melampous was not in Argos at the time when Proitos' daughters went mad. The poet thus called on Artemis to intervene.

However, given Bakchylides' emphasis on the madness of Proitos' daughters specifically, if he also believed (as he may well have done) that Melampous migrated to Argos quite later, the upshot is clearly two extraordinary cases of feminine madness in the city of Argos. This would certainly be a remarkable thing, but then again we have frequently witnessed the need for this kind of mythic doubling before.

As for Bakchylides' poetic program, his priorities become increasingly clear in terms of the politics of poetic patronage that guided creativity in the epinician genre[860]. Briefly, it should suffice to point out in the present context that thematically *Ode Nine* and *Ode Eleven* both invoke well-known myths commensurate with the patriotic pride of the particular athletic victor in whose honor they were composed.

So, for example, it is altogether appropriate that *Ode Nine*, which was written for Automedes of Phliasia (a city just a short distance to the northwest of the cult center of Zeus at Nemea where the athletic competitions were held[861]), incorporated the legend of the *Seven Against Thebes* and acknowledged the story of the Nemean Games' foundation, which was the standard overture to that first tragic assault, certainly by the time Bakchylides was writing[862]. From this vantage point, therefore, it is again no surprise to witness Melampous' genealogical legacy in a poem for a victor who hailed from Phliasia, considering that Melampous' migration to Argos prefigured the Theban wars as far back as Homer, and Phliasia, itself, by virtue of its location, automatically invoked the first Theban War.

Likewise, *Ode Eleven*, which was composed for Alexadamos of Metpontion, relies on the numinous powers of Artemis in a way that may be peculiar to Bakchylides, but nonetheless accords especially well with the organization of civic ritual in Alexadamos' native city. At Metapontion, the goddess Artemis presided over a major temenos in the heart of the city, and was worshipped at San Biagio, on the outskirts, as well[863]. Thus, her persona loomed large in the rhythm of sacred ceremony in the place Bakchylides was commissioned to honor on behalf of Alexadamos, the recipient of this ode[864].

Therefore, all things considered, it is very likely the case that Bakchylides was taking creative advantage of a popular mythological trend that promoted the down dating of Melampous' position in the legendary sequence of events at Argos, and involved his temporal disassociation from the period when Proitos was king. Moreover, this possibility in turn suggests that Melampous' removal to a subsequent point in time afforded the poet the opportunity to recast the myth of the madness of the *Proitides* to embrace and to glorify the civic pride of the Achaian colonists of Metapontion[865]. The repositioning of Melampous must be addressed in detail.

Comparing Diodoros with Pausanias, Melampous may be seen moving further and further from the reign of King Proitos in the direction of the Trojan War. So, in Diodoros, the Argive women go mad and Melampus is summoned to affect a cure in the reign of Anaxagoras, son of Megapenthes, who was generally known as a son of Proitos. In Pausanias, also, the Argive women go mad in the reign of Anaxagoras. Anaxagoras, however, is this time described as a son of Argeios (a figure unheard of elsewhere), son of Megapenthes, who was, in turn, the son of Proitos. Accordingly, Melampous' migration to Argos is postponed by two generations in Diodoros, and in Pausanias, postponed by three[866]. This introduces a mythologically concrete explanation for the atrophy of the madness of Proitos' daughters, and hence the substitution of Proitos' daughters' madness with the madness of a group of generic Argive women, but it also introduces the fundamental question as to why these adjustments were being made.

Meanwhile, Melampous' migration intercepts with yet another legendary event that comes to the fore in the below-cited excerpts, namely the idea that Proitos' brother, Akrisios, and through him, his grandson Perseus, initially controlled the city of Argos, at a time when Proitos and his descendants were stationed in the neighboring city of Tiryns[867]. This arrangement, however, was later reversed when Perseus negotiated an exchange of kingdoms with Megapenthes, son of Proitos. Thereupon, from the time of that exchange of realms, Perseus' descendants commanded Tiryns, which was previously Proitos' family' stronghold, and, founding Mykenai in the process, Perseus abandoned the city of Argos to the control of Proitos' line. This purported exchange shows signs of standardization in Bakchylides and in Herodotos, since related mythological symptoms suggest its influence where it does not point-blank appear, and this means it is probably safe to say that the exchange was current by the fifth century[868].

In this context, the story customarily put forth to justify this exceptional exchange of kingdoms appears to combine a mix of old and new elements that gained widespread acclaim in reinterpreted form. Mainly, although we have seen that from a structural standpoint, any assortment of reasons might perform this function with no substantial effect on the set stream of events, here consistent allegiance to the idea that Akrisios died in a discus competition – where Perseus' aim went badly awry killing his grandfather (viz. Akrisios) as an oracle once predicted, way back in the days before Perseus was born[869] – employs the standard motif of oracular fulfillment (as familiar from Herodotos as it is from Homer) in a way that may well reflect rudimentary elements of the earliest strata of Danae's biography. Adding to the antiquity of oracular predestiny as an abiding traditional motif, the unexpected insistence that the fatal discus match took place at Larissa, in southeastern Thessaly[870], enhances the prospect of an old localization linked to the early adventures of Akrisios' line and having nothing to do with the city of Argos[871]. By contrast, however, the curious invocation of Perseus' feelings of personal shame for bringing about his grandfather's death stands out as an incongruous motivation or, at least, an untraditional type of root cause for Perseus' decision to give up his kingdom and take control of the Proitid heartland instead[872].

At any rate, the point is that Melampous' connection with Anaxagoras as opposed to Proitos, himself, and its explanatory relevance to the rise of the afflicted generic Argive women combines with the tale of the exchange of kingdoms to expose the strategic fabrication of Akrisios' role as an early Argive king. The logic of this indictment runs as follows.

When one asks, why Melampous came to be down dated, and why Pausanias decided to insert the otherwise unknown figure Argeios in between Megapenthes and Anaxagoras, while simultaneously seeking the motivation behind this very unusual exchange of kingdoms, the one mythic objective capable of addressing the confluence of these features that cluster together in contra-distinction to the remnants of early epic is a concerted effort to place the line of Akrisios within the boundaries of the Argive state. As it happens, explicit information concerning the early lineage of Proitos of Argos is, unfortunately, unavailable. However, the line of Proitos, as it came to be known, posits six generations from Proitos to Troy, which may well include at least one added figure (viz. Megapenthes or Anaxagoras)[873], ostensibly prompted by Melampous down dating. Otherwise Proitos lineage accords reasonably well with the genealogies attributed to Melampous and Bias, which led to the Trojan War in five and in four generations, respectively[874], with the evidence on Melampous stemming back to Homer[875]. Yet when the line of Akrisios is added into the mix with Akrisios in the role of Proitos' brother, a conspicuous rift enters into the framework – for the line of Akrisios takes five generations to reach Herakles' parents, Amphitryon and Alkmene, placing Herakles in the sixth generation and, therefore, at a point when the other three lines have already lived out the Trojan War. Notwithstanding, the Trojan War was unconditionally held to postdate Herakles' death.

Given this situation, down dating Melampous by two generations amounts to a quick and very effective fix that enhanced the integrity of the line of Akrisios, which was otherwise seriously out of sync. And while this measure certainly assuaged the problem, it was not good enough in the eyes of Pausanias, who detected the significant further advantage of adding yet another generation so Herakles could line up with Kapaneus of Argos, rather than with Sthenelos, Kapaneus' son, who was a famous Trojan War hero. Then pursuing the whole matter down as far as the *return of the Herakleidai*, again through the addition of Argeios, Pausanias aptly situated the "Dorian invasion," when the Heraklid Temenos seized the province of Argos, three generations after the Trojan War, in accordance with leading popular standards[876].

As far as the purported exchange of kingdoms, this story arose logically as a tactic designed to circumvent the received tradition with the integration of the line of Akrisios in mind. For early epic demanded, in no uncertain terms, that the lines of Proitos, Melampous, and Bias be stationed in Argos before the Theban Wars, which presupposed the established *tripartite division*, while the designated Argive contingent leaders at Troy, insured that it was indeed the province of Argos that Melampous' arrival divided into three. On this count, it is clear that the need to authenticate the Argive status of the Perseid/Pelopid line inspired the very ingenious claim that going back to the time of Akrisios, Perseus' line held power in Argos, antedating the advent of Protid sovereignty. Thus, the Perseids were as native as native could be and relocated only later on, when the exigencies surrounding an ancient oracle led Perseus, quite of his own accord, to transfer the family line to Tiryns, founding Mykenai in the process. This of course made it possible to believe that Agamemnon himself was a bona fide Argive ruler.

We see here the intricate problem of mythic Argos stripped down to its most basic political rationale, which is corroborated at random by all available testimony from early Greek epic to later Greek myth. Moreover, the ambiguity as to exactly where the great Argive families were actually ruling (viz. out of Argos, Mykenai, or Tiryns?) that surfaces prominently in the dramatic texts is less of a wonder than a situation inspired by the foregoing state of affairs. Beyond this, in a more general way, the topography of sovereignty in the kingdom of Argos was clearly the locus of a great clash between traditional and contemporary mythic prerogatives.

Consequently, in the end it would seem that the hypothesis with which this long exercise started has a very great deal to recommend it. In conjunction with its attendant restructuring tactics – the *regenerative strategy* and *mythological theft*, to which we may now justifiably add the general run of tribal migration stories – the idea that the mythic figure Aiolos, the eponymous figurehead of the Aiolic East Greeks who lived in the region round about the city of Troy was at one time the greatest of mythic progenitors, stands out as a cogent mythological precept with persuasive historical means of support. In close contact early on with major eastern metropoleis, the East Greek Aiolians evidently devised a major conceptual legacy for themselves. Their legacy, though their own, was discernibly based on cross-culturally standard methods of genealogical reckoning that had long since become the dominant medium for the narrative validation of cultural identity. The ingenuity and magnitude of the resulting charter, combined with its virtuoso expression through the preservation of the Homeric poems, ultimately engaged the non-Aiolic Greek world over the course of the ensuing centuries in a quest to adapt this inherited legacy to changing political specifications and volatile new configurations of power.

It is my experience, as I have attempted to show, that the Aiolic hypothesis makes it possible to enter the otherwise seemingly inscrutable world of Greek mytho-genealogical structure. This structure in its totality turns out to be a viable and informative historical document that in its own meta-empirical way traces the rise of the archaic Greek city-states.

---

[822] The following list of lost ancient texts dealt with the seer Melampous' life story, and the related life stories of his descendants: In epic: the *Melampodia, Thebais, Epigoni,* and *Alkmaionis,* and Steisichoros' *Eriphyle.* In drama: Aischylos' *Nemea, Hypsipyle, Epigoni, Argeiai, Eleusinioi.* Sophokles' *Epigoni, Alkmaion,* and satirical *Salmoneus* and *Amphiaraos.* Euripides' *Alkmaion is Psophis, Alkmaion in Korinth,* plus additional *Alkmaion* plays attributed to Agathon and to Achaios, and an *Eriphyle* attributed to Asklepiades.

[823] Salmoneus was one of the great heroic malefactors that were inevitably struck down by the gods, in his case by Zeus (Hes fr 15, 30; ApB 1.9.7 included below).

[824] We may note in this context another Enipeus, a tributary of the Alpheus River in the western Peloponnese (e.g. W. Hazlitt 1851/1995). This alternative river, no doubt connects rather nicely with story that Salmoneus founded a city in Elis named after himself (DS 4.68 and ApB 1.9.7 cited below; specifically in Pisatis according to Strabo 8.3.31). While it is difficult to assess the antiquity of this claim, the Enipeus that flows from the peaks of Mt. Orthrys is, generally speaking, a much stronger candidate for the protagonist in Tyro's life story, since this Eneipeus succinctly invokes the geopolitical heritage of the whole family line.

[825] Again, Od.11.235-259.

[826] Od.15.223-234; Phereky. FGrHist. 3F117; Pindar *Pyth*.4.124-154; DS 4.68 (see below); ApB 1.9.9-11 (see below); Paus.2.28.4 (see below), 4.2.5.

[827] So also, 8.6.10 in *Appendix A* below.

[828] On the results of Blegen's excavations at Pylos see, Carl W. Blegen and Marion Rawson, *The Palace of Nestor at Pylos in Western Messenia.* 3 vols. Princeton: 1966-1973. For the contemporary implementation of the Messenian claim to Homeric Pylos see, for example, R. Hope Simpson and J.F. Lazenby Oxford 1970. The map of *Mainland Greece* published in R. Fagles translation of the *Iliad* is also indicative of the same trend.

[829] e.g. Il.2.591-602, 5.541-549, 11.710-728, Od.15.292-300, where the emphasis is on the Alpheios River and the central west coast of the Peloponnese.

[830] So, Agamemnon's attempt to win back Achilles with an extensive kingdom on the Messenian Gulf (Il.9.149-157; see also Str.8.5.8; ApB 1.9.4; Paus.4.2.4-4.3.1).

[831] Σ Od.11.326; Hes fr 62 MW.

[832] Od.11.281-292; 15.223-255.

833 Reports that this cattle rightfully belonged to Tyro, who initially resided with her uncle Deion after her father Salmoneus' death, until Deion married her off to her uncle Kretheus, may well explain the curious presence of ἄτη and an Ἐρίνης in the *Odyssey's* narrative on Melampous' role in performing the task that enabled him to win Pero's hand in marriage on behalf of his brother rather than for himself (Od.15.223-240; Phereky. FGrHist 3F33; Σ Od. 11.290). According to this reasoning, the wrongful withholding of the ancestral herd by Deion's descendants in Phylake activated the vengeance of an Erinys, who was responsible for both Neleus' demand as well as Melampous' infatuation. The menacing forces of retribution that initially activated the Erinys' wrath were, therefore, assuaged by the cattle's retrieval.

834 So in the passages cited below, Bakchylides names Hera, Diodoros, Dionysos, while Apollodoros cites Hesiod for Dionysos, and cites Akousilaos for Hera.

835 viz. Stenelos (line of Proitos), Eurylaos (line of Bias) and Diomedes (line of Bias through marriage). On this distribution and also the Argive-Theban Wars, see Il.2.559-568, 572, Il. 4.365-410, Il.5.799-845, Il.10.283-294, Il.23.344-345, 676-681.

[836] Minor variations inevitably occur. So, for example, in the passages cited below, Diodoros has Salmoneus marry one Alkidike, daughter of Aleos, who was in turn a son of Apheidas, son of Arkas, of the developed Arkadian line. This assertion is repeated by Apollodoros with no mention of Alkidike's mythological heritage, and probably represents a duplicate claim indicative of considerable popular currency. Its novelty, however, is hardly subject to doubt (on the evidence for the novelty of the Arkadian line, see mythic-theft-type-one, example three, above). Also in Diodoros, the assertion that Melampous' son Antiphates married Zeukippe, a daughter of the Spartan Hippokoon (a son of Tyndareos of dubious antiquity), stands out as a post-Homeric Peloponnesian innovation above for reasons enumerated above (mythic-theft-type-two, example two). Moreover, Diodoros' further claim that Melampous' grandson Oikles married Hypermestra, daughter of *Thespios* (i.e. rather than Thestios) is either an error or a deliberate gloss designed to reinforce his Athenian proclivities, which are readily transparent upon close inspection and touched on briefly above in the section on Iolaos where Athenians and Thespians are involved. Diodoros further provides an excellent example of the tendency to conflate Amphion of Orchomenos (son of Iasos and father of Chloris at *Odyssey* 11.281-286; her sister marries Pelias at ApB 1.9.10) with Amphion of Thebes, the brother of Zethos, famous for jointly building the ancient city's foundations. In Apollodoros, the eponymous Mantineus, whose daughter Aglaia is said to have married Abas of Argos (viz. father of Proitos and Akrisios) stands out as a typical innovation, which reoccurs again in Diodoros minus any paternal identification (so, the reverse distribution of information encountered with Alkidike as mentioned above). Likewise, the assertion that Nestor married Anixibia, the daughter of an obscure figure named Kratieus stands in contradiction to the Odyssey's Eurydike, daughter of Klymenos (3.453). For what it is worth Klymenos was the name of a son of Oineus of Kalydon and another Aiolic figure in the line of Athamas. Particularly conspicuous in Apollodoros is the pairing of Amythaon and Idomene, daughter of Pheres, on the one hand (1.9.11), though later, Amythaon is paired again with Idomene, who is this time the daughter of the Argive Abas (2.2.2). In the second case, therefore, Idomene was a sister of Proitos and Akrisios, and she is credited with the medicinal skills assigned to Agamede, Augeias' daughter at *Iliad* 11.738-740. More generally, the addition, here and there, of formerly unknown legendary figures is a fairly conspicuous general trend that naturally facilitated genealogical innovations, and can at times be shown to purposefully suppress older yet no longer favored progeny. This trend is exemplified in Diodoros with the addition of Manto and Pronoe among the offspring of Melampous (which was evidently not unique to him cf. Hes fr 136 MW; Phereky. FGrHist 3F115), by Aristomachos at Apollodoros 1.9.13, and, in general throughout the *Bibliotheka* where long lists of progeny make an appearance (so, that of Neleus and Chloris at 1.9.9), since typically some are quite well-known while others are altogether unknowable (Pausanias' additions are dealt with at length below. For Manto, daughter of Teiresias, cf. G.L. Huxley 1969: 47,164 and M. Davies 1989: 30 on Σ AR 1.308b, which cites the epic *Epigoni*). Finally, there is a major collateral sequence that was clearly tacked on to this lineage complex without profoundly affecting its basic structure. This is namely the lineage that appears in the *Ehoiai* (in very fragmented form Hes fr 136 MW) as well as Pherekydes (3F115), and was later transmitted by Pausanias (1.43.5) that appended a lineage of Korinthian seers onto the inherited line of Melampous as inspired by *Iliad* 13.660-672, where Euchenor, son of Polyidos, a seer from Korinth, meets his death at the hands of Paris (see also M. West 1985: 79-81).

[837] For a comprehensive account of the surviving ancient narratives, see Gantz 1993: 502-528. More on this also below.

[838] e.g Hekataios FGrHist 1F102c; Thouky.2.68. Amphilochos does not appear in the *Iliad*, though he was later transformed into a Trojan War hero as were the sons of Theseus too, for example. In this regard he was later attached to the adventures of Calchas in Asia Minor with a party of surviving Trojan War heroes (compare Proklos' ΝΟΣΤΟΙ with ApE 6.2).

[839] So reciprocally, Adrastos himself was the sole survivor of the first expedition. Aigialeus was later granted a son Kyanippos, who registers in a series of lineage extensions developed in connection with the *Return of the Herakleidai*.

840 So, Proklos' ΧΡΗΣΤΟΜΑΘΙΑ ΠΕΡΙ ΤΩΝ ΚΥΠΡΙΩΝ. Oxonii 1810; M. Davies 1988, 1989; D. Obbink and M. West 2006. As T. Gantz points out, Diktys of Krete reports that Diomedes carried Thersandros body to safety, a detail more than likely reminiscent of their parallel status in the family structure (Dictys 2.2; Gantz 579).

841 I refer to the order of the excerpted passages, set out chronologically in the appendix.

842 Though no specific kinship relation is stated.

843 "...τε ἴδον στυγερήν τ' Ἐριφύλην, ἥ χρυσὸν φίλου ἀνδρὸς ἐδέξατο τιμήεντα."

844 Daughter of Ares & Aphrodite at *Theogony* 934-937 and, therefore, evidently a goddess herself.

845 For the necklace of Harmonia, the earliest evidence is artistic, so for example, as Pausanias reports on the chest of Kypselos 5.17.7-8. See also LIMC s.v. Eriphyle / Amphiaroas; Hellanikos FGrHist 4F98. On the feud between Polyneikes and his brother Eteokles that led to Polyneikes expulsion from Thebes, see especially, Aischylos *Hepta* 631—650 (with Phereky.FGrHist. 3F96); Sophokles *Oidipous at Kolonos* 392-420; Euripides *Phoinissai* 1-87; DS 4.65.1; ApB 3.6.1. That Thersandros, son of Polyneikes, mimicked his father's strategy in using the robe of Harmonia to bribe Eriphyle to send her sons to Thebes is first attested in Hellanikos (FGrHist 4F98; so also ApB 3.7.2). The antiquity of this notion defies assessment, yet it is far from essential to the basic plot structure.

846 So, Il.2.559-568.

847 So, also Od.15.241-247 and Pindar *Nemean 9* as cited below. To the well-documented conflict between Adrastos and Amphiaraos involving Eriphyle, the scholia to *Nemean* 9.30 add that Amphiaraos killed Adrastos' father Talaos, and Pausanias' description of the Amyklai throne reports a fight between Amphiaraos and Lykourgos, son of Pronax, that Tydeus and Adrastos intervened to break up (3.18.12). Pronax, like Adrastos, and the *Iliad*'s Mekisteus was regarded as another son of Talaos (viz. son of Bias) who, as the Pindar scholia report, ruled in Argos before his death, which evidently sparked off competition between Amphiaraos and Adrastos in some versions. This accords, for example, with Pindar's *Nemean 9* where the sons of Talaos were supreme before they were overpowered by Amphiaraos. And this could perhaps, though far from necessarily, relate to the murder of Talaos, although such a murder may well be expected to lead Amphiaraos into exile. And while Adrastos' exile to Sikyon is repeatedly supported, beginning with the Homeric *Catalogue of Ships*, we are far less informed about other family conflicts beyond the vague sense that there was more to the story; some of these features were early and others later embellishments. In any event, Pronax was often later considered to have fathered Lykourgos, a priest of Nemean Zeus, whose infant son Opheltes' accidental death (he was killed by a snake bite) became the celebrated incident that stood behind the legendary foundation of the Nemean Games at the time of the first Argive assault against Thebes. Judging from Pausanias, it seems that in some parts of the Peloponnese Lykourgos' wife was identified as Eurydike, daughter of Adrastos (5.17.7-8). And though she did not remain standard elsewhere as such, this information may well be relevant to the skirmish depicted on the Amyklai throne. Meanwhile, however, Apollodoros asserts that Lykourgos the priest of Nemean Zeus was actually the son of Pheres of Thessaly (1.9.14 viz. not a son of Pronax of Argos at all), which may not be unrelated to the role of Hypsipyle, Jason's former lover, in the events that unfolded at Nemea. But it is also self-evident that the Nemean Games' foundation could not have played a part in the early epic perspective, since the games were not founded until the mid-sixth century. This, of course, however, does not preclude an early cluster of legends involving a priest of Nemean Zeus, in which case the son of Pheres designation would be the more likely authentic match, leaving Pronax' antiquity an open question, or certainly his son Lykourgos' role in the prelude to the first Argive-Theban war. Overall, it seems clear that Bias' son Talaos bore a number of sons in addition to Adrastos (viz. surely Mekisteus, possibly Pronax, and also Parthenopais as treated above), and that various tensions between the two houses associated with Melampous' cure furthered the progression of mythic events, creating an important and memorable saga. Yet somewhat suspect in all this is the intimation of violent conflict over the throne (i.e. in Pindar as cited below), because the whole point of the tripartite division was the allocation of a substantial realm for each of the ruling families involved. This type of emphasis again raises the issue of overcrowding in mythic Argos attendant on post-Homeric reinterpretation, especially the absorption of Perseus line. On the legendary foundation of the Nemean Games, cf. T. Gantz 1993: 510-512.

848 The marriage of Oineus of Kalydon to Periboia, daughter of Hipponoos, father of Kapaneus, of the Proitid line represents yet another prior connection between the genealogies of Argos and Aitolia (e.g. Hes fr 12 MW).

849 On Hypermestra, see for example, Paus.2.21.2). For Tydeus' marriage, Il.14.121; On Tydeus' exile: Hes fr 10a 51-57 OCT; ApB 1.8.5, citing the *Alkmaionis*; Relevant to Polyneikes' marriage, Hes fr 192 MW; Deipyle and Argeia were generally named from Pherekydes onward, so FGrHist 3F122. Notably, however, Pausanias witnessed Eurydike and Demonassa on the chest of Kypselos (5.17.7-8). For further narratives, see Euripides' *Phoinissai* 408-434, *Hiketides* 131-161, and later, Statius' *Thebaid* (1.390-347) and Apollodoros (3.6.1).

850 Od.15.244-246; Pindar *Ol.*6.8-14, *Pyth.*8.35-55; *Nem.*9.16-27, Nem.10.7-9; Aischylos *Hepta* 597-626; Sophokles *Elektra* 837-840; Euripides *Hiketides* 925-927. On the Oracle of Amphiaraos at Oropos, see Hdt.1.46, 49, 52, 8.134; Str. 9.1.22; A. Schachter 1981, s.v. *Amphiaraos*.

851 Naturally, the identity of the *epigoni* originates with the identity of their fathers. As T. Gantz points out, the surviving accounts of the participants in the first Argive attack against Thebes exhibit a degree of variation, while the earliest lists date from the Classical Period. A survey of these lists admits two possibilities: that the number seven was not a traditional designation, but rather a number that was later incorporated by the tradition, or that the number seven was indeed old and authoritative, but became problematic when new personalities generated an excess number of participants, spawning an ongoing variety of opinions as to who would command priority status and which early claimants ought to be hedged out. Pindar's description of seven pyres burning outside the ramparts of Thebes (*Nem*.9.22-24, above; notably *not* on the outskirts of Athens cf. Euripides *Hiketides*; Isokrates *Panegyr*. 55, 64,; Paus.1.39.2 with 1.14.2) would seem to assume nine participants in total, since Adrastos survived and Amphiarios was miraculously swallowed up by the earth. Even so, this number could well stem from either of the above mentioned possibilities. Likewise, Pausanias assertion that there were indeed more than seven well-known combatants in spite of the title of Aischylos' play (2.20.5) could also result from either progression because it is clear that by the early fifth century there was already an excess number of candidates. The extant lists have been meticulously compiled by Timothy Gantz on pp. 514-519 and 522-525. Overall, they exhibit the following patterns, which may best be perceived from the vantage point of the allocation that surfaces in three plays: Aischylos *Hepta* 397-625 / Sophokles *Oidipous at Kolonos* 1503-1513 / Euripides *Hiketides* 857-932. All agree on: 1. Polyneikes son of Oidipous / 2. Tydeus son of Oineus / 3. Kapaneus son of Hipponoos (line of Proitos) / 4. Amphiaraos son of Oikles (line of Melampous) and 5. Adrastos, son of Talaos (line of Bias). However, in these three plays Adrastos serves as an escort as opposed to an active warrior, though including him yields five consistent participants who remain consistent in other accounts. Notably in this vein, Euripides' *Phoinissai* (89-181) substitutes Adrastos for Eteoklos (son of Iphis) granting Adrastos warrior status instead of having him simply accompany the army. And this practice is followed by Diodoros (4.65.4-5), Statius' *Thebaid* (4.32-250) and Apollodoros (3.6.3). As Gantz points out, this was most likely Adrastos' original role, though clearly having him serve as escort rather than warrior readily facilitated an added space in the roster of seven combatants. It is also worth noting, in this regard, that Eteoklos son of Iphis was gradually phased out from the time of Euripides' *Phoinissai* onward, though in the same playwright's *Hiketides* not only Eteoklos, but his father and his sister play significant dramatic roles. Eteoklos reappears on a monument at Delphi, commissioned by the Argives using Theban sculptors, where he replaces the Arkadian Parthenopaios (Paus.10.10.3). Otherwise, he basically disappears from the record. Consistently elsewhere these same five figures produce the following offspring: 1. Thersandros, son of Polyneikes / 2. Diomedes, son of Tydeus / 3. Sthenelos, son of Kapaneus / 4. Alkmaion & Amphilochos, sons of Amphiaraos / 5. Aigialeus, son of Adrastos.
The following personalities are contested participants: 1. Parthenopais, son of Atalanta, (viz. the Arkadian), though elsewhere a son of Talaos (line of Bias e.g. Paus.2.20.5). His son is variously cited as Promachos (Paus.2.20.5), Stratolaos (Σ Il.4.404-407) or Tlesimenes or Biantes (Hyg. *Fab*.71) / 2. Eteoklos son of Iphis (generally attributed to the line of Proitos, though his genealogy remains somewhat obscure). Eteoklos' son scarcely appears in the sources, but he is called Medon in the scholia to Sthenelos' speech in *Iliad* book four. This name is suspicious in and of itself since the *Iliad*'s Medon, who was doubtless well-known, was the half-brother of Aias, son of Oileus (Il.13.694-697, 15.332-336). Eteoklos himself was understood as Kapaneus' brother-in-law, and appears as his nephew as well, in an instance where Iphis and Kapaneus are brothers (Paus.6.17.6). His sister Euadne, Kapaneus' wife, was renowned for throwing herself on her husband's funeral pyre (Euripides *Hiketides* 990-1071; 1031-1044 for Iphis, father of Eteoklos and Euadne). Euadne shows signs of considerable antiquity, yet she was also subject to competing genealogies (so, Pindar *Ol*.6). / 3. Hippomedon appears either as a son of Talaos (*Oidipous at Kolonos* 1507), a son of Aristomachos, son of Talaos (ApB 1.913, 3.7.1), or a son of a sister of Adrastos (Paus.10.10.3). In spite of his popularity in the extant sources, Hippomendon's identity is mythologically, the weakest of the recorded sons of Talaos, which may mean that he was a strategic substitution for an old but later less-favored counterpart / 4. Last but not least among the contested figures was Mekisteus, son of Talaos whose son Eurylaos was a representative of the contingent from Argos in the *Iliad* (2.676-680, 23.676-680). Interestingly enough, though Mekisteus and Eurylaos were incontrovertibly old traditional figures, ostensibly involved in the Argive-Theban wars, the evidence shows that they were frequently censored by everyone other than the Argives (Paus.2.20.5, 10.10.4, however, see Hdt.5.67 and Paus.9.18.1). In the end what we see are five consistent participants with four recurrent contenders for the two remaining available posts. One of these, if the *Iliad* is any guide, ought to be Mekisteus, son of Talaos, and his son Eurylaos in the next generation. This leaves Eteoklos, Parthenopais, and Hippomedon in competition for the one available space in the event of an ancient roster of seven, or otherwise resulting in a total of nine, commensurate with Pindar's seven pyres (unless, by chance, Adrastos was in fact, traditionally an escort rather than a warrior, which would leave room for one more out of the remaining two in the case of an authentic legendary seven, but would fudge the connection with Nemean 9). Barring serious extenuating circumstances, which can be mythically substantiated in a number of cases (viz. Alkmaion, Amphilochos, Aigialeus), it is clear that the next mission of the *epigoni* was to join Agamemnon's expedition to Troy. In this regard, for what it is worth, the destinies of the sons of the three contested protagonists involved in the first expedition to Thebes (viz. excluding Eurylaos, son of Mekisteus) cannot be traced either to events at Troy or to the intervening period.

852 For the historical standpoint, cf. F.H. Stubbings, CAH II.2 1975: 165-169; For more recent suspicions as to its validity, cf. A. Schachter, *Phoinix* 21 1967: 1-10; W. Burkert 1992:106-114; K. Dowden 1992: 68-70.

853 On the integrity of the episode in the *Odyssey*, which was previously challenged by a number of theorists (e.g. U. von Wiliamowitz-Moellendorff 1927: 148ff. and D.L. Page 1954: 84ff.; G.S. Kirk 1962: 240ff.),see A. Heubeck 1954: ch. 2 and B. Fenik 1974: 233-244).

854 On the subject of Sikyon, the emergence of an autonomous genealogical line involving Lysimache, daughter of Polybos, the Sikyonian king, is fairly suspect on a number of grounds. In the scholia to *Nemean 9*, the fourth-century writer, Menaichmos of Sikyon is cited for Lysimache, daughter of Polybos and wife of Talaos (viz. son of Bias; FGrHist 131F5), a notion later echoed by Pausanias, who calls this woman Lysianassa (2.6.3). The *Nemean 9* scholia also report that others considered Lysimache to be Adrastos' wife, whom he ostensibly had occasion to marry at the time he sought refuge in that city on account of internal conflict at Argos. While it cannot be determined whether Homeric epic acknowledged a Sikyonian ruling family that reigned under the authority of the house of Perseus, and accordingly, later, under Agamemnon, the introduction of Polybos seems more likely the product of subsequent mythological thinking aimed at liberating the polis of Sikyon from under the authority of the house of Pelops and the authority of Argos itself. In this context, the story of Thyestes in Sikyon (mainly via Hyg. *Fab*.88, also the title of one of Sophokles' plays) that we are scarcely informed about, may well derive in its basic outline from an old epic point of view, judging, for example, from a fourth-century krater described by Gantz that depicts Adrastos ruling in Sikyon with his wife Amphithea at a time when Pelops' son Thyestes was also active in the Peloponnese (1993: 550) and also obliquely supported by Isocrates who links Adrastos with the end of Eurystheus' reign (e.g. *Panegyr*.54-56). It is also relevant that Apollodoros describes a woman named Lysimache as the daughter of Melampous' son Abas, who married Bias' son Talaos, generating, as cited above: Adrastos, Parthenopais, Pronax, Mekisteus, Aristomachos, and Eriphyle. And while it is fairly clear that Melampous' son Abas represents an innovation himself (e.g. Paus.1.43.5), Apollodoros has Adrastos marry Amphithea, the daughter of his brother Pronax, which yields a set of endogamous marriages with no Sikyonian lineage anywhere in sight. Accordingly, as far as we can tell, Adrastos' early epic association with Sikyon may not have been based on established lineage ties, but may have been simply an accommodation made at the discretion of the house of Perseus (or conceivably, the house of Pelops). Beyond this, if the connection was fortified genealogically, our access to early tradition fades out.

855 As mentioned above, on this topic see especially, Hes Fr 136 MW; Phereky. FGrHist 3F115; Paus.1.43.5.

856 11.92-112.

857 9.10-26.

858 Conspicuously here, the god Dionysos instigates the Argive women's affliction, which mirrors Diodoros 4.68, above.

859 viz. here, in Bakchylides' *Ode Eleven* and Apollodoros 2.2.2, but also in Pherekydes, so FGrHist 3F114.

860 On this topic, see for example, F.J. Nisetich 1980: intro; A.P. Burnett 1985; L. Kurke 1991, and in C. Dougherty and L. Kurke, eds. 1993; and, in general, the work of T.K. Hubbard.

861 Paus. 2.12.3, 2.14.2-3.

862 Again, this was the story of the infant Opheltes (son of Lykourgos, the priest of Nemean Zeus), who suffered a fatal snake bite as the Argive army approached. This event was interpreted as a very bad omen, but inspired no realistic thought of retreat in spite of persistent warnings from the seer Amphiaraos. The army paused to commemorate the death of the child, who was ceremoniously re-named Archemoros, signaling the *beginning of doom* for the Argives. For more on this episode, see Gantz 1993: 510-512.

863 11.113-124. For recent discussions on the political and territorial relationship between urban and extra-urban sanctuaries, initiated by F. Polignac in his influential 1984 publication: *La Naissance de la Cité grecque*, see, I. Malkin's critique and F. Polignac's updated assessment in B. Alroth and P. Hellstrom, eds. 1996.

864 On Artemis at Metapontion, cf. A.P. Burnett 1985: 101 n. 8; L. Cerchiai, L. Jannelli, and F. Longo, eds. 2002: 130-143. See Burnett, ch. 7 for another interpretation of Bakchylides' Eleventh Ode.

865 The colonists from Achaia, it should be noted, readily identified themselves with the original meaning of the word, which is to say, with the image of Achaian identity as expressed in the Homeric poems in contrast to the run of post Trojan War legends that later came to define the province of Achaia and the ancestry of its contemporary inhabitants (viz. the Dorian and Ionian migration narratives). These, the historical Achaians, likewise adopted into their overall public self-image, though there is little doubt that in the order of things the Homeric vision was the earlier prototype first employed by the colonists of Magna Graecia. Its continued tenacity is evident in this context. See, J.M. Hall 2002: 58-65.

866 See attached charts, Appendix B.

867 As Strabo emphasizes, Argos, Tiryns, and Mykenai were remarkably close to one another, so close as to require special explanation as to their status as administrative strongholds in two separate kingdoms. Though Strabo skillfully glosses over the matter, he is no doubt thinking in mytho-genealogical terms, namely along the same lines as the rest of the cited passages. In general, the division of Argos between the brothers, Proitos and Akrisios, is either characterized by fraternal hostility (so in Apollodoros, stemming back to the womb and resulting in Proitos' exile to Lykia, his subsequent return with Lykian reinforcements, and his conquest and fortification of Tiryns; see also Bakchylides' *Ode Eleven*, above) or by an amicable apportionment of Argive territory (so, Paus.2.16.2, below). The walls of Tiryns, astonishing to this day, were held to have been constructed by the Kyklopes, often specifically on Proitos' behalf.

868 So, for instance, in Herodotos, the appearance of the generic Argive women, Bakchylides' emphasis on the great feud that arose between Proitos and Akrisios, and to cite an example from outside the selected texts, the assertion that occurs in the Hesiodic *Aspis* stating that after killing Alkmene's father, Elektryon, Amphitryon fled to Thebes from the city of Tiryns (77-82).

869 e.g. Phereky. FGrHist 3F10.

870 So Phereky. FGrHist 3F12; ApB 2.4.4; Sophokles wrote a play entitled *Larisaioi*, which no doubt focused on these events. For more coverage on the life stories of Perseus and Danae, see Gantz 1993: 299-311.

871 Hyginus, notably, transferred the competition to Seriphos (*Fab.* 63), the island that became central to the adventures of Perseus and Danae when they were cast out of Argos by Akrisios and set to out sea in a floating chest. It is not unreasonable, however, to suspect that this eventually popular setting was not original to early epic. For related later renditions with some exceptional features cf. Ovid *Met.*5.236-241; Hyg *Fab* 244.

872 So, ApB 2.4.4; Paus.2.16.3 (below).

[873] The later addition of at least one generation is suggested, for example, by the line of Bellerophon as it is depicted in the *Iliad*. This line runs from Bellerophon's father Glaukos, to Glaukos of Lykia, who confronts Diomedes, in four generations, where Bellerophon is ostensibly portrayed as a younger contemporary of King Proitos (Il.6.119-236). Such an addition is also suggested by the effects of moving Melampous' migration to the reign of Anaxagoras, since on account of that move the line of Proitos would come up significantly short, were it any shorter than it presently is. This pattern, accordingly, zeros in on the circumstances conducive to such an addition, whereas Pausanias, as noted above and below, saw fit to add yet another generation.

[874] viz. including Melampous and Bias, themselves.

[875] In *Odyssey* book 15, as cited below.

[876] Beyond adding Argeios, Pausanias also included a figure named Alektor, who takes the place of the well-known Hiponoos (viz. son of Anaxagoras, father of Kapaneus and, at times, also father of Iphis as well, in turn, the father of Euadne, Kapaneus' wife), whose daughter Periboia was known as Tydeus' mother (cf. Hes fr 12 MW; Σ Il.2.564). Whether in so doing he meant to imply that this was the Alektor mentioned in the *Odyssey* (4.10-12), whose daughter married Megapenthes, son of Menelaos, by a slave woman, is pretty much anyone's guess. In any case, it can at least be said that Pausanias acknowledged two Megapenthes: Megapenthes of Argos (viz. son of Proitos, e.g. 2.16.3, 2.18.1-6) and Megapenthes of Sparta (viz. son of Menelaos, e.g. 2.18.6, 3.18.13, 3.19.9).

BIBLIOGRAPHY

Abramson, H. 1981. "A Hero Shrine for Phrontis at Sounion." *California Studies in Classical Antiquity* 12: 1-19.

Ackerman, H.C. and J.R. Gisler, eds. 1981-1999. *Lexicon iconographicum mythologiae classicae*. [LIMC] 18 vols. Zürich: Artemis.

Adkins, A.W.H. 1971. "Homeric Values and Homeric Society." *Journal of Hellenic Studies* 91: 1-14.

___. 1960. *Merit and Responsibility*. Oxford: Clarendon Press.

Alcock, Susan E. and Robin Osborne, eds. 1994. *Placing the Gods: Sanctuaries and Sacred Space in Ancient Greece*. Oxford: Clarendon Press.

Alden, M.J. 1996. "Genealogy as Paradigm: the Example of Bellerophon." *Hermes* 124.3: 257-263.

Allen, T.W. 1924. *Homer: The Origins and Transmission*. Oxford: Clarendon Press.

___. 1921. *The Homeric Catalogue of Ships*. Oxford: Clarendon Press.

___. 1913a. "The Canonicity of Homer." *Classical Quarterly* 7.4: 221-233.

___. 1913b. "Pisistratus and Homer." *Classical Quarterly* 7.1: 33-51.

___. 1912. "Lives of Homer I & II." *Journal of Hellenic Studies* 32: 250-260; 33: 19-26.

___. 1911. "Homerica I. The Acheans." *Classical Review* 25.8: 233-236.

___. 1910. "The Homeric Catalogue." *Journal of Hellenic Studies* 30: 292-322.

___. 1909. "Argos in Homer." *Classical Quarterly* 3: 81-98.

___. 1908. "The Epic Cycle I & II." *Classical Quarterly* 1 & 2: 64-74 / 81-88.

___. 1907. "The Homeridae." *Classical Quarterly* 1: 135-143.

___. 1906. "Μυρμιδόνων Πόλις." *Classical Review* 20.4: 193-201.

Alroth, Brita and Pontus Hellström, eds. 1996. *Religion and Power in the Ancient Greek World: Proceedings of the Uppsala Symposium*. Motala, Sweden: Motala Grafiska AB.

Alty, J.H.M. 1982. "Dorians and Ionians." *Journal of Hellenic Studies* 102: 1-14.

Anderson, Michael J. 1997. *The Fall of Troy in Early Greek Poetry and Art*. Oxford: Clarendon Press.

Andersen, O. and M. Dickie, eds. 1995. *Homer's World: Fiction, Tradition, Reality*. Bergen: Norwegian Institute at Athens.

Anderson, Greg. 2000. "Alcmeonid Homelands, Political Exile, and the Unification of Attica." *Historia: Zeitschrift für alte Geschichte* 49.4: 387-412.

Anderson, J.K. 1954. "A Topographical and Historical Study of Achaea." *Annual of the British School at Athens* 49: 72-92.

Andrewes, A. 1956. *The Greek Tyrants*. London: Hutchinson University Library.

___. 1949. "The Corinthian Actaeon and Pheidon of Argos." *Classical Quarterly* 43: 70-78.

___. 1951. "Ephoros Book I and the Kings of Argos." *Classical Quarterly* 45: 39-45.

Antonaccio, Carla M. 1995. *An Archaeology of Ancestors: Tomb Cult and Hero Cult in Early Greece*. London: Rowman & Littlefield Publishers.

Apthorp, M.J. 1980. *The Manuscript Evidence for Interpolation in Homer*. Heidelberg: Carl Winter Universitätsverlag.

Armstrong, C.B. 1969. "The Casuality Lists in the Trojan War." *Greece & Rome* 16.1: 30-31.

Athens Comes of Age: From Solon to Salamis. 1978. Papers of a Symposium Sponsored by the Archaeological Institute of America, Princeton Society and the Department of Art and Archaeology, Princeton University. Archaeological Institute of America Publications.

BIBLIOGRAPHY

Aubet, Maria E. 2001. *The Phoenicians and the West: Politics, Colonies and Trade.* 2nd ed. Cambridge: Cambridge University Press.

Bakhuizen, S.C. 1976. *Chalcis-In-Euboea: Iron and Chalcidians Abroad.* Leiden: E.J. Brill.

Barron, J.P. 1974. "New Light on Old Walls: The Murals of the Theseion." *Journal of Hellenic Studies* 92: 20-45.

___. 1964. "Religious Propaganda of the Delian League." *Journal of Hellenic Studies* 84: 35-48.

___. 1962. "Milesian Politics and Athenian Propaganda." *Journal of Hellenic Studies* 82: 1-6.

Barthes, Roland. 1972. *Mythologies.* Trans. Anette Lavers. New York: Noonday Press.

Beloch, K.J. 1912-1927. *Griechishe Geschichte.* 2nd ed. 4 vols. Berlin: de Gruyter, 1967.

Bérard, Claude, ed. 1989. *A City of Images: Iconography and Society in Ancient Greece.* Trans. Deborah Lyons. Princeton: Princeton University Press.

Bernabé, A. 1987. *Poetarum epicorum Graecorum: testimona et fragmenta.* Stuttgart: B.G.Teubner.

Bernal, Martin. 1987. *Black Athena: The Afroasiatic Roots of Classical Civilization.* New Brunswick, NJ: Rutgers University Press.

Beye, Charles R. 1964. "Homeric Battle Narrative and Catalogues." *Harvard Studies in Classical Philology* 68: 345-373.

___. 1961. "A New Meaning for ΝΑΥΣ in the Catalogue." *American Journal of Philology* 82: 370-378.

Bill, Clarence P. 1930. "The Location of the Palace of the Atridae in Greek Tragedy." *Transactions of the American Philological Association* 41: 111-129.

Birchall, A. and R.A. Crossland, eds. 1974. *Bronze Age Migrations in the Aegean: Archaeological and Linguistic Problems in Greek Prehistory.* Park Ridge, NJ: Noyes Press.

Bittlestone, Robert with James Diggle and John Underhill. 2005. *Odysseus Unbound: the Search for Homer's Ithaka.* Cambridge: Cambridge University Press.

Blackman D.J. 1969. "Plautus and Greek Topography." *Proceedings of the American Philological Association* 100: 11-22.

Blegan, Carl W. and Marion Rawson. 1966-1973. *The Palace of Nestor at Pylos in Western Messenia.* 3 vols. Princeton: Princeton University Press.

Bloom, Harold. 1987. *Homer's Iliad: Modern Critical Interpretations.* New York: Chelsea House Publishers.

Blümer, Wilhelm. 2001. *Interpretation archaischer Dichtung: die mythologischen Partien der Erga Hesiods.* Münster: Aschendorff.

Boardman, John.1999. *The Greeks Overseas: Their Early Colonies and Trade.* 4th ed. London: Thames and Hudson.

___. 1972. "Herakles, Peisistratos and Sons." *Revue Archaeologique* Fasc. 1: 57-72.

___. 1965. "Herakles, Peisistratos and Eleusis." *Journal of Hellenic Studies* 95:1-12.

___. 1957a. "Early Euboian Pottery and History." *Annual of the British School at Athens* 52: 1-29.

___. 1957b and H. W. Parke. "The Struggle for the Tripod and the First Sacred War." *Journal of Hellenic Studies* 77.2 276-282.

Boegehold, Alan L. and Adele C. Scafuro, eds. 1994. *Athenian Identity and Civic Ideology.* Baltimore: Johns Hopkins University Press.

Boer, W. Den. 1954. *Laconian Studies.* Amsterdam: North-Holland Publishing Co.

Bonnefoy, Yves. 1992. *Mythologies: Dictionnaire des mythologies et des religions des sociétés traditionnelles du monde antique.* Trans. Gerald Hingisblum. Chicago : University of Chicago Press.

Bosworth, Brian A. 2003. "Plus ça change.... Ancient Historians and their Sources." *Classical Antiquity* 22.2: 167-197.

Bowra, C.M. 1935. *Early Greek Elegists*. Cambridge, MA: Harvard University Press.

___. 1934 "Stesichorus in the Peloponnese." *Classical Quarterly* 18.2: 115-119.

___. 1930. *Tradition and Design in the Iliad*. Oxford: Clarendon Press. Rpt. Westport, CT: Greenwood Press, 1977.

Bradeen, Donald W. 1947. "The Lelantine War and Pheidon of Argos." *Transactions of the American Philological Association* 78: 223-241.

Braswell, B.K. 1971. "Mythological Innovation in the *Iliad*." *Classical Quarterly* 21: 16-26.

Bremmer, Jan. 1998. "Greek Cultic Poetry: Some Ideas Behind a Forthcoming Edition."*Mnemosyne* 51.5: 513-524.

___. 1997. "Myth as Propaganda: Athens and Sparta." *Zeitschrift Für Papyrologie Und Epigraphik* 117: 9-17.

___. 1994. *Greek Religion. Greece & Rome: New Surveys in the Classics*, #24. Oxford: Oxford University Press.

___. 1987. ed. *Interpretations of Greek Mythology*. London: Croom Helm.

Briggs, Ward W. and William M. Calder III, eds. 1990. *Classical Scholarship: A Biographical Encyclopedia*. Garland reference library of the humanities: vol. 928. New York: Garland Publishers.

Brijder, H.A.G. 1984. *Ancient Greek and Related Pottery: Proceedings of the International Base Symposium in Amsterdam 12-15 April 1984*. Amsterdam: Allard Pierson series, vol. 5.

Broadbent, Molly. 1968. *Studies in Greek Genealogy*. Leiden: E.J. Brill.

Buck, Carl Darling. 1955. *The Greek Dialects*. Rpt. of *Introduction to the Study of the Greek Dialects*. New York, 1910. Chicago: University of Chicago Press.

Buck, Robert J. 1979. *A History of Boeotia*. Edmonton: University of Alberta Press.

Buitron-Oliver, Diana, ed. 1991. *New Perspectives in Early Greek Art. Symposium Papers* 6. Washington: National Gallery of Art.

Burckhardt, Jacob. 1998. *The Greeks and Greek Civilization*. Oswyn Murray ed., Trans. Sheila Stern. New York: St Martin's Press.

Burgess, Jonathan S. 2001. *The Tradition of the Trojan War in Homer and the Epic Cycle*. Baltimore: Johns Hopkins University Press.

____. 1996. "The Non-Homeric Cypria" *Transactions of the American Philological Association* 126: 77-99.

Burkert, Walter. 1992. *The Orientalizing Revolution: Near Eastern Influence on Greek Culture in the Early Archaic Age*. M.E. Pinder and Walter Burkert trans. Cambridge: Harvard University Press.

____. 1985. *Greek Religion*. J. Raffan Trans. Cambridge: Harvard University Press.

____. 1979. *Structure and History in Greek Mythology and Ritual*. Berkeley: University of California Press.

____. 1970. "Jason, Hypsipyle, and New Fire at Lemnos: A Study in Myth and Ritual." *Classical Quarterly* 64: 1-16.

Burn, A.R. 1929. "The So-Called 'Trade-Leagues' in Early Greek History and the Lelantine War." *Journal of Hellenic Studies* 49: 14-37.

Burnett, Anne Pippin. 1985. *The Art of Bacchylides*. Cambridge, MA: Harvard University Press.

Burstein, Stanley M., Ramsay MacMullen, Kurt A. Raaflaub and Allen M. Ward . 1997. *Ancient History: Recent Work and New Directions*. Regina Books: Claremont, CA.

Bury, J.B. 1937. *A History of Greece to the Death of Alexander the Great*. 2nd ed. New York: Random House.

Buxton, Richard, ed. 1999. *From Myth to Reason? Studies in the Development of Greek Thought*. Oxford: Oxford University Press.

____. 1994. *Imaginary Greece: The Contexts of Mythology*. Cambridge: Cambridge University Press.

____. 1992. "Imaginary Greek Mountains." *Journal of Hellenic Studies* 112: 1-15.

Cairns, Douglas L. 2001. *Oxford Readings in Homer's Iliad.* Oxford University Press.

Calder, William M. III and David A. Traill, eds. 1986. *Myth, Scandal, and History: The* Heinrich Schliemann Controversy and a First Edition of the Mycenaean Diary. Detroit: Wayne State University Press.

Calame, Claude. 1989. *Métamorphoses du mythe en Grèce antique.* Genève: Labor et Fides.

Cancik, Hubert and Helmuth Schneider, eds. 1996-2003. *Der neue Pauly: Enzyklopadie der Antike.* Stuttgart: J.B. Metzler.

___. 2002- *Brill's New Pauly: Encyclopaedia of the Ancient World.* English Edition. Christine F. Salazar and Francis G. Gentry, eds.

Carpenter, Thomas H. and Christopher A. Faraone, eds. 1993. *Masks of Dionysus.* Ithaca, NY: Cornell University Press.

Carter, Jane B. and Sarah P. Morris. 1995. *The Ages of Homer: A Tribute to Emily Townsend Vermeule.* Austin: University of Texas Press.

Cartledge, Paul, ed. 1985. *Crux: Essays Presented to G.E.M. de Ste. Croix on his 75th Birthday. History of Political Thought* 6.1-2. London: Duckworth / Imprint Academic.

___. 1982. "Sparta and Samos: A Special Relationship." *Classical Quarterly* 32.2: 243-265.

___. 1980. "The Peculiar Position of Sparta in the Development of the Greek City-State." *Proceedings of the Royal Irish Academy* 80c.6: 91-108.

___. 1979. *Sparta and Lakonia: A Regional History 1300-362 B.C.* London: Routledge & Kegan Paul.

Casanova, Angelo. 1979. "Catalogo, Eee e Grandi Eee nella tradizione ellenistica." *Prometheus: Rivista quadrimestrale di studi classici.* 5.3: 217-240.

Cassola, Fillipo. 1953. "Le genealogie mitiche e la coscienza nazionale greca." *Rendiconti della Accademia di Archeologia Lettere e Belle Arti."* 35: 279-304.

Castriota, David. 1992. *Myth, Ethos, and Actuality: Official Art in Fifth Century B.C. Athens.* Madison: University of Wisconsin Press.

Cawkwell, G.L. 1993. "Sparta and Her Allies in the Sixth Century," *Classical Quarterly* 43.3: 364-376.

Cerchiai, Luca, Lorena Janelli and Fausto Longo. 2002. *The Greek Cities of Magna Graecia and Sicily.* Los Angeles: J. Paul Getty Museum.

Chadwick, H. Munro. 1912. *The Heroic Age.* Cambridge: Cambridge University Press.

Chadwick, John. 1973. *Documents in Mycenaean Greek.* 2nd ed. Cambridge: Cambridge University Press.

___. 1972 "The Mycenaean Documents." In W.A. McDonald and G.R. Rapp, eds. *The Minnesota Messenia Expedition: Reconstructing a Bronze Age Regional Environment.* Minneapolis: University of Minnesota Press.

Childs, William A.P. 1993. "Herodotus, Archaic Chronology, and the Temple of Apollo at Delphi." *Jahrbuch des deutschen archäologischen Instituts* 108 Berlin: Walter de Gruyter.

Clay, Jenny Strauss. 2005. *Hesiod's Cosmos.* Cambridge: Cambridge University Press.

___. 1998. "What the Muses Sang: *Theogony* 1-115." *Greek Roman and Byzantine Studies* 29.4: 323-333.

___. 1989. *The Politics of Olympus. Form and Meaning in the Major Homeric Hymns.* Princeton: Princeton University Press.

Clogg, Richard. 1992. *A Concise History of Greece.* Cambridge: Cambridge University Press.

Cohen, David. 1991. *Law, Sexuality, and Society: The Enforcement of Morals in Classical Athens.* Cambridge: Cambridge University Press.

Cohen, Ivan M. 1986. "The Hesiodic *Catalogue of Women* and the *Megalai Ehoiai.*" *Phoenix* 40.2 127-142.

Coldstream, J.N. 2003. *Geometric Greece: 900-700 B.C.* 2nd ed. London: Routledge.

___. 1976. "Hero Cults in the Age of Homer." *Journal of Hellenic Studies* 96: 8-17.

___. 1968. *Greek Geometric Pottery: A Survey of Ten Local Styles and Their Chronology.* London: Methuen.

Collard, C., M.J. Cropp and K.H. Lee. 1997. *Euripides Selected Fragmentary Plays, Vol. I.* Warminster: Aris & Phillips Ltd.

Combellack, Frederick M. 1976. "Homer the Innovator." *Classical Philology* 71.1: 44-55.

___. 1965. "Some Formulary Illogicalities in Homer." *Transactions of the American Philological Association* 96: 41-56.

___. 1950. "Contemporary Unitarians and Homeric Originality." *American Journal of Philology* 71.4: 337-364.

___. 1948. "The Identity and Origin of Eurychus in the Ships' Catalogue of Hyginus." *American Journal of Philology* 69 1948: 190-196.

Conacher, D.J. 1996. *Aeschylus: The Earlier Plays and Related Studies.* Toronto: University of Toronto Press.

___. 1987. *Aeschylus' Oresteia: A Literary Commentary.* Toronto: University of Toronto Press.

Connelly, Joan Breton. 2007. *Portrait of a Priestess: Women and Ritual in Ancient Greece.* Princeton: Princeton University Press.

___. 1996 "Parthenon and Parthenoi: A Mythological Interpretation of the Parthenon Frieze." *American Journal of Archaeology* 100.1: 53-80.

Connor, W.R. 1993. "The Ionian Era of Athenian Civic Identity." *Proceedings of the American Philosophical Society* 137.2: 194-206.

___. 1987. "Tribes, Festivals, and Processions: Civil Ceremonial and Political Manipulation in Archaic Greece." *Journal of Hellenic Studies* 109: 40-50.

Cook, R.M. 1983. "Art and Epic in Archaic Greece." *Bulletin Antieke Beschaving: Annual Papers on Classical Archaeology* 58: 1-10.

___. 1962. *The Greeks in Ionia and the East*. London: Thames and Hudson.

___.1946. "Ionia and Greece in the Eighth and Seventh Centuries." *Journal of Hellenic Studies* 66: 67-98.

___. 1937. "The Date of the Hesiodic Shield." *Classical Quarterly* 31: 204-214.

de Coulanges, Numa Denis Fustel .1864. *La cité antique*. Trans. A. Momigliano and S.C. Humphreys. Baltimore: Johns Hopkins University Press:1980.

Coulson, William and Olga Palagia, eds. 1993. *Sculpture from Arkadia and Laconia: Proceedings of an International Conference at the American School of Classical Studies at Athens April 10-14, 1992*. Oxbow, Monograph 30.

Crielaard, Jan P., ed. 1995. *Homeric Questions: Essays in Philology, Ancient History and Archaeology, Including the Papers of A Conference Organized by the Netherlands Institute at Athens (15 May 1993)*. Amsterdam: J.C. Gieben.

Davies, Malcolm. 1991. *Trachiniae*. Oxford: Clarendon Press.

___. 1989a. *The Greek Epic Cycle*. London: Duckworth.

___. 1989b. "The Date of the Epic Cycle." *Glotta* 67.1-2: 89-100.

___. 1988. *Epicorum Graecorum Fragmenta*. Göttingen: Vandenhoeck and Ruprecht.

Davison, J.A. 1955. "Peisistratus and Homer." *Transactions of the American Philological Association* 86: 1-21.

Depew, Mary and Dirk Obbink, eds. 2000. *Matrices of Genre: Authors, Canons and Society*. Cambridge, MA: Harvard University Press.

Desborough, V. 1972. *The Greek Dark Ages*. London: Ernest Benn Limited.

Descceudres, J-P., ed. 1990. *Greek Colonists and Native Populations*. Oxford: Clarendon Press.

Detienne, Marcel and J-P Vernant, eds. 1989. *The Cuisine of Sacrifice Among the Greeks*. Trans. P. Wissing. Chicago: University of Chicago Press. Trans. of *La cuisine du sacrifice en pays grec*. Paris: Editions Gallimard, 1979.

___. 1986. *The Creation of Mythology*. Trans. M. Cook. Chicago: University of Chicago Press. Trans. of *L'invention de la mythologie*. Paris, 1981.

___. 1957. Diamantopoulos, A. "The Danaid Trilogy of Aeschylus." *Journal of Hellenic Studies* 77.2: 220-229.

Diehl, Ernestus. 1949-1952. *Anthologia lyrica Graeca*. 3 vols. 3rd ed. Leipsig: B.G. Teubner.

Dietrich, B.C. 1988. "Divine Personality and Personification." *Kernos* 1: 19-28.

Dodds, E.R. 1951. *The Greeks and the Irrational*. Berkeley: University of California Press.

Donlan, Walter. 1989. "The Unequal Exchange between Glaukos and Diomedes in Light of the Homeric Gift-Economy." *Phoenix* 43.1: 1-15.

___. 1985. "The Social Groups of Dark Age Greece." *Classical Philology* 80.4: 293-308.

Dörpfeld, Wilhelm. 1927. *Alt-Ithaka ein Beitrag zur Homer-Frage: Studien un Ausgrabungen aus der Insel Leukas-Ithaka*. Munich: R. Uhde.

Dougherty, Carol and Leslie Kurke, eds. 1993. *Cultural Poetics in Archaic Greece: Cult, Performance, Politics*. Cambridge: Cambridge University Press.

Dowden, Ken. 1992. *The Uses of Greek Mythology*. London: Routledge.

Drachmann, A.B. 1922. *Atheism in Pagan Antiquity*. Copenhagen: Gyldendal.

___. 1903-1927. *Scholia vetera in Pindari carmina*. 3 vols. Leipsig: B.G. Teubner.

Drews, Robert. 1988. *The Coming of the Greeks: Indo-European Conquests in the Aegean and the Near East.* Princeton: Princeton University Press.

———. 1983. *Basileus: The Evidence for Kingship in Geometric Greece.* New Haven: Yale University Press.

———. 1979a. "Argos and Argives in the *Iliad*." *Classical Philology.* 74.2: 111-135.

———. 1979b. "Phoenicians, Carthage and the Spartan Eunomia." *American Journal of Philology* 100.1: 45-58.

———. 1976. "The Earliest Greek Settlements on the Black Sea." *Journal of Hellenic Studies* 96: 18-31.

———. 1973. *The Greek Accounts of Eastern History.* Washington D.C. Center for Hellenic Studies.

———. 1965. "Assyria in Classical Universal Histories." *Historia: Zeitschrift für alte Geschichte* 14: 129-142.

Dunbabin, T.J. 1957. *The Greeks and Their Eastern Neighbors: Studies in the Relations Between Greece and the Countries of the Near East in the Eighth and Seventh Centuries.* London: Unwin Brothers Ltd.

———. 1948. "The Early History of Corinth." *Journal of Hellenic Studies* 68: 59-69.

Easterling, P. and J.V. Muir, eds. 1985. *Greek Religion and Society.* Cambridge: Cambridge University Press.

———. 1982. ed. *Trachiniae.* Cambridge: Cambridge University Press.

Edmonds, L., ed. 1990. *Approaches to Greek Myth.* Baltimore: Johns Hopkins University Press.

Edwards, Mark W. 1990. "Neoanalysis and Beyond." *Classical Antiquity* 9.2: 311-325.

———. 1980. "The Structure of Homeric Catalogues." *Transactions of the American Philological Association* 110: 81-103.

Edwards, Ruth B. 1979. *Kadmos the Phoenician: A Study in Greek Legends and the Mycenaean Age.* Amsterdam: Adolf M. Hakkert.

Emlen, Julia, Anthony Molho, and Kurt Raaflaub, eds. 1991. *City States in Classical Antiquity and Medieval Italy*. Stuttgart: Franz Steiner Verlag.

Emlyn-Jones, C.J. 1980. *The Ionians and Hellenism*. London: Routeledge.

Erbse, Hartmut. 1969-1988. 7 vols. *Scholia Graeca in Homeri Iliadem*. Berlin: Walter de Gruyter.

Farnell, L.R. 1896-1934. 5 vols. *The Cults of the Greek States*. Oxford: Clarendon Press.

___. 1921. *Greek Hero Cults and Ideas of Immortality*. Oxford: Clarendon Press.

Fenik, Bernard. 1986. *Homer and the Nibelungenlied: Comparative Studies in Epic Style*. Cambridge, MA: Harvard University Press.

___. 1978. ed. *Homer: Tradition and Invention*. Leiden: E.J. Brill.

___. 1974. *Studies in the Odyssey. Hermes Zeitschrift für Klassische Philologie*. Einzelschriften Heft 30. Wiesbaden: Franz Steiner Verlag.

___. 1968. "Typical Battle Scenes in the Iliad." *Hermes* 21.

Ferguson, William S. 1938. "The Salaminioi of Heptaphylai and Sounion." *Hesperia* 8.1: 1-74.

Ferrari, Gloria. 2002. "Myth and Genre on Athenian Vases." *Classical Antiquity* 22.1: 37-54.

___. 2000. "The *Ilioupersis* in Athens." *Harvard Studies in Classical Philology* 100: 119-150.

Fick, August. 1886. *Die homerische Ilias*. Göttingen: Vandenhoeck und Ruprecht.

___. 1883. *Die homerische Odyssee*. Göttingen: R. Peppmüller.

Figueira, Thomas J. 1993. *Excursions in Epichoric History: Aiginetan Essays*. Lanham, MD: Rowman & Littlefield, Inc.

Finkelberg, M. 2005. *Greeks and Pre-Greeks: Aegean Prehistory and the Greek Heroic Tradition*. Cambridge: Cambridge University Press.

___. 2003. and Guy G. Stroumsa, eds. *Homer, the Bible, and Beyond: Literary and Religious Canons in the Ancient World*. Leiden: Brill.

___. 2000. "The *Cypria*, the *Iliad*, and the Problem of Multiformity in Oral and Written Tradition." *Classical Philology* 95.1: 1-11.

___. 1998. "The Geography of the *Prometheus Vinctus*." *Rheinisches Museum für Philologie* 141.2: 119-141.

___. 1994. "The Dialect Continuum of Ancient Greek." *Harvard Studies in Classical Philology* 96: 1-36.

___. 1991. "Royal Succession in Heroic Greece" *Classical Quarterly* 41.2: 303-316.

___. 1988. "Ajax's Entry in the Hesiodic *Catalogue of Women*." *Classical Quarterly* 38.1: 31-41.

Finley, M.I. 1986. *The Use and Abuse of History*. London: Hogarth Press.

___. 1981. *Economy and Society in Ancient Greece*. London: Chatto & Windus.

___.1964. J.L. Caskey, G.S. Page, D.L. Page. "The Trojan War" *Journal of Hellenic Studies* 84: 1-20.

___. 1957. "Homer and Mycenae: Property and Tenure." *Historia: Zeitschrift für alte Geschichte* 6: 133-159.

___. 1954. *The World of Odysseus*. 2nd ed. London: Penguin, 1991.

Fisher, Nick and Hans van Wees. 1998. *Archaic Greece: New Approaches and New Evidence*. London: Duckworth.

Foley, Helene P. 2001. *Female Acts in Greek Tragedy*. Princeton: Princeton University Press.

___. 1985. *Ritual Irony: Poetry and Sacrifice in Euripides*. Ithaca: Cornell University Press.

Foley, John M. 1999. *Homer's Traditional Art*. University Park: Pennsylvania State University Press.

Fontenrose, Joseph. 1988. *Didyma: Apollo's Oracle, Cult, and Companions*. Berkeley: University of California Press.

___. 1974. "Work, Justice, and Hesiod's Five Ages." *Classical Philology* 69.1: 1-16.

———. 1968. "The Hero as Athlete." *California Studies in Classical Antiquity* 1: 73-104.

———. 1959. *Python: A Study of Delphic Myth and its Origins.* Berkeley: University of California Press.

———. 1948. "The Sorrows of Ino and of Procne." *Transactions of the American Philological Association* 79: 125-167.

Forbes Irving, P.M.C. 1990. *Metamorphosis in Greek Myths.* Oxford: Clarendon Press.

Fornara, Charles W. 1983. *The Nature of History in Ancient Greece and Rome.* Berkeley: University of California Press.

Forrest, W.G. 1968. *A History of Sparta: 950-192 BC.* Rpt. London: Duckworth, 1980.

———. 1957. "Colonization and the Rise of Delphi" *Historia: Zeitschrift für alte Geschichte* 6: 160-175.

Foster, Benjamin R. 1995. *From Distant Days: Myths, Tales and Poetry of Ancient Mesopotamia.* Bethesda, Maryland: CDL Press.

Fowler, Robert L., ed. 2004. *The Cambridge Companion to Homer.* Cambridge: Cambridge University Press.

———. 1998. "Genealogical Thinking, Hesiod's *Catalogue*, and the Creation of the Hellenes." *Proceedings of the Cambridge Philological Society* 44: 1-19.

Fränkel, Hermann F. 1973. *Early Greek Poetry and Philosophy.* Trans. Moses Hadas and James Willis. New York: Harcourt Brace Jovanovich.

Frost, Frank J. 1990. "Peisistratos, the Cults and the Unification of Attica." *Ancient World* 21.1.

Gantz, Timothy. 1993. *Early Greek Myth: A Guide to Literary and Artistic Sources.* 2 vols. Baltimore: Johns Hopkins University Press.

———. 1980. "The Aischylean Tetralogy: Attested and Conjectured Groups." *American Journal of Philology* 101.2: 133-164.

Garland, Robert. 1992. *Introducing New Gods: The Politics of Athenian Religion*. London: Duckworth.

Garvie, A.F. 1969. *Aeschylus' Supplices: Play and Trilogy*. Cambridge: Cambridge University Press.

Geddes, A.G. 1984. "Who's Who in Homeric Society?" *Classical Quarterly* 34.1: 17-36.

Gerson, L.P. 1990. *God and Greek Philosophy: Studies in the Early History of Natural Theology*. London: Routledge.

Giovannini, A. 1969. *Etude historique sur les origines du catalogue des vaisseaux*. Berne: Editions Francke.

Golden, Mark and Peter Toohey, eds. 1997. *Inventing Ancient Culture: Historicism, Periodization and the Ancient World*. London: Routledge.

Goldhill, Simon and R. Osborne, eds. 1999. *Performance Culture and Athenian Democracy*. Cambridge: Cambridge University Press.

Gomme, A.W. 1937. *Essays in Greek History and Literature*. Oxford: Basil Blackwell.

____. 1913. "The Legend of Cadmus and the Logographoi I & II." *Journal of Hellenic Studies* 33: 53-72, 223-245.

Goody, Jack and S.J. Tambiah. 1973a. *Bridewealth and Dowry. Cambridge Papers in Social Anthropology 7*. Cambridge: Cambridge University Press.

____. 1973b. ed. *The Character of Kinship*. Cambridge: Cambridge University Press.

____. 1968. ed. *Literacy in Traditional Societies*. Cambridge: Cambridge University Press.

Gorman, Vanessa B. 2001. *Miletos, the Ornament of Ionia*. Ann Arbor: University of Michigan Press.

Graf, Fritz. 1993. *Greek Mythology an Introduction*. Trans. Thomas Marier. Baltimore: Johns Hopkins University Press.

Graham, A.J. 1992. "Abdera and Teos." *Journal of Hellenic Studies* 112: 44-73.

___. 1983. *Colony and Mother City in Ancient Greece*. 2nd ed. Chicago: Aris Publishers.

___. 1971 "Patterns in Early Greek Colonization." *Journal of Hellenic Studies* 91: 35-47.

Gray, D.H.F. 1958. "Mycenaean Names in Homer." *Journal of Hellenic Studies* 78: 43-48.

Green, Peter. 1997. *The Argonautika*. Berkeley: University of California Press.

___. 1984. *Lesbos and the Cities of Asia Minor*. Austin, TX: Dougherty Foundation.

Greenhalgh, P.A.L. 1972. "Patriotism in the Homeric World." *Historia: Zeitschrift für alte Geschichte* 21.3: 528-537.

Griffin, Audrey. 1982. *Sikyon*. Oxford: Clarendon Press.

Griffin, Jasper. 1986. "Words and Speakers in Homer." *Journal of Hellenic Studies* 106: 36-57.

___. 1977. "The Epic Cycle and the Uniqueness of Homer." *Journal of Hellenic Studies* 97: 39-53.

Griffith, Mark and Donald J. Mastronarde, eds. 1990. *Cabinet of the Muses: Essays on Classical and Comparative Literature in Honor of Thomas G. Rosenmeyer*. Atlanta: Scholars Press.

___. 1983. Aeschylus: *Prometheus Bound*. Cambridge: Cambridge University Press.

Gruen, Eric. 1993. "Cultural Fictions and Cultural Identity." *Transactions of the American Philological Association* 123: 1-14.

Guthrie, W.K.C. 1971. *The Sophists*. Cambridge: Cambridge University Press.

___. 1954. *The Greeks and Their Gods*. Boston: Beacon Press.

Habicht, Christian. 1985. *Pausanias' Guide to Ancient Greece*. Berkeley: University of California Press.

Hack, R.K. 1929. "Homer and the Cult of Heroes." *Transactions of the American Philological Association* 60: 57-74.

Hägg, Robin, ed. 1992. *The Iconography of Greek Cult in the Archaic and Classical Periods.* Athens: Centre d'Etude de la Religion Grecque Antique.

___, Nanno Marinatos and Gullög C. Nordquist, eds. 1988. *Early Greek Cult Practice: Proceedings of the Fifth International Symposium at the Swedish Institute at Athens, 26-29 June, 1986.* Stockholm: Paul Astroms Forlag.

Hall, Edith. 1989. *Inventing the Barbarian: Greek Self-definition Through Tragedy.* Oxford: Clarendon Press.

___. 1988. "When Did the Trojans Turn into Phrygians? Alcaeus 42.15." *Zeitschrift für Papyrologie und Epigraphik* 73: 15-18.

Hall, J.M. 2002. *Hellenicity: Between Ethnicity and Culture.* Chicago: University of Chicago Press.

___. 1997. *Ethnic Identity in Greek Antiquity.* Cambridge: Cambridge University Press.

___. 1995. "How Argive was the 'Argive' Heraion: the political and cultic geography of the Argive plain 900 – 400 BC." *American Journal of Archaeology* 99: 577-613.

Hallager, Erik, Birgitta Hallager and Maria Vlassakis. 1992. "New Linear B Tablets From Khania." *Kadmos* 31.1: 61-87.

Halliwell, Stephen. 1984. "Plato and Aristotle on the Denial of Tragedy." *Proceedings of the Cambridge Philological Society* 30: 49-71.

Hallo, William W. & William K. Simpson. 1971. *The Ancient Near East.* Harcourt Brace Jovanovich.

Hamilton, Richard. 1989. *The Architecture of Hesiodic Poetry.* Baltimore: Johns Hopkins University Press.

Hammond, N.G.L. 1976. *Migrations and Invasions in Greece and Adjacent Areas.* Park Ridge, NJ: Noyes Press.

Hansen, Mogens Herman. 1993. *The Ancient Greek City-State: Symposium on the Occasion of the 250th Anniversary of The Royal Danish Academy of Sciences and Letters July, 1-4 1992.* Copenhagen: Det Kongelige Danske Videnskabernes Selskab.

Harder, Annette. 1985. *Euripides' Kresphontes and Archelaos: Introduction, Text and Commentary. Mnemosyne Supplentum* 87. Leiden: E.J. Brill.

Harris, William V. 1989. *Ancient Literacy*. Cambridge, MA: Harvard University Press.

Harrison, Thomas, ed. 2002. *Greeks and Barbarians*. Edinburgh: Edinburgh University Press.

Havelock, Eric A. 1982. *The Literate Revolution in Greece and Its Cultural Consequences*. Princeton: Princeton University Press.

___. 1963. *Preface to Plato*. Cambridge, MA: Harvard University Press.

Hazlitt, William. 1851. *The Classical Gazetter: A Dictionary of Ancient Sites*. Rpt. 1995. London: Guernsey Press.

Henige, David, P. 1974. *The Chronology of Oral Tradition: Quest for a Chimera*. Oxford: Clarendon Press.

Herington, C.J. and J. Scully, Trans. 1975. Aeschylus' *Prometheus Bound*. New York: Oxford University Press.

Herman, G. 1990. "Patterns of Name Diffusion Within the Greek World and Beyond." *Classical Quarterly* 40.2: 349-363.

___. 1987. *Ritualized Friendship and the Greek City*. Cambridge: Cambridge University Press.

Herzfeld, Michael. 1981. *Ours Once More: Folklore, Ideology, and the Making of Modern Greece*. Austin: University of Texas Press.

Heubeck, Alfred. 1988-1992. *A Commentary on Homer's Odyssey*. 3 vols. Oxford: Clarendon Press.

___. 1954. *Der Odyssee-Dichter und die Ilias*. Erlangen: Druck von Junge & Sohn.

Higbie, Carolyn. 2002. "Diomedes' Genealogy and Ancient Criticism." *Arethusa* 35: 173-188.

Hobsbawm, Eric and Terence Ranger, eds. 1983. *The Invention of Tradition*. Cambridge: Cambridge University Press.

Hodder, Ian. 1992. *Theory and Practice in Archaeology*. London: Routledge.

Holley, N.M. 1949. "The Floating Chest." *Journal of Hellenic Studies* 49: 39-47.

Hooker, J.T. 1979. "New Reflections on the Dorian Invasion." *Klio* 61.2: 353-360.

___. 1976. *Mycenaean Greece*. London: Routledge & Kegan Paul.

Hope Simpson, R and J.F. Lazenby. 1970. *The Catalogue of Ships in Homer's Iliad*. Oxford: Clarendon Press.

Hornblower, Simon. 2004. *Thucydides and Pindar: Historical Narrative and the World of Epinikian Poetry*. Oxford: Oxford University Press.

___. 1994, ed. *Greek Historiography*. Oxford: Clarendon Press.

Hubbard, Thomas K. 1992. "Remaking Myth and Rewriting History: Cult Tradition in Pindar's *Ninth Nemean*." *Harvard Studies in Classical Philology*. 94: 77-111.

___. 1991. "Theban Nationalism and Poetic Apology in Pindar. *Pythian 9.76-96*." *Rheinisches Museum für Philologie* 134: 22-38.

___. 1987. "Two Notes on the Myth of Aeacus in Pindar." *Greek, Roman & Byzantine Studies* 28: 5-22.

Humphreys, S.C. 1978. *Anthropology and the Greeks*. London: Routledge.

Hurt, H.V. and J. Pinsent, eds. 1992. *Homer 1987: Papers of the Third Greenbank Colloquium*. Liverpool: Liverpool Classical Papers 2.

Hunter, Richard, ed. 2005. *The Hesiodic Catalogue of Women*. Cambridge: Cambridge University Press.

Huxley, G.L. 2006. "Olympiad Dating" Rev. of *Discrepancies in Olympiad Dating and* Chronological Problems in Archaic Peloponnesian History, by P-J Shaw. Classical Review 56.1: 148-151.

___. 1978. "Portus Persicus." Philologus 122.1.

___. 1975. "The Malian Boat: Aristotle F 544." *Philologus* 119.1.

___. 1969. *Greek Epic Poetry from Eumelos to Panyassis*. Cambridge, MA: Harvard University Press.

___. 1969. "Aigai in Alkaios." *Greek, Roman, and Byzantine Studies* 10.1: 5-11.

___. 1967. "A Problem in the Kypria." *Greek Roman and Byzantine Studies* 8: 25-27.

___. 1966. "The Numbers in the Homeric Catalogue of Ships." *Greek Roman and Byzantine Studies* 7: 313-318.

___. 1961. *Early Sparta*. Cambridge, MA: Harvard University Press.

Jacoby, Felix. 1949. *Atthis: The Local Chronicles of Ancient Athens*. Oxford: Clarendon Press.

___.1947a. "Some Remarks on Ion of Chios." *Classical Quarterly* 41.1-2: 1-17.

___.1947b. "The First Athenian Prose Writer".*Mnemosyne* 3.13: 13-64.

___.1923-1958. *Die Fragmente der griechischen Historiker*. Berlin: Weidmann.

Janko, Richard. 1998. "The Homeric Poems as Oral Dictated Texts." *Classical Quarterly* 48.1: 1-13.

___. 1990. "The *Iliad* and it Editors: Dictation and Redaction." *Classical Antiquity* 9.2: 326-356.

___. 1986. "The Shield of Heracles and the Legend of Cycnus." *Classical Quarterly* 36.1: 38-59.

___. 1982. *Homer, Hesiod and the Hymns: Diachronic Development in Epic Diction*. Cambridge: Cambridge Univ. Press.

Jeffery, L.H. 1976. *Archaic Greece: The City States c.700-500 B.C.* New York: St. Martin's Press.

___. 1965. "The Battle of *Oinoe* in the Stoa Poikile: A Problem in Greek Art and History." *Annual of the British School at Athens* 60: 41-57.

___. 1961. *The Local Scripts of Archaic Greece: A Study of the Origin of the Greek Alphabet and Its Development from the Eighth to the Fifth Centuries B.C.* Oxford: Clarendon Press.

Johansen, H. Friis and E.W. Whittle. 1980. *Aeschylus - The Suppliants*. 3 vols. Copenhagen: I Kommission hos Gyldendalske Boghandel.

Jones, Nicholas P. 1980. "The Order of the Dorian Phylai." *Classical Philology* 75.3: 197-215.

Jones, P.V. 1992. "The Past in Homer's Odyssey." *Journal of Hellenic Studies* 112: 74-90.

Kagan, D. 1982. "The Dates of the Earliest Coins." *American Journal of Archaeology* 86: 343-360.

Kampitsis, Ioannis. 1975. *Μινυάδες και Προιτίδες: Τα μυθολογικά δεδομένα. Επιστημονική Επετηρίδα Φιλοσοφικής Σχολής* 3. Δωδώνη: Πανεπιστημίο Ιωαννίνων.

Kannicht, Richard. 1982. "Poetry and Art: Homer and the Monuments Afresh." *Classical Antiquity* 13.1: 70-86.

Kearns, Emily. 1989. *The Heroes of Attica*. London: Institute of Classical Studies Bulletin Supplement 57.

Kebric, Robert B. 1983. *The Paintings in the Cnidian Lesche at Delphi and Their Historical Context. Mnemosyne Supplementum 80*. Leiden: E.J. Brill.

Kelly, Thomas. 1976. *A History of Argos to 500 B.C.* Minneapolis: University of Minnesota Press.

___. 1974. "Argive Foreign Policy in the Fifth Century B.C." *Classical Philology* 69.2: 81-99.

___. 1970a. "Did the Argives Defeat the Spartans at Hysiae in 669 B.C.?" *American Journal of Philology* 91.1: 31-42.

___. 1970b. "The Traditional Enmity between Sparta and Argos: the birth and development of a myth." *American Historical Review* 75.4: 971-1003.

Kinkel, G. 1877. *Epicorum Graecorum Fragmenta*. Leipsig: B.G. Teubner.

Kirk, G.S. 1985-1993. *The Iliad: A Commentary*. 6 vols. Cambridge: Cambridge University Press.

___. 1974. *The Nature of Greek Myths*. London: Penguin.

___. 1972. "Greek Mythology: Some New Perspectives." *Journal of Hellenic Studies* 92: 74-85.

___. 1964. and J.E. Raven, eds. *The Presocratic Philosophers*. Cambridge: Cambridge University Press.

___. 1962. *The Songs of Homer*. Cambridge: Cambridge University Press.

Knox, Bernard. 1990. Introduction. *The Iliad of Homer*. Trans. Robert Fagles. New York: Viking Penguin.

___. 1979. *Word and Action: Essays on the Ancient Theatre*. Baltimore: Johns Hopkins University Press.

Koster, W.J.W. 1960-1977. *Scholia in Aristophanem*. 4 vols. Groningen: Bouma's Boekhuis B.V.

Kron, Uta. 1976. "Die zehn attischen Phylenhoren: Geschichte, Mythos, Kult, und Darst." *Mitteilunges des Deutschen Archäologischen Instituts. Athenische Abteilung. Beiheft: 5*. Berlin: Mann.

Kullman, Wolfgang. 1984. "Oral Poetry Theory and Neoanalysis." *Greek, Roman, and Byzantine Studies* 25: 307-324.

___. 1960. *Die Quellen der Ilias*. *Hermes* Einzelschriften 14. Wiesbaden: F. Steiner.

Kurke, Leslie. 1991. *The Traffic in Praise: Pindar and the Poetics of Social Economy*. Ithaca: Cornell University Press.

Kurtz, Donna and Brian Sparkes. 1982. *The Eye of Greece: Studies in the Art of Athens*. Cambridge: Cambridge University Press.

Lang, Andrew. 1906. *Homer and His Age*. Rpt. New York: AMS Press, 1968.

Lang, Mabel L. 1994. "Lineage-Boasting and The Road Not Taken." *Classical Quarterly* 44.1: 7-16.

___. 1989. "Unreal Conditions in Homeric Narrative." *Greek, Roman, and Byzantine Studies* 30.1: 5-26.

Langdon, Susan, ed. 1993. *From Pasture to Polis: Art in the Age of Homer*. Columbia, MO: University of Missouri Press.

Larson, Jennifer. 1995. *Greek Heroine Cults*. Madison: University of Wisconsin Press.

Larson, Stephanie. 2007. *Tales of Epic Ancestry: Boiotian Collective Identity in the Late Archaic and Early Classical Periods*. Stuttgart: Franz Steiner Verlag.

___. 2000. "Boiotia, Athens, the Peisistratids, and the *Odyssey's* Catalogue of Heroines." *Greek Roman and Byzantine Studies* 41: 193-222.

Latacz, Joachim. 2003. *Homers Ilias. Gesamtkommentar*. Munich/Leipzig: K.G. Saur.

___. 2001. *Troia und Homer: Der Weg zur Losung eines alten Ratsels*. Berlin: Koehler & Amelang.

___. 1996. *Homer: His Art and His World*. Trans. James P. Holoka. Ann Arbor: University of Michigan Press.

Lattimore, Richmond. 1964. *Story Patterns in Greek Tragedy*. Ann Arbor: University of Michigan Press.

Leaf, Walter. 1915. *Homer and History*. London: Macmillian.

___. 1912. *Troy: A Study in Homeric Geography*. London: MacMillan.

___. 1910. "Hesiod and the Dominions of Aias." *Classical Review* 24.6: 179-180.

Leduc, Claudine. 1992. "Marriage in Ancient Greece." in P.S. Pantel, ed. Trans. A. Goldhammer *A History of Women in the West*, vol.1. part 2. ch.5. Cambridge, MA: Harvard University Press.

Lehmann, Gustav A. 1980. "Der *Erste Heilige Krieg* – Eine Fiktion. *Historia: Zeitschrift für alte Geschichte* 29.2: 242-246.

Leick, Gwendolyn. 2001. *Mesopotamia: The Invention of the City*. London: Penguin.

Lemerle, Paul. 1971. Trans. H. Lindsay and A. Moffatt. *Byzantine Humanism: The First Phase*. Australian Association for Byzantine Studies 3. Canberra, 1986.

Lenz, John R. 1993. "Kings and the Ideology of Kingship in Early Greece (c. 1200-700 B.C.): Epic, Archaeology and History." Diss. Columbia University.

Léveque, Pierre. 1988. "Pandora ou la terrifiante féminité." *Kernos* 1: 49-62.

Lévi-Strauss, Claude. 1966. *The Savage Mind*. Chicago: University of Chicago Press.

___. 1955. "The Structural Study of Myths." *Journal of American Folklore* 68: 428-444.

Lesky, Albin. 1961. *Göttliche und menschliche Motivation im homerischen Epos*. Heidelberg: C. Winter.

Lincoln, Bruce. 1997. "Competing Discourses: Rethinking the Prehistory of *Mythos* and *Logos*." *Arethusa* 30.3: 341-367.

___. 1994. *Authority: Construction and Corrosion*. Chicago: University of Chicago Press.

Lloyd, Alan B., ed. 1996. *Battle in Antiquity*. London: Duckworth.

Lobel, E. and D.L. Page, eds. 1955. *Poetarum Lesbiorum Fragmenta*. Oxford: Clarendon Press.

Long, A.A. 1970. "Morals and Values in Homer." *Journal of Hellenic Studies* 90: 121- 39.

Loraux, Nicole. 1981. *Les Enfants d'Athéna: idées athéniennes sur la citoyenneté et la division des sexes*. Paris: F. Maspero.

Lorimer, H.L. 1950. *Homer and the Monuments*. London: Macmillian & Co.

Lord, Albert B. 1971. "Homer, the Trojan War and History." *Journal of the Folklore Institute* 8: 85-92.

___. 1960. *The Singer of Tales*. Cambridge, MA: Harvard University Press.

___. 1953. "Homer's Originality: Oral Dictated Texts." *Transactions of the American Philological Association* 84: 124-134.

___. 1951. "Composition by Theme in Homer and Southslavic Epos." *Transactions of the American Philological Association* 82: 71-101.

Louden, Bruce. 2006. *The Iliad: Structure, Myth, and Meaning*. Baltimore: Johns Hopkins University Press.

Lowenstam, Steven. 1995. "The Sources of the Odysssey Landscapes." *Echos du Monde Classique* 39.14: 193-226.

___. 1993. "The Arming of Achilleus on Early Greek Vases." *Classical Antiquity* 12.2: 199-218.

___. 1992. "The Uses of Vase-Depictions in Homeric Studies." *Transactions of the American Philological Association* 122: 165-198.

Luce, J.V. 1978. "The *Polis* in Homer and Hesiod." *Proceedings of the Royal Irish Academy* 78.1.

MacDowell, Douglas M. 1963. *Athenian Homicide Law in the Age of the Orators*. Manchester: Manchester University Press.

Mackie, C.J. 2001. "The Earliest Jason. What's in a Name?" *Greece & Rome* 48.1: 1-17.

Mackinnon, J.K. 1978. "The Reason for the Danaids' Flight." *Classical Quarterly* 28.1: 74-82.

Macleod, Roy, ed. 2002. *The Library of Alexandra: Centre of Learning in the Ancient World*. London: I.B. Tauris.

Malkin, Irad, ed. 2001. *Ancient Perceptions of Greek Ethnicity*. Cambridge, MA: Harvard University Press.

___. 1998. *The Returns of Odysseus*. Berkeley: University of California Press.

___. 1994. *Myth and Territory in the Spartan Mediterranean*. Cambridge: Cambridge University Press.

Mann, Rupert. 1994. "Pindar's Homer and Pindar's Myths." *Greek Roman and Byzantine Studies* 35.4: 313-337.

Matthews, Victor J. 1975. *Panyassis of Halikarnassos: text and commentary*. *Mnemosyne Supplementum 33*. Leiden: E.J. Brill.

Merkelbach, R. and M.L. West. 1990. *Fragmenta Selecta*. 3rd ed. *Oxford Classical Texts* [OCT]. Oxford: Clarendon Press.

___. 1967. *Fragmenta Hesiodea*. Oxford: Clarendon Press.

Mieroop, van de, M. 1997. *The Ancient Mesopotamian City*. Oxford: Clarendon Press.

Miller, D. Gary. 1982. *Homer and the Ionian Epic Tradition: Some Phonic and Phonological Evidence Against an Aeolic Phase*. Innsbruck: Beiträge zur Sprachwissenschaft 38.

Miller, J.F. 1993. "The Shield of Argive Abas at Aeneid 3.286." *Classical Quarterly* 43.2: 445-450.

Mills, Sophie. 1997. *Theseus, Tragedy and the Athenian Empire*. Oxford: Clarendon Press.

Mitten, D.G., J.G. Pedley and J.A. Scott, eds. 1972. *Studies Presented to George M.A. Hanfmann*. Mainz: P. Verlag.

Momigliano, A.D. 1994. *Studies on Modern Scholarship*. Trans. T.J. Cornell. G.W. Bowerstock and T.J. Cornell, eds. Berkeley: University of California Press.

Mondi, Robert. 1984. "The Ascension of Zeus and the Composition of Hesiod's *Theogony*. *Greek Roman and Byzantine Studies* 25.4: 325-344.

Moon, Warren G. 1983. *Ancient Greek Art and Iconography*. Madison: University of Wisconsin Press.

Morris, Ian and Barry Powell, eds. 1997. *A New Companion to Homer*. Leiden: Brill.

___. 1994, ed. *Classical Greece: Ancient Histories and Modern Archaeologies*. Cambridge: Cambridge University Press.

___. 1988. "Tomb cult and the 'Greek Renaissance': The Past in the Present in the Eighth Century B.C." *Antiquity* 62: 750-761.

___. 1986. "The Use and Abuse of Homer." *Classical Antiquity* 5.1: 81-138.

Morrison, J.S. 1942. "Meno of Pharsalus, Polycrates, and Ismenias." *Classical Quarterly* 36: 57-78.

Mosshammer, Alden A. 1979. *The Chronicle of Eusebius and the Greek Chronographic Tradition.* London: Associated University Presses.

Muellner, Leonard. 1990. "The Simile of the Cranes and Pygmies: A Study of Homeric Metaphor." *Harvard Studies in Classical Philology* 93: 59-101.

Murray, Oswyn and Simon Price, eds. 1990. *The Greek City from Homer to Alexander.* Oxford: Clarendon Press.

Myres, John L. 1958. *Homer and His Critics.* London: Routledge & Kegan Paul.

___. 1930. *Who Were the Greeks.* Rpt. New York: Biblo and Tannen, 1967.

___. 1907. "A History of Pelasgian Theory." *Journal of Hellenic Studies* 27: 170-225.

Nagy, Gregory. 2001. "Homeric Poetry and Problems of Multiformity: The Panathenaic Bottleneck." *Classical Philology* 96.2: 109-119.

___. 1990. *Greek Mythology and Poetics.* Ithaca: Cornell University Press.

___. 1979. *The Best of the Achaeans: Concepts of the Hero in Archaic Greek Poetry.* Baltimore: Johns Hopkins University Press.

Neils, Jennifer. 1987. *The Youthful Deeds of Theseus.* Rome: G. Bretschneider.

Nilsson, Martin P. 1932. *The Mycenaean Origin of Greek Mythology.* New York: Norton.

Nisetich, Frank J. 1980. *Pindar's Victory Songs.* Baltimore: Johns Hopkins University Press.

Notopoulos, James A. 1951. "Continuity and Interconnexion on Homeric Oral Composition." *Transactions of the American Philological Association* 82: 81-101.

Obbink, D. 2006. "A New Archilochus Poem." *Zeitschrift für Papyrologie und Epigraphik* 156: 1-9.

___. 1996. *Philodemus on Piety*. Oxford: Oxford Clarendon Press.

O' Brien, Michael J. 1988. "Pelopid History and the Plot of Iphigenia in Tauris." *Classical Quarterly* 38.1 98-115.

Osborn, Robin. 1996. *Greece in the Making: 1200 – 479 B.C.* London: Routledge.

Page, Denys L. 1962. *Poetae melici Graeci*. [PMG] Oxford: Clarendon Press.

___. 1959. *History and the Homeric Iliad. Sather Classical Lectures* 31. Berkeley: University of California Press.

___. 1955. *The Homeric Odyssey. Mary Flexner lectures, delivered at Bryn Mawr College*. Oxford: Clarendon Press.

___. 1951. *Alkman/Partheion*. Oxford: Clarendon Press.

Parke, H.W. 1988. *Sibyls and Sibylline Prophecy in Classical Antiquity*. London: Routledge.

___. 1985a. *The Oracles of Apollo in Asia Minor*. London: Croom Helm.

___. 1985b. "The Massacre of the Branchidai" *Journal of Hellenic Studies* 105: 59-68.

___. 1967. *Greek Oracles*. London: Hutchinson Ltd.

Parker, Robert. 1996. *Athenian Religion: A History*. Oxford: Clarendon Press.

___. 1984. "The Herakleidai at Thorikos." *Zeitschrift für Papyrologie und Epigraphik* 57: 59.

___. 1983. *Miasma: Pollution and Purification in Early Greek Religion*. Oxford: Clarendon Press.

Parry, Adam. 1972. "Language and Characterization in Homer." *Harvard Studies in Classical Philology* 76: 1-22

___. 1966. "Have We Homer's Iliad?" *Yale Classical Studies* 20: 177-216.

Parry, Milman. A. Parry, ed. 1971. *The Making of Homeric Verse*. Oxford: Oxford University Press.

Pearson, Lionel. 1987. *The Greek Historians of the West: Timaeus and His Predecessors*. Atlanta, GA: Scholars Press.

___. 1962. "The Pseudo-History of Messenia and its Authors" *Historia: Zeitschrift für alte Geschichte* 11: 397-426.

___. 1942. *Local Historians of Attica*. Rpt. Atlanta: Scholars Press, 1981.

Pelliccia, Hayden. 1997. "As Many Homers As You Please." *New York Review of Books*, Nov. 20.

Pengalase, Charles. 1994. *Greek Myths and Mesopotamia: Parallels and Influence in the Homeric Hymns and Hesiod*. London: Routledge.

Peradotto, John. 1990. *Man in the Middle Voice: Name and Narration in the Odyssey*. Princeton: Princeton University Press.

Perlman, Paula. 2000. *City and Sanctuary in Ancient Greece: The Theorodokia in the Peloponnese. Hypomnemata: Untersuchungen zur Antike und zu ihrem Nachleben* 121. Göttingen: Vandenhoeck and Ruprecht.

Pettersson, Michael. 1992. *Cults of Apollo at Sparta: The Hyakinthia, the Gymnopaidiai and the Karneia*. Stockholm: Paul Aströms förlag.

Pfeiffer, Rudolf. 1968. *History and Classical Scholarship from the beginnings to the end of the Hellenistic Age*. Oxford: Clarendon Press.

Piérart, Marcel, ed. 1992. *Polydipsion Argos : Argos de la fin des palais mycéniens à la constitution de l'Etat classique. Bulletin de Correspondance Hellénique*. Supplément 22. Fribourg: Editions Universitaires.

Platnauer, Maurice, ed. 1954. *Fifty Years of Classical Scholarship*. Oxford: Basil Blackwell.

Polignac, François de 1984. *La Naissance de la cité grecque*. Paris: Editions La Découverte. Rpt.. *Cults, Territory and the Origins of the Greek City-State*. Trans. J. Lloyd. Chicago: University of Chicago Press, 1995.

Poole, William. 1994. "Euripides and Sparta" in A. Powell and S. Hodkinson, eds. *The Shadow of Sparta*. London: Routledge.

Popham, M.R., P.G. Kalligas, and L.H. Sackett, eds. 1990. *Lefkandi II: The Protogeometric Building at Tomba*. London: Thames and Hudson.

———. 1983. Popham, M., L.H. Sackett and E. Touloupa. "The Hero of Lefkandi." *Antiquity* 56: 169-174.

———. 1980. Popham, M.R., P.G. Kalligas, and L.H. Sackett, eds. *Lefkandi I: The Iron Age*. London: Thames and Hudson.

Powell, Barry. 1991. *Homer and the Origin of the Greek Alphabet*. Cambridge: Cambridge University Press.

———. 1989. "Why Was the Greek Alphabet Invented? The Epigraphical Evidence." *Classical Antiquity* 8.2: 321-350.

Pozzi, Dora C. and John M. Wickersham, eds. 1991. *Myth and the Polis*. Ithaca, NY: Cornell University Press.

Preller, Ludwig and Carl Robert. 1894-1926. *Griechische mythologie*. 4th ed. 3 vols. Berlin: Weidmann.

Price, T.H. 1973. "Hero-Cult and Homer." *Historia: Zeitschrift für alte Geschichte* 22: 129-144.

Prichard, James B. 1969. *Ancient Near Eastern Texts Relating to the Old Testament*. 3rd ed. Princeton: Princeton University Press.

Propp, Vladmir. 1968. Trans. Laurence Scott. 2nd ed. *Morphology of the Folktale*. Austin: University of Texas Press.

Querbach, C.J. 1985. "Hesiod's Four Races." *Classical Journal* 81: 1-12.

Radt, S. 1985. *Tragicorum Graecorum fragmenta*. vol. 3 Aeschylus. Göttingen: Vedenhoeck & Ruprecht.

Redfield, James M. 1994. *Nature and Culture in the Iliad: The Tragedy of Hector*. 2nd ed. Durham: Duke University Press.

Reeder, Ellen D., ed. 1995. *Pandora: Women in Classical Greece*. Baltimore, MD: Walters Art Gallery in association with Princeton University Press.

Renner, Timothy. 1978. "A Papyrus Dictionary of Metamorphoses." *Harvard Studies in Classical Philology* 82: 277-293.

Rich, John and Graham Shipley, eds. 1993. *War and Society in the Greek World*. London: Routledge.

Robinson, Eric W. 1997. *The First Democracies: Early Popular Government Outside Athens. Historia: Zeitschrift für alte Geschichte.* Enizelschriften 107. Stuttgart: Franz Steiner Verlag.

Robertson, Martin. 1975. *A History of Greek Art.* London: Cambridge.

Robertson, Noel. 1992. *Festivals and Legends: The Formation of Greek Cities in the Light of Public Ritual.* Toronto: University of Toronto Press.

___.1984. "The Ritual Background of the Erysichthon Story." *American Journal of Philology* 105.4: 369-408.

___. 1978. "The Myth of the First Sacred War." *Classical Quarterly* 28.1: 38-73.

Roebuck, Carl. 1961. "Tribal Organization in Ionia." *Transactions of the American Philological Association* 92: 495-507.

___. 1959. *Ionian Trade and Colonization.* Rpt. Chicago: Ares, 1984.

___. 1951. "The Organization of Naucratis." *Classical Philology* 46: 212-220.

Roisman, Joseph. 1984-1986. "The Image of the Political Exile in Archaic Greece." *Ancient Society* 15-17: 23-32.

Roller, Lynn E. 1981. "Funeral Games in Greek Art." *American Journal of Archaeology* 85.2: 107-119.

Roscher, W.H., ed. 1884-1937. *Ausführliches Lexikon der griechischen und römischen Mythologie.* Leipzig: B.G. Teubner.

Rose, H.J. 1959. *A Handbook of Greek Mythology.* New York: E.P. Dutton & Co.

Rose, V. 1886. *Aristotelis qui ferebantur librorum fragmenta.* Leipsig: B.G. Teubner.

Rosenmeyer, Thomas G. 1957. "Hesiod and Historiography." *Hermes* 85: 257-285.

Rosivach, Vincent J. 1987. "Autochthony and the Athenians." *Classical Quarterly* 37.3: 294-305.

Rowe, C.J. 1983. "Archaic Thought in Hesiod." *Journal of Hellenic Studies 103:* 124-135.

Rubino, C.A. and C.W. Shelmerdine, eds. 1983. *Approaches to Homer.* Austin: University of Texas Press.

Rusten, J.S. 1980. "The Return of the Heracleidai." *Zeitschrift für Papyrologie und Epigraphik* 40: 39-42.

Rutherford, Ian. 2001. *Pindar's Paeans: A Reading of the Fragments with a Survey of the Genre.* Oxford: Oxford University Press.

Rutherford, Richard B. 1996. *Homer. Greece & Rome: New Surveys in the Classics* #26. Cambridge: Cambridge University Press.

Rutherford, William G. 1896. *Scholia Aristophanica.* 3 vols. London: Macmillian.

Rzach, Alosius. 1902. *Hesiodi Carmina.* Leipzig: B.G. Teubner.

Sacks, Kenneth S. 1990. *Diodorus Siculus and The First Century.* Princeton: Princeton University Press.

Said, Suzanne. 1977. "Les Combats de Zeus et Le Problèm des Interpolations dans La Thégonie D'Hésiode." *Revue des études grecques* 430-431: 183-210.

Sale, William M. 1994. "The Government of Troy: Politics in the *Iliad*." *Greek Roman and Byzantine Studies* 35.1: 5-102.

___. 1989. "The Trojans, Statistics, and Milman Parry." *Greek Roman and Byzantine Studies* 30.3: 341-410.

Salmon, J.B. 1984. *Wealthy Corinth: A History of the City to 338 BC.* Oxford: Clarendon Press.

Scaife, Ross. 1995. "The *Kypria* and its Early Reception." *Classical Antiquity* 14: 164-191.

Schachter, A. 1981-1994. *Cults of Boiotia.* 3 vols. *Bulletin Supplements* 38.1-3. London: Institute of Classical Studies.

___. 1967. "The Theban Wars." *Phoenix* 21: 1-10.

Schefold, Karl. 1992. *Late Archaic Greek Art.* Trans. Alan Griffiths. Cambridge: Cambridge University Press.

___. 1966. *Myth and Legend in Early Greek Art.* Trans. Audrey Hicks. New York: H.N. Abrahms.

Scherratt, E.S. 1990. "Archaeology and the Homeric Question" *Antiquity* 64: 807-824.

Schibli, Hermann S. 1990. *Pherekydes of Syros*. Oxford: Clarendon Press.

Schwartz, E. 1891. *Scholia in Euripidem*. vol.2. Rpt. Berlin: Walter de Gruyter, 1966.

Scodel. Ruth. 1992. "The Wits of Glaucus." *Transactions of the American Philological Association."* 122: 73-84.

___. 1982. "The Achaean Wall and the Myth of Destruction." *Harvard Studies in Classical Philology* 86: 33-50.

Scott, John A. 1965. *The Unity of Homer*. New York: Biblo and Tannen.

Seaford, Richard. 1994. *Reciprocity and Ritual: Homer and Tragedy in the Developing City-State*. Oxford: Clarendon Press.

___. 1987. "The Tragic Wedding." *Journal of Hellenic Studies* 107: 106-130.

Sealey, Raphael. 1983. "The Athenian Courts for Homicide." *Classical Philology* 78.4: 275-296.

___. 1976. *A History of the Greek City States: 700-338 B.C.* Berkeley: University of California Press.

___. 1957. "From Phemios to Ion." *Revue des études grecques* 70: 312-351.

Segal, Robert A. 2004. *Myth: A Very Short Introduction*. Oxford: Oxford University Press.

Severyns, A. 1938-1963. *Researches sur la Chrestomathie de Proclos*. Paris: Société d' édition Les Belles lettres.

Shapiro, H.A. 1992. "Theseus in Kimonian Athens: The Iconography of Empire." *Mediterranean Historical Review* 7.1.

___. 1989. *Art and Cult Under the Tyrants in Athens*. Mainz, Verlag Philpp von Zabern.

___. 1984a. "Herakles, Kyknos and Delphi." *Proceedings of the first International Syposium on Ancient Greek and Related Pottery*.

___. 1984b. "Herakles and Kyknos." *American Journal of Archaeology* 88.4: 523-529.

Shipley, Graham. 1987. *History of Samos: 800-188 BC.* Oxford: Clarendon Press.

Sifakis, G. M. 1997. "Formulas and their relatives: a semiotic approach to verse making in Homer and modern Greek Folksongs." *Journal of Hellenic Studies* 117: 136-153.

Silk, M.S. 1985. "Heracles and Greek Tragedy." *Greece and Rome* 32.1: 3-22.

Slatkin, Laura M. 1991. *The Power of Thetis: Allusion and Interpretation in the Iliad.* Berkeley: University of California Press.

Smith, O.L., ed. 1977. *Scholia metrica anonyma in Euripidis Hecubam, Orestem, Phoenissas. Opuscula Graecolatina 10.* Copenhagen: Institute for Classical Philology.

Snell, B. 1971-2004. *Tragicorum Graecorum Fragmenta* 5 vols. Göttingen: Vandenhoeck & Ruprecht.

Snodgrass, A.M. 2006. *Archaeology and the Emergence of Greece.* Ithaca, NY: Cornell University Press.

___. 1998. *Homer and the Artists: Text and Picture in Early Greek Art.* Cambridge: Cambridge University Press.

___. 1980. *Archaic Greece: the age of experiment.* Berkeley: University of California Press.

___.1974. "An Historical Homeric Society?" *Journal of Hellenic Studies* 94: 114-125.

___.1971. *The Dark Age of Greece: an archaeological survey of the eleventh to the eighth centuries B.C.* Edinburgh: Edinburgh University Press.

Solmsen, F. 1990. *Hesiodi: Theogonia. Opera et Dies. Scutum.* 3rd ed. *Oxford Classical Texts* [OCT]. Oxford: Clarendon Press.

___. 1982. "The Earliest Stages in the History of Hesiod's Text." *Harvard Studies in Classical Philology* 86: 1-31.

___. 1949. *Hesiod and Aeschylus*. Rpt.1995. Ithaca: Cornell University Press.

Sourvinou-Inwood, Christine. 1991. *Reading Greek Culture: Texts and Images, Rituals and Myths*. Oxford: Clarendon Press.

___. 1986. "Crime and Punishment: Tityos, Tantalos, and Sisyphos in *Odyssey 11*." Bulletin of the Institute of Classical Studies – University of London 33: 37-58.

___. 1979. *Theseus as Son and Stepson: A Tentative Illustration of Greek Mythological Mentality*. University of London Institute of Classical Studies: Bulletin Supplement 40.

___. 1971. "Theseus Lifting the Rock and a Cup Near the Pithos Painter." Journal of Hellenic Studies 91: 94-109.

Spaeth, Barbette S. 1991. "Athenians and Eleusinians in the West Pediment of the Parthenon." *Hesperia* 603: 332-362.

Starr, C.G. 1965. "The Credibility of Early Spartan History." *Historia: Zeitschrift für alte Geschichte* 14: 257-272.

Steiner, Deborah T. 1997. "Greek Letters: Review of Barry Powell's Homer and the Origin of the Greek Alphabet" *Arion* 3rd series 5.1: 233-241.

___. 1995. "Stoning and Sight: A Structural Equivalence in Greek Mythology." *Classical Antiquity* 14.1: 193-211.

Szegedy-Maszak, Andrew. 1978. "Legends of the Greek Lawgivers." *Greek Roman and Byzantine Studies* 19.3: 199-209.

Taplin, Oliver. 1992. *Homeric Soundings: The Shaping of the Iliad*. Oxford: Clarendon Press.

Tersini, Nancy D. 1987. "The Unifying Themes in the Sculpture of the Temple of Zeus at Olympia." *Classical Antiquity* 6.1: 139-159.

Thalmann, William G. 1984. *Conventions of Form and Thought in Early Greek Epic Poetry*. Baltimore: Johns Hopkins University Press.

___. 1978. *Dramatic Art in Aeschylus's Seven Against Thebes*. New Haven: Yale University Press.

Thomas, Carol G. 1993. *Myth Becomes History: Pre-Classical Greece.* Claremont, CA: Regina Books.

Thomas, Rosalind. 1992. *Literacy and Orality in Ancient Greece.* Cambridge: Cambridge University Press.

Thompson, Wesley E. 1967. "The Marriage of First Cousins in Athenian Society." *Phoenix* 21.4: 273-282.

Tigerstedt, E.N. 1965. *The Legend of Sparta in Classical Antiquity.* Stockholm: Almquist and Wiksell.

Toher, Mark. 1989. "On The Use of Nicolaus' Historical Fragments." *Classical Antiquity* 8.1: 159-172.

Tomlinson, R.A. 1972. *Argos and the Argolid: from the end of the Bronze Age to the Roman Occupation.* Ithaca, NY: Cornell University Press.

Trigger, Bruce G. 2006. *A History of Archaeological Thought.* 2nd ed. Cambridge: Cambridge University Press.

Tsountas, Christos and J.I. Manatt. 1897. *The Mycenaean Age: A Study of the Monuments and Culture of Pre-Homeric Greece.* Rpt. 1969 Chicago: Argonaut Press.

Ulf, Christoph. 1990. *Die homerische Gesellschaft: Materialien zur analytischen Beschreibung and historischen Lokalisierung.* Munich: C.H. Beck.

van Wees, Hans. 1994. "The Homeric Way of War: the *Iliad* and the Hoplite Phalanx (I & II)." *Greece & Rome* 41.1: 1-18 & 41.2: 131-155.

___. 1992. *Status Warriors: War, Violence, and Society in Homer and History.* Amsterdam: J.C. Gieben.

Vermule, Emily. 1964. *Greece in the Bronze Age.* Chicago: University of Chicago Press.

Vernant, J-P. 1980. Trans. Janet Lloyd. *Myth and Society in Ancient Greece.* Sussex (orig. Paris: F. Maspero, 1974).

___. 1968 ed. *Problèmes de la guerre en Grèce ancienne.* Paris: Mouton & Co.

Vian, Francis. 1965. "Mélampous et les Proitides.' *Revue des études anciennes* 67: 25-30.

___. 1963. *Les origines de Thebes: Cadmos et les Spartes*. Paris: C. Klincksieck.

Vidal-Naquet, Pierre. 1986. *The Black Hunter: Forms of Though and Forms of Society in the Greek World*. Trans. Andrew Szegedy-Maszak. Baltimore: Johns Hopkins University Press. Trans of *La chasseur noirs: Formes de pensées et formes de société dans le monde grec*. Paris: F. Maspero, 1981.

Visser, Eduard. 1997. *Homers Katalog der Schiffe*. Stuttgart: B.G. Teubner.

Visser, Margaret. 1984. "Vengeance and Pollution in Classical Athens." *Journal of the History of Ideas* 45.2: 193-206.

Vlassopoulos, Kostas. 2007. *Unthinking the Greek Polis: Ancient Greek History Beyond Eurocentrism*. Cambridge: Cambridge University Press.

von Fritz, Kurt. 1947. "Pandora, Prometheus, and the Myth of the Ages." *Review of Religion* 5.2: 227-260.

Wace, A. & F. Stubbings, eds. 1962. *A Companion to Homer*. London: Macmillan.

Wade-Gerry, H.T. 1958. *Essays in Greek History*. Oxford: Basil Blackwell.

___. 1952. *The Poet of the Iliad*. Cambridge: Cambridge University Press.

___. 1949. "A Note on the Origin of the Spartan Gymnopaidiai." *Classical Quarterly* 43: 79-81.

Walcot, P. 1979. "Cattle Raiding, Heroic Tradition, and Ritual: The Greek Evidence." *History of Religions* 18.4: 326-351.

___. 1966. *Hesiod and the Near East*. Cardiff: University of Wales Press.

___. 1961. "The Composition of the Works and Days." *Revue des Etudes Grecques*. 74: 1-19.

Ward, A.G. ed., 1970. *The Quest for Theseus*. New York: Praeger.

Wardman, A.E. 1960. "Myth in Greek Historiography." *Historia: Zeitschrift für alte Geschichte* 9: 403-413.

Wendel, Carl .1932. *Die überlieferung der scholien zu Apollonios von Rhodes. Abhandlungen der Gesellschaft der Wissenshaften zu Göttingen – Philologische – Historische Klasse* 3.1. Berlin: Weidmannsche buchhandlung.

West, M.L. 2006. "Archilochus and Telephos." *Zeitschrift für Papyrologie und Epigraphik* 156: 11-17.

___. 2003. *Greek Epic Fragments*. Cambridge, MA: Harvard University Press.

___. "The Invention of Homer." *Classical Quarterly* 49.2: 364-382.

___. 1997. *The East Face of Helicon: West Asiatic Elements in Greek Poetry and Myth*. Oxford: Clarendon Press.

___. 1995. "The Date of the *Iliad*." *Museum Helveticum* 52.4: 203-219.

___. 1994. "Ab ovo." *Classical Quarterly* 44.2: 289-307.

___. 1988. "The Rise of Greek Epic." *Journal of Hellenic Studies* 103: 151-172.

___. 1985a. *The Hesiodic Catalogue of Women: Its Nature, Structure, and Origins*. Oxford: Clarendon Press.

___. 1985b. "The Hesiodic Catalogue: New Light on Apollo's Love-Life." *Zeitscrhift für Papyrologie und Epigraphik* 61: 1-7.

___. 1983a. *The Orphic Poems*. Oxford: Clarendon Press.

___. 1983b. "The Hesiodic Catalogue: Xouthids and Aiolids." *Zeitschrift für Papyrologie und Epigraphik* 53: 27-30.

___. 1978. *Hesiod Works & Days*. Oxford: Clarendon Press.

___. 1966. *Hesiod Theogony*. Oxford: Clarendon Press.

Whitehead, David, ed. 1994. *From Political Architecture to Stephanus Byzantius*. Historia Einzelshriften 87. Stuttgart: Steiner Verlag.

___. 1986. *The Demes of Attica: 508/7 – ca. 250 B.C.* Princeton: Princeton University Press.

Whitley, James. 1991. *Style and Society in Dark Age Greece*. Cambridge: Cambridge University Press.

___. 1988. "Early States and Hero Cults: A Re-Appraisal." *Journal of Hellenic Studies* 108: 173-182.

Wilamowitz-Moellendorff, Ulrich von. 1927. *Die Heimkehr des Odysseus*. Berlin: Weidmann.

___. 1884. *Homerische Untersuchungen.* Berlin: Wiedmann.

Wilkins, John. 1993. *Euripides Heraclidae with Introduction and Commentary.* Oxford: Clarendon Press.

___. 1990. "The Young of Athens: Religion and Society in *Herakleidai* of Euripides." *Classical Quarterly* 40.2: 329-339.

Will, Edouard. 1955. *Korinthiaka: recherches sur l'histoire et la civilization de Corinth des origins aux guerres mediques.* Paris: E. de Boccard.

Willcock, Malcolm M. 1990. "The Search for the Poet Homer." *Greece & Rome* 37.1:1-13.

___. 1976. *A Companion to the Iliad.* Chicago: University of Chicago Press.

___. 1970. "Aspects of the gods of the *Iliad.*" *Bulletin of the Institute of Classical Studies* 17: 1-10.

___. 1964. "Mythological Paradeigma in the *Iliad.*" *Classical Quarterly* 14: 141-154.

Wilson, N.G. 1983. *Scholars of Byzantium.* London: Duckworth.

Winkler, J.J. and F.I. Zeitlin, eds. 1990. *Nothing to Do with Dionysos? Athenian Drama in Its Social Context.* Princeton: Princeton University Press.

Winnington-Ingram, R.P. 1983. *Studies in Aeschylus.* Cambridge: Cambridge University Press.

___. 1980. *Sophocles: An Interpretation.* Cambridge: Cambridge University Press.

___. 1961. "The Danaid Trilogy of Aeschylus." *Journal of Hellenic Studies* 81: 141-152.

Wolf, Fredrich August. 1795. *Prolegomena ad Homerum.* Anthony G. Grafton, Glenn W. Most and James E.G. Zetzel trans. Princeton: Princeton University Press, 1985.

Woolley, Leonard. 1959. *A Forgotten Kingdom: Results Obtained from the Excavations of Two Mounds, Atchana and Al Mina in the Turkish Hatay.* London: M. Parrish.

Yamagata, N. 1997. "ἄναξ and βασιλεύς in Homer" *Classical Quarterly* 47.1: 1-14.

Zeitlin, Froma I. 1996. *Playing the Other: Gender and Society in Classical Greek Literature*. Chicago: University of Chicago Press.

APPENDIX A: THE LEGEND OF THE TRIPARTITE DIVISION OF ARGOS

Odyssey 11.281-297.

Καὶ Χλῶριν εἶδον περικαλλέα, τήν ποτε Νηλεὺς γῆμεν ἑὸν διὰ κάλλος, ἐπεὶ πόρε μυρία ἕδνα, ὁπλοτάτην κούρην Ἀμφίονος Ἰασίδαο, ὅς ποτ᾽ ἐν Ὀρχομενῷ Μινυείῳ ἶφι ἄνασσεν· ἡ δὲ Πύλου βασίλευε, τέκεν δέ οἱ ἀγλαὰ τέκνα, Νέστορά τε Χρόνιόν τε Περικλύμενόν τ᾽ ἀγέρωχον. τοῖσι δ᾽ ἐπ᾽ ἰφθίμην Πηρὼ τέκε, θαῦμα βροτοῖσι, τὴν πάντες μνώοντο περικτίται· οὐδ᾽ ἄρα Νηλεὺς τῷ ἐδίδου ὃς μὴ ἕλικας βοῦς εὐρυμετώπους ἐκ Φυλάκης ἐλάσειε βίης Ἰφικληείης ἀργαλέας· τὰς δ᾽ οἶος ὑπέσχετο μάντις ἀμύμων ἐξελάαν· χαλεπὴ δὲ θεοῦ κατὰ μοῖρα πέδησε, δεσμοί τ᾽ ἀργαλέοι καὶ βουκόλοι ἀγροιῶται. ἀλλ᾽ ὅτε δὴ μῆνές τε καὶ ἡμέραι ἐξετελεῦντο ἂψ περιτελλομένου ἔτεος καὶ ἐπήλυθον ὧραι, καὶ τότε δή μιν ἔλυσε βίη Ἰφικληείη, θέσφατα πάντ᾽ εἰπόντα· Διὸς δ᾽ ἐτελείετο βουλή.

'And I saw Chloris, surpassingly lovely, the one whom Neleus married for her beauty, giving numberless gifts to win her. She was the youngest daughter of Iasos' son Amphion, who once ruled strongly over Orchomenos of the Minyai. So she was queen of Pylos and she bore him glorious children, Nestor and Chromios and proud Periklymenos. Also she bore that marvel among mortals, majestic Pero, whom all the heroes round about courted, but Neleus would not give her to any, unless he could drive away the broad-faced horn-curved cattle of strong Iphikles out of Phylake. It was hard to do, and only the blameless seer Melampous undertook it, but he was bound fast by the hard destiny of the god, and the painful fetters on him, and the loutish ox herds. But when the months and the days had come to an end, and the year had gone full circle and come back with the seasons returning, then strong Iphikles released him, when he had told him all the prophecies he knew; and the will of Zeus was accomplished."

APPENDIX A

Odyssey 15.222-258..

ἤ τοι ὁ μὲν τὰ πονεῖτο καὶ εὔχετο, θῦε δ' Ἀθήνῃ νηΐ πάρα πρυμνῇ· σχεδόθεν δέ οἱ ἤλυθεν ἀνὴρ τηλεδαπός, φεύγων ἐξ Ἄργεος ἄνδρα κατακτάς, μάντις· ἀτὰρ γενεήν γε Μελάμποδος ἔκγονος ἦεν, ὅς πρὶν μέν ποτ' ἔναιε Πύλῳ ἔνι, μητέρι μήλων, ἀφνειὸς Πυλίοισι μέγ' ἔξοχα δώματα ναίων· δὴ τότε γ' ἄγγων δῆμον ἀφίκετο, πατρίδα φεύγων Νηλέα τε μεγάθυμον, ἀγαυότατον ζωόντων, ὅς οἱ χρήματα πολλὰ τελεσφόρον εἰς ἐνιαυτὸν εἶχε βίῃ. ὁ δὲ τῆος ἐνὶ μεγάροις Φυλάκοιο δεσμῷ ἐν ἀργαλέῳ δέδετο, κρατέρ' ἄλγεα πάσχων εἵνεκα Νηλῆος κούρης ἄτης τε βαρείης, τήν οἱ ἐπὶ φρεσὶ θῆκε θεὰ δασπλῆτις Ἐρινύς. ἀλλ' ὁ μὲν ἔκφυγε κῆρα καὶ ἤλασε βοῦς ἐριμύκους ἐς Πύλον ἐκ Φυλάκης καὶ ἐτίσατο ἔργον ἀεικὲς ἀντίθεον Νηλῆα, κασιγνήτῳ δὲ γυναῖκα ἠγάγετο πρὸς δώμαθ'. ὁ δ' ἄλλων ἵκετο δῆμον, Ἄργος ἐς ἱππόβοτον· τόθι γάρ νύ οἱ αἴσιμον ἦεν ναιέμεναι πολλοῖσιν ἀνάσσοντ' Ἀργείοισιν ἔνθα δ' ἔγημε γυναῖκα καὶ ὑψερεφὲς θέτο δῶμα, γείνατο δ' Ἀντιφάτην καὶ Μάντιον, υἷε κραταιώ. Ἀντιφάτης μὲν ἔτικτεν Οἰκλῆα μεγάθυμον, αὐτὰρ Οἰκλείης λαοσσόον Ἀμφιάραον, ὃν περὶ κῆρι φίλει Ζεύς τ' αἰγίοχος καὶ Ἀπόλλων παντοίην φιλότητ'· οὐδ' ἵκετο γήραος οὐδόν, ἀλλ' ὄλετ' ἐν Θήβῃσι γυναίων εἵνεκα δώρων. τοῦ δ' υἱεῖς ἐγένοντ' Ἀλκμαίων Ἀμφίλοχός τε. Μάντιος αὖ τέκετο Πολυφείδεά τε Κλεῖτόν τε· ἀλλ' ἦ τοι Κλεῖτον χρυσόθρονος ἤρπασεν Ἠὼς κάλλεος εἵνεκα οἷο, ἵν' ἀθανάτοισι μετείη· αὐτὰρ ὑπέρθυμον Πολυφείδεα μάντιν Ἀπόλλων θῆκε βροτῶν ὄχ' ἄριστον, ἐπεὶ θάνεν Ἀμφιάραος· ὅς ῥ' Ὑπερησίηνδ' ἀπενάσσατο πατρὶ χολωθείς, ἔνθ' ὅ γε ναιετάων γαντεύετο πᾶσι βροτοῖσιν.

τοῦ μὲν ἄρ' υἱὸς ἐπῆλθε, Θεοκλύμενος δ' ὄνομ' ἦεν, ὃς τότε Τηλεμάχου πέλας ἵστατο· τὸν δ' ἐκίχανεν σπένδοντ' εὐχόμενόν τε θοῇ παρὰ νηΐ μελαίνῃ, καί μιν φωνήσας ἔπεα πτερόεντα προσηύδα·

So, while he was busy with prayer and sacrifice to Athena beside the stern of the ship, there came to him an outlander from Argos, where he had killed a man; now he was a fugitive. He was a prophet, and by blood was the stock of Melampous. Melampous once had lived in Pylos, at home in his high house; but then he came to the land of other men, fleeing his country and great-hearted Neleus, the proudest of men living, who until a year was fulfilled kept much of his substance by force, for Melampous meanwhile in the halls of Phylakos was held in constraint of wearisome bondage, suffering strong pains for the sake of Neleus' daughter, and the bitter infatuation which the goddess Erinys, wrecker of houses, inflicted upon him. Yet he escaped death, and drove away the loud-lowing cattle from Phylake to Pylos, and achieved the unjust labor godlike Neleus imposed on him, and led back the lady to his brother's house; but he himself went to horse-pasturing Argos, since now it was ordained for him that he should live there and be lord over many Argives. And there he too married a wife and established a high-roofed house, and had children, Mantios and Antiphates, strong sons. Antiphates had a son; this was great hearted Oikles. His son was Amphiaraos, leader of storming armies, whom Zeus of the aegis loved in his heart, as did Apollo, with every favor, but he never came to the doorsill of old age, but perished in Thebes, because his wife had been bribed with presents. He in turn had sons, Amphilochos and Alkmaion. The children born to Mantios were Polypheides and Kleitos, but Dawn of the golden throne carried Kleitos away, because of his beauty, so that he might dwell among the immortals; but Apollo made high-hearted Polypheides a prophet, and far the best among mortals, after Amphiaraos had died. He, angered with his father, in Hyperesia lived and was lord, and there he was a prophet for all men. It was this man's son, by name Theoklymenos, who now came to Telemachos and stood near, and there he found him pouring libation and praying beside his fast black vessel.

R. Lattimore, Trans.

Bacchylides *Ode* 11.37-126.

For Alexidamos, son of Phaiskos of Metapontion.

νῦν δ' Ἄρτεμις ἀγροτέρα
χρυσαλάκατος λιπαρὰν
Ἡμ]έρα τοξόκλυτος νίκαν ἔδωκε.
τ]ᾶι ποτ' Ἀβαντιάδας
 β]ωμὸν κατένασσε πολύλ-

APPENDIX A

λ[ι]στον εὔπεπλοί τε κοῦραι·

τὰς ἐξ ἐρατῶν ἐφόβησε<ν>
  παγκρατὴς Ἥρα μελάθρων
Προίτου, παραπλῆγι φρένας
  καρτερᾶι ζεύξασ' ἀνάγκαι·
παρθενίαι γὰρ ἔτι
  ψυχᾶι κίον ἐς τέμενος
πορφυροζώνοιο θεᾶς·
φάσκον δὲ πολὺ σφέτερον
πλούτωι προφέρειν πατέρα ξανθᾶς παρέδρου
σεμνοῦ Διὸς εὐρυβία.
  ταῖσιν δὲ χολωσαμένα
στήθεσ<σ>ι παλίντροπον ἔμβαλεν νόημα·
φεῦγον δ' ὄρος ἐς τανίφυλλον
  σμερδαλέαν φωνὰν ἱεῖσαι,

Τιρύνθιον ἄστυ λιποῦσαι
  καὶ θεοδμάτους ἀγυιάς.
ἤδη γὰρ ἔτος δέκατον
  θεοφιλὲς λιπόντες Ἄργος
ναῖον ἀδεισιβόαι
  χαλκάσπιδες ἡμίθεοι
σὺν πολυζήλωι βασιλεῖ.
νεῖκος γὰρ ἀμαιμάκετον
βληχρᾶς ἀνέπαλτο κασιγνήτοις ἀπ' ἀρχᾶς
Προίτωι τε καὶ Ἀκρισίωι·
  λαούς τε διχοστασίαις
ἤρ<ε>ιπον ἀμετροδίκοις μάχαις τε λυγραῖς,
λίσσοντο δὲ παῖδας Ἄβαντος
  γᾶν πολύκριθον λαχόντας

Τίρυνθα τὸν ὁπλότερον
κτίζειν, πρὶν ἐς ἀργαλέαν πασεῖν ἀνάγκαν·

Ζεύς τ' ἔθελεν Κρονίδας
τιμῶν Δαναοῦ γενεὰν
 καὶ διωξίπποιο Λυγκέος
παῦσαι στυγερῶν ἀχέων.
 τεῖχος δὲ Κύκλωπες κάμον
ἐλθόντες ὑπερφίαλοι κλεινᾶι π[όλ]ει
κάλλιστον, ἵν' ἀντίθεοι
ναῖον κλυτὸν ἱππόβοτον
Ἄργος ἥρωες περικλειτοὶ λιπόντες,
ἔνθεν ἀπεσσύμεναι
 Προίτου κυανοπλόκαμοι
 φεῦγον ἄδματοι θύγατρες.

τὸν δ' εἷλεν ἄχος κραδίαν, ξεί-
 να τέ νιν πλᾶξεν μέριμνα·
δοίαξε δὲ φάσγανον ἄμ-
 φακες ἐν στέρνοισι πᾶξαι.
ἀλλά νιν αἰχμοφόροι
 μύθοισί τε μειλιχίοις
 καὶ βίαι χειρῶν κάτεχον.
τρισκαίδεκα μὲν τελέους
μῆνας κατὰ δάσκιον ἡλύκταζον ὕλαν
φεῦγόν τε καὶ Ἀρκαδίαν
 μηλοτρόφον· ἀλλ' ὅτε δὴ
 Λοῦσον ποτὶ καλλιρόαν πατὴρ ἵκανεν,
ἔνθεν χρόα νιψάμενος φοι-
 νικοκ[ραδέμνο]ιο Λατοῦς

κίκλη[ισκε θύγατρ]α βοῶπιν,
 χεῖρας ἀντείνων πρὸς αὐγὰς
ἱππώκεος ἀελίου,
 τέκνα δυστάνοιο λύσσας
πάρφρονος ἐξαγαγεῖν·
 θύσω δέ τοι εἴκοσι βοῦς

APPENDIX A

ἄζυγας φοινικότριχας.'
τοῦ δ' ἔκλυ' ἀριστοπάτρα
θηροσκόπος εὐχομένον· πιθοῦσα δ' Ἥραν
παῦσεν καλυκοστεφάνους
 κούρας μανιᾶν ἀθέων·
ταὶ δ' αὐτίκα οἱ τέμενος βωμόν τε τεῦχον,
χραῖνόν τέ μιν αἵματι μήλων
 καὶ χοροὺς ἵσταν γυναικῶν.

ἔνθεν καὶ ἀρηιφίλοις
ἄνδρεσσιν <ἐς> ἱπποτρόφον πόλιν Ἀχαιοῖς
ἕσπεο· σὺν δὲ τύχαι
ναίεις Μεταπόντιον, ὦ
 χρυσέα δέσποινα λαῶν·
ἄλσος δέ τοι ἱμερόεν
 Κάσαν παρ' εὔυδρον πρόγο-
νοι ἐσσάμενοι Πριάμοι' ἐπεὶ χρόνωι
βουλαῖσι θεῶν μακάρων
πέρσαν πόλιν εὐκτιμέναν
χαλκοθωράκων μετ' Ἀτρειδᾶν. δικαίας
ὅστις ἔχει φρένας, εὑ-
 ρήσει σὺν ἅπαντι χρόνωι
 μυρίας ἀλκὰς Ἀχαιῶν.

But now Artemis of the woods with her golden distaff,
the Gentle One, the famous archer,
has awarded him this dazzling victory.
To her once, Proitos, Abas' son, the king of Tiryns set up an altar,
where many prayers would be offered,
he and his beautifully-robed daughters,
whom mighty Hera had driven out
of their grand palace in fear,
yoking their minds to a violent obsession:
maidens still, they entered the sanctuary

of the purple-belted goddess to boast
that their father was richer by far than holy Zeus' consort.
In a snit, then she put a crazy thought
into their heads, and they scurried off
to the woods and the mountainsides,
uttering high shrill screams,
strangers now to civilization, cities,
Tiryns and its familiar god-built streets.
This was the tenth year
since the bronze-armored heroes,
fearless in battle, and their much-envied
king had left Argos, the city loved
by the gods, and lived in Tiryns.
An insurmountable strife between the brothers,
Proitos and Akrisios, had grown up
from a trivial start. With outrageous
feuding and grievous battles,
they were ruining their people,
who, in desperation, begged the sons
of Abas, with that land so rich in barley,
that the younger of the two should be permitted
to found a city in Tiryns,
before they were all destroyed.
And Zeus son of Kronos, honored
his blood-kin, Danaos,
and his nephew and son-in-law,
the horse-driving Lynkeus.
And the god was willing to relieve their hateful troubles.
So the mighty Kyklopes came,
and labored hard to build
a magnificent wall for the radiant
city, where the godlike heroes lived,
having left behind them horse-pasturing
Argos. From this Tiryns it was
that the dark-haired daughters of Proitos
rushed in their wild flight. And woe
overcame Proitos' heart, and the eerie thought

APPENDIX A

struck him – that he would plant
his double-edged sword deep in his chest.
But his loyal spearmen restrained him,
with gentling words and the force
of their strong hands. For a year and a month,
his daughters roamed and wandered
like wild beasts in the forest's shadows
and fled through the sheep-nourishing fields
of Arkadia's hills. When their father came
at last to Lusus' stream, he washed himself
in its water and called on Leto's daughter,
Artemis, who wears the crimson headdress.
Imploring the ox-eyed goddess, he stretched
his hands to the sun's rays and asked
that she deliver his poor daughters
from the grip of their dreadful madness.
"I will sacrifice to you twenty red-backed oxen,
never yoked," he said. And the huntress goddess,
hearing his prayer, interceded with Hera,
who relieved the god-forsaken girls
of their madness. In thanks for this
they build her a sanctuary and an altar
they stained red with the blood of sheep,
and they founded a women's chorus
to chant never-ending prayers.
From there you accompanied the brave
Achaian men to Metapontion,
their horse-nurturing city;
where, fortunate, you dwell, the people's
mistress. A lovely grove near Casas'
fair waters they dedicated to you,
when in the fullness of time,
by the will of the blessed gods, they sacked
with the bronze-armored sons of Atreus,
Priam's far-off well-built city
at Troy. Any fair-minded judge
would have to admit the proposition

that, throughout time, there have been
deeds of valor, more than a man can number,
done by the stalwart Achaians.
David R. Slavitt, Trans.

Pindar *Nemean* 9.11-26.

ὃς τότε μὲν βασιλεύων κεῖθι νέαισί θ' ἑορταῖς
ἰσχύος τ' ἀνδρῶν ἁμίλλαις ἅρμασί τε γλαφυροῖς ἄμφαινε
κυδαίνων πόλιν.
φεῦγε γὰρ Ἀμφιαρῆ ποτε θρασυμήδεα καὶ δεινὰν στάσιν
πατρῴων οἴκων ἀπό τ' Ἄργεος· ἀρχοὶ δ' οὐκ ἔτ' ἔσαν Ταλαοῦ
παῖδες, βιασθέντες λύᾳ.
15 κρέσσων δὲ καππαύει δίκαν τὰν πρόσθεν ἀνήρ.
ἀνδροδάμαντ' Ἐριφύλαν, ὅρκιον ὡς ὅτε πιστόν, δόντες
Οἰκλείδᾳ γυναῖκα, ξανθοκομᾶν Δαναῶν ἔσσαν μέγιστοι καὶ ποτε
ἐσ <λὸν ἐς> ἑπταπύλους Θήβας ἄγαγον στρατὸν ἀνδρῶν
αἰσιᾶν
οὐ κατ' ὀρνίχων ὁδόν· οὐδὲ Κρονίων ἀστεροπὰν ἐλελίξαις
οἴκοθεν μαργουμένους
20 στείχειν ἐπώτρυν', ἀλλὰ φείσασθαι κελεύθου.
φαινομέναν δ' ἄρ' ἐς ἄταν σπεῦδεν ὅμιλος ἱκέσθαι
χαλκέοις ὅπλοισιν ἱππείοις τε σὺν ἔντεσιν· Ἰσμηνοῦ δ' ἐπ'
ὄχθαισι γλυκὺν
νόστον ἐρεισάμενοι λευκανθέα σώματ' ἐπίαναν καπνόν·
ἑπτὰ γὰρ δαίσαντο πυραὶ νεογυίους φῶτας·
ὁ δ' Ἀμφιάρῃ σχίσσεν κεραυνῷ παμβίᾳ
25 Ζεὺς τὰν βαθύστερνον χθόνα, κρύψεν δ' ἅμ' ἵπποις,
δουρὶ Περικλυμένου πρὶν νῶτα τυπέντα μαχατὰν θυμὸν
αἰσχυνθῆμεν.

He (viz. Adrastos) was king at the time in Sikyon,
and with new festivals,
the trial of men's strength
and speed of wrought chariots,

he glorified the city, and gave it a name among men,
all in thanks for his escape –
he had come there fleeing dread Amphiaraos
and the deadly strife at home in Argos.
For the sons of Talaos, crushed in that struggle,
were princes no more. The man of greater might
puts an end to the order of old.

But the sons of Talaos, betrothing
Eriphyla the man-subduer
as a pledge of trust to Oikles' son,
once more were the mightiest of the fair-haired Danaans,
and in time they led a host of men
to seven-gated Thebes.
No propitious omens sent them on their way,
nor did Kronos' son,
hurling the lightning bolt,
bid them, in their madness, to set forth from home –
rather to refrain from going.

But they were massed together,
hastening to sure disaster
with brazen arms and caparisoned steeds:
yielding up all hope of a sweet return,
they fattened the white bloom of smoke
with their corpses;
by the banks of Ismenos,
seven pyres fed on their youthful flesh.
But with all-powerful thunder
Zeus cleft the deep-breasted earth for Amphiaraos
and hid him from sight chariot and all,

before the spear of Periklymenos
could strike him in the back
and shame his warrior spirit.
F.J. Nisetich, Trans.

Herodotos 9.33-35.

Ὡς δὲ ἄρα πάντες οἱ ἐτετάχατο κατὰ ἔθνεα καὶ κατὰ τέλεα, ἐνθαῦτα τῇ δευτέρῃ ἡμέρῃ ἐθύοντο καὶ ἀμφότεροι. Ἕλλησι μὲν Τεισαμενὸς Ἀντιόχου ἦν ὁ θυόμενος·

οὗτος γὰρ δὴ εἵπετο τῷ στρατεύματι τούτῳ μάντις· τὸν ἐόντα Ἠλεῖον καὶ γένεος τοῦ Ἰαμιδέων [Κλυτιάδην] Λακεδαιμόνιοι ἐποιήσαντο λεωσφέτερον. Τεισαμενῷ γὰρ μαντευομένῳ ἐν Δελφοῖσι περὶ γόνου ἀνεῖλε ἡ Πυθίη ἀγῶνας τοὺς μεγίστους ἀναιρήσεσθαι πέντε. ὁ μὲν δὴ ἁμαρτὼν τοῦ χρηστηρίου προσεῖχε γυμνασίοισι ὡς ἀναιρησόμενος γυμνικοὺς ἀγῶνας, ἀσκέων δὲ πένταεθλον παρὰ ἓν πάλαισμα ἔδραμε νικᾶν Ὀλυμπιάδα, Ἱερωνύμῳ τῷ Ἀνδρίῳ ἐλθὼν ἐς ἔριν. Λακεδαιμόνιοι δὲ μαθόντες οὐκ ἐς γυμνικοὺς ἀλλ᾽ ἐς ἀρηίους ἀγῶνας φέρον τὸ Τεισαμενοῦ μαντήιον, μισθῷ ἐπειρῶντο πείσαντες Τεισαμενὸν ποιέεσθαι ἅμα Ἡρακλειδέων τοῖσι βασιλεῦσι ἡγεμόνα τῶν πογέμων. ὁ δὲ ὁρέων περὶ πολλοῦ ποιευμένους Σπαρτιήτας φίλον αὐτὸν προσθέσθαι, μαθὼν τοῦτο ἀνετίμα, σημαίνων σφι ὡς, ἤν μιν πολιήτην σφέτερον ποιήσωνται τῶν πάντων μεταδιδόντες, ποιήσει ταῦτα, ἐπ᾽ ἄλλῳ μισθῷ δ᾽ οὔ. Σπαρτιῆται δὲ πρῶτα μὲν ἀκούσαντες δεινὰ ἐποιεῦντο καὶ μετίεσαν τῆς χρησμοσύνης τὸ παράπαν, τέλος δὲ δείματος μεγάλου ἐπικρεμαμένου τοῦ Περσικοῦ τούτου στρατεύματος κατaίνεον μετιόντες. ὁ δὲ γνοὺς τετραμμένους σφέας οὐδ᾽ οὕτω ἔτι ἔφη ἀρκέεσθαι τούτοισι μούνοισι, ἀλλὰ δεῖν ἔτι τὸν ἀδελφεὸν ἑωυτοῦ Ἡγίην γίνεσθαι Σπαρτιήτην ἐπὶ τοῖσι αὐτοῖσι λόγοισι τοῖσι καὶ αὐτός [γίνεται]. ταῦτα δὲ λέγων οὗτος ἐμιμέετο Μελάμποδα, ὡς εἰκάσαι βασιληίην τε καὶ πολιτηίην αἰτεομένους. καὶ γὰρ δὴ καὶ Μελάμπους τῶν ἐν Ἄργεϊ γυναικῶν μανεισέων, ὥς μιν οἱ Ἀργεῖοι ἐμισθοῦντο ἐκ Πύλου παῦσαι τὰς σφετέρας γυναῖκας τῆς νούσου, μισθὸν προετείνατο τῆς βασιληίης τὸ ἥμισυ. οὐκ ἀνασχομένων δὲ τῶν Ἀργείων ἀλλ᾽ ἀπιόντων, ὡς ἐμαίνοντο πλεῦνες τῶν γυναικῶν, οὕτω δὴ ὑποστάντες τὰ ὁ Μελάμπους προετείνατο ἤισαν δώσοντές οἱ ταῦτα. ὁ δὲ ἐνθαῦτα δὴ ἐπορέγεται ὁρέων αὐτοὺς τετραμμένους, φάς, ἢν μὴ καὶ τῷ ἀδελφεῷ Βίαντι μεταδῶσι τὸ τριτημόριον τῆς βασιληίης, οὐ ποιήσειν τὰ βούλονται. οἱ δὲ Ἀργεῖοι ἀπειληθέντες ἐς στεινὸν καταινέουσι καὶ ταῦτα. ὡς δὲ καὶ Σπαρτιῆται, ἐδέοντο γὰρ δεινῶς τοῦ Τεισαμενοῦ, πάντως συνεχώρεόν

APPENDIX A

οἱ. συγχωρησάντων δὲ καὶ ταῦτα τῶν Σπαρτιητέων, οὕτω δὴ πέντε σφι μαντευόμενος ἀγῶνας τοὺς μεγίστους Τεισαμενὸς ὁ Ἠλεῖος, γενόμενος Σπαρτιήτης, συγκαταιρέει. μοῦνοι δὲ δὴ πάντων ἀνθρώπων ἐγένοντο οὗτοι Σπαρτιήτῃσι πολιῆται. οἱ δὲ πέντε ἀγῶνες οἵδε ἐκένοντο, εἷς μὲν καὶ πρῶτος οὗτος ὁ ἐν Πλαταιῇσι, ἐπὶ δὲ ὁ ἐν Τεγέῃ πρὸς Τεγεήτας τε καὶ Ἀργείους γενόμενος, μετὰ δὲ ὁ ἐν Διπαιεῦσι πρὸς Ἀρκάδας πάντας πλὴν Μαντινέων, ἐπὶ δὲ ὁ Μεσσηνίων ὁ πρὸς Ἰσθμῷ· ὕστατος δὲ ὁ ἐν Τανάγρῃ πρὸς Ἀθηναίους τε καὶ Ἀργείους γενόμενος [οὗτος δὲ ὕστατος] κατεργάσθη τῶν πέντε ἀγώνων.

When Mardonius' dispositions were complete, with the national contingents all in their respective places in the line, both armies, on the following day, proceeded to offer sacrifice. the man who officiated for the Greeks was Tisamenos, the son of Antiochos, who was serving with the army in the capacity of diviner. He came originally from Elis and belonged to the Klytiad family of the Iamidae, but the Lacadaemonians had adopted him as one of themselves, under the following circumstances. Having no children, he had gone to Delphi to consult the oracle on the subject, and the Priestess, in her reply, told him that he was destined to win the "five greatest contests". Failing to understand the meaning of this prophecy, he went into training for athletics under the impression that that was the kind of "contest" he was to win, and actually came within a single event of winning the Olympic pentathlon against Hieronymos of Andros. The Lakedaimonians, however, realized that the word "contests" in the oracle referred not to athletics but to war, and attempted to induce him, by the offer of a wage, to become joint leader with their Heraklid kings in the conduct of their wars. Tisamenos saw that the Spartans were extremely anxious to get his support, and consequently raised his price, indicating that he would do as they asked only if they made him a Spartan citizen with full civic rights. Otherwise he would have nothing to do with the proposal. The first effect upon the Spartans of Tisamenos' demand was indignation, and they stopped asking for his services; but later on, under the terrible threat of the Persian invasion, they again sought him out and agreed to his terms. Tisamenos, however, seeing that they had come round, declared that he was no longer satisfied with the original conditions, but must have his brother Hagias too, made a citizen of Sparta with the same rights as himself. In making this demand Tisamenos was following the example of Melampous – if one can compare a demand for citizenship with a demand for a throne. For Melampous, it will be remembered, when he was fetched by the Argives from Pylos and offered a fee to restore their women, who had all gone mad, to sanity, claimed half the kingdom as payment for the service. The Argives thought the demand a monstrous one, and left him: but later, when more of their women caught the disease, they brought themselves to consent and went back to Melampous to promise what he asked. Thereupon, Melampous, seeing they had come round to his terms, reached out for a bit more, and refused to perform the service they wanted unless they gave, in addition, one-third of the kingdom to his brother Bias. The Argives, who were in dire straits, had to consent to this too. It was just the same with the Spartans – they needed Tisamenos badly, and consequently gave him everything he asked for. The result was that this man from Elis, having become a citizen of Sparta, helped the Spartans, in his capacity as diviner, to win five "contests" of the greatest importance. (Tisamenos and his brother were the only two foreigners ever to be made Spartan citizens.) They were the following: first, the battle of Plataia, which I am about to describe; second, the fight at Tegea against the Tegeans and Argives: third, at Dipaces against the combined forces of Arkadia, excluding Mantinea; fourth, against the Messenians at Ithome, and last, against the Athenians and Argives at Tanagra.

 A. De Selincourt, Trans.

 The battles of Tegea and Dipaces occurred c.473-470; not much is known of them. For battle of Ithome c. 465-460 cf. Thouky.I. 101-3, Tanagra occurred in 457 cf. Thouky.I.107-8.

Diodoros Sikelos 4.68.

Τούτων δ' ἡμῖν διευκρινημένων, πειρασόμεθα διελθεῖν περὶ Σαλμωνέως καὶ Τυροῦς καὶ τῶν ἀπογόνων ἕως Νέστορος τοῦ στρατεύσαντος ἐπὶ Τροίαν. Σαλμωνεὺς γὰρ ἦν υἱὸς Αἰόλου τοῦ Ἕλληνος τοῦ Δευκαλίωνος· οὗτος δ' ἐκ τῆς Αἰολίδος ὁρμηθεὶς μετὰ πλειόνων Αἰολέων ᾤκισε τῆς Ἠλείας παρὰ τὸν Ἀλφειὸν ποταμὸν πόλιν καὶ ἐκάλεσεν ἀφ' ἑαυτοῦ Σαλμωνίαν. γήμας δ' Ἀλκιδίκην τὴν Ἀλέου ἐγέννησε θυγατέρα τὴν προσαγορευθεῖσαν Τυρώ, κάλλει διαφέρουσαν. τῆς δὲ γυναικὸς Ἀλκιδίκης ἀποθανούσης ἐπέγημε τὴν ὀνομαζομένην Σιδηρώ· αὕτη δὲ χαλεπῶς διετέθη πρὸς τὴν Τυρώ, ὡς ἂν μητρυιά. μετὰ δὲ ταῦτα Σαλμωνεύς, ὑβριστὴς ὢν καὶ ἀσεβής, ὑπὸ μὲν τῶν ὑποτεταγμένων ἐμισήθη, ὑπὸ δὲ Διὸς διὰ τὴν ἀσέβειαν ἐκεραυνώθη. τῇ δὲ Τυροῖ, παρθένῳ κατ' ἐκείνους τοὺς χρόνους οὔσῃ, Ποσειδῶν μιγεὶς παῖδας ἐγέννησε Πελίαν καὶ Νηλέα. ἡ δὲ Τυρὼ συνοικήσασα Κρηθεῖ ἐτέκνωσεν Ἀμυθάονα καὶ Φέρητα καὶ Αἴσονα. Κρηθέως δὲ τελευτήσαντος ἐστασίασαν περὶ τῆς βασιλείας Πελίας τε καὶ Νηλεύς· τούτων δὲ Πελίας μὲν Ἰωλκοῦ καὶ τῶν πλησίον χωρίων ἐβασίλευσε, Νηλεὺς δὲ παραλαβὼν Μελάμποδα καὶ Βίαντα τοὺς Ἀμυθάονος καὶ Ἀγλαΐας υἱοὺς καὶ τινας ἄλλους τῶν Ἀχαιῶν Φθιωτῶν καὶ τῶν Αἰολέων ἐστράτευσεν εἰς Πελοπόννησον. καὶ Μελάμπους μὲν μάντις ὢν τὰς Ἀργείας γυναῖκας μανείσας διὰ τὴν Διονύσου μῆνιν ἐθεράπευσεν, ἀντὶ δὲ ταύτης τῆς εὐεργεσίας χάριν ἔλαβε παρὰ τοῦ βασιλέως τῶν Ἀργείων Ἀναξαγόρου τοῦ Μεγαπένθους τὰ δύο μέρη τῆς βασιγείας· κατοικήσας δ' ἐν Ἄργει κοινὴν ἐποιήσατο τὴν βασιλείαν Βίαντι τῷ ἀδελφῷ. γήμας δὲ Ἰφιάνειραν τὴν Μεγαπένθους ἐτέκνωσεν Ἀντιφάτην καὶ Μαντώ, ἔτι δὲ Βίαντα καὶ Προνόην· Ἀντιφάτου δὲ καὶ Ζευξίππης τῆς Ἱπποκόωντος Οἰκλῆς καὶ Ἀμφάλκης ὑπῆρξαν, Οἰκλέους δὲ καὶ Ὑπερμνήστρας τῆς Θεσπίου Ἰφιάνειρα καὶ Πολύβοια καὶ Ἀμφιάραος ἐγένοντο. Μελάμπους μὲν οὖν καὶ Βίας καὶ οἱ ἀπ' ἐκείνων οὕτω τῆς ἐν Ἄργει βασιλείας μετέσχον, Νηλεὺς δὲ μετὰ τῶν συνακολουθησάντων παραγενόμενος εἰς Μεσσήνην πόλιν ἔκτισε Πύλον, δόντων αὐτῷ τῶν ἐγχωρίων. ταύτης δὲ βασιλεύων καὶ γήμας Χλῶριν τὴν Ἀμφίονος τοῦ Θηβαίου, παῖδας ἐγέννησε δώδεκα, ὧν ἦν πρεσβύτατος μὲν Περικλύμενος, νεώτατος δὲ Νέστωρ ὁ ἐπὶ Τροίαν στρατεύσας.

Now that we have examined these matters we shall endeavor to set forth the facts concerning Salmoneus and Tyro and their descendants as far as Nestor, who took part in the campaign against Troy. Salmoneus was a son of Aiolos, who was the son of Hellen, who was the son of Deukalion, and setting out from Aiolis with a number of Aiolians he founded a city in Eleia on the banks of the river Alpheius and called it Salmonia after his own name. And marrying Alkidike, the daughter of Aleos (of Arkadia), he begat by her a daughter who was given the name Tyro, a maiden of surpassing beauty. When his wife Alkidike died Salmoneus took for a second wife Sidero as she was called who treated Tyro unkindly, as a step-mother would. Afterwards Salmoneus, being an overbearing man and impious, came to be hated by his subjects and because of his impiety was slain by Zeus with a bolt of lightning. As for Tyro, who was still a virgin when this took place, Poseidon lay with her and begat two sons, Pelias and Neleus. Then Tyro married Kretheus and bore Amythaon and Pheres and Aison. But at the death of Kretheus a strife over the kingship arose between Pelias and Neleus. Of these two Pelias came to be king over Iolkos and the neighboring districts, but Neleus, taking with him Melampous and Bias, the sons of Amythaon and Aglaia and certain other Achaians of Phthiotis and Aiolians, made a campaign to the Peloponnese. Melampous, who was a seer, healed the women of Argos of the madness which the wrath of Dionysos had brought upon them, and in return for this benefaction he received from the king of the Argives, Anaxagoras the son of Megapenthes, two-thirds of the kingdom; and he made his home in Argos and shared the kingship with Bias his brother. And marrying Iphianeira, the daughter of Megapenthes he begat Antiphates and Manto, and also Bias and Pronoe; and of Antiphates and of Zeukippe the daughter of Hippokoon[877], the children were Oikles and Amphalkes, and to Oikles and Hypermnestra, daughter of Thespios, were born Iphianeira, Polyboia and Amphiaraus. Now Melampous and Bias and their descendants shared in the kingship in Argos, as we have stated, but Neleus, when he had arrived in Messene together with his companions founded the city of Pylos, the natives of the region giving him the site. And while king of this city he married Chloris, the daughter of Amphion the Theban, and begat twelve sons, the oldest of whom was, Periklymenos and the youngest Nesor who engaged in the expedition against Troy.

C.H. Oldfather, Trans.

APPENDIX A

Strabo 8.6.10.

Ἄργος δὲ καὶ τὸ πεδίον λέγεται παρὰ τοῖς νεωτέροις, παρ' Ὁμήρῳ δ' οὐδ' ἅπαξ· μάλιστα δ' οἴονται Μακεδονικὸν καὶ Θετταλικὸν εἶναι.

10. Τῶν δ' ἀπογόνων τοῦ Δαναοῦ διαδεξαμένων τὴν ἐν Ἄργει δυναστείαν, ἐπιμιχθέντων δὲ τούτοις τῶν Ἀμυθαονιδῶν, ὡρμημένων ἐκ τῆς Πισάτιδος καὶ τῆς Τριφυλίας, οὐκ ἂν θαυμάσειέ τις, εἰ συλλενεῖς ὄντες οὕτω διείλοντο τὴν χώραν εἰς δύο βασιλείας τὸ πρῶτον, ὥστε τὰς ἡγεμονίδας οὔσας ἐν αὐταῖς δύο πόλεις ἀποδειχθῆναι πλησίον ἀλλήλων ἱδρυμένας, ἐν ἐλάττοσιν ἢ πεντήκοντα σταδίοις, τό τε Ἄργος καὶ τὰς Μυκήνας, καὶ τὸ Ἡραῖον εἶναι κοινὸν ἱερὸν ἀμφοῖν τὸ πρὸς ταῖς Μυκήναις, ἐν ᾧ τὰ Πολυκλείτου ξόανα, τῇ μὲν τέχνῃ κάλλιστα τῶν πάντων, πολυτελείᾳ δὲ καὶ μεγέθει τῶν Φειδίου λειπόμενα. κατ' ἀρχὰς μὲν οὖν τὸ Ἄργος ἐπεκράτει μᾶλλον, εἶθ' αἱ Μυκῆναι, μείζονα ἐπίδοσιν λαβοῦσαι διὰ τὴν τῶν Πελοπιδῶν εἰς αὐτὰς μεθίδρυσιν· περιστάντων γὰρ εἰς τοὺς Ἀτρέως παῖδας ἁπάντων, Ἀγαμέμνων ὢν πρεσβύτερος, παραλαβὼν τὴν ἐξουσίαν, ἅμα τύχῃ τε καὶ ἀρετῇ πρὸς τοῖς οὖσι πολλὴν προσεκτήσατο τῆς χώρας· καὶ δὴ καὶ τὴν Λακωνικὴν τῇ Μυκηναίᾳ προσέθηκε. Μενέλαος μὲν δὴ τὴν Λακωνικὴν ἔσχε, Μυκήνας δὲ καὶ τὰ μέχρι Κορίνθου καὶ Σικυῶνος καὶ τῆς Ἰώνων μὲν τότε καὶ Αἰγιαλέων καλουμένης, Ἀχαιῶν δὲ ὕστερον, Ἀγαμέμνων παρέλαβε. μετὰ δὲ τὰ Τρωικὰ τῆς Ἀγαμέμνονος ἀρχῆς καταλυθείσης, ταπεινωθῆναι συνέβη Μυκήνας, καὶ μάλιστα μετὰ τὴν τῶν Ἡρακλειδῶν κάθοδον. κατασχόντες γὰρ οὗτοι τὴν Πελοπόννησον ἐξέβαλον τοὺς πρότερον κρατοῦντας, ὥσθ' οἱ τὸ Ἄργος ἔχοντες εἶχον καὶ τὰς Μυκήνας συντελούσας εἰς ἕν· χρόνοις δ' ὕστερον κατεσκάφησαν ὑπ' Ἀργείων, ὥστε νῦν μηδ' ἴχνος εὑρίσκεσθαι τῆς Μυκηναίων πόλεως. ὅπου δὲ Μυκῆναι τοιαῦτα πεπόνθασιν, οὐ δεῖ θαυμάζειν, οὐδ' εἴ τινες τῶν ὑπὸ τῷ Ἄργει καταλεγομένων ἀφανεῖς νῦν εἰσιν. ὁ μὲν δὴ Κατάλογος ἔχει οὕτως· οἳ δ' Ἄργος τ' εἶχον Τίρυνθά τε τειχιόεσσαν Ἑρμιόνην τ' Ἀσίνην τε, βαθὺν κατὰ κόλπον ἐχούσας, Τροιζῆν' Ἠιόνας τε καὶ ἀμπελόεντ' Ἐπίδαυρον, οἵ τ' ἔχον Αἴγιναν Μάσητά τε, κοῦροι Ἀχαιῶν. τούτων δὲ περὶ μὲν τοῦ Ἄργους εἴρηται, περὶ δὲ τῶν ἄλλων λεκτέον.

11. Τῇ μὲν οὖν Τίρυνθι ὁρμητηρίῳ χρήσασθαι δοκεῖ Προῖτος καὶ τειχίσαι διὰ Κυκλώπων,

After the descendants of Danaus succeeded to the reign of Argos, and the sons of Amythaon, who were emigrants from Pisatis and Triphylia, became associated with these, one should not be surprised if, being kindred, the at first so divided the country into two kingdoms that the two cities in them which hold the hegemony were designated as the capitals, though situated near one another, at a distances of less than fifty stadia, I mean Argos and Mykenai, and that the Heraion near Mykenai was a temple common to both. In this temple are the images made by Polykleitos, in execution the most beautiful in the world, but in costliness and size inferior to those by Pheidias. Now at the outset Argos was more powerful, but later Mykenai waxed more powerful on account of the removal thereto of the Pelopidai; for, when everything fell to the sons of Atreus, Agamemnon, being the elder, assumed supreme power, and by a combination of good fortune and valour acquired much of the country in addition to the possessions he already had; and indeed he also added Lakonia to the territory of Mykenai. Now Menelaos came into possession of Lakonia, but Agamemnon received Mykenai and the regions as far as Korinth and Sikyon and the country which at that time was called the country of the Ionians and Aigialians but later the country of the Achaians. But after the Trojan times, when the empire of Agamemnon had been broken up, it came to pass that Mykenai was reduced, and particularly after the return of the Herakleiai; for when these had taken possession of the Peloponnesos they expelled its former masters, so that those who held Argos also held Mykenai as a component part of one whole. But in later times Mykenai was razed to the ground by the Argives, so that today not even a trace of the city of the Mykenaians is to be found. And since Mykenai has suffered such a fate, one should not be surprised if also some of the cities which are catalogued as subject to Argos have now disappeared. Now the *Catalogue* contains the following: "And those who held Argos, and Tiryns of the great walls, and Hermione and Asine that occupy a deep gulf, and Troizen and Eiones and vine-clad Epidauros, and the youths of the Achaians who held Aigina and Mases." But of the cities just

431

named I have already discussed Argos, and now I must discuss the others. 11 Now it seems that Tiryns was used as a base of operations by Proitos and was walled by him through the aid of the Kyklopes…

H.L. Jones, Trans.

Apollodoros 1.9.7 – 1.9.14.

7. Σαλμωνεὺς δὲ τὸ μὲν πρῶτον περὶ Θεσσαλίαν κατῴκει, παραγενόμενος δὲ αὖθις εἰς Ἦλιν ἐκεῖ πόλιν ἔκτισεν. ὑβριστὴς δὲ ὢν καὶ τῷ Διὶ ἐξισοῦσθαι θέλων διὰ τὴν ἀσέβειαν ἐκολάσθη · ἔλεγε γὰρ ἑαυτὸν εἶναι Δία, καὶ τὰς ἐκείνου θυσίας ἀφελόμενος ἑαυτῷ προσέτασσε θύειν, καὶ βύρσας μὲν ἐξηραμμένας ἐξ ἅρματος μετὰ λεβήτων χαλκῶν σύρων ἔλεγε βροντᾶν, βάλλων δὲ εἰς οὐρανὸν αἰθομένας λαμπάδας ἔλεγεν ἀστράπτειν. Ζεὺς δὲ αὐτὸν κεραυνώσας τὴν κτισθεῖσαν ὑπ' αὐτοῦ πόλιν καὶ τοὺς οἰκήτορας ἠφάνισε πάντας.

8. Τυρὼ δὲ ἡ Σαλμωνέως θυγάτηρ καὶ Ἀλκιδίκης παρὰ Κρηθεῖ [τῷ Σαλμωνέως ἀδελφῷ] τρεφομένη ἔρωτα ἴσχει Ἐνιπέως τοῦ ποταμοῦ, καὶ συνεχῶς ἐπὶ τὰ τούτου ῥεῖθρα φοιτῶσα τούτοις ἐπωδύρετο. Ποσειδῶν δὲ εἰκασθεὶς Ἐνιπεῖ συγκατεκλίθη αὐτῇ· ἡ δὲ γεννήσασα κρύφα διδύμους παῖδας ἐκτίθησιν. ἐκκειμένων δὲ τῶν βρεφῶν, παριόντων ἱπποφορβῶν ἵππος μία προσαψαμένη τῇ χηλῇ θατέρου τῶν βρεφῶν πέλιόν τι τοῦ προσώπου μέρος ἐποίησεν. ὁ δὲ ἱπποφορβὸς ἀμφοτέρους τοὺς παῖδας ἀνελόμενος ἔθρεψε, καὶ τὸν μὲν πελιωθέντα Πελίαν ἐκάλεσε, τὸν δὲ ἕτερον Νηλέα. τελειωθέντες δὲ ἀνεγνώρισαν τὴν μητέρα, καὶ τὴν μητρυιὰν ἀπέκτειναν Σιδηρώ· κακουμένην γὰρ γνόντες ὑπ' αὐτῆς τὴν μητέρα ὥρμησαν ἐπ' αὐτήν, ἡ δὲ φθάσασα εἰς τὸ τῆς Ἥρας τέμενος κατέφυγε, Πελίας δὲ ἐπ' αὐτῶν τῶν βωμῶν αὐτὴν κατέσφαξε, καὶ καθόλου διετέλει τὴν Ἥραν ἀτιμάζων.

9. ἐστασίασαν δὲ ὕστερον πρὸς ἀλλήλους, καὶ Νηλεὺς μὲν ἐκπεσὼν ἧκεν εἰς Μεσσήνην καὶ Πύλον κτίζει, καὶ γαμεῖ Χλωρίδα τὴν Ἀμφίονος, ἐξ ἧς αὐτῷ γίνεται θυγάτηρ μὲν Πηρώ, ἄρρενες δὲ Ταῦρος Ἀστέριος Πυλάων Δηίμαχος Εὐρύβιος Ἐπίλαος Φράσιος Εὐρυμένης Εὐαγόρας Ἀλάστωρ Νέστωρ Περικλύμενος, ᾧ δὴ καὶ Ποσειδῶν δίδωσι μεταβάλλειν τὰς μορφάς, καὶ μαχόμενος ὅτε Ἡρακλῆς ἐξεπόρθει Πύλον, γινόμενος ὁτὲ μὲν λέων ὁτὲ δὲ ὄφις ὁτὲ δὲ μέλισσα, ὑφ'

Ἡρακλέους μετὰ τῶν ἄλλων Νηλέως παίδων ἀπέθανεν. ἐσώθη δὲ Νέστωρ μόνος, ἐπειδὴ παρὰ Γερηνίοις ἐτρέφετο· ὅς γήμας Ἀναξιβίαν τὴν Κρατιέως θυγατέρας μὲν Πεισιδίκην καὶ Πολυκάστην ἐγέννησε, παῖδας δὲ Περσέα Στράτιχον Ἄρητον Ἐχέφρονα Πεισίστρατον Ἀντίλοχον Θρασυμήδην.

10. Πελίας δὲ περὶ Θεσσαλίαν κατώκει, καὶ γήμας Ἀναξιβίαν τὴν Βίαντος, ὡς δὲ ἔνιοι Φυλομάχην τὴν Ἀμφίονος, ἐγέννησε παῖδα μὲν Ἄκαστον, θυγατέρας δὲ Πεισιδίκην Πελόπειαν Ἱπποθόην Ἄλκηστιν.

11. Κρηθεὺς δὲ κτίσας Ἰωλκὸν γαμεῖ Τυρὼ τὴν Σαλμωνέως, ἐξ ἧς αὐτῷ γίνονται παῖδες Αἴσων Ἀμυθάων Φέρης. Ἀμυθάων μὲν οὖν οἰκῶν Πύλον Εἰδομένην γαμεῖ τὴν Φέρητος, καὶ γίνονται παῖδες αὐτῷ Βίας καὶ Μελάμπους, ὃς ἐπὶ τῶν χωρίων διατελῶν, οὔσης πρὸ τῆς οἰκήσεως αὐτοῦ δρυὸς ἐν ᾗ φωλεὸς ὄφεων ὑπῆρχεν, ἀποκτεινάντων τῶν θεραπόντων τοὺς ὄφεις τὰ μὲν ἑρπετὰ ξύλα συμφορήσας ἔκαυσε, τοὺς δὲ τῶν ὄφεων νεοσσοὺς ἔθρεψεν. οἱ δὲ γενόμενοι τέλειοι παραστάντες αὐτῷ κοιμωμένῳ τῶν ὤμων ἐξ ἑκατέρου τὰς ἀκοὰς ταῖς γλώσσαις ἐξεκάθαιρον. ὁ δὲ ἀναστὰς καὶ γενόμενος περιδεὴς τῶν ὑπερπετομένων ὀρνέων τὰς φωνὰς συνίει, καὶ παρ' ἐκείνων μανθάνων προύλεγε τοῖς ἀνθρώποις τὰ μέλλοντα. προσέλαβε δὲ καὶ τὴν διὰ τῶν ἱερῶν μαντικήν, περὶ δὲ τὸν Ἀλφειὸν συντυχὼν Ἀπόλλωνι τὸ λοιπὸν ἄριστος ἦν μάντις.

12. Βίας δὲ ἐμνηστεύετο Πηρὼ τὴν Νηλέως· ὁ δὲ πολλῶν αὐτῷ μνηστευομένων τὴν θυγατέρα δώσειν ἔφη τῷ τὰς Φυλάκου βόας κομίσαντι αὐτῷ. αὗται δὲ ἦσαν ἐν Φυλάκῃ καὶ κύων ἐφύλασσεν αὐτὰς οὗ οὔτε ἄνθρωπος οὔτε θηρίον πέλας ἐλθεῖν ἠδύνατο. ταύτας ἀδυνατῶν Βίας τὰς βόας κλέψαι παρεκάλει τὸν ἀδελφὸν σαλλαβέσθαι. Μελάμπους δὲ ὑπέσχετο, καὶ προεῖπεν ὅτι φωραθήσεται κλέπτων καὶ δεθεὶς ἐνιαυτὸν οὕτω τὰς βόας λήψεται. μετὰ δὲ τὴν ὑπόσχεσιν εἰς Φυλάκην ἀπῄει καί, καθάπερ προεῖπε, φωραθεὶς ἐπὶ τῇ κλοπῇ δέσμιος ἐν οἰκήματι ἐφυλάσσετο. λειπομένου δὲ τοῦ ἐνιαυτοῦ βραχέος χρόνου, τῶν κατὰ τὸ κρυφαῖον τῆς στέγης σκωλήκων ἀκούει, τοῦ μὲν ἐρωτῶντος πόσον ἤδη μέρος τοῦ δοκοῦ διαβέβρωται, τῶν δὲ ἀποκρινομένων λοιπὸν ἐλάχιστον εἶναι. καὶ ταχέως ἐκέλευσεν αὐτὸν εἰς ἕτερον οἴκημα μεταγαγεῖν, γενομένου δὲ τούτου μετ' οὐ πολὺ συνέπεσε τὸ οἴκημα. θαυμάσας δὲ Φύλακος, καὶ μαθὼν ὅτι ἐστὶ μάντις ἄριστος, λύσας

APPENDIX A

παρεκάλεσεν εἰπεῖν ὅπως αὐτοῦ τῷ παιδὶ Ἰφίκλῳ παῖδες γένωνται. ὁ δὲ ὑπέσχετο ἐφ᾽ ᾧ τὰς βόας λήψεται. καὶ καταθύσας ταύρους δύο καὶ μελίσας τοὺς οἰωνοὺς προσεκαλέσατο· παραγενομένου δὲ αἰγυπιοῦ, παρὰ τούτου μανθάνει δὴ ὅτι Φύλακός ποτε κριοὺς τέμνων ἐπὶ τῶν αἰδοίων παρὰ τῷ Ἰφίκλῳ τὴν μάχαιραν ᾑμαγμένην ἔτι κατέθετο, δείσαντος δὲ τοῦ παιδὸς καὶ φυγόντος αὖθις κατὰ τῆς ἱερᾶς δρυὸς αὐτὴν ἔπηξε, καὶ ταύτην ἀμφιτροχάσας ἐκάλυψεν ὁ φλοιός. ἔλεγεν οὖν, εὑρεθείσης τῆς μαχαίρας εἰ ξύων τὸν ἰὸν ἐπὶ ἡμέρας δέκα Ἰφίκλῳ δῷ πιεῖν, παῖδα γεννήσειν. ταῦτα μαθὼν παρ᾽ αἰγυπιοῦ Μελάμπους τὴν μὲν μάχαιραν εὗρε, τῷ δὲ Ἰφίκλῳ τὸν ἰὸν ξύσας ἐπὶ ἡμέρας δέκα δέδωκε πιεῖν, καὶ παῖς αὐτῷ Ποδάρκης ἐγένετο. τὰς δὲ βόας εἰς Πύλον ἤλασε, καὶ τῷ ἀδελφῷ τὴν Νηλέως θυγατέρα λαβὼν ἔδωκε. καὶ μέχρι μέν τινος ἐν Μεσσήνῃ κατῴκει, ὡς δὲ τὰς ἐν Ἄργει γυναῖκας ἐξέμηνε Διόνυσος, ἐπὶ μέρει τῆς βασιλείας ἰασάμενος αὐτὰς ἐκεῖ μετὰ Βίαντος κατῴκησε.

13. Βίαντος δὲ καὶ Πηροῦς Ταλαός, οὗ καὶ Λυσιμάχης τῆς Ἄβαντος τοῦ Μελάμποδος Ἄδραστος Παρθενοπαῖος Πρῶναξ Μηκιστεὺς Ἀριστόμαχος Ἐριφύλη, ἣν Ἀμφιάραος γαμεῖ. Παρθενοπαίου δὲ Πρόμαχος ἐγένετο, ὃς μετὰ τῶν ἐπιγόνων ἐπὶ Θήβας ἐστρατεύθη, Μηκιστέως δὲ Εὐρύαλος, ὃς ἧκεν εἰς Τροίαν. Πρώνακτος δὲ ἐγένετο Λυκοῦργος, Ἀδράστου δὲ καὶ Ἀμφιθέας τῆς Πρώνακτος θυγατέρες μὲν Ἀργεία Δηιπύλη Αἰγιάλεια, παῖδες δὲ Αἰγιαλαὺς καὶ Κυάνιππος.

14. Φέρης δὲ ὁ Κρηθέως Φερὰς ἐν Θεσσαλίᾳ κτίσας ἐγέννησεν Ἄδμητον καὶ Λυκοῦργον.

Salmoneus at first lived in Thessaly, but later went to Elis and there built a city. He was arrogant and wished to make himself the equal of Zeus and was punished for this lack of reverence. For he said that he himself was Zeus, removed the god's sacrifice and ordered men to sacrifice to him. Dragging bronze cauldrons behind his chariot with dried skins tied over the tops of them he claimed he made thunder, and hurling burning torches in the air he said that he made lightning. Zeus struck him with a thunderbolt and utterly destroyed the city he had founded, with all its inhabitants.

8. Tyro, the daughter of Salmoneus and Alkidike, was reared by Kretheus, the brother of Salmoneus, and fell in love with the Enipeus River. She continually visited its flowing stream and lamented there. Poseidon in the form of Enipeus made love with her. She gave birth secretly to two sons and exposed them. As the babies were lying out in the open, some horsemen passed by and a mare grazed one of them with her hoof, making a bruise on its face. One of the horsemen took up the children and reared them, calling the one with the bruise Pelias (Livid) and the other Neleus. When they were grown they found their mother and killed their stepmother, Sidero, for they knew that she had mistreated their mother. They set out after her and caught her in the grove of Hera, where she had fled. Pelias slaughtered her at the altars themselves and made a general practice of dishonoring Hera.

9. Later, the brothers quarreled with each other and Neleus went in exile to Messene, founded Pylos and married Chloris, the daughter of Amphion. She bore him a daughter, Pero, and sons named Tauros, Asterios, Pylaon, Deimachos, Eurybios, Epilaos, Phrasios, Eurymenes, Evagoras, Alastor, Nestor, and Periklymenos. Poseidon gave to Periklymenos the ability to change his shape. When Herakes sacked Pylos, Periklymenos changed himself into a lion, into a snake, and then into a bee, but died even so at Herakles' hands with the rest of Neleus' sons. Nestor alone was saved since he was reared among the Gerenians (cf.2.7.3). He married Anaxibia, the daughter of Kratieus. By her he had daughters named Pisidike and Polykaste, and sons named Perseus, Stratichos, Aretos, Echephron, Pisistratos, Antilochos and Thrasymedes.

10. Pelias settled in Thessaly and married Anaxibia, the daughter of Bias, or as some say, Phylomache, the daughter of Amphion. By her he had a son Akastos, and daughters named Pisidike, Pelopia, Hippothoe and Alkestis.

11 Kretheus founded Iolkos and married Tyro, the daughter of Salmoneus, who bore him sons named Aison, Amythaon, and Pheres. Amythaon lived in Pylos and married Idomene, the daughter of Pheres, by whom he had sons named Bias and Melampous. Melampous lived in the country. In front of his house there grew a hollow oak which was a lair for snakes. Melampous' servants killed the snakes, but he gathered wood for a fire, burned them, and reared their young. When

they were grown they came to him while he slept, one at each shoulder, and cleaned his ears with their tongues. He arose, frightened, but was able to understand the voices of birds flying overhead. Learning the future from them he foretold it to men. He learned also the art of divination by means of sacrifices and, meeting Apollo at the Alpheus River, was afterwards and excellent seer.

12. Bias sought to marry Pero, the daughter of Neleus. Since many wanted to marry her, Neleus said that he sould giver her to the man who brought him the cattle of Phylakos. They were in Phylake guarded by a dog which neither man nor animal could approach. When Bias was unable to steal them he asked his brother to help him. Melampous then went to Phylake and, as he had foretold, was caught in the act of stealing the cattle and imprisoned in a cell. When nearly a year had passed he heard worms talking in the wood of the ceiling. One asked how much of the beam had been eaten through and the others answered that only a very little of it was left. Melampous immediately demanded to be transferred to another cell. Shortly after this was done, the roof of the first cell collapsed. Phylakos was amazed, and when he learned that Melampous was a famous seer, he freed him and summoned him to tell how his son Iphiklos might have children. Melampous promised to tell him in return for the cattle. After he sacrificed and cut up two bulls he called the birds to himself. He learned from a vulture that once when Phylakos was castrating rams he laid the still bloody knife beside Iphiklos, and that the child became frightened and ran away. Phylakos then stuck a knife in a sacred oak and it was swallowed up and hidden by the bark. The vulture said that if he found the knife, scraped off the rust and gave it to Iphiklos in a mixture to drink for ten days, he would have a son. After he learned this Melampous found the knife, scraped off the rust and gave it to Iphiklos to drink for ten days. Iphiklos then had a son, Podarkes. Melampous drove the cattle to Pylos, received the daughter of Neleus and gave her to his brother. He lived in Messene for a time, but when Dionysos drove the women of Argos mad, Melampous restored them to sanity in return for a part of the kingdom and lived there with Bias.

13. To Bias and Pero a son, Talaus, was born. He married Lysimache, the daughter of Abas, Melampous' son, and by her he had Adrastus, Parthenopaeus, Pronax, Mekisteus, Aristomachos, and

Eriphyle, whom Amphiaraus married. Parthenopais had a son, Promachos, who went with the Epigoni on the expedition against Thebes (cf.3.7.2), and Mekisteus had a son, Eurylaos, who went to Troy. Pronax had a son, Lykourgos, and Adrastos and Amphithea, the daughter of Pronax, had daughters named Argia, Deipyle, and Aigialia, and sons named Aigialeus and Kyanippos.

14. Pheres, the son of Kretheus, founded Pherae in Thessaly and had sons named Admetos and Lykourgos.

Apollodoros 2.2.1 – 2.2.2.

Λυγκεὺς δὲ μετὰ Δαναὸν Ἄργους δυναστεύων ἐξ Ὑπερνήστρας τεκνοῖ παῖδα Ἄβαντα. τούτου δὲ καὶ Ἀγλαΐας τῆς Μαντινέως δίδυμοι παῖδες ἐγένοντο Ἀκρίσιος καὶ Προῖτος. οὗτοι καὶ κατὰ γαστρὸς μὲν ἔτι ὄντες ἐστασίαζον πρὸς ἀλλήλους, ὡς δὲ ἀνετράφησαν, περὶ τῆς βασιλείας ἐπολέμουν, καὶ πολεμοῦντες εὗρον ἀσπίδας πρῶτοι. καὶ κρατήσας Ἀκρίσιος Προῖτον Ἄργους ἐξελαύνει. ὁ δ᾽ ἧκεν εἰς Λυκίαν πρὸς Ἰοβάτην, ὡς δέ τινές φασι, πρὸς Ἀμφιάνακτα· καὶ γαμεῖ τὴν τούτου θυγατέρα, ὡς μὲν Ὅμηρος, Ἄντειαν, ὡς δὲ οἱ τραγικοί, Σθενέβοιαν. κατάγει δὲ αὐτὸν ὁ κηδεστὴς μετὰ στρατοῦ Λυκίων, καὶ καταλαμβάνει Τίρυνθα, ταύτην αὐτῷ Κυκλώπων τειχισάντων. μερισάμενοι δὲ τὴν Ἀργείαν ἅπασαν κατῴκουν, καὶ Ἀκρίσιος μὲν Ἄργους βασιλεύει, Προῖτος δὲ Τίρυνθος. καὶ γίνεται Ἀκρισίῳ μὲν ἐξ Εὐρυδίκης τῆς Λακεδαίμουος Δανάη, Προίτῳ δὲ ἐκ Σθενεβοίας Λυσίππη καὶ Ἰφινόη καὶ Ἰφιάνασσα. αὗται δὲ ὡς ἐτελειώθησαν, ἐμάνησαν, ὡς μὲν Ἡσίοδός φησιν, ὅτι τὰς Διονύσου τελετὰς οὐ κατεδέχοντο, ὡς δὲ Ἀκουσίλαος λέγει, διότι τὸ τῆς Ἥρας ξόανον ἐξηυτέλισαν. γενόμεναι δὲ ἐμμανεῖς ἐπλανῶντο ἀνὰ τὴν Ἀρλείαν ἅπασαν, αὖθις δὲ τὴν Ἀρκαδίαν καὶ τὴν Πελοπόννησον διελθοῦσαι μετ᾽ ἀκοσμίας ἁπάσης διὰ τῆς ἐρημίας ἐτρόχαζον. Μελάμπους δὲ ὁ Ἀμυθάονος καὶ Εἰδομένης τῆς Ἄβαντος, μάντις ὢν καὶ τὴν διὰ φαρμάκων καὶ καθαρμῶν θεραπείαν πρῶτος εὑρηκώς, ὑπισχνεῖται θεραπεύειν τὰς παρθένους, εἰ λάβοι τὸ τρίτον μέρος τῆς δυναστείας. οὐκ ἐπιτρέποντος δὲ Προίτου θεραπεύειν ἐπὶ μισθοῖς πηλικούτοις, ἔτι μᾶλλον ἐμαίνοντο αἱ παρθένοι καὶ προσέτι μετὰ τούτων αἱ λοιπαὶ γυναῖκες· καὶ γὰρ αὗται τὰς οἰκίας ἀπολιποῦσαι τοὺς ἰδίους ἀπώλλυον παῖδας καὶ εἰς τὴν ἐρημίαν ἐφοίτων. προβαινούσης δὲ ἐπὶ πλεῖστον τῆς συμφορᾶς, τοὺς αἰτηθέντας μισθοὺς ὁ Προῖτος ἐδίδου. ὁ δὲ ὑπέσχετο θεραπεύειν ὅταν ἕτερον τοσοῦτον τῆς γῆς ὁ ἀδελφὸς αὐτοῦ λάβῃ Βίας. Προῖτος δὲ εὐλαβηθεὶς μὴ βραδυνούσης τῆς θεραπείας αἰτηθείη καὶ πλεῖον, θεραπεύειν συνεχώρησεν ἐπὶ τούτοις. Μελάμπους δὲ παραλαβὼν τοὺς δυνατωτάτους τῶν νεανιῶν μετ' ἀλαλαγμοῦ καί τινος ἐνθέου χορείας ἐκ τῶν ὀρῶν αὐτὰς εἰς Σικυῶνα συνεδίωξε. κατὰ δὲ τὸν διωγμὸν ἡ πρεσβυτάτη τῶν θυγατέρων Ἰφινόη μετήλλαξεν· ταῖς δὲ λοιπαῖς τυχούσαις καθαρμῶν σωφρονῆσαι συνέβη. καὶ ταύτας μὲν ἐξέδοτο Προῖτος Μελάμποδι καὶ Βίαντι, παῖδα δ' ὕστερον ἐγέννησε Μεγαπένθην.

Lynkeus ruled Argos after Danaos and by Hypermestra had a son Abas. He and Aglaia, daughter of Mantineus, had two sons named Akrisios and Proitos. They quarreled with each other even in the womb, and when they were grown, fought over the kingship, inventing the shield in the course of their battle. Akrisios won and drove Proitos out of Argos. Proitos went to Lycia and to the court of Iobates, or, as some say, of Amphianax, and married his daughter who was named Antia according to Homer (Il.6.160), but Stheneboia according to the tragedians (but cf. 3.9.1). His father-in-law with an army of Lycians restored him to his own country and Proitos then seized Tiryns, the walls of which the Kyklopes built for him.

2. Akrisios and Proitos divided the Argive land between themselves, the former ruling Argos, the latter Tiryns. Akrisios had Danae by Eurydike, the daughter of Lakedaimon, and Proitos had Lysippe, Iphinoe, and Iphianassa by Stheneboia. When Proitos daughters were grown they went mad because they refused to accept the rites of Dionysos, according to Hesiod, but according to Akousilaos because they mocked the wooden statue of Hera. After going insane they wandered through all the Argive country, passed through Arkadia and the rest of the Peloponnese, and ran with abandon through the desert. Melampous promised to cure the women in return for a third of the rule. He was the son of Amythaon and Abas' daughter Idomene, a seer and the first to use drugs and cathartics in the practice of medicine. When Proitos refused treatment at such a

high price, his daughters became yet more insane and in addition the rest of the women went mad along with them. Moreover, they left their houses, killed their own children, and went to the desert. Not until the situation was at its worst did Proitos agree to the price demanded. Now, however, Melampous promised to cure the madness only on condition that his brother Bias receive as much territory as he. Proitos, fearing that Melampous would exact an even higher price if treatment were delayed, agreed to these terms. Melampous then took with him the strongest of the young men and by means of shouts and a certain inspired dance chased the women from the mountains to Sikyon. During the pursuit Iphione, the oldest of Proitos daughters, died. The two remaining were purified and regained their sanity. Proitos gave them to Melampous and Bias to marry and later had a son Megapenthes.

Apollodoros 2.4.1.

Ἀκρισίῳ δὲ περὶ παίδων γενέσεως ἀρρένων χρηστηριαζομένῳ ὁ θεὸς ἔφη γενέσθαι παῖδα ἐκ τῆς θυγατρός, ὅς αὐτὸν ἀποκτενεῖ. δείσας δὲ ὁ Ἀκρίσιος τοῦτο, ὑπὸ γῆν θάλαμον κατασκευάσας χάλκεον τὴν Δανάην ἐφρούρει. ταύτην μέν, ὡς ἔνιοι λέγουσιν, ἔφθειρε Προῖτος, ὅθεν αὐτοῖς καὶ ἡ στάσις ἐκινήθη· ὡς δὲ ἔνιοί φασι, Ζεὺς μεταμορφωθεὶς εἰς χρυσὸν καὶ διὰ τῆς ὀροφῆς εἰς τοὺς Δανάης εἰσρυεὶς κόλπους συνῆλθεν. αἰσθόμενος δὲ Ἀκρίσιος ὕστερον ἐξ αὐτῆς γεγεννημένον Περσέα, μὴ πιστεύσας ὑπὸ Διὸς ἐφθάρθαι, τὴν θυγατέρα μετὰ τοῦ παιδὸς εἰς λάρνακα βαλὼν ἔρριψεν εἰς θάλασσαν. προσενεχθείσης δὲ τῆς λάρνακος Σερίφῳ Δίκτυς ἄρας ἀνέτρεφε τοῦτον.

When Akrisios asked the oracle how to have male children the god replied that his daughter Danae would bear a son who would kill him. Fearing this, Akrisios constructed and underground chamber of bronze in which he guarded his daughter. Some say that Proitos, however, seduced her (and that from this arose the quarrel between him and Akrisios). Others say that Zeus changed himself into liquid gold and flowed through the roof into Danae's womb, in this way having intercourse with her. Akrisios later found out about Perseus, the son she gave birth to. He refused to believe that she was seduced by Zeus, so he put her and her son into a chest and cast them into the sea. The chest was carried to Seriphos where Dictys recovered it and reared Perseus.

Apollodoros 2.4.4.

Περσεὺς δὲ μετὰ Δανάης καὶ Ἀνδρομέδας ἔσπευδεν εἰς Ἄργος, ἵνα Ἀκρίσιον θεάσηται. ὁ δὲ <τοῦτο μαθὼν καὶ> δεδοικὼς τὸν χρησμόν, ἀπολιπὼν Ἄργος εἰς τὴν Πελασγιῶτιν ἐχώρησε γῆν. Τευταμίδου δὲ τοῦ Λαρισσαίων βασιλέως ἐπὶ κατοιχομένῳ τῷ πατρὶ διατιθέντος γυμνικὸν ἀγῶνα, παρεγένετο καὶ ὁ Περσεὺς ἀγωνίσασθαι θέλων, ἀγωνιζόμενος δὲ πένταθλον, τὸν δίσκον ἐπὶ τὸν Ἀκρισίου πόδα βαλὼν παραχρῆμα ἀπέκτεινεν αὐτόν. αἰσθόμενος δὲ τὸν χρησμὸν τετελειωμένον τὸν μὲν Ἀκρίσιον ἔξω τῆς πόλεως ἔθαψεν, αἰσχυνόμενος δὲ εἰς Ἄργος ἐπανελθεῖν ἐπὶ τὸν κλῆρον τοῦ δι' αὐτοῦ τετελευτηκότος, παραγενόμενος εἰς Τίρυνθα πρὸς τὸν Προίτου παῖδα Μεγαπένθην ἠλλάξατο, τούτῳ τε τὸ Ἄργος ἐνεχείρισε. καὶ Μεγαπένθης μὲν ἐβασίλευσεν Ἀργείων, Περσεὺς δὲ Τίρυνθος, προστειχίσας Μίδειαν καὶ Μυκήνας. ἐγένοντο δὲ ἐξ Ἀνδρομέδας παῖδες αὐτῷ, πρὶν μὲν ἐγθεῖν εἰς τὴν Ἑλλάδα Πέρσης, ὃν παρὰ Κηφεῖ κατέλιπεν (ἀπὸ τούτου δὲ τοὺς Περσῶν βασιλέας λέγεται γενέσθαι), ἐν Μυκήναις δὲ Ἀλκαῖος καὶ Σθένελος καὶ Ἕλειος Μήστωρ τε καὶ Ἠλεκτρύων, καὶ θυγάτηρ Γοργοφόνη, ἣν Περιήρης ἔγημεν.

Perseus hurried to Argos with Danae and Andromeda to see Akrisios. When he learned that they were coming he left Argos in fear of the Oracle (that Danae's son would kill him[878]) and went to the land of the Pelasgians. Teutamides, king of Larissa, held athletic games in honor of his father who had died and Perseus came to participate in them. Competing in the pentathlon he hurled the discus, struck Akrisios on the foot, and killed him instantly. Perseus realized that the prophesy had been fulfilled. He buried Akrisios outside the city but was ashamed to return to Argos to claim the inheritance from his grandfather, so he went instead to Proitos' son Megapenthes at Tiryns and exchanged Argos for Tiryns with him. Megapenthes then ruled Argos and Perseus, Tiryns. He also fortified Midea and Mykenai.

Before Perseus came to Greece, Andromeda bore him a son Perses (whom he left with Kepheus) from whom the kings of Persia are said to be descended. In Mykenai she bore to him sons named Alkaios, Sthenelos, (Heleus, Mester) and Elektryon, and a daughter Gorgophone whom Perieres married.

M. Simpson, Trans.

Pausanias. 2.16.1-4.

Ἄργος δὲ Φορωνέως θυγατριδοῦς βασιλεύσας μετὰ φορωνέα ὠνόμασεν ἀφ' αὑτοῦ τὴν χώραν. Ἄργου δὲ Πείρασος γίνεται καὶ Φόρβας, Φόρβαντος δὲ Τριόπας, Τριόπα δὲ Ἴασος καὶ Ἀγήνωρ. Ἰὼ μὲν οὖν Ἰάσου θυγάτηρ, εἴτε ὡς Ἡρόδοτος ἔγραψεν εἴτε καθ' ὃ λέγουσιν Ἕλληνες, ἐς Αἴγυπτον ἀφικνεῖται· Κρότωπος δὲ ὁ Ἀγήνορος ἔσχε μετὰ Ἴασον τὴν ἀρχήν, Κροτώπου δὲ Σθενέλας γίνεται, Δαναὸς δ' ἀπ' Αἰγύπτου πλεύ. σας ἐπὶ Γελάνορα τὸν Σθενέλα τοὺς ἀπογόνους τοὺς Ἀγήνορος βασιλείας ἔπαυσεν. τὰ δὲ ἀπὸ τούτου καὶ οἱ πάντες ὁμοίως ἴσασι, θυγατέρων τῶν Δαναοῦ τὸ ἐς τοὺς ἀνεψιοὺς τόλμημα καὶ ὡς ἀποθανόντος Δαναοῦ τὴν ἀρχὴν Λυγκεὺς ἔσχεν. οἱ δὲ Ἄβαντος τοῦ Λαγκέως παῖδες τὴν βασιλείαν ἐνείμαντο, καὶ Ἀκρίσιος μὲν αὐτοῦ κατέμεινεν ἐν τῷ Ἄργει, Προῖτος δὲ τὸ Ἡραῖον καὶ Μιδείαν καὶ Τίρυνθα ἔσχε καὶ ὅσα πρὸς θαλάσσῃ τῆς Ἀργείας· σημεῖά τε τῆς ἐν Τίρυνθι οἰκήσεως Προίτου καὶ ἐς τόδε λείπεται. χρόνῳ δὲ ὕστερον Ἀκρίσιος Περσέα αὐτόν τε περιεῖναι πυνθανόμενος καὶ ἔργα ἀποδείκνυσθαι, ἐς Λάρισαν ἀπεχώρησε τὴν ἐπὶ τῷ Πηνειῷ. Περσεὺς δὲ--ἰδεῖν γὰρ πάντως ἤθεγε τὸν γονέα τῆς μητρὸς καὶ λόγοις τε χρηστοῖς καὶ ἔργοις δεξιώσασθαι--ἔρχεται παρ' αὐτὸν ἐς τὴν Λάρισαν· καὶ ὁ μὲν οἷα ἡλικίᾳ τε ἀκμά, ων καὶ τοῦ δίσκου χαίρων τῷ εὑρήματι ἐπεδείκνυτο ἐς ἅπαντας, Ἀκρίσιος δὲ λανθάνει κατὰ δαίμονα ὑποπεσὼν τοῦ δίσκου τῇ ὁρμῇ. καὶ Ἀκρισίῳ μὲν ἡ πρόρρησις τοῦ θεοῦ τέλος ἔσχεν, οὐδὲ ἀπέτρεψέν οἱ τὸ χρεὼν τὰ ἐς τὴν παῖδα καὶ τὸν θυγατριδοῦν παρευρήματα· Περσεὺς δὲ ὡς ἀνέστρεψεν ἐς Ἄργος--ᾐσχύνετο γὰρ τοῦ φόνου τῇ φήμῃ--, Μελαπένθην τὸν Προίτου πείθει οἱ τὴν ἀρχὴν ἀντιδοῦναι, παραλαβὼν δὲ αὐτὸς τὴν ἐκείνου Μυκήνας κτίζει. τοῦ ξίφους γὰρ ἐνταῦθα ἐξέπεσεν ὁ μύκης αὐτῷ, καὶ τὸ σημεῖον ἐς οἰκισμὸν

APPENDIX A

ἐνόμιζε συμβῆναι πόλεως. ἤκουσα δὲ καὶ ὡς διψῶντι ἐπῆλθεν ἀνελάσθαι οἱ μύκητα ἐκ τῆς γῆς, ῥυέντος δὲ ὕδατος πιὼν καὶ ἡσθεὶς Μυκήνας ἔθετο τὸ ὄνομα τῷ χωρίῳ.

Argos, the grandson of Phoroneus, succeeding to the throne after Phoroneus, gave his name to the land. Argos begat Peirasos and Phorbas, Phorbas begat Triopas, and Triopas begat Iasos and Agenor. Io, the daughter of Iasos, went to Egypt, whether the circumstances be as Herodotos records or as the Greeks say. After Iasos, Krotopos, the son of Agenor, came to the throne and begat Sthenelas, but Danaos sailed from Egypt against Gelanor, the son of Sthenelas, and stayed the succession to the kingdom of the descendants of Agenor. What followed is known to all alike: the crime the daughters of Danaos committed against their cousins, and how, on the death of Danaos, Lynkeus succeeded him. But the sons of Abas, the son of Lynkeus, divided the kingdom between themselves; Akrisios remained where he was at Argos, and Proitos took over the Heraeum, Mideia, Tiryns and the Argive coast region. Traces of the residence of Proitos remain to the present day. Afterwards Akrisios, learning that Perseus himself was not only alive but accomplishing great achievements, retired to Larisa on the Peneus. And Perseus, wishing at all costs to see the father of his mother and to greet him with fair words and deeds, visited him at Larisa. Being in the prime of life and proud of his inventing the quoit, he gave displays before all, and Akrisios, as luck would have it, stepped unnoticed into the path of the quoit. So the prediction of the god to Akrisios found its fulfillment, nor was his fate prevented by his precautions against his daughter and his grandson. Perseus, ashamed because of the gossip about the homicide, on his return to Argos induced Megapenthes, the son of Proitos to make an exchange of kingdoms; taking over himself that of Megapenthes, he founded Mykenai. For on its site the cap (mykes) fell from his scabbard, and he regarded this as a sign to found a city. I have also heard the following account. He was thirsty, and the thought occurred to him to pick up a mushroom (mykes) from the ground. Drinking with joy water that flowed from it, he gave to the place the name of Mykenai.

Pausanias 2.18.4-9.

Μόνους δὲ Ἑλλήνων οἶδα Ἀργείους ἐς τρεῖς βασιλείας νεμηθέντας. ἐπὶ γὰρ τῆς ἀρχῆς τῆς Ἀναξαγόρου τοῦ Ἀργείου τοῦ Μελαπένθους μανία ταῖς γυναιξὶν ἐνέπεσεν, ἐκφοιτῶσαι δὲ ἐκ τῶν οἰκιῶν ἐπλανῶντο ἀνὰ τὴν χώραν, ἐς ὃ Μελάμπους ὁ Ἀμυθάονος ἔπαυσε σφᾶς τῆς νόσου, ἐφ᾽ ᾧ τε αὐτὸς καὶ ὁ ἀδελφὸς Βίας Ἀναξαγόρᾳ τὸ ἴσον ἕξουσιν. ἀπὸ μὲν δὴ Βίαντος βασιλεύουσι πέντε ἄνδρες **ἐπὶ γενεὰς τέσσαρας ἐς Κυάνιππον τὸν Αἰγιαλέως, ὄντες Νηλεῖδαι τὰ πρὸς μητρός, ἀπὸ δὲ Μελάμποδος γενεαί τε ἓξ καὶ ἄνδρες ἴσοι μέχρις Ἀμφιλόχου τοῦ Ἀμφιαράου**[879]· τὸ δὲ ἐγχώριον γένος οἱ Ἀναξαγορίδαι βασιλεύουσι πλέον. Ἶφις μὲν γὰρ ὁ Ἀλέκτορος τοῦ Ἀναξαγόρου Σθενέλῳ τῷ Καπανέως ἀδελφοῦ παιδὶ ἀπέλιπε τὴν ἀρχήν· Ἀμφιλόχου δὲ μετὰ ἅλωσιν Ἰλίου μετοικήσαντος ἐς τοὺς νῦν Ἀμφιλόχους, Κυανίππου δ᾽ ἄπαιδος τελευτήσαντος, οὕτω Κυλαράβης ὁ Σθενέλου μόνος τὴν βασιλείαν ἔσχεν. οὐ μέντοι παῖδας κατέλιπεν οὐδ᾽ οὗτος, ἀλλὰ Ὀρέστης ὁ Ἀγαμέμνονος τὸ Ἄργος κατέσχε παροικῶν τε ἐγγὺς αὐτῷ καὶ ἄνευ τῆς πατρῴας ἀρχῆς προσπεποιημένος μὲν Ἀρκάδων τοὺς πολλούς, παρειληφὼς δὲ καὶ τὴν ἐν Σπάρτῃ βασιλείαν, συμμαχικοῦ δὲ ἐκ Φωκέων ἀεί ποτε ἐπ᾽ ὠφελείᾳ ἑτοίμου παρόντος. Λακεδαιμονίων δὲ ἐβασίλευσεν Ὀρέστης Λακεδαιμονίων ἐφέντων αὐτῷ· τοὺς γὰρ Τυνδάρεω θυγατριδοῦς τὴν ἀρχὴν ἔχειν ἠξίουν πρὸ Νικοστράτου καὶ Μεγαπένθους Μενελάῳ γεγενημένων ἐκ δούλης. Ὀρέστου δὲ ἀποθανόντος ἔσχε Τισαμενὸς τὴν ἀρχήν, Ἑρμιόνης τῆς Μενελάου καὶ Ὀρέστου παῖς. τὸν δὲ Ὀρέστου νόθον Πενθίλον Κιναίθων ἔγραψεν ἐν τοῖς ἔπεσιν Ἠριγόνην τὴν Αἰγίσθου τεκεῖν. ἐπὶ δὲ τοῦ Τισαμενοῦ τούτου κατίασιν ἐς Πελοπόννησον Ἡρακλεῖδαι, Τήμενος μὲν καὶ Κρεσφόντης Ἀριστομάχου, τοῦ τρίτου δὲ Ἀριστοδήμου προτεθνεῶτος εἵποντο οἱ παῖδες. Ἄργους μὲν δὴ καὶ τῆς ἐν Ἄργει βασιλείας ὀρθότατα ἐμοὶ δοκεῖν ἠμφισβήτουν, ὅτι ἦν Πελοπίδης ὁ Τισαμενός, οἱ δὲ Ἡρακλεῖδαι τὸ ἀνέκαθέν εἰσι Περσεῖδαι· Τυνδάρεω δὲ καὶ αὐτὸν ἐκπεσόντα ἀπέφαινον ὑπὸ Ἱπποκόωντος, Ἡρακλέα δὲ ἔφασαν ἀποκτείναντα Ἱπποκόωντα καὶ τοὺς παῖδας παρακαταθέσθαι Τυνδάρεῳ τὴν χώραν· τοιαῦτα δὲ καὶ περὶ τῆς Μεσσηνίας ἕτερα ἔλεγον, παρακαταθήκην Νέστορι δοθῆναι καὶ ταύτην ὑπὸ Ἡρακλέους ἑλόντος Πύλον.

ἐκβάλλουσιν οὖν ἐκ μὲν Λακεδαίμονος καὶ Ἄργους Τισαμενόν, ἐκ δὲ τῆς Μεσσηνίας τοὺς Νέστορος ἀπογόνους, Ἀλκμαίωνα Σίλλου τοῦ Θρασυμήδους καὶ Πεισίστρατον τὸν Πεισιστράτου καὶ τοὺς Παίονος τοῦ Ἀντιλόχου παῖδας, σὺν δὲ αὐτοῖς Μέλανθον τὸν Ἀνδροπόμπου τοῦ Βώρου τοῦ Πενθίλου τοῦ Περικλυμένου. Τισαμενὸς μὲν οὖν ἦλθε σὺν τῇ στρατιᾷ καὶ οἱ παῖδες ἐς τὴν νῦν Ἀχαΐαν· οἱ δὲ Νηλεῖδαι πλὴν Πεισιστράτου--τοῦτον γὰρ οὐκ οἶδα παρ᾽ οὕστινας ἀπεχώρησεν--ἐς Ἀθήνας ἀφίκοντο οἱ λοιποί, καὶ τὸ Παιονιδῶν γένος καὶ Ἀλκμαιωνιδῶν ἀπὸ τούτων ὠνομάσθησαν. Μέλανθος δὲ καὶ τὴν βασιλείαν ἔσχεν ἀφελόμενος Θυμοίτην τὸν Ὀξύντου· Θυμοίτης γὰρ Θησειδῶν ἔσχατος ἐβασίλευσεν Ἀθηναίων.

The Argives are the only Greeks that I know of who have been divided into three kingdoms. For in the reign of Anaxagoras, son of Argeious, son of Megapenthes, the women were smitten with madness, and straying from their homes they roamed about the country, until Melampous the son of Amythaon cured them of the plague on condition that he himself and his brother Bias had a share in the kingdom equal to that of Anaxagoras. Now descended from Bias five men, Neleids on their mother's side, occupied the throne for four generations down to Kyanippos, son of Aigialeus, and descended from Melampous six men in six generations down to Amphilochos, son of Amphiaraos[880]. But the native house of the family of Anaxagoras ruled longer than the other two. For Iphis, son of Alektor, son of Anaxagoras, left the throne to Sthenelos, son of Kapaneos, his brother. After the capture of Troy, Amphilochos migrated to the people now called the Amphilochians, and, Kyanippos having died without issue, Kylarabes, son of Sthenelos, became sole king. However, he too left no offspring, and Argos was seized by Orestes, son of Agamemnon, who was a neighbor. Besides his ancestral dominion, he had extended his rule over the greater part of Arkadia and had succeeded to the throne of Sparta; he also had a contingent of Phokian alles always ready to help him. When Orestes became king of the Lakedaimonians, they themselves consented to accept him; for they considered that the sons of the daughter of Tyndareos had a claim to the throne prior to that of Nikostratos and Megapenthes, who were sons of Menelaos and a slave woman. On the death of Orestes, there succeeded to the throne, Tisamenos, the son of Orestes and of Hermione, the daughter of Menelaos. The mother of Penthilos, the bastard son of Orestes, was, according to the poet Kinaithon, Erigone, the daughter of Aigisthos. It was in the reign of Tisamenos that the Herakleidai returned to the Peloponnese; they were Temenos and Kresphontes, the sons of Aristomachos, together with the sons of the third brother, Aristodemos, who had died. Their claim to Argos and to the throne of Argos, was, in my opinion, most just, because Tisamenos was descended from Pelops but the Herakleidai were descendants of Perseus. Tyndareos himself, they made out, had been expelled by Hippokoon and his sons, and given the land in trust to Tyndareos. They gave the same kind of account about Messenia also, that it had been given in trust to Nestor by Herakles after he had taken Pylos. So they expelled Tisamenos from Lakedaimon and Argos, and the descendants of Nestor from Messenia, namely Alkmaion, son of Sillos, son of Thrasymedes, Peisistratos, son of Peisistratos, and the sons of Paion, son of Antilochos, and with them Melanthos, son of Andropompos, son of Boros, son of Penthilos, son of Periklymenos. So Tisamenos and his sons went with his army to the land that is now Achaia. To what people Peisistratos retreated I do not know, but the rest of the Neleidai went to Athens, and the clans of the Paionidai and of the Alkmaionidai were named after them. Melanthos even came to the throne, having deposed Thymoites the son of Oxyntes; for Thymoites was the last Athenian king descended from Theseus.

 W.H.S. Jones, Trans.

---

[877] i.e. brother of Tyndareos.

[878] ApB 2.4.1

[879] See below for a modification of Jones' translation of this passage.

APPENDIX A

[880] This translation appears to warrant modification where the line of Melampous is concerned. As far as I can tell, what Pausanias means in the phrase that reads "six men in six generations," is rather, six men, likewise in four generations, picking up the four from the previous statement that concludes his assessment of Bias family line, and applying it also to the line of Melampous. There are two main reasons this must be so, in addition to the participle βασιλεύουσι. First, the fact that six generations did not exist between Melampous and Amphilochos, who was the seer's great-great-grandson so any direct progression would reach him in four. And secondly, since charting genealogies by reigning rulers as opposed to, straightforwardly, by generations was a typical practice used by Pausanias in his treatment of the pre-histories of individual poleis, which also afforded maximum flexibility in terms of systematizing various traditions. On these grounds, it is best to conclude, that this presentation records an unstated sequence of six Melampid rulers at Argos, rather than a straightforward genealogical sequence. Mythologically also, this makes considerable sense, seeing that Pausanias acknowledged a non-Homeric son of Melampous named Abas (1.43.5, in addition to Mantios who replaced Antiphates), whose descendants became influential in Korinth, while it was popular to consider Alkmaion the leader of the second expedition to Thebes that was conducted by the Epigoni (e.g. ApB 3.7.2), and otherwise, certainly, an Argive ruler, if due to the matricide, only for a brief period.

APPENDIX B: ARGIVE GENEALOGIES

Tripartite Division of Argos.
Exhibit B1: the three Argive lines plus the line of Akrisios.

The following genealogies are generally standard. The lines of Melampous and Bias are customarily uneven. Proitos' line as it stands is significantly longer, and Akrisios' line is longer still, since it does not make it down to Herakles' generation until the other three lines have lived out the Trojan War. The additional length of the line of Proitos disappears in *Exhibit B*, below, when Melampous and Bias are matched up with Anaxagoras rather than Proitos, rendering Proitos' line rather short by comparison (viz. Sthenelos is lined up with the protagonists of the first Theban War). This problem is alleviated by Pausanias, as set out in *Exhibit C*.

MELAMPOUS	BIAS	PROITOS	AKRISIOS
ANTIPHATES		MEGAPENTHES	DANAE
OIKLES	TALAOS	ANAXAGORAS	PERSEUS
AMPHIARAOS	ADRASTOS/ERIPHYLE	HIPPONOOS	ELEKTRYON
*ALKMAION/AMPHILOCHOS	*AIGIALEUS	KAPANEUS	ALKMENE
		*STHENELOS	**HERAKLES**

- *active at the time of the Trojan War.
- Hyllos (like Herakles' son Tlepolemos) must be dated to the Trojan War era, though he was not a participant in the Trojan War.

APPENDIX B

Tripartite Division of Argos.
Exhibit B2. Melampous and Bias migrate to Argos in the reign of Anaxagoras (e.g. Diodoros 4.68)

Columns 1, 2, and 3 illustrate the effects of placing Melampous' cure in the reign of Anaxagoras following, Diodoros 4.68. Namely, the lineage of Melampous and Bias are brought more appropriately into alignment with the lines of Proitos and Akrisios (taken together), considering also that Melampous' cure necessarily had to take place after the alleged exchange of kingdoms between Perseus and Megapenthes. Quite likely also, this move provoked the lengthening of Proitos early epic lineage, which nonetheless comes up relatively short, whereas before the adjustment this same stemma suggests an excess of characters (so *Exhibit A*, above). Pausanias' account of the post Trojan War figures involved in *Return of the Herakleidai* are reproduced below the dotted line in order to demonstrate the effects of Pausanias' adjustments in *Exhibit B3*. Excluding Orestes, these figures represent the post-Homeric mainland standardization of *Return of the Herakleidai*.

		PROITOS	AKRISIOS
		MEGAPENTHES	DANAE
MELAMPOUS	BIAS	ANAXAGORAS	PERSEUS
ANTIPHATES		HIPPONOOS	ELEKTRYON
	TALAOS		
OIKLES		KAPANEUS	ALKMENE
AMPHIARAOS	ADRASTOS/ERIPHYLE	*STHENELOS	**HERAKLES**
*ALKMAION/AMPHILOCHOS	*AIGIALEUS	KYLARBES	*HYLLOS
	---------------------------	(ORESTES)	KLEODAIOS
	KYANIPPOS	(TISAMENOS)	ARISTOMACHOS
			TEMENOS

APPENDIX B

Tripartite Division of Argos.
Exhibit B3: Following Pausanias 2.18.4-8.

There, Argeios is added to the Protid line, Alektor is substituted for Hipponoos, and Melampous again arrives in the reign of Anaxagoras. The addition of Argeios makes it possible for Herakles to line up with Kapaneus, which places him suitably in the pre-Trojan War era, while Melampous' arrival in the reign of Anaxagoras, which has now been effectively moved down one notch, makes it possible for the Heraklid Temenos to line up with Orestes' son Tisamenos three generations after the Trojan War.

		PROITOS	AKRISIOS
		MEGAPENTHES	DANAE
		ARGEIOS	PERSEUS
MELAMPOUS	BIAS	**ANAXAGORAS**	ELEKTRYON
MANTIOS/ABAS		ALEKTOR	ALKMENE
	TALAOS		
OIKLES		KAPANEUS	**HERAKLES**
AMPHIARAOS	ADRASTOS/ERIPHYLE	*STHENELOS	*HYLLOS
*ALKMAION/AMPHOLOCHOS	*AIGIALEUS	KYLARBES	KLEODAIOS
	KYANIPPOS	(ORESTES)	ARISTOMACHOS
		(TISAMENOS)	**TEMENOS**

Three Cardinal Divisions of Ancient Greek Identity

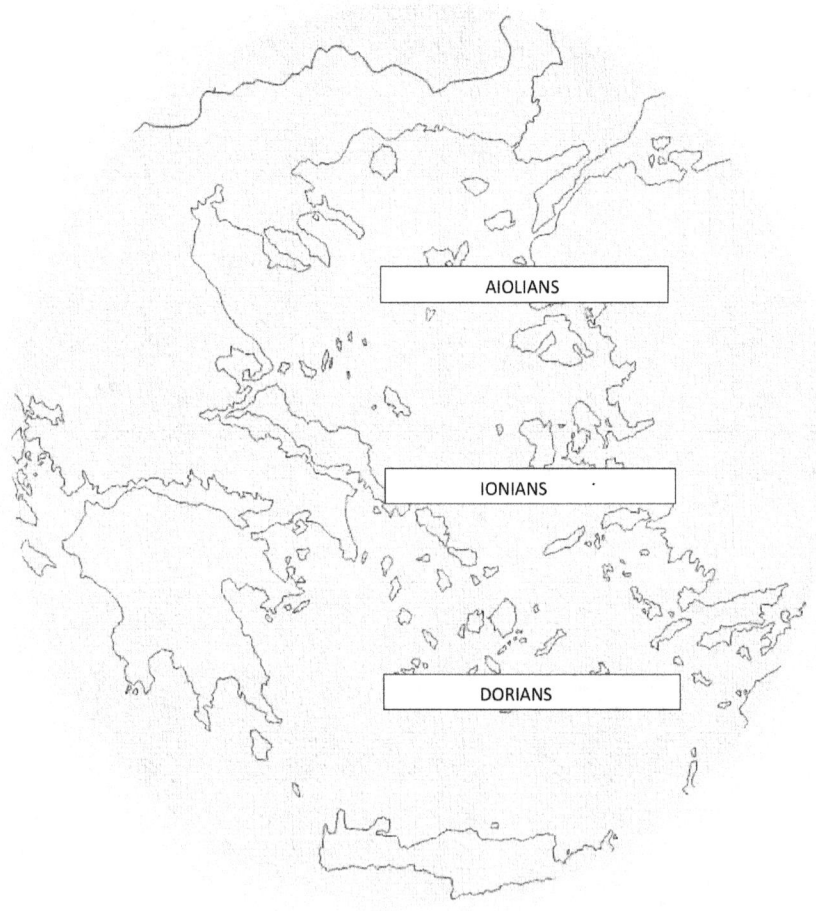

ABOUT THE AUTHOR

Zoe Alexandra Pappas, Ph.D. is a native New Yorker with multiple degrees from Columbia University where she focused on the confluence of humanities disciplines and various applications of systems and set theory. As an independent historian, logician, and analyst, she is the founder and president of *Mytho Logic Inc.* – an institution devoted to isolating and correcting misunderstandings based on ill-founded knowledge of the everyday forces of cause and effect. First and foremost, however, *Mytho Logic* was founded to advance the publication of – "Genealogy and Identity: The Genealogical Evidence for the Appropriation of Early East Greek Mythology by the Mainland Greek City-States in the Archaic Period" – a unique assessment of the Hellenic mythological heritage focused at once on historical context and on the internal genealogical structures intrinsic to the ancient mythic stories themselves. *KnowledgeTech: Techniques for Learning* is now the curriculum development and teaching arm of *Mytho Logic's* commitment to inherent creativity and the promotion of intellectual excellence, so oftentimes left involuntarily dormant in individuals and communities locally and worldwide.

www.ingramcontent.com/pod-product-compliance
Lightning Source LLC
Chambersburg PA
CBHW071115080526
44587CB00013B/1350